THE
ACTIVE
SOCIETY

Amitai Etzioni

THE
ACTIVE
SOCIETY

A Theory of Societal and Political Processes

Collier-Macmillan Limited, London

The Free Press, New York

The Free Press
A DIVISION OF THE MACMILLAN COMPANY
866 Third Avenue, New York, New York 10022

Collier-Macmillan Canada Ltd., Toronto, Ontario

Library of Congress Catalog Card Number: 68-10791

First Free Press Paperback Edition 1971

For the Active Ones

In particular my students at Columbia and at Berkeley

Daughter: A flower child is a young person belonging to a new generation which is very idealistic and thoughtful. They believe in love, beauty, peace, understanding, freedom, sharing and helping each other. Flower children are trying to change the world with these ideas.

Mother: We tried to point out to her that the flower children and the hippies are not creative persons, not really doing anything useful.

—*The New York Times*, Oct. 19, 1967, p. 52

Preface

THE MODERN period ended with the radical transformation of the technologies of communication, knowledge, and energy that followed World War II. A central characteristic of the modern period has been continued increase in the efficacy of the technology of production which poses a growing challenge to the primacy of the values these means are supposed to serve. The post-modern period, the onset of which may be set at 1945, will witness either a greater threat to the status of these values by the surging technologies or a reassertion of their normative priority. Which alternative prevails will determine whether society is to be the servant or the master of the instruments it creates. The active society, one that is master of itself, is an option the post-modern period opens. An exploration of the conditions under which this option might be exercised is the subject of this endeavor.

The theory presented here combines analytical and historical perspectives: It contains an analysis of the active quality and its components, and a set of hypotheses about the historical circumstances under which societies or sub-societies (ethnic groupings, classes) acquire varying degrees of self-control. As an analytic conception, the active society is a model to which the actual composition of various societies and sub-societies can be compared and with whose help they can be dissected. The historical context in which the active option arises, and hence of this study, is contemporary civilization and its transformation.

In one sense, all societies have entered the post-modern period, for none has escaped the impact of the new technologies. At the same time, societies differ significantly in the degree to which they have faced the challenge of modernity and in their access to the options the post-modern period offers. For industrialized societies, the question is one of regaining self-control as they transform. For industrializing societies, it is a question of moving toward the active society while avoiding at least some of the strains of modernization.

This study of the active society seeks to lay the foundations for a theory of macroscopic action. We say *foundations* because our knowledge is too limited and the task of building a comprehensive theory is too demanding for any one mason to lay much more than a base. We focus on *macroscopic* action because much of the theoretical work so far has limited itself largely to the analysis of either micro-units or of "universal" properties which are common to all units. Social and political processes, however, draw heavily on macro-units which have properties and processes and, hence, a theoretical status of their own. Finally, our emphasis is on *action* because much of existing theory views social and political processes as static or, if dynamic, as passive rather than active. The civil rights movement in the United States, decolonization and modernization drives in new nations, trans-national social movements, and, above all, the shift to the post-modern era provide prime illustrations of our propositions.

As no society is yet active, our study draws on an analysis of the constraints on activation in existing societies and the partial successes in their transformation. Modern democracies fall short of the active ideal-type, particularly in their low capacity to change; totalitarian societies fail to keep their goals and even more so their procedures responsive to their members. Among the post-modern societies the Scandinavian nations and, even more, Israel seem to have come relatively closer to an active society, a society responsive to its changing membership, one engaged in an intensive and perpetual self-transformation. As the active society is best depicted as a macroscopic and permanent social movement, the examination of social movements is of particular interest.

Our theory seeks to reconcile three approaches to the study of society. We wish to illustrate that a social science theory can be scientifically valid, can be intellectually relevant, and can serve as a springboard for active participation.

Factual statements and value judgments can be systematically articulated without being fused or confused. Sociological imagination can enrich rather than replace social science. We reject the idea that there is no more to social analysis than neutral research, just as we reject the notion that the truth value of a statement is measured by the service it renders to the advancement of a cause.

While we have sought to free ourselves from traditional disciplinary boundaries, the need to consider both sociological and political science was inescapable. Sociologists deal with collectivities and societies; administration and government are a major concern of political scientists. Since we are interested in the governance of societal processes, we have constructed a theory that draws upon both disciplines.

This author was engaged in a similar effort in two previous books, one dealing with control mechanisms (or complex organizations) and one with the changing relations among societies.* To some extent, the present volume is the culmination of a project that began with the preparation of the first of these books in 1958.

The foundations of a theory of macro-action, we shall see, are different from theories that treat their subjects as passive. There are, however, three major common foundations of this and previous theoretical endeavors. (1) Cybernetics, the study of steering, is essential if the ways social units act in unison and transform themselves are to be understood. (2) A study of collectivities, societies, and their bonds is necessary if the forces that limit societal steering as well as provide the "materials" it guides are to be explored. (3) Finally, a traditional concern of political science, power, must be included. If the first approach studies the social mind and nerves, and the second deals with the social bone structure, this last analyzes the social muscles.

As in any work that deals with the foundations of a distinct theoretical approach, much space is devoted here to general considerations. While this volume contains numerous propositions (in the technical sense of the term), its main thrust is to provide a theoretical framework within which additional propositions can be formulated and data codified. This volume assumes a division of labor that ought to be made explicit: a division between those who specialize in developing theories and those who deal with empirical verification. The linking of theory and research involves the meeting of two genders; the *fusion* of the two is much more difficult to come by and is no more creative.

Since the empirical validity of many of the propositions presented here can be determined only after some research, the question arises as to what stan-

---

* Amitai Etzioni, *A Comparative Analysis of Complex Organizations* (New York: The Free Press, 1961); and *Political Unification: A Comparative Study of Leaders and Forces* (New York: Holt, Rinehart & Winston, Inc., 1965).

dards other than plausibility were used in choosing propositions.* In part, the answer lies in an effort to make the propositions consistent with each other and with existing theory, but this is not much help since much of existing theory itself is not verified. The problem is accentuated where we break relatively new theoretical ground because there are few landmarks to guide us. What we have attempted to do is (1) to advance propositions on such a level as to facilitate verification, which makes our theory more synthesizing and less analytic than many; (2) to use relatively operational terms for which empirical indicators have already been specified or can be readily determined. In general, we have referred the reader to studies that have operationalized the concepts used here rather than entered into methodological discussions; in a few instances, when such studies were not available, we have suggested indicators. (3) We have included only propositions of which we are not aware that there is a conflicting body of data or which explained why we still hold to our proposition despite some counter-evidence. We have not reviewed existing literature but instead refer to one or more review works as well as original studies. These works include references to additional studies examined but not cited here.

Theories are the product of collective efforts. The new theory advanced here has many roots in the past, cited below; it is thus at best partly new. Moreover, like all theories, it is inherently incomplete; it must be continually revised and expanded. Above all, the power of the propositions this theory generates have yet to be tested in empirical research and in social action. In short, this endeavor is just a link in a chain that has no end.

For reasons that will become evident later, many of the propositions and perspectives advanced here rest upon statements of degree. Several of the chief variables represent varying mixtures of basic elements. If reduced to black-and-white dichotomies, much of what follows is turned meaningless or false.

Behind the theoretical and methodological considerations of the following pages lie a dilemma and an image. The dilemma is similar to one Freud perceived in individual conduct: How is a man's future controlled? How can his history be made less by fate and more by rational, yet spontaneous, action? We ask similar questions about the social actor: How is he guided? What extends or curtails his self-control? How authentic it is? Answering these questions requires an understanding of how societal units move and transform, a theory of society and its political organization.

The image which often appeared to me as these pages were written was that of an ocean liner propelled by an outboard motor, requiring not only more drive but also reconstruction while continuing to sail the high seas. Social

---

* Where the propositional nature of a statement is not evident from the context, the phrases "we suggest" and "we expect" are used to indicate the hypothetical status of the statement.

scientists, especially those dealing with macroscopic action, participate in this reconstruction. And we are all aboard.

Plan of the Book

The first part of this volume has the shape of ever-narrowing circles, starting with the normative assumptions of the active society (Chapter 1), followed by a brief exploration of some of the philosophical premises of theories of action (Chapter 2), a discussion of methodological aspects of theories of macro-action (Chapter 3), and one of the substantive, meta-theoretical assumptions of such endeavors (Chapter 4). It closes with a presentation of the basic concepts of the theory presented here (Chapter 5).

The study of the elements of the active orientation and of the movement toward an active society is built around two subjects: the instruments of societal control, and the processes of consensus formation. The second and third parts deal with the cybernetic and power aspects of societal control. The fourth part is relatively synthesizing, adding a study of consensus-formation to the study of societal control and thus enabling us to explore the active quality, which rests upon a combination of the ability to control and the capacity to form consensus. The last part deals with the transformation of the relationship among societies from tribalistic divisions toward communal unity, thus adding the study of the transformation of the boundaries of society to that of its structure. The epilogue is concerned with distinguishing inauthentic (or pseudo) activation from the real quality, and the role of projects in disalienation and authentication.

A. E.

Acknowledgments

THE FIRST notes which eventually led to the writing of this book were taken in 1958 when I joined the faculty of Columbia University. In the following six years, as the volume of notes swelled, I benefited—at one point or another—from discussion of the subjects explored here, with all the members of the Department of Sociology at Columbia University and Professor William T. R. Fox of its Department of Public Law and Government.

The writing of the book itself lasted about three years, most of the first of which was spent at the Center for Advanced Study in the Behavioral Sciences, without whose help this book would never have been drafted. I am much indebted to the Center's staff, in particular to the comments of Miriam Gallaher, and to the patience with which Dorothy Brothers typed two preliminary drafts of the manuscript. The administrative magic of Ralph W. Tyler, Preston Cutler, and Jane A. Kielsmeier allowed me to devote my full time to the book. Among the Fellows from whose comments I particularly benefited, were Robert P. Abelson, Ernest W. Adams, William P. Alston, Norman Cohn, Franco Ferrarotti, Stanley Hoffmann, William J. McGuire, Nelson W. Polsby, Donald R. Reich, Percy H. Tannenbaum, Martin A. Trow, and Richard A. Watson. In the second year of the project I was the recipient of a Social Science Research Council faculty research grant. In the third year I benefited from a grant from the National Science Foundation (GS-1475) devoted to the extension of this project in the methodological direction. Charlotte A. Fisher typed, with unmatched speed and accuracy, three verions of this volume.

When I worked on the first outline of this volume, I discussed it with two of my students, Sarajane Heidt and Martin Wenglinsky, who had not met before. When the book went to press Jane and Marty had been married for more than a year. During the whole period I benefited from their comments. Jane worked with me on a week-to-week basis and proved a most valuable assistant. She assisted in every aspect of this work from setting the table of contents to moving commas around. Marty's suggestions were much less frequent but similarly helpful. Robert McGeehan, a young political scientist, usefully commented on each chapter. I also benefited from the assistance of Audrey Chapman, Frederick DuBow, Charlotte Fishman, Nancy Gertner, Barry Greenberg, Victor Hausner, Elaine Hoiska, William L. Johnson, Joseph J. Karlesky, Kenneth Laudon. Peggy McClure, Barbara Mitrani, Linda Thalberg. Lydia Redlbacher, Paul Ritterband and Harriet Zuckerman commented on parts of the manuscript. I especially benefited from discussing my ideas with Daniel Bell and William J. Goode.

OUTLINE TABLE OF CONTENTS

Analytical Table of Contents

PART FOUR

SOCIETAL CONSENSUS AND RESPONSIVENESS

PART FIVE

BEYOND TRIBALISM

EPILOGUE

THE
ACTIVE
SOCIETY

CHAPTER 1

The Active Orientation:

Introduction

THE RISE of natural science is often mistakenly viewed as the great turning point in the history of man's conception of himself, as a Copernican revolution in reverse, one in which man regains his central place as he learns to master nature.[1]* Actually, according to even the more optimistic assumptions of natural scientists, man is only able to learn the laws of nature and to use them for his own purposes. He advances by riding the natural current but is unable to modify even the weakest laws of nature.[2] The world is as much "given" for a positivist, secular scientist as it was for a high priest of the medieval church. Men may be able to decipher nature's secret code and thus gain access to the contents of her safe, but they cannot reset the code. Thus, despite all the secularization of Western thought, this central concept of man is still that of a passive observer in a world not of his making and not under his control.

The rise of psychoanalytic thought cleared the way for an authentically

---

* Reference notes for this chapter appear on page 16.

active view of man. According to psychoanalytic theories, man is able, if at great pain and by great endeavor, not only to understand himself but also to transform himself, to free himself from his own past and to set a new course of action. The psychoanalytic active orientation is, however, highly atomistic and soon encounters its own fundamental limitation. Psychoanalysis concedes that in fact man is unable to set himself free; he needs the helping hand of an already free man. Freudian psychoanalysis produces the intellectually tortuous notion of a caste of high priests who have been freed by a succession of higher ranking priests, the first of whom—the founder of the line—commanded a superior power; *he* was able to set himself free.[3] With this kind of capacity to liberate, handed down from analyst to analyst and from them to their select patients, most of the world is left passive, as those saved must be reached one by one. Actually, we shall attempt to show, no man can set himself free without extending the same liberty to his fellow men, and the transformation of self is deeply rooted in the joint act of a community transforming itself. The self which is to be activated is neither the center nor the appendage of the individual self, but rather the self of a social collectivity. (A social collectivity has a self, not as a reified or metaphysical category but as the carrier of an active orientation. Collectivities can set goals, commit themselves to their realization, and pursue them.)

To be Is to be Social

Man is *not* unless he is social; what he is depends on his social being, and what he makes of his social being is irrevocably bound to what he makes of himself.* He has the ability to master his internal being, *and the main way to self-mastery leads to his joining with others like himself in social acts.* Potentially, every man is free to choose; social laws, unlike those of nature, can be flaunted and, above all, rewritten. In fact, however, social laws penetrate individual existence so deeply that most escapes are limited in scope and often lead from compliance with one set of laws to even fuller compliance with another. The confines of social life are frequently composed of other people in the same predicament; hence, in principle, the transformation of social life can be propelled by give-and-take among the subjects themselves. While individual action is possible, it cannot be understood

---

* Our position on the social category is close to that of Martin Buber, especially as stated in the second edition of his *I and Thou* (New York: Charles Scribner's Sons, 1958). In a postscript to this edition, Buber writes: "... we are no longer concerned with the threshold, the preliminal and the superliminal of mutuality, but with mutuality itself as the door into our existence." (p. 131.) For a comparison of this position with that of G. H. Mead, see Paul Pfuetze, *The Social Self* (New York: Bookman Associates, 1954), especially pp. 229–297. For a more extreme, sociologistic position, see John Dewey, "Social as a Category," *The Monist*, Vol. 38 (1938), pp. 161–177.

except against the background of the social action of which it is a part, on which it builds, or against which it reacts.

The social self, however, is not a random combination of persons; it is structured and its movements are organized. The social entity is not an oppressive reality, hovering above the individual, constraining his acts. It is far more penetrating than this, for it is part of what he views as his irreducible self, encompassing his streaks of disaffection and rebellion as well as his periods of compliance. The individual can more readily participate in transforming a social entity, making it closer to his image, than he can engage in a fully individualistic act. It is here that the idea of an individual activist, a fearless hero who masters his fate,[4] completely fails to grasp societal reality and fails to provide a viable alternative to totalitarianism. There simply are not enough Atlases on which to rest a socio-political theory. We concur here with Wolin:

> Kierkegaard's lonely, desperate "leap" to God, Nietzsche's solitary superman struggling against the toils of a mediocre bourgeois world, Sorel's "myth" of the spontaneous general strike by a proletariat welded to unity only by an heroic impulse—these were all last-ditch efforts to secure some place for unorganized individual action. They were last gasps of a romanticism to expire. . . ."[5]

There is, of course, much individualistic and detached intellectual activity, but social change is chiefly propelled by social selves, by acting collectivities.* Individuals participate, some even lead others, but the vehicle of change is a social grouping.

Active versus Passive

Social scientists have generally regarded social combinations in terms of two opposing modes of relating man to man; one in which man views man

---

* A deep tension between the Western tendency to stress individual autonomy and to recognize the social prerequisites of action runs through much of the writing on this subject. The following selection is rather typical in its attempt both to do justice to the facts of social life and to reflect the belief in individualism. "The individual is never wholly absorbed in his society, wholly responsive to it, wholly accounted for by it. . . . Even if he yearns for total absorption, total surrender, he never fully attains it. Unlike the cells of the organism, the individual is a self-directing unit, with some kind or degree of autonomy." Robert M. MacIver, *The Web of Government* (New York: The Free Press, 1965), p. 412. The effect of the passage is achieved by the words "wholly," "total," "fully," and "some kind or degree." They allow at one and the same time the recognition that there is little room for individualistic action (which is a widely recognized fact) and the implication that there is a capacity for individualistic action (which is a value of the author). The same passage, reporting the same facts but without the individualistic undertone, would read: The individual is almost completely absorbed in the society, responsive to it, and accounted for by it. . . . If he yearns to, he can achieve almost total absorption, etc. Later in the book (p. 413) the author stresses individual reflection—this, we hold, may be more autonomous than action but is of little sociological consequence unless it is translated into action, and this in turn must be social action.

as instrument, the other as purpose. But in both the *Gesellschaft* and the *Gemeinschaft* orientations which, behind various conceptual masks, have dominated the social sciences up to now,* the societal combination—as in our allegorical safe—is assumed to be set. Even the historical shift from one to the other is viewed, by and large, as given. Modernization is a recent example of the concept of social process as ongoing: something that happens; it cannot be halted.[6]

Our active–passive dimension cuts across these traditional social science categories. The active (or passive) social unit may be a community or an association. The distinction creates a new dimension in the most basic view of man in society: That of an actor standing above and beyond the ongoing processes and seeking to bring them under his scrutiny and control. *To be active is to be in charge;* to be passive is to be under control, be it of natural processes, of social waves and streams, or—of active others. To hold that the social self may be thought of as a self able to reset its own code is not to deny the significance of the *Gemeinschaft* and *Gesellschaft* tradition. The fact is, however, that social laws *can* be altered. It is here that we find the key to a secular conception of man—in the ability of men, by changing their social combinations, to change themselves, to be the creator.

The Components of the Active Orientation

A full measure of the active orientation cannot be attained by the unchecked restructuring of social patterns but by achieving a balanced combination of all its elements and by broadening the circle of those who share in the orientation. The active orientation has three major components: a self-conscious and knowing actor, one or more goals he is committed to realize, and access to levers (or power) that allow resetting of the social code. (We repeat that the active self as a rule is not an individual, since one man is

---

* The extent to which this dichotomy has dominated sociological thought is apparent when the pairs of contrasting terms used by various leading sociologists are listed next to each other. As is well known, it was mechanical and organic solidarity for Durkheim; organic and mechanic for Toennies; status and contract for Maine; community and society for MacIver; folk versus urban society for Redfield. In the works of many other anthropologists as well as sociologists the terms used are "primary" and "secondary" groups. In the sociology of organizations the dichotomy appears as formal versus informal. Much of the contrast made between traditional and modern societies has a similar connotation. Weber's bureaucratic or legal–rational society is *Gesellschaft* in a different garb. The root of Parsons' pattern-variables is in this tradition; universalism, specificity, neutrality, and so on, are the *Gesellschaft* side, while their opposition—particularism, diffuseness, affectivity, and so forth—represent the *Gemeinschaft*. "Note on *Gemeinschaft* and *Gesellschaft*," Talcott Parsons, *The Structure of Social Action* (New York: The Free Press, 1937), pp. 686–694. Expressive and instrumental phases, "warm" and "cool" relations, draw on this distinction, which in turn is probably a latter-day derivative of a tradition that opposed rational and non-rational modes of social conduct.

generally unable to transform collectivities, but a combination of persons who jointly activate their social grouping and thus alter their collective life and their individual selves.)

Without consciousness, the collective actor is unaware of his identity, his being acted upon, his ability to act, and his power; he is passive, like a sleeping giant. Without commitment to a purpose, action lacks direction and merely drifts.[7] Without power, the most incisive and sharply focused awareness or the firmest commitment will not yield more action than a derailed train.[8] To be active is to be aware, committed, and potent.

Freedom to act is not without constraints. *There is no action without counteraction*, and each generation's action faces the remains of earlier generations' failures as well as their successes. Social action often spells conflict, loss, and sorrow. Nor would an unrestrained action by any one actor do much more than reduce whatever safeguards there are against turning other actors—and the acting self—into instruments. The penalty for excessive action, whether it takes the form of collectivization, regimentation, or welfare-state paternalism, is not much lower than—and in some cases surpasses—that of inaction.

Constraints on action involve not only insufficient knowledge and awareness, slackening commitment, or failing power; they are, in part, self-imposed restraints because in each act the active self must balance potential cost against prospective gain and weigh the risks of misjudging one or both. A primary problem of modern society was precisely its failure to make such supervision of action coextensive with its capacity to act. Not the dearth of instruments but the paucity of guidance characterized modern society.

The active man is a self-restraining one; each of the components of the active orientation requires this. To know is to delay action until information is collected and processed. To be committed is to defer rewards in favor of higher realization of goals. To apply power for activation, we shall see, is to use it within limits determined by and in the service of shared values and not individually held ones. As each of these components conflicts somewhat with the others, restraint is also a prerequisite of a balanced combination. Nor are spontaneity and control necessarily opposed; a gain in authentic expression is often a gain in self-control, both for a person and for society.

The Rise of Social Options

In his pains to master his fate, man is reaching a new phase in which his ability to obtain freedom, as well as his ability to subjugate others, is greatly extended. Both of these build on his increasing capacity to transform social bonds rather than accommodate to, or merely protest, the social patterns he encounters. The post-modern period will be marked, in addition to a continued increase in the potency of instruments available and an exponential growth of knowledge, by man's potential ability to control both. An active society, one which realizes this potential, would differ most from modern societies in this key way: It would be a society in charge of itself rather than unstructured or restructured to suit the logic of instruments and the interplay of forces that they generate. Hence, while this study substantively focuses on the transition from modern to post-modern society and the conditions for the rise of an active society, formally, it seeks to develop a theory of societal self-control.

When society is made not only more malleable, but also more responsive to its members, it is made more receptive to its own values. There has never been a society that does not fall far short of its values. There is a universal, unbridgeable gap between societal ideals and the societal reality of vested interests, status constellations, and power politics. An increase in social malleability extends new opportunities for fuller realization of a society's values. Activating a society and heightening its responsiveness to its members are the most effective ways of assuring the use of the new options for realization of values rather than for further objectivization of social relations.

There are now fewer barriers confronting the social self in its self-oriented activity. The expansion of man's knowledge of himself and his power over himself is an expansion of his options, but this in itself does not guarantee a fuller realization of his multiple values. The expected unlocking of the biological code will impose a whole new set of options that may be used to curtail the freedom of man.[9] Additional advances in social engineering—such as chemical control of behavior, or wide-scale, effective, subliminal advertising, now in early experimental stages[10]—raise the possibility of man's reduction to a non-conscious, a-normative, passive object. They would provide, in addition to the option of undermining the objective basis of life (an option already generated by the natural sciences), the possibility of maintaining man as a physical and biological entity while entirely controlling his subjective faculties, i.e., completing the objectivization of his life. An increase in options is an expansion of the freedom to choose, but this includes the choice to destroy everything, even freedom itself.

The reduction of man uncovered by earlier generations in the realm of property relations, where improved capacity to produce was combined with the increased option to objectivize, was a forewarning of the potential cost that might be charged against an increase in social options. The claim that this early and relatively primitive objectivization would cease if control of the new means of production were turned over to the collectivity has proved false. Instead it was combined with greater objectivization in other realms as well as production. In all post-modern societies, the reduction of man is a multiple affliction, appearing in all societal sectors from education to politics. Hence activization, if it is to be effective, must be comprehensive; it must not promote progress (or the hope of progress) in one sector by adding to the objectivization of others.

Active is Public

If the new social options are to further the realization of values and not provide new means for their restriction, new energy must be injected into societal activities. Harnessing societal energy is the sociological equivalent of the physicists' harnessing of nuclear energy. Unleashed in an explosion, it becomes the most destructive force known. Released gradually and employed in man's service, it becomes a most potent tool. Latent in the societal molecules, the collectivities, is enough energy to achieve a broad realization of values. What should be studied are ways of mobilizing and channeling this latent energy.

Unlike the release of the energy locked in physical molecules, the release of social energy requires not the smashing of the unit but its transformation. On the one hand, the social unit has to be maintained, even strengthened, for we know that without these units, the individual's emotional stability, the pluralistic society's political effectiveness, and the foundations of cultural heterogeneity all are eroded. On the other hand, the social units can be active participants in a society only to the degree that they transform into public energy some of the energy they and their members generate in their private pursuits. True, to a significant degree social assets can be built up by member units seeking to attain their private goals, but expanding the scope of societal action demands public energy. (This includes not just economic assets, but also such factors as loyalties, time, and psychic energy.) Thus, the active society has written on its door the Greek motto: An idiot is a man who is completely private.

The active society would be closer than modern society to the city-state in the intensity and breadth of its political life. In the active society, as compared to a modern one, a higher ratio of assets would be invested in political action, and intellectual reflection would have a higher, more public status. The status of political and intellectual activity combined would approximate the status of economic processes in modern societies.

To be Active Is to be Responsive

In the realm of machines, there are two so-called revolutions: mechanization of work and mechanization of control of the machines that work. In the social realm, a similar, two-step development may be recognized. The first societal revolution came with the development of the corporation, or modern organization in general, which provided the sociological machine, the more effective way of "getting things done." The second societal revolution involves the control by second-order organizations of first-order organizations which do the work—in other words, the introduction of a comprehensive overlayer of societal guidance.

The cybernetic analogy has a basic limitation: The machines that are controlled have no political power and no ethical status. Societal guidance differs from the overlayer which automation imposes on machines in that it has itself two layers; control and responsiveness. One layer controls the member units, specifying their commitment to the values of society. The other layer's function is to insure the responsiveness of the control to the members of society. Weakness of the first layer causes drifting, with the society moving wherever the vectors of corporate ambition (or somnolence) push it; the weakness of the second layer implies either internal rigidities in the mechanism or subjugation of most members by some who monopolize access to societal control centers.

The multiplication of controls and an increase in their effectiveness need not imply that the active society will be one of prescriptive regulation. Additional control on one level might facilitate reduced control on another. Basically, if the societal overlayer is responsive to the membership, control need not be stringent. In that sense, the shift to an active society would be like the shift from coal to electricity as a source of energy; it would allow less concentration of the labor force "under one roof," as more work can be carried out in the natural social units. Similarly, greater responsiveness, with the qualifications spelled out below, entails reduction of both the corporate bodies' need to "make" people comply and the state's need to combat the consequences of alienation. There is, thus, an inverse relationship between alienation and responsiveness.

Providing the conditions for mobilization of its members (the other side of increased responsiveness), is to society what psychoanalysis is to a person. It is an attempt to unlock the combinations formed under the impact of past events, to remove distortions thus accumulated, and to make for a less costly accommodation to the environment. Such mobilization serves to increase spontaneity within the limits of the constraints of society in its particular historical stage.

The end of the quest for control of modernity comes into view as societal control gains in responsiveness. There can be little success in attempts to undo modernity itself; we cannot abolish science and we cannot return to a pre-nuclear or pre-industrial age any more than Adam could return the half-eaten apple to the tree of knowledge. Nor can one sustain any illusions about the happy craftsman in the medieval guild or the happy native in the bush.[11] And if given the option to return, most men would not.

Increased knowledge and consciousness, a deepening participation in the public sphere, a decline in the obsession with material assets and rewards, and growth in the effectiveness of societal controls—all these require a greater reliance on symbols and a smaller role for objects in societal life. This increased symbolization of societal processes, we shall see, makes society more malleable, more given to guidance and less given to objectivization. Further, the strains of scarcity can be reduced more readily, since symbols—unlike objects—can be given away and still be retained.

As the role of symbols and symbol processing would be much greater in an active society than in a modern one, understanding and improving the social units that specialize in the processing of symbols and their relations to the centers of control are integral parts of the analysis of and transition toward the active society. A study of the intellectual's place in the political process of post-modern societies, as well as a study of the regulation of scientific endeavor, can no longer be treated as an isolated subject, an exploration of a detached activity. The intensified effect of the natural and social sciences on society must find a corollary in an intensified study of societal guidance, if either science or society is to continue to evolve.

A Historical Perspective

A study of the active society must combine a contextual approach with a genetic one. In the contextual (or *gestalt*) approach, active societal units, their components, and their combinations are abstracted from any specific historical period. More active units are compared to less active ones. The relations among the components of the active orientation are related to each other in a theoretical model which may be applied to social units in different societies, cultures, and ages. There are, for instance, active units in any modern society, and one expects to find some passive ones in the more active societies.

But this also is a genetic study, one whose historical perspective is not modernization but the transition from the modern to the post-modern period. While there is a variety of modern societies, the values and institutions of all of them grant a high priority to the logic of instrumentality in the realms of production and administration, education and research. Similarly, although the post-modern period will surely know more than one type of society, due to various technological and intellectual advances all these societies will share in a much higher potential capacity to introduce societal control.

The advent of the post-modern period has been marked by the rapid rise of a new technology of knowledge, which serves data collection and analysis, simulation, and systems analysis. It has been said that the computer is to the production of knowledge what the steam engine was to production of materials.[12] This is a fair, only slightly exaggerated, comparison, even if one relies on more conservative estimates of computer capacities.[13] The exponential growth of social science has been illustrated by the often quoted statement that "90 to 95 per cent of all the behavioral scientists who ever lived are now alive."[14] In the first two decades of the post-modern period, investment in research and development has grown much more rapidly than GNP, especially in modernized countries.[15] The rapid construction of organizations specializing in the production and processing of knowledge is a post-modern parallel to economic development which characterized modernization. As a result, society has much more information about itself, a development which generates a whole new set of options for societal control, new decisions to be made, and a new range of processes to be guided.

Also growing is an awareness of the ability to restructure society and of how to go about it at a smaller societal cost. Western nations have gained confidence in their capacity to control societal processes with the wide use of Keynesian and other controls for preventing wild inflations and deep depressions and for spurring economic growth. Limited attempts to alter the distribution of wealth, to modify relationships among status groups such as races, to build up community bonds among nations, and to foster mental health, while all were much less successful, still constitute recent examples of the growing daring of Western social engineering. The more mature Communist nations, starting with an unrestrained optimism about their capacity to remake societies, have learned to conduct their transformation efforts more realistically and at less cost.

Whether this potential increase of societal control will be actualized, and above all, whether it will be accompanied by more authentic participation of a greater ratio of the members of society or a greater concentration of power in the hands of a few is much less evident. The transition to the post-modern period has begun; its continuation, barring a major nuclear war, is more or less a foregone conclusion. However, whether the societies of the post-modern period will realize the active option is difficult to foresee, and to what degree societal life will become distorted before the capacity for self-correction rises is hard to tell.

The "cyborg,"[16] a combination of a living organism with one or more mechanical systems, provides a core-image of an imbalance that the post-modern period inherited from its predecessor. Although a driver and a car constitute a very simple cyborg, the term specifically refers to more permanent and intimate combinations of man and machine, such as artificial lungs, hearts, and kidneys, which are provided by medical technology. These and other innovations are expected to extend and rejuvenate the life of the body. However, almost no progress is being made in developing an artificial brain. An old brain in a young body well symbolizes the end product of a period highly endowed with muscles but lagging in development of societal guidance.

We shall see that there are also significant imbalances in the development of the new capacities. The gap between information collection and analysis, for instance, seems large and expanding. The amount of well-analyzed societal information not "digested" by decision-makers seems also high. And well-informed decision-makers often seem quite unable to mobilize the members of society, while others are unresponsive to their needs. Thus, the new knowledge and increased capacity for control may be coupled either with inadequate political skill or with a political will that is too narrowly based.

This study focuses on ways in which the active society differs from non-active, post-modern societies as well as modern ones, provides indicators of a transition in an active direction, and suggests conditions under which this transition may be initiated, advanced, accelerated, or blocked.

To Transform is to Shift Boundaries

The transition from the modern to the post-modern period tends to be viewed as if the action unit will remain the same. But just as the transition from the medieval state to the modern one involved a change of actor from feudal manor to national state, so the transition to the post-modern age might well require a rise of a new action unit.

Deliberate fragmentation of society, favored by the neoanarchists, provides no solution to the problems of modernity or the new era.[17] Actually, some of our most burning problems emanate precisely from tribalism, which in both its primitive and modern forms tends to handle non-members not just as means (which, after all, command some respect, some maintenance) but as consumable, perishable objects.

Many values to which societies under study ascribe, especially stable peace, cannot be realized unless tribalism is superseded at least to a degree. Therefore, the drive to achieve fuller realization of values requires not just a change in the quality of society—an increase in the efficacy of control and responsiveness—but also a change in the boundaries of the units of control and of responsiveness. The national society, a concentration of societal guidance in the hands of a nation-state, is a limited historical phenomenon, not only because it was little known until three hundred years ago, but also because its decline seems already to have begun. In the post-modern period, marked changes in societies' boundaries for partial pooling of control activities are to be expected. Some of these changes have already taken place. More can be anticipated in the next generation, and still more, we shall see, can be brought about by an active society.

An intimate link exists between the nature of man and the nature of the social grouping which commands his prime loyalty and which is the center of his public life. As the illiterate man and his primitive tribe go hand in hand, as the warring knight can hardly be understood outside the context of many small, feuding fiefs, so the active citizen—conscious, engaged, and politically effective—can hardly be depicted outside an active society. Since the active society will be a post-nationalist one, the active citizen will be a cosmopolitan one.

The needs for higher levels of responsiveness and for more encompassing control units are related; earlier empires failed to provide for either and consequently foundered. Nor do contemporary quasi-empires fulfill this demand. Increased intra-unit responsiveness is required before inter-unit control overlayers can be unified sufficiently to provide more encompassing and viable communities. The frequent failure of attempts at unification in Latin America, Africa, the Middle East, and Eastern Europe illustrates this point.

Active for What?

When activation is elevated to an ideological level, there is a danger that it will become an unethical and an anti-intellectual force. Various fascist traditions, for instance, display an element of "act now, think later," a degradation of moral judgment and rational reflection in favor of "pure" drives. Mussolini said, "Fascism desires an active man, one engaged in activity with all his energies."[18] And his Minister of Education and chief fascist theoretician added, ". . . Fascism returns to the most rigorous meaning of Mazzini's 'Thought and Action,' whereby the two terms are so perfectly coincident that no thought has value which is not already expressed in action."[19] Nothing could be further from our concept of the active orientation. The active orientation contains as autonomous elements both normative and intellectual components: commitment and consciousness; these guide the third component, power. Dissociated from the first two, action becomes a blind, brute force, at best indiscriminate and at worst destructive.

We do maintain that action, guided by consciousness and the actor's values, has a value in itself. Even by the most technical sociological definitions, a commitment to a value that is not activating, which has no consequence in action, is really no commitment at all.[20] Students of ethics may debate whether or not hypocrisy, by reflecting at least verbal homage to a pretended value, indicates the existence of a normative commitment. But we shall see that inauthentic commitments more often stand in the way of an active society than outright rejection and alienation. Furthermore, action is a good indicator of what the commitments actually are; an actor faces many demands and many claims but it is his action which reveals to others, and often to himself, where he stands and for what he stands.[21]

The value of action stands out when its opposite—passivity, acquiescence, being acted upon without reacting—is explored. While complete passivity is rare, a high degree of inactivity is quite common in the period of mass persuasion, consumption obsession, and political inefficacy. The resurgence of autonomous reflection, normative concerns, and political potency, therefore, are the values of action and of activation.

Activation of self injects new energy into the pursuit of values; it is the opposite of lip service, of Sunday religion. It is true that mobilization of one side often triggers a counter-mobilization of the other.[22] Nevertheless, as we shall see, an active society, one in which all major groups actively participate in public life, is a society whose values are more fully realized than those of less active ones. This is because many values are inherently dependent on an active society in that they either assume community-wide participation as part of their very definition (political democracy, for example), or such participation is a prerequisite for their realization (as in the case of distributive justice).

The prominent position of the active orientation in our approach reflects our observation that most societies are short not on values but on their realization; most are committed, in one degree or another, to sets of values that few would seek to improve upon. The Soviet constitution, for example, lists many liberties, from freedom of religious worship to freedom of assembly, including even freedom of press and speech.[23] The American creed, as Myrdal points out, is quite egalitarian. What they tend to lack most is effectual commitment. The study of the active society is, therefore, the study of a society engaged in realizing *its* values and an exploration of the barriers which deter societies from realizing these values and investigating ways to accelerate their fulfillment.

One may point to racist South Africa or even Nazi Germany and ask what activation of their values would encourage. But no society is further from active than one whose structure is imposed on its members and that must build a wall or a war between itself and the outside world to maintain its stronghold. To be active is to be responsive, and an oppressive society is unresponsive by definition and hence reduces its members to passivity. While no existing society is fully responsive or free, and hence its full normative stature cannot be expected to be unveiled until it is fully activated, in those societies where there is a measure of responsiveness, it allows the values of the members to be expressed and built upon in a movement toward higher realization. By contrast, the values of the members of a tyrannical society are, in effect, unknown. The members of such a society, caught in a web of inauthentic mobilization in support of unethical positions, may seem to support its tyranny, but, as we shall argue in detail below, such mobilization tends to be relatively superficial and tenuous.*

Nor is there any other ground on which to answer the question "active for what?" than: for the uninhibited, authentic, educated expression of an unbounded membership. Other answers, from elitist to anarchistic, have, of course, been offered, but they all seem to us less adequate for reasons often cited. Our main concern here is consequently for the societal and political conditions under which history will be made more responsive to man, and not a search for new normative criteria to which history may be brought to respond.

Values and Structure

The dynamic study of the realization of values points to a comparative exploration of societal structures. Values not mediated through concrete social structures tend to become tenuous, frail, and, in the long run,

---

*We do not take here an optimistic view of human nature in the sense that were the members free to express themselves, they would seek only values of which we approve. But we expect that in a society which is responsive to its members and which uses its educational capacity, in the broadest sense of the term, to elevate their expressions of themselves, lies a possibility for fuller realization.

insupportable. Although verbal formulations may remain, authentic commitment is gradually eroded. To borrow a distinction, the loss of a visible community entails the loss of the invisible one. Thus, though every church might be torn down and new ones built, there is no escape from erecting edifices if values are to be served.[24]

The sociological question, therefore, is not *if* structures are necessary but *which* structures are necessary. An active society's reply is new; it does not involve escape from anomie or *Gesellschaft* into a pseudo-*Gemeinschaft* or "quest for community." The idea of community for community's sake is a retreat from engagement, consciousness, and effective action; a return to passivity is a trap into which many social movements have fallen. At the same time, the answer does not lie with those who are willing to sacrifice man on the altar of mankind and reduce him, through even deeper objectivization, in order to better serve "his" cause. The active society, the association of members who treat each other as goals and non-members as if they were members, offers a basis for social action in which values are realized without humanity being objectivized.

The foundation of the active orientation of a societal unit is neither metaphysical nor psychological but structural; we can point to sub-units, processes, and access to resources devoted to maintaining the orientation. Moreover, the tendency toward social entropy, the tendency to return to passivity, has a structural source: It intensifies when the investment in a unit's controlling overlayer is declining. Thus, the effort to activate, and, by implication, the quest for realization of values, is inevitably also an exploration of and search for an active structure.

A Dynamic Social Contract

While the active community subscribes to a social contract, it is not signed once-and-for-all to escape a natural state, nor does it entail the signatories' resignation to the political protectorate of the state or to a kind of Lockean passive tranquility. It is not a fixed agreement but one open to amendment, revision, and reformulation. The changing forces are the rise of new social groups out of passivity, the spread of consciousness, the expansion of social options, the growth in membership bound by a contract, and—most gradually we shall see—a decline in the emphasis on material wealth in favor of increased symbolization of society.

Social science came into being with the decline of the belief in a natural social order determined by a superior force, with the search for a secular explanation of societal structure. That is, structure was still largely viewed as given, for the artifacts of past actions seemed like parts of nature and the ebb and flow of historical tides appeared inevitable. Theories of action, on the other hand, ought to view the societal order as a flux, as a structure whose dynamics are to be understood *and* marshalled, as an organizational pattern.

In the process of societal activation, not only do more people gain a share in the society, thereby reconstituting its structure, but the members themselves are also transformed; they advance along with the society that they are changing. The dynamic relationship thus holds not just between rising groups and the establishment but between the personalities of yesterday and tomorrow, although in a narrow biological and historical sense these are the "same" persons.[25] Mankind is continually redefining itself, but this redefinition is tenuous unless it is recorded in social tablets. There is a need for dynamic interchange between personal self-realization and societal activation. A general will exists which, though not standing above the members, is not merely their reflection at each point in time. Members who are active change the societal structure, advance the general will, *and*, in turn, rely on the changed structure in advancing themselves. The social embodiment of values has an element of objectivization, but it also enables each member to lift himself. Human beings cannot reweave anew the normative fabric of society each morning; institutionalization is both inevitable and necessary. A delicate balance is required between a general will that is too weak to serve as a solid base for societal growth and one that is too powerful and unresponsive to the members' endeavors to introduce change.

The dynamic social contract thus stands between the chaotic state of nature and a stifling will imposed on the members, and its dynamic quality protects society from Lockean conservatism. For the active society, this spells a changing normative and political consensus, one whose growing value realization hinges on a continual interplay between members and structure.

A Role for Social Science

Knowledge of society in general and systematic verified knowledge in particular affect each of the components that constitute the active orientation. As a source of factual information and analytic perspective, social science is a part of the process that provides social units with consciousness. The effect of invalid information or faulty analysis is that consciousness will be misdirected or blurred or both.

As an intellectual process overlaying normative commitments, as a critical evaluator of existing social combinations, as an explorer of alternative combinations and their transformation, the social sciences are able to clarify basic commitments and to make them more realistic and, thus, more sustained. In this way, the social sciences may come to share in social activation. The weaker intellectually the social sciences and the more hidden or lacking their normative implications, the more utopian, erratic, and short-lived will be society's and their active orientation.

Finally, to know is to have power, and social knowledge is a source of power over society. The more malleable society becomes, and the more valid and comprehensive the social sciences become, the greater will be their potential power. It is for this reason that an active orientation among social scientists assumes increasing importance. The public status of social knowledge is only a partial safeguard against the possibility that social science will become a more and more potent tool of the few against the many, increasing the power of the mighty and the vulnerability of the weak. An active orientation of social scientists, while providing no guarantee that the social sciences will not be reduced to such a tool, is one safeguard against this contingency. Not only public availability but also what is being made available distinguishes between a tool which is useful chiefly for bureaucratic purposes and one that will contribute to any collectivity's efforts at self-realization.

One need not believe in the omnipotence of science or advocate social engineering to see that the social sciences have a growing part to play in societal activation and transformation. The question is how competent, public, and responsive to society and not just some of its members will be their use. That they will be used, and increasingly, is predetermined.

Seen from this viewpoint, ours is a study of the conditions, components and, above all, the dynamics of an active social self. Our perspective is that of a social self as an object of transformation (a common sociological tradition) *and* as a subject who maintains an active orientation (an important tradition of political science). Our study systematically combines these two perspectives: It is the exploration of a society that knows itself, is committed to moving toward a fuller realization of its values, that commands the levers such transformation requires, and is able to set limits on its capacity for self-alteration—lest it become self-mutilation. This would be an active society.

NOTES

1. For a typical though sophisticated expression of this view, see Johan Huizinga, "Naturbild und Geschichtsbild im Achtzehnten Jahrhundert," *Parerga* (Amsterdam: Pantheon-Verlag, 1945), pp. 149 ff.

2. Ernest Nagel, *The Structure of Science* (New York: Harcourt, Brace & World, 1961), pp. 378–379, 594–595, and Henri Poincaré, "The Evolution of Laws," in his *Mathematics and Science: Last Essays* (New York: Dover Publications, 1963), pp. 1–14, esp. pp. 13–14.

3. Reinhard Bendix refers to this as the "recruitment" problem. *Social Science and the Distrust of Reason* (Berkeley: University of California Press, 1951), p. 17. This criticism holds less for important segments of contemporary writings on psychoanalysis; see for instance Abraham H. Maslow, *Toward a Psychology of Being* (Princeton, N.J.: Van Nostrand, 1962), esp. pp. 168–205.

4. Karl R. Popper, *The Open Society and Its Enemies* (Princeton, N.J.: Princeton University Press, 1963), II, pp. 275–276. See also Ayn Rand, *Atlas Shrugged* (New York: Random House, 1957).

5. Sheldon S. Wolin, *Politics and Vision* (Boston: Little, Brown & Company, 1960), p. 423. Wolin adds, "Nowhere was the anguishing tension between the

world of organization and the creative individual more clearly revealed than in the thought of Max Weber."

6. The point was somewhat emphatically made by Sorokin: "Like a log on the brink of Niagara Falls, we are impelled by unforeseen and irresistible socio-cultural currents, helplessly drifting from one crisis and catastrophe to another." Pitirim A. Sorokin, *The Crisis of Our Age* (New York: E. P. Dutton & Co., 1941), p. 130. See also *Social and Cultural Dynamics* (New York: Bedminster Press, 1962), IV, p. 768. ". . . an argument against industrialization in general is now futile, for the world has firmly set its face toward the industrial society, and there is no turning back." Clark Kerr, John T. Dunlop, Frederick Harbison, Charles A. Myers, *Industrialism and Industrial Man* (New York: Oxford University Press, Galaxy Books, 1964), p. 15. ". . . I am firmly convinced that the democratic revolution which we are now beholding is an irresistible fact, against which it would be neither desirable nor prudent to contend, . . ." Alexis de Tocqueville, *Democracy in America* (New York: Vintage Books, Knopf, 1945), II, p. vi.

7. For a comparison of an active with a passive self, both lacking commitment (or, in the author's term, both "despairing" selves), see S. Kierkegaard, *The Sickness unto Death* (Princeton: Princeton University Press, 1941), pp. 410–413.

8. Everett W. Knight, *The Objective Society* (New York: Braziller, 1960), p. 45.

9. On recent developments see Theodosius Dobzhansky, "Changing Man," *Science*, Vol. 155, (27 January 1967), pp. 409–415; T. M. Sonneborn (ed.), *The Control of Human Heredity and Evolution* (New York: Macmillan, 1965); John A. Moore, *Ideas in Modern Biology* (Garden City, N.Y.: Natural History Press, 1965).

10. On subliminal advertising see Alvin W. Rose, "Motivational Research and Subliminal Advertising," *Social Research*, Vol. 25 (1958), pp. 271–284; Perrin Stryker, "Motivation Research," *Fortune*, Vol. 53 (June 1956), pp. 144–147; Ross Wilhelm, "Are Subliminal Commercials Bad?," *Michigan Business Review*, Vol. X (1958), pp. 26–29; Joseph H. Voor, "Subliminal Perception and Subception," *Journal of Psychology*, Vol. 41 (1956), pp. 437–458.

On chemical control of behavior, see an authoritative collection of essays, *The New Chemotherapy in Mental Illness*, edited by Hirsch L. Gordon (New York: Philosophical Library, 1958), especially essays by Harold E. Himwich and Edward B. Truitt, Jr.

11. For a study of what a day was like in the middle ages, see Peter Laslett, *The World We Have Lost* (New York: Charles Scribner's Sons, 1965). This book draws on a large number of new sources that came to light after 1959. See also Prosper Boissonade, *Life and Work in Medieval Europe* (New York: Harper & Row, 1964), pp. 102–118, 132–149; Henry Osborn Taylor, "The Spotted Actuality" in his *The Medieval Mind* (Cambridge, Mass.: Harvard University Press, 1959), I, pp. 487–509; Herbert J. Muller, *Uses of the Past* (New York: Oxford University Press, Galaxy Books, 1952), pp. 235–249.

12. Gilbert Burck, *The Computer Age and its Potential for Management* (New York: Harper & Row Torchbooks, 1965), pp. 1–2.

13. John T. Dunlop (ed.), *Automation and Technological Change* (Englewood Cliffs, N.J.: Prentice-Hall, 1962). See esp. chapters by Floyd C. Mann, Melvin Anshen, and Francis Bello.

14. Robert K. Merton, "The Mosaic of the Behavioral Sciences," in Bernard Berelson (ed.), *The Behavioral Sciences Today* (New York: Harper & Row, 1964),

p. 249. See also Derek J. Price, "The Exponential Curve of Science," *Discovery*, Vol. 17 (1956), pp. 240–243.

15. In 1945 the United States Gross National Product was $212 billion and expenditures for research and development totalled $1.520 billion. In 1964 the GNP was $628.7 billion whereas estimated funds for research and development were $18.780 billion. Thus whereas the GNP increased by less than three times, research and development grew more than twelve times. (Although funds are usually higher than expenditures, the difference is not large enough to affect our conclusion.) United States Bureau of the Census, *The Statistical Abstract of the United States: 1959* (Washington, D.C.: Government Printing Office, 1959), p. 495 and 1966, pp. 320, 322 and 543.

16. It is an "exogenously extended organizational complex functioning as an integrated homeostatic system unconsciously." This term was coined by Manfred E. Clynes and Nathan S. Kline. "Cyborgs and Space," *Astronautics*, Vol. 5 (1960), p. 27.

17. For this mood see Norman O. Brown, *Life Against Death* (Middletown, Conn.: Wesleyan University Press, 1959); Paul Goodman, *People or Personnel* (New York: Random House, 1963); and various essays in Paul Goodman (ed.), *The Seeds of Liberation* (New York: Braziller, 1965).

18. Mussolini, *The Doctrine of Fascism*, quoted in Carl Cohen, *Communism, Fascism, and Democracy* (New York: Random House, 1962), p. 350. See also Ernst Nolte, *Three Faces of Fascism* (New York: Holt, Rinehart & Winston, 1966).

19. Giovanni Gentile, *The Philosophic Basis of Fascism*, quoted in Cohen, *op. cit.*, p. 365.

20. Clyde Kluckhohn and others, "Values and Value-Orientations," in Talcott Parsons and Edward A. Shils (eds.), *Toward a General Theory of Action* (Cambridge, Mass.: Harvard University Press, 1952), p. 395. The study of attitudes has been criticized as incomplete, even misleading, unless attitudes, as predispositions to act, are compared to action.

21. This point is a central observation of Jean-Paul Sartre, *L'existentialisme est un Humanisme* (Paris: Nagel, 1960).

22. "Sides" here refers not just to various collectivities but also to various sides of a personal self. Nietzsche, who stressed the role of action in sustaining commitment, ties it too closely to facing an external adversary. See "Homer's Contest" in Walter A. Kaufmann (ed.), *The Portable Nietzsche* (New York: Viking Press, 1954), pp. 32–39. Albert Camus returns to this issue: "No" says the conqueror, "don't assume that because I love action I have had to forget how to think." *The Myth of Sisyphus and Other Essays* (New York: Vintage Books, 1955), p. 62.

23. Constitution of the USSR as amended by the Supreme Soviet on February 25, 1947.

24. Here lies one of the greatest shortcomings of neo-anarchist and some existentialist philosophies, in which "hell" is other people and social structure (or the "One") is necessarily inauthentic. See Martin Heidegger, *Sein und Zeit* (Tübingen: M. Niemeyer, 1957), pp. 61 ff. See also Ludwig Binswanger, *Being in the World*, Preface and Introduction by Jacob Needleman (New York: Basic Books, 1963), pp. 127–128.

25. Cf. Christian Bay, *The Structure of Freedom* (Stanford: Stanford University Press, 1958), p. 15.

PART ONE

FOUNDATIONS

FOR A THEORY OF

MACROSCOPIC ACTION

CHAPTER 2

The Realm of Action

and Its Laws

U NDERLYING ANY THEORY is a set of assumptions about the nature of the phenomena under study and their relation to the observing and reflecting mind. These assumptions may be implicit, vague, and eclectic, but they nevertheless affect the specific propositions advanced. Although this is not the place to present a philosophy of action, we shall briefly review the assumptions on which our theory of action is based.

Differential Malleability

Beyond the Antinomy of Idealism and Realism

The traditional dichotomy of Western philosophy between subject and object depicts a passive self. Philosophers have disputed the criteria for valid knowledge and debated whether or not the subject can know the objective world, but both the realist and idealist protagonists of this ontological and epistemological dispute have tended to view the subject as unable to alter the object.* Whatever the object is—a thing unto itself or sense data—it is treated as given. We may ignore it, we may misconceive it, but we cannot change it. For some, the God who molded the world also programmed the subject's ability to perceive it. Others have viewed man as an object among objects, a spirit among spirits, or an agent able to know others not by opening windows in his closed capsules but rather by studying its interior. Still, his capsule, as well as the others', is pre-designed. Even when to know good meant to do good, what there was to know and do was pre-arranged.

This traditional dichotomy has several important intellectual implications. By extricating the soul from the collapse of the body, it makes personal survival following bodily death understandable. It promotes various versions of ascetic morality such as inhibition and suppression of natural urges and, thus, won the endorsement of the mainstreams of both Christianity and Cartesian rationalism. Finally, it implies that the methods of inquiry applied to natural science cannot be applied to man and society; nature and society are two distinct and unbridgeable worlds.[1]†

The core problem for a philosophy of action is an explication of the capacity to act. To act requires some knowledge, but to know the world does not assume active participation in determining what the world is like. We, therefore, seek to account for the circumstances under which an actor can guide his own action, is blocked by past actions he cannot undo, and to account for the degree of his awareness of such barriers and of his relations to them. This is not just a socio-political question but also a more fundamental one of what the world is assumed to consist of and what, apart from any specific historical limitation, the basic limits of such a capacity to act might be.

Our starting point is a concept that cuts across the dichotomy of idealism versus realism, the concept of a controlled act. Our primary assumption is that there is an agent who can act in the world. We assume that this agent has a map of symbols that refers to a non-symbolic world, a map that is at

---

* Kantians may argue that although the "thing in itself" is forever unknowable, man, in perceiving an object, alters it. The alteration takes place internally—i.e., in the perceiver's consciousness—but nevertheless it reflects an active man. It seems to us that such an argument confuses the term "object" as referring to sense data with "object" as a mental construct. The latter "object" (or better, percept) is understood and analyzed sense data; that is, sense data carved out with the tools of our mind. The resulting conceptions in part reflect, to be sure, our faculties and dynamics. But sense data stripped of interpretation (which, paradoxically, we cannot experience but which we may be able to conceive analytically) are utterly given for the idealist disciples of Kant, and are the door to the thing-in-itself for his non-idealist followers—but that thing-in-itself in turn is given. Thus, by both Kantian schools, the world, whatever is meant by this term, is given. Moreover, man's faculties, the foundations of whatever activeness there is, are also viewed as completely given.

† Reference notes for this chapter appear on page 36.

least partly valid, and that his combinations of symbols (such as his *decisions* to act) affect the non-symbolic world. We further assume that he, in turn, is able to recognize the impact he has made—i.e., record it on his symbol map. Thus, this philosophy of action assumes an ability to move between the symbolic and the non-symbolic worlds. It makes its primary postulate the very transition that traditional Western philosophies find so difficult: from the *decision* to move to the *act* of moving; from the inner world to the outer one.[2] Our most basic unit, action, has elements of and consequences in both realms, though it is not coextensive with either.

For the philosophy of action, the concepts of social action—"we" and "they"—have the same stature as the "I" that is so central in the individualistic Cartesian tradition. Psychogenetically, all three concepts are learned from the socio-cultural environment, and which one is learned first depends on the particular culture. If there is any feature common to all human groupings, it seems likely that it is a sense of a "we" (for instance, in the mother–child relationship) which precedes that of an individualistic "I."[3] From an epistemological viewpoint, there is little reason to believe that we have a better or more valid insight into "I" than into "we"; both are abstractions.[4] Skinner has pointed out that when we "observe" our own private experience, we are primarily *talking* about such inner events. But we learn to talk about them by accepting, usually uncritically, the conventions of the language of those around us. So, in fact, we are still relying upon others' perceptions of our overt behavior and its observable antecedents when we first learn to describe our own inner experience.[5] We probably have at least as many misconceptions about ourselves as about others' selves, and while our intuitive sense of ego may be stronger than our sense of alter, the validity of this intuition is no more self-evident.

What is the importance of these or any other empirical observations for conclusions about the nature of man? First, such observations, especially anthropological ones, were and are used to support conflicting philosophical positions. Secondly, a philosophy whose conclusions conflict with empirical observations has at least some explaining to do. Thirdly, as we shall see, the primary sphere for action is found in societal projects, not personal ones. Hence, individualistic philosophies, which make an ego the primary unit of their systems, will not do as a basis for a study of action, and a corrective is needed. Martin Buber took a major step toward such a corrective in the statement that "I" and "Thou" are two poles of an interpersonal relation; without each other, they do not make sense even analytically.[6] In principle, the agent of our philosophy of action is, hence, not an individual or a collectivity but whatever the seat of action may be. Whether this is an "I" acting in its capacity as an integral part of an I–Thou relationship (and, hence, inevitably involving the other) or a more collective "We" is a secondary question. As long as we make action and actors our primary concepts, our approach is unmarred by the egocentric view of the world.

The Actor in the World

The capacity to act is the key assumption, the foundation, of our theoretical structure. In the following chapters, we inquire into the conditions under which action is more encompassing, effective, transforming; we explore the forces which constrict action and distort it. But throughout the work, we build on the assumption that action is possible, and, hence, that there is an element of choice which can be projected into our world.

The world, the sum total of all that is subject to action, is differentiated according to the degree to which it is responsive to action. We join those who have revived and revised the Aristotelian idea of arranging existences in a hierarchy with dead matter at the bottom, living matter metabolically interacting with the environment just above it, the moving, perceiving animal world next, and, finally, on top, man as the maker of symbols.[7] Each higher existence includes the lower one and is not exhausted by its distinguishing, "emergent" property. Man is, thus, the most encompassing being and has an existence on all levels.

We are dealing with these existences in terms of matter (dead or living), action, and symbols. The basis of our division is malleability, the differential ability of an actor to alter the varying patterns he encounters. Although we grant no special status to any one segment of the world, we expect some segments to be more malleable than others. Man seems most free to set and reset the combination of ideas and ideals, the relatively pure symbolic world, which is the least bound by sense data. He seems most limited in setting and resetting the laws of matter (or nature); not only can he more readily think about a horse with wings than produce one, but the laws of nature are immutable in a way that holds for no combination of symbols or social law.*

Finally, the realm of action itself seems to have an intermediary status between the realm of symbols and the realm of nature. Here, the actor faces the consequence of past actions which have been objectivized, often in the form of institutions, *as if* they were states of nature. But the patterns of action can be restructured—not as readily, it seems, as symbols but more readily than nature. Man can write laws; he commands the potential of social compliance—though rarely, if ever, can he achieve the complete compliance of social combinations with his laws. As he can change the laws of social "nature," he thus makes its study one that will never be completed.[8] *This*

---

* The above statements hold for combinations of concepts (in the realm of ideas) and for the revision of the rules governing such combinations. To emphasize the ability to reset these rules, various writers have compared the rules of mathematics to rules of games in which we try to play out our hand now by one set of rules and another time by a different one. Each of the three realms seems to contain some procedures that define the rules for setting rules; how these relate to each other and how relatively malleable are these procedures are questions that cannot be explored within the limits of this study.

order of relative malleability—symbols, action, objects—is a working assumption of our study.

A passive man or society may be said to be objectivized in the sense of being treated like an object. But even the most passive man retains at least some potential activation. He may, therefore, be object-like, but he is not an object as long as he is not dead.

Whereas the capacity to act is itself an inherent part of human potential, the extent of the capacity is historically bound. It changes with the actor's awareness of his capacity, with the scope and validity of his knowledge of the world, and with his power to modify both. In this respect, there appear to have been two historical, "secular"* trends since the rise of modernity. First, the scope of action seems to have grown at the expense of the two other realms; that is, more natural objects and more symbols have become subjects of action. Secondly, the pattern of action itself has become more changeable.

The three major disciplines of knowledge—the humanities, the social sciences, and the natural sciences—have arranged themselves roughly along the malleability differential. There seems also to be an association between the extent to which a sphere is active and the empirical validity of the discipline studying it. It is commonly accepted that the disciplines dealing with what we refer to here as the more malleable elements are less "scientific" than those dealing with the less malleable elements. This sometimes is regarded as a temporary difference, the implication being that once the social sciences have attained the same research investment in man-years as the natural sciences, they, too, will come of age scientifically. It follows, however, from the preceding line of analysis, that inherent differences in the subject matter of the three disciplines are likely to keep their scientific natures distinct even if investments were somehow to be equalized.

A confusion arises when the social sciences and the study of human behavior are conceived as coextensive. Man, unlike symbols and objects, is not limited to one segment of the world; he is not just the product or the creator of action. His unique characteristic is that he exists in all three realms and is subject to their respective dynamics. Hence, attempts to explain human behavior only through the sciences of objects[9] or as a symbolic process[10] are a priori segmental.

Insofar as we are dealing with a theory of the realm of action, we study man as an initiator of action, as an object of his action and that of other actors, and as subject to "objective" social processes. But this is not to deny the effect of processes of the other two realms on man in the third world, that of action. Indeed, most contemporary social science theories, reacting against earlier reductionism, have too narrowly limited the role of nature and

---

* Secular trends is used throughout this volume in the statistical sense to refer to trends which despite some "ups" and "downs" show a general tendency.

symbolic processes in shaping the realm of action. Under the influence of Max Weber, the independent role of symbols (especially ideas) has regained much recognition, but the role of nature usually is regarded as merely setting some very broad limits within which man is free to fix his social life according to his ideas and needs. Actually, there is growing evidence that behavior may be more specifically and to a far greater extent affected by biological and chemical factors than much theoretical writing in social science assumes.[11] If such factors are not studied here, this is not to imply that they are unimportant.

While some social science theories have neglected the effect of non-social factors on action, others make studies of the social behavior of animals a major source for the study of action.[12] Although man is not uniquely a social creature, action is uniquely a creation of man. Whatever other differences there are between men and animals, animal social life differs most significantly from man's precisely in terms of malleability, for the social structure of animal societies is largely inherited (i.e., given). Hence, in the study of human behavior, we focus on a distinctly human characteristic: malleable relations among actors; thus, the world of social *action* does require a distinct discipline.

The realm of action is broader than that of social action. In social action, both the actor and the object of his action are human; in other kinds of action, the actor is human but the object is not. But, as action toward non-human objects (material objects and symbols) is affected by the social relations among actors in much the same way as action whose objects are actors, we treat all these kinds of actions jointly as the realm of action or the social world.[13]

Symbolic and Mechanical Processes

Processes in each of the three realms are subject to different sets of laws which are related to the extent to which each realm is responsive to action. The basic contrast is between mechanistic laws that govern the relations among material objects and laws that govern the relations among symbols. To explore the difference between the two kinds of laws would take us far afield.[14] It suffices to say here that relations among symbols, such as in those in a mathematical equation, do not exist in space and time and, hence, are not affected by the constraints of space and by temporal processes that affect material objects. Relations among symbols are also free from scarcity, a central attribute of the world subject to mechanical logic. Symbols can be shared and retained; the teacher is not less knowledgeable after he "imparts" his knowledge to his class.

While symbols are not subject to mechanical laws, they are subject to some laws of their own. Internal consistency is probably the most important and evident of these. The numerous "laws" of mathematics and logic may be viewed as various elaborations on this most central rule of the symbolic world. We refer here not to a psychological need for consistency on the part of the person or persons who hold symbolic statements (a need that is in the third realm, the world of action), but to the relationship among the symbols themselves which can be characterized and rearranged, drawing on the laws of consistency intrinsic to the symbolic world.

The realm of action is one in which the laws of objects and of symbols are intertwined. In the realm of action, men relate through filters of symbols. In the realm of objects, men affect each other directly, as when air polluted by one is inhaled by another. In the realm of symbols, relations are almost as direct.* The relations of man to man in the realm of action (or social world) take place in accordance with an intertwined set of laws, the mechanic *and* the symbolic ones.

This statement, central to any action theory,[15] has been questioned from two sides. On the one hand, there are still those who seek to study human relations in the social realm as they study relations in nature—in a purely mechanistic way. This is to the logic of social science what biological and chemical reductionism are to social realism. Attempts at social and political application of mechanistic cybernetics are the most recent examples.[16] Actually, the cybernetic application has been to such a degree associated with the mechanistic view of man that the possibility of its integration into a philosophy of action, one that recognizes a realm subject to joint symbolic and mechanical explanation, has been ignored. Hence, one of the incidental effects of this volume may be to illustrate that a cybernetic theory need not be mechanistic. On the other hand, there are those who go to the opposite extreme, seeing little importance in the mechanical aspects of action and viewing interpretative explanations by the actor as the key variable. This is to the intertwined logic of social science what cultural reductionism is to the social realm. Such a symbolistic position is approximated by quite a few psychoanalytically oriented theoreticians and is still found among social scientists.

The varying positions toward the role of symbols can be illustrated by divergent interpretations given to a well-known statement by W. I. Thomas: "If men define situations as real, they are real in their consequences."[17] The statement has a certain ambiguity: Some give it a more symbolistic, others a more "objective" interpretation. According to a symbolistic view, the statement can be understood to suggest that what really is out there does not matter because the reaction (and the reaction to the reaction, hence

---

* While a symbol can be related directly to a symbol, like two notes in a tune, they always require an objective material carrier such as air waves or pages of a book. The carrier's importance, however, is small, as a symbolic relation can be readily transferred to another carrier with little alteration of its meaning and because the effects of a communication are largely determined by its substance rather than by the nature of the carrier.

all interaction) is determined by the interpretation of what is there. When a man approaches and extends his hand, a fellow man, in our culture, will shake it if he interprets this as a friendly gesture. He may run away if he views the same gesture as an attack. To stretch the point, a man may try to shake a hand even when none has been offered, as long as he defines the situation as one in which there is a hand out there trying to reach his.

Among the numerous sociologists who refer to Thomas' statement, several come close to such a symbolistic interpretation. For instance, two sociologists have stated:

> Human Behavior can be accounted for only in terms of interplay between attitudes and values . . . subjective desires are what usually determine the way in which (the) individual reacts to external influences.[18]

Another suggests that in Thomas' system

> . . . the subject may perceive a number of elements in a situation which cannot be demonstrated to exist scientifically; but if they exist subjectively, behavior will depend upon this version of the situation.[19]

The point these views have in common is that no direct effect of "reality" is explicitly recognized. It is not pointed out, for instance, that a locked jail door has social consequences no matter what meaning the inmates give the fact that the door does not open. In addition, the effect of objective factors on the interpretation is also not made explicit, as if the actor is equally free to impose any interpretation that he chooses (e.g., the door is really open, or being imprisoned is a widely recognized honor).

In contrast, the following treatment of the Thomas dictum takes into account both the symbolic and the mechanical aspects of action: "We may therefore conclude that if people define situations as real, whether or not they are, their behavior will be altered" (i.e., not determined, but affected by the interpretation); and, "we do not suggest, however, that a person's definition of the situation is totally unrelated to the reality of the situation."[20]

An actor may respond to "pure" symbols which have no natural base apart from their carrier. This could mean either that the symbol exists only in the actor's own mind, or that it is shared by at least some of the other actors in the given situation. Or an actor may respond to a symbol that has some objective correlative beyond its mere carrier. In the first case, only the interpretation applies; in the second, both symbolic and mechanical processes affect the action.[21]

An illustration may help to bring into relief this crucial distinction between symbolistic and social interaction. When forces of the Soviet Union shot down an American airplane in 1963 during a period of détente, the event had no effect on United States military or economic capabilities; and, though it occurred in the mechanical world in the sense that bullets ripped the plane, its socio-political consequences were completely dependent on the interpretation given the occurrence (i.e., on what normative symbol was assigned and how this symbol related to other symbols). In this case, the United States government and press first presented the incident as a violation of the détente spirit, which in itself was a symbolic state; later, the incident was reinterpreted as an "honest" mistake, and its effect on the détente was defused.[22] However, had Soviet forces destroyed on the same day four hundred American long-range missiles, the event—whatever the interpretation given to it—would have curtailed United States capacity to act in the world of objects. And, as is often the case when an "objective" change is involved, there would have been less leeway for interpretation, although the interpretation given would still have mattered. Thus, in the social realm, the logics of objects and of symbols are coeffective.

This is the point at which practically all sociological discussions end. But as our central interest is the malleability of the world of action, we must take the next step and ask: To what degree is the realm of action given? Where is it open to intervention? How do processes that are under the control of an actor differ from those that are ongoing?

The Capacity to Control

The Control of Action

The malleability of the world provides only a potential for action; it is the capacity of the actor in which the realization of potential is deposited. *Control is possible in principle because, on the one hand, the units of action, while they exist in the mechanical world, also respond to symbols.* It is as if each unit of action learned a code that enables it to respond to signals of a controlling agent. At the same time, this control is not exempt from mechanical laws.

Each of the basic elements of the control processes, which are also the components of the active orientation, has both mechanical and symbolic aspects. *Knowledge* is a set of symbols whose dynamics are subject to the laws of the symbolic world; at the same time, processing and using it incur costs in the mechanical world which are affected by developments in it. Costs are incurred, for instance, in the collecting, processing, storage, and application of information.

Commitments are "energized" symbols. They couple one or more sets of images (such as included in purposes) reflected in the messages carried by the communication networks of the committed unit, with an allocative pattern of its energy. This reveals an assignment of some of its energy to the realization or support of the images to which the unit is committed. The images come under the laws of the symbolic realm; the psychic, social, or other sources and forms of energy are subject to those of the mechanical realm.

Power includes one kind that is based on the manipulation of symbols to which the subjects are committed, while two other kinds are based on the exploitation of objects in the mechanical world, specifically the means of violence and material objects. Threats to use these two kinds of power are symbolic, but the capacity to threaten is related, however loosely, to their mechanical components.* To conclude that just because there is no one-to-one association between the symbolic and the non-symbolic aspects of power there is no association at all, or that in relations among actors power can be understood as either symbolic or mechanical, is to fail to understand the essence of control and action and, hence, of social and political reality.

We view processes in the world of action as divided into two basic kinds: those which control and those which are controlled.[23] This division is based on the central criterion of our approach to the study of action, the malleability differential. We suggest that controlling processes, as a whole, are more responsive to the laws of symbolic relations than controlled ones.

Beyond this primary division, a secondary one seems useful: a view of the controlling processes as an overlayer that rests on top of a controlled underlayer. We note that the two layers are not coextensive; some processes are uncontrolled. The ratio of those which are controlled to those which are not provides a crude measure of the degree to which a unit is controlled. We say "crude" because a fuller measure takes into account various attributes of the controlling overlayer itself.

The controlling overlayer consists of two major, analytically distinct segments. The first is composed of the *symbolic-control*† *processes* such as the processing of information, synthesis, and decision-making, all of which are explored below. These processes, if the dynamics of the carriers of symbols are disregarded, are subject to symbolic laws. The second major segment is composed of the *processes of implementation* which serve as a bridge between the symbolic-control processes and those being controlled, using both symbolic components (e.g., the communication of signals) and objects in the mechanical world (e.g., goods and services). Both provide "hooks" which the controlling overlayer implants in the controlled underlayer and which are used to guide it. To be able to direct, to guide, or to transform a controlled unit, the overlayer must have some means of reaching the unit, of transmitting its signals, of enforcing them if a response is not obtained, and of recording the effects of its efforts.[24]

The importance of all this for the active orientation is to emphasize that although the incomplete and often limited realization of values is in part the result of both natural and social environmental constraints, *it is in part determined by the degree and quality of the controlling overlayer of the acting unit.* True, control itself is not generated in a social vacuum: It is itself

---

* For a definition of power, a classification, and a fuller discussion of the points raised here, see below Chapters 13 and 14.

† There may also be symbolic processes that are under control or uncontrolled.

affected by environmental forces. The environment, however, is not impervious to the acting self; it is partly molded or chosen by it. Under any given set of environmental conditions, *actors differ significantly in their levels of self-control and realization, a fact attributable to factors and processes that are in part internally set.* This assumption of an actor who is in part free to formulate and implement his line of action in the social world is at the heart of our approach, and the theory which follows seems to us to suggest that it is a fruitful one.

Control of Controls

If the capacity to control assures a measure of activation, the development of this capacity greatly affects the extent, scope, and quality of activation. Man is not merely able to stand above the ongoing processes and review them, to choose between alternative courses of action and implement the choice. He also has the potential capacity to choose among criteria of choices, and to impose controls on controls.

Actually, we shall see that the controlling overlayer of social action may be split into more than two sub-layers: There can be a review of reviews of control, and so on. The number of sub-layers indicates the sophistication of the controlling overlayer. The limitation on the number of sub-layers of control of controls is practical, not theoretical. The level of activeness a social unit attains and the degree to which it realizes its values (as against the degree to which it helps to realize the values of other social units) are significantly affected not only by its total investment in control as against action, but also by the internal structure and quality of the controlling overlayer itself. To put it differently, *there is an association between the quality of a social unit's control and the degree to which it is subject to symbolic as opposed to mechanical logic.* All other things being equal, social units whose ratio of investment in control over action is the same but which have a more "sophisticated" controlling overlayer are freer to realize their values and less subject to their environment.

We say "all other things being equal" not only because differences in environment affect the utility of varying degrees of sophistication of controlling overlayers but, most of all, because differences in upward flows—from the membership of a social unit to its controlling overlayers—greatly affect the effectiveness of its control. To emphasize this point, we refer to the combined sources of social regulation and change, the downward and the upward flows, as social *guidance*, while we reserve the term social control for downward flows and consensus-formation for upward ones. While the distinction between control and consensus-formation is an analytic one, as no social unit has one without also having the other, the differences in the degree of the mix are most important for understanding social regulation and change.

The limit inherent in the concept of control is that it has costs in terms of both the energy its exercise drains from the ongoing action and that which is spent to realize its directives. As in the relations between superego and ego, activation is constricted not only because of lack of guidance, but also because of excessive control. Much of the following deals with specific control arrangements and compares their relative effectiveness. But these are all varying accommodations to the basic inherent limitation: As control gives form, it also eats into the substance.

Here is a basic difference between the social and natural worlds. Many contemporary social scientists, especially in the United States but increasingly in Western Europe, have argued that both worlds are subject to the same canons of science. While this may be valid on a high level of abstraction, it is not the case when the specific logic of each world is considered. The world of nature knows no split between review processes and those under review. It has no symbolic overlayer and no set of processes that guides another set toward realization of a state of affairs first formulated symbolically by the first set.

The fact of societal self-control cannot be understood in terms of mechanical logic because it cannot account for the formulation of basically new purposes, just as the laws of the symbolic realm cannot explain how new symbols affect processes in the world of objects. Both kinds of explanations must be drawn on simultaneously in order to analyze social processes.

This combination is a unique quality of the social realm and a unique subject of social science. Various positivist philosophers have argued that because a computer acts "reflectively" or has a consciousness, man, having similar qualities, can be fully explained in mechanical terms.[25] But the fact that man can construct a machine that acts on two levels—that is, controls itself—only suggests that the artifacts of social action are to be studied as following in part social logic rather than merely as aspects of the mechanical world. Man can introduce into the relations among objects some of his own capacity for symbolization and transcendence, a capacity not found in the physical and chemical worlds and present only in very rudimentary forms among the higher levels of animal life. Although the relations among objects can be "humanized" to a degree, this surely does not demonstrate that man is machine-like.

A Transcendental Capacity

Man as an active creature has a capacity to project himself into the future by projecting a future and by pulling himself toward it. In the process, he changes both his environment and himself. In this context, the term *transcendental* acquires a clear reference and becomes an integral part of a social science perspective. The processes that constitute a controlling overlayer can design a state before it exists and can attempt to bring about its realization. When the design is first formulated, it may have no more reality than a port marked on a map, and no more compelling power; still, once the image is set, it can be used to guide action toward it. Ultimately a ship may anchor at that port. Thus, we view all social units, not just organizations, as at least potentially commanding a controlling overlayer that can assist the unit to transcend itself.

Inherent in purposes are images of a future to which implementation processes are committed. We, thus, avoid the prevalent mistake of considering purposes as themselves future states of affairs, a line of reasoning which opens such an analysis to the positivist criticism that it can be conducted only in a *post hoc* fashion. Purposes are present and past commitments to images of a future. Whether or not these purposes will be realized depends on many other factors, but guiding images qualify as purposes whether or not they are realized. Hence, no knowledge of the future as it will actually be is assumed in this definition.[26]

Purposes, however, are not merely symbolic statements. Future images become purposes only when energy is committed to them, when the controlling overlayer "gears" a segment of the controlled processes to the realization of these images. In order to transcend itself, then, a social unit must have one or more images to whose realization it is actively committed.

These images may be of a changed environment, a different self, or both. In any event, a controlling overlayer that includes a symbolic component is assumed. Without it, a collectivity can neither form an image of what it is not, nor guide itself toward such an image. While all social units have at least a potential capacity to transcend themselves, far from all social units realize it, and among those which do, some transcend more than others. The more effective the control a social unit gains of its environment and of itself— the more transcendental it becomes—the more able it is to realize its future images.

The assumption of social units' ability to transcend themselves, we have seen, requires no assumption of any knowledge of the future. One can, however, add the notion of a degree of knowledge of the "real" future and still maintain an empirical conception of transcendence. Many actors set goals with some regard to the future as they expect it to be, and their expectations are partly based on valid information. In that sense, they anticipate the future, are able to orient themselves toward it, and use it in setting their purposes* and in moving toward them.

Introducing the setting of purposes and, hence, of values (one criterion for the selection of purposes) brings up another major connotation of the transcendental—namely, judging existing reality in terms of its complete form. Here, the transcendental tradition is associated with "negative"

---

* This entails their ability to take into account the effect of their action and transcending capacity on this future.

philosophy[27] which views reality as inferior in terms of unrealized, "pure" values. The prevailing reaction of social science in the West, following positivist philosophy, was to refrain from any systematic attempt to evaluate normatively social science data, and thus to forgo this aspect of transcendental analysis along with the others. It seems to us that transcendental judgments can be divested of the notion of an absolute set of values in terms of which social processes are to be judged; such values seem unavailable to most social scientists.[28] At the same time, relying for transcendental analysis on a particularistic set of values, that of one or a group of social scientists, is also to no avail because it tends to reduce sociology to an ideology. Still, we hold, a transcendental analysis can be conducted completely openly, building on the values to which the social unit under study is actively committed but disregarding the parochial, tribalistic limits within which it expresses them. Thus, for instance, a social scientist might well not have an absolute definition of justice and might refrain from using his own; it might, however, be induced from the societal concept of justice—not, let us say, the definition of it rendered by American Southern segregationalists, but rather the common concept which underlies their definition and that of other American collectivities, stripping it of the limitation to whites or Americans only. Universalizing the values of the subjects provides an Archimedial standpoint for a critical yet objective social science.

Manifest Goals

For the same reasons that it is fruitful to view social units as able to transcend themselves, it is also helpful to re-include *manifest purposes*, purposes the social actor himself is aware he is committed to, *as an explanatory principle* in the study of social and political processes. Actually, this line of analysis never was completely lost to sociology, but its theoretical legitimacy needs to be restored.

Studies which explain voting or purchasing behavior by the explanations provided by the respondents themselves, without probing into latent motivations, meanings, or predispositions, are part of the tradition of manifest analysis. The mark of these studies is not the use of manifest data itself, but the reliance, for analytic purposes, on factors of which the respondents are themselves aware. One well-known example of the use of such an approach is Weber's explanation of the formation and persistence of bureaucratic organization in terms of its efficiency.[29]

The rise and decline of this principle, we shall see, follows a "natural history" shared by several other key concepts in this work and hence deserves a brief comment. Explaining actions in terms of manifest purposes originally carried a heavy metaphysical baggage of teleology.[30] Purposes were viewed as having a reality and, above all, a force of their own. They were credited with the ability to compel imperfect forms of reality to move toward fuller realization, i.e., themselves. Sociology generally came to reject teleological explanations on the grounds that there is no evidence for the existence of such a force and that its assumption is not heuristically necessary. Instead, manifest functions were involved as consequences in ongoing systems of which the actor was aware[31] but not as images of a future state that he knows he is trying to bring about. Moreover, the main lines of sociological analysis focused on latent functions. Behavior that seemed irrational when examined on a manifest level was found to serve functions unbeknown to the actor. The attempt to move away from the obvious—i.e., what the respondents themselves knew—put a premium on latent analysis. For some social scientists, latent analysis served a debunking purpose; manifest reasons were challenged as concealing the true reasons. Consequently, the manifest category has fallen into almost complete disuse on the theoretical level. Our theory of action combines the two traditions, drawing on both latent and manifest analysis, without introducing the metaphysical overtones of earlier philosophies.*

Symbols, Objects, and Energy

In accounting for the capacity to act, we have drawn so far on the traditional conceptions of symbolic and mechanical laws, relating these concepts to the third, "mixed" realm of social action and within it, differentiating the controlling, controlled, and uncontrolled processes. We shall see below that it is fruitful, in addition, to draw on an energy model for the study of societal action, control, and change. Were the energy model merely a heuristic device, its ontological implications would be of little interest. But, as we shall see, the model works too well, is too isometric with our theory of action, to be treated simply as a convenient analogy.[32]

It should, hence, be noted that while we use here the language of symbols and objects, these have energy corollaries. Symbols gain a role in social action precisely because they are "energized"—command psychic and social resources, including control of objects. Objects, in turn, can be readily viewed as forms of stored energy which can be released and thus transformed into social action. (In the natural sciences, sub-atomic particles and electrons are concepts that remind us that the border between matter and energy may be much more fluid than we tend to assume.) We shall see below the

---

* We shall encounter this three-step development again: A concept takes on metaphysical overtones, it is rejected and falls into disuse, and then it is reintroduced without such overtones. A period of disuse is apparently needed to divest a concept of its original metaphysical assumptions. We might call the whole process a "divesting procedure." Here we attempted to divest "transcendental" and manifest categories of metaphysical overtones. The concept of "charisma" has already undergone this process and "national character" ought to be similarly divested of metaphysics and re-fused as a social science concept.

implications of this view for a theory of societal processes and political organization. Its relevance for the age-old controversies between materialism and idealism need not be pursued here; suffice it to state that the present study supports the proposition that there is a basic unity behind the varying manifestations. Concepts such as symbols and material objects are used because they refer to important differences in manifestation, which have properties of their own. That the underlying elements are identical explains—on the level of a principle, rather than as an *ad hoc* finding—why one manifestation which appears different from another may not be intrinsically so. Societal units, we shall see, may be viewed as containing an unprocessed energy; following activation, which entails the transformation of these units, this energy is available for kinetic usages, for societal action. The processed energy available to any one unit may be channeled (or committed) to alternative societal usages. Throughout this volume, cost is used to refer to loss of kinetic energy, the result of prolonged storage (i.e., inaction), flow to another unit, or consumption by alternative actions of the same units. Both the realization of societal goals and the activation of units consume energy; at the same time, one of the major goals to which energy can be committed is the attainment of additional resources from which energy can be derived, or to the change of existing patterns of allocation and thus to the shifting of commitment.

We have explicated the assumptions on which the capacity to act and to control rest, its differential character, and the key conceptions a theory of action and control can build upon. We turn now to ask: Who is the actor?

NOTES

1. See Stuart Hampshire, *Thought and Action* (New York: Viking Press, 1960), pp. 98–99. Gilbert Ryle, *Dilemmas* (Cambridge, Eng.: Cambridge University Press, 1954). For recent works that take a similar position, see Hans Jonas, *The Phenomenon of Life* (New York: Harper & Row, 1966) and Marjorie Grene, *The Knower and the Known* (London: Faber & Faber, Ltd., 1966).

2. This position is presented by Heidegger in his *Sein und Zeit, op. cit.* The traditional dilemma has not lost its fascination. See, for instance, Max Black, "Making Something Happen" in Sidney Hook (ed.), *Determinism and Freedom in the Age of Modern Science* (New York: New York University Press, 1958), esp. p. 15.

3. The absence of the notion of an autonomous individual among the Greeks is supported by the observation that they have no concept or word for privacy. Definition of self is made in terms of affiliation in membership groups. Ernestine Friedl, "The Role of Kinship in the Transmission of National Culture to Rural Villages in Mainland Greece," *American Anthropologist*, Vol. 61 (1959), p. 34. The Greek term *philotimo*, to experience oneself as a member of a group, has no English equivalent. See Dorothy Lee, "View of Self in Greek Culture," in her *Freedom and Culture* (Englewood Cliffs, N.J.: Prentice-Hall, 1959), pp. 141–143. Alvin W. Gouldner, *Enter Plato: Classical Greece and the Origins of Social Theory* (New

York: Basic Books, 1965), p. 347. See also J. L. Fischer, "Words for Self and Others in Some Japanese Families," *American Anthropologist*, Special Publication, Part 2, Vol. 66 (1964), pp. 115–126 and James H. S. Bossard, *The Sociology of Child Development* (New York: Harper & Row, 1948), pp. 35–40. A theoretical argument of why this might be the case was advanced by Talcott Parsons and Robert F Bales in *Family, Socialization and Interaction Process* (New York: Free Press, 1955), pp. 134 ff.

4. Cf. Stuart Rice, *Quantitative Methods in Politics* (New York: Knopf, 1928), pp. 19–24. See also C. H. Warriner, "Groups are Real: A Reaffirmation," *American Sociological Review*, Vol. 21 (1956), pp. 549–554.

5. These points, made in the works of both G. H. Mead and Jean Piaget, were recently stressed by B. F. Skinner in his "Behaviorism at Fifty," *Science*, Vol. 140 (1963), pp. 951–958, esp. p. 956.

6. Martin Buber, *I and Thou, op. cit.* Mead stresses in his four books the centrality of the act, and sees both the "I" and consciousness as emerging from social communication.

7. See Hans Jonas, *The Phenomenon of Life, op. cit.*, pp. 157–175, and Jacob Bronowski, *The Identity of Man* (Garden City, N.Y.: Natural History Press, 1965).

8. Durkheim suggested in his early writings that social reality is as constraining as physical reality. Emile Durkheim, *De la Division du Travail Social* (Paris: Alcan, 1926), p. 335 f. On this point see Edward A. Tiryakian, *Sociologism and Existentialism* (Englewood Cliffs, N.J.: Prentice-Hall, 1962), p. 22. In his later work Durkheim recognized the greater flexibility of social constraints. *The Elementary Forms of Religious Life* (New York: Free Press, 1965). On this point see Talcott Parsons, *The Structure of Social Action* (New York: Free Press, 1949), pp. 378–390.

9. For mechanistic theories of human behavior see the writings of such behaviorists as John B. Watson, *Behaviorism* (Chicago: University of Chicago Press, 1960), and Paul Edwards, "Hard and Soft Determinism," in Hook, *Determinism and Freedom . . . , op. cit.*, pp. 104–143. For one of the most explicit presentations of the underlying assumptions, see Albert Paul Weiss, *A Theoretical Basis of Human Behavior* (Columbus, Ohio: R. G. Adams & Co., 1925).

10. " 'Social systems' are essentially *symbolic* systems, or what I have called elsewhere 'eiconic' systems" (quotation marks in original). Kenneth E. Boulding, "Political Implications of General Systems Research," *General Systems Yearbook*, Vol. 6 (1961), p. 2. The major contemporary sociologist whose basic approach is emanationist and idealistic is Pitirim A. Sorokin. Among contemporary political scientists, see Murray Edelman, *The Symbolic Use of Politics* (Urbana, Ill.: University of Illinois Press, 1964). For other "symbolistic" works, see Kenneth Burke, *Permanence and Change*, 2nd edition (Los Altos, Calif.: Hermes, 1954). Burke was much influenced by the works of Edward Sapir and I. A. Richards. For a recent review work along this tradition, see Hugh Dalziel Duncan, *Communication and Social Order* (New York: Bedminster Press, 1962). See also Alfred North Whitehead, *Symbolism, Its Meaning and Effect* (New York: Macmillan, 1927).

11. On this point see Bruce K. Eckland, "Genetics and Sociology: A Reconsideration," *American Sociological Review*, Vol. 32 (1967), pp. 173–194. A sample of recent findings illustrates this general point: Persons who undergo heart

surgery frequently experience temporary insanity while recovering. Thirty cases of mental derangement were reported from among 79 adults who had undergone such surgery between January, 1962 and June, 1965. See Donald S. Kornfeld, Sheldon Zimberg, and James R. Malm, "Psychiatric Complications of Open-Heart Surgery," *New England Journal of Medicine*, Vol. 273 (August 5, 1965), pp. 287–292. Wagner H. Bridger found significant character differences among 300 newborn babies he studied. "Individual differences in behavior and autonomic activity in newborn infants," paper presented at the ninety-second meeting of the American Public Health Association, New York City, October, 1964. See also Wagner H. Bridger and Morton F. Reiser, "Psychophysiologic Studies of the Neonate: An Approach Toward the Methodological and Theoretical Problems Involved," in *Psychosomatic Medicine*, New Series Vol. 21 (1959), pp. 265–276. For a case study of mental illness caused by a metabolic disorder, see Ida Macalpine and Richard Hunter, "The 'Insanity' of King George III: A Classic Case of Porphyria," *British Medical Journal*, Vol. 1 (1966), pp. 65–71. See William E. Bunney, Jr. and John M. Davis, "Bireoubephrine in Depressive Reactions," *Archives of General Psychiatry*, Vol. 13 (1965), pp. 484–494. On the renewed interest in physiology since about 1950, see Ernest R. Hilgard in Berelson (ed.), *The Behavioral Sciences Today*, *op. cit.*, p. 44. For discussion of biochemistry and generation of mental disease, see Part II of Don D. Jackson, *The Etiology of Schizophrenia* (New York: Basic Books, 1960).

12. The prevalence of animal studies in some branches of psychology needs no documentation. For recent non-psychological studies see William Etkin (ed.), *Social Behavior and Organization Among Vertebrates* (Chicago: University of Chicago Press, 1964), especially articles by F. A. Beach, "Biological Bases for Reproductive Behavior," pp. 117–142, and N. Tinbergen, "The Evolution of Signaling Devices," pp. 206–230. See also Irven DeVore (ed.), *Primate Behavior: Field Studies of Monkeys and Apes* (New York: Holt, Rinehart & Winston, 1965).

13. On the same point, stressing the difference between meaningful behavior (action) and other behavior, see Max Weber, *The Theory of Economic and Social Organization*, trans. by A. M. Henderson and Talcott Parsons (New York: Free Press, 1947), pp. 110–117. See also Lester F. Ward, *Dynamic Sociology* (New York: Appleton-Century-Crofts, Inc., 1883), Vol. II, pp. 376–385.

14. On this difference see Pitirim A. Sorokin, *Social and Cultural Mobility* (New York: Free Press, 1937), Vol. II, p. 258. See also pp. 3–60. For a recent discussion of the two kinds of laws, see E. F. O'Doherty, "Logic of the Social Sciences," *The Sociological Review*, New Series, Vol. 1 (1953), pp. 49–64. Morris R. Cohen, in arguing "that when A is the cause of B, A is also a means of bringing about B as an end," points out that man can be conceived as subject to two different kinds of dynamics. *Reason and Nature*, rev. ed. (New York: Free Press, 1953), p. 342. But note that his second, non-mechanic dynamics differs from that of a theory of action. It is transcendental in the traditional sense of the term. For a less traditional use of the concept, see pp. 120–122 below. On the nature of social laws, Sidney Hook, *The Hero in History* (New York: John Day, 1943), pp. 250–259.

15. Here we take as our starting point the tradition social science most owes to Max Weber. See *The Theory of Social and Economic Organization*, *op. cit.*, p. 88, *passim*. Alfred Schutz, *Der sinnhafte aufban der sozialen Welt* (Wien: Springer Verlag, 1932).

16. "The cybernetical model reduces animal nature to the two terms of sentience and motility. . . . A feedback mechanism may be going, or may be at rest: in either state the machine exists." Jonas, *Phenomenon of Life, op. cit.*, p. 126. See also H. C. Rieger, "The Mechanics of Bureaucracy: An Essay in Social Cybernetics," *The Indian Journal of Public Administration*, Vol. 12 (1966), pp. 175–194, esp. p. 184; and G. A. Miller, E. Galanter, K. H. Pribram, *Plans and the Structure of Behavior* (New York: Holt, Rinehart, & Winston, 1960).

17. William I. Thomas and Dorothy S. Thomas, *The Child in America: Behavioral Problems and Programs* (New York: Knopf, 1928), p. 572.

18. Meyer Weinberg and Oscar E. Shabat, *Society and Man* (Englewood Cliffs, N.J.: Prentice-Hall, 1956), p. 188.

19. Edmund H. Volkart, *Social Behavior and Personality: Contributions of W. I. Thomas to Theory and Social Research* (New York: Social Science Research Council, 1951), p. 14; see also p. 5. "It was no longer what actually existed that seemed most important: it was what men thought existed." H. Stuart Hughes, *Consciousness and Society* (New York: Knopf, 1958), p. 66. Thomas D. Eliot paraphrases the dictum as follows: "The way in which people define situations determine their attitudes, their conception of their roles, and therefore their acts under the given conditions." See his "A Criminological Approach to the Social Control of International Aggressions," *American Journal of Sociology*, Vol. 58 (1953), p. 513. A "modernization" and further popularization of Thomas' thesis in a symbolistic interpretation is found in the work of Marshall McLuhan, who sees man as creating communicative tools and thus defining the environment, his perception, and through them, himself. *Understanding Media: The Extensions of Man* (New York: McGraw-Hill, 1964).

20. Alvin W. and Helen P. Gouldner, *Modern Sociology* (New York: Harcourt, Brace & World, 1963), p. 555. See also Margaret W. Vine, *An Introduction to Sociological Theory* (New York: Longmans, Green & Co., 1959).

21. For additional discussion, see below, pp. 332–342.

22. Amitai Etzioni, "Anatomy of an Incident," *Columbia Journalism Review*, Vol. 3 (1964), pp. 27–31.

23. The concept of control may well one day provide the elusive key to a unified behavioral science. Clark Kerr, drawing on his contact with a large variety of disciplines, pointed to its pivotal position. See his *The Uses of the University* (Cambridge, Mass.: Harvard University Press, 1964), pp. 119–120. On its rising role in biology, see Sonneborn, *The Control of Human Heredity and Evolution, op. cit.*

24. Note that we are dealing here with the control of action processes. When the controlled processes are those of machines, chemical processes, or symbolic processes such as the work of a computer, the relative weight of mechanical and symbolic components in the controlling process is different.

25. On this issue see Kenneth M. Sayre and Frederick J. Crosson (eds.,) *The Modeling of the Mind: Computers and Intelligence* (Notre Dame, Indiana: University of Notre Dame Press, 1963), esp. Michael Scriven, "The Mechanical Concept of Mind," pp. 243–254. In a "postscript" the author argues that computers are "in fact" conscious. John Lucas argues for the other side, that there is a difference in principle, in his "Minds, Machines, and Gödel," *op. cit.*, pp. 255–271. Alan Gauld, "Could a Machine Perceive?," *British Journal for the Philosophy of Science*, Vol. 17 (1966), pp. 44–58.

26. Georges Sorel, *Reflections on Violence*, trans. by T. E. Hulme (London: George Allen & Unwin Ltd., 1915), pp. 136 ff.

27. See Herbert Marcuse, *Reason and Revolution* (Boston, Mass.: Beacon Press, 1960), p. 26.

28. Leo Strauss is an exception. See his *Natural Right and History* (Chicago: University of Chicago Press, 1953).

29. Weber, *The Theory of Economic and Social Organization, op. cit.*, p. 337. This observation of Weber's position was made by Alvin W. Gouldner, *Patterns of Industrial Bureaucracy* (New York: Free Press, 1954), p. 25. Gouldner himself studies chiefly the latent functions.

30. On teleology, see Ward, *Dynamic Sociology, op. cit.*, Vol. 2, Chapter XI, esp. p. 100.

31. See Robert K. Merton, *Social Theory and Social Structure*, rev. ed. (New York: Free Press, 1957), p. 51. Manifest functions are discussed as including subjective motivations, needs, *and* purposes; *op. cit.*, pp. 61 ff. For our purposes, it is useful to treat manifest purposes as a distinct category. See also Dorothy M. Emmet, *Function, Purpose, and Powers* (New York: St. Martin's Press, 1958), pp. 107–108.

32. Elizabeth Duffy's *Activation and Behavior* (New York: Wiley & Sons, 1962) contains propositions, expressed in terms of physiological variables, which are isometric to several of the key propositions present in Chapter 15 of this book, expressed in terms of macro-sociological variables.

CHAPTER 3

The Languages of Societal Analysis:

Methodological Assumptions

MUCH OF HISTORY is a story of the games and fights of social giants, and much of what society is reflects their doings. Armies and churches, tribes and classes, these are the actors of the social world. To understand history or society, these giants and their interaction must be studied. An analytic approach that is confined to an atomistic exploration of these actors would contain only a fragment of reality. This is not to say that macroscopic analysis can afford to ignore the advances made by modern social science, which are often microscopic in orientation, nor that it should revert to the vague, ideological, often untestable, grand "theories" of pre-sociological ages. What is wanted, rather, is an expansion of the scope of general theory and the addition of a new subdiscipline—macro-sociology—which would focus on societies, their components, and their changing combinations in the way micro-sociology specializes in studying relations within small groups. This and the following chapter deal respectively with the methodological and substantive assumptions of such a macro-sociology. We deal here with languages in which divergent theories could be formulated employing the same sets of assumptions. Our specification of these assumptions into a distinct theory of macro-sociology begins in Chapter 5.

The claim that a distinct theory for macroscopic analysis is needed has often been challenged; therefore, we shall proceed step by step to support this claim. It might be argued simply on pragmatic grounds that such an addition is fruitful, but more needs to be said about what we mean by fruitfulness. A second line of support draws on formal logic, specifically on the relations among units, variables, and emergent properties. Exploring these first briefly will allow us in the following section to treat formally both the differences between micro- and macro-analysis and their relationship to analytic frameworks that explain social data by non-social theories, especially those of personality. (Readers who are not interested in methodological formalities or who are already in agreement that macro-sociology is needed may do well to turn to the next chapter.)

Some Preliminary Considerations

The Test of Fruitfulness

Theory construction is a process in which concrete data are "broken down" into abstract components and reintegrated on still more abstract levels. While analysis and synthesis are universal features of theory-building, the number of tiers among which analysis and synthesis are spread differs significantly. Much arbitrariness seems justified both in selecting tiers and in fixing the divisions between them; they need only be consistent with each other—i.e., what is defined as being on one level must not be defined in the same theory as being on another.*

The relativity of the framework is inevitable. What in one theory is part of the definition of a concept (lower tier) may be conceived as an independent factor (higher tier) in another. A high degree of face-to-face communication, for example, is sometimes seen as a defining characteristic of small groups. In some other theoretical work, however, it is viewed as a factor in group formation. This is quite proper, so long as face-to-face communication is not used both ways in the same theory. Ultimately, though, the arbitrariness of theory construction is limited by the theory's usefulness in explaining empirical data; some divisions are more fruitful than others.

The criterion of fruitfulness, however, is in itself somewhat arbitrary. One might view a productive theory as one that helps to explain a body of data. But the procedures for measuring the degree of "fit" between theory and data are not beyond controversy, and the body of data against which a

---

* In addition, it seems advisable that definitions should not violate disciplinary traditions unless there is a strong and demonstrable reason. Otherwise communication within a discipline is unnecessarily hampered.

theory is tested is often redefined when the theory runs into difficulties in explaining the data. This is like an airline that claims its flights usually arrive "on time" but changes the expected time of arrival when they are delayed. Thus, one might set out to formulate a general sociological theory but test it on nothing more complex than small groups, or one might build a decision-making theory that will account mainly for routine decisions and define all the many categories of decisions the theory does not fit as non-routine.* The test of the fruitfulness of a macro-sociological or political theory is how well it explains the main variance in the data about societies, their chronologies, their relations to each other and to their component parts. Theories that do less may be internally consistent and empirically valid but they are not fruitful and therefore are irrelevant.

Levels of Analysis, Units, and Variables

The main division of theory drawn upon here is a simple one between lower and higher levels of abstraction. *Units* of analysis are on lower levels; variables which characterize these units or their combinations are on higher ones. For example, a group is a unit; integration is a variable. It should be emphasized that the lower levels of analysis, as well as the higher ones, are constructs. The units are more "real" than the variables only insofar as they are *relatively* more concrete, but they are not found in nature any more than are the variables. Theory construction proceeds by projecting higher levels onto lower ones (e.g., groups are characterized as more or less integrated) and by systematically advancing propositions about the relations among units or among variables.

For much of the contemporary theoretical work in sociology and social anthropology, *role* is the basic unit; personality and group are viewed as combinations of roles.[1]† Many writers, however, argue or assume that

---

* "The sort of simple, explicit model which operations researchers are so proficient in using can certainly reflect most of the significant factors influencing traffic control on the George Washington Bridge, but the proportion of the relevant reality which we can represent by any such model or models in studying, say, a major foreign-policy decision, appears to be almost trivial." Charles Hitch, "Operations Research and National Planning—A Dissent," *Operations Research*, Vol. 5 (1957), p. 718.

Occasionally, the theory turns out to work well for an important *sub-category* of the body of data, which can be delineated. In that case the theory's power is actually high, and only the claim for generality is weak. Some theorems of contemporary economics are a case in point; they are said to work well for "the economies of all but developing nations." See, for instance, Dudley Seers, "The Limitations of the Special Case," *Bulletin of the Oxford University Institute of Economics and Statistics*, Vol. 25 (1963), pp. 77–98. Then too as we attempted to show in an earlier publication, much of organizational theory applies well only to highly bureaucratized organizations. *A Comparative Analysis of Complex Organizations, op. cit.*, pp. 23–27.

† Reference notes for this chapter appear on page 56.

groups are less real than individuals, thus implying that theories should use individuals as the primary unit.[2] For us, groups and personalities are equally analytic; both are conceptual abstractions from sense data about behavior. For example, in the case of a white man striking a Negro, this behavior in itself is not more individual than it is social, or more psychological than it is sociological. Such observable items are broken into various components merely for purposes of analysis. We might be interested in whether or not these actors are members of the same group, or in the effect of this behavior on some aspect of their personalities. The empirical and conceptual procedures we will use to examine both kinds of questions are basically the same. Personality has no privileged status.[3]

Moreover, it has proved useful to view the same item of behavior from both sociological and psychological perspectives with each accounting for part of the variance in the actual behavior. Single items of behavior having proven too small to use as the basic unit for most analytic purposes, clusters of behaviors are used instead and are referred to as roles.[4] Roles are combined into personalities and into social units; i.e., each role can be studied as a component of both. All those roles carried out by one biological actor constitute a "personality"; the combination of complementary roles carried out by two or more such actors make up a social unit.[5]

In both personalities and social units there is, in addition to roles, some non-institutionalized behavior, a "free-floating" psychic or social energy.[6] The scope of this behavior is small in well integrated societies. It is greater in anomic societies, in periods of crisis, and for persons whose socialization has been defective or is incomplete.

To conceive of an *individual* as a member of a social group gives priority to the concept of the individual and makes the social group a second-order concept.[7] This makes little sense from the viewpoint of role-theory. Members of groups are "segments" of individuals or roles. Similarly, the personality is composed of the same "segments." Thus, both concepts are of the same order of abstraction, and role—not the individual—is the basic unit.

Viewing a person as an abstraction runs counter to commonsense notions that associate personality with the biological individual and, hence, view a person as more concrete than a group.[8] Actually, there is nothing especially abstract about a concept of a role; it is well-anchored in empirical observation: We do not encounter an "individual"; we meet only segments of persons. We are never introduced to John Doe as a totality but rather to a co-worker, a new neighbor, or a fellow commuter. When we get to know John Doe—after we have been exposed to several segments of his personality, as we learn about his other roles or see him in several of them—we piece together an image of him as a person. First, though, we know him in a role and not as a man. Thus, the concept of role is less an artificial construct and has more direct empirical anchoring than is often recognized.

For the purposes of our analysis, one other basic concept is needed along with role, personality, and social unit, that of control. We defined control as the process of specifying preferred states of affairs and revising ongoing processes so as to move in the direction of these preferred states. As the theory is developed in later chapters, variables are introduced to characterize these processes.

Emergent Properties

Variables, it is widely recognized, may be properties either of units or of their relations. For example, a group may be highly integrated internally, but its level of integration with other groups may be low. Beyond this elementary distinction, it is often useful to distinguish between units, sub-units, and supra-units. Each of these entities displays properties of its own and of its relations with other entities on the same level (e.g., one supra-unit to another), as well as with entities on different levels. The properties of atoms and of inter-atom relations are on one level—those of molecules are on another. The properties added (or removed) by a transition from one level to another are "emergent properties" from the viewpoint of the other level.[9] The transition from role analysis to group analysis illustrates this point. Assume that we are studying marriage compatibility. We may study the role of wife (or husband) internally: How compatible are various segments of the role? Or, externally, what is the degree of articulation between the two marital roles; e.g., how compatible are the expectations the husband has of his wife with her expectations of him? All this, however, still amounts to the study of the properties of roles and inter-role relations; it is not an analysis of the family as a social group or supra-unit. We shift our theoretical focus from a unit to a supra-unit when we view the family not as a mere combination of roles, but as an entity having a structure and processes of its own. The added variables that characterize the family per se, such as having a democratic or authoritarian structure, are emergent properties.*

We refer to the properties of the relationships between two or more units on the same level—e.g., two sub-units or two units—as *inter-unit* variables; and to the properties of inter-level relations, such as between a unit and a sub-unit or a supra-unit and a unit, as *hierarchical* variables. The key difference between them is that inter-unit variables do not assume that the elements are "within" each other, and, hence, as between two groups, their

---

* Thus, we answer in the affirmative "the controversial question . . . whether there are attributes of groups not definable in terms of either the behavior of the individuals composing the group or the relations between these individuals or both." May Brodbeck, "Methodological Individualisms: Definition and Reduction," *Philosophy of Science*, Vol. 25 (1958), p. 2. For one of the best recent treatments of micro-theory see Joseph Berger, Bernard P. Cohen, J. Laurie Snell, and Morris Zelditch, Jr., *Types of Formalization in Small-Group Research* (Boston: Houghton Mifflin, 1962).

relations are external. Hierarchical variables, on the other hand, take the opposite tack—relations are internal with one entity encompassing the other.

While one might treat both relationships in terms of exchange or input–output, disregarding the differences between inter-unit and hierarchical contexts entails overlooking essential differences in the nature of these exchanges. How great the omission is depends on the specific use the entities make of their boundaries, especially how much of a barrier these boundaries are made to be. We shall have a chance to deal with such thresholds below when we explore mechanisms of control and processes of integration. Suffice it to say that the actions of a unit in isolation are not identical with those of a unit that is a member of a supra-unit. The latter is less autonomous in the methodological sense of the term; its properties account for less of the variance of the action under study. The properties of the supra-units set limits

INTER-UNIT RELATIONS   HIERARCHICAL RELATIONS

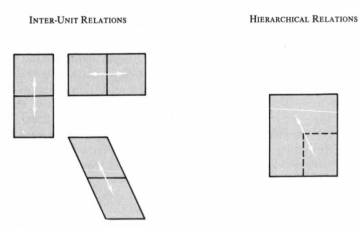

on the variance of the properties of the member units. This does not hold for the relations among units (*or* among sub-units, *or* among supra-units). Thus, the degrees of integration of a supra-unit (for instance, the United States in the first decades of the Union) and of its member units are intimately related, but those of two units (e.g., United States and the Soviet Union) in an inter-unit relationship are not directly related (though, like any other property, degree of integration of one unit may constitute a relevant environmental property for another unit).[10] It follows that unless we have a theory which encompasses the properties of supra-units so that we can form propositions as to which emergent properties we are to hold constant, even the relations among properties of units and of inter-unit relations cannot be adequately analyzed.

Inter-unit states may be *described*, and even explained in part, without introducing the concept of emergent properties; it is not the recognition of distinct inter-unit states that introduces a new level of analysis, but rather the proposition that these states cannot be explained in full without adding a distinct set of variables. Nor is there any *necessary* relation between the amount of interaction among a given set of units and the explanatory power of a supra-unit containing these units. There may be, for instance, a comparatively high level of transaction between two nations; however, most of it may be explained in terms of the properties of nations and their relations rather than by the properties of supra-national organizations. Empirically, though, there seems to be an association; when the volume of transactions is high, the probability that supra-unit variables will account for more of the variance also increases.[11]

Universals, Micro-, and Macro-Properties

The explanatory power of hierarchical variables in accounting for the variance in any particular body of data cannot be determined a priori or formally. We suggest that it is fruitful to proceed with a hierarchical theory which views societies as units that have sub-units and supra-units. As the sub-units of society themselves may be viewed as supra-units of lower level units and sub-units, we refer to the first set of entities—that of the societies as units, supra-units, and their sub-units—as the macroscopic level of sociological theory. In the following pages, we shall first explore the relationship of this level to the microscopic and universal levels; a subsequent section takes up the relationship between our inter-level differentiation and the distinction between inter-unit and hierarchical relations.

Three Kinds of Variables

An underlying proposition of this work is that it is productive for sociopolitical analysis to treat data about societies, their components, and their combinations as distinct phenomena whose variance cannot be explained satisfactorily on the basis of the properties and relations of lower level units such as small groups and individual roles. Variations in the economy of a nation, for example, can be explained only partially in terms of the behavior of myriads of firms and families and their relations. Similarly, it is insufficient to analyze national politics solely in terms of voters and interest groups. We refer to the emergent properties used in analyzing societal data as macro-properties and to the sub-theory constructed from their combinations as macro-theory, as distinct from micro-theory which deals with inter-personal behavior and small groups. (When discussing the substantive rather than the methodological aspect of the macro-level, we refer to societal level, societal properties, societal units, etc. Although the term "societal" is archaic, it serves well to distinguish macro- from micro-data, both of which are "social."*)

The classification of variables, however, is not exhausted by this distinction. Some variables are not predicated on micro- or macro-units, but can be used to characterize both kinds of units; we refer to these as *universal* variables. The distinction, for instance, between predisposition and action seems to be universal and can be usefully applied to personalities, roles, small groups, and societies (though with diminishing returns as we move down this list).† On the other hand, the institutionalized control of the means of violence is largely a macro-variable; it has only minimal application in micro-theory and next to none in intra-role and intra-personality analysis.

It might be argued that such a division of variables is unnecessary because most variables are universals. (Either macro-behavior is explained by micro-properties and their relations, or micro- and macro-sub-theories are assumed to be isometric and explainable by one, universal, set of variables.) It seems to us, however, that the question of the relative theoretical power of universal versus micro- and macro-variables cannot be answered a priori. This work proposes not only that macro-variables are irreducible, but that their theoretical significance is considerable. Moreover, even if the propositions advanced in the following chapters (many of which are on the macroscopic level) prove to be invalid, the failure to do so may be held only against this macro-theory, whereas if they hold up—even after revision, reformulation, and elaboration—this would support the claim that macroscopic theory is needed.

Merton, answering the criticism that sociologists tend to specialize in the study of trivial phenomena and neglect significant historical processes, pointed to the fact that the study of the trivial fruit fly led to the understanding of some general laws of genetics.[12] Similarly, we can study the universal properties of interaction in any instance of interaction, even in the small-talk of college freshmen. (And, just as fruit flies are in ample supply, students are more accessible than, say, generals.) But just as the anatomy of elephants cannot be studied by dissecting fruit flies, so, too, the morphology of macroscopic social units cannot be effectively explored by studying the structure of small groups.‡ Societies, we hold, have emergent properties

---

* The term societal has been used traditionally, though not exclusively, to refer to macro-social data. More recently, it has been thus used by Ralph H. Turner in a book review of Talcott Parsons' *Social Structure and Personality* (New York: Free Press, 1964) in *American Sociological Review*, Vol. 30 (1965), p. 789.

† If a variable is universal only to sociology—e.g., institutionalization—it is applicable to small groups and societies and roles (which are a universal unit) but not to personality. If a variable is universal for social science—e.g., norms—it is applicable to personality as well.

‡ Making the same point with reference to individuals, Barton stated: "Random sampling of individuals is a sociological meatgrinder. You can study mice or frogs by putting them through a hamburger machine and looking at every hundredth cell under a microscope, but you tend to lose information about anatomy and physiology that way.

which are not isometric with those of small groups. Thus, the methodological contingencies of a *full* theory of societies (and of polities) seem to necessitate the addition of a sub-theory to deal with macro-properties.

Micro- and Macro-Social Units Defined

The distinction between micro- and macro-units is widely used in biology, economics, and many other disciplines. Which *social* units are micro- and which macroscopic? There are two ways to answer this question. One is to denote the main units in each of the two categories. The other is to find a characteristic that would distinguish the two kinds. Using the first approach, we suggested that societies, their major components (e.g., classes), and their combinations (e.g., various international bodies) be treated as macro-units.* Friendship groups, work-teams, and families might be viewed as the chief micro-units. Units not specifically named may be said to belong to the category of the listed unit they most resemble (e.g., ethnic groups are like classes and, hence, are macro-units). Units that are more complex than small groups but less complex than sub-societies, especially complex organizations and communities, may be viewed as a third, intermediate category.

The second approach seems to us more satisfactory, though it leads to similar results. Macro-units (of sociology) are defined as all those units the majority of whose consequences affect one or more societies,[13] their combinations, or their sub-units. The time period must be specified because acts that have mainly microscopic consequences in one period may have macroscopic ones in a later period and vice versa. The cut-off point selected depends on the problem being considered. While consequences of the actions of social units cannot be readily counted, it seems that most consequences of many social units are either of one or the other kind, which makes differentiation easier. Those units whose consequences are less concentrated may have to be classified as intermediary cases rather than classified according to a count that would require classifying each and every consequence. Our definition is a functional one in the sociological sense of the term—that is, a definition according to the consequences the units have for a system. Here the system is a macroscopic framework, that of a society. Classes, ethnic groups, and social movements, are obviously macroscopic. Communities and complex organizations are macroscopic to the degree they significantly influence societies, their components, and their combinations—and not if they have no such influence. Thus, General Motors is a macroscopic

---

Structure and function get lost, and we are left with cell biology." Allen H. Barton, "Personal Influence Revisited," a paper delivered to the Market Research Council, New York, May 20, 1966, p. 1.

* In line with the denotative approach, societies would be characterized as a unit like the American, French or British Society.

company, whereas the neighborhood grocery store is not. A family might be macroscopic—if it is an emperor's family, for example—but most families are not.*

We have examined elsewhere in greater detail the suggestion that one may learn about macro-units by studying micro-units, an approach held for instance by those who conduct small-group experiments to explore international relations.[14] The main justification for such procedure is the heuristic value that studies of micro-units have for the exploration of macroscopic ones, and not the validation of propositions about macroscopic processes on the microscopic level. This argument, though, raises two questions: First, why do those who conduct these studies use methods whose special power is validation rather than discovery? Second, why is so little attention paid to the macroscopic validation of propositions derived from studies of micro-units?

Part of the difficulty arises because some social scientists still do not face the question of the units of analysis and, by discussing "man," shift back and forth between statements whose only referent can be a personality system or a small group and statements about nations and societies; often, one statement implies an independent variable which is microscopic and a dependent one which is macroscopic, without any hint as to what the inter-level mechanism may be.[15] Among those who do recognize the differences in the units of analysis, there are some who justify such inter-level jumps by suggesting either that the microscopic and macroscopic units are isometric (which denies the existence of emergent properties), or by assuming that there is a close if not one-to-one link between processes on both levels. Thus, national leadership is assumed to be highly responsive to public opinion or public opinion highly influenced by national leadership, and, hence, fluctuations in personal attitudes are studied to predict national conduct. Actually, the tightness of the relationship among the processes of the various units is a matter that must be established empirically and cannot be decided *ex cathedra*. As far as the evidence available allows one to reach a conclusion, it suggests that there is considerable inter-level freedom,[16] thus strengthening the argument for a distinct macroscopic analysis.

Two Kinds of Reductionism

Social science analysis has, for the last generation, been under considerable pressure to move toward psychologistic reductionism and micro-analysis. There are several sources of this tendency. The absorption of

---

* "But do not the families significantly affect society?" it may be asked. The answer, as we see it, is that each family does not, and the variables which account for the accumulated effects of the families *in toto*, are not attributes of the individual families. Thus, for instance, the "decline" of the traditional family may be said to enhance modernization,

psychological frames of reference and terminology into the mainstream of Western, especially American, culture makes this kind of reductionism natural; to stand outside one's culture requires a constant effort.[17] Further, the anthropomorphic character of language encourages the formulation of statements about macro-units in personality terms (e.g., "the United States was humiliated"). The relative ease with which personal and micro- as compared to macro-behavior can be observed is an additional factor. And the great demand in the West for psychological and micro-social knowledge with regard to such matters as marketing, election campaigns, labor relations, and other corporate and administrative needs has heightened this tendency, whereas the countries that are most active on a macro-level (Communist and developing countries) have invested much less in modern sociological analysis.* Finally, macro-analysis is more likely to lead to social criticism, and, hence, it became unpopular in periods when such criticism was suppressed.

Our macroscopic approach is based on the non-reductionist position that societal units are fruitfully viewed as having emergent properties. This is not to fall into the opposite trap, to imply that societal behavior can be fully explained by emergent macroscopic variables and theories. Obviously, geographical, biological, psychological, and other factors partially explain societal behavior, and, in principle, no concrete item of behavior is fully explained by any one discipline or theory. The non-reductionist position holds only that (a) an important segment of the variance in societal behavior can be explained only by macro-factors (and *this* is what is irreducible to other variables), and (b) these factors and the relations among them constitute a distinct sub-theory within the theory of action.

There are two different kinds of macroscopic emergent properties which, when ignored, make for two kinds of reductionism: The first reductionism does not separate sociology from psychology and from social psychology, whereas the second fails to distinguish macro- from micro-sociology. The first kind, the reduction to psychology, occurs much more frequently among philosophers and psychologists than sociologists and political scientists. Members of the latter disciplines tend to understand that their methodological claim to distinct disciplinary status is predicated on the existence of emergent properties on a level of analysis distinct from that of personality.[18] Still, psychological reductionism is not dead in the social sciences themselves,

---

but if we seek to explain the causes of this decline, the answer will not be found in the family as a unit. Its transformation is only an intervening variable between modernization and some other, usually, macroscopic variables. If intra micro-unit variables were the factor, how are we to explain that myriad units are changing—in the same way— simultaneously?

* The last two factors, though, appear to be changing, in that the West is becoming more active on the societal level, and both planning and developing societies are becoming more interested in modern sociology.

though it is much more widely practiced than subscribed to as a methodological position.[19] Among contemporary sociologists, no less a scholar than George Homans holds a reductionist position.[20] An anthropologist reported in 1965 that as "we have so often been told, cultural phenomena must, in the final analysis, be explained in psychological terms."[21] And David Bidney has stated, "sociologists and anthropologists, who are interested in social behavior and its products, cannot investigate their data except with reference to actual human organisms."[22]

Most sociologists and political scientists who are non-reductionist in their methodological positions agree that both theoretical anchoring and methodological manipulation are needed before universal concepts and data about member-units can become part of micro- or macro-analysis.[23] Thus, a family's or a nation's attitudes are not the arithmetical sum of those of the members, but are in part the result of processes the social unit brings to bear on its members. Though the study of the attitudes of persons has no less theoretical status than that of a family or nation, sociology and political science begin when universal social science building blocks are combined into the study of micro- or macro-social units and processes, and when the social consequences are studied separately from personal and interpersonal ones. Unfortunately, this central point is frequently ignored in the research of even those who subscribe to it in the abstract. A significant portion of sociological and political science empirical research is reductionistic–psychologistic.*

If the border separating studies of personality from those of social units is recognized but often trespassed, that which separates microscopic from macroscopic social analysis is frequently not even recognized. Hence, we stress the second kind of emergent properties, those which are within the realm of sociology and political science; their neglect does not render these

---

* This point was made by V. O. Key, Jr., *The Responsible Electorate* (Cambridge: Harvard University Press, 1966), pp. 3–5 and *passim*. See also "Foreword" by Arthur Maass, *op. cit.*, p. ix. Many tables in which quantitative data are reported and which have the appearance of providing sociological analysis actually provide psychological interpretations. For instance, a table showing that x per cent of middle-class members hold attitude y, which is in conflict with attitude z, is reductionist when the conflict is conceived, as it usually is, as intra-personal and thus the *explanation* is psychological. Such data become sociological once sociological variables are included in the analysis. This tends to require the addition of data on properties of the social units themselves (which can be derived from data about members or directly collected).

Coleman, making a related point, stresses the role of aggregate data. "In general, the attempt to develop formal group-level relations directly, without recourse to individual behavior, may pose considerable difficulty. Unless precise quantitative data exist, the form of the group-level relation, and the operational meaning of the concepts, may have to be quite arbitrary. But by moving from the individual level to that of the group, the operational meaning of the concepts is well specified, and the form of the relation derives from the more easily verifiable individual-level relations." *Introduction to Mathematical Sociology*, *op. cit.*, pp. 251–252.

disciplines impossible but largely curtails their richness and potency. While the first kind of emergent properties sets the social universe of discourse apart from the others, the second separates the analysis of macro-units and processes both from that of micro-units and processes and from that of universal elements.

There are several reasons why the microscopic study of societal phenomena is not satisfactory. First, as we have suggested, part of societal variance is explainable only by macro-factors. Secondly, because the life-span of most micro-units is short (as a rule, even shorter than the lifetimes of their members), it is on a macro-level that long-term, historically significant, forces tend to operate and their effects become most visible. Moreover, change any member of a work team, a friendship group, or even a family, and (even where there is considerable institutionalization) significant variations in the social structure and process of the micro-unit would appear. The same would not be true of a macro-unit, however, for the strength and consequences of social forces are considerably greater on this level.

Finally, it is on the macro-level that the main assets and instruments of history-making lie, particularly where modern and especially where post-modern societies are concerned. From permanent armies to large-scale taxation, from mass media to mass political parties—these factors are not controlled by micro-units. It is on the macro-level that we find the greatest range of options for self-oriented change. (When an individual, family, clique, or some other micro-unit affects processes on the macro-level, it, of course, gains historical significance. "Histories" of other individuals, personal genealogies, or the records of the genesis of micro-units have little interest for societal analysis unless they are used as data for macro-analysis either by some method of aggregation of a large number of such personal or micro-"histories" or by considering a few of them as typical of many others.[24] In either case, each individual "history" is not important for societal analysis. History is to be viewed technically as a set of macroscopic processes.)

Macro–Micro Threshold and Hierarchical Relations

What are the relationships of our distinction between micro- and macro-units to that between supra-units and units? The first pair of concepts presents an absolute, "fixed" distinction, as by definition consequences for a small group are under no condition macroscopic, and those for a society are not microscopic. On the other hand, the second distinction provides a relative frame-of-reference which can be shifted up or down to suit the analysis; what is a unit for one study may be a sub-unit or supra-unit for another.

There is no one-to-one relationship between supra-units and macro-units, or sub-units and micro-units. All three levels—sub-units, units, and supra-units—may be part of a macroscopic analysis (e.g., studying the relationships between the United Nations, regional organizations, and the member nation-states), part of a micro-analysis (e.g., the relationships between a role, a sub-family such as siblings, and a family), or may bridge both kinds of analysis. Or, to put it differently, the application of the term supra-unit suggests that there is an emergent property, a property above and beyond those of the units and the inter-unit relations, but this property may not be macroscopic. There are other emergent properties in the social realm than the micro–macro pair. We have singled this out for the purposes of our study; the unit–supra-unit differentiation serves to relate the macro–micro pair to a larger logical category of hierarchical relations among units.

Another reason why it seems useful to maintain an absolute distinction beside a relative one is that we seek to advance the proposition that macro-behavior is to be explained in part only by micro-theories. If "macroscopic" were a relative concept, like the relation of a supra-unit to a unit, we could not even formulate such a proposition; what is macro-analysis in one study would be micro-analysis in another.

Micro–Macro Distinction and Middle-Range Theories

Having related our two criteria, we refer them now to a third, well established, criterion: How does the distinction between micro- and macro-theory relate to that between grand theories and theories of the middle range? Middle-range theory refers to distinct sub-sets of variables. These may be distinguished by their level of abstraction; grand (universal) theory uses variables that could apply to all other analytic categories, whereas middle-range theories make no such claim. Bales' interaction-categories and Parsons' pattern-variables, for example, are perceived as characterizing any act, while the distinction between traditional, charismatic, and legal authority obviously is not. Thus, "grand theory" may be used to refer to the universal variables applicable in all sub-fields of a discipline, while "middle-range" theory uses specialized sets (such as economic, educational, and political variables) for various bodies of concrete data.

In addition, variables may be differentiated by the kind of unit to which they are applied. This generates two middle-range sub-theories, micro- and macro-, and one "grand" sub-set, the universal variables which apply to both kinds of units. (The suggestion that theories are best pieced together rather than cast all at once in one grand mold or derived from the top[25] applies to all these categories of sub-theories.)

Finally, it should be noted that there is no necessary theoretical relation between the size of a unit and the macro–micro distinction, even though empirically macro-units tend to be larger than micro ones. It is possible for a macro-unit to be smaller; some universities, for instance, have more effect on national action than some business corporations which are much larger. To take the point one step further, the study of most small groups is microscopic, but that of national elites, for example, tends to be part of macroscopic analysis.

In this chapter, we discussed the reasons we hold that a distinct sub-theory of macroscopic units and processes is both needed and feasible, and what its relations to other analytic efforts might be. We turn next to explore the substantive assumptions of macro-analysis.

Appendix: The State of Macro-Analysis in the Various Social Sciences

Most social sciences do not distinguish between micro- and macroscopic units and sub-theories. Some so clearly focus on one kind of unit that the distinction seems unnecessary or not relevant. The subject matter of psychology is personality, which is neither a micro- nor a macro-social unit; political science's subject matter is macroscopic, though the tendency toward psychological reductionism and micro-politics seems to be on the rise.[26] To the degree that anthropology is concerned with preliterate societies, the difference between micro- and macro-units seems to present itself less than it would in the study of modern societies, and it is rarely observed. Interest in the transition from man to Man, which disregards both the micro–macro and the psycho-social thresholds, is still more common in this discipline than in most others,[27] and is probably most often found in psycho-analytic writing about societal behavior. In sociology, the micro–macro threshold was much ignored during the last generation, especially in America, and since World War II has been largely ignored in Europe. This neglect, however, has been pointed out forcefully over the last decade, and there has been some gain both in macro-sociology and in recognition of the threshold.[28]

The micro–macro distinction is established in economics, with studies of business firms usually being treated as micro-economics and those of the national economy as macro-economics.[29] It would appear, however, that the concept of emergent properties has not been fully recognized. Boulding, for example, views macro-economics as the *study of aggregates*, while micro-economics is seen as dealing with member items (individual industries, particular commodities). This amounts to inter-unit analysis without introducing emergent properties. It is small wonder, therefore, that he finds it "difficult" to explain why "many propositions which are true of individuals or of small groups turn out to be untrue when we are considering the system as a whole."[30]

The terms macro- and micro- when used are, as a rule, defined by denotation.[31] The distinction between universals and micro- and macro-emergent properties is not drawn; universals and micro-variables are often collapsed into one category, which leads to the inference that since some of these "micro-variables" apply also to the macro-level, the distinction between macro- and micro-analysis is not valid. Often, even when the difference between *behavior* on the two levels is clearly recognized, as with regard to individual versus national debt, the theoretical distinction is less widely utilized.[32]

The distinctions we advance here seem to be of value for all social sciences. For psychology, their employment would more clearly focus the question of whether a society can be studied as isometric with personality. In political science, they would clarify the difference between aggregate studies of voters, their personalities and friendship patterns, on the one hand, and those of national political processes on the other. Above all, they would better prepare sociology (though other changes are needed as well) for historical analysis and for the presentation of an action theory of society.

NOTES

1. We follow here the "universal" theory of action as developed by Ralph Linton, Robert K. Merton, and Talcott Parsons.

2. While many sociologists view this issue as dated in various sister disciplines, it is quite alive. See F. A. V. Hayek, "Scientism and the Study of Society," *Economica*, N.S. 9 (1942), pp. 267–291; N.S. 10 (1943), pp. 34–63; N.S. 11 (1944), pp. 27–39; J. W. N. Watkins, "The Principle of Methodological Individualism," *British Journal for the Philosophy of Science*, Vol. 36 (May 1952), pp. 186–189; May Brodbeck, "On the Philosophy of the Social Sciences," *Philosophy of Science*, Vol. 21 (1954), pp. 140–156; L. J. Goldstein, "The Two Theses of Methodological Individualism," *British Journal for the Philosophy of Science*, Vol. 9 (1958), pp. 1–11; Abraham Kaplan, *The Conduct of Inquiry* (San Francisco: Chandler, 1964), pp. 80–82; Donald T. Campbell, "Common Fate, Similarity, and Other Indices of the Status of Aggregates of Persons as Social Entities," *Behavioral Science*, Vol. 3 (1958), pp. 14–25. See also Robert M. MacIver, *The Web of Government, op. cit.*, p. 416.

3. This point was stressed by Skinner, "Behaviorism at Fifty," *op. cit.*

4. Ralph Linton defined *role* as "the dynamic aspect of a status. . . . When [an actor] puts the rights and duties which constitute the status into effect [i.e., behaves] he is performing a rôle." *The Study of Man* (New York: Appleton-Century-Crofts, 1936), p. 114. He defined "status" as "a position in a particular pattern" (*ibid.*, p. 113) and not as a rank. See T. R. Sarbin, "Role Theory," in Gardner Lindzey (ed.), *Handbook of Social Psychology* (Cambridge, Mass.: Addison-Wesley, 1954), Vol. I, pp. 223–258. For recent discussions of "role" see Neal Gross, Ward S. Mason, Alexander W. McEachern, *Explorations in Role Analysis; Studies of the School Superintendency Role* (New York: Wiley & Sons, 1958), esp. Chap. 2, and J. Milton Yinger, *Toward a Field Theory of Behavior* (New York: McGraw-Hill, 1965), Chap. 6.

5. This definition of a social unit is similar to Robert K. Merton's definition of a role-set: "That complement of role-relationships in which persons are involved by virtue of occupying a particular social status." "The Role-Set: Problems in Sociological Theory," *British Journal of Sociology*, Vol. 8 (1957), p. 110. The main difference is that role-set is defined from the viewpoint of an actor, the occupant of

the role; the social unit is defined from the viewpoint of an observer, looking at the combinations of the roles, so to speak, from the side. Unless the role *occupant* is a sociologist, a role-set and a social unit perspective will differ substantially.

6. For additional discussion, see Dennis H. Wrong, "The Oversocialized Conception of Man in Modern Sociology," *American Sociological Review*, Vol. 26 (1961), pp. 183–193 and Herman Turk, "An Inquiry into the Undersocialized Conception of Man," *Social Forces*, Vol. 43 (1965), pp. 518–521.

7. Peter M. Blau, who follows a different theoretical track, sees "microstructures" as composed of individuals. *Exchange and Power in Social Life* (New York: Wiley & Sons, 1964), p. 24; see also pp. 253, 283. May Brodbeck states: "A group is an aggregate of individuals standing in certain descriptive relations to each other" in "Methodological Individualisms," *op. cit.*, p. 2. The same position is taken by Jurgen Ruesch: "The Social System is the actual habitual network of communication between people," in Roy R. Grinker (ed.), *Toward a Unified Theory of Human Behavior* (New York: Basic Books, 1956), p. 328. See also Muzafer Sherif, "Introduction" to John H. Rohrer and Muzafer Sherif, *Social Psychology at the Crossroads* (New York: Harper & Row, 1951), esp. pp. 2–3. These references are merely illustrative. We have found in literally scores of textbooks and monographs an explicit or implicit assumption that the individual is a more concrete and hence a more basic concept than "group," and that groups are made of individuals.

8. ". . . societal concepts are not capable of being 'pointed to,' " Maurice Mandelbaum, "Societal Facts," in Patrick Gardiner (ed.), *Theories of History* (New York: Free Press, 1959), p. 486. Mandelbaum discusses this position but does not hold it himself.

9. On emergent properties, see Ernest Nagel, "Wholes, Sums, and Organic Unities," *Philosophical Studies*, Vol. 3 (1952), pp. 17–32. See also Talcott Parsons, *The Structure of Social Action* (New York: Free Press, 1937), pp. 33 ff. "One of the special problems which is peculiar to sociology and some·disciplines in natural science is the existence of multiple-level systems of relations. A variable which characterizes a group will affect some attribute of individuals within the group, and these attributes in turn will affect the attribute of the group," James S. Coleman, *Introduction to Mathematical Sociology* (New York: Free Press, 1964), p. 241. Abraham Edel, "The Concept of Levels in Social Theory," in Llewellyn Gross (ed.), *Symposium on Sociological Theory* (New York: Harper & Row, 1956), pp. 167–195.

10. For an extension of this discussion and illustrative material, see the author's *Political Unification, op. cit.*

11. For a concrete example, see below, pp. 373.

12. Robert K. Merton, "Notes on Problem-Finding in Sociology," in Robert K. Merton, Leonard S. Broom, Jr., L. Cottrell (eds.), *Sociology Today* (New York: Basic Books, 1959), p. xxvi.

13. Societies are defined as self-sufficient social systems. See Talcott Parsons et al. "Some Fundamental Categories of the Theory of Action: A General Statement," in Talcott Parsons and Edward A. Shils, (eds.), *Toward a General Theory of Action* (Cambridge, Mass.: Harvard University Press, 1952), p. 26.

14. Amitai Etzioni, "Social Psychology of International Relations," in *Handbook of Social Psychology*, Elliott Aronson and Gardner Lindzey (eds.), rev. ed. (Reading, Mass.: Addison-Wesley, Forthcoming).

15. See *ibid.* for references and examples.

16. *Ibid.* See also below, 163–168.

17. On the place of individualism in the Anglo-Saxon societal perspective, see Adamantia Pollis, "Political Implications of the Modern Greek Concept of Self," *British Journal of Sociology*, Vol. 16 (1965), p. 30.

18. This was recently discussed by Blau, *Exchange and Power in Social Life, op. cit.*, p. 3. See also Parsons, *The Structure of Social Action, op. cit.*, p. 734 and *passim.*

19. For an economist's discussion of this point, see Everett E. Hagen, *On the Theory of Social Change: How Economic Growth Begins* (Homewood, Ill.: Dorsey Press, 1962), esp. 36–49.

20. "Let us get men back in, and let us put some blood in them . . . no matter what we say our theories are, when we seriously try to explain social phenomena by constructing even the veriest sketches of deductive systems, we find ourselves in fact, and whether we admit it or not, using what I have called psychological explanations." George Homans, "On Bringing Men Back In," *American Sociological Review*, Vol. 29 (1964), pp. 816–817, from his Presidential Address to the American Sociological Association. Timothy C. Brock, a psychologist, seconds these words in his "Double-talk and Mother-wit," *Contemporary Psychology*, Vol. 10 (1965), p. 460. For a moderate defense of reductionism, see Catton, *From Animistic to Naturalistic Sociology, op. cit.*, pp. 302–316. Emile Durkheim, who advanced powerful arguments against psychological reductionism, came close to being a socio-cultural reductionist. See *Sociologie et Philosophie* (Paris: Presses Universitaires de France, 1951), pp. 33 ff.

21. David Kaplan, "The Superorganic: Science or Metaphysics?," *American Anthropologist*, Vol. 67 (1965), p. 959. See also p. 961.

22. David Bidney, *Theoretical Anthropology* (New York: Columbia University Press, 1953), p. 46. See also p. 78. Cf. to a fine non-reductionist case study, *Navajo Witchcraft*, by Clyde Kluckhohn. Kluckhohn studies the interrelationship between personality needs, stratification, and societal patterns. (See papers of the Peabody Museum, 22, No. 2, 1944.)

23. On the methodological steps, see Paul F. Lazarsfeld and Herbert Menzel, "On the Relation Between Individual and Collective Properties," in Amitai Etzioni (ed.), *Complex Organizations: A Sociological Reader* (New York: Holt, Rinehart & Winston, 1961), pp. 422–440. See also James S. Coleman, "Relational Analysis: The Study of Social Organizations with Survey Methods," Etzioni, *ibid.*, pp. 441–452. See also Erwin K. Scheuch, "Cross-National Comparisons Using Aggregate Data: Some Substantive and Methodological Problems," in Richard L. Merritt and Stein Rokkan, *Comparing Nations* (New Haven: Yale University Press, 1966), pp. 131–167. Cf. Anatol Rapoport, "Uses and Limitations of Mathematical Models in Social Science," in *Symposium on Sociological Theory*, Llewellyn Gross (ed.), (New York: Harper & Row, 1959), pp. 348–372.

24. For a fine example of the second use, see Sigmund Diamond, *The Reputation of the American Businessman* (Cambridge, Mass.: Harvard University Press, 1955). For a discussion of the use of mass personal documents, see Robert Angell, "A Critical Review of the Development of the Personal Document Method in Sociology, 1920–1950," in Louis Gottschalk, Clyde Kluckhohn, and Robert Angell, *The Use of Personal Documents in History, Anthropology, and Sociology* (New York: Social Science Research Council, 1945), Bulletin 53, pp. 177–232. For an argument

that personal histories per se are of sociological importance, see C. Wright Mills, *The Sociological Imagination* (New York: Grove Press, Inc., 1959), pp. 159–164.

25. Merton, *Social Theory and Social Structure, op. cit.*, pp. 5–10.

26. This is a central thesis of Wolin's *Politics and Vision, op. cit.* See esp. pp. 407–434. See also Key, *The Responsible Electorate, op. cit.*

27. David Kaplan, "The Superorganic. . .," *op. cit.*, p. 961, and his "Personality and Social Structure," in Joseph B. Gittler (ed.), *Review of Sociology* (New York: Wiley & Sons, 1957), pp. 87–121, esp. 113.

28. In 1967, for the first time in its history, a plenary session of the American Sociological Association was devoted to macro-sociology. Papers were presented by Talcott Parsons, Paul F. Lazarsfeld, and Amitai Etzioni. See also Wilbert E. Moore, "Global Sociology: The World as a Singular System," *American Journal of Sociology*, Vol. 71 (1966), pp. 475–482. See also references cited in footnote 31 below.

29. Many textbooks of economics include micro-economics and macro-economics sections. Robert Heilbroner, *Understanding the Macro-economics* (Englewood Cliffs, N.J.: Prentice-Hall, 1965) is devoted to the second category.

30. Kenneth E. Boulding, *Economic Analysis* (New York: Harper & Row, 1955), pp. 237–238.

31. Among the sociologists who use the term are the following: Robert K. Merton and Bernard Barber refer to "macro- and micro-sociological perspectives of knowledge" in their "Sorokin's Formulations in the Sociology of Science," Philip J. Allen (ed.), *Pitirim A. Sorokin in Review* (Durham, N.C.: Duke University Press, 1963), p. 338; macro-sociology is referred to by Werner Stark, *The Sociology of Knowledge* (London: Routledge & Kegan Paul, 1958), p. 28, also in reference to the sociology of knowledge. Stein Rokkan and Henry Valen refer to a macro-variable in their "Parties, Elections, and Political Behavior in the Northern Countries: A Review of Recent Research," in Otto Stammer (ed.), *Politische Forschung* (Cologne: Westdeutscher Verlag, 1960), p. 110. Milbrath, *Political Participation, op. cit.*, p. 5, refers to "macro" as "the behavior of the larger political system." Bo Anderson dedicated an article to "Erik Allardts Makrosociology," *Sociolozik Forshung*, Vol. 1 (1966), pp. 22–31. Philip E. Slater devotes a book to the study of small groups which he entitles *Microcosm* (New York: Wiley & Sons, 1966). Stein Rokkan and Angus Campbell compare "micropolitics" to "macropolitics" in "Norway and the United States of America," *International Social Science Journal*, Vol. 12 (1960), p. 69. See also Fred W. Riggs, "International Relations as a Prismatic System," *World Politics*, Vol. 14 (1961), pp. 144–181; Gabriel A. Almond and Sidney Verba, *Civic Culture* (Boston: Little, Brown, 1965), pp. 30–35; and Blau, *Exchange and Power in Social Life, op. cit.*, pp. 24–25 ff.; James S. Coleman, "Research Chronicle: Adolescent Society," in Philip E. Hammond, *Sociologists at Work* (New York: Basic Books, 1964), p. 186, discusses "macro-structure." See also Edward A. Shils, "The Calling of Sociology," in Talcott Parsons et al. (eds.), *Theories of Society* (New York: Free Press, 1961), Vol. II, p. 1444, and Scott Greer, "The Social Structure and Political Process of Suburbia," *American Sociological Review*, Vol. 25 (1960), pp. 514–526, esp. 515.

32. Milton Friedman has most sharply voiced the case for methodological individualism in economic theory. See his *Essays on Positive Economics* (Chicago: University of Chicago Press, 1953), pp. 3–46. See also Frank H. Knight, *Ethics of Competition* (New York: Harper & Row, 1936).

CHAPTER 4

The Languages of Societal Analysis:

Substantive Assumptions

WHAT CONCEPTIONS underlie the various theories concerning the properties and dynamics of society? How must these conceptions be modified before a theory of macro-action can be advanced? These are the questions this chapter attempts to answer. A theory that is quite satisfactory for explaining micro-action may be inadequate to account for macro-action, and one that explains micro-dynamics with one set of assumptions (e.g., laws of symbolic relations) may use another set (e.g., mechanistic) for macro-dynamics. As a consequence, there is a need to explore the conceptions with direct reference to the level of analysis with which we are concerned—macro-analysis. Because our subject matter is societal and political processes rather than, let us say, economic ones, macroscopic analysis here *ipso facto* means societal and political analysis. In this chapter, we first review three prevailing approaches or "languages,"[1]*

---

* Reference notes for this chapter appear on page 83.

each of which has been used to formulate a variety of theories about macro-action; we then outline the foundations of a fourth approach, the one we favor.

Three Prevailing Languages

The three major languages (or meta-theories) of social science we will consider are the atomistic, the collectivistic, and the voluntaristic. The macro-atomistic approach views societal properties and processes as the consequences of mechanistic relations among a large number of micro-units. The collectivistic viewpoint, in contrast, explains such societal states as the consequences of quasi-organic relationships among the components of a societal whole. Finally, the macro-voluntaristic approach tends to view societal states as if they were the expressions of one macroscopic will or mind.

These three approaches are logically exhaustive in terms of the possible combinations of macroscopic hierarchical relations:[2] The atomistic view stresses attributes of units and inter-unit relations to the neglect of supra-unit properties. The voluntaristic orientation focuses on a supra-unit and tends to neglect unit properties and inter-unit relations. The collectivistic approach studies both units and supra-units. Thus, the first approach tends to be highly *fragmental*; the second *monolithic*; and the third, concerned with the relations of the parts to a whole—which it views as largely given—may be characterized as *quasi-organic*.

These three approaches differ according to whether or not and where they see a capacity for an active orientation. The atomistic approach, in its pure form, provides no such macro-capacity; it sees only microscopic actors who relate to each other in mechanistic ways. The collectivistic approach views relations among the parts of the societal whole either as given, or as changing only as a result of historical, cultural, or environmental forces over which the collectivity has no control. If the atomistic approach sees the locus of the active orientation as being in micro-units, the collectivistic approach does not even grant the existence of such an orientation. While symbolic interpretation plays an important role in explaining the bonds which tie the parts to the collective whole, the study of their function and dynamics tends to assume that these, too, are given or change because of forces uncontrolled by the collective actors. In contrast, the voluntaristic approach gives excessive attention to the active capacity. In its pure form, it recognizes few permanent limitations inherent in the actor and even fewer inherent in his social environment.

Although the users of the various languages are not necessarily aware of or motivated by them, the differences in approach have significant ideological implications. Both atomistic and collectivisitic approaches tend to have conservative implications, for they do not view societal processes as open to deliberate guidance. They see no societal villains and no macro-heroes. Voluntaristic theories, on the other hand, tend to point to one or more macro-actors, such as a domestic elite or a foreign power; the ideological implications of this approach depend on the actor specified by the particular theory.

We will now examine in more detail these three societal conceptions. We suggest that a convergence of the collectivistic and voluntaristic approaches provides the foundations for a more satisfactory theory of societal action, and that the atomistic approach adds a model which is applicable to a sub-set of societal properties and processes.

We treat all three of the conceptions, it should be stressed, as ideal types; few theories and even fewer empirical studies draw exclusively on one language of societal analysis. Many theoretical works and empirical studies, however, can be readily classified in terms of the language on whose concepts and assumptions they primarily draw, explicitly or implicitly. Many others can be characterized in terms of their relative reliance on one of these three languages. We cannot overemphasize that the purpose of the following discussion is not to review studies and their findings or to summarize scores of theoretical works, but to illustrate three common languages of social science and a fourth which arises out of their convergence.

The Atomistic, Aggregate Approach

The atomistic approach, in its pure form, recognizes macro-states but not macro-action or actors; it explains the state of the society, economy, or polity in terms of the properties, relations, or actions of the micro-units, rather than in terms of their supra-unit, macroscopic relations. There is no systematic place for a societal actor; whenever he is arbitrarily introduced, he affects the inter-unit state by acting like any one micro-unit in an aggregate of such units.[3]

The full-competition model of economics is a well-known application of an atomistic conception. The state of the national economy is explained in terms of the actions or decisions of numerous persons, families, or firms. To the degree that government appears in such an economic model at all, it is viewed as another member unit which acts in the unguided market which is itself an aggregation of myriad microscopic decisions.

Many economic studies are based on assumptions quite different from those of a full-competition model, but they still draw heavily on the basic atomistic-aggregate concept. Examples of these are analyses of the ways in which consumers, families, or farmers react to government-applied Keynesian controls. These micro-units are seen as acting on the basis of their individual qualities or judgments or their inter-relations, but not on the basis of macro-properties or processes. In contrast, many studies of monopolies, price leadership, labor relations, and the economics of development are much less affected by the atomistic approach and draw more upon other languages of societal analysis discussed below.*

The balance-of-power theory of international relations also uses an atomistic language.[4] The state of international affairs is viewed as determined by the actions of the various units (nation-states).† War, should it occur, is the result of an "upset" in the balance, which, in turn, is explained by the emergence of a new coalition between the units, by changes in the power of some units, or by the appearance of new units in the particular historical situation. However, no collectivistic supra-unit is assumed to have the capacity to correct the balance. Even when a balancer is introduced, it is seen as merely one more unit whose self-interest dictates weighing one side of the scale to safeguard the balance, rather than as a supra-unit force. It is somewhat like a rook moving to prevent a checkmate, with all the figures knowing and observing the rules of the game but with no player to guide them.

When international organizations are introduced into this picture, they are credited with some collective regulatory function, but this capacity is seen as so limited that most of the variance of international conditions and developments is still explained atomistically. In contrast, studies concerned with the evolution of regional communities which deal with powerful, institutionalized, non-rational bonds among nations (or at least among their elites)—for instance, shared conservative values, aristocratic upbringing, and

---

* Even here atomistic perspectives are far from unknown. "When economists build models of growth, they typically do not give explicit independent roles to the ability or motivation to solve problems of public policy. For most existing economic theories, public decision-making lies entirely outside the realm of economic analysis—as when certain basic decisions are relegated to the shadowy worlds of 'pre-conditions' to economic growth—or public decision-making in appropriate quantity and quality is viewed as an automatic by-product of economic processes which are impelled by the 'classic' outputs of capital, labor, and natural resources, to which technical progress and education have lately been added. Private decision-making has fared somewhat better since it has been dealt with through the concept of entrepreneurship. But the entrepreneur of formal price theory is conceived of as springing into action as soon as his calculations tell him that a profit can be made. His ability to calculate and his motivation to achieve profits are never in doubt." Albert O. Hirschman, *Journeys Toward Progress* (Garden City, N.Y.: Doubleday Anchor Books, 1965), p. 19.

There are strong atomistic elements in positivistic (or naturalistic) sociology. See Stuart C. Dodd, *Dimensions of Society* (New York: Macmillan, 1942); William R. Catton, Jr., *From Animistic to Naturalistic Sociology* (New York: McGraw-Hill, 1966), esp. pp. 257–284. For a recent political science example, see James M. Buchanan, "An Individualistic Theory of Political Process," *Varieties of Political Theory*, David Easton (ed.) (Englewood Cliffs, N.J.: Prentice-Hall, 1966), pp. 25–37. On this approach see Paul Meadows, "Organization Theory and the Atomistic Models," in his "The Metaphors of Order: Toward a Taxonomy of Organization Theory," in Llewellyn Gross (ed.), *Sociological Theory: Inquiries and Paradigms* (New York: Harper & Row, 1967), pp. 91–95.

† This particular application of the atomistic approach differs from the others discussed here in that the units themselves are macroscopic by definition. But the relations among them are studied in a fragmental, mechanistic, inter-unit fashion.

tastes among diplomats in the century of peace[5]—shift the focus from atomistic to collectivistic analysis. The same holds for studies of empires and quasi-empires.[6]

Capitalist economies and the relations among nation-states may be *relatively* appropriate subjects for atomistic analysis, since the relevant data may be explained to a greater extent by inter-unit factors than the data describing many other sub-societal, societal, and intersocietal relations. Atomistic conceptions, however, have also been applied to such societal processes as domestic politics and inter-unit unification, and in these cases they seem much less appropriate.

An example of this is veto-group analysis of national politics, which attempts to explain the macro-behavior of legislative output and executive policies in terms of the relations among political groups, their qualities and dynamics. Relatively little independent explanatory power is granted to national institutions themselves, to national leadership, or to ruling classes. A major outcome ascribed to the aggregate of the actions of the veto groups is blockage, stalemating the polity. Whatever national action does occur cannot, within the limits of this approach, be credited to (or blamed on) any one group or coalition of groups, because all groups affect the national action, like vectors feeding into a vector-diagram.[7]

Veto-group studies of domestic politics differ from interest-group studies in that the latter see specific groups as promoting specific macroscopic acts— e.g., a specific law. Such a view may still be highly atomistic so long as little weight is granted to macroscopic factors to account for the general legislative output (there are one or more "atoms" that largely account for each legislative act).[8] Less atomistic studies of domestic politics give a relatively larger role to shared values, presidential leadership, the specific institutional structure, and other societal factors.[9] Non-atomistic studies of domestic politics, to the degree that they deal with interest-groups at all, see these groups as considerably affected by the cultural, societal, and economic structures of the specific society under study.[10]

Attempts to determine on the basis of transactional analysis the nature and dynamics of bonds that tie units into communities—whether these be nations, suburbs, or tribes—are other examples of the atomistic approach. The transactions studied include telephone calls, letters, telegrams, trade, and tourism. Macro-properties (e.g., the integration of communities) are perceived as the product of transactions among the units, not as the result of a supra-unit action. In general, the more transactions that occur, the more the units are viewed as related, and the more the supra-unit—the community— is seen as integrated.[11]

It might be argued that there is no contradiction between explaining macro-action by societal factors *and* as the outcome of myriad individual decisions, since macro-processes set the context in which micro-decisions are made. But atomistic models do not see the situation in this way; if they did, macro-variables would be included and the relative weight of societal factors as compared to micro-choices considered. Typical atomistic studies describe only the properties of the micro- or individual decision-makers and their interrelations and focus their *explanatory* eye on micro- and individual factors, deflecting it from macro-factors. (Of course, an occasional study that uses atomistic language introduces a macro-variable, but it enters in an *ad hoc* fashion and not as an integral part of the atomistic theory.) Thus, atomistic theories in their pure form cannot be said to adhere to either an active or a passive conception on the macroscopic level because they do not recognize this as a distinct level of analysis. They are, so to speak, pre-active.

The Collectivistic, System Approach

The collectivistic approach recognizes a macroscopic supra-unit which has properties and dynamics of its own. The central assumption of this approach is that the units under study hang together and are tied to each other with powerful bonds. The resulting entity has a "structure," "pattern," or "character," or provides a "*gestalt*" or a "context," the term used depending upon the specific theory. In this sense, collectivistic language is the opposite of the atomistic approach in which, "to put it more generally, we tend to think of *things* not *relations*, of *items* but not *context*, of *dualities* rather than a *field*."[12]

It may appear that collectivistic language and system analysis are one and the same. A system is defined as a relationship in which changes in one or more component parts initiate changes in the other component parts, and these changes, in turn, produce changes in the parts in which the original changes occurred.[13] The structure is the specific form of the relationship among the parts at a given point in time. Actually, the concept of system has been used in two rather different ways in social science, a terminological confusion that has caused much theoretical confusion. Many social scientists, especially sociologists and anthropologists, use "system" as a *supra-unit* concept; others, especially "general system" theorists, use it as an *inter-unit* concept.[14] The definition of system as a feedback relationship covers both usages. The concept is employed rather loosely to include almost all relationships—those in which there is a powerful integrating mechanism that counters centrifugal forces (as in a community), those in which the units are only interdependent (as in a pure market relationship), and those in which the relationships are only situational (in that the environment has features that bind the units in a feedback relationship).[15] Thus, relations as different as those between lovers and those among unacquainted drivers have been characterized as systems.[16]

A survey of works in the intellectual tradition that brought about the use of the system concept in social science suggests that implicit in the term is a relationship which is much more collectivistic than the formal definition of a feedback relationship indicates. "System" in this tradition is used to advance the proposition that the units under study are not merely related but are related in a hierarchical, supra-unit fashion. The main point is that a unit, a member of the system, does not respond directly to a stimulus input from the environment but rather in accord with the system's level of integration and, above all, structure. Supra-unit bonds are assumed to have a distinct analytic status. The term "system," when used in this way, highlights the quasi-organic nature of societal entities which do not merely adapt to their environments or behave in accord with the stimulus-response model, but react creatively on the basis of their "character."

The latter-day dilution of the term "system" so that it sometimes implies a supra-unit and sometimes only atomistic relations results in the partisans of both usages being critical of each other. Those who view a system as having a supra-unit quality tend to feel that other users are applying the term loosely while inter-unit theorists criticize the unstated hierarchical assumptions of the supra-unit users.* Ideally, the best way to resolve the situation would be to define "system" exclusively as a pattern of feedback relations, either with or without a supra-unit centripetal mechanism. But the prevailing usages seem too widely held to be open to correction in that way. Hence, we shall use the terms "supra-unit" and "inter-unit" to characterize the two kinds of system relationships. ("System" will be used to denote feedback relations when it does not matter whether the pattern is hierarchical or inter-unit.)

The collectivistic approach is in the supra-unit tradition of system analysis; it explains macro-action by the fact that units hang together to make up a macroscopic supra-unit, and by the particular structure of the "whole" thus created. But while the collectivistic approach sees the social unit as capable of reacting creatively to external stimuli, it does not systematically recognize a capacity of the societal actor to change himself or to restructure internal relations on either the supra-unit or the member unit level.

An analogy frequently drawn in collectivistic writings may help to illustrate this point. Systems' pattern-maintenance is frequently compared to the capacity of a body to maintain its temperature despite changes in the environmental temperature. The internal thermostat functions within given limits; if strained—let us say, by overloading—the mechanism will break and the actor will "die"—that is, the boundary between the actor and the environment will disappear. From then on, the temperature of the unit will reflect that of the environment.[17] Collectivistic theories do not assume, to stay with our example, that the body can reset its thermostat or restructure its anatomy so as to make changes in itself part of its active response to the environment. Changes *are* assumed to take place in the actor (e.g., as the body

---

* For additional discussion, see Appendix of Chapter 5.

ages, a society tends to bureaucratize and lose its flexibility and legitimacy), but the actor is considered unable to control these internal changes even partially. The routinization of charisma—the turning of a spontaneous, active social movement into a rigid bureaucracy—is not willed by its participants; it is a process that occurs because of forces beyond their control, often even against their wishes.[18] Ethnic relations, for example, have been viewed as moving through a four-phase "natural history," from conflict through competition and cooperation to assimilation, whether the ethnic groups involved desire such change or not.[19]

The typical definitions of social system recognize no differences between animal and human societies. The relevant difference between the two kinds of societies is that for the former, division of labor, and hence, "roles" and structure are largely given and transmitted from generation to generation by a biological mechanism, whereas in human societies, they are transmitted by social processes and are, therefore, open to resetting by the members, acting collectively. This essential difference in malleability is not adequately taken into account by the collectivistic view.

Several sociologists have come to view personalities, small groups, and societies as evolving genotypically, as "differentiating"—first bifurcating and then redividing four ways.[20] This illustrates the "social forces" orientation implicit in the collectivistic language: Processes unfold without any active member control. No unit or supra-unit is assumed to have a capacity to stop— or accelerate—differentiation. Social systems are viewed as biological ones in which a rise in temperature, let us say, triggers a higher rate of counteracting perspiration, without there being any possibility of a deliberate decision to use some alternative mechanism, to deliberately search for more effective mechanisms when available ones are strained, or to anticipate future overloading and prepare adequate responses in advance.

Although biology is the source of this analogy, sociologists, using the differentiation model, have tended to ignore biologists' concern with how the differentiation process is guided.[21] Instead of an active capacity, many collectivistic theories tend to assume, on the social as well as on the biological level, a process of Darwinian selection that eliminates those units which do not fulfill the functional prerequisites.[22] That is, social units that do not command the necessary mechanisms "die"; they fail to maintain their boundaries. The units we encounter do, it is said, satisfy these prerequisites.

Such a quasi-organic model may be suitable for studying primitive societies, although even many of these seem to have elements of an active orientation, a capacity to learn collectively from experience and to introduce some changes into their societal pattern.[23] Surely a language for theorizing about societal action must take into account the fact that very few societies disintegrate, and that most societies have the capacity to change themselves to some degree. We need not assume that societies use a refined sociological theory as the basis of their action to suggest that they have *some* sociological insight which has *some* validity and upon which they act *to a degree*. Further, while some societal units score very low on these dimensions, this certainly does not justify omitting these dimensions from a general theory of societies. The concepts of manifest goals, societal guidance, transcendence, and the active orientation, however, are not part of the collectivistic language. Ongoing processes are central to it; parts "work" on each other, groups "interrelate" or "interact," and, as if on their own, forces of deviancy are said to "generate" forces of social control.

The Voluntaristic Approach

The voluntaristic approach focuses on a societal actor who, in principle, is able to remold his world at will. Limitations on his freedom are recognized, but these are viewed as abnormalities, restrictions of his true capacity, or residues of earlier periods. Highly voluntaristic works were more common in earlier times—in the days when Greek philosophers believed that to know good would suffice to bring it about, in the Age of Enlightenment, and in the heyday of utopian socialism.[24] While Marxism is far from a voluntaristic theory, the optimism with which Chinese—and to a lesser degree, Soviet— leaders approach the recasting of their societies suggests that they adhere to a highly voluntaristic version of Marxism, even if they believe that the changes they are attempting to implement are historically necessary. Voluntaristic views of society still have considerable ideological and popular appeal in the West, an appeal which is reflected in the widespread belief that if the government (or the President) would only put its mind and power to removing a particular evil, that evil would be banished.

Voluntarism was at the center of a major school of international relations which believed that changes in international law, charters, and international organizations could fundamentally alter international reality, an approach which has not died out despite potent criticism. Voluntarism is also at the root of a major school of public administration, the "formal-organization" approach, the "balanced approach" to master planning in economics, as well as cybernetics and game-theory.

Most voluntaristic theories are a-structural: Their actor is a man (a great man), or a group of men who act like one man (the power elite), or Man writ large—"American sensibilities were offended"—as though societies or corporations were giant-sized individuals.[25] This a-structural language makes it easier to perceive the social body as monolithic and avoids the questions of what mechanisms provide for action in unison, what binds the "atoms," and what allows restructuring of their relations and dynamics.[26]

Similarly, the a-structural view does not take into account the fact that societal units are composed of many sub-units and actors, and that the action of any one of them—if it is to have macroscopic consequences—requires either winning the others' support or forcing their compliance. This sets sharp limitations on any one actor's ability to act and on the ability of all of them to act together at the same time. Discerning few external or internal constraints on action, the voluntarists' view is hyper-active. The constraints it does recognize are introduced as *ad hoc* limitations on the applicability of this perspective, which do not require its modification.

There are two major voluntaristic approaches: One views the societal actor as if he were a non-rational being, and the other views him as if he were rational. The non-rational voluntaristic approach perceives societal units as acting like macro-persons—responding to drives, emotions, and beliefs.[27] Since these are beyond the actor's control, this version has a passive element. Its voluntarism lies in its explanation of societal behavior as the response to one actor's drives and urges. Many psychoanalytic interpretations of national conduct, some psychological writings on societal action, and earlier anthropological and sociological views of national character are representative of this approach.[28]

Rationalistic voluntarism is more activist: It assumes that the macro-actor is not only free to compel his "body" to express his will, emotions, and urges but is also able to modify his will in accord with information gained and by sequential reasoning.[29] Man, it is conceded, does not always act rationally, but this is due to limitations on his knowledge, on his capacity to analyze, and on his decision-making model. Provided with better information, computers, and models, Man would not only think but would also act more rationally.* Value and power conflicts, it is held, can be solved through arbitration, mediation, negotiation, or by "splitting the difference."[30] In short, no permanent or major limitations on the active orientation are recognized; the world is seen not as an atom-filled container or a quasi-organic tissue but as the product of an omnipotent agent.

Varying degrees of rationalistic voluntarism can be found in administrative science and branches of political science. In studies of administration, it is most evident in the scientific management approach[31] and in some schools of decision-making.[32] Although never as popular in political science as it was in economics, rationalistic voluntarism was quite important before World War II, particularly in the field of international law and organization.[33]

Hans Morgenthau, who has contributed significantly to the reduction of voluntarism in political science, depicts its rationalistic version as follows:

> One [school] believes that a rational and moral political order, derived from universally valid abstract principles, can be achieved here and now. It assumes the essential goodness and infinite malleability of human nature, and blames the failure of the social order to measure up to the rational standards on lack

---

* The word "better" is used inasmuch as many theories in this area prescribe how the actor ought to behave; i.e., they hope to provide the model for his more rational behavior.

of knowledge and understanding, obsolescent social institutions, or the depravity of certain isolated individuals and groups. It trusts in education, reform, and the sporadic use of force to remedy these defects.[34]

The influence of rationalistic voluntarism has waned during the last three decades, although it often survives in a diluted form in which more extensive *ad hoc* limitations on rationality and the freedom to act are recognized. Recently, however, the rationalistic model has seen a measure of revival.[35] In part, this is associated with attempts to use computers to explain macro-behavior (although the association is historical rather than necessary), to apply game theory and other rationalistic models to military strategy and foreign policy,[36] and to study macro-social behavior with some of the less structural cybernetic models.[37] Rationalism and hyperactivism enter here with their stress on the role of communication. When communication links have been laid out effectively and given valid information inputs, the actors are expected to move toward their goals. This is a variant of a psycho-analytic belief in the power of increased and effective communication.[38] Thus, despite much criticism, rationalistic conceptions have been revived in the study of administration, are being tried out in political science, and are being viewed with renewed interest in sociology. These are only in part independent developments; they also reflect the penetration of models from economics into fields where they seem less suitable.

A Language for Societal Action

We will now outline the language we prefer. In part it grows out of a convergence of the collectivistic and the voluntaristic traditions, particularly as applied to cybernetics. To these, the concepts of power analysis must be added before we have a language rich enough to formulate a theory which deals with the major societal variables. To refrain from having to state that the approach we favor is one of collectivistic–voluntaristic-power analysis, we refer to it as a *language of societal action* and to the theory advanced with the terms of this language as a *theory of societal guidance*.

The Convergence of Collectivism and Voluntarism

The language of societal action advanced here renders the collectivistic approach more active and the voluntaristic one less hyper-active. In collectivistic language social units are assumed to be bound into supra-units in such a way that no unit can move significantly without the movement of the others. Furthermore, the supra-unit has a structure of its own which limits the movement of all the units together. To correct this passive view, we draw on the cybernetic voluntaristic approach for a conception of societal units which have controlling overlayers that reach into the member-units (i.e., sub-units), affecting them and responding to them. Thus, to the collectivistic assumption of the "stickiness" of societal units and ongoing processes, we add the conception of mechanisms that are able to guide macroscopic processes and changes.

While the language of societal action draws on voluntaristic concepts, it rejects the hyper-active postulate of voluntarism. We view constraints on societal action as neither tentative nor abnormal, but as an integral part of our meta-theoretical perspective. These constraints arise in part from the fact that each macro-action unit is composed of a multitude of micro-units whose relations and actions affect macro-action; we also assume that, as a rule, there is more than one societal actor—i.e., that there is more than one macro-unit which is endowed with the capacity to act and, hence, also with the capacity to limit actions of other units. In addition, the actors are usually related in ways not subject to their control. In this sense, a collectivistic element is added to voluntarism in constructing a language of societal action.

The drama of societal activation lies in the struggle between the forces which attempt to actualize the potential capacity to act and the pressures toward passivity which, in themselves, can be analyzed largely in terms of a collectivistic system approach.* Similarly, the effects of the actor on other actors and their effects on him are subject to system analysis. What the collectivistic action-theories neglect, however, are the sources and bases of guided effort. These theories do not ask systematically which actors, using what means and pursuing what goals, can change the structure of the system and its boundaries. Collectivistic theories do not systematically differentiate between units which have poor capacities for knowledge-analysis and those which have sophisticated capacities, between those with a high degree of commitment and those with a low one, between passive units and active ones.

The language of societal action differs from the collectivistic one in that it seeks to systematically explore the nature of the societal capacity to act, what such a capacity specifically entails, under what conditions it evolves, and what constraints it faces. While obviously not all societal units are active, we do suggest that an effective theory of societal processes must include concepts that allow for such a capacity; otherwise, passive and active units cannot be differentiated and compared. The question of whether or not societal units have an active capacity cannot even be phrased unless the language of societal action includes these concepts.

---

* Modernization (i.e., the transition from pre-modern to modern societies), transformation from modern to post-modern societies and from post-modern to active societies,[39] and unification of political units that were previously more autonomous are particularly suited for this convergence approach because the relationship between controlling overlayers and societal processes is particularly conspicuous.

While the language of societal action draws on voluntaristic concepts to characterize some aspects of societal activeness, it differs from them in assuming that societal control is both rational and non-rational, and that societal control is not necessarily highly unified or coordinated and is more internally differentiated than the analogy to a person implies. Actually, it might be argued that the control mechanisms of societal units are not sufficiently unified to justify referring to them as "actors" without introducing unwarranted voluntaristic assumptions. Whether or not the controls of a specific societal unit are united enough to allow the member units to act in unison is an empirical question. We suggest, however, that the executive branches of the governments of most modern states were, and those of most post-modern states are, sufficiently unified for them usefully to be regarded as constituting one controlling overlayer. The same holds for the judicial branch, even though the unifying mechanism was and is often cultural rather than organizational. Some legislatures qualify while others may not; national organizations such as labor unions and armies obviously do. To state that a societal unit has a controlling overlayer does not imply that the overlayer is centralized or that the level of internal conflict is low; to act in unison does not require a high degree of unity.

Another reason for the inclusion of a voluntaristic element in a language of societal (macroscopic) action is that the range of societal options seems much more extensive than the range of personal ones. A collectivity can learn more rapidly than any person (e.g., by hiring experts),* it usually has a longer life span, it often has more assets, and—especially when it commands an organizational network—it can more readily change parts than a person can restructure his personality, not to mention his body. Hence, a voluntaristic element seems particularly useful in macroscopic analysis.

So far, we have seen that the language of societal action is "in-between" the voluntaristic and collectivistic languages, for it emerges out of the convergence of both. But in its acceptance of the morphological (or structural) view, the societal-action perspective is closer to the collectivistic than to the voluntaristic approach. Societal action cannot be explained without indicating the various positions of the societal actors in a given field and outlining the relations among them—i.e., without outlining the structure. Similarly, it must be recognized that leadership (or elites)—an element of all controlling overlayers—constitutes a differentiated structure, and that there are many layers of followers "packed" into collectivities and sub-collectivities, which have their own structures. Thus, control mechanisms themselves have structural bases, and their consequences are to be studied in terms of their effects on the actors' positions and relations (i.e., in structural terms). Of particular significance for the present approach is the structural

---

* A person can also retain an expert, but the expert does not become part of his *internal* system and structure.

base of societal guidance. We hold that a societal unit may have one or more sub-units (or overlayers) which enable the unit as a whole to use knowledge, to be committed to one or more policies, and to guide its action toward its realization.

The structural element of the language of societal action distinguishes this approach from system analysis that is conducted in atomistic terms. Such analysis applies a system perspective on one level and atomistic-aggregate, unstructured analysis on all the others. Most input–output and exchange theories qualify by determining, on the highest level of generalization, the functional prerequisites of a system, and then pointing to aggregate exchanges between elites and masses of individuals or among sub-systems, as meeting these functional needs.[40] We seek to advance propositions as to which social units and sub-units specialize in the service of the various functions (though, of course, all units contribute to more than one functional need) *and* about the relations among the units, which make up the societal structure.

Finally, we must introduce the conception of power. We have already seen that our conception of the active orientation draws on *cybernetic* components (e.g., the capacity to use knowledge and to calculate) which are relatively rational and on a capacity to *commit* which has strong non-rational aspects, especially those related to leadership characteristics and values. To these components *power* is added, which is intrinsically neither rational nor irrational. (A major part of the following discussion is devoted to each of these three elements.)

Power as a relational and relative concept assumes that those actors subject to control themselves have varying control capacities, though, by definition, they are less effective than those in control of a particular supra-unit(s). Active units are not assumed to command a superior control mechanism or to be able to drown out other units and force their own way; rather, the capacity to act is to be studied in the context of other units which are in principle similarly endowed. Second, active units are not assumed to be those that suppress their members by powerful controls, but those that have more effective consensus-formation mechanisms, which—as we shall see—are needed for effective and authentic activation of the members *and* of the societal units. It is through consensus-formation that the collectivistic "drag" on action is reduced and the capacity of supra-units to act is enhanced (above and beyond their controlling capacities). Third, societal units frequently face their own pasts as a barrier or cost; changes can be made, but the energy spent in doing so is drawn from the amount available for action directly related to the actors' goals. Thus, we do not assume a capacity for facile action, even where there is an effective guidance mechanism. It was to stress this assumption that we entitled our theory one of societal guidance; societal guidance differs from societal control in that it also includes consensus-formation.

An Illustration

The difference between earlier theories and our approach to the study of action may be illustrated by the difference between the concepts of integration, a key concept of the collectivistic approach, and societal action, central to our approach. Integration characterizes the degree to which the components of a system are bound together. A certain degree of integration is a prerequisite for societal action, for if a unit's bonds are very weak, its members will not be able to act in unison; i.e., the unit will cease to be a unit and will become instead an aggregate of smaller units. But even a highly integrated unit is not necessarily active. Without a controlling overlayer a societal grouping may rise in a stratification structure or change its internal make-up in response to external forces or to the power of other active groupings, but as a unit it will be unable to assume an active stance.* And, conversely, a very active social unit may be integrated only to a limited degree. In fact, it could be argued that a low level of integration enhances a unit's malleability, which, in turn, increases its activation potential. Modernization, for instance, seems to proceed more easily in less than fully integrated regions of a country, all other things being equal (though not in highly disintegrated regions.)

Studies that approach political action from a voluntaristic viewpoint tend to fall into the opposite trap of not taking into account sufficiently the degree of integration. This is particularly true for studies of interest groups. Actually, these groups are sometimes highly integrated and sometimes aggregates, and their political action differs considerably according to their degree of integration, a fact that is not duly recognized in many interest-group studies.[41] This leads to an underestimation of the latitude of an interest group's leadership when the group's membership is poorly integrated, and an overestimation of this factor when it is highly integrated. The same limitation is found in the studies of the relations between public opinion and decision-making elites which view the public as several aggregates, such as more-and-less-educated or more-and-less-committed citizens, disregarding the fact that public opinion is, to a considerable degree, generated in societal units in which an educated and committed minority may lead the rest of the members.[42] In short, the integration of units and their degree of activation are related, but far from identical; a comprehensive theory of societal action must include both and explore their effects on each other.

---

* Hannah Arendt's discussion of "the power generated when people gather together and 'act in concert' " typically confuses this critical distinction between social integration and social action. *The Human Condition* (Chicago: University of Chicago Press, 1958), p. 220.

The Place of Atomistic Sub-Sets

The macro-action approach draws largely on collectivistic and voluntaristic conceptions; the atomistic approach is useful chiefly for the study of an important sub-set of societal entities: inter-unit and/or intra-unit relations when the supra-units which contain these units are weak. Examples of such societal entities include free enterprise markets, interstate relations under relatively "ideal" balance-of-power conditions, "segmental" intertribal relations, and societal entities whose fabrics are so weak that families (or even individuals) interact as if no political organization or societal bonds exist.[43] An atomistic model is also relevant where supra-units set sharp limits on inter-unit relations but leave them relatively unguided within those limits, as, for instance, some kinds of private enterprise in state-controlled economies. These societal situations deserve attention because, aside from being interesting in themselves as representing part of societal reality, they highlight the nature of all other kinds of societal supra-units. What is needed, though, and what atomistic theories do not provide is a theory able to deal with the relations of both weak and powerful supra-units.[44]

To put the same point differently, while some societal processes may be atomistic, many important ones cannot be fruitfully analyzed or understood without assuming a supra-unit with a controlling capacity. For instance, in some societies economic processes are built into other societal relations and require no specialized societal control. This seems to be the case for the exchange relations Malinowski described.[45] Modern economies, however, invariably have a segregated, macroscopic controlling overlayer. Integration of racial groups in a society, to take another example, may be in part atomistic, the result of myriad interactions between members of the various groupings. But, again, it is common for post-modern societies to attempt to influence the process, either by accelerating it (as in Israel) or by hindering it (as in South Africa). Thus, inter-unit relations, even when they can be studied in part by an atomistic theory, must also be approached with a language which recognizes societal supra-units, both because these units account for part of the variance and because they tend to set a context, however weak, for the part for which they do not account. Finally, there is one process which, for reasons which are explored below, cannot be conceived at all without a language which contains supra-units and the components of an active orientation, namely, the political process.

We outlined the ways in which the convergence of collectivistic and voluntaristic assumptions provides for a language of societal action, and indicated the place of atomistic assumptions within such a context. The same convergence encompasses the prevailing traditions of contemporary political science and sociology. We are unable to construct our work within the limits of one discipline because societal action and guidance deals both with political *and* societal processes.

Societal and Political Processes

Political processes, as we see it, have two societal functions: to combine sub-units into a societal unit, to make out of parts a whole, and to guide societal action toward the realization of societal values as expressed *via* the political processes. Thus, the concept of political process provides an answer to the question of how, empirically, a societal "will" is expressed. If these processes are distorted, we shall see, the expression of the members' needs will also be distorted. The service of both functions assumes some awareness of the societal whole *and* its parts, a measure of responsiveness to the members' needs, and some command of power and its purposive exercise. In short, we assume that for a societal entity to exist, political processes are required. We further assume that political processes are the main control mechanism of societal action. (They may be inadequate or distorting but their effect remains the central one.) Hence, the study of the interplay between guidance processes and ongoing ones, between activation and passivity, is an indispensable component of any theory that can hope to account for societal action.

Because the prevailing sociological tradition is collectivistic and several major schools of political science are relatively voluntaristic, the language of societal action must draw on both these disciplines and bridge this interdisciplinary border. More specifically, the societal-action approach draws on the sociological perspective in making societal units rather than individuals or political units the core units of analysis, and in viewing both their internal make-up and their relations as having the qualities of a system. But neither the societal units nor the relations among them are assumed to be given or to change only as the result of ongoing processes. (While some societal units do have a highly "fixed" structure and accommodate to ongoing processes with little self-control, a full socio-political theory—which has to encompass modern society as well as primitive and historical ones and has to deal with religious and social movements, political parties, complex organizations, and states as well as with ethnic groupings and classes, and with the interaction between more active and more passive sub-units—must include, on the most basic level, the concept of a unit capable of a measure of self-guidance, an active societal unit.) Some societal units may have very little self-control, others a great deal, and still others an intermediate amount. While there can be a societal unit without a controlling overlayer, a theory of societal processes without one is markedly incomplete.

The language of societal action draws on political science for its greater concern with the malleable and active aspects of societal units than is common in prevailing sociological theories. Political science deals to a large extent with states rather than societies, with administration rather than informal organization, with parties rather than ethnic groupings or classes, and with voting rather than interaction.[46] In recent years, however, political scientists have become increasingly concerned with the limitations societal bonds impose on macro-action,[47] and some sociologists have become more interested in guidance mechanisms. Thus, a line of analysis has been evolving that bridges the traditional gap between these two disciplines.[48] The present endeavor grows out of this convergence and explicates some of its assumptions.

The need to augment sociological-collectivistic approaches arises out of the recognition that macro-units are not only bound to each other or "interacting," but also guide themselves vis-à-vis each other *and* their shared relationships. The courses they take, while in part determined by other units' movements, are also affected by their accurate or inaccurate interpretation of those movements, by their decisions about how to react, and by collectively determined policies. That this is the case could not be better known; what is less well known is that the prevailing sociological theories do not provide the analytic tools to explain these aspects of macroscopic data. Thus, concepts which sociological-collectivistic analyses tend not to use play a key role in our language of societal action. First among these are the concepts necessary to explore an active orientation: Information, consciousness, decision-making, policy, and strategy.*

----

* The concepts listed are not treated in the leading theoretical books and textbooks of sociology. Thus, for instance, an examination of the index of eight books of Parsons published between 1937 and 1964, shows that consciousness appears only twice (in *The Structure of Social Action, op. cit.*, referring to Durkheim's "collective-consciousness.") Decision-making and information are treated in the study of complex organizations but not in that of collectivities or societies. Policy and strategy are not explored. In Merton's revised edition of *Social Theory and Social Structure, op. cit.*, consciousness appears in discussions of Marx's concept of false consciousness. Decision-making, information, and strategy are not treated. Charles P. Loomis' review of modern theories (*Modern Social Theories*, 2nd edition, Princeton: Van Nostrand, 1965) and his own theoretical work (*Social Systems: Essays on Their Persistence and Change*, Princeton: Van Nostrand, 1960) list one of these concepts (decision-making); the others do not appear. Among textbooks, Leonard S. Broom and Philip Selznick's *Sociology*, revised edition (New York: Harper & Row, 1963) mentions one of these concepts once; Kingsley Davis' *Human Society* (New York: Macmillan, 1953) not once (consciousness is listed in the personal but not the social sense); none appears in Harry M. Johnson's *Sociology* (New York: Harcourt, Brace & World, 1960); and none in one of the best readers in elementary sociology, that of Logan Wilson and William L. Kolb (*Sociological Analysis*, New York: Harcourt, Brace & World, 1949). "The persistence of evolutionary, biologistic, instinctivist theories in French, British, and American sociology (even in Sumner and Park) obstructed the formulation of a socio-logical theory in which knowledge and decision were important categories." Edward A. Shils in Talcott Parsons et al., *Theories of Society* (New York: Free Press, 1961), Vol. II, p. 1434. These sociological works are not criticized for not covering elements they never attempted to cover; rather, the areas they exclude serve to illustrate what the prevailing sociological traditions considered outside their proper domain.

A Dynamic Perspective

Societal Change and the Active Orientation

Collectivistic approaches, as we saw, tend to see societal constraints as given, while societal-action analyses view the same constraints as in part the results of past actions and, thus, in part, choices.[49] Understanding the latter requires examination of the routes followed as well as of the alternatives weighed but rejected, available but ignored.

The inclusion of the *unchosen* alternatives in societal guidance analysis has three advantages. It depicts more accurately the extent of man's freedom. It helps reveal the qualities of the guidance mechanisms, which is of explanatory and predictive value since the more we know about the reasons alternatives were misjudged, well chosen, or disregarded, the better we understand what happened and what is likely to happen the next time choices are made. Finally, viewing constraints as in part the results of past actions alerts analysts to their dynamic quality and to the possibility of overcoming them. The study of how they were erected suggests how they may be restructured.[50] All this suggests that societal determinism, even if conceived only as a heuristic device, has undesirable side-effects; it renders the theory and the theoretician more passive than the facts warrant.

A theory of societal guidance seeks to make societal analyses not merely more dynamic, a need which has often been recognized, but also more active. These terms, it should be stressed, are not the same. As long as change is viewed as the "natural" outgrowth of ongoing processes such as institutionalization, the phase movement, or differentiation, we have the elements of a dynamic system analysis without a conception of an active orientation. A theory of guidance asks how a given actor guides a process and how he changes a unit's structure or boundaries. The main differences are not between change and no-change, but between guided changes and ongoing processes whether they involve change or not.*

Finally, the morphological perspectives which collectivistic and societal-action approaches adopt differ in this dimension. In the collectivistic approach, structure characterizes the specific relationships among the member units. The theory of societal guidance asks, in addition, how a given structure was modelled, how it is maintained, how it can be altered, where are the seats of power, who commands knowledge, and who has the capacity to commit. In short, it seeks to discover who controls the societal processes and under what conditions any and all of these features can be altered.

---

* The distinction between guided and unguided is an analytic continuum. Each process may be scored as more versus less guided and may have sub-processes that vary in the degree to which they are guided.

A Functional–Genetic Approach

The theory of societal guidance draws on both functional and genetic conceptions in that it uses a concept of alternative contributions to a system as well as a temporal perspective.[51] (We use "genetic" rather than "historical" because we reserve the term "history" for macroscopic, societal genetics.)* The earlier functional approach of Malinowski and Radcliffe-Brown, which is still occasionally confused with the latter-day Mertonian functional analysis by some critics,[52] made several assumptions that gave functional analysis a static and conservative flavor. But these assumptions are not inherent in the approach.[53] There is no need to assume that every item of behavior has a function, or that functional consequences are normatively preferable to dysfunctional ones.[54] Giving full status to functional alternatives and distinguishing them systematically from functional equivalents[55] allows us to see how new alternatives are introduced, how weight is shifted from one alternative to another, and how structure changes.

Over the last decade, the notion that social sciences may rely on two theories, one of statics and one of dynamics, has gained a measure of popularity. This notion draws on an analogy to physics, in which both beam and wave theories of light are used simultaneously. But in both fields such a bifocal approach is actually a measure of despair for the lack of a theory which might unite all processes. We shall attempt in the remainder of this chapter to suggest why such despair may be premature.

Most functional analysis, even in its later metamorphosis, is still collectivistic, emphasizing the interdependence of the members of an existing system. While it is a useful tool for the conceptualization of supra-units, it adds little to the study of inter-unit relations when the system's bonds are weaker and to the study of the conditions under which supra-units evolve from inter-unit relations. Above all, while it can define the conditions under which a structure will be disbanded, it has no systematic answer to the question of which new societal structure will appear instead.

One significant advance, still within the collectivistic· tradition of functionalism, is to be found in those theories which contain a limited universe of possible structures and rules of transformation; this allows one to suggest—when a specific structure disbands—which other patterns the system may take, and which patterns are most likely to evolve.[56] However, to link the functional analysis of systems with that of guided change, two

---

* In using genetic models it is important to distinguish between them as heuristic devices and as hypotheses about real processes. Hobbes' explanation of the social contract as involving a transition from a natural to a societal state is viewed as heuristic device by generous critics and as an hypothesis by less friendly ones. The same may be said about the treatments of Freud's cultural genetics and Mead's genesis of the personal self. Blau's genetic assumptions (in his *Exchange and Power, op. cit.*) seem to be heuristic; ours are propositional.

capacities must be assumed: (a) The capacity of the overlayer of a unit to design a future structure (the degree to which such a design specifies answers which meet known functional prerequisites tells a good deal about how "realistic" the unit is), and (b) the capacity of the unit to transform its system in line with the design.

By adding the concept of options to functional analysis, we add the notion that some alternatives are more readily available than others. We note next that as a rule no two options have the same societal costs and consequences. These, in turn, are affected by earlier choices and by opportunities which were neglected. These guidance concepts serve to link a genetic with a structural-functional approach, and a more historical with a more analytical one.* This provides the conceptual formulation for our opening hypothesis, that the active society is an option of the historical transition from the modern to the post-modern era. It is an option in the sense that nothing in its design violates any functional *prerequisites*, although its realization entails a choice among several sets of functional *alternatives* and a fundamental societal *change*.

The course of action a societal unit follows is not viewed as leading mechanically from one stage to another. On the contrary, at each stage an actor under study is viewed as having had other options of which he was aware, unaware, or partially aware; such "symbolic" factors as the degree of his awareness and the quality of his decision-making do affect his history. Every actor is assumed to have some options; the extent of these options seems greater in later historical periods than in earlier ones.† While we hold that this moderated voluntarism can be justified by empirical findings, it is also essential to note that without such assumptions about the nature of the relationship between societal actors and history, there is no objective base for a critical, transcendental stand.

How the options which were not exercised and the intra-overlayer processes which affected the choices are to be analyzed is far from self-evident.

---

* The idea of linking a general and abstract theory with a study of the particular and concrete, of the historical, is age-old. John Stuart Mill explored this possibility in his discussion of the concept of "*axiomata media*" in his *A System of Logic* (New York: Harper & Bros., 1850), Vol. II, Book 6, Chapter 5, Section 5, pp. 544–545. Karl Mannheim revived this idea and specifically related it to modern social science in his *Man and Society in an Age of Reconstruction* (New York: Harcourt, Brace & World, 1940), pp. 173–190. It was further explored by Adolf Löwe, *Economics and Sociology* (London: Allen & Unwin, 1935), and in a little known article by Talcott Parsons reviewing this effort, "Book Reviews," *American Journal of Sociology*, Vol. 43 (1937), pp. 477–481, as well as by C. Wright Mills, *The Sociological Imagination, op. cit.*, pp. 149 ff. Most of these works focus on the general virtues of relating the two perspectives; we further suggest the utility of tying the genetic historical approach to a version of functional analysis and attempt later in this volume to lay out some of the details of such an approach.

† Marx referred to a period of "necessity" to be followed by a period of "freedom," making the contrast too strong and the jump too sharp but pointing in a similar direction to the one suggested here.

History can be studied as a sequence of events, and the effects of earlier events on later ones can be explored without viewing these events as in part the outcome of controlling processes and societal choices. But such an actorless history would underestimate societies' ability to transform themselves, would omit an important segment of what *did* happen, and neglect some of the most significant insights the past may provide for the future.

As far as functional models are concerned, one can use several system referents arranged along a time dimension and ask what functions an item in one system serves for the transformation toward, and for the maintenance of, a later system. In particular, the comparison of synchronic and future systems seems useful.[57]

As far as guidance is concerned, the properties of the societal overlayers are to be explored to advance propositions about the degree to which their qualities affect the creation and exploitation of new options.* This assumes a cybernetic capacity on the societal level, societal power, and consensus-formation. As we shall see in detail below, our difference from cybernetic theory on this point is rather considerable. Cybernetics has often been characterized as the study of controlling heavy energy-expending units (those which do the "work") by low energy units (the controlling ones), because it is assumed that direction relies on information and communication of cognitive signals[58] which require only relay energy. We shall argue below that these signals must either be backed by energy (i.e., power), or they must begin not with downward controlling signals but with signals worked out with those to be controlled, in an authentic consensus-forming process. At the same time, cybernetics does not answer the question of what propels basic changes, while the present approach points to the exercise of power or authentic consensus-formation as the energizers of societal transformations.

While we are not concerned with this question here, it seems that the study of personality and individual behavior may also benefit from greater use of the conception of an active orientation. Widely held theories of social control imply that actors conform or deviate, reward or punish automatically, according to some internalized norms and psychological needs. But the actors are in part conscious of their behavior and choose here not to respond and there to deliberately "overreact," here to punish and there to forgive. Therefore, they can be fruitfully compared not just in terms of their values, the degree to which they have internalized them, and the extent of their assertiveness or submissiveness but also in terms of the degree to which they

---

* Here are two links to dialectic analysis: (a) the view of societies as exhausting more versus less of their potential, and (b) the level of realization of the existing options may well be lower at the end of a period than at its beginning, and, therefore, the process is dialectic rather than unilinear if more than one period is taken into account. Pierre L. van den Berghe, "Dialectic and Functionalism: Toward a Theoretical Synthesis," *American Sociological Review*, Vol. 28 (1963), pp. 695–705.

are conscious of what they are doing, to what theories of social control *they* subscribe, and what strategies they adopt.[59]

A collectivistic reductionist may argue that reactions to deviant acts, such as forgiveness or punitiveness, are defined by norms and values which are internalized and institutionalized just like those that define which acts are deviant and which are conforming. In part, this is a question for empirical research; that is, are the norms and values that affect the intensity and modes of commitment and sanctioning as socio-culturally imprinted as the substance of the norms and values on which these are predicated, or is there here a greater number of individual and micro-unit options? More important for the present discussion is that, however they are determined, these norms and values constitute a second-order set on top of the controlled one. The first set defines what is a deviation, and the second defines various ways of reacting to it. In any event, sanctioning is not automatic and the choices made on the second (controlling) level are one significant factor in determining the socio-cultural imprinting. For instance, if the choice made is frequently to forego sanctioning, this may lead to a loosening of the standards, or to new efforts to imprint them, or to some other action; but whatever it is, the accumulation of choices has an effect on the socio-cultural imprinting and not only the other way around. A theory of personality may also benefit from assuming a degree of malleability and from using the concepts of cybernetic overlayers working on underlayers of ongoing processes, combining a guidance and a functional–genetic perspective.[60]

What is widely referred to as a social action theory is actually a collectivistic theory.[61] As a theory which is universal in its structure, it recognizes an actor who sets goals and chooses among means. (That the actor is free to choose between compliance to and violation of norms is not systematically taken into account, even on this level.) No parallel is found in the study of small groups, collectivities, societies, or social units in general. In exploring these, a collectivistic model is followed. The stress on the role of ideas and values makes the "universal" theory of action non-mechanistic but not a theory of societal (macroscopic) action, not to mention guidance. Values introduce the element of interpretation; i.e., units do not affect each other directly but through filters of interpretation of each other's behavior. But these interpretations themselves are viewed as related in a collectivistic manner.[62] Science, religion, philosophy, and ideology are "sub-systems"; they are differentiated, they "interact," and so on. But no actor or combination of actors guides these processes, even in part.

A theory that takes an active view of symbolic processes would include a conception of the capacity of the actors to guide in part the direction in which ideas develop and the ways in which sub-systems of symbols relate to each other. Most important, it would take a much less "tight" view of the relations among normative themes and between them and the societal structures. Most normative systems most of the time can be used to legitimize two or more societal structures. Which of the alternative themes is chosen, which option is exercised, depends in part on the societal actors. This is not to suggest that the normative systems provide no constrictions or can be readily manipulated. The range of options available is limited, some alternatives have less legitimating power than others, and some are more costly to establish than others.[63] Symbolic systems are not to be viewed as monolithic or as quasi-organic webs but as sets of options. Typical collectivistic studies tend to view man as preferring what he ought to prefer and choosing what he must choose; when he deviates, the direction, scope, and substance of his deviation are also conceived as predetermined. Voluntarism allowed for is thus illusory, and options are not an integral part of the perspective. This is not a valid view of individual actors and, above all, of combinations of them.

The forerunner of a societal guidance inter-disciplinary theory which draws on a functional–genetic language may well be found in a major line of development in organizational analysis. Here, the interaction between what is referred to as formal and informal relations, control structure and participants, rational orientations and collectivities, has long been the focus of two traditions whose convergence provides a language for theories of macro-action.[64] Here is a typical statement, which stands for scores of others that could be cited, from a recent work in the sociology of complex organizations:

> ... the leader is an agent of institutionalization, offering a guiding hand to a process that would otherwise occur more haphazardly, more readily subject to accidents of circumstances and history. This is not to say that the leader is free to do as he wishes, to mold the organization according to his heart's desire, restrained only by the quality of his imagination and the strength of his will.[65]

The application of such a statement to societal actors is less automatic than it may seem.[66] The role of leadership in a society is, under most historical situations, much more limited than that of leadership in many corporations. The form may also be quite different, with control centers—such as the White House staff or planning agencies—taking over large segments of the functions fulfilled in organizations by leading personalities. In general, however, there is much promise in the application of the sociology of organizations to the study of society; it has combined the voluntaristic and collectivistic traditions more systematically than have societal studies, and post-modern society is becoming more and more like a very complex organization.

NOTES

1. For a methodological treatment, see Paul F. Lazarsfeld and Morris Rosenberg, "Introduction" to the volume they edited *The Language of Social Research* (New York: Free Press, 1957), pp. 15–18.

2. See Chap. 3, pp. 45–46, on hierarchical relations.

3. "The Negro masses ... still serve white people but they no longer trust, respect, nor love them. ... And with the breakdown of faith in the integrity of the

white power structure there is a concomitant loss of respect for law as an effective means of social change. This, I submit, is the main reason why the Negro revolt has come now and as it has." Louis E. Lomax, *The Negro Revolt* (New York: Harper & Row, 1962), p. 77. Each Negro is viewed in this typical statement, as interacting with a white man, and—with the "white power structure."

4. There are numerous interpretations of the balance-of-power conception. See Ernst B. Haas, "The Balance of Power as a Guide to Policy Making," *Journal of Politics*, Vol. 15 (1953), pp. 370–398; Paul Seabury (ed.), *Balance of Power* (San Francisco: Chandler, 1965); F. H. Hinsley, *Power and the Pursuit of Peace: Theory and Practice in the History of Relations between States* (Cambridge, England: Cambridge University Press, 1963). These need not concern us here, since the assumptions spelled out below appear in most of them.

5. Henry A. Kissinger, *A World Restored* (Boston: Houghton Mifflin, 1957), pp. 7–85, 319–321, 329–330. See also Edward V. Gulick, *Europe's Classical Balance of Power* (Ithaca, N.Y.: Cornell University Press, 1955), pp. 4–5, 10–24.

6. For references and discussion, see below, pp. 583–586.

7. For a presentation of this approach, see David Riesman, in collaboration with Reuel Denney and Nathan Glazer, *The Lonely Crowd* (New Haven: Yale University Press, 1950), pp. 244–254 and 266. For critiques, see Ralf Dahrendorf, "Democracy without Liberty," and William Kornhauser, " 'Power Elite' or 'Veto Groups'?" in Seymour M. Lipset and Leo Lowenthal, *Culture and Social Character* (New York: Free Press, 1961), pp. 175–206 and pp. 252–267 respectively. See also Ernest S. Griffith, *Impasse of Democracy* (New York: Harrison-Hilton Books, Inc., 1939).

8. Earl Latham, *The Group Basis of Politics* (Ithaca, N.Y.: Cornell University Press, 1952). See also William H. Riker, *The Theory of Political Coalitions* (New Haven: Yale University Press, 1962).

9. David B. Truman, *The Governmental Process* (New York: Knopf, 1951). Charles E. Lindblom, *The Intelligence of Democracy* (New York: Free Press, 1965).

10. Lewis Anthony Dexter, "What Do Congressmen Hear: The Mail," *Public Opinion Quarterly*, Vol. 20 (1957), pp. 16–27; Bernard C. Cohen, *The Influence of Non-governmental Groups on Foreign Policy Making* (Boston: World Peace Foundation, 1959).

11. See on transactional analysis, Karl W. Deutsch and I. Richard Savage, "A Statistical Model of the Gross Analysis of Transactional Flows," *Econometrica*, Vol. 28 (1960), pp. 551–572; Karl W. Deutsch, "Shifts in the Balance of Communication Flows: A Problem of Measurement in International Relations," *Public Opinion Quarterly*, Vol. 20 (1956), pp. 143–160; and Karl W. Deutsch, "Transaction Flows as Indicators of Political Cohesion," in Philip E. Jacob and James V. Toscano (eds.), *The Integration of Political Communities* (Philadelphia: Lippincott, 1964), pp. 75–97; Llewellyn Gross, "A Transactional Interpretation of Social Problems," in Llewellyn Gross (ed.), *Sociological Theory: Inquiries and Paradigms* (New York: Harper & Row, 1967), pp. 315–331.

12. Daniel Bell, preface to Sir Leon Bagrit, *The Age of Automation* (New York: Mentor, 1965), p. xix.

13. On this concept see Ludwig von Bertalanffy, "General System Theory," *General Systems*, Vol. 1 (1956), pp. 1–10; W. R. Ashby, "Principles of the Self-Organizing System," in Heinz M. von Foerster and George W. Zopf, Jr. (eds.),

Principles of Self-Organizations: Transactions (New York: Pergamon Press,. 1962), pp. 255–278; Talcott Parsons and Neil J. Smelser, *Economy and Society* (New York: Free Press, 1956), pp. 8–9, 14–15; Morton A. Kaplan, *System and Process in International Politics* (New York: Wiley & Sons, 1957), pp. 4–5; Charles B. Robson, "Der Begriff des 'Politischen Systems' " ("The Concept of 'Political System' "), *Kölner Zeitschrift für Soziologie und Sozialpsychologie*, Vol. 17 (1965), pp. 521–527; J. P. Nettl, "The Concept of System in Political Science," *Political Studies*, Vol. 14 (1966), pp. 305–338. For similar definitions and a bibliography of related works, see James G. Miller, "Living Systems: Basic Concepts," *Behavioral Science*, Vol. 10 (1965), pp. 193–237. See also Neal Gross et al., *Explorations in Role Analysis, op. cit.*, p. 53.

14. The supra-unit concept is referred to as a "natural system model" by Alvin W. Gouldner, "Organizational Analysis," Merton, Broom, and Cottrell, *Sociology Today, op. cit.*, Vol. II, pp. 400–407. On an inter-unit concept of systems, see Bertalanffy, "General System Theory," *op. cit.*

15. For instance, when density is high, the probability that the movement of one unit will affect that of another and that this in turn will affect the first one is high.

16. Robert Herman and Keith Gardels, "Vehicular Traffic Flow," *Scientific American*, Vol. 209 (1963), pp. 35–43, esp. pp. 35–36. Arthur L. Stinchcombe, "A Parsonian Theory of Traffic Accidents," a paper presented to the annual meeting of the American Sociological Association in Miami, Florida, September 1966.

17. Walter B. Cannon, *The Wisdom of the Body*, rev. ed. (New York: Norton, 1963), pp. 177 ff.

18. According to Durkheim, the division of labor varies directly with the volume and density of societies, and, if it progresses in a continuous manner in the course of social development, this is because societies become regularly denser and generally more voluminous. Emile Durkheim, *The Division of Labor in Society*, trans. by George Simpson (New York: Free Press, 1933), p. 262. See also references in footnote 6, Chapter 1.

19. Robert E. Park and Ernest W. Burgess, *Introduction to the Science of Sociology* (Chicago: University of Chicago Press, 1924), pp. 504–784. For other "collectivistic" works on ethnic relations, see the works of E. Franklin Frazier, in particular *The Negro in the United States* (New York: Macmillan, rev. ed., 1957), and Tamotsu Shibutani, Kian M. Kwan, and Robert H. Billigmeier, *Ethnic Stratification: A Comparative Approach* (New York: Macmillan, 1965).

20. ". . . after the first internalized social object has been established, the process of differentiation of the personality system proceeds by the 'splitting' of each of these internalized objects into two." Talcott Parsons and Robert F. Bales, *Family, Socialization, and Interaction Process, op. cit.*, p. 29. See also T. Parsons, "Some Considerations on the Theory of Social Change," *Rural Sociology*, Vol. 26 (1961), pp. 219–239; Amitai Etzioni, "The Functional Differentiation of Elites in the Kibbutz," *American Journal of Sociology*, Vol. 64 (1959), pp. 476–487 and S. N. Eisenstadt, "Social Change, Differentiation, and Evolution," *American Sociological Review*, Vol. 29 (1964), pp. 375–386.

21. On the guidance of biological systems, see James D. Watson, *Molecular Biology of the Gene* (New York: Benjamin, 1965), pp. 416–425; Philip E. Hartman and Sigmund R. Suskind, *Gene Action* (Englewood Cliffs, N.J.: Prentice-Hall,

1965), pp. 141–146. See also Arnold W. Ravin, *The Evolution of Genetics* (New York: Academic Press, 1965).

The main debate was historically between the preformists and the epigenesists. The first argued that the initial undifferentiated cells include, as a *sub*-unit, a differentiated guidance mechanism (or code), capable of guiding the differentiation of the *unit* itself. The opposition disagreed but suggested no alternative mechanism. Among the preformists were Bonnet, Hallee, and Halpighi; among the epigenesists were Harvey, Wolff, and Goethe. For a sociological application, see Amitai Etzioni, "The Epigenesis of Political Communities at the International Level," *American Journal of Sociology*, Vol. 68 (1963), pp. 407–421.

22. For a discussion of this point, see Anatol Rapoport, "Mathematical, Evolutionary, and Psychological Approaches to the Study of Total Societies," in Samuel Z. Klausner (ed.), *The Study of Total Societies* (Garden City, N.Y.: Doubleday, 1967), pp. 123 ff; and A. G. Jacobson, "Inductive Processes in Embryonic Development," *Science*, Vol. 152 (1 April 1966), pp. 25–34.

23. See, for instance, Lloyd A. Fallers, *Bantu Bureaucracy* (Chicago: University of Chicago Press, 1965), and L. Pospisil, "Social Change and Primitive Law: Consequences of a Papuan Legal Case," *American Anthropologist*, Vol. 60 (1958), pp. 832–837.

24. The founders of the *kibbutz* movement, probably the most extensive socialist utopian experiment, were highly optimistic about their capacity to remold man and society. On this and other Utopian settlements, see Martin Buber, *Path to Utopia* (Boston: Beacon Hill, 1958).

25. For a discussion of a suggestion to consider the state as a person, see James M. Buchanan, "The Pure Theory of Government Finance," *Journal of Political Economy*, Vol. 57 (1949), pp. 496–505. Harold G. Nicolson laments the passing of classic diplomacy in these terms in his *The Evolution of Diplomatic Method* (London: Constable, 1954). ". . . statesmen under the pressure of necessity turn the steering wheel in a direction which will destroy the ship of state in a titanic collision instead of bring it into the harbor of peace." Quincy Wright, "International Conflict and the United Nations," *World Politics*, Vol. 10 (1957), p. 33. Wright is referring here Lewis F. Richardson.

26. "Wars," says the UNESCO Constitution, "begin in the minds of men." *Ibid.*, p. 26. Philip Selznick discusses the view of the business executive as a man who can mold his corporation "according to his heart's desire." See his *Leadership in Administration* (New York: Harper & Row, 1957), pp. 26–28; see also p. 60.

27. For a review of works in this line, see Lucian W. Pye, "Personal Identity and Political Ideology," *Behavioral Science*, Vol. 6 (1961), pp. 205–221. The development in the work of Harold D. Lasswell from a more to a less voluntaristic conception is discussed (especially pp. 206–207). See also Nathan Leites, "Psychocultural Hypotheses about Political Acts," *World Politics*, Vol. 1 (1948), pp. 102–119.

28. Otto Klineberg, *The Human Dimension in International Relations* (New York: Holt, Rinehart & Winston, 1964). Among the writings in this vein are the works of Erich Fromm, Erik H. Erikson, Jerome Frank, Abraham Kardiner, and Heinz Hartman. For critical discussions, see Frank Riessman and S. M. Miller, "Social Change Versus the 'Psychiatric World View'," *The American Journal of Orthopsychiatry*, Vol. 34 (1964), pp. 29–38, and Kenneth N. Waltz, *Man, the State, and War* (New York: Columbia University Press, 1959). On the concept of national

character, see Emily M. Nett, "An Evaluation of the National Character Concept in Sociological Theory," *Social Forces*, Vol. 36 (1958), pp. 297–303.

29. For the psychological assumptions behind this approach in political science, see Thomas I. Cook, "Democratic Psychology and Democratic World Order," *World Politics*, Vol. 1 (1949), pp. 553–564.

30. J. B. Scott, *Law, the State, and the International Community* (New York: Columbia University Press, 1939). For a more sophisticated approach, see Elmore Jackson, *Meeting of Minds* (New York: McGraw Hill, 1952). Most writings in the "conflict resolution" and "problem solving" traditions are voluntaristic, often to a high degree.

31. Luther H. Gulick and L. Urwick (eds.), *Papers on the Science of Administration* (New York: Institute of Public Administration, Columbia University, 1937). For more recent work, see John M. Pfiffner and Frank P. Sherwood, *Administrative Organization* (Englewood Cliffs, N.J.: Prentice-Hall, 1960), esp. Chapter 6.

32. See Martin Shubik (ed.), *Game Theory and Related Approaches to Social Behavior* (New York: Wiley, 1964) and Jacob Marschak and Leonid Hurwicz, *Games and Economic Behavior* (Chicago: Cowles Commission for Research in Economics, 1946). See also James M. Buchanan and Gordon Tullock, *The Calculus of Consent: Logical Foundations of Constitutional Democracy* (Ann Arbor: University of Michigan Press, 1962), Gordon Tullock, *The Politics of Bureaucracy* (Washington, D.C.: Public Affairs Press, 1965), and Duncan Black, *The Theory of Committees and Elections* (Cambridge, England: Cambridge University Press, 1958). For a study of "group" behavior explained in terms of individualistic goals, see Mancur Olson, Jr., *The Logic of Collective Action* (Cambridge, Mass.: Harvard University Press, 1965).

33. For a recent study, see Anthony Downs, *An Economic Theory of Democracy* (New York: Harper & Row, 1957). See also William J. Baumol, *Welfare Economics and the Theory of the State* (London: Longmans, Green, 1952). For one of the most encompassing expressions of this tradition, see the work of Quincy Wright, especially his *A Study of War* (Chicago: University of Chicago Press, 1965), Chapter 29, "International Organization and War," pp. 1043–1078. See also K. C. Wheare, *Federal Government* (New York: Oxford University Press, 1964, 4th ed.). For a major critique, see E. H. Carr, *The Twenty Years' Crisis*, second edition (New York: St. Martin's Press, 1956). Charles S. Hyneman, in *The Study of Politics* (Urbana: University of Illinois Press, 1959), Chapter 3, further analyzes this approach.

34. Hans J. Morgenthau, *Politics Among Nations* (New York: Knopf, 1954), p. 3. See also his *Scientific Man vs. Power Politics* (Chicago: University of Chicago Press, Phoenix Edition, 1965), p. 14 ff. Here Morgenthau occasionally draws near the opposite trap, an irrationally governed world (e.g., pp. 153–167). Waltz notes that "Morgenthau sees 'the ubiquity of evil in human action' arising from man's ineradicable lust for power and transforming 'churches into political organizations . . . revolutions into dictatorships . . . love for country into imperialism.' " *Ibid.*, pp. 194–195, quoted in Waltz, *Man, the State and War, op. cit.*, p. 24.

35. Herbert A. Simon, *Models of Man* (New York: Wiley, 1957), and also his second edition of *Administrative Behavior* (New York: Macmillan, 1957). See also works by Olson and by Downs cited above.

36. Thomas C. Schelling, *The Strategy of Conflict* (Cambridge, Mass.: Harvard University Press, 1960), is most often cited in this context.

37. J. G. Miller, "Toward a General Theory for the Behavioral Sciences," *American Psychologist*, Vol. 10 (1955), pp. 513–531; Charles R. Dechert, "The Development of Cybernetics," *The American Behavioral Scientist*, Vol. 8 (1965), pp. 15–20; Rieger, "The Mechanics of Bureaucracy," *op. cit.* For works relating this approach to organizational analysis, see Lucien Mehl, "La Cybernétique et l'Administration," *Revue Administrative*, 58 (1957), pp. 410–419, and Georges Langrod, "Les Applications de la Cybernétique à l'Administration Publique," *International Review of Administrative Sciences*, 24 (1958), pp. 295–312. In recent years there has been a growing interest in this approach in the Soviet Union. See Aksel I. Berg (ed.), *Kibernetiku na Sluzhbu Kommunizmu* (Moscow–Leningrad, 1961); English translation, U.S. Joint Publications Research Service, *Cybernetics at the Service of Communism* (Washington, 1962). For earlier, basic works, see Arturo Rosenblueth, Norbert Wiener, and Julian Bigelow, "Behavior, Purpose, and Teleology," *Philosophy of Science*, Vol. 10 (1943), pp. 18–24, and Norbert Wiener, *Cybernetics* (New York: Wiley & Sons, 1948).

38. Norman Abramson, *Information Theory and Coding* (New York: McGraw-Hill, 1963); Richard L. Meier, "The Measurement of Social Change," 1959 *Proceedings of the Western Joint Computer Conference*, pp. 327–331; E. N. Gilbert, "Information Theory after 18 Years," *Science*, Vol. 152 (15 April 1966), pp. 320–326. See also Fred S. Grodins, *Control Theory and Biological Systems* (New York: Columbia University Press, 1963), pp. 16–26.

39. For a fine article applying a societal guidance view to modernization, see Harold D. Lasswell, "The Policy Sciences of Development," *World Politics*, Vol. 17 (1965), pp. 286–309. For a good overview of other approaches and numerous references, see Robert A. Packenham, "Approaches to the Study of Political Development," *World Politics*, Vol. 17 (1964), pp. 108–120.

40. For major works in system theory, varying in the emphasis on structural aspects, see sociological works—Talcott Parsons and Neil J. Smelser, especially their *Economy and Society*, *op. cit.*, and recent works by Eisenstadt and by Blau, which combine an output–input exchange analysis with varying degrees of structural analysis. Peter M. Blau, *Exchange and Power*, *op. cit.*; S. N. Eisenstadt, *Essays on Comparative Institutions* (New York: Wiley, 1965), pp. 16 ff. In political science, see David Easton, *A Systems Analysis of Political Life* (New York: Wiley & Sons, 1965); Gabriel A. Almond, "A Developmental Approach to Political Systems," *World Politics*, Vol. 17 (1965), pp. 183–214.

41. See, for example, the discussion of interest groups in Arthur F. Bentley, *The Process of Government*, new ed. (Evanston, Ill.: The Principia Press of Illinois, 1949), pp. 203–212, especially p. 211; J. Leiper Freeman, *The Political Process* (New York: Random House, 1965), pp. 5–11. David Easton complained: "In political science research workers tend to lump all social aggregates together as though for purposes of research no one aggregate was different from another." *The Political System* (New York: Knopf, 1953), p. 181. Truman, on the other hand, takes the degree of integration of an interest "group" into account. See his *The Governmental Process op. cit.*, esp. pp. 156–187. See also Harmon Zeigler, *Interest Groups in American Society* (Englewood Cliffs, N.J.: Prentice-Hall, 1964), cf. Joseph La Polombara, *Interest Groups in Italian Politics* (Princeton: Princeton University Press, 1964). Studies of both kinds are included in Henry W. Ehrmann (ed.), *Interest Groups on Four Continents* (Pittsburgh, Penn.: University of Pittsburgh Press, 1958).

42. For a study of the differences between leadership and followers which recognizes the non-aggregate quality of the various publics, see Samuel A. Stouffer, *Communism, Conformity, and Civil Liberties* (Garden City, N.Y.: Doubleday, 1955).

43. For a case study, see Edward C. Banfield, *The Moral Basis of a Backward Society* (New York: Free Press, 1958). See also footnote 3, Ch. 5.

44. David Easton made this point in the context of criticizing some anthropologists for having two theories, one for state and one for state-less tribes. See his "Political Anthropology" in Bernard J. Siegel (ed.), *Biennial Review of Anthropology* (Stanford: Stanford University Press, 1959), p. 235. See also Chadwick F. Alger, "Comparison of Intranational and International Politics," *American Political Science Review*, Vol. 57 (1963), pp. 414–419.

45. Bronislaw Malinowski, *Argonauts of the Western Pacific* (New York: E. P. Dutton, 1961), pp. 85 ff.

46. There are, of course, different schools and traditions in political science, although many of them are macroscopic. In recent decades, however, a strong atomistic trend has developed which focuses on "the study of *individuals* rather than larger political units" (italics in original). Robert A. Dahl, "The Behavioral Approach in Political Science: Epitaph for a Monument to a Successful Protest," *American Political Science Review*, Vol. 55 (1961), p. 766. Dahl quotes David Easton, *The Political System, op. cit.*, pp. 201–205, to the same effect. See also David B. Truman, "The Implications of Political Behavior Research," *Items* (SSRC), Vol. 5 (December 1951), pp. 37–39.

47. Actually, one political scientist, Manfred Halpern, argued that political science went so far in this direction that it lost its power as an autonomous discipline and became submerged in sociology: "The tendency of sociologists and anthropologists to think of political systems as embedded in social systems . . . has also led to the habit (though it did not need to do so) of viewing the political system as merely derived from society. . . . Political scientists themselves have contributed to this diminution of political analysis by uncritically accepting this prevailing structural functional habit . . ." "Toward Further Modernization of the Study of New Nations," *World Politics*, Vol. 17 (1964), p. 163.

48. Two works that approach the center of this convergence are Seymour M. Lipset, *Political Man* (Garden City, N.Y.: Doubleday, 1960), which advances the tradition surprisingly far with little self-conscious methodological or rigid theoretical framework, and Karl W. Deutsch, *The Nerves of Government, op. cit.* (which still has a strong voluntaristic-rationalistic accent). See also John A. Porter, *The Vertical Mosaic: An Analysis of Social Class and Power in Canada* (Toronto, Canada: Toronto University Press, 1965) and Franz Schurmann, *Ideology and Organization in Communist China* (Berkeley: University of California Press, 1966). Carl J. Friedrich (*Man and His Government, op. cit.*) represents the convergence from the political science side, on a textbook level; Gabriel A. Almond, Sidney Verba, and James S. Coleman bring to the tradition a social–psychological dimension, as does Lucian W. Pye, *Politics, Personality, and Nation Building* (New Haven: Yale University Press, 1962). David Apter, *The Politics of Modernization* (Chicago: University of Chicago Press, 1965), Lloyd Fallers, *Bantu Bureaucracy, op. cit.*, and Morris Janowitz, *The Military in the Political Development of New Nations* (Chicago: University of Chicago Press, 1964) are coming to the convergence from a "social

forces" or system theory direction. Alain Touraine's concept of *actionalisme* approaches the same perspective from a more socio-philosophical tradition. See his *Sociologie de l'Action* (Paris: Editions du Seuil, 1965). From the cybernetic direction, see Alfred Kuhn, *The Study of Society: A Unified Approach* (Homewood, Ill.: Richard D. Irwin, Inc., 1963). See also S. F. Nadel, *The Theory of Social Structure* (New York: Free Press, 1958), esp. pp. 128 and 153.

Non-dogmatic Marxist analysis provides important elements for a theory of societal action. Cf. Parsons "The Point of View of the Author," Max Black (ed.), *The Social Theories of Talcott Parsons* (Englewood Cliffs, N.J.: Prentice-Hall, 1961), p. 362, and Seymour M. Lipset, "The Sociology of Marxism," *Dissent*, Vol. 10 (1963), pp. 59–69.

49. Robert M. MacIver states that ". . . the social structure is for the most part created. . . . Unlike the physical nexus [the social type of causal nexus] does not exist apart from the objectives and motives of social beings" and requires a methodological strategy that fits the distinctiveness of social events. *Social Causation* (Boston: Ginn, 1942), pp. 20–21. Weber, of course, took a similar stand in his concept of social action as "meaningful behavior," and it also lies at the root of Parsons' theory of social action. But neither explains what mechanisms exist through which the structure of a society is "created"; what they do discuss is how it evolves.

"Much political research tends to approach political institutions and structures as established social artifacts rather than as the direct outcomes of human actions and reactions." Jacob and Toscano, *Integration of Political Communities, op. cit.*, p. 212.

This issue has been often focused around the analysis of revolutions. Crane Brinton stated: "To sum the matter up in a metaphor: the school of circumstances regards revolutions as a wild and natural growth . . . outside human planning; the school of plot regards revolutions as a forced and artificial growth. . . . Actually, we must reject both extremes, for they are nonsense, and hold that revolutions do grow from seeds sown by men who want change . . . but that the gardeners are not working against Nature . . . and that the final fruits represent a collaboration between men and Nature." *Anatomy of Revolution* (New York: Prentice-Hall, 1938), pp. 89–90. Cf. to James H. Meisel, *Counter-Revolution: How Revolutions Die* (New York: Atherton, 1966): ". . . All contribute to it but without intending to. One cannot agree to make a revolution. Nor is it necessary." (p. 21.) He refers, to the same effect, to Eugen Rosenstock-Huessy, *Die europaeischen Revolutionen und der Charakter der Nationen* (Stuttgart: W. Stollhammer, 1951), p. 80. For an example of a recent study of societal change as an ongoing process, see Albert Sireau, *Culture et Peuplement* (Louvain: Éditions Nauwelaerts, 1965).

50. Leach provides a fine illustration of this approach. He deals with a society where property is held by unilineal descent groups. Each individual belongs to one and only one such group. But he can choose which of his kinship lines to use, according to his conception of his interests. See E. R. Leach, "On Certain Unconsidered Aspects of Double Descent Systems," *Man*, No. 214 (1962), pp. 130–134. Leach showed the same choice pattern between aristocratic and egalitarian principles in determining one's position in his *Political Systems of Highland Burma* (Cambridge: Harvard University Press, 1954). What makes all this "historical" is that the accumulation of choices in one category tends to shift the society in one

direction, at least for a given period. See also David Matza's important study of the alternatives open to deviants, *Delinquency and Drift* (New York: Wiley & Sons, 1964) and Theodore Abel, "The Element of Decision in the Pattern of War," *American Sociological Review*, Vol. 6 (1941), pp. 853–859.

51. On the temporal dimension, see essays included in J. T. Fraser (ed.), *The Voices of Time* (New York: Braziller, 1966), especially in Part IV. The genetic approach is conceived in a similar way to ours by Lawrence Nabers, "The Positive and Genetic Approaches," in Sherman Roy Krupp (ed.), *The Structure of Economic Science: Essays on Methodology* (Englewood Cliffs, N.J.: Prentice-Hall, 1966), pp 68–82.

52. See, for instance Carl G. Hempel, "The Logic of Functional Analysis," in Llewellyn Gross (ed.), *Symposium on Sociological Theory* (New York: Harper & Row, 1959), pp. 271–307; John Rex, *Key Problems of Sociological Theory* (London: Routledge & Kegan Paul, 1961), pp. 60–77. See also Walter Buckley, "Structural–Functional Analysis in Modern Sociology," in Howard Becker and Alvin Boskoff (eds.), *Modern Sociological Theory in Continuity and Change* (New York: Holt, Rinehart & Winston, 1957), pp. 236–259.

53. William Flanigan and Edwin Fogelman, "Functionalism in Political Science," in Don Martindale (ed.), *Functionalism in the Social Sciences*, Monograph 5 (1965), in a series sponsored by the American Academy of Political and Social Sciences, pp. 111–126.

54. Merton, *Social Theory and Social Structure*, rev. ed., *op. cit.*, p. 52.

55. Etzioni, *A Comparative Analysis of Complex Organizations*, *op. cit.*, p. 78.

56. Morton A. Kaplan, "Essential Rules and Rules of Transformation," in Amitai and Eva Etzioni (eds.), *Social Change: Sources, Patterns, and Consequences* (New York: Basic Books, 1964), pp. 476–480.

57. On the concept of future systems as a functional frame of reference and two examples of empirical studies, see Amitai Etzioni, *Studies in Social Change* (New York: Holt, Rinehart & Winston, 1966), especially pp. 3–7, 112, 196.

58. "In 'Look out! A car is coming at you!'—the very small amount of vocal energy would trigger off a large amount of energy in the companion who is acting as the receiving system." (Here the author refers to Aaron V. Cicourel, *Method and Measurement in Sociology*, New York: Free Press, 1964). "... a minute amount of structured energy or matter from one component of a higher system is able to 'trigger' selectively a large amount of activity or behavior on other components in the system." Walter Buckley, *Sociology and Modern Systems Theory* (Englewood Cliffs, N.J.: Prentice-Hall, 1967). Quoted respectively from pp. 47 and 48. See also John T. Dorsey, Jr., "An Information-Energy Model," in F. Heady and C. L. Stokes (eds.) *Papers in Comparative Public Administration* (Ann Arbor, Mich.: Institute of Public Administration, The University of Michigan, 1962), pp. 37–57.

59. Erving Goffman, *The Presentation of Self in Everyday Life* (Garden City, N.Y.: Doubleday, 1959) is a fine study of such strategies, although he does not view them as conscious efforts. David Matza's significant study of deviant behavior explicitly faces the question of the deviant's relative freedom. See his *Delinquency and Drift*, *op. cit.*, especially pp. 27–29. Howard S. Becker studies deviancy as a career in which the deviant builds up an increasing commitment to his line of deviancy; in similar processes, conforming actors build up a commitment to their respective vocations. This study implies a significant measure of freedom to choose

among alternative deviant careers as well as more and less deviant conduct, similar in scope to that available to those who choose among vocational specializations. See his *Outsiders: Studies in the Sociology of Deviance* (New York: Free Press, 1963).

60. For two examples of a societal guidance approach to psychology, see Gordon Allport, "The Psychology of Participation," *The Psychological Review*, Vol. 53 (1945), pp. 117–132 and Henry A. Murray and Clyde Kluckhohn, "Outline of a Conception of Personality," in Clyde Kluckhohn and Henry A. Murray with the collaboration of David M. Schneider (eds.), *Personality in Nature, Society, and Culture*, rev. and enl. (New York: Knopf, 1953), pp. 18–19.

61. See, for instance, Parsons' main theoretical works; several of his later essays, especially on organizations, add a voluntaristic element and, thus, move toward the same convergence as discussed here. Talcott Parsons, "Suggestions for a Sociological Approach to the Theory of Organizations," *Administrative Science Quarterly*, Vol. 1 (1956), pp. 63–85 and pp. 225–239.

62. Normative systems, we shall see, are also viewed as changing collectivistically and, therefore, cannot be assigned a cybernetic role. Cf. Talcott Parsons, *Societies: Evolutionary and Comparative Perspectives* (Englewood Cliffs, N.J.: Prentice-Hall, 1966), esp. pp. 11–14. "In Devereux's contribution, much is made of Parsons' adoption of a 'postulate of voluntarism' with its corollary that 'action' is governed by subjective orientations and is therefore in some fundamental sense a structure of meanings. . . . I think this is quite correct. Here, as at many other points, Parsons is primarily interested in the postulates of sociology. But this is something very different from a theory of action. . . . A true theory of social action would say something *about* goal-oriented or problem-solving behavior, isolating some of its distinctive attributes, stating the likely outcomes of determinate transformations." Philip Selznick, "The Social Theories of Talcott Parsons," Review Article, *American Sociological Review*, Vol. 26 (1961), pp. 932–935, quoted from page 934. The book reviewed is *The Social Theories of Talcott Parsons: A Critical Examination*, edited by Max Black (Englewood Cliffs, N.J.: Prentice-Hall, 1961). The article referred to is Edward C. Devereux, Jr., "Parsons' Sociological Theory," *ibid.*, pp. 1–63.

63. We stress legitimation because of our interest in socio-political processes. Similar questions might be raised with regard to other cultural elements, although there, of course, cultural autonomy may be greater or smaller.

64. Amitai Etzioni, *Modern Organizations* (Englewood Cliffs, N.J.: Prentice-Hall, 1964), pp. 32–49.

65. Philip Selznick, *Leadership in Administration: A Sociological Interpretation*, *op. cit.*, p. 27. For a systematic attempt to integrate the underlying conceptions of Weber and Lasswell, see Giulio Bolacchi, *La Struttura Del Potere* (Roma: Edizioni Ricerche, 1964), esp. pp. 14–28.

66. For a discussion of the philosophical implications and an annotated bibliography, see Lancelot Law Whyte, *Essay on Atomism: From Democritus to 1960* (Middletown, Conn.: Wesleyan University Press, 1961). The relationship of atomism to exchange analysis is most evident in Marcel Mauss, *Essai Sur Le Don*, first published in 1925, trans. by I. Cunnison as *The Gift* (New York: Free Press, 1954). The best known recent works in the exchange tradition in sociology are those of George C. Homans, *Social Behavior: Its Elementary Forms* (New York:

Harcourt, Brace & World, 1961), and Peter M. Blau, *Exchange and Power in Social Life, op. cit.* On the relationship between functionalism and exchange, see Eugene V. Schneider and Sherman Krupp, "An Illustration of the Use of Analytical Theory in Sociology: The Application of the Economic Theory of Choice to Non-economic Variables," *The American Journal of Sociology*, Vol. 70 (1965), pp. 695–703.

CHAPTER 5

A Theory of Societal Guidance:

Basic Elements

THE NORMATIVE, philosophical, and metatheoretical assumptions of a language of societal action have been explored in the preceding chapters; now we turn to the basic elements of a specific theory of macro-action, societal guidance. The statements advanced here attempt to answer two key questions: Who are the carriers and regulators of societal action, and what are the relations among them?

The social sciences developed with the search for a secular explanation of societal order.[1]* Having rejected supranatural explanations and, with them, the authority of the church and of absolute monarchy as the source of order, the social sciences developed concurrently with the rise of the industrial middle class and the nation-state and sought a new account of a new society.

Many socio-political theories take some form of social order as their starting point and seek to examine the conditions under which that order arose and the factors that undermine it or account for its transformation.

---

* Reference notes for this chapter appear on page 125.

Studies of the transitions from a *Gemeinschaft* to a *Gesellschaft* and from a conflict-ridden to a conflict-free society are well-known examples. For general theoretical purposes, however, it seems useful to take as an analytic starting point the state of *social entropy*,* in which no social bonds are assumed and no social order is posited. Any social order is considered a counter-entropic arrangement that requires explanation.

However, the major question for us is not only under what conditions an order is established, but also under what conditions an order is advanced which allows for more actualization of the social potential than other social orders. The terms "social potential" and "actualization" may at first seem reminiscent of unempirical and vague philosophical statements. We shall see, however, that they have as much a place in a social science theory as such terms as "system" and "structure." And these terms are used here in much the same sense as they are in one of the "harder" sciences, thermodynamics.[2]

Three Kinds of Social Relations†

Social Entropy: A Null Hypothesis

For general theoretical purposes, it seems productive to start the analysis of social order with a set of biological units which are assumed to have a human potential but which remain, in actuality, animal-like—without training for symbolic communication and interpretation, for social life—unless a set of social processes occurs. This assumption of social entropy highlights our premise that activation of the social potential and, in this sense, the establishment of social order are "unnatural" in that their introduction and maintenance require continual effort.

Complete social entropy, however, is of little interest for macro-theory. In the following discussion we therefore assume that the *basic* processes of socialization and institutionalization as well as the generation of micro-cohesion occur. Our discussion focuses on the conditions of *societal* as distinct from *social* activation and order. Societal order requires not only that biological units come to play roles and that these roles are institutionalized into micro-units, but also that micro-units relate to macro-units and that

---

* Entropy is used in the natural sciences to refer to the ultimate state of inert uniformity of component elements, the absence of form and of differentiation. "Complete sociocultural conformity may be compared to a state of entropy which follows upon the leveling down of differences in a closed system." Bidney, *Theoretical Anthropology, op. cit.*, p. 376. Our use is analytic; for a genetic approach, see Frank Hole, "Investigating the Origins of Mesopotamian Civilization," *Science*, Vol. 153 (1966), pp. 605–611.

† The term social rather than societal is used to indicate that the following statements belong to the segment of theory which deals with universal variables and not just macro-variables.

the macro-units relate to each other. These relations can then be compared in order to ascertain which kinds of relations actualize more of the societal potential. Societal entropy occurs when the societal structure breaks down and there occurs no societal actualization; each man or family must fend for itself.[3]

A Classification of Social Relations

There are three basic* analytic ways in which social atoms may be built into social molecules: A relationship may be normative, utilitarian, or coercive. A normative relationship entails shared values and norms; the relating actors treat each other as goals, and their mutual commitments are non-rational. Utilitarian relations entail a complementary interest; the actors treat each other as means, and commitments are rational. Coercion entails the use, or the threatened use, of means of violence by one actor against one or more other actors. Actors treat each other as objects, and the commitment may be either rational or non-rational. Concrete relations are frequently a mixture of the three kinds. However, one tends to dominate, as in the relationship between a mother and a child, two traders, and a criminal and his victim, or, to turn to macroscopic examples, between the leaders and the followers of a social movement, between two nation-wide corporations, and between an occupation force and the populace.

The three basic social bonds[4] differ in the ways in which they relate the member units of the systems they create. Cooperation is more likely to occur within the first, contained conflict within the second, and uncontained conflict within the third. While it is true that some of the most bitter conflicts are fought over normative differences and in normative terms, the conflicts occur not among those who share the particular normative bond but rather among those who do not share the basic or specific values contested. On the other hand, those who have complementary or competing utilitarian interests, as in market relations, still share a utilitarian bond.

Similarly, it might be asked whether or not those subject to coercion are always in open conflict with those who apply it. First, it should be stressed that we are dealing with probabilities. We expect only that uncontained conflict will be more frequent in coercive relations than in the other two kinds. Secondly, most relations are mixed, and therefore many relationships that at first seem coercive may actually contain significant utilitarian and normative elements—e.g., relationships between slaves and masters, both on the dyadic interpersonal level and between two classes. Finally, when a relationship is built relatively heavily on coercion, uncontained conflict, while

---

* Basic because they belong to the universal theory of action; they apply to the relationships among microscopic as well as macroscopic units and can be used to characterize states of personalities.

likely to occur, eventually may not be manifest immediately, since those subject to coercion, while highly alienated and inclined to rebel, will often suppress or repress their attitudes until an opportunity for rebellion arises and means are available.[5]

Physical scientists have wondered how order is possible if the world is moving toward entropy. According to one position, anti-entropy is possible in principle, as increases in knowledge reduce random action. According to a second position, anti-entropy is basically not possible; progress in one sub-world necessarily entails the reduction of order (or increased entropy) in one or more other sub-worlds. In the societal world this would mean that gains in the integration of one sub-system are made at the cost of disintegration in others.

To extend this point, we suggest, in opposition to the integrationist model, that each of the three basic relationships serves as a base of both integration and cleavage, and that the very act of binding is also an act of setting a boundary. Shared values and sentiments, it is true, lead to the formation of cohesive groups, but unless the group is mankind as a whole, each membership also generates a non-membership and, thus, potential outgroups. Whether a shared value provides order or disorder is largely a question of perspective; for instance, the nationalism which helped the unification of the German states also generated new cleavages in Europe and deepened old ones. Similarly, complementary or competing interests form bonds, but they often also lead to the formation of a counter-interest group of those who do not share in the relationship. Finally, force may bind those who exercise it as well as those which are subject to it; but it also tends to specify one or more groupings who are not parties to the coercive relationship. They may range from spectators to allies of the oppressor or the oppressed; whatever their position, however, it is different from that of the parties directly involved. Thus, force, too, separates as it relates.

Cohesive Units and Organizational Networks

To avoid the pitfalls of assuming integrated social units where there are none, we start with the null hypothesis that all roles are unrelated, with no normative, utilitarian, and coercive bonds. Against this background, social units stand out as clusters of roles which are more related to each other than would be expected on a random basis. When the relationship is loose (i.e., the difference from randomness is small), it seems best to avoid terms that evoke highly integrated images such as "group" or "community"; we use "social units" as the generic term and "societal units" for macroscopic ones. When the relationship is tighter, we refer to "cohesive units."

The most important cohesive societal units are collectivities and societies. A collectivity is to a theory of societal guidance what a role is to a theory of action—i.e., the basic unit of analysis. A society is a cohesive supra-unit whose member units are collectivities. We turn now to explore our basic units, their composition and internal processes, and their relations to each other. The criteria for selecting definitions and the substantive questions behind the various propositions are—how is the active potential of a society realized? How is a societal category transformed into a cohesive and organized political unit? And, how do such units relate to each other to form, dissolve, or re-form more encompassing societal entities?

Definition of Collectivities

A *collectivity* is a macroscopic unit that has a potential capacity to act by drawing on a set of macroscopic normative bonds which tie members of a stratification category. Roughly, a collectivity is both a large small-group and a class. Unlike the cohesion of a small-group, the cohesion of a collectivity is not based on face-to-face contact. Unlike class position in the stratification structure, the position of a collectivity is not necessarily horizontal nor is its prime base necessarily economic. Its position may be vertical (as when collectivities are ecologically based), or diagonal (as is the case for many ethnic groupings in the United States). Thus, a major common base may be shared values and not just interests.

Normative bonds are part of the definition of a collectivity because units which lack those are unstable and cannot serve as the building stones of a theory. As Durkheim pointed out, any contractual relationship requires a precontractual underpinning; i.e., societal bonds that are only utilitarian (not to mention only coercive) are inherently unstable. Units that command only strong utilitarian bonds (e.g., a high level of financial transactions among the members) may break up when, following a change in the environment, culture, or make-up of the actors, the relation no longer "pays." If some units that are linked by a high level of transactions maintain a stable bond despite such changes, this is not because the transactions bind them firmly, but because the units are also tied by normative bonds.*

Collectivities need to be characterized morphologically—i.e., in terms of their loci in a societal structure; otherwise they remain curiously unanchored and tend to make a theory atomistic and aggregative. The specification of two structural positions, we suggest, is most useful for a theory of societal guidance: the place in the societal allocation of assets, or in the stratification structure; and the place in the societal distribution of power, or in the political organization. We turn now to provide such morphological anchoring for our key concepts.[6]

---

* Whether these bonds grow out of the utilitarian transactions themselves, or precede them, or come from another source does not detract from the inherent instability of the utilitarian element of the relationship.

Collectivities and Their Stratification Base

It seems useful to view categories (or aggregates) of *social* units as "untreated" matter, which, if properly processed, can yield varying degrees of *societal* action, the macrosociological equivalent of kinetic energy. From this viewpoint collectivities are "half-processed," midway between stratification categories and organized collectivities. That is, if the members of a societal category (defined by their place in a societal structure and, hence, their stratification position) are to act in unison, forming a collectivity increases their potential capacity to do so. This, however, is only one step toward *having macroscopic consequences*; additional processing is needed.*
Having similar, as distinct from shared, interests or values does not provide an actualized capacity to act in unison.† Under most circumstances, with charismatic situations (mass behavior) constituting the main exception, only collectivities with organizational arms or organizations which have mobilized a collectivity base are sufficiently activated to induce macroscopic effects.[7]

Which stratification categories will actually form collectivities is difficult to specify because a set of social units may be divided into a limitless number of categories. By comparison, collectivities are much less numerous and much more concrete; often actors are aware of them and react to them.‡ This is not to suggest that any category may be transformed into a collectivity. Each person and micro-unit has a variety of statuses. Which of these will serve as bases for collectivities depends in part on the nature of these statuses. For instance, societal units whose members are concentrated ecologically are expected to serve more readily as a base for formation of collectivities than those which are not. Second, cohesion-formation is affected by the ways in which similar statuses are used; selective processes of collectivity-formation occur which decrease the social distance in one direction at the cost of increasing it in others.

---

* Aggregates of units which are concentrated in an ecological area or within the boundaries of an organization (to which they do not belong and into which they are not integrated) are somewhat less unprocessed than mere stratification categories because the transition from such an aggregate to a collectivity is, we suggest, less costly in societal terms than if the process must start with a mere category.

† The difference between *similar* (or other "background" traits) and *shared* values should be stressed. Often, collective bonds are expected to grow out of homogeneous backgrounds without an expenditure of societal energy. Actually, these similarities are only potentials for collective bonds (i.e., categories) which need to be processed. For instance, members must be made aware of their similarity before it becomes a shared characteristic.

‡ As the number of categories that are actually "processed" to form collectivities is very small in comparison to the universe of categories, it is much easier methodologically to move from collectivities to categories than vice versa. That is, it is much easier to determine what stratification statuses the members of a collectivity share than to predict which of a given set of status categories will serve as a basis for forming a collectivity.

Macroscopic Formation of Cohesion

Collectivities are often defined in such a way that it is impossible to distinguish them from small groups.[8] Such a definition is achieved in part by not granting the concept a structural stratification anchoring and in part by not indicating the mechanisms for macroscopic cohesion-formation. As there are several terms for micro-units whose members share normative bonds (such as cohesive, primary, or face-to-face groups), and as there is no term for cohesive macroscopic units, it seems advisable to reserve "collectivities" for this purpose.

To discover the ways in which the members of a macroscopic stratification unit acquire the normative bonds which give macro-units at least some of the solidarity of cohesive micro-units, we must take into account that a collectivity is composed not of individuals but of sub-collectivities which, in turn, contain cohesive micro-units not randomly aggregated; i.e., the collectivity has an internal structure of its own. The cohesion of a collectivity cannot be based on face-to-face interaction, informal communications, or interpersonal contacts among the members. For micro-units to be bound into sub-collectivities and collectivities, loyalties developed in cohesive micro-units must be extended. Such extensions of loyalties depend upon the following factors: (a) the leaders of the micro-units, of the sub-collectivities, and of the collectivity itself, (b) shared values and symbols, and (c) institutionalized intra-collectivity communication channels.*

Several characteristics of macroscopic cohesion-formation are of special interest. First, the extension of loyalties is not based on a charismatic relationship in the traditional sense of the term. Membership in collectivities is not atomized, and there is no one "great" leader who directly interacts with the followers; a collectivity is not a mass movement. On the contrary, there are usually a number of leaders of varying stature and status, none of whom is "great." Second, the interaction between these leaders and the member units is institutionalized, as are the relations among the leaders themselves.

While the leadership network is hierarchical, it is not necessarily monocentric. There is often more than one hierarchy in a collectivity and two or more centers of leadership. Such a leadership pattern will still make for one collectivity so long as these centers share the same basic values and there is some form of coordination among them. Thus, for instance, American Jewry has a variety of religious organizations but no one supreme center;

---

* While each sub-unit can be integrated into more than one unit and supra-unit, the normative bonds of the sub-units seem frequently limited to one or two collectivities or supra-collectivities.[9] Normative bonds are usually arranged in a hierarchy, so that even when they are numerous, they vary in intensity, with one or two having a clear priority. For instance, working-class organizations may have a national and an international class commitment, but usually the national is predominant.

yet the extent of coordination and of shared basic values seems sufficient for it to qualify as one collectivity.

While values and symbols play a significant role in cohesion-formation, the leadership network, we suggest, is the primary mechanism for extending loyalties from member-units to the supra-unit. This proposition draws on the psychological theorem that values and symbols are abstractions to which commitments are made through an interpersonal relationship between a leader and his followers. Such commitments are likely to be made between persons who are closely related, with one higher and one lower in status (e.g., father and son, priest and parishioner, officer and soldiers) when those higher in status have either personal or official leadership qualities or both.

Not least among the factors determining the level of macro-cohesion are the processes which affect the cohesive relationship *among the leaders themselves*. Leadership-cohesion is achieved by interpersonal contacts among the leaders, by training various leaders at the same institutions (e.g., Oxford and Cambridge), by their relating to a smaller set of higher-ranking leaders who in turn are in personal contact with each other, and by various kinds of gatherings which provide occasions for interpersonal contact.

All this is not to suggest that contacts among the member-units of a collectivity are exclusively limited to contacts among their leaders. There is also some direct personal interaction among the members of different micro-units and sub-collectivities (e.g., national conventions of religious groups) and interaction through the collectivity's formal communication media (e.g., the Negro press).[10]

These various cohesion-formation mechanisms are needed not only because the number of members is great, but also because most collectivities —unlike cohesive micro-units—are ecologically dispersed. Collectivities are almost never ecologically concentrated in modern or post-modern societies.* Sub-collectivities tend to be ecologically concentrated (e.g., Harlem for Negro-Americans) but less often and to a lesser degree than micro-units. A sub-collectivity may crystallize around local core-institutions, such as churches or clubs. Thus, although its members may be dispersed ecologically, their social space will be concentrated by modern means of transportation and communication which help to confine their normative interaction to contact with each other.

Three clarifications should be added. First, a collectivity is often multi-faceted (or broad in scope) in the sense that members who share one status (e.g., ethnic) will tend also to share others (e.g., religious), though there will always be numerous dimensions on which the members differ significantly.

---

* The main exception to this rule is collectivities whose stratification base is vertical; i.e., those whose defining status base is ecological. These are usually the least "modern" sector of the society under study.

Secondly, even for those categories which a collectivity does mobilize, there is almost invariably a significant unmobilized segment. As we are interested less in stratification per se than in a theory of the relations between the stratification structure and societal and political action, we are exploring the relationship between categories and collectivities chiefly with regard to their consequences for such action. To keep the function of cohesion-formation distinct from the organization of collectivities for purposes of societal or political action, we refer to networks whose main function is to sustain the normative bonds of the members of a collectivity as *associations*. Fraternities and social clubs are typical examples. We refer to the other kind of network simply as *organizations*. While a concrete societal unit may serve both associational and organizational functions, one or the other is often dominant. For example, Sigma Pi Phi, a Negro fraternity, is mainly associational,[11] while CORE is primarily an instrument of societal and political action.

Much of the foregoing discussion also applies to combinations of collectivities and to societies. A society can be viewed as a supra-collectivity to the extent that it commands the same cohesion-formation mechanisms as collectivities.[12] We shall see later that a society is more than a macroscopic cohesive supra-unit, however, both because it has integrative mechanisms which generally are not available to member collectivities, and because it tends to be broader in scope. For present purposes, though, it suffices to treat society as a supra-collectivity—that is, as another potential base of macroscopic action.

Macroscopic cohesion-formation processes provide stratification units with bonds among their members which enhance their potential capacity to act in unison. But how, specifically, does one cohesive societal unit act in relation to another, and under what conditions is such action macroscopic in its consequences?

Interaction of Cohesive Societal Units

Cohesive societal units interact in three main ways: (a) Members may interact *directly* with one another, across unit boundaries. The interaction may be among individuals, micro-units, or sub-collectivities (or collectivities, if we are dealing with societies). It is not merely inter-member interaction but macroscopic interaction to the extent that the norms and sanctions which regulate it are significantly affected by societal factors.[13]

(b) Members of two societal units may react to symbols of one another and to impersonal communications from or about each other without any interpersonal interaction or communication.[14] This may be referred to as *symbolic* interaction.

(c) Finally, cohesive societal units may interact via the institutional or organizational apparatus of the interacting units or of a supra-unit, as when the leaders of two racial groupings arrange a joint prayer in which both groupings participate. This may be referred to as *representational* interaction.[15]

Collectivities almost never interact the way football teams meet in the field, with all members participating, and societies are even less likely to interact frontally than collectivities. Practically all societal units are internally differentiated in terms of their relations with other units. The same is true with regard to active alteration of the relationship between a unit and its sub-units; this responsibility, too, is unevenly distributed among the members. Hence, internal differentiation affects all aspects of macro-interaction.

A central hypothesis of this study is that *direct interaction among the members of two or more macro-cohesive units is relatively infrequent, and that which does occur tends to have few macroscopic consequences.* For example, Negroes and whites interact directly much less frequently with each other than with members of their own collectivity. And when they do interact across collectivity boundaries, such interaction occurs largely in secondary relationships which have relatively limited normative force and even less macroscopic impact. While direct interactions provide a resource upon which macroscopic processes draw (and which they affect), we suggest that *direct interactions are not the main explanation for most macro-dynamics.*

Cross-unit *symbolic interactions* are frequent in modern and post-modern societies, *but we expect that they, too, will tend to have limited consequences for macro-processes.* On the other hand, structural and organizational factors in macro-interaction are expected to have a more significant effect on macro-processes, under most circumstances, than the other kinds of factors, and possibly greater effects than both of them combined.

Cohesive Units and Organizational Networks

To actualize its action potential, any macro-cohesive unit, however well integrated,[16] requires additional "processing" by one or more organizations. We turn first to explore this aspect of activation in collectivities and then in societies.

COLLECTIVITIES AND ORGANIZATIONS

A collectivity has an energy potential which, in itself, is unusable; unless transformed into kinetic energy, it is free-floating and cannot be applied to affect either external or internal states. Hence, it is at best "shorthand" to say, for instance, that a class or ethnic grouping "demands" or "rises." The referent is usually to one or more organizations (such as a political party or labor union), their varying combinations, or a social movement. This is more than a terminological quibble. The organizational network is often *much* narrower in scope than the collectivity that is being processed, as measured (a) in the number of statuses per person or social unit involved, (b) in terms of the membership recruited, and (c) in the assets mobilized. (This holds for the transformation of static energy into kinetic energy in nature as well.) An analysis of macroscopic interaction on the basis of potentials rather than energy actually mobilized, is, therefore, misleading.

In short, from the viewpoint of a theory of societal guidance, a collectivity without organization is passive. While an increase in its associational activities may increase its cohesion and, thus, its action potential, such an increase by itself does not enlarge the collectivity's actual societal impact. Analysis of organizational processing is essential for determining how much of the potential impact is actualized and what forces and processes account for the magnitude of the proportion, two questions central to this study.

Conversely, can organizations act without a collectivity base? Should we focus on organizations as the societal instruments "of getting things done?" While all organizations constitute control networks, they vary in their need for a cohesive base and in their capacity to mobilize consensus.[17] Several scholars, especially of the Human Relations tradition, hold that there is a universal theory of organizations and tend to imply that all organizations need to mobilize the commitments of their members and to relate them to a cohesive unit. In contrast, we suggest that organizations be classified as we have classified social relations—as predominantly coercive, utilitarian, or normative in the control of their participants.[18] These kinds of organizations are expected to differ in their need for a cohesive base. When the means of control are predominantly coercive, as in traditional prisons, effectively functioning organizations do not have to gain the involvement of the inmates, nor, usually, are they able to. When the organizations' means are normative, as in most religious or educational organizations, they cannot function effectively unless consensus is established and commitment mobilized.[19] Utilitarian organizations, such as factories, require less consensus-formation and mobilization of commitments than normative organizations but more than coercive ones.

While the mobilization of consensus does not necessarily depend on a cohesive underlayer (consensus can be marshaled in an atomistic mass situation, drawing on charismatic leadership), mobilization without this underlayer is expected to be inherently unstable. Charismatic activation is analogous to a short-circuit in mobilizing static energy: It generates very high flows, but for a short time. As a rule, effective consensus-building entails the organization's articulation with a cohesive societal unit (or sub-unit). Hence, we suggest, effective normative organizations frequently have a collectivity base, effective utilitarian organizations have such a base less frequently, and effective coercive organizations lack these bases completely (though they often lead to the formation of a counter-collectivity, an inmate community or a colonial society.)[20] In short, while collectivities as a rule do not act macroscopically without organization, we suggest that some kinds of organizations can—and others cannot—act without a cohesive base.

The phrase "cohesive base of an organization" covers a large variety of possible relations. Besides organizations without cohesive bases and cohesive societal units without organizational "processing," the main possible combinations are the following:

(a) *A cohesive unit may serve as a recruiting ground for one or more organizations* (a recruiting ground not just for members but also for funds and loyalties). Such activation is invariably partial; there are frequently more members in this kind of cohesive unit than there are members in "its" organizations (e.g., members in labor unions vs. in the working class). What makes such organizations "belong to" a collectivity or sub-collectivity is, first of all, the absence of other organizations (having a macro-action function) that mobilize more of the unit's members and commitments. Secondly, when a collectivity's interests and values are compared to organizational policies, the policies of "representative" organizations are expected to "fit" better than those of other organizations.[21]

A COLLECTIVITY AND ITS ORGANIZATIONS

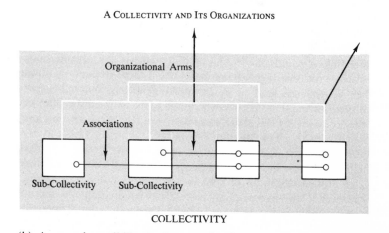

COLLECTIVITY

(b) A second possibility is that *membership in an organization serves as the basis for associational activities*, and thus, a cohesive unit is built around the organization. An army stationed overseas is a case in point. Here, the autonomy of the societal unit will tend to be comparatively small, while the power of the organization as compared to that of other organizations will tend to be great. (This, we shall see, has significant consequences as organizations tend to be more control-oriented and provide for less consensus-formation than collectivities.)

(c) Finally, *some organizations bridge or "cross-cut" a variety of cohesive units*, drawing on persons, micro-units, or sub-collectivities in several collectivities but not serving as a main channel of activation for any one societal unit. The effectiveness of such organizations in mobilizing consensus and in precipitating societal action has not been determined; we suggest, tentatively, that these cross-cutting organizations are generally less effective than representative organizations or those which have a clear cohesive base.

We are concerned with specifying some of the major elements of a theory of societal guidance. It is not our purpose in this chapter, therefore, to explore the full range of relationships between cohesive units and organizations, but only to stress that these relationships may vary considerably, that organizations per se provide mainly control networks and not consensus-formation structures, and that cohesive units without organizations are, in general, unable to engage in societal action.* The nature of the articulation of cohesive units with organizations determines, to a large degree, whether or not and for what purposes potential societal energy is mobilized, and to what degree the societal unit is active.

SOCIETY AND STATES

Much of what has been said about the relationship between collectivities and organizations may be applied to the relationship between societies and states.† A society without a state is largely passive, and a state without a societal base is a control network with only a limited capacity for the mobilization of consensus.[22] Our null hypothesis for organizations and collectivities was that they are not necessarily coextensive and that instances of their coincidence need to be explained. Similarly, our null hypothesis about societies and states is directly opposed to the nationalistic, ethnocentric treatment of societies and states as coextensive; they often are not, and it is when they are that an explanation is required.

The state may be defined as a supra-organization;[23] other organizations are units within its context. Like other organizations, the state has written by-laws, an explicit definition of who is and who is not a participant, and specifications of various participant roles. There is a division of labour among levels of government and between agencies, "hierarchization," lines of communication, authority, and decision-making. As in all organizations, the state's pyramidal pattern does not preclude the possibility of the partial autonomy of sub-units, though—in a fashion typical of other organizations— sub-unit autonomy tends to exist within limits set by the overriding unit. It is important to remember that a supra-unit relationship—the way in which the state relates to member units—is hierarchical in the logical sense of the

---

* The formation of consensus requires the generation of non-rational commitments, a task at which cohesive units are more effective than organizations. The combination of cohesive units and organizations produces the most effective guidance system, drawing on both control networks and consensus-building structures as well as utilitarian and normative processes.

† Statements about the state refer to modern and post-modern states. They hold, but to a lesser degree, for states of earlier societies. Among these, the statements are expected to hold more for bureaucratic societies, such as ancient China, than for such feudal societies as medieval Europe.

term; the supra-unit sets a context which constrains members or provides a base for them to build on. However, these relationships are often not hierarchical in the bureaucratic sense of the term. For example, while the relationship of federal agencies to the American state (the supra-unit) is hierarchical in the bureaucratic sense, its relationship to labor unions is not.

The state is more a mechanism of "downward" political control than a mechanism of "upward" societal consensus-formation.* A comparison of a federal agency with a political party or an interest group highlights the difference between organizations which primarily carry downward flows and those which primarily carry upward ones. While the distinction between upward and downward flows is analytic—since most networks carry some of each kind—most networks specialize in one of the two and may be characterized accordingly. We shall use the term *control networks* to refer to those networks in societies or collectivities which are used primarily for downward political flows, and *consensus-formation processes* or structures for those specializing in upward ones.

Just as a society is not merely a supra-collectivity, so, too, a state is more than a supra-organization. First, whereas organizations, almost without exception, mobilize only a part of the membership of the collectivity they "represent," state mobilization tends to be much more universal, as it creates at least a minimal organizational role—that of "citizen"—for most members of the relevant societal unit. Second, whereas most organizations are in at least limited competition with others attempting to mobilize the same collectivity, the state claims and maintains a comparatively effective monopoly in some areas of societal activity and is intolerant of competition in several others. Finally, the state relies on coercion for control purposes, whereas most organizations do not unless they either are part of the state or have gained from it the right to coerce.

The control capacity of the state is higher when it or other forces have weakened various member cohesive units, and/or when the state elites and staff have become a cohesive unit themselves (often by fusing with another organization such as the dominant political party or the military).

It has often been argued that it is meaningless to ask about the relations between society and state because one is a part of the other.[24] In part, this is a matter of definition; as understood here, the society is a collectivity of collectivities and the state is an organizational framework of society. Thus, there is little difficulty in conceptualizing the relationship between the two or, for that matter, between the whole (if one wishes to view the society–state as such) and its parts (the state's relations to other societal elements).

---

* Consensus-formation as well as mobilization is explored in detail in Chapters 15–18. Suffice it to say here that the term refers to a wide range of "participation" or "upward" relationships, and not only to activities explicitly or exclusively aimed at building consensus.

Moreover, some rather important insights for a theory of societal guidance can be gained by viewing society and the state as two analytic concepts applied to the same phenomena. This will become evident later when we discuss inter-societal boundaries and tribalism. Suffice it to say here that often in pre-modern periods (and, to a lesser but still important degree, in the modern and post-modern world) societies and states are not coextensive, either because they do not have the same membership, or because those who control the state are not members of the society. This occurred in colonial situations, where the organizational machinery of one society was controlled by another; in situations in which the state encompassed two or more societies—e.g., the Austro-Hungarian empire; and when one society was found in two or more states, as in post-World War II Germany and, to a lesser degree, in Korea and perhaps even in Vietnam.[25] In short, the relations of states and societies is analogous to those of organizations and collectivities: A state may "represent" a society; it may serve as a base around which a society develops; or it may cut across several societies.

COHESION AND CONTROL

Collectivities and societies on the one hand and organizations and states on the other are often treated as two distinct types of societal units. The first pair of concepts evokes images of relatively passive units, while the second pair implies units able to gain at least a measure of self-control. The first pair is said to have a structure, a term which connotes a stable if not a static pattern; the second tends to be viewed as more malleable.

From the viewpoint of a theory of societal guidance, a societal unit may have varying combinations of both cohesive relations and control networks. An active unit has a greater amount of both elements. Cohesive units without control networks lack the capacity for self-control and, hence, are passive. Organizations or states without a cohesive base have at best a deficient ability to build consensus. They can serve as coercive or utilitarian organizations but not as effective tools of societal and political action, which require a strong normative element. A theory of societal guidance sees societal units as an organized collectivity or society (if the cohesive element is strong); as an organization or supra-organization with a cohesive underlayer (if the organizational element is strong); or as various other mixes. Thus, we are dealing with a continuum of societal units that differ in their malleability, control capacities, and ability to build consensus, rather than with two distinct kinds of units.

Once we view societal units in this way, it becomes clear that the stronger the control component, all other things being equal, the less "structured" and more malleable the unit is likely to be.* The foundations of cohesive

---

* This relationship is expected to hold so long as the increase in the control component does not reach a level at which the cohesive base is undermined.

units are non-rational bonds, while those of control networks have a stronger calculative element. Cohesive units define statuses, control networks—roles; cohesive units tend to be broad in scope, control networks—narrow. All these control factors make a unit more malleable, more "organizational," and, thus, potentially more capable of self-control.

To put it differently, passive and active units have hierarchical relations, normative patterns, and regulated behavior. In the more passive units these appear respectively as structures, culture (or sub-culture), and institutionalized norms; in the more active units they take the forms of organizational networks, codes, and rules. The first set of terms connotes given properties; the second implies means and techniques of societal action that can be changed relatively freely. It is important, though, to note that this is a continuum, that each societal unit is partly given and partly malleable, and above all, that *each unit may become less structured and more organized,* and *vice versa.*

Consensus-Formation

		+	−
Controlling Overlayer	+	active societal units	control networks (normative, utilitarian, coercive*)
	−	cohesive units	categories (and aggregates)

* Normative, utilitarian, and coercive refer to the typical means of control and are ordered in this way because of differences in consensus, as discussed above.

Societal units may be thus viewed in terms of a "two-dimensional activeness space." They may be characterized as commanding varying degrees of controlling and consensus-forming capacities. Above all, it is important to note that there is no necessary contradiction between cohesive units and control networks; both are important for increasing the societal capacity to act, and active units command both cohesive and control elements.

The Slanting Effect of Control Networks

The mobilization of cohesive units does not only free latent energy; processing alters the nature of the action finally taken. Control networks do not merely raise the level of activation but also alter the direction of theunit's commitment. Their specific effect depends on factors such as the internal patterning of the networks, the societal background of the organizational or state staff and leadership (which are never randomly drawn from the societal units which are activated), and their ideology.[26]

The societal guidance view differs both from those views which, in line with collectivistic analysis, expect organizations largely to reflect the societal and cultural "background," and from voluntarists who expect them to be relatively free to act, disregarding their ties to their societal base. Similarly, the state is seen as having relatively little autonomy when it acts primarily as a referee among societal units or is under the control of a few of them and serves as a tool against the others. But in all cases, including the latter, *the state never merely reflects societal consensus* (or that of those who use it); it always has a power and a perspective of its own. Like all organizational tools it not only serves a master but also affects what he is able and intends to do.

In summary, we have been concerned with the foundations of societal order and the units of macroscopic action. Our discussion points to two main factors: *the integration of units into collectivities and societies, and the linking of units by control networks into organizations and states.* The two modes are not mutually exclusive; many units are related in both ways. The relations, though, are not necessarily coextensive; a control supra-unit and an integrative one may form systems that differ in their boundaries. Similarly, divisions inside the controlling overlayers and inside the controlled action underlayers may not be coextensive; one control unit may direct processes in two or more action units or sub-units (see below, discussion of external and system elites), and one action unit may be controlled by two or more overlayer units. The resulting *imbalances* are a major line of explanation for the decline of one order and the rise of another—i.e., for change. Since imbalances and new balances are in part the result of guided efforts, societal guidance is an indispensable concept for a theory of societal change.

Both integration and control may be normative, utilitarian, or coercive. While any concrete relation may mix all six analytic combinations, we expect that one combination will tend to prevail in any one relationship. This is not to suggest that all are equally frequent; coercion, we expect, is more likely to be used as a means of control than of integration, while normative bonds seem to play a relatively more central role as a means of integration.

The same theoretical dimension, activation, expresses itself differently on various analytic levels. The most basic distinction is between processed and unprocessed energy (which applies to the realms of nature and social relations). The second is an analytic distinction between controlling overlayers and action underlayers (which applies only to social action and the world structured by it). On the third level are societal (macroscopic) concepts which include collectivities and organizations as units and societies and states as supra-units; or, more analytically, cohesive relations and control networks may be characterized by their respective hierarchical relations, as structures or organizational patterns.

Two other pairs of concepts introduced below—assets and power, and class and elite—tie the basic dimension to concepts of stratification and political processes. The complete structure is represented in the following table:

unprocessed free-floating (latent, potential) energy	processing capacity, yielding committed (manifest, mobilized) energy
action underlayer	controlling overlayer
collectivity	organization
society	state
cohesive relations	control networks
societal structure	organizational pattern
assets	power
class	elite

We cannot over emphasize that while passive attributes appear on the left hand side of the chart, those on the right hand side are not active attributes; only when they are combined with the "passive" base is the active quality generated. To what degree and under what conditions this occurs are what the theory of societal guidance seeks to establish.

To advance a theory of societal guidance, the relationship between the two aspects of the basic dimension of activeness needs to be conceptualized. In part, this is achieved by the concepts defining the types of societal units which draw on varying "mixes" of these elements. More analytically, we draw on the distinction between consensus-formation and implementation processes. Consensus-formation refers to a process whose base is in the cohesive relations but which affects the control networks; implementation, on the other hand, originates in the control networks and affects the cohesive relations. Like the preceding distinction, this pair of concepts is also analytic, since a concrete unit may serve both processes; most units, though, tend to specialize in one or the other.

While all these concepts refer to bridges between the overlayers and the underlayers of one and the same unit, integration refers to bonds that make of units (not layers) a supra-unit. Control appears in both schemes, for it serves to define the overlayer as against the underlayer of a unit and the links of one or more units (or layers) to each other or to a supra-unit. We now turn from the internal relations of a unit to explore the bonds and links which relate social units to each other, curbing or extending their capacity to act but never leaving it unaffected.

Action Autarky and Control Autonomy:
Two System Relationships

The boundaries of social units and supra-units, the limits of whatever order they supply and the bases for action they provide, have been difficult for social scientists to delineate. One main source of difficulty is the attempt, in line with the integrationist model, to define one boundary for each social system. The criteria used for such a definition include convention (i.e., agreement among the subjects about who belongs and who does not), legal norms, and political considerations.[27]

We assume that a social system may have more than one boundary, and that the boundaries need not be coextensive. Systems appear in a theory of societal guidance primarily in the relationship of the units that make up the action underlayer (which is more or less integrated), and in the relationship of the components of the controlling overlayer (which is more or less centralized). The first concept of system represents the collectivistic element—the second, the cybernetic one. In addition, we suggest, it is productive to distinguish between normative, utilitarian, and coercive boundaries of both the controlling overlayer and the action underlayer. A case study of almost any historical society (from nineteenth century B.C. China to nineteenth century A.D. Germany) or developing society (from Brazil to Nepal) will help to illustrate the differences among these boundaries and the importance of including the possibility of partial "cross-cutting" as a central concept of a theory of societal guidance. Communities of those who share an ideology, trade with each other, and enhance each other's security often are not coextensive; and those who control any one of these, may have little power over the others. If the relations among the units of action and control are to be specified in greater detail, a conceptualization of varying, partially "cross-cutting" bondages and linkages is required. To advance in this direction, a distinction within controlling overlayers must first be recognized.

Control Centers and Implementation

Controlling overlayers tend to have two kinds of sub-units: control centers (their "heads") and implementation mechanisms (their "bodies"). *Control centers* are units which direct the controlling overlayers and processes by (a) processing incoming knowledge, (b) making major decisions, especially among alternative policies and strategies, and (c) issuing signals to the body of the controlling overlayer and to the collectivities. All these activities entail the processing of symbols. *Implementation mechanisms* link the control centers with the action units under control. Analytically, there are two kinds of implementation processes—(a) those which generate power to support the signals issued by the control centers, and (b) those which carry communication signals from the centers to the collectivities, feedbacks from the action units and the mechanisms themselves to the centers, and the input of "raw" (unprocessed) knowledge. The implementation processes are comparatively more mechanical than those which take place in the control centers because while the use of objects is central for the application of power, it is marginal for intra-center processes.

The upward (or feedback) communications carried by the implementation mechanisms and those carried by consensus-formation processes and structures should be carefully distinguished, for if they are not, the analytic distinction between controlling overlayers and guidance systems becomes blurred. To illustrate the difference: Corporation headquarters usually constitute a control center; upward reports by foremen on workers' morale are implementation feedbacks; the representative functions of labor union stewards are part of the consensus-formation processes. In a role or a micro-unit, all these kinds of communications may occur jointly. In a small shop a chat between the boss and his workers may encompass all three. However, in macroscopic units the three functions tend to be served by segregated processes and units. In the following discussion, these functions are discussed analytically and synthetically. Part II of the book focuses on variables that characterize the control centers of societal units, Part III centers on imple-mentation mechanisms, while Part IV considers consensus-formation. Power appears in the discussions of implementation (Chapters 13 and 14) and of consensus-formation (Chapters 16–18).

Elites and Collectivities

An *elite* is a societal control center; it specializes in the cybernetic functions of knowledge-processing and decision-making, and in issuing controlling signals for societal units. The term "elite" is preferred over "leadership" because elite refers to a societal sub-unit and not to personal qualities. The members of an elite may or may not have leadership qualities.[28] The ability of an elite to function may rest largely on the positions of the members and the technologies and assets available to them, and not on their personalities. There is no implicit assumption here that an elite is necessarily "elitist."[29] Elitism is a dimension by which elites can be characterized, and is not part of their definition. An elite may be highly representative, open, or changeable.

Elites are not a stratification concept.[30] Although their members may be drawn primarily from one class and may serve that class's interests, elites are never a ruling class. "Ruling class" is a term which combines stratification and control referents and, in this sense, is a political concept; it suggests that there is a class which is closely associated with a state-controlling elite. As we see it, classes (or, more generally, collectivities) and elites are never coextensive. There are invariably segments of a collectivity which have no control func-tions, and, almost without exception, some members of the elites are drawn from the other classes, at least those members who occupy lower organiza-tional ranks. Class is a status concept; elite is a role concept. The members of a class (as a collectivity) are by definition cohesive; those of an elite may be cohesive but not as a matter of definition. It should also be noted that elites may rise in any collectivity, not merely the "ruling" (or, upper) one, and that the relations between elites and societal units may exhibit all the various imbalances between control networks and cohesive units discussed above.

Kinds of Elites

From the viewpoint of the analysis of controlling overlayers, the following distinctions among elites seem productive:

(a) *External versus internal elites.*[31] An *external elite* is not integrated into the supra-unit, while an *internal elite* is a member of such a supra-unit. To develop this conceptualization, it should be noted that there are two main ways to introduce a supra-unit on top of a set of units: (1) to integrate the units by drawing on various combinations of the three major kinds of bonds discussed above; and (2) to link them by a control network using various combinations of the three kinds of control means. Both types of supra-units often coexist, but the integrated supra-unit and the control supra-unit need not be coextensive. When the control system is not coextensive with the integrated supra-unit, the elite(s) (as control centers are by definition) will be partially or wholly external. When there is more than one control network or more than one elite in a network controlling the same societal unit, some elites may be internal and some external.

When an elite is external, the controlling overlayer and the consensus-formation processes are separated. A central proposition of a theory of societal guidance follows from these premises: When elites are external (or when some are internal and some external), societal guidance is less effective and the societal unit is less active than when all the elites are internal. The process by which the control exercised by external elites is shifted to internal ones is referred to as "internalization," and the opposite process is referred to as "externalization."

(b) Internal elites may be either unit-elites or system-elites. *Unit-elites* are control centers that are monopolized by one or a few member-units (the term "monopolized" refers to the responsiveness of the elite to the demands of the member units and not necessarily to the societal origin of the members of the elite, the circles they frequent, the views they hold, etc.). *System-elites* are responsive to most if not all of the member units. As no elite is ever completely responsive to one unit or equally responsive to all of them, the difference between unit and system elites is to be viewed as a relative one. While internal elites may be unit- or system-elites, external elites are, as a rule, unit-elites so far as the system they control is concerned.[32]

(c) Elites may be characterized by the kind of activities they control as either *specific* or *general*. And, if specific, the elites may be classified according to the nature of the activity—economic, educational, religious, and so on—that they control. Unless otherwise specified, the term "elite" is used here to refer to generalized control—i.e., to the encompassing organizational or political control center of a societal unit.

(d) Elite control may be highly specific or may merely define limits within which the subjects' conduct may vary. We refer to these two kinds of control as *prescriptive* and as *contextuating*, and to the dimension as the degree of specification (of control). There are close associations between this dimension of control and democratic versus totalitarian elites, "indicative planning" (or "programming") versus totalistic planning, and the levels of responsiveness achieved and alienation produced, all of which are explored below.

Autarky versus Autonomy

To complete our discussion of the ways in which societal units relate to each other, the relationship of dependence versus independence needs to be specified. The main point here is that *units which appear independent from an integrative viewpoint may not be independent actors from a societal guidance perspective.* The degree of dependency of one unit on another has been discussed in the social science literature in a variety of terminological garbs ranging from subjugation to sovereignty. Two main dimensions of this relationship, we suggest, must be kept distinct: functional dependency and subordination.[33]

An *autarkic* societal unit is one whose activities meet all the basic functional needs of the unit.* Autarky (i.e., functional self-sufficiency) assumes that the societal unit is broad in scope, encompassing all three kinds of relationships and acting as an integrated system in all of them. The activeness of such an autarkic unit is quite a different question. This depends on the autonomy of the unit and the extent to which its activities are self-controlled. All the basic functional needs of a societal unit may be served; yet, the society may be no more self-controlled than the pampered son of domineering parents. In short, the autarky and the autonomy of a societal unit vary independently.

From a narrow functional viewpoint, it does not matter who controls an activity so long as the various needs are fulfilled. Thus, for instance, a country needs oil; the oil wells may be drilled by private indigenous corporations, by a government company, or by a foreign-based corporation. Though the location of control is likely to have secondary effects on the fulfilling of other functions (e.g., encouragement of indigenous investment, costs of production, etc.) as well as on the supply function itself; the questions of whether or not the oil needs of the country are fulfilled and who controls the drilling are analytically distinct. Interesting issues are raised by the effects of the two sets of factors on each other—e.g., will foreign control lead to more oil production in the short run (i.e., should a society trade some loss of autonomy for more autarky); what effects will such a trade have on political autonomy, and so on. While

---

* The concept of autarky was used historically to refer to self-sufficient units, especially self-sufficient economies. It is often associated with the mercantilist approach. Though the basic image it evolves is correct, we seek to divest the concept of the secondary connotation which implies a self-controlled (nationalistic) economy, because in this sense, autarky and autonomy become synonymous.

autarky (self-sufficiency in activities) and autonomy (self-control) are associated empirically, they do not necessarily co-vary. A high input of assets, as long as it is under the control of the receiving unit, does not necessarily reduce the unit's autonomy, although, in effect, it often does. High degrees of autarky may coexist with low degrees of autonomy, as when a subsistence economy is under tight foreign control.

Fulfilling the needs of a societal unit assures its survival and possibly its effectiveness, while the autonomy of a unit affects its capacity to set its goals and its capacity for self-directed transformation. This question is relevant to both internal–external relations and intra-system relations; in the former, control of a unit may rest with non-members, and in the latter, an internal elite may be more responsive to some members than to others, misrepresenting the distribution of needs in the system. We shall see below that imbalances of either kind cause dysfunctions of their own. Full autarky and autonomy, on the other hand, may decrease intra-unit strains but increase inter-unit ones. The substantive question of which constellations make for effective intra-unit and supra-unit bonds that allow for active communities as well as sub-communities, is explored later (especially Part V). Here, formal aspects of these concepts are explored.

In Dynamic Perspective

Autonomy Imbalances: Their Dynamics and Their Correlates

The degree of autonomy (or self-control) of a societal unit is not necessarily the same for all activities. There are several typical profiles of unbalanced autonomy. One is the combination of relatively high autonomy in normative activities with considerably less autonomy in utilitarian ones. An example, drawn from studies of inmate communities in custodial prisons, may help to illustrate this point.

Inmates' utilitarian activities (e.g., forced labor) are tightly controlled by the guards, as are the allocation of food, clothing, and residence. Cohesion-building activities (e.g., games), the carriers of normative integration, are much more self-determined, though they are affected by assignments to cells and wards in accordance with external criteria. Inmates commonly succeed in enforcing their norms and "wash out" most normative effects of the prison. The autonomy of the inmate community is thus unbalanced, and, as a consequence, the inmates cannot be certain that the allocation of material rewards will agree with their values and symbolic rewards. This gives their community a dual stratification structure and increases the probability of deviancy. Those who prefer to sacrifice the symbolic rewards (e.g., being favorably regarded by inmates) in favor of increasing their material comfort (e.g., by cooperating with the guards) have an opportunity to do so. In fully autonomous communities, material and symbolic rewards, utilitarian and normative stratification, support rather than undermine each other. Hence, in custodial prisons, there are pressures to balance the levels of autonomy. In part this is achieved by inmates' attempts to control the utilitarian means (e.g., the smuggling in of food from the outside and *sub rosa* production of whiskey), by their reallocating material rewards initially allocated by the guards, and by "fixing" (i.e., influencing the guards to allocate rewards in line with the inmates' scale of values, stratification, and power structure). Most colonial societies had less utilitarian than normative autonomy, and one reason for their national independence movements was to balance these autonomies (in addition to increasing each of them).

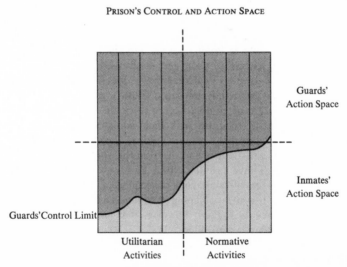

PRISON'S CONTROL AND ACTION SPACE

The same analytic scheme applies to a large variety of other situations. On the micro-dynamics level, adolescence is marked by rising normative autonomy coupled with comparatively high utilitarian dependency on parents. Tension increases when the criteria of utilitarian input and allocation do not fit the autonomous identity and symbolic conception the adolescent has evolved in the normative realm. The pressure is toward internalization of utilitarian control—first, by seeking to "reallocate" that which is allocated by the parents (reduce the specification of control), and soon by some autonomous input as well. The tension is rarely completely resolved before the young person gains employment and a home of his own—i.e., when his utilitarian autonomy approximates his normative autonomy.

The transition from partial normative autonomy (or from partial utilitarian dependency) to full normative and utilitarian autonomy typically involves two major changes: (a) the focus of conflict shifts, at least in part, from internal–external relations to inter-units ones; and (b) the extent of the emphasis on normative activities lessens. The basic reason for both of these changes is that the criteria and control codes of utilitarian and normative activities are inevitably in conflict to some degree, and the more fully developed each set of activities, the more the criteria and codes are likely to conflict. The basic utilitarian orientation is the rationality of means; the basic normative orientation is non-rationality of purposes.

So long as utilitarian activities are controlled by an external elite, a societal unit can stress normative considerations, disregarding to a considerable degree utilitarian needs as well as the need to harmonize utilitarian and normative criteria, which tends to entail some sacrifice of rationality. This is analogous to the idealism of an adolescent who relies for the satisfaction of his utilitarian needs on his well-to-do parents.

As the levels of autonomy in the control of the two sets of activities (utilitarian and normative) come into balance, the conflict between external and rising internal elites is often reduced, but the level of conflict among member-elites, such as businessmen and intellectuals, army and unions, is expected to rise. This is often explained by the loss of a common enemy, as when an imperial power withdraws and a country gains independence. But the same internalization of conflict occurs when the external elite is not an enemy (e.g., in parents' relations with their adolescent children). We also expect that when the transition is more gradual, the internalized conflict will be smaller, and that anticipatory socialization (in which the unit is prepared for the transition) will have a similar effect. This is not to suggest that having a common enemy has no intra-systemic consequences for the relations among those who face it or that the weakening of common enemies does not increase intra-unit conflict. We do suggest, however, that more importance is attributed to this factor than is warranted.

Two other correlates of newly-acquired balanced autonomy, we suggest, are an intensification of political activity in which differences among sub-units are worked out, and a reduction of the emphasis on normative activities. The latter is illustrated by the decline in normative activities of adolescents who begin raising families and holding jobs, the decline of ideological commitment in new nations following independence, and the New Economic Policy (NEP) in Russia following the revolution.

The twin concepts of functional autarky and control autonomy cast some new light on a related question: the conditions under which people rebel or revolt. Common sense suggests that the most oppressed peoples are the most likely to revolt. Social scientists have replaced this notion with the proposition that when total oppression is lessened by some amelioration of conditions, demands rise, and violent uprisings are likely to occur if the increasing pressure for additional concessions is not met. It also has been suggested that imbalances in the available assets and not the absence of these assets are the key variable.

A societal guidance perspective suggests two additions, if not revisions, to this proposition. First, it suggests that part of the variance in revolutionary potential is the result of imbalances in self-control rather than assets. Thus, the French Revolution, for instance, cannot be explained merely by the fact that some improvement in the French peasant's standard of living was not followed by further improvement; it was also the refusal to allow the peasants to continue to increase their participation in the political consensus-formation and, hence, societal guidance processes that triggered the revolution.

So far we have considered changes in control that involved the addition of utilitarian to already-existing normative autonomy. The opposite process, in which autonomous utilitarian units internalize normative controls, may be illustrated by examining new administrative (or organizational) units which acquire a cohesive base and normative activities. A study of a national church structure, for example, shows that it was first organized for strictly administrative purposes, leaving all normative activities *and* controls to local congregations. Slowly it acquired a measure of *national* control over the *local* normative activities and began to develop some national normative activities.[34]

We make no evolutionist assumption that unbalanced autonomies of either kind and the tensions or conflicts generated by them are always or even frequently resolved. Various environmental factors may "freeze" an imbalance. Moreover, an imbalance may be aggravated rather than resolved. A study of a factory that was well integrated into a community shows that when it was purchased by a company outside the community, a control imbalance was generated. Both utilitarian and normative activities continued to be carried out locally, but the new management, which controlled the utilitarian processes of the factory, was not subject to the normative bonds of the local community in the same way that the old management had been. This led to a conflict in the form of a strike. New balance was achieved by organizing the workers into a national labor union in which they faced the association of manufacturers and worked out their differences by drawing on the normative supra-units, the national society, of which *both* were members.[35]

Finally, an imbalance may develop not between a collectivity and a non-member elite but between a collectivity and its sub-collectivities. This is likely to occur when the collectivity is a new one and its system-elites are established by the upward transfer of control of the sub-collectivities' activities, as well as by the generation of some new collective activities. This tends to happen when social units are partially or wholly merged, whether they be corporations, nations, tribes, or other kinds of units.

So far we have discussed societal units subject to external control which come to internalize control, building up and balancing their self-control. A parallel process is the loss of control by an external elite, a process to which there have been important differences in the reactions of external elites. Britain, France, and Belgium differ markedly in the gradualness of their decolonization, in the degree to which control of other societies was a basis of their internal order, and in their capacity not only to tolerate the pulling away of the dependent societies but also to free themselves from their own dependence on the fruits of external control. Britain is usually viewed as the most successful on all these counts. In France the loss of colonies is associated, first, with political instability, and, later, with the semi-authoritarian regime of De Gaulle. In Belgium this process was followed by an intensification of internal conflict between the two main linguistic–cultural collectivities. It is of interest to note that Britain had previously—with the rise of the industrial bourgeoisie and later the working class—been more successful than France and Belgium in reallocating internal control.[36] Thus, there seems to be a generic capacity for control readjustment that is higher in some societies than in others.

Change and Transformation

Internalization or externalization of control, increases in the balance and extent of self-control of normative and utilitarian activities, unification of two or more units through the formation of an integrative and/or a control supra-unit—these are all processes that assume a capacity for societal change. But the active capacity is more than the capacity to change, for changes may occur merely in response to ongoing processes inside or outside the unit. Hence, the importance of the distinction between societal units with a capacity to transform themselves and units which are merely changeable.

When the controlling overlayers of societal units are very weak, the action of the units, like ships in tow, can largely be explained by the action and control of other units. Some other units have limited measures of self-control; they are like ocean liners propelled by outboard motors. Then there are units which have more effective mechanisms of self-control; these are societal units which are able to guide their own actions and, to a degree, deliberately transform themselves, coming closer to their self-image and to a "creative" response* to their environmental and internal challenges.

The concept of transformability is central to this study. It implies a much more active orientation than the system concept of homeostasis or even the concept of ultra-stability in cybernetics. A social unit is *homeostatic* so long as it is able to generate forces that allow it to maintain its boundaries and pattern within a given limit of variability and in the face of environmental

---

* A "creative" response is both adaptive and in accord with the unit's needs and "character." Compare these statements to a stimulating but organistic discussion of "super-elasticity and regeneratives span" in Arthur Koestler, *The Act of Creation* (New York: Macmillan, 1964), pp. 450–452.

challenges. It is *ultra-stable* if it is able to change some of its mechanisms for maintaining itself and its pattern when confronted with challenges that would strain to the breaking point its homeostatic mechanisms as previously set. A societal unit has *transformability* if it also is able to set—in response to external challenges, in anticipation of them, as or a result of internal developments—a new self-image which includes a new kind and level of homeostasis and ultra-stability, and is able to change its parts and their combinations as well as its boundaries to create a new unit. This is not a higher-order ultra-stability but an ability to design and move toward a *new* system *even if the old one has not become unstable.* It is an ability not only to generate adaptive changes or to restore new stability to an old unit, but also to bring about a new pattern, new parts, and, hence, a new society.

Adaptation to the environment may serve as the occasion for a transforming change, particularly among more creative units (for instance, Japan's industrialization following the Western challenge in the mid-nineteenth century). However, the full measure of transformability is not realized until a unit can transform its internal structure and its boundary-relations with other units in response to its internal needs, searching for a more effective way of meeting them under the given environmental conditions and seeking to move toward a greater realization of the values to which it subscribed or of new values to which it has become committed. Such *self-triggered* transformability is a "higher" and less common level of activeness than *environmentally-triggered* transformation. The more it is achieved, the more societal actors may be considered their own masters.

Seen from a different perspective, it might be said that transformation serves to correct or to avoid basic malformations, faulty integrations, and fundamentally unresponsive structures. Transformation, therefore, frequently requires dissolving a unit's old structure and building a new one, at least—considerable de-differentiation and then re-differentiation in accord with new patterns. The more differentiated a structure has become, the greater the need for regression if it is to be transformed. In the process, latent capacities of the unit, which were hidden or suppressed by its old structure, often become available for societal action. In this sense, the unit may be said to have been rejuvenated.

In society, as in the personality, such regression (or de-differentiation) is not without the danger "of not coming back," of preferring the less differentiated state. Hence, the period of the greatest societal malleability (the period between two structures) also contains the greatest risks of rise in societal entropy. For example, social movements, instead of leading to a New Jerusalem, may drift into self-oriented and hedonistic behavior. But when transformation is completed rather than trapped midway, societal creativity will be unusually high.

We stated earlier that the functional analysis employed here differs from traditional functional analyses in that it includes a genetic perspective. We now add that this genetic focus encompasses the transformation of systems and not merely changes "in the system." When this perspective is applied to macroscopic units, our study becomes historical, for the question before us is not only under what conditions passive units are transformed into more active ones, but also the extent of societies' passivity at various time periods and the degree to which they have become activated over time. The analysis of a fully active society provides the design of a future-system; the functional prerequisites of such a society, and the morphological and historical conditions under which it may be achieved, are explored below.

In the following chapters we study the specific components of controlling overlayers and consensus-formation processes and explore the ways in which differences in these components affect the extent to which a societal unit is active. It is a central proposition of the theory of societal guidance that differences in control and consensus account for a significant part of the variance in societal activeness and in the transformability of various societal units in general and toward an active society in particular.

Before we proceed, it should be stressed once more than the following discussion advances propositions and is not concerned with the review or presentation of data.[37] The following chapters are analytic, dealing with one major independent variable at a time; hence, the propositions presented should be read as if they were prefaced by "all other conditions being equal." The claim that differences in the guidance (control and consensus) mechanisms are important for explaining differences in societal activeness does not imply that these mechanisms account for most of the variance. All we suggest is that they account for a significant part of the variance, and, hence, a theory that excludes them is seriously deficient. We also argue that with the rise of modernity, and even more so as we move into the post-modern period, guidance factors have become more significant.

Each component of societal guidance mechanism is studied in the following chapter from the following viewpoints: (a) the controlling *functions* it fulfills; (b) the *processes* it uses; (c) the *structure* of the *units* which specialize in serving the particular function(s); (d) the *relations* between these units and other units;* and (e) changes in all these over time, i.e. *genetically.*

An underlying assumption of all that follows is that without special processes and units, without effort and investment, a unit cannot gain or maintain an active orientation; entropy develops, and the societal unit gradually becomes more passive, its course more determined by other, more active units and non-social environments. To be passive is natural; it is activeness that requires effort and explanation.

---

* The study of processes is more encompassing than the study of the units, because processes link a much larger universe of actions to the service of a function. Education, for instance, is carried out not only in schools (units primarily devoted to education) but also in factories (e.g., in foremen–workers relations).

Appendix: Concrete versus Abstract Units and Systems

An important characteristic of systems analysis, its advocates claim, is that it does not reify its constructs, does not succumb to the fallacy of misplaced concreteness.[38] The system, they stress, is an abstraction. Its units are analytic conceptions; their attributes and, thus, their relations are variables. The educational sub-system, for example, is not to be confused with the school "system"; schools have economic, political, educational, stratificational, and other elements, and other sub-systems have educational elements. The educational sub-system is an abstraction of these educational elements which have certain properties in common—for instance, the pattern-variables they tend to emphasize.

Warnings against reification are stern. Failure to avoid this pitfall, we are told, "is what lies at the basis of many deep-rooted errors, especially in social science."[39] And it is said that "it is the essence of science, thus, to be systematic, and to be systematic requires it to be highly abstract and to see similar properties in what are apparently diverse objects."[40] The wages of the sin of reification committed in the first chapter of many books have confounded the analysis in the third and fourth chapters.

When the abstract concept of system is used, it should be noted, the components of the system *cannot interact*; they can only correlate. In abstract system language it makes no sense to state that an actor "responded" or "reacted" to a rise in integration, interaction, or other such concepts, as these are concepts of the observer and not descriptive of units in the observed world, the world of action. Descriptions of action and of concrete factors that an actor reacts to can be analyzed by the use of these variables; but the action concepts and the observer's variables will never be coextensive unless the observer commits the "sin" of reification. In terms of an abstract system's variables, the concepts descriptive of action are synthesized composites. There is no action in abstract systems, and abstract systems can record action only indirectly, following analysis—i.e., abstraction and fragmentation into constructs.

If the shift between concrete observations and abstract system variables could be accomplished with assurance and economy, this way of relating observations and abstract concepts would have much to recommend it. Actually, abstract systems analysis is of so much potential value that it must be retained even if such a transition is achieved only with considerable difficulty, as is the case in most of the social sciences. Action-oriented research requires a theoretical framework which draws on the abstract concepts of systems analysis but, at the same time, is more closely related to observations, concrete data, and the orientations of a concrete actor. (In terms of the present analysis, the distinction between control and consensus as two-system build-ing processes should be viewed as analytic; the concepts of the active orientation—knowledge, commitment, and power—which take into account the actor's viewpoint, are more concrete.)

Abstraction is not simply to be omitted; even everyday language contains numerous abstractions, and these affect concrete actors. *The question, therefore, is not one of a dichotomy but rather of degree and quality: how abstract and what kind of abstraction?* The concepts of the language of societal action include a sub-set that is relatively more concrete and synthesized than those of abstract (analytic) system language and is more coextensive with the concepts of the actor himself.[41] For example, the terms community, nation, action, mobilization, policy, in addition to knowledge, commitment, and power are used as explications of terms used by the actors.[42] Furthermore, these relatively concrete terms are central to our analysis and are not merely lower-level concepts which are to be analyzed by fragmentation. Their varying combinations characterize societal units and their actions.[43]

Science requires abstraction, but whether it is to be high- or low-level abstraction and whether concepts are to cut across or to be coextensive with action terms are open questions which are best answered according to which language yields the most fruitful theories. The theory of societal guidance outlined in the following chapters is an attempt to add to highly abstract systems analysis a related but more concrete set of concepts and theorems. Should this endeavor be said to have a theoretical formulation more like that of medicine (as an "applied" science) rather than physics (an analytic discipline), we certainly would not consider this comparison invidious.

Some support for our position that more concrete, synthesized underpinnings are needed for systems theories may be seen in the fact that the widest usage of "social system" is the reified one, despite abstract definitions (and admonitions against such use). Scholarly works have been treating the factory rather than production activities as a social system,[44] the school rather than the educational system,[45] and the mental hospital rather than "pattern-maintenance, tension–management."[46] Moreover, social systems have been regularly characterized as concrete phenomena. Two sociologists point out, in a typical statement, that "a social system may be considered as concrete, or a cooperative social structure, such as a football team, a Farm Bureau local, a family, a church congregation, a school, or even a silo-filling ring."[47] One distinguished social scientist explicitly raised the possibility of deliberate reification.[48]

We use a relatively synthesized concept of social system, along with the one referred to above as an analytic social system (i.e., relatively abstract). A synthesized social system is defined similarly to an abstract system—as a relationship in which changes, in one or more members initiate changes in all the others, which, in turn, have feedback effects on the member in which the changes were initiated. The only difference is that the members of synthesized social systems are not high-level abstractions but relatively concrete units such as collectivities and societies. It should be noted that neither the analytic nor the synthesized conception of social system refers to only one instance of feedback between members; some degree of continuity must exist in the feedback and, of course, in the membership of a system. And "constituting a system" is treated as a proposition subject to empirical test; any two units do not necessarily form a system. When the actors are less related, when there is no feedback effect or only a sporadic and inconsequential one, we shall refer to the relationship as a "situation."

Societal units, we suggest, often "behave" as if they were linked in a system fashion. We have a system, for instance, if a civil-rights movement activates northern liberals who form one of the groups that affect federal action, which, in turn, affects white southerners who affect the civil-rights movement, including its relations with northern liberals. But unlike the analytic system, which is composed of variables, this system is composed of collectivities, organizations, movements, and government agencies. Furthermore, these units *act* on each other, and their actions can be recorded and in part explained in terms of the units, and not just in terms of changes in the rates of abstract variables. Finally, the bonds that tie the units into concrete systems are often observable; for example, the state—in the concrete sense of courts, police, and federal agencies—is a primary system link.

We, thus, use, to some extent, concepts similar to those which societal actors use, perceive, and to which they respond. Though this synthesizing approach may have some disadvantages (which can be avoided, at least partially, by maintaining an overlayer of more analytic concepts), it has two obvious advantages: It makes theory more operational, which means that it is easier to identify indicators for the concepts, thus making the theory more verifiable; and it makes the transition from findings to policy more feasible. In short, it makes the theory itself more active.

NOTES

1. Georg Simmel, "Ekkurs über das Problem: Wie ist Gesellschaft möglich?" *Soziologie* (Leipzig: Duncker & Humblot, 1908), Chap. I. See also Nisbet, *The Sociological Tradition, op. cit.,* pp. 21–23.

2. Such terms are also found in physiology. See Elizabeth Duffy, "The Concept of Energy Mobilization," *Psychological Review,* Vol. 58 (1951), pp. 30–40, and, by the same author, "The Psychological Significance of the Concept of 'Arousal' or 'Activation,' " *Psychological Review,* Vol. 64 (1957), pp. 265–275. John C. Eccles, "Interpretation of Action Potentials Evoked in the Cerebral Cortex," *Electroencephalography and Clinical Neurophysiology,* Vol. 3 (1951), pp. 449–464.

3. It is reported that such a state is approximated by several tribes. See R. F. Fortune, "Arapesh Warfare," *American Anthropologist,* N.S. 41 (1939), pp. 22–41 and Gertrude E. Dole, "Anarchy without Chaos: Alternatives to Political Authority among the Kuikuru," in Marc J. Swartz, Victor W. Turner, and Arthur Tuden (eds.) *Political Anthropology,* (Chicago: Aldine Publishing Company, 1966), pp. 73–87. Alexander Mintz, "Non-Adaptive Group Behavior," *The Journal of Abnormal*

Social Psychology, Vol. 46 (1951), pp. 150–159, shows in laboratory conditions how panic brings about reduction of cooperation and an everyone-for-himself attitude. Banfield shows that there is little "moral fabric" in a southern Italian town above and beyond the family level. Banfield, *The Moral Basis of a Backward Society, op. cit.* Lewis M. Killian shows how sociability regresses when disaster strikes an American city. "The Significance of Multiple-Group Membership in Disaster," in Dorwin Cartwright and Alvin Zander (eds.), *Group Dynamics* (New York: Harper & Row, 1953), pp. 249–256.

4. Kenneth E. Boulding, *The Organizational Revolution* (New York: Harper & Row, 1953), p. xxxi; Reinhold Niebuhr, "Coercion, Self-Interest, and Love," *ibid*, pp. 228–244; Franz L. Neumann, "Approaches to the Study of Political Power," *Political Science Quarterly*, Vol. 65 (1950), p. 168; John R. Commons, *Legal Foundations of Capitalism* (Madison: University of Wisconsin Press, 1957), pp. 47–64; Morris Janowitz, *The Professional Soldier* (New York: Free Press, 1960), p. 258.

5. These matters are discussed in detail in Chapters 13 and 14, which deal with power and its relationship to activation.

6. For additional discussion of the two dimensions and their relations, see Chapters 13 and 14.

7. Lenin emphasized the organizational aspect while Marx was more concerned with the stratification aspects. See Wolin, *Politics and Vision, op. cit.*, pp. 423–427.

8. Parsons states, "A collectivity is a concrete system of interacting human individuals, of persons in roles." Talcott Parsons, *Structure and Process in Modern Societies* (New York: Free Press, 1960), p. 171. See also Talcott Parsons, *The Social System* (New York: Free Press, 1951), p. 41; and Parsons and Shils, *Toward a General Theory of Action, op. cit.*, pp. 192–194. See also Blau, *Exchange and Power in Social Life, op. cit.*, pp. 285–286.

9. One of the best studies of the extension of loyalties is Edward A. Shils and Morris Janowitz, "Cohesion and Disintegration in the Wehrmacht in World War II," *Public Opinion Quarterly*, Vol. 12 (1948), pp. 280–315. For additional illustrations and discussion, see Chapter 15.

10. The Sunday and night rates for long-distance telephone calls in the United States dropped to a point where in 1965 leaders of local chapters of the Students for a Democratic Society began using the telephone on a massive scale to "keep in touch" nationally.

11. E. Franklin Frazier, *Black Bourgeoisie* (New York: Free Press, 1957), p. 94.

12. The stratification base of society depends on its position in the global distribution of assets. See Gustavo Lagos, *International Stratification and Under-developed Countries* (Chapel Hill: University of North Carolina Press, 1963), esp. pp. 128–162; Johan Galtung, "A Structural Theory of Aggression," *Journal of Peace Research*, No. 2 (1964), pp. 95–119; Irving L. Horowitz, *Three Worlds of Development* (New York: Oxford University Press, 1966), esp. pp. 20–24.

13. For a discussion of a large variety of possible interactions which fall in this category and for reference to relevant studies, see Manford H. Kuhn, "Major Trends in Symbolic Interaction Theory in the Past Twenty-five Years," *The Sociological Quarterly*, Vol. 5 (1964), pp. 61–84.

14. For an empirical study of such interaction, see Dina A. Zinnes, "A Comparison of Hostile Behavior of Decision-Makers in Simulate and Historical

Data," *World Politics*, Vol. 18 (1966), pp. 474–502. For seven articles on national and international images, see Part I of Herbert C. Kelman (ed.), *International Behavior* (New York: Holt, Rinehart & Winston, 1965).

15. Herman Turk and Myron J. Lefcowitz, "Towards a Theory of Representation Between Groups," *Social Forces*, Vol. 40 (1962), pp. 337–341.

16. Actually, a very highly integrated unit may spend so much of its assets and energy on associational activities and on cohesion building, that it will be left with little for societal action.

17. The relations between consensus-formation and collective base are further explored below.

18. Etzioni, *A Comparative Analysis . . ., op. cit.*, pp. 23–67.

19. Kenneth B. Clark discusses the need for Negro churches to maintain their ties with the Negro community in order to act effectively. *Dark Ghetto* (New York: Harper & Row, 1965), pp. 182–184.

20. Some data in support of this proposition is reviewed in Etzioni, *A Comparative Analysis . . ., op. cit.*, pp. 160–172.

21. Discussion of the relation of national policies to "the national interest" illustrates how a large variety of policies may be convincingly shown to "fit" a particular interest. Hence, mobilization seems to be a better criterion of "representation" than "fit" between interests and policy.

22. We argue in detail below that the notions of "mass" mobilization and charismatic compliance are unduly atomistic and do not account for the activation of most societies most of the time.

23. Weber, *The Theory of Social and Economic Organization*, translated by A. M. Henderson and Talcott Parsons, *op. cit.*, p. 154. Dahrendorf, *Class and Class Conflict in Industrial Society, op. cit.*, pp. 290–292, stresses the state's organizational character. Note that we deal here only with the domestic state. See also Rupert Emerson's discussion of the "state" and the "nation" in *From Empire to Nation* (Boston: Beacon Press, 1962), pp. 114–119, 133–139.

24. Lasswell's definition of a state makes it coextensive with that of society, which in turn appears more like an undifferentiated social–psychological micro-unit than a collectivity of collectivities. *Psychopathology and Politics* (Chicago: University of Chicago Press, 1930), pp. 240 ff. Cf. Talcott Parsons, *Structure and Process in Modern Societies, op. cit.*, pp. 180–181.

25. For some data on the degree to which these may be considered "one" society, see Bruce Sievers, "The Divided Nations: International Integration and National Identity," *Stanford Studies of the Communist System, Research Paper No. 11*, 1966.

26. Lipset made this point in reference to the resistance to social governments by the civil servants of Saskatchewan, Canada. See his *Agrarian Socialism* (Berkeley: University of California Press, 1950), pp. 255–275. Stouffer, *Communism, Conformity, and Civil Liberties, op. cit.*, showed the leadership of organizations to be more liberal than the rank and file (esp. pp. 29–36). See also Wilson, *Negro Politics: The Search for Leadership, op. cit.*, pp. 91 and 130; Dahrendorf, *Class and Class Conflict in Industrial Society, op. cit.*, pp. 184–185; Truman, *The Governmental Process, op. cit.*, p. 322; and Friedrich, *Man and His Government, op. cit.*, p. 150. The organizational effect is not necessarily in the liberal direction. Robert Michels saw the leadership as having a conservative effect on Social–Democratic

parties and unions in his *Political Parties* (New York: Free Press, 1966). The AMA staff and oligarchy is reported to be further to the right than the average member. Oliver Garceau, *The Political Life of the American Medical Association* (Cambridge, Mass.: Harvard University Press, 1941), pp. 113–115. Dr. Milford Rouse, the president-elect of the AMA (who took office in June, 1967), is a former director of the H. L. Hunt Life-Line Foundation, which even *Time* described as "ultra-right" (July 8, 1966, p. 42).

27. These are said to come into play "wherever there exists a sharp decline in the power of the government of the system to influence action." Robert A. Dahl, *Modern Political Analysis* (Englewood Cliffs, N.J.: Prentice-Hall, 1963), p. 23. Dahl reviews the various definitions and provides the political one cited above.

28. *Ibid.*, p. 17.

29. Cf. a discussion of leadership by Talcott Parsons in his review of C. Wright Mills' *The Power Elite* in *World Politics*, Vol. 10 (1957), pp. 123–143. We concur with Bell who pointed out that the concept of elite may lead one to view political life as more monopolized and monolithic than the data justify. Daniel Bell, *The End of Ideology* (New York: Free Press, 1960), pp. 45–52. But lacking a more suitable term, we try to "divest" this one. See also Suzanne Keller, *Beyond the Ruling Class* (New York: Random House, 1963), pp. 19–22 and T. B. Bottomore, *Elites and Society* (New York: Basic Books, 1964), esp. 18–41.

30. For a fine review of the conceptual traditions and confusion of stratification and political factors, see T. B. Bottomore, *Elites and Society*, *op. cit.* For an earlier work, see James H. Meisel, *The Myth of the Ruling Class* (Ann Arbor: University of Michigan Press, 1958). Both authors suggest that the concept of elites is not useful and tend towards a joint stratification–political analysis. This holds also for C. Wright Mills' main works. We follow the bifocal approach, adhered to by Aron and Bendix (though neither makes the particular political concept of elite a center of his analysis). See Raymond Aron, "Social Structure and the Ruling Class," *British Journal of Sociology*, Vol. 1 (1950), pp. 1–16 and 126–143; Reinhard Bendix, "Social Stratification and Political Power," *American Political Science Review*, Vol. 46 (1952), pp. 357–375. See also Urs Jaeggi, *Die Gesellschaftliche Elite: Eine Studie zum Problem der Sozialen Macht* (Bern: Paul Haupt, 1960); Hans P. Dreitzel, *Elitebegriff und Sozialstruktur* (Stuttgart: Ferdinand Enke, 1962).

31. We draw here on the difference between external and internal aspects of a social unit as developed by George C. Homans, *The Human Group* (New York: Harcourt, Brace & World, 1950), p. 90.

32. These may be the system-elite of some other system. Thus, for instance, imperialist governments fulfill an external-elite function for colonial societies and are unit-elites for them, even if they are freely elected in the metropolitan country, because from the viewpoint of the controlled system the imperialist government is disproportionately responsive to the metropolitan country and external to the colonial system.

33. *The Sociology of Georg Simmel*, translated, edited, and introduced by Kurt H. Wolff (New York: Free Press, 1950), pp. 250–253, 268–272. See also Leopold von Wiese, adapted and amplified by Howard Becker, *Systematic Sociology* (New York: Wiley & Sons, 1932). pp. 12 ff.

34. Paul M. Harrison, *Authority and Power in the Free Church Tradition* (Princeton: Princeton University Press, 1959).

35. W. Lloyd Warner and J. O. Low, *The Social System of a Modern Factory* (New Haven: Yale University Press, 1947).

36. David Thomson, *The Democratic Ideal in France and England* (Cambridge, England: Cambridge University Press, 1940).

37. Marion J. Levy, Jr., stressed the "right" of the theoretician to thus specialize, in *Modernization and the Structure of Societies, op. cit.,* pp. 6–7.

38. Parsons, *The Structure of Social Action, op. cit.,* pp. 34–35, 71 and *The Social System, op. cit.,* p. 5.

39. Parsons, *The Structure of Social Action, op. cit.,* p. 29.

40. Bernard Barber, "Tension and Accommodations Between Science and Humanism," *American Behavioral Scientist,* Vol. 7 (1963), p. 5–6.

41. There are many other uses of the system concept that need not detain us here. However, one that is close to the notion of abstract system used above should be mentioned. Some philosophers and sociologists use "system" to denote a deductive structure. In this sense, mathematical theories constitute systems. See, for instance, Morris R. Cohen's *Reason and Nature* (New York: Free Press, 1953), pp. 108–114. The difference between this concept of system and our concept of an abstract system is that these are "purely" derived systems while ours are in part induced ones; they are purely logical, while ours are theoretical (i.e., logico-empirical.) The concepts of deductive systems can be more abstract than those of theoretical ones without causing the loss-of-reality they tend to affect theories with. The same holds for Miller's distinction between conceptual and concrete systems. See Miller, "Living Systems: Basic Concepts," *op. cit.,* pp. 201–209.

42. On the procedures of explication, see Rudolf Carnap, *Meaning and Necessity* (Chicago: University of Chicago Press, 1956), p. 8. Paul F. Lazarsfeld and Morris Rosenberg (eds.), "General Introduction" in their *The Language of Social Research: A Reader in the Methodology of Social Research* (New York: Free Press, 1955), p. 2.

43. Marion J. Levy, Jr. distinguishes between analytic and concrete structure along similar lines. *The Structure of Society* (Princeton: Princeton University Press, 1952), pp. 88–90.

44. Warner and Low, *The Social System of a Modern Factory, op. cit.*

45. C. Wayne Gordon, *The Social System of the High School* (New York: Free Press, 1957).

46. See William A. Caudill, *The Psychiatric Hospital as a Small Society* (Cambridge, Mass.: Harvard University Press, 1958), esp. pp. 3–5.

47. C. P. Loomis and J. A. Beegle, *Rural Social Systems* (New York: Prentice-Hall, 1950), p. 3–7. See also Alex Inkeles, "Some Sociological Observations on Culture and Personality Studies," in Kluckhohn and Murray, *Personality in Nature, Society and Culture, op. cit.,* p. 582; John P. Clark, "Measuring Alienation Within a Social System," *American Sociological Review,* Vol. 24 (1959), pp. 849–850.

48. Ernst B. Haas, "System and Process in the International Labor Organization," *World Politics,* Vol. 14 (1962), p. 323. Friedrich also states that systems are "real." *Man and His Government, op. cit.,* pp. 24–25. Haas proceeds by treating the International Labor Organization as a system. See his *Beyond the Nation-State* (Stanford: Stanford University Press, 1964), esp. pp. 86–87. For Haas' view of systems see esp. pp. 53–54. On the other hand, the system analysis of David Easton and Gabriel A. Almond is more of the analytic, non-reifying kind.

PART TWO

CYBERNETIC

FACTORS

INTRODUCTION

Our exploration of the factors which affect the capacity of a societal unit to guide its actions begins with cybernetic factors—with properties of the steering mechanisms, especially of the control centers. The role of knowledge in societal guidance is discussed (Chapters 6 to 10), followed by a study of societal decision-making (Chapters 11 and 12).

The sociology of knowledge has traditionally been part of the "universal" sector of sociological theory.* Its key propositions apply to persons, small groups, or classes, with little systematic differentiation or treatment of emergent properties of macroscopic units.[1]† Our analysis focuses on these properties from the perspective of a theory of societal guidance. No attempt is made to study societal knowledge from other macroscopic viewpoints—for instance, from a purely collectivistic one.

The societal guidance approach to knowledge deals with four main theoretical dimensions: (a) the relation among the various symbols and sets of symbols that constitute knowledge—i.e., intra-knowledge relations; (b) the relation between knowledge as a symbolic system and the external world; (c) the intra-societal organization of the relations between the production and the consumption of knowledge; and (d) the effects of differences in the possession and organization of knowledge on the relations between societal actors.

These four dimensions are derived from a cybernetic analogy: The knowledge unit is a sub-unit of the controlling overlayer which regulates societal processes. The four dimensions cover (a) the internal makeup of the knowledge sub-unit; (b) its relations to the more encompassing unit (the control overlayer); and (c) the role of knowledge in the relation of the control overlayer to the societal unit as a whole. Finally, (d) the model covers the role of knowledge in the relation of the societal unit to other societal units and to more encompassing societal supra-units.

Each of these dimensions is illustrated below with a discussion of one or two specific issues. No attempt is made to review all or even many of the issues involved in these questions. Rather, our purpose is to use specific examples to illustrate the

---

*"True, we have a so-called sociology of knowledge. Yet, with very few exceptions, the discipline thus misnamed has approached the problem of the social distribution of knowledge merely from the angle of the ideological foundation of truth in its dependence upon social and, especially, economic conditions, or from that of the social implications of education, or that of the social role of the man of knowledge."

Alfred Schutz, "The Well-Informed Citizen, an Essay on the Social Distribution of Knowledge", in his *Collected Papers II, Studies in Social Theory*, Arvid Brodersen, editor. (The Hague: Martinus Nijhoff, 1964), p. 121.

† Reference notes for this Introduction appear on page 134.

theoretical dimensions. The first part of Chapter 6 attempts a functional definition of knowledge and its characterization. The second part of Chapter 6 and Chapters 7, 8, and 9, each deal respectively with one of the four dimensions delineated above.

Knowledge[2] is one factor which significantly affects the action and reaction of societal units; it frees them from responding blindly to their environment or reacting "automatically" according to their characters. While all societal units have some knowledge of each other and of themselves, there are great differences in the volume, validity, and consistency of their collective knowledge, as well as in the degree to which they use whatever knowledge they command in their collective action.

THE DIMENSIONS OF A MACRO-SOCIOLOGY OF KNOWLEDGE

    a Intra-knowledge relations

    b Knowledge and reality

    c Relations between knowledge
       producers and other controlling
       units

    d Knowledge's effect on societal
       action and interaction

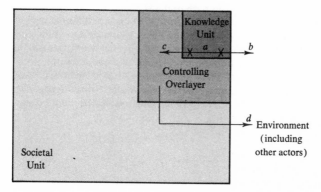

From an analytic viewpoint, societal knowledge not only affects the societal processes as a major component of the controlling overlayer but also is affected by the patterns and flows of ongoing societal processes. That is, societal knowledge is a major source of a society's capacity to organize itself but is itself affected by societal constraints.

From a historical viewpoint, the societal foundations of knowledge are changing: Post-modern societies and collectivities increasingly use knowledge to shape their relations to each other and to guide their own transformations. Because of this trend (however uneven it may be), the significance of knowledge as a variable which partially explains differences in societal conduct is increasing. In particular, the differences in the societal *organization* of the production and utilization of knowledge are of increasing importance in determining the realization of macroscopic goals.

Finally, the unequal distribution of knowledge-resources among societal units increasingly affects their relations to one another—whether these are suppressive, exploitive, or cooperative. Processes long considered largely the domain of economic and coercive factors are increasingly influenced by the allocation, withholding, and management of knowledge.

NOTES

1. For studies reviewing the earlier field, see Jacques J. Maquet, *The Sociology of Knowledge* (Boston: Beacon Press, 1951), and Werner Stark, *The Sociology of Knowledge* (London: Routledge & Kegan Paul, 1958). For an analytic review of the major classical sociological perspectives, see Robert K. Merton's well-known essay, "The Sociology of Knowledge" in his *Social Theory and Social Structure* (New York: Free Press, rev. ed., 1957), pp. 456–488. See also Karl Mannheim's *Ideology and Utopia*, translated by Louis Wirth and Edward A. Shils (New York: Harcourt, Brace & World, 1936). For a review and critique of the traditional concerns of sociology of knowledge and a suggestion that it ought to be concerned with "the social construction of reality," a process in which "everyone in society participates," see Peter L. Berger and Thomas Luckmann, *The Social Construction of Reality: A Treatise in the Sociology of Knowledge* (Garden City, N.Y.: Doubleday, 1966), esp. pp. 11–14. See also Schutz, *Der Sinnhafte Aufbau der Sozialen Welt, op. cit.*, and Talcott Parsons, "An Approach to the Sociology of Knowledge," *Transactions of the Fourth World Congress of Sociology* (Louvain: International Sociological Association), 1959, Vol. 4. Some studies have examined the production of knowledge in micro-structures (e.g., leadership of scientific work teams). Only recently has the macroscopic organization of science become a central topic of socio-political interest. See Don K. Price, *The Scientific Estate* (Cambridge, Mass.: Harvard University Press, 1965). Bernard Barber and Walter Hirsch (eds.), *The Sociology of Science* (New York: Free Press, 1962). Other works are cited below.

2. For definition, see p. 137.

CHAPTER 6

Knowledge

as a Societal Factor

C AN KNOWLEDGE be viewed as a societal resource? What functions does it fulfill for societal actors? To what extent are societal actors able to gain a valid view of their environment and of themselves? How do their various items of knowledge relate to each other? These are the questions we attempt to explore in this chapter.

A Functional Analysis of Societal Knowledge

Knowledge as a Societal Property

Societal units produce knowledge and use it collectively. Knowledge does not exist only in the minds of individuals; like other societal assets, knowledge is stored in collective facilities (from libraries to computer tapes), is made available for collective action (as when an organization retains experts), and is shifted from the service of one societal goal to the service of another e.g., by transferring a large contingent of laboratory employees from the service of the United States Army to that of the National Aeronautics and Space Agency (NASA).[1]* Though knowledge is an unusual asset in that it is a set of symbols rather than objects, we suggest that it is nevertheless fruitful to view it as an asset and to study the production, processing, and consumption of knowledge as societal activities. In some senses, societal actors use knowledge in much the same way as persons: Their internal structures often bias their views of the world and of their changing places in it, and they misunderstand each other and react in "unrealistic" ways. The quality of societal knowledge is affected by its societal base—by the degree of political autonomy of its producers, the level of public financing of knowledge-production, and the institutionalization of lines of communication between the sources of new knowledge and the centers of power.

Functions of Knowledge

Knowledge is a set of symbols that serves two societal functions. First, it provides a *relation to reality* by containing information about the non-social environment, other actors, and the actor himself. Second, knowledge, in conjunction with religion and ideology, provides "meaning," an important bond that ties actions and actors to one another[2] and affects societal commitments. Meaning is derived by interpreting facts cognitively and by evaluating them in normative terms, a function we refer to as *evaluative interpretation.*†

All societal actors have a capacity for reality-testing: That is, they revise their knowledge to some degree in accord with their experience. In this sense, they are not basically different from scientists who revise their theories on the basis of data. Not only do societal actors revise their knowledge, but scientists also do not readily discard a theory when faced with "stubborn" facts, nor do they "adhere" to a theory only for "relevant" reasons.[3] There are two main differences between societal actors and scientists: (a) The societal actors' procedures for collecting and revising knowledge are comparatively loose and informal. (b) Societal actors are relatively more concerned with the interpretive aspect of their knowledge, which tends to be incompatible with giving *primary* consideration to reality-testing. While actors do differ significantly in the degree to which they are able to face reality, in effect, no actor's knowledge escapes considerable evaluative interpretation.

Because of their great concern with interpretation, societal actors commonly perceive the symbolic realm differently from two major traditions of philosophical and social scientific thought, positivism and pragmatism.

---

* Reference notes for this chapter appear on page 151.

† We use the term evaluative (normative) interpretation to distinguish this kind of meaning from factual interpretation, conducted by logical or methodological procedures. This distinction is an analytic one; both kinds of interpretation are often interwoven.

Adherents of these traditions tend to differentiate sharply between value-judgments and factual statements. Factual statements are viewed as assisting in reality-testing; value-judgments are seen either as signs of confusion and ignorance and, therefore, non-productive, or as constituting a myth, religion, or ideology which is useful but has no reality-testing value, and thus, to be sharply distinguished from factual statements.

Apart from the question of whether or not this sharp separation of values and facts is an adequate basis for social science, we suggest that *the knowledge used by societal actors commonly mixes information* (factual statements) *with evaluative interpretation* (itself a mixture of cognitive and normative statements). This is not to say that societal actors confuse *pure* normative systems, such as religion or ideology, with information; value-judgments *are* set aside. Societal actors, especially modern ones, are aware that appeals to action because "it is for your country" or "it is just" are not part of knowledge.* But what most societal actors use as knowledge, we suggest, includes a mixture of facts and common sense, science and folklore, empirical observations, insights, and evaluations.†

---

* This statement can be empirically tested. One could, for instance, show a number of statements to samples of educated and uneducated citizens and ask them to separate those dealing with facts from those dealing with "opinions." We expect that at least the first group would be able to sort out the "pure" value-judgments from statements mixing value-judgments with information, although we would expect the latter to be classed together with "pure" information (factual statements).

† The following example stands for many that could be cited:

"Public controversy has surrounded the proposal to construct a branch of the Cook County Hospital on the South Side in or near the Negro area. Several questions of policy are involved in the matter, but the ones which have caused one of the few *public* debates of an issue in the Negro community concern whether, or to what extent, building such a branch would result in an all-Negro or 'Jim Crow' hospital and whether such a hospital is desirable as a means of providing added medical facilities for Negro patients. Involved are both an issue of *fact* (whether the hospital would be segregated, intentionally or unintentionally, as a result of the character of the neighborhood in which it would be located) and an issue of *value* (whether even an all-Negro hospital would be preferable to no hospital at all in the area). In reality, however, the factions have aligned themselves in such a way and the debate has proceeded in such a manner that the fact issue and the value issue have been collapsed into the single question of whether to build or not to build. Those in favor of the proposal will argue that the facts do not bear out the charge of 'Jim Crowism'—'the proposed site . . . is not considered to be placed in a segregated area for the exclusive use of one racial or minority group'; or 'no responsible officials would try to develop a new hospital to further segregation'; or 'establishing a branch hospital for the . . . more adequate care of the indigent patient load, from the facts thus presented, does not represent Jim Crowism.' At the same time, these proponents argue that whatever the facts, the factual issue is secondary to the overriding consideration that 'there is a here-and-now need for more hospital beds. . . . Integration may be the long-run goal, but in the short run we need more facilities.' " James Q. Wilson, *Negro Politics* (New York: Free Press, 1960), p. 189.

For a treatment of knowledge as combining factual and normative elements see Franco Ferrarotti, *Max Weber e il Destino della Ragione* (Bari Editor: Laterza, 1965).

The major reason for the mixing of factual statements with value-judgments is that facts without normative interpretations are of limited societal or political utility. From a macroscopic viewpoint, the fact that one technology, for instance, is more efficient than another is of little interest if the superior technology violates the religious values of a collectivity, the national self-image of a society, or the political commitments of an elite.* We expect, therefore, that societal decision-makers will view new technologies in terms of both their efficiency and their normative merits. And the organization of societal knowledge is greatly affected by the needs and perspectives of societal decision-making.

To the degree that both functions of knowledge can be served by the same new "bit" of knowledge, i.e.—if the item both increases the reality of the actor's knowledge *and* supports his evaluative interpretations—there are relatively few barriers to macroscopic learning. But when an increase in validity is at the expense of a societal interpretation which, let us say, protects a collectivity's share of the societal allocation of assets, a compromise is often worked out between the service of the two needs. In the long run, new information is not necessarily disregarded, but it may be temporarily neglected, diluted, or distorted in favor of maintaining the prevailing evaluative interpretations.

While actors differ in the degree to which they have valid knowledge, can determine the extent to which their knowledge is valid, sacrifice facts for interpretation or vice versa, and use information in guiding their actions, even the most learned societal actor seldom has more than a fraction of the relevant information he theoretically could use. The study of knowledge and action, therefore, is concerned with *relative* degrees of ignorance, confusion of fact and half-fact, and dissociation of societal intellect from the societal guidance of action.

These considerations, often neglected by the partisans of the new technology of knowledge, explain why the growing improvement in the societal capacity to collect and analyze information has had a lesser effect on the "reality" of societal action than would be expected from an analysis of the new technology's capacity.[4] This phenomenon resembles the previously found "artificial" restriction of output: It has been shown that production is more in accord with the outputs set by the workers' norms than in accord with their physiological capacities. The degree to which the knowledge produced is valid and the extent to which that knowledge is utilized are only partially determined by the technical capacity to collect and process valid knowledge; they are also determined by the social definitions of how much

---

* Quantitative considerations should be taken into account here. Thus, if a new technology is clearly superior, and the norm it violates is weak and marginal, the technology may well be adopted. But this does not change the basic observation that the technology must first be evaluated from both viewpoints if a societal actor is to consider such adoption.

information is desired, what questions are to be submitted to research, and which findings are to be accepted, suppressed, or disregarded. This may be called the "artificial" restriction of information.

Such restriction is a basic fact of societal life. While one can alter the mixture—that is, increase the information component and change the specific meaning given to a societal fact—the societal need for the evaluative interpretation of facts and not just for "pure" value-judgments seems to be universal. Thus, as distinct from Marx, we submit that while the interpretation of any actor—including the proletariat—may be replaced, all societal actors are "interpreting." It is this interpretation which bridges knowledge and values, as it bridges knowledge and interests.

This limitation of reality-testing, we suggest, is not pathological but appears in "normal" societal units. They are "normal" in that even though there are strong constraints on reality-testing, these constraints do not prevent the functioning of the units. Pathological units are those whose reality-testing is constricted to the point that they are able to accommodate to changes in the environment only at a very high cost. While there are few social-science studies of societal units that are pathological by this criterion, several good descriptive reports are available. One concerns the manner in which Senator Barry Goldwater and his staff directed the 1964 Republican presidential campaign.[5] They repeatedly violated most of the rules of effective political conduct, and, despite continued feedback information from public opinion polls and press reports to the effect that their unorthodox approach was failing, they grew even more committed to it.*

The Low Validity of Societal Knowledge

To a greater extent than individuals, societal actors can function for long periods of time with little empirically valid social knowledge.† There are four reasons that the reality-testing of macroscopic actors is particularly limited:

1. The reality-testing of an individual is reinforced by the actors with whom he interacts relatively closely. Macro-actors, as a rule, are less closely related to each other. A person unable to distinguish green from red will normally be corrected by others. It should be noted that such a person may not be empirically wrong but may only be "out of line" socially.[6] Pressure to

---

* It may be argued that Goldwater was acting rationally and was responding to the feedback information—in accord with a goal not of winning the election but of educating the American people to the conservative creed. But he and his staff gave many indications of believing that their strategy would win the election, and whatever their goals, from the viewpoint of the Republican Party and its institutionalized goals, the strategy was deficient in reality-testing.

† Empirically valid knowledge and knowledge that is reality-tested are the same thing. Empirical validation does not necessarily involve scientific procedures; trial-and-error, for instance, is a primitive but relevant method. For a discussion of validity, see below pp. 143–4.

"realign," therefore, serves as a means of social rather than environmental reality-testing. It is this social reality-testing that macro-actors tend to lack, for a nation can be "color-blind" for many years and yet continue to insist that other nations are in the wrong.[7] Since there is comparatively little supranational interaction or joint action, there is relatively little agreement about facts or pressure to reach such agreement.*

If one person mistakenly views another as hostile, there are corrective mechanisms available, both "interwoven" ones, such as in the relations with a trusted friend, and "segregated" ones, such as those provided by a psychotherapist. But on the intra-societal level—among classes, tribes, or races in the many poorly integrated societies—and particularly among nations, there are few corrective mechanisms. There are friendships among macro-actors; Britain, for instance, since 1945 has often acted as a trusted reality-testing friend for the United States. The ability of one actor to do this for another, however, depends on the strength of the integrative bonds between them, but these bonds are commonly weaker among macro-actors than among individuals or micro-units.

The closest approximation (on the macroscopic level) to psychotherapy seems to be the experience of a crisis, one which actors with low reality-testing capacities are likely to undergo, particularly if they act in a rapidly changing environment.[8] Like a speeding motorist who suddenly senses that his steering wheel is inoperative, to "experience a crisis" means that with comparative suddenness the decision-making sub-units of a societal unit realize that the unit's ability to adapt has been sharply curtailed. A crisis, obviously, has a "therapeutic" effect only if it forces adaptations previously avoided, including the revision of knowledge. On the other hand, macro-actors, like individuals, may react to a crisis by "regressing," by adhering more closely to the same course of action, ritualistically repeating their earlier moves, often with increased rigidity.[9]

2. Macro-actors have a greater capacity than other actors to alter their environments, and hence, rather than adjusting their knowledge to social reality, they can often change the reality to fit their preconceptions or misconceptions. Nations, for example, may generate wars to confirm their perceptions of hostile neighbors.

3. A third reason for expecting societal actors to be less "realistic" and more interpretive in their uses of knowledge is that the relations between elites and societal units have greater "slack" than those between the cybernetic mechanisms and action-underlayers of persons or micro-units (to the degree that they command such mechanisms at all). A national elite can maintain an invalid image in the minds of the citizens, especially in situations of comparatively little inter-elite competition, such as when there is a bi-

---

* Micro-actors fall between persons and macro-actors on this dimension, because they are, on the average, more integrated than macro-actors but less so than most persons.

partisan or "consensus" foreign policy.* Such "schizophrenia" is much less common in "normal" persons and small groups, because the control mechanisms and the action underlayers are less segregated.

4. Finally, if knowledge is to be an attribute of a societal unit, it must be shared by at least the main centers of guidance, often by the majority of the active members, and occasionally by all the members. Sharing a sub-unit's knowledge with the other relevant sub-units so that it becomes unit-knowledge is a major task for societal guidance, but much less so for persons and small groups. The degree to which a societal unit's knowledge is *shared* among the elites and the various publics is a key criterion by which to measure *societal* knowledge.[10] Although we expect a greater sharing of knowledge to be associated with a greater capacity to act, *high knowledge sharing—even among or within elites—is not common, and its absence does not prevent a unit from acting in unison.* The capacity to act is often preserved through the sharing of knowledge regarding specific acts, even though there might be little consensus on policy or values.

To put the matter succinctly, a confused societal actor, in whom different images of the world and himself are in conflict, can still function quite effectively. Hence, the term "societal" knowledge should not conjure up simply images of science, information, or openmindedness—although these are included—as it may be more likely to resemble thick, foggy, and multi-layered filters through which societal actors relate to one another and to themselves.

Societal Structure and Validity

The structure of a societal unit affects the degree to which its knowledge is invalid and the direction in which it is slanted. While all societal units have a need for evaluative interpretation, the specific direction of the slanting and the degree to which knowledge is unrealistic depend considerably on the particular values, structure, and organization of the societal unit under study. The way in which these factors affect the manifest use of knowledge by societal units is analogous to the way in which a person's subconcsious influences his use of knowledge. Also, like psychotherapists, social scientists or critics who attempt to unveil the underlying societal dynamics confront, at least initially, resistance and rejection, because the exposure of latent factors threatens those who benefit from the promotion of false images.

---

* Holding such a false image may seem "realistic" for the elite and "unrealistic" for the societal unit, for if the elite allowed a more valid interpretation to gain hold, it might lose its controlling position. But such a statement which confuses two frames of reference is an error which undermines the essence of functional analysis. One needs to distinguish between the needs of the societal unit and the needs of an elite. If the images that an elite promotes are false, this reduces the reality-testing of the societal unit it leads, whatever the consequences of such a reduction for the elite itself.

Moreover, various processes of selection, especially a differential recruitment to politics, seem to place some personality types in controlling positions more than others. This appears to result in a correlation between power and the possession of certain psychological characteristics.[11] Of special interest to a theory of societal guidance are those analyses which seek to determine the conditions under which elites have a greater personal capacity to absorb valid knowledge, are psychologically freer to experiment, and are able to communicate new knowledge to non-elites. The psychological composition of the non-elites becomes proportionately more consequential as the mechanisms that make the controlling position of the few dependent on their responsiveness to the many become more powerful.

Finally, the ability of a societal unit to know is significantly affected by the technology of knowledge, especially by the availability of computers. Though this technology may be available to individuals or to micro-units, it is much more often a property of macro-units. While such a technology and its components are external to the personality of an individual and to the structures of most micro-units, they can be highly integrated into macrosystems. Consequently, even if all individuals had the same capacity to know, we would have to consider their places in the societal organization of the production of knowledge and their consumption or "access" rights before we could determine their relative knowledge and their ability to affect societal action by the use of knowledge.

The answer to the question of how a collectivity learns is often given in atomistic–individualistic terms—e.g., by the members enrolling in a training course. This assumes that new knowledge enters a collectivity via the members' personalities. A collectivity, however, can learn more rapidly by importing experts or by buying a library. Similarly, while it is difficult for a person to unlearn invalid knowledge, a collectivity can do so with relative ease— e.g., by changing the experts it consults or by reprogramming the computers. That a societal unit has a relatively greater ability to accumulate knowledge than a person and to use more of it simultaneously is evident. Societal units, thus, possess more knowledge than is available to any one member (or even to all members combined). Actually, a so-called "knowledgeable" person is often someone with access to a societal source of information or to facilities for collection and analysis of information that are not his own.

There may seem to be a contradiction between these statements and the preceding discussion of the relatively less realistic societal, as compared to personal, knowledge. But the contradiction is only apparent; societal actors, we suggest, command much greater amounts of knowledge than persons (or micro-units), but their knowledge is of "poorer" quality; that is, it tends to be less realistic or, at least, more difficult to correct. It is the greater amount which allows societal actors to a degree, to make up for the poorer quality of their knowledge. We turn next to explore the relations among the items of knowledge a societal actor commands and the processes which affect these relations. These are processes which significantly affect, within the limits of societal knowledge, the quality of that knowledge.

Intra-Symbolic Relations: The Role of Synthesis

The relations among the symbols which constitute societal knowledge significantly affect the contribution of the knowledge to the actor's reality-testing and evaluative interpretation. In this section we illustrate the study of these internal relations of societal knowledge and their effect on societal guidance by exploring two specific theoretical issues: (a) the level of synthesis, and (b) the balance among the different components of societal knowledge. As we shall see, if the actor's capacity to synthesize is small, or his knowledge is imbalanced, he may command a good deal of information but know little and have only a fragmented view of the world and of himself. Other dysfunctions occur, however, if synthesizing is excessive.

The Function of Synthesis

Both information and evaluation tend to be produced bit by bit. This is obvious for information, which is usually produced in the form of discrete facts. It is less obvious for evaluation, which is by definition a process of assessing items by relating them to broader contexts of a cognitive, normative, or esthetic nature. However, evaluation, too, is often highly fragmented. Items are frequently evaluated in terms of a single dimension without the construction of an index, or—its intellectual equivalent—an over-all evaluation of their worth. The dysfunction of such evaluation is that items assessed as valuable may actually be so only if complementary items are also available. The determination of the availability of necessary corollary items is in part a question of the comprehensive collection of information. Evaluative synthesis, however, depends on the interrelation and joint evaluation of those complementary facts available to an actor.

For knowledge to be usable, as a rule, bits must be organized into more encompassing contexts. We shall refer to this process as synthesizing and to the result as synthesis.* Synthesis is a matter of degree; no actor relates all his fragments of knowledge well to all the others, but some have them more organized than others.

To assess the level of knowledge-synthesis, the following three dimensions should be taken into account: (a) The number of bits which are encompassed

---

* Synthesis and context are not synonyms; the former is a property of the latter. A context is the frame of reference within which bits are related. Synthesis refers to the degree to which the bits have been tied to the frame and the extent to which the whole context is well-structured. The synthesis of a context may, thus, be high or low.

in a particular knowledge context determines the size of the "job" the synthesizing process is required to do. Generally, it is more difficult to relate a large number of fragments than it is to deal with a smaller number. When, however, there are very few fragments—as in some archaeological investigations—it becomes difficult, if not impossible, to construct a composite picture. (b) The number of the bits systematically related to one context or another is a measure of how much of the synthesizing "job" is being done. Since in all knowledge-processing the integration of bits may be carried out in more than one context at a time, we also need to assess (c) the degree to which the contexts are related to each other to make up a knowledge system. In most knowledge systems, we suggest, bits are more integrated into sub-systems than the sub-systems are integrated into systems; there are, however, significant differences in the degree of synthesis of sub-systems into systems. High synthesis of knowledge is achieved only when bits are well integrated into contexts and contexts into knowledge systems.

The boundaries between contexts are usually substantive; knowledge is organized, for instance, into distinct contexts regarding nature and society. Social scientists have attempted to divide knowledge analytically into purely cognitive and purely evaluative contexts. As we suggested earlier, societal actors do not as a rule thus divide their synthesizing processes. Actors' syntheses typically mix cognitive and evaluative interpretation in each single context and in their combination into knowledge systems.

While analytic segregation on one level—that of bits into contexts—does not prevent the synthesis of contexts into knowledge systems that societal actors can use, segregation on both levels reduces the applicability of knowledge to societal action. Modern societies and, to a greater extent, large segments of scientific communities are among the actors who, we suggest, approximate such two-level analytic segregation. No actor can be highly active unless his knowledge-synthesis bridges this analytic gap which is a legacy of the modern period.

Deficient versus Excessive Synthesis

The starting point of the theory of societal guidance for the study of knowledge-synthesis is that bits are not integrated into contexts unless investments are made and efforts are undertaken to achieve such integration. That is, our null hypothesis is that no synthesis will occur. In practice, of course, rudimentary synthesis is built into socialization and into language itself; our concern is with macroscopic synthesis and its organization by societal actors.

In exploring the effects of the particular synthesizing capacities of a societal actor, it is essential to hold them analytically separate from the number of bits introduced. This is necessary since, like other processing capacities, what is sufficient for one level of input may be inadequate for a significantly higher level and excessive for a much lower one. We will now examine briefly the kinds of dysfunctions that occur when synthesizing capacities and knowledge input are seriously imbalanced.

When the synthesizing capacity of an actor is low, the greater his input of knowledge, the greater we expect his disorientation to be. The actor's view of the world, of himself, and of processes and changes will be splintered—clear in spots but vague in its totality.[12]

When knowledge input is limited, *ad hoc* and informal synthesis may be possible, provided for the societal unit by processes in a leader's mind or in a committee meeting. But when the input is voluminous and the evaluation is complicated, these mechanisms become flooded.[13] This is true not only of persons but also of control centers, organizations (e.g., army headquarters) and national governments (e.g., the White House). The problem of twentieth-century historians and of contemporary social science is often not the lack but rather the abundance of information. Moreover, deficient synthesis may be the unwitting result of inadequate knowledge-processing, or it may even be a deliberate strategy of elites who fear the picture a fuller synthesis might produce.

Whatever the particular history of deficient synthesis, the dysfunctions are the same. A common reaction to deficient synthesis is for the controlling unit to bury itself in detail and to neglect the longitudinal and lateral reviews of knowledge systems.[14] It is widely agreed, for instance, that the United States Department of State has much more effective planning capacities for dealing with single, isolated acts than for formulating over-all policy.[15] NASA spends much more money collecting information than analyzing it; it has accumulated, for example, many pictures of cloud formations but has put the information contained in these pictures to little use.[15a] Similarly, President Johnson was deeply involved in such details of the Vietnam War as how high the bombers flew and the size of the bombs they used, but he was criticized for not paying more attention to the wider political context.[16] There is reason to believe that this is a general pattern of the Anglo-Saxon collective use of knowledge,[17] having deep historical and philosophical roots.[18]

When cognitive and evaluative syntheses are highly segregated, a societal actor tends to act like a person whose affect has become dissociated from his cognitive processes; i.e., he is unaware of the moral implications both of his cognitive plans for action and of the information he gains about the outcomes of his acts. The dissociation of military thinking from political and normative evaluations, is a well-known societal parallel.[19] Here, one may refer to societal schizophrenia; the outcome is analogous though the mechanisms are different.

All this does not mean that the more that knowledge is synthesized, the greater will be the effectiveness of an actor. Over-synthesis does occur and has dysfunctions of its own. Scholasticism represents a low input of information and over-interpretation. Continental thinking, especially French rationalism, exhibited similar qualities.[20] We expect that actors who use over-synthesized knowledge will suffer from poor reality-testing, not unlike that of actors who do not synthesize sufficiently. Whether this leads to hyperactivism, resignation, or other kinds of ineffectual guidance has yet to be explored.

The Prevalence of Ineffective Synthesis

While we do argue that a highly active societal unit needs a capacity for synthesis that matches the other elements of the controlling overlayer, especially the level of knowledge input, we do not suggest that a high capacity for synthesis is common. Actually, only a few of the more organized post-modern units seem to command effective synthesizing units; many otherwise well-organized societal units have only a limited synthesizing capacity.

One of the most deep-seated fallacies in social science is the rationalist assumption of a high degree of consistency in the interpretations produced by societal units. Intellectuals value internal consistency highly; a rational person does not hold conflicting views simultaneously. Hence, when partially incompatible information or ideas are found to be held by a public (or an individual), the explanation is usually in terms of distorting psychological processes or conflicting economic and social interests. Actually, this incompatibility is in part an artifact of overly abstract system analysis. When the unit of study is arbitrarily imposed in such a way that it cuts across meaningful societal boundaries, it is not surprising that the defined "public" holds conflicting views; in fact, some views are held by one societal grouping and some by another.

Second, even when a public is defined in terms of a meaningful societal unit, one which has some integrative processes, incompatible information is still likely to be held by various sub-units. We expect that many collectivities (as well as individual members) routinely and "normally" hold bits of information that are less than fully synthesized. Even highly systematic ideological systems, which are more synthesized but to which few societal units adhere, are not free from all such contradictions. Synthesis is, therefore, to be treated as a continuous and not a dichotomous variable. Some actors have more than others, few have much, and the main societal need is for a level of synthesis that matches other knowledge-capacities.

A Structural Perspective

The internal makeup of the controlling overlayer affects the extent to which a societal actor is able to synthesize.* Some controlling overlayers provide only one level of control comprised of the immediate review and

---

* See Chapter 2, pp. 31–32 on the internal structure of the overlayer.

direction of supervised processes. Other overlayers, however, are split into two (or more) sub-layers which relate to each other in a similar way that controlling overlayers relate to controlled societal processes. Thus, there are second-order review units which analyze the work of the first-order review units, and so on. The relative investment in second-order review units and processes as against first-order ones (e.g., in research and planning as against direct supervision of processes) is a structural expression of the relative weight given to synthesis. We saw that the United States Department of State has been viewed as having a deficient capacity to synthesize. In line with this proposition, we find a structural parallel: an investment in research and development that is one of the smallest among agencies in the federal government.[21]

The deeper causes of "flooding"—i.e., high knowledge input coupled with low synthesizing capacities—are not to be found in the strategy followed by the sub-units but rather in the organizational structure itself. Flooding, we suggest, is likely to occur when higher-ranking units, entrusted with control functions, command fewer cybernetic resources than the lower-ranking units under their "control." A discrepancy is, thus, generated between formal authority and the capacity to regulate, at least as far as knowledge synthesis is concerned. The White House Office of Science and Technology, for example, has a much smaller staff and budget than the headquarters of the agencies it supposedly oversees.[22] In social science research, it is much easier to acquire funds for the collection of information than for its analysis.[23] Furthermore, much more information is collected by questionnaire surveys than is ever analyzed, even superficially.[24]

Intra-organizational conditions that make for high knowledge input (in terms of the number of bits) and low synthesis and, therefore, low knowledge include the following: (a) When there is a considerable pressure to complete a study or report in a short time, the collection of data, which is an early step, is rarely curtailed as much as synthesis, which necessarily is undertaken closer to the deadline. (b) A shortage of resources has similar effects because the closer the project is to completion, the greater the budget pressures tend to be. (c) Data collection seems to require less skill and to be more easily mechanized than the more complex operation of synthesis, so a shortage of professional personnel encourages low synthesis. Skilled professional personnel is especially necessary for the higher levels of synthesis as distinct from half-processing such as classification and tabulation. (d) Political pressures inside the organization, between the political head and the staff, and from the outside, tend to mute conclusions, and hence, synthesizing. All these factors are reported to have hindered such projects as the report of the Warren Commission concerning the assassination of President Kennedy,[25] the work of the National Commission on Technology, Automation and Economic Progress,[26] and the McCone Commission report on the 1965 Watts riots in Los Angeles.[27]

The effect of intra-knowledge relations on societal action was illustrated by the discussion of the synthesis of bits and of contexts of knowledge. A second illustration of this dimension and its societal significance is derived from a brief examination of the relations among the main components of knowledge.

Intra-Symbolic Relations: The Sub-Systems of Societal Knowledge

All knowledge is a simplification—a reduced, schematic abstraction from a richer, less ordered, more concrete reality. Knowledge is to the world what a map is to the road: It reports some details to the neglect of many others, and the signs must be understood before it is of any use at all. There is always the possibility of another selection, which may better serve a particular societal need, and many alternate choices might be made if other needs (e.g., reality-testing) were paramount.

From this viewpoint, science is not basically different from other knowledge sub-systems. While it draws on statements that are empirically validated, their truth is not only relative and tentative, but they also do not escape the reduction of reality entailed in selectivity. The societal importance of the scientific approach to knowledge-formation—as opposed to other approaches—is dependent on the rank given to reality-testing in the scale of societal values. Even a very high ranking, however, does not alter the position of science as one approach to reality among many—highly favored in the modern period, and, for reasons we shall discuss shortly, of less value for an active society.

While all approaches toward reality are basically relativistic and segmental, it is useful to compare their respective merits. A common fallacy in such comparisons is to view the basis of selection of one particular approach as the criterion for evaluation of all others. Thus, if we use as our criterion the empirical validity of isolated bits, some models of empirical research will score high, since this is their special quality; if we take the extent of emotional content, some forms of poetry score high. Therefore, it seems more productive to use criteria derived from the functional needs to be served rather than from the disciplines serving them, and to use a combination of criteria for assessment which will cover all the basic societal needs for knowledge rather than subordinate assessment to any one need.

The following criteria are suggested for comparing the extent to which the societal knowledge of various actors services their needs for reality-testing and evaluative interpretation. We do not attempt to explore the many ramifications of selection criteria; we seek mainly to illustrate the multi-criterion approach. Drawing on the preceding discussion, we suggest that societal knowledge can be fruitfully compared according to the extent to which (a) it is *empirically valid* (bit by bit); (b) the various contexts are *synthesized*;

(c) reality-testing and evaluation are *fused* in the same contexts or *segregated*, and, if segregated into separate contexts, whether these contexts are linked or unrelated; and (d) whether or not it is *encompassing* in terms of coverage of the subjects-areas, in which the unit is acting.

We expect that in primitive knowledge, reality-testing and evaluation are highly fused; in modern knowledge, they are relatively segregated and unrelated; and in active knowledge, they are less segregated and much more related. Post-modern knowledge, from this point of view, falls between the modern and the active; it seems somewhat more synthesized and its contexts are somewhat more related than modern knowledge[28] but much less so than an active society would require.

There is a universal tendency in the production of knowledge to trade empirical validity for coverage and vice versa. Although this choice is not always necessary—some bodies of knowledge may be both more empirically valid and more encompassing than others—there are great difficulties in attempting to increase knowledge simultaneously on any two dimensions. Since different skills are often required for each dimension, the tendency is to specialize in the advancement of one to the neglect of the others. Such specialization may be functional, as in other forms of the division of labor, but only under the same conditions, i.e., so long as one specialization does not undermine the others, *and* the "products" of the various specialized units are related. Except for some attention to inter-unit articulation, entire organizations may specialize in one pursuit with little concern for the others. Societal knowledge needs can still be served, however, as long as there are some units that concern themselves with synthesis. A dysfunctional situation is expected where the ideologies that legitimate the work of the various specialized units undermine the rationale for the work of other specialized units or the synthesizing units. In this sense, the empiricist viewpoint, which stresses "hard" facts and downgrades other intellectual efforts, and the humanistic stance, which associates empirical research with escape from evaluative responsibilities, are both dysfunctional. The consequences of these ideologies are relatively minor when they serve only to boost the efforts of their respective knowledge-processing units. They become serious, however, to the extent that by affecting the allocation of resources, manpower, societal attention, and, above all, the general cultural ethos, public knowledge, and political decision-making. Then they undermine the service of the other knowledge functions and the synthesis of the various specialized efforts.

The need for knowledge to be encompassing is often particularly challenged; in fact, a narrow focus is often considered an essential prerequisite for the effective production of knowledge. While bits may certainly need to be highly specific, knowledge, as we see it, rests in the contexts. And as the contexts and knowledge systems become more encompassing, the more easily will the societal needs for knowledge be fulfilled. Moreover, because it covers more societal needs (which are both determined and expressed by societal values), a more encompassing context or sub-system of knowledge is necessarily more value-relevant. This is not to question the functional need of science for freedom from societal pressures or the normative right of scientists to pursue the values institutionalized in their collectivity which promote the search for empirical validity and cognitive interpretation. It must be noted, however, that the societal values and those of scientific collectivities are only partially compatible. In the scientific collectivity's scale of values, coverage tends to rank low; on the other hand, societal units, while served by the enhanced reality-testing which their scientific sub-units provide, do have a need for coverage. This is evident both in the dialogue between society and the scientific collectivities (which occasionally becomes a conflict) over what is a proper balance and in the society's turning to producers of knowledge other than scientists. This is the societal reason that poets writing about nature, psychoanalysts writing about society, and literary critics writing about international relations have knowledge functions. Their concepts are more encompassing, closer to the world of action, and more evaluative than those of science. The poet who telescopes an earthquake or the bombing of Hiroshima into a few rhymes provides a less analytic and less accurate but a more intimate and expressive view than a researcher approaching the same phenomenon.[29] Because it tends to ignore frequency distributions and comparative dimensions, the psychoanalytic image of society is often low in terms of empirical validity. It does provide, however, a more inclusive and affective communication of, let us say, the feelings of a Negro-American in a Chicago slum or a Jew in a German concentration camp.[30] And these perspectives are a part of societal knowledge just as much as the more empirical components.

The knowledge required by an active societal unit is more encompassing and synthesized than that required by passive participants. The more malleable a societal unit, the greater will be its need for an over-all design to guide its efforts toward its environment and toward itself. So long as the actions of a societal unit are limited, so long as it is more determined than determining, the results of a disproportionate stress on empirical validity are relatively less consequential. The sub-units will still hold together because of ongoing processes or external pressures; the future will not be anticipated in any encompassing way, but even if it were, there would be little the unit could do. Moreover, the danger of generating critical imbalances by utilizing spotty knowledge to guide uneven efforts is relatively small. Of course, a relatively passive unit could realize more of its goals if the elements of its knowledge were more balanced, but when the other components of the active orientation are lacking, unbalanced knowledge is less detrimental than it is to a more active unit. We expect that a systematic comparison of the use of knowledge in traditional (undeveloped) societies with that of transitional (developing) societies would illustrate this point.

Finally, in comparison with modern and post-modern societies, an active society is more concerned with the expressive aspects of societal life and its holistic pattern. These in turn are more effectively expressed by the "telescoping" elements of societal knowledge than they are by the more empirical elements. Consequently, an active society must invest relatively more effort in satisfying the demands of coverage than those of other aspects of knowledge.

The study of macro-action seeks to contribute to the societal knowledge an active society will require, although as a scientific discipline, even when it is more fully developed, it will still be unable to serve as the only tool of such knowledge. Nevertheless, because it is relatively more encompassing (by including macroscopic emergent properties), relatively more interpretative (by including historical perspectives), and more value-relevant than the empiricist approaches to social science, we expect macro-analysis to be an effective tool of the societal knowledge of an active society.

NOTES

1. See Major General John B. Medaris, *Countdown for Decision* (New York: Putnam's Sons, 1960), pp. 256–269.

2. See discussion of symbolic versus mechanic relations in Chapter 2.

3. The relevant reasons for holding a theory in the face of opposing facts are (1) additional data may explain the discrepancy, and (2) it may be more productive to hold a theory and a few "exceptions" than to sacrifice a theory that explains a major body of data. Irrelevant reasons for holding to a theory include status considerations and habits of thought. On this point, see Thomas S. Kuhn, *The Structure of Scientific Revolutions* (Chicago: University of Chicago Press, 1962), pp. 63–65. That the difference between a scientist's knowledge of the world and that of any man is only one of degree and not a dichotomous opposition is pointed out by George A. Kelly, *The Psychology of Personal Construct* (New York: Norton, 1955), Vol. I, pp. 5 ff. See also Howard Baumgartel, "Some Human Problems in Interpersonal Communication," *Journal of Communication*, Vol. 14 (1964), pp. 180–182. For additional discussion, see I. B. Cohen, "Orthodoxy and Scientific Progress," *Proceedings of the American Philosophical Society*, Vol. 96 (1952), pp. 505–512, and Barber, "Resistance by Scientists to Scientific Discoveries," *op. cit.*, pp. 596–602.

4. For an extreme expression see Marshall McLuhan, who summarizes his anticipations in these words: "The computer, in short, promises by technology a Pentecostal condition of universal understanding and unity. The next logical step would seem to be . . . to by-pass languages in favor of a general cosmic consciousness which might be very like the collective unconscious dreamt of by Bergson." Marshall McLuhan, *Understanding Media, op. cit.*, p. 80.

Herbert A. Simon takes a comparatively more moderate stand. In a statement made in 1957, he contended that "there are now in the world machines that think, that learn and that create. Moreover, their ability to do these things is going to increase rapidly until—in a visible future—the range of problems they can handle will be coextensive with the range to which the human mind has been applied." Simon optimistically predicted that within ten years a digital computer would be the world's chess champion, would "discover and prove an important new mathematical theorem," and would "write music that will be accepted by critics as possessing considerable aesthetic value." He also predicted "that within ten years most theories in psychology will take the form of computer programs, or of qualitative statements about the characteristics of computer programs." H. A. Simon and Allan Newell, "Heuristic Problem Solving: The Next Advance in Operations Research," *Operations Research*, Vol. 6 (January–February, 1958), pp. 1–10, quoted from p. 7 and p. 8.

In a later paper, Hubert L. Dreyfus contested Simon's estimation of the future of digital computers. Dreyfus contended that "there does exist a boundary to possible progress in the field of artificial intelligence: given the nature of the information to be processed, the contribution of the uniquely human forms of information processing [fringe consciousness, essence/accident discrimination, and ambiguity tolerance] which we have considered are indispensable, since they alone provide access to information inaccessible to a mechanical system." Hubert L. Dreyfus, "Alchemy and Artificial Intelligence," paper based on an informal talk presented at The RAND Corporation in August, 1964, p. 65, and see p. iii.

5. Richard Rovere, *The Goldwater Caper* (New York: Harcourt, Brace & World, 1965).

6. See Wynona S. Garretson, "The Consensual Definition of Social Objects," *The Sociological Quarterly*, Vol. 3 (1962), pp. 107–113.

7. For a specific case of "blindness" in macro-actors, in Britain's view of Kenya, see Clyde Sanger, "The Transformation of Jomo Kenyatta," *The Reporter*, Vol. 34 (March 10, 1966), pp. 37–39. For a more detailed discussion, see Carl G. Rosberg, Jr. and John Nottingham, *The Myth of "Mau Mau": Nationalism in Kenya* (New York: Praeger, 1966).

8. This proposition is illustrated by the pre-war preparations for both world wars and the realities of those wars. See Cyril Falls, *The First World War* (New York: Longmans, 1960), esp. pp. 13–21 and *passim*; B. H. Liddell Hart, *A History of the World War: 1914–1918* (London: Faber & Faber, 1934), pp. 67–77 and *passim*.

9. A good example are strategies of attrition adopted by all the main belligerents in World War I. See Falls, *The First World War, op. cit.*, esp. pp. 165–178. See also Guy Chapman, *A Passionate Prodigality* (New York: Holt, Rinehart & Winston, 1966). For other studies of crises and the reaction of macro-actors, see Charles A. McClelland, "Action Structures and Communication in Two International Crises: Quemoy and Berlin," *Background*, Vol. 7 (February, 1964), pp. 201–215. See also Edward Weintal and Charles Bartlett, *Facing the Brink, An Intimate Study of Crisis Diplomacy* (New York: Charles Scribner's Sons, 1967).

10. For a detailed discussion, using complex organizations as the unit, see Etzioni, *A Comparative Analysis . . ., op. cit.*, pp. 128 ff.

11. For a theoretical discussion, see Harold D. Lasswell, *Psychopathology and Politics* (Chicago: University of Chicago, 1930), pp. 53–55. See also Herbert McClosky, "Conservatism and Personality," *American Political Science Review*, Vol. 52 (1958), pp. 27–45. On the correlation between personality variables and political conduct, see Alex Inkeles, "National Character and Modern Political Systems," in Francis L. K. Hsu (ed.), *Psychological Anthropology* (Homewood, Ill.: Dorsey, 1961), pp. 172–208.

12. Regarding the attack on Pearl Harbor, one author has suggested that ". . . most people had come to believe that what had happened was that the different items of information that might have revealed the Japanese intention to attack at Pearl Harbor had come across the desks of top officials in disordered fragments, and that these hard-pressed and overworked officials, responsible for so many things besides estimating the intentions of the Japanese, never had time to correlate the odds and ends of information and thus make their meaning apparent." See Roger Hilsman, *Strategic Intelligence and National Decisions* (New York: Free Press, 1956), p. 23.

13. As an example of flooding, competitors bidding for the 900-passenger C-5A transport submitted to Federal Aviation Agency experts proposals that amounted to 240,000 pages, a 480-volume bookshelf that weighed 35 tons. See *Newsweek*, July 18, 1966, p. 13.

14. Lateral and longitudinal are used throughout this volume as in Mark Lefton and William R. Rosengren, "Organizations and Clients: Lateral and Longitudinal Dimensions," *American Sociological Review*, Vol. 31, (1966), pp. 802–810.

15. See Subcommittee on National Security Staffing and Operations, "Administration of National Security: Basic Issues," a study submitted to the Committee on Government Operations, United States Senate (Washington, D.C.: Government Printing Office, 1963), esp. pp. 6–16.

15a. This observation is based on the *Bulletin of the Atomic Scientists*, Vol. 17 (January, 1961) p. 39, and private communication with NASA officials.

16. James Reston, *The New York Times*, July 31, 1966. For this point concerning President Kennedy, see Reston, *The New York Times*, December 29, 1961.

17. For a discussion of the "American idiosyncrasy in favor of the immediately practical and against the general-theoretical," see Fritz Machlup, *The Production and Distribution of Knowledge in the United States* (Princeton, N.J.: Princeton University Press, 1962), p. 202. See also Stanley Hoffmann, "Restraints and Choices in American Foreign Policy," *Daedalus*, Vol. 91 (1962), pp. 668–704.

18. Karl R. Popper, *The Open Society and Its Enemies*, Vol. II (Princeton, N.J.: Princeton University Press, 1963), esp. pp. 259–265.

19. See James L. McCamy, "The Administration of Foreign Affairs in the United States," *World Politics*, Vol. 7 (1955), pp. 315–325. See also John J. McCloy, *The Challenge to American Foreign Policy* (Cambridge, Mass.: Harvard University Press, 1953).

20. For a discussion of the differences between the traditions of Anglo-Saxon "pragmatism" and French "rationalism" as they relate to differences in economic planning, see Andrew Shonfield, *Modern Capitalism: The Changing Balance of Public and Private Power* (New York: Oxford University Press, 1965), pp. 151–175.

21. In fiscal year 1965, the Department of State spent $10.9 million on research and development, while NASA spent $4,555 million for the same purpose. The figures exaggerate the difference because State Department research requires less investment per bit of information than that of NASA where expensive hardware is required. But the difference seems to hold even if one takes this factor into account. For the data, see the National Science Foundation Report, *Federal Funds for Research, Development, and Other Scientific Activities, Fiscal Years 1965, 1966, and 1967*, Vol. 15 (Washington, D.C.: Government Printing Office, 1966), p. 83,

table C-3. See also Roger Hilsman, *To Move a Nation* (Garden City, N.Y.: Doubleday, 1967), p. 26–27, 63–73.

22. The size of the staff of the OST was about 30 men (NASA headquarters has several thousands). See the report prepared by the Science Policy Research Division of the Congressional Library's Legislative Reference Service for the Military Operations Subcommittee of the House Committee on Government Operations, *The Office of Science and Technology* (Washington, D.C.: Government Printing Office 1967), esp. pp. 41–47. See also Philip H. Abelson, "The Office of Science and Technology," *Science*, Vol. 156 (1967), p. 173.

23. A cursory examination of grants awarded by the National Institutes of Health, the National Science Foundation and the Agency for International Development in the period from 1960 to 1964 supports this conclusion, which barely needs documentation.

24. A degree of "over-collection" is unavoidable and even necessary. The reference here is to the neglect of analysis beyond this built-in limitation. Among those who pointed out the tendency to collect data but not to analyze them, see W. C. H. Prentice, "Too Many Surveys," *Science*, Vol. 151 (March 4, 1966), pp. 1034–35; R. C. Amara, "Data Collection and Systems Analysis," *Science*, Vol. 152 (April 22, 1966), p. 450.

25. Edward Jay Epstein, *Inquest: The Warren Commission and the Establishment of Truth* (New York: Viking Press, 1966). *Newsweek*, June 13, 1966, pp. 36–38, reports interviews with members of the staff of the commission which supported some of Epstein's conclusions and questioned others. By and large, however, they did not challenge his characterization of the conditions in which the Commission worked.

26. Daniel Bell, "Government by Commission," *The Public Interest*, No. 3 (Spring, 1966), pp. 3–9.

27. Robert Blauner, "Whitewash Over Watts," *Trans-action*, Vol. 3 (March–April, 1966), pp. 3–9, 54.

28. A comparison of the view of bit learning by children in the work of two influential educationalists, Piaget and Bruner, is instructive. Piaget, of the last generation of the modern era, stressed bit by bit learning, while Bruner emphasized contextuating education. See Jean Piaget, *The Language and Thought of the Child* (New York: Harcourt, Brace & World, 1926) and Jerome S. Bruner, *The Process of Education* (Cambridge, Mass.: Harvard University Press, 1965).

29. For the argument that poetry is capable of knowledge, see Archibald MacLeish, "Why Do We Teach Poetry?," *Atlantic Monthly*, Vol. 197 (March, 1956), pp. 48–53.

30. Numerous volumes have been written on this subject. One that pays much attention to the dimensions here discussed is Jacques Barzun, *Science: The Glorious Entertainment* (New York: Harper & Row, 1964).

CHAPTER 7

Societal Knowledge

and Collective Reality-Testing

T HE KNOWLEDGE societal units command significantly affects their collective action, but societal units are internally differentiated—what one sub-unit may know, another often does not. In particular, the knowledge available to expert and control units is likely not to be available to other members. As the support of the membership affects the societal capacity to act and to guide, the disposal of obsolescent knowledge of the membership (especially of the relatively active members) and the sharing of new knowledge within it significantly affect the activeness of societal units. We now seek to outline the conditions under which societal actors can improve their collective reality-testing and the degree to which they can transform these very conditions. To illustrate this dimension of the societal guidance of knowledge, we focus on one issue: The determinants of the costs of revising societal knowledge.

Symbols and the Outside World: An Example

The Costs Tend to be High

Societal knowledge has economic, psychological, and political costs.* The "transportation" of knowledge inside one person is rarely studied; it is common to assume that it is instantaneous and costless. This is clearly not the case for societal actors. Knowledge gained by one part of the macro-unit is not readily available to other parts without special investments and efforts. Elites, we suggest, often learn more rapidly than non-elites (though there are important differences within both of these categories). They are therefore confronted with the dilemma of either acting without sharing newly acquired knowledge with non-elites (and of accepting the risk of a "backlash" if and when the discrepancy between their modified policy and public knowledge becomes visible), or of educating the non-elites, which requires expenditures, delays in action, and political risks because the non-elites, alerted by the educational campaign, may marshall an effort to block the proposed change in policy.

A theory of the societal guidance of knowledge seeks to combine a study of the costs of "transportation" with a study of the costs of overcoming resistance to change. Many societal images are institutionalized, and, consequently, their modification requires investments similar to those required for other institutional changes. In this context, the power of political elites and the mass media is often greatly overestimated. How much of an investment an elite must make to change a given societal image varies greatly with differences in (a) the substance of the image (e.g., domestic vs. foreign); (b) the societal conditions (e.g., a well-integrated vs. an anarchic system); (c) the size of the active publics; and (d) the degree to which the elite monopolizes the means of communication. In general, however, except for rare and brief charismatic situations, even when other conditions are quite "favorable" to change, significant alterations in the images of non-elites are costly. Nations do not readily "change their minds" nor classes their orientations.

The relative emphasis on "transportation" costs as compared to the costs of change is a good indicator of the meta-theoretical position of a particular work or theory. Voluntaristic theories tend to stress transportation costs, on the rationalistic assumption that once valid information reaches the members of a society, the change will be relatively "automatic." Thus, for instance, it was believed that informing the public of the hazards of smoking would lead to a significant reduction in smoking. On the other hand, most contemporary sociologists tend to assume resistance to change and neglect the costs of "transportation." A contemporary sociologist, unfamilar with the field of birth control, would tend to assume that the main reason for not

---

* All references to costs, unless otherwise specified, are from the viewpoint of the acting societal unit, i.e., resources used and no longer available for its action.

adopting contraceptive devices is motivational or cultural and would pay little attention to the inadequacy of the information.[1]* Our attempt to give similar weights to both kinds of costs is based on our combination of voluntaristic and collectivistic assumptions discussed above.

The Internal Structure of Societal Knowledge

In guiding societal action and in adjusting the related knowledge, elites face costs from two sources. Some of these costs originate in the non-symbolic realm and range from printing books to maintaining microwave relay stations. The nature of these costs is quite evident. This is less true, however, of the costs which are generated by the internal coherence of societal knowledge and its structure as a symbolic system. In exploring these costs, theories which take into account the fact that symbolic systems have a tendency toward internal consistency and thus, a collectivistic aspect, seem more useful than those which treat the symbolic realm as an aggregation of symbolic items.[2] Among those analyses which do take consistency into account are studies which, stressing inter-item relations, examine the effects of change in one item on changes in others but do not apply a supra-unit conception.[3] In contrast, we suggest, it is fruitful to view societal knowledge as having a hierarchical structure which provides a contexuating orientation for bits (or items) of knowledge. The bits are more concrete, specific, and cognitive than the contexts. A fact is a bit; a theory is a context. An attitude is a bit; a world view is a context. This internal composition seems to hold constant for systems of knowledge which vary significantly in their degree of validity. This is not to suggest that all societal knowledge is thus organized; there are unstructured areas and aggregates of bits in-between organized fields. The following discussion deals with organized societal knowledge which, we suggest, is commonly held by members of the relatively active publics[4] and elites of modern and post-modern societies—in their views of themselves and of the other main actors.

Several writers on public opinion have recently emphasized the non-ideological orientation of the public.[5] These views of public opinion do not necessarily conflict with our own, as they differentiate between the active and passive publics and show that the active members of society—even if they include only 7 to 16 per cent of the voters—have a systematic view of both domestic and foreign affairs.† Also these studies, reacting to earlier assumptions about an informed electorate (which includes the passive majority),

---

* Reference notes for this chapter are on page 168.

† We focus in the following discussion on knowledge citizens have with regard to political matters, because this sector of citizens' knowledge has been most systematically studied and is most relevant to societal action. It seems that the same findings would apply to other sectors but this is a largely unexplored area.

may be underestimating the role of public opinion by setting up rather strict criteria for what is "ideological." A person who holds to a vague general position, e.g., a liberal one, which he is unable to articulate with much clarity, may nevertheless be quite "ideological." It might be useful to reserve the term ideological positions for relatively explicit and systematic positions. But we must then recognize that many of those who are not ideological by this definition, the same studies show, do have a cognitive and an evaluative position, e.g., are liberal or conservative on domestic issues, though their position is a vague one. We discuss below the political consequences of these positions, but first a little more should be said about their internal makeup.

We expect that under most circumstances the relationship between the bits of knowledge and the context will be loose; that is, bits can be changed at relatively low cost as long as the new ones fit the existing context. For example, many Americans in the late 1940s and through most of the 1950s believed that the Soviet Union was a militarily aggressive and expansionist force (a contextuating orientation). Several bits of knowledge, such as the subjugation of Czechoslovakia in 1948 and the suppression of the Hungarian rebellion in 1956, were part of the "evidence" on which the overriding idea rested, although, in its rejection of totalitarianism, the context clearly had a normative foundation. Other people held the same contextuating orientation but supported it by other bits, such as Soviet intervention in Poland and East Germany in 1953 and Premier Khrushchev's 1959 "We shall bury you" speech at the United Nations.

Contextuating orientation refers to the supra-unit relations among the bits; we use the active form—"contextuating"—to stress the fact that these relations are, in part, open to guided change.

A typical contextuating orientation does not depend on any specific bit or group of bits. Some bits can be removed with little effect on the orientation, while others may be added but have only a declining marginal effect on an established orientation. If all bits are removed—let us say, because they are shown to be invalid—and no new ones are supplied, the orientation may still be maintained on normative grounds alone. But, we expect, this would strain the contextuating orientation and leave it potentially open to rapid and low-cost transformation.[6] (The relationships between facts and theories have a similar pattern, except that here the procedures for relating bits to the context, for introducing new bits, and for removing old bits are more formal, explicit, and public.)

Once again, a thermodynamic analogy seems appropriate. We expect the transformation of a contextuating orientation to resemble the transformation of solid matter into a liquid. First, investment of energy yields manifest results—the temperature of the body which is being heated rises; but, after a while, a point is reached at which an additional investment of energy yields no increase in temperature, and the body seems to "resist" the transformation. Much continued "heating" (or activation) is necessary before a threshold of transformation is reached, after which the body becomes a liquid and the temperature again rises relatively rapidly.

This analogy is used to suggest that societal knowledge will tend to change not atomistically but under the impact of contextuating orientations. The following propositions, if verified, would support our view of the contextual organization of knowledge: (a) It is more costly to change a contextuating orientation than to replace a bit that fits an orientation with another that does not, and the latter, in turn, is more costly than replacing a bit that fits with another which also fits.[7] (b) Bits can be removed at relatively low cost as long as the context is not challenged, but such removal has few action consequences because support for a course of action tends to be based on the context and not on the bits. (c) When the contextuating orientation is strained by the *continual* removal of bits, the cost of removing additional bits is expected to rise. If efforts to change are still continued, the cost will continue to rise sharply until a tipping point is reached beyond which the old contextuating orientation will collapse. And it will then be relatively inexpensive to reorganize the particular field.*

It is relatively inexpensive for an elite to introduce a new contextuating orientation in areas in which none has been established. Up to the mid-1950s, outer space was such an unimprinted field. When it first received wide public attention with the orbiting of a Soviet satellite in October, 1957, most Americans had few established notions about space.[8] Thus, it was comparatively easy for Presidents Eisenhower and Kennedy to establish a context for it into which later bits could be fit.[9]

What holds for providing a contextuating orientation for a previously unstructured field is true as well for additional specification of a previously vague field, though we suggest it is somewhat more costly to provide an orientation here because even the vague context means that there are some limitations, some resistances, and therefore, some costs. Since the advent of the post-modern age, various federal and private welfare agencies in the United States have quite deliberately structured an image of the aged as "senior citizens." At the beginning of that period, only a vague image of "old people" existed. Social scientists and welfare agencies argued that aging people, whose number had grown because of improved health services, had a poorly structured role. When the aged retired, many became alienated and engaged in deviant personal and political behavior.[10] Some even died younger, on the average, than the aged who were employed. Through processes which need not be discussed here, American welfare

---

* In one *gestalt* experiment, a subject wears "goggles fitted with inverted lenses and initially sees the entire world upside down. At the start his perceptual apparatus functions as it had been trained to function in the absence of goggles, and the result is extreme disorientation, an acute personal crisis. But after the subject has begun to learn to deal with his new world, *his entire visual field flips over*, usually after an intervening period in which vision is simply confused." Kuhn, *The Structure of Scientific Revolutions, op. cit.*, p. 111.

agencies, in conjunction with commercial interests and social scientists, set out to create a more articulate image of old age as another stage in the process of "growth." It became viewed as a time for leisure and a socially active life.[11] The relatively low cost of this venture is apparent if we compare it, for instance, to efforts to change the societal image of the Jew.[12] It is much less costly to construct a new context or to "specify" one than to transform an institutionalized context.

The Kennedy Experiment: An Illustration

The costs of altering an institutionalized context are illustrated by the introduction of a foreign policy of *détente* in 1963–1964. We have chosen this particular example because there are few studies of changes of societal contexts[13] and because we are familiar with this case from our own work.[14] On June 10, 1963, President Kennedy announced the initiation of a major change in the foreign policy of the United States; he called it "a strategy for peace." Whether he was trying to exacerbate already tense relations between China and Russia, was interested simply in solidifying the policy of peaceful coexistence, or was spurred by various combinations of these and other motives, is open to question. Nonetheless, Kennedy, it seems to us, was aiming at a extensive *détente*. This entailed a considerable change in the "Cold War" context to which much of the nation had been committed since the late 1940s.

The President pointed out in his speech initiating the new policy that "constructive changes" had taken place in the Soviet Union, which "might bring within reach solutions which now seem beyond us." Stressing that the Cold War should not be viewed as immutable, he added that "our problems are man-made . . . and can be solved by man." United States policies, Kennedy declared, must be constructed so "that it becomes in the Communists' interests to agree to a genuine peace," a statement which implied that American policies were not yet so designed, and, more importantly, that the Western nations could live in peace with the Communist countries. He also asked the American people to "re-examine" their attitudes toward the USSR and the Cold War—that is, to be willing to alter their images of others and of themselves. In short, he was questioning the core of the Cold War context.

In the three months following this speech, Kennedy suggested that the United States and Russia explore the stars together. Moreover, the United States sold $65 million worth of wheat to the USSR, the two nations initiated a partial nuclear test ban treaty, and several other "coexistence" measures were agreed upon or discussed. Whatever the international significance of these measures, they created a new mood in the United States as expressed in the newspapers and public opinion polls. The change was achieved, in part, through a great public debate on the basic assumptions of a *détente* policy, a debate that centered around two issues: ratification of the test ban treaty and initiation of the wheat agreement. For more than two months, these issues occupied much of the time and space devoted to foreign policy in the mass media and in Congress.

By late October, 1963, President Kennedy retarded his attempt to change the image of the USSR and of American–Soviet relations. Fewer *détente* measures were initiated; Soviet initiatives were turned down; and negotiations over measures already under consideration (especially an air travel and a consular treaty) were drawn out. Reasons for the slowdown are open to conflicting interpretations. Kennedy seems to have realized, to put it in our terminology, how strongly the old context was institutionalized and how costly it would be to change. At first, he tried to retain the support of the old context as he began to institute the new one, but when such straddling became difficult, he withdrew, at least temporarily.

Kennedy began to recognize the cost of change before October, 1963. The test ban treaty had to be ratified by the Senate, and various pressure groups actively agitated against it. Kennedy seemed increasingly concerned with the political cost of his *détente* policy. His re-election might have depended lárgely upon his ability to appeal to voters who were conservative in matters of foreign policy; liberals were already on his side or were at least likely to prefer him over prospective Republican candidates. Well aware of President Wilson's blunder, Kennedy did not wish to sign a treaty which the Senate might not ratify.

Before he would sign it and until it was ratified, Kennedy had to invest much time and effort if the necessary support for the test ban treaty were to be obtained. His efforts included sending numerous experts to testify before Congress and an appeal for support from prominent citizens' committees and clergymen. He personally coordinated the testimonies of administration representatives before Congress. But Kennedy seemed to sense that presenting the treaty as an item in a new context, as part of the "strategy for peace," entailed considerable political risk. He therefore related the test ban to the old context as well, arguing that the treaty, in effect, was a bit that fitted into the Cold War context.* Similarly, the American–Soviet wheat agreement was first introduced as a tension-reducing step but was thereafter increasingly presented as a Cold War measure which would point out Russian agricultural deficiencies.

If approval for the test ban treaty and wheat agreement were to be gained, this mixture of contexts was probably the most expedient way to proceed.

---

* His experts pointed out that the United States had tested twice as many weapons as the Russians, and hence, a "freeze" was to America's advantage. Moreover, the United States was interested mainly in the miniaturization of warheads, a process which could be undertaken through the underground testing not forbidden by the treaty. Altogether, it was argued, the treaty would give the United States a unilateral military advantage.

In terms of changing the earlier context, however, this straddling of old and new was ineffectual. In retrospect, it seems that Kennedy initially under-estimated both the costs of changing the public's image and the political risks involved. Another major cost involved a strain on the relationships between the Unites States and some of its allies.

The Kennedy experiment illustrates our conception of the costs of chang-ing societal knowledge and the factors anchoring institutionalized contexts. These include: (a) psychological forces (i.e., challenging a context generates strains in those who believe in it because of the insecurity caused by the transition); (b) economic vested interests (some industries, unions, and armed services that objected actively to the *détente* stood to lose because of it); and (c) political forces—attempting to shift to a new context in a pluralistic society allows the opposition to identify itself with the old context and to charge the supporter of the new context with inconsistent and unjustifiable if not treasonable tendencies. This is not to suggest that a contextual transforma-tion was not possible, in this situation; our purpose is rather to highlight what its costs would have been and to illustrate a fallacy of the voluntaristic approach to societal knowledge.

Toward a Societal Guidance Perspective of Knowledge

The State of the Field

Additional research is needed about societal contexts and the conditions under which they may be transformed. At the present time, there is a large body of literature on public opinion and attitude change, but it offers little systematic analysis of the costs of the adjustment of societal knowledge. How does most of this literature differ from the research required by the theory presented here? First, most of the data deal with individual attitudes, accounting for their changes in terms of intra-personality or micro-unit processes.* This may be viewed as the atomistic approach to the study of societal knowledge. A second approach, more often pursued by historians,

---

* The large and rapidly growing literature on attitudes and inter-attitude relations, tensions, and changes deals almost exclusively with psychological mechanisms. The strains inherent in holding a bit that does not suit a context have been explored but are viewed as internal to their personalities or to small groups. Few studies examine situations in which some sub-units of a collectivity hold bits which do not fit, while other sub-units reinforce the context. Cases in which the leadership holds one and the members the other, are simi-larly rarely analyzed. For a review of the relevant psychological literature, see Roger Brown, *Social Psychology* (New York: Free Press, 1965), esp. pp. 549–609; Herbert I. Abelson, *Persuasion: How Opinions and Attitudes Are Changed* (New York: Springer Publishing Co., 1959); Theodore M. Newcomb, *Social Psychology* (New York: Dryden Press, 1950). See also works cited below Chapter 7, footnote. 5. See esp. Campbell. et al., *The American Voter, op. cit.*, p. 521.

is a collectivist–holistic study of the "mood" or "mind" of a period, in which changes are explained chiefly in terms of ongoing processes.[15] Finally, voluntaristic studies have focused on the role of mass persuasion or propaganda in changing individual attitudes (toward such things as buying an investment bond or surrendering during a war)[16] but rarely on their role in changing entire contexts.

Elites, Publics, and Knowledge-Adjustment

Societal guidance studies of revisions of contextuating orientations may be analytically divided into (a) studies which deal primarily with downward adjustments, such as the Kennedy experiment, and (b) studies which focus on upward adjustment, in which a change in the direction of the societal action follows rather than precedes changes in the relevant publics or collectivities.[17] Upward changes (explored below when we deal with the processes of consensus-formation),[18] allow the controlling mechanisms to alter the societal course with little cost to the guiding elites. On the other hand, such upward flows may encourage or even force changes which the elites do not prefer, thus imposing some costs of their own.

A question often raised substantively finds an analytic base here: To what degree do elites and to what degree do "the people" set the societal images which affect the ways in which societal actors view others and themselves? At one time, a relatively naïve democratic theory was held in which political elites were seen as representatives of public views. The reaction against this theory emphasized that (a) the elites affect the perspectives of the publics and therefore the "instructions" the publics give the elites, or (b) that most of the public has only vague knowledge of what elites do and make their political choices on other bases. This may be an over-reaction, however, and a third, synthesizing view is needed, one which recognizes a more active role for the elites than the first approach and a more active role for the publics than the second. The third approach, to which we adhere, does not mechanically combine the populist and elitist views but suggests, in essence, that *the elites are relatively free to set the societal course so long as such changes either entail only bit changes in the societal knowledge of the publics (especially the relatively active ones) or relate to areas in which public knowledge was previously unorganized. When, however, elites initiate changes that fall outside the boundaries of institutionalized contexts* (especially in democratic pluralistic societies), *the "backlash" is likely to be powerful, and consequently, elites, if they wish to remain in control, must either change the contexts or avoid contextual—i.e., fundamental—changes.*[19] Many of the same respondents, who—survey studies show—do not know much about their Congressman, his position or voting record, will both know and react when he "steps out of line" to a degree as voting against the defense budget, for the 1964 civil rights bill (if he is a Southerner), and so on. If he does stay within—admittedly vague—limits, most voters seem to care little what specific positions he takes.

Here, the problem of democracy in the post-modern age of mass information about a large variety of societal actions finds a pragmatic solution: The citizen, even the active one, cannot hope to command all the relevant information. He, in effect, grants the elites a considerable measure of freedom to act (in most areas), and becomes relatively more active only when these acts fall outside his contextual limits. The implied imperative—that an elite is not to change *fundamentally* a line of societal action without first informing and winning the consent of the publics—is a realistic prerequisite because it correctly recognizes the political importance of the publics, as well as their limitations. The imperative is also realistic in that although it is impossible to inform even the active publics about all changes, it seems feasible to inform them about contextual ones.

By allowing the experts and the elites the freedom of specification within the contexts set by means of consensus-building processes, such a combination of monopolization of bit-knowledge with a broad sharing of contextuating knowledge provides a pragmatic base for a democratic process. On the other hand, this very arrangement turns into a political block to transformation when the elites approach with a paralyzing fear any change of direction which requires a change of context and consequently, public education. If, in addition, the intellectuals' capacity to initiate contextual transformation is seriously inhibited, the polity is likely to be democratic only in the sense of representing obsolescent *status quos*. The notion that contexts are changed only with difficulty does suggest that they cannot be readily manipulated, but it does not imply that they need not—at turning points—be confronted.

To return to our basic concern, it may be argued that a public's orientations have been largely determined by the earlier actions of one or more elites, and as a result, that the limitations encountered by elites are largely of their own making. First, however, such ongoing societal processes as education and informal communication also contribute to these limitations. Second, although the previous actions of elites have an effect on the publics, so also do the previous upward efforts of the publics have an effect on elites. The genetic and the functional perspectives should not be confused: The fact that an elite helped to shape an orientation historically does not mean that it is free to remold it at a later point. Third, *fundamental* changes in lines of action —which, we suggested, entail at least some mobilization of the support of the active publics—require greater efforts in pluralistic societies than in more monolithic ones, but they are needed in both kinds of societies. (The basic reasons for the higher costs of mobilization in democratic societies are that (1) the level of communication "noise" is louder and so a campaign must be "pitched higher" to be noticed at all, and (2) attempted changes of context tend to mobilize counter elites to champion and thus reinforce the old context. The reasons that more monolithic regimes still require the mobilization of consensus are explored below.)

The distinction between active and passive publics seems particularly useful here, in that changing the contextuating orientations held by the more active publics is likely to impose significantly higher costs on the elites than changing those of the more passive publics. While an elite does incur costs when its comes into conflict with the orientations of passive publics, these costs are likely to be lower, less visible, and less immediate than the costs imposed by a conflict with the active publics. If a policy violates the context of an active public, the latter is likely to protest, shift its votes, reduce its campaign contributions, and otherwise exert *political* counter-pressures. While these pressures will be most immediately experienced by the relevant elite, mechanisms (embedded in the political institutions) for dealing with such pressure are available. The "protest" of passive publics—which arises when their less well-bounded and less well-organized but nevertheless effective contexts are violated—takes the form of reduced productivity, less conscientious tax-paying, immigration, or other similar societal costs. These affect the elites less directly than a loss of political support but are also more difficult to handle, for they are less visible and not channeled into political institutions.

Finally, much has been made out of the fact that most voters' decisions are more affected by party loyalties and candidate personalities than by the issues at hand or the candidates' record. But it should be noted that the parties, even American ones, do provide a cognitive and normative context.* When a party violates the voters' contexts, many do shift and vote for the other's party candidate, as the 1964 elections showed, when many Republicans voted for Johnson against Goldwater. More importantly, while the passive publics have little direct knowledge of issues and candidates' record, we suggest that they do rely on members of the active publics for leadership, who are in turn better informed and more ideological.

Future studies are needed to explore systematically the following factors which affect the costs of changing an institutionalized context: (a) the amount of effort invested in the context's initial introduction; (b) the latent

---

* The following is a conclusion of a study of party leaders and followers: "Although it has received wide currency, especially among Europeans, the belief that the two American parties are identical in principle and doctrine has little foundation in fact. Examination of the opinions of Democratic and Republican leaders shows them to be distinct communities of co-believers who diverge sharply on many important issues. . . . Republican and Democratic leaders stand furthest apart on the issues that grow out of their group identification and support—out of the managerial, proprietary, and high-status connection of the one, and the labor, minority, low-status, and intellectual connections of the other." Herbert McClosky, Paul J. Hoffmann, and Rosemary O'Hara, "Issue Conflict and Consensus Among Party Leaders and Followers," *American Political Science Review*, Vol. 54 (1960), pp. 406–427, quoted from pp. 425–426.

interests it serves; (c) the degree to which it has become "unrealistic"; (d) the kinds of reinforcing mechanisms that have been built around it (e.g., mass media support); and (e) the length of time it has been reinforced. The Cold War orientation, for instance, was initially established with considerable effort to replace the earlier 1945 conception of collective security under the United Nations, rapid American disarmament, and a partial return to isolationism. It took much more than an article by George Kennan on containment and a major speech to Congress by President Truman for the Cold War orientation to provide the context of the new American world view.[20] In addition to such international events as the establishment of Communist governments in Eastern Europe and Soviet intervention in Turkey, Iran, Greece, and especially in Prague, a considerable American governmental effort was required to "sell" the containment policy to the American people in 1946–1947.[21] Since that time, it has not only been reinforced but has become a *cliché* on the basis of which newspaper editorials, news stories, and radio and television programs are written and interpreted. Many politicians build their campaigns around it, and it is ritually evoked in July 4th speeches, commencement exercises, and so on. For a decade and a half, only a very small and ineffectual minority rejected this context; politicians who challenged it were usually voted out of office or not elected, and intellectuals who questioned it were often considered disloyal or misguided. Thus, it is not surprising that President Kennedy could not change this context in three months.[22]

Changing a Contextuating Orientation

The conditions under which a context is or is not amenable to change include factors beyond the control of any and all elites. It has been suggested, for instance, that the typical personalities of the members of a collectivity affect the degree of ridigity with which it adheres to contextuating orientations. Rigid adherence may affect costly change and sudden "tipping," whereas more flexible adherence may encourage a less costly and more gradual transformation.[23]

While the personalities of the members of the various collectivities are largely "given" from a societal guidance viewpoint, there is an element of choice in the strategy adopted by the elite. The choice appears in the following development: An elite introduces a new policy; in an effort to legitimate it, the elite shares with the public a number of new bits of information (e.g., data illustrating the plight of the poor in the United States). Since the costs and risks of an outright confrontation with the old context (e.g., anti-welfare state) are high, the new bits are introduced as fitting the old context (in this case, as minor corrections to a free enterprise economy) in the hope that they will accumulate and win acceptance before they are "roofed" with a new context. Many members of the non-elite accept the new bits as consonant with the old context and are not aware of their new generalized meaning; they receive a sudden jolt, however, when either the leading elite or an opposing elite calls attention to the new contextuating meaning of the recently-introduced bits. At this point, public resentment of the concealment often appears,[24] and, thus, when it is felt that the old context has been challenged, the strategy of the bit-by-bit introduction of a change is unsuccessful.

The alternative strategy is to confront the contextuating orientation directly before many new bits are introduced. This strategy requires considerable investment and is especially likely to backfire if the elites underestimate the costs and/or stop midway in their campaign, because the stereotypes are then challenged but not destroyed. On the other hand, if the stereotypes are overcome, the need to move step-by-step, bit-by-bit is also overcome, and the introduction of a new orientation and related policy changes can be rapid and fundamental.

Affecting these dynamics is the fact that the contextuating orientation often focuses around a contextuating key symbol. While this holds for many individual orientations, especially among less-educated individuals or groups, it seems to be even more characteristic of societal knowledge, for here consensus is of the essence, and consensus on many items and assumptions is difficult to obtain. Contexts are thus built around a few highly abstract notions and a symbol, such as Pearl Harbor (sneak attack), Munich (appeasement), or Little Rock (the domestic use of federal force). New bits are readily absorbed if they can be tied to one of these contextuating symbols. For example, it was argued that the test ban treaty would be another Munich which exposed the country to a new Pearl Harbor, and that new civil rights legislation would bring about another Little Rock.

These contextuating symbols have special potency because they arise from shared collective experiences which intensely influence the societal unit's members and which are reinforced by the mass media, commemorations, political speeches, and repeated allusions. Contextuating symbols, once institutionalized, are a powerful force for supporting the knowledge *status quo*, for there are usually few experiences of similar potency on the side of societal change. (On the other hand, when a new experience does support change, as Pearl Harbor supported Roosevelt in his efforts to gain American support for the United States' entry into World War II, deep-seated contexts, such as isolationism, give way more readily.)[25]

When no experience on the order of a Pearl Harbor or a Little Rock exists, the struggle to alter a contextuating orientation occasionally brings about efforts to create events which will achieve the same effect; these have been referred to as "pseudo-events."[26] The civil rights movement in 1963 and 1964, for instance, effectively used such pseudo-events as sit-ins and pray-ins to make the Negro plight more visible. Although this has yet to be explored, it seems to be true that symbols which telescope collective experiences are more commonly negative than positive, perhaps because they develop from crises. Another hypothesis in need of exploration is that it seems less difficult to alter collective images in favor of greater inter-group hostility (war, racial conflict) than to induce inter-group cooperation (e.g., the Atlantic Alliance, racial reconciliation).

In short, societal knowledge is much more than a set of images in people's minds.[27] It has social, economic, and political foundations, and both societal learning and unlearning involve a process of institutional change which—like other societal processes—is in part ongoing and in part guided.

Much has been written about the relationships between the policies which elites introduce, their contextuating orientations, and the orientations of various publics. Our purpose here was not to review the existing literature or to outline future research. We sought rather to illustrate a formal dimension and a substantive–theoretical issue. The formal dimension is the conditions under which the revision of societal knowledge is possible; the substantive issue is the costs of changing the level of collective reality-testing, e.g., in the development of United States foreign policy. Since a societal unit is not a monolith, the internal distribution of knowledge within it—in particular, among the elites and the various publics—is expected to have significant consequences for the quality and changeability of societal knowledge. On the one hand, the elites are like drivers who keep their eyes on the road and change their direction as they see its turns; on the other hand, the passengers have their own views of the road and of the driving. While their influence on any one turn is often minimal, they may replace the drivers when the driving falls out of the context of their expectations. The drivers, in anticipation of such a possibility, do alter their driving *and* work to change the contexts which govern the passengers' perspectives. This is achieved in part by altering the preferences of the passengers and in part by altering the information they gain and their evaluation of that information. We, therefore, sought to explore some of the effects of the elites' actions on the societal knowledge of the members, the ramifications of changes in the members' knowledge on the elites' capacity to guide, and the costs incurred by a "change of course."

NOTES

1. On the importance of information, see Bernard Berelson et al., *Family Planning and Population Programs* (Chicago: University of Chicago Press, 1966), pp. 292–293 and *passim*. A qualitative report suggests that mothers did not go to a clinic because they did not have anything "decent" to wear; i.e., the information that this was not necessary had not reached them. See Hannah Lees, "The Negro Response to Birth Control," *The Reporter*, May 19, 1966, p. 47.

2. Robert P. Abelson, "Modes of Resolution of Belief Dilemmas," *Journal of Conflict Resolution*, Vol. 3 (1959), pp. 343–352; Robert P. Abelson and Milton J.

Rosenberg, "Symbolic Psychologic; A Model of Attitudinal Cognition," *Behavioral Science*, Vol. 3 (1958), pp. 1–13; Leon Festinger, *A Theory of Cognitive Dissonance* (New York: Harper & Row, 1957); Milton J. Rosenberg, Carl I. Hovland, William J. McGuire, Robert P. Abelson and Jack W. Brehm, *Attitude Organization and Change* (New Haven: Yale University Press, 1960); Milton J. Rosenberg, "A Structural Theory of Attitude Dynamics," *Public Opinion Quarterly*, Vol. 24 (1960), pp. 319–340.

3. See, for example, Charles E. Osgood and Percy H. Tannenbaum, "The Principle of Congruity in the Prediction of Attitude Change," *Psychological Review*, Vol. 62 (1955), pp. 42–55. For discussion and references to other works, see Roger Brown, *Social Psychology* (New York: Free Press, 1965), esp. pp. 558–573.

4. We prefer the term active public as distinct from attentive public because we are referring to those citizens who are not only politically informed and aware but also act politically (e.g., vote, make campaign contributions, protest). The basic distinction is made in Almond, *The American People and Foreign Policy, op. cit.*, pp. 138–139. See also Floyd H. Allport, "Toward a Science of Public Opinion," *Public Opinion Quarterly*, Vol. 1 (1937), pp. 7–23.

5. Evidence on the infrequency of "ideological" thinking among the voters is presented in Campbell, et al, By the criteria used, the authors were able to classify only 3.5 per cent of the voters as "ideological" and 12 per cent as "near-ideological." Angus Campbell, Philip E. Converse, Warren E. Miller, and Donald E. Stokes, *The American Voter* (New York: Wiley & Sons, 1960), p. 249. Warren E. Miller and Donald E. Stokes, "Constituency Influence in Congress," *American Political Science Review*, Vol. 57 (1963), pp. 45–56. Philip E. Converse, "The Nature of Belief Systems in Mass Publics," in David E. Apter (ed.), *Ideology and Discontent* (New York: Free Press, 1964), pp. 206–261; Angus Campbell, Philip E. Converse, Warren E. Miller, Donald E. Stokes, *Elections and the Political Order* (New York: Wiley & Sons, 1966); William N. McPhee and William A. Glaser (eds.), *Public Opinion and Congressional Elections* (New York: Free Press, 1962). Additional materials were published in William N. McPhee, *Formal Theories of Mass Behavior* (New York: Free Press, 1963), Chapters 2 and 4.

According to one study, the overwhelming majority of American youth (all but 5 per cent) manifested "a coherent political orientation." See Richard Centers, "Children of the New Deal: Social Stratification and Adolescent Attitudes," *International Journal of Opinion and Attitude Research*, Vol. 4 (1950), p. 331, quoted in Herbert H. Hyman, *Political Socialization; A Study in the Psychology of Political Behavior* (New York: Free Press, 1959), pp. 62–63.

6. Our discussion here draws on Ernest R. Hilgard, *Theories of Learning* (New York: Appleton-Century-Crofts, 2nd ed., 1956), pp. 222–257; David Katz, *Gestalt Psychology: Its Nature and Significance* (Baltimore: Ronald Press, 1950); and Wolfgang Kohler, *Gestalt Psychology* (New York: Liveright, 1929). See also Brown, *Social Psychology, op. cit.*, pp. 547–609; Theodore M. Newcomb, *Social Psychology* (New York: Dryden Press, 1950), pp. 118, 126–132, 194–262; and W. J. H. Sprott, *Social Psychology* (London: Methuen & Co., 1952), pp. 20–30, 70–86.

7. On the instability of bits which do not fit, see Jeanne Watson, "Some Social and Psychological Situations Related to Change in Attitude," *Human Relations*, Vol. 3 (1950), pp. 15–56. Cf. George H. Smith and Joel Dobin, "Information and Politico-Economic Opinions," *Public Opinion Quarterly*, Vol. 12 (1948), pp. 731–

733. See also Robert E. Lane and David O. Sears, *Public Opinion* (Englewood Cliffs, N.J.: Prentice-Hall, 1964), p. 12.

8. Donald N. Michael, "The Beginning of the Space Age and American Public Opinion," *Public Opinion Quarterly*, Vol. 24 (1960), p. 574.

9. Samuel Lubell, "Sputnik and American Public Opinion," *Columbia University Forum*, Vol. 1 (Winter, 1957), pp. 15–21.

10. On political deviant behavior of senior citizens, see Sheldon L. Messinger, "Organizational Transformation: A Case Study of a Declining Social Movement," *American Sociological Review*, Vol. 20 (1955), pp. 3–10, and Frank A. Pinner, Paul Jacobs, Philip Selznick, *Old Age and Political Behavior* (Berkeley: University of California Press, 1959).

11. See Wilbert E. Moore, "Aging and the Social System," in his *Order and Change: Essays in Comparative Sociology* (New York: Wiley & Sons, 1967), pp. 234–250, and Edna Wasser, *Creative Approaches in Casework with the Aging* (New York: Family Service Association of America, 1966). See also Margaret Blenkner, *Serving the Aging*, (New York: Community Service Society of New York, 1964) and Jerome Kaplan (ed.), *Social Welfare of the Aging* (New York: Columbia University Press, 1962).

12. See Charles Herbert Stember, "The Recent History of Public Attitudes," and John Higham, "American Anti-Semitism Historically Reconsidered," in Charles Herbert Stember and others, *Jews in the Mind of America* (New York: Basic Books, 1966), pp. 29–234, 237–258. On the Negro, see Harold Isaacs, *The New World of Negro Americans* (New York: Viking Press, 1964).

13. We elaborate this point below, Chapter 7.

14. For much additional discussion and documentation for the statements made here, see Amitai Etzioni, "A Psychological Approach to Change," in *Studies in Social Change* (New York: Holt, Rinehart & Winston, 1966), pp. 79–109. For background see Theodore C. Sorensen, *Kennedy* (New York: Harper & Row, 1965), esp. Ch. 25. Arthur M. Schlesinger, Jr., *A Thousand Days* (Boston: Houghton Mifflin, 1965), esp. pp. 888–923.

15. Wilbur J. Cash, *The Mind of the South* (New York: Doubleday, 1954), Henry Steele Commager, *The American Mind* (New Haven: Yale University Press, 1952). Such studies are more common among historians than survey analysts, but the former tend to omit the quantitative aspects. Hopefully, a combination of perspectives, essential for the macro-analysis of knowledge, will gradually become more common. Among studies that approximate such a combination from a survey viewpoint, see Lee Benson, "Research Problems in American Political Historiography," in Mirra Komarovsky (ed.), *Common Frontiers of the Social Sciences* (New York: Free Press, 1957), pp. 113–183. For a structural viewpoint, see Daniel Lerner, *The Passing of Traditional Society* (New York: Free Press, 1958).

16. Edward A. Shils and Morris Janowitz, "Cohesion and Disintegration in the Wehrmacht in World War II," *Public Opinion Quarterly*, Vol. 12 (1948), pp. 281–315. Dorwin Cartwright, "Some Principles of Mass Persuasion: Selected Findings of Research on the Sale of United States War Bonds," *Human Relations*, Vol. 2 (1949), pp. 253–267.

17. Case studies of both are included in Elmer E. Cornwell, Jr., *Presidential Leadership of Public Opinion* (Bloomington, Ind.: Indiana University Press, 1965).

18. See Chs. 17 and 18.

19. Sayre and Polsby state, ". . . in a wide range of community situations, participation in decision-making is limited to a relatively few members of the community, but only within the constraints of a bargaining process among competing elites and of an underlying consensus supplied by a much larger percentage of the local population, whose approval is often costly to secure." Wallace S. Sayre and Nelson W. Polsby, "American Political Science and the Study of Urbanization," in Philip M. Hauser and Leo F. Schnore (eds.), *The Study of Urbanization* (New York: Wiley & Sons, 1965), p. 132.

20. George F. Kennan, "The Sources of Soviet Conduct," *Foreign Affairs*, Vol. 25 (1947), pp. 566–582. "Recommendations on Greece and Turkey, Message of the President to the Congress," *Department of State Bulletin*, Vol. 16 (1947), pp. 534–537.

21. President Truman requested $400 million in military and economic aid for Greece and Turkey. "But to get the aid request approved by Congress, it would be necessary to 'scare hell out of the country to get the measure through' was the advice of Senator Arthur H. Vandenberg at the time—the President framed his doctrine in rousing ideological terms that seemed to commit American power against all forms of Communist 'coercion.' " See John W. Finney "Truman Doctrine, 20 Years Old, Faces Reappraisal," *The New York Times*, March 12, 1967, p. 18.

22. For additional details, see Etzioni, "A Psychological Approach to Change," *op. cit.*

23. See, for instance, Milton Rokeach, *The Open and Closed Mind* (New York: Basic Books, 1960), esp. pp. 138 ff. See also O. J. Harvey (ed.), *Experience, Structure, and Adaptability* (New York: Springer Publishing Co., 1966).

24. See William Kornhauser, *The Politics of Mass Society* (New York: Free Press, 1959), p. 61.

25. See also the role of the note sent in 1917 by the German Foreign Minister Zimmermann, proposing an alliance with Mexico and Japan in the event the United States entered the war, on mobilizing American public support for precisely such an act. Arthur S. Link, *Wilson: Campaigns for Progressivism and Peace* (Princeton: Princeton University Press, 1965). pp. 342–346. See also R. Ernest Dupuy: *5 Days to War, April 2–6, 1917* (Stackpole Books, 1967).

Soviet advances in Eastern Europe spurred a change in the thinking of many Americans. Indicating bipartisan support for the new policy, in June, 1948, the Senate passed the well-known Vandenberg resolution which laid a foundation for the post-war American involvement in Western Europe. See John W. Spanier, *American Foreign Policy Since World War II* (New York: Praeger, 1960), pp. 45–46.

26. Daniel J. Boorstin, *The Image* (New York: Atheneum, 1962), pp. 9–12.

27. Cf. Frederick S. Dunn, *War and the Minds of Men* (New York: Harper & Row, 1950), *passim*.

CHAPTER 8

Knowledge and Power

As IS WELL KNOWN, kings do not make philosophers and philosophers do not make kings. Or, as a modern-day sociologist would put it, the functional prerequisites of power and of knowledge are incompatible. Beginning with the structural differentiation of the two, we ask—how does the relationship between the centers of societal control and the societal units which specialize in the production of knowledge affect societal activeness? The answer, we shall see, is affected by the organization of the production of knowledge itself, by the structure of access to power, and by the provision for fundamental overview. The main actors involved seem to be political elites, intellectuals, experts, and the various publics. Their mutual relations must be taken into account in any study of knowledge and power.

The Interaction Between Knowledge and Control

An·analysis of the relationships between units that specialize in the production and processing of knowledge and units that head the controlling overlayers of societies may benefit from the combination of cybernetic analysis with the study of power hierarchies which has been developed in the analysis of complex organizations.[1]* It has been suggested that (a) the authority of knowledge and the authority of control are best kept structurally segregated and (b) the specific nature of the relations between the two kinds of authority significantly affects the efficacy of complex organizations.[2] Here we explore the relations between knowledge and control on the societal level. While these are examined in structural–organizational terms, the normative implications of varying arrangements are evident.

Segregation of the Two Knowledge Functions

According to a widely held organizational viewpoint, the quality of societal knowledge is considerably affected by the degree to which the societal services devoted to reality-testing and evaluative-interpretation are segregated, and by the ways in which the units that specialize in serving these functions are linked.[3] Primitive actors—including not only preliterate tribes, but also collectivities in post-modern societies which have poor knowledge-facilities—are said to keep the services of the two functions meshed. The elders, be they tribal chiefs or leaders of old-fashioned labor unions,[4] are the source of collective information about what the world is like, how it functions, *and* how it should be collectively interpreted.

A high degree of segregation, it is suggested, makes for greater division of labor, thus allowing for greater specialization. The segregation of staff from line and of collectors and assessors of intelligence from policy makers has been advocated for complex organizations.[5] On the societal level, modernization has been said to require the segregation of academic and professional ("expert") elites from their political counterparts.[6]

In this structural segregation—along functional rather than collectivity lines—the knowledge elites, as the centers of societal reality-testing, are viewed as dealing primarily with information, while political decision-makers (with the help of ideological elites) are more concerned with societal interpretations. It is often suggested in this context that the immunity of professionals and the academic community from political and economic sanctions is a prerequisite for their unconstrained testing of reality; this defers the responsibility for dealing with societal needs, values, and power to the political elites.[7] Finally, it is proposed that societal units are more effective if, as autonomous as the knowledge elites may be, the political elites have a clearly superior rank, since they are in charge of the encompassing societal action.[8]

This widely held model has two limitations. First, it stresses the problem of segregation but underemphasizes the means by which information and

---

* Reference notes for this chapter appear on page 190.

evaluative interpretation are to be related (other than by granting superiority to one kind of elite over another).[9] Second, it is too abstract to provide a productive model for describing the effects of inter-elite relations on the societal use of knowledge, as it is primarily a prescriptive scheme which defines the way things ought to be. It expresses the value of freeing scientists from a concern with the societal implications of their findings and legitimates the decision-making elites' claim that they ought to maintain superior rank. This model also suggests that the reduction of conflicts between the knowledge and power elites can occur through this sharp segregation of the sides which rarely view the world within the same contextuating orientations.

The actual pattern of relations between key sources of new information, new interpretations, and decision-making is itself a major subject on which only a few illustrative observations can be made here. First, while the segregation model may prescribe the societal conditions most favorable to basic research, most of the information used by post-modern societies is "applied" and only indirectly based on basic research. If federal obligations for research are taken as a rough indicator, the United States committed $1,689.9 millions in 1965 to basic research and $12,909.7 millions to applied research and development.[10] Most of the applied information is gathered and used by engineers, x-ray technicians, social workers, and so on, whose norms and needs differ greatly from those of the basic researchers. A considerable degree of contextuating control seems to inflict surprisingly little damage on their work. Applied research has been carried out quite effectively even in totalitarian societies.[11] Political supervision of and intervention in such work, even in Stalin's day, may be less stringent than was once believed but are much greater than the amounts which the segregation model assumes that research can tolerate.[12]

Second, there is also significantly less segregation on the opposite score: As the custodians of reality-testing, the producers of information participate much more actively in recasting political orientations than the segregation model suggests.[13] New information is introduced into the political process through numerous mechanisms other than the ubiquitous, non-directive, classified, expert's report left on the decision-maker's desk.

Experts are able to support almost any side in most political contests with testimony before executive or legislative committees, sometimes by drawing on different sets of facts, but much more commonly by giving different cognitive and evaluative interpretations to available facts. Conflicting interpretations about the danger of fallout from thermonuclear bombs, the probabilities of surviving a nuclear attack, and the effects of medicare are among the better-known examples.[14] The Armed Services support advisory corporations, whose studies support and sometimes even extend the basic contextual positions of the Services, even though they may differ about details.[15] Industries maintain public relations divisions to magnify and interpret "their" experts' findings on cancer and tobacco, vitamins and growth, drugs and pregnancy.[16] The effectiveness of experts, somewhat like that of attorneys, is determined not only by the amount of their evidence but also by the skill with which they present it, the resources they command, and the acuteness of their political perceptions.[17] Therefore, it is not that one group of experts presents the facts and the other perpetrates falsehoods, but rather that matters often involve questions which, even if an impartial and expertly trained judge were available, cannot be readily decided on the basis of information alone.[18]

It might be argued that while the predictions and advice of experts generally cannot be evaluated when they are first given, those experts who are proved correct gradually acquire more status and following, while those who are shown to be wrong are rejected. Although such societal "editing" of experts has not been systematically studied, we suggest that even *post hoc* selection is more limited in extent and efficacy than is often assumed. Occasionally, a clear test of a highly specific problem is possible, and some experts are shown to be correct while others are discredited—e.g., Admiral Rickover's arguments in favor of the feasibility of building nuclear-powered submarines. Knowledge concerning societal actors and their properties, however, tends to be far less verifiable and more time-consuming in its testing. Therefore, a "wrong" approach often outlives the experts who advocated it. The differences between "right" and "wrong" approaches are not clearly defined but are usually a matter of being less or more effective. The tests of the relative effectiveness of such matters as foreign aid, civil rights legislation, or police codes are, as a rule, difficult to establish, ambiguous, and open to different expert interpretations.[19] Because of the high costs of allowing "their" experts to be discredited, political elites tend not only to defend them partisanly but even attempt to prevent their evaluations.[20] The politicalization of the "editing" of experts who have access to power also works in reverse: Effective experts go unheard while less knowledgeable ones receive an audience because of such outright political factors as the change of an administration or the majority in a legislature. We do not argue that uninformed men usually serve as counselors while experts are ignored. We simply submit that the selection of the experts whose advice is introduced into the societal decision-making processes is a complex, partly evaluative and partly political process. Structurally, the processes of societal reality-testing and evaluation are interwoven rather than segregated, just as information and interpretation as symbolic systems are mixed in the societal mind.

Pluralistic Input

What, then, leads to a more effective societal organization of knowledge input? One frequently given answer posits pluralism both in production and in input. It is suggested, all other things being equal, that as one knowledge-elite (or school of thought) increasingly monopolizes either the production of knowledge in a particular field or the access to a decision-making elite, the actor's reality-testing will tend to become less effective. In organizational terms, this means that the less restricted the *participation* in the contest among knowledge producers which have political access, the more effective will be the knowledge *supply*; and the less politically-based the decisions regarding the *outcomes* of the knowledge contest, the more effective will be the societal course followed. It cannot be stressed enough, however, that this is a matter of degree; given the concern with societal needs other than reality-testing, considerable politicalization of the knowledge supply and of decision-making is to be expected even among comparatively effective actors.

It is also necessary to recognize that the pluralism of the production of knowledge rests on more than the institutionalization of the proper values. It is not only affected by "background" conditions, such as Calvinism or free enterprise economics, but it is also affected by the societal organization, especially by the distribution of relevant resources. For instance, the proposal to establish a cabinet-level United States Department of Science has not received wide approval because it would too greatly concentrate the sources of support for the production of knowledge.[21] A scientist who is refused support from one agency should always have another source of support to which he can turn, although, of course, the mere existence of two or more sources of support does not suffice if one school of thought controls the allocation of resources by all the sources. Thus, not only does a degree of pluralism in regard to sources of support, training, and affiliation seem a prerequisite for the relatively effective use of knowledge, but also a measure of conflict among the various sources of support seems necessary.

Furthermore, the position which favors pluralistic input is held not only for the societal organization of knowledge-production; it is advanced for the intra-governmental production of knowledge as well. One of the arguments for intelligence collection by the three Armed Forces, the CIA, and the State Department is that combining these services into one intelligence agency would undermine the pluralistic production of this form of knowledge. (We, of course, do not imply that the number of agencies must be large or that some additional coordination of their efforts would be detrimental to the quality of the knowledge produced.)

The significance of the distributive patterns of knowledge-producing resources should not be underestimated. While a great mind might generate a great idea under most conditions, there seems to be a positive association— especially in the applied fields—between investment (not only of funds but also of the number and quality of personnel and organizational talents and efforts) and the level and quality of knowledge output. This is not to suggest that by merely increasing investment in, let us say, cancer research, the problem would be solved more quickly. Some areas of research are already "flooded," while in others some basic questions must be answered before much additional progress can be anticipated. But while there is no one-to-one correlation between investment and results, in many cases the amount of investment does make a significant difference.[22]

Second, pluralism cannot be maintained when one area is given all the resources it needs while the others starve. The knowledge contest then becomes like a court fight between a battery of corporation lawyers and a young man from the Legal Aid Society. That is, if the case is an open-and-shut one, the latter man may win, but under most circumstances—when experience, the capacity to gather evidence, and the power of the presentation matter—he is more likely to lose because of his lower capacity either to amass the necessary facts or to make them visible and accessible to the judge and jury—i.e., to the decision-makers.

More active units, we suggest, have a more egalitarian pattern of investment in the various areas as well as of access to control centers of the various knowledge-producing units than is prescribed by the prevailing goal-priorities and societal power-relations. This serves as a guarantee that alternatives which have no immediate appeal and little power but may have merit will not be drowned out and also allows for anticipation. Thus, the access to decision-making centers of societies is so organized that deprived collectivities are heard long before they command sufficient power to force attention. Such societies also organize their knowledge input so that they are aware of gathering clouds on the international horizon long before the storm is blowing down their gates. Those actors who are unable to study, understand, and deal with systems whose patterns differ from their own priorities and power structures are precisely those who are untransformable, while those actors whose knowledge production is relatively detached from their existing societal structures are those one would expect to be most able to anticipate, recast, survive, and grow.

The pluralistic organization of knowledge production and of its input into the societal decision-making process is expected to be more effective than monopolization not only for societal reality-testing but also for evaluative interpretation. Focusing on one substantive issue—the structural-organizational base of societal criticism—we now turn to explore the organization of knowledge from this second functional viewpoint.

Communities-of-Assumptions

Societal actors, as we have seen, tend to view the world and themselves with contextuating eyes. While "lack of enclosure" is an institutionalized value for the knowledge collectivities themselves (academic communities, learned societies), consensus has an instrumental value for the political elites, aside from the degree of validity of the knowledge. A major task of any political elite is to construct a whole from societal parts; dissensus is costly and hinders the elite's ability to fulfill this function. And while consensus is not necessarily favorable to an elite in power, dissensus rarely is, for fragmentation of the political base and conflict within it tend to weaken the elite's capacity to guide.

When a societal unit faces a crisis which threatens some of its main values or its survival, pressure to cling to interpretations which had previously gained elite and/or majority support often increases, even though such a crisis may highlight the unreality of these interpretations. That is, we expect that societal actors, like persons, will often become increasingly ritualistic rather than innovative under pressure. This will express itself in the repetition of acts that have already failed and in an obsessive rejection of criticism.[23]

The elites of most modernized societal units are influential in determining whether or not a particular situation is a crisis, e.g., how dangerous are city riots or the gold outflow. And, one major reason for identifying crises is the elites' concern with their own positions. There is, therefore, pressure to limit new interpretations to those which fit the prevailing context not just during a crisis imposed on the system from outside but also in the course of pseudo-crises generated by an elite and by its interpretation of the situation.

The contextuating pressure of the control centers is directed above all toward knowledge and communication units which are able to provide and spread conflicting interpretations. It is not that political elites do not desire more valid and encompassing knowledge; some leaders, such as Roosevelt, are reported to have encouraged conflict among their staffs to increase the quality of the knowledge with which they were provided.[24] But whenever such conflicts reach a level which challenges the basic interpretive assumptions of an elite or of the societal unit, there tends to be resistance to basic innovations which may transform the prevailing context. This pressure for preserving the basic consensus is even further accentuated because the criteria for distinguishing the valid from the invalid are more vague on the contextual level than when bits are considered. Such vagueness increases the desire for a "community of assumptions" within which interpretations are confined.

A *community-of-assumptions* may be defined as the set of assumptions shared by the members of a societal unit which sets a context for its view of the world and itself.[25] A community-of-assumptions differs from a context in that a context is a symbolic system while a community-of-assumptions is a combined societal and symbolic one; that is, a community-of-assumptions is a context internalized and institutionalized by a societal unit. A context may be held by only a few leaders or by a small sub-unit of the members, but a community-of-assumptions exists only if it is shared at least by the elites and the active members of a societal unit. There are often several contexts in the symbolic world of any societal unit but only one or two communities-of-assumptions.

A community-of-assumptions may be limited by subject. Such communities may define the context for viewing only the external world or the internal world as well. However, we expect them to contextuate the orientation toward outsiders more than toward members, whether it be the orientation of the United States toward other nations (as compared to the United States' orientation toward sub-societies), or the orientation of one ethnic group toward others—e.g., Negroes toward whites as compared to Negro sub-groupings. Intimacy makes enclosure difficult. While this makes the transformation of internal (and self) images easier than the transformation of images of outsiders, it also means that internal (and self) images are more vague and less agreed upon. This is one factor that hampers self-oriented action as compared to action oriented toward others.

Some social scientists have suggested that a community-of-assumptions is a prerequisite for an effectively integrated elite or a cohesive societal unit; others have pointed out that those in control of the United States Armed Services, for instance, have no shared "mentality," and, hence, elites do not require a community-of-assumptions.[26] We suggest that the answer may lie in between these two positions. While not all elites also constitute communities-of-assumptions, even about external images, and while different bits may be held by members of an elite or by elites and their publics, they may nonetheless share a community-of-assumptions. Thus, the three Armed Services may have conflicting estimates of a potential enemy's capacities, and some generals may be Democrats while others are Republicans, but the fact that most share the Cold War perspective is sufficient for them to be able to work effectively in unison. And those elites which do not share a community-of-assumptions may exist but are less effective controlling agents.

Communities-of-assumptions are usually held without awareness* of their hypothetical nature. Many actors assume that the world really is the way their internalized and institutionalized images depict it; they do not see their images as a set of assumptions shared by their community but of undetermined validity.† The presence of some diversity of interpretation(s) within the community-of-assumptions itself further obscures the community's existence, since concepts, views, and facts which appear subject to dissent conceal that dissent is tolerated only within the limits of fundamentally

---

* "...what is most surprising to a new arrival in Saigon is the general unawareness, almost innocence, of how what 'we' are doing could look to an outsider." Mary McCarthy, "Report from Vietnam: I. The Home Program," *The New York Review of Books*, Vol. 8 (April 20, 1967), pp. 5–11, quoted from p. 5.

† The mechanisms which enforce a community-of-assumptions are not different from other aspects of societal control. Discussing the ways in which scientists are kept from exploring topics "too far off," despite a formal ideology of unrestricted freedom to explore, a *Science* reporter stated: "It appears that a major influence in keeping an investigator from being carried too far off the track of relevant research is, as Baker put it, 'the cultural influence of the community.' Getting the glazed-eye treatment from colleagues is an effective way of keeping researchers from going too far afield." John Walsh, "Bell Labs: A System Approach to Innovation is the Main Thing," *Science*, July 22, 1966, p. 395.

the same interpretations. It is difficult to determine the extent to which such communities act as blindfolds of which the elites as well as the active publics are unaware. However, it is likely that the elites who generated these communities-of-assumptions are themselves caught up in them to some extent; *and*, in addition, the elites often seem bound into a community-of-assumptions which substantively differs from that of their subjects but is similar in its constricting effect. Not the least of these communities is the elites' contextuating view of what their subjects believe and will tolerate and what courses of action they view as out-of-context and, therefore, as unacceptable.

A community-of-assumptions is not necessarily a dysfunctional phenomenon. Given the high number of possible basic positions and sub-positions, decision-making elites would obviously be overloaded and paralyzed if they had to examine the full range of policy alternatives each time they acted. The same holds for the publics. It is very difficult to work out a consensus about assumptions among the various Armed Services, governmental agencies, Congress, and publics on any given line of policy. And when such a consensus is finally reached, undoing it is an expensive process. Actually, the costs are usually so high that it "pays" a societal unit to lose some of its reality-adjusting capacity and to maintain a set of assumptions that do not "fit" well rather than to change them frequently. Only when the community-of-assumptions prevents learning long after the reality has changed significantly is a point reached at which the community's costs in terms of a loss of reality-testing outweigh its gains in terms of reduction of conflict and reinforcement of solidarity and "meaning."

It may seem that the more active societal units are those which more successfully determine the stage at which the costs of maintaining the community-of-assumptions outweigh the gains. This capacity, however, assumes (a) that the actor is aware of the existence of the community-of-assumptions, (b) a highly refined analytic ability to determine the relative costs and gains, and (c) the availability of an alternative set of assumptions to replace the old ones when their costs become unacceptable.

Actually, societal actors per se rarely calculate in this manner. Societal units that are effective from this viewpoint seem to be those *whose organization of knowledge includes an institutionalized provision for revision of the community-of-assumptions*. Such organization requires one or more structural positions whose functions are (a) to remain outside the community-of-assumptions in order to be able to analyze and evaluate information on the basis of *different sets of assumptions*, and (b) to exert pressure on elites and/or publics to *change* the communities-of-assumptions, especially as their relations to reality become more distant. The point is that the process by which new orientations enter and become established is a political one. Ideas per se have no societal power, and new ideas, especially contextuating ideas that may serve as the basis of a community-of-assumptions, do not enter into a societal system because the elites or active publics suddenly feel that new contextuating orientations are needed or are more valid or meaningful than the established ones. The process tends rather to be one of a societal conflict between the elites in power and the knowledge-producing elites that promote alternative assumptions (often in coalition with competing political elites). As a result, the sub-units charged with maintaining alternative orientations and "opening" communities-of-assumptions have a mobilization function as well as a symbolic-interpretative one. While we shall see that a considerable amount of such mobilization is carried out by other sub-units, the critics themselves must give their criticism enough of a societal push to get it off the ground before even favorable winds can carry it.

In short, it is unlikely that societal actors will act effectively without communities-of-assumptions, for, while such communities delay reality-testing, they contribute to consensus building, and thus, to action in unison. Therefore rather than seeking the conditions under which there will be no such communities, a task which seems utopian as well as unconducive to an active orientation, we explore, instead, the conditions under which communities-of-assumptions are kept relatively "flexible" and transformable. The answer is given in morphological rather than genetic terms; that is, it seems to lie in the availability of a particular kind of knowledge-producing sub-unit—one that is outside the community-of-assumptions, able to exert pressure on the societal unit (or its elites), and is a permanent feature of the societal organization of knowledge.

The Societal Need for Fundamental Criticism

Fundamental criticism is the function of those sub-units whose task is to overview the communities-of-assumptions and challenge them when they become detached from reality. Since such criticism challenges not bits— which could be changed within the existing community-of-assumptions—but the context, we refer to it as fundamental criticism ("radical" criticism would also be an appropriate term). The function of bit-criticism differs from that of fundamental criticism: When the disparity between reality and a community-of-assumptions is not great, bit-criticism enhances reality-testing within the limits of a community-of-assumptions and, thus, strengthens the community in the sense that the "same" context is shown capable of adaptation. When the community's detachment from reality is considerable, however, bit-criticism is dysfunctional because it tends to conceal the disparity and to delay overdue transformation.

Two main structural conditions seem necessary for the provision of fundamental criticism: (a) the critical sub-units must operate even when there is no need or opportunity for the transformation of a community-of-assumptions. Effective societal guidance systems, like other effective systems, require a measure of redundancy, that is, some duplication is required if the relevant function is to be fulfilled. The reason for "redundancy" in this particular case is that the system most in need of fundamental criticism is also likely to be most resistant to it and least inclined to make the structural arrangements necessary for the cultivation of such criticism. To the degree that these arrangements are available, they seem to have been institutionalized before a loss-of-reality crisis occurred. Secondly, the availability of alternative fundamental interpretations (i.e., potential communities-of-assumptions) when the prevailing one is broken or weakened requires their preparation *before* the event, which, in turn, necessitates prolonged efforts to synthesize large bodies of knowledge and mobilize initial support.

(b) A value of tolerance for such criticism must be included as part of the *established* community-of-assumptions—a tolerance for basically divergent viewpoints and institutions outside of the community. Scientific metatheories do, to a degree, maintain such assumptions. They are rarely maintained in political systems, however, although liberal and social-democratic ideologies do have some such notions.

The function of fundamental criticism differs according to the state of the societal unit and of its community-of-assumptions. Units that are well integrated by other criteria are also likely to have communities-of-assumptions promoted by and supporting the elites in power. In this kind of unit, the promotion of an alternative set of assumptions takes the form of criticism. In less integrated units, fundamental criticism is often part of the competition over which assumptions should serve as the community-of-assumptions. In the process of nation-building, this is often closely related to the struggle over national identity. Criticism here serves to guard against premature enclosure and the quick acceptance of older assumptions as a basis for the new community. Thus, both when there is an established community-of-assumptions and when one is just being evolved, fundamental societal criticism has a central function.

Intellectuals, Experts, and Political Elites

Post-Modern Criticism: A Morphological Perspective

The critical function requires one or more sub-units relatively immune from societal pressure which allow for and even reward the questioning of a supra-unit's basic assumptions. Such immunity may be the accidental outgrowth of other arrangements; for instance, the granting of relative autonomy and access to the centers of power to units engaged in long-run planning or research and development (R & D), tends to provide the sociological conditions under which fundamental criticism may be institutionalized. In the courts of kings in earlier periods, some religious functionaries and jesters had such an institutionalized role.[27]

Which societal sub-units are likely to fulfill the critical function in the post-modern period? The answer varies with the kind of society. In pluralistic societies, the fourth estate, the free press, was viewed as the depository of the function of fundamental criticism, but there is little empirical research on the degree to which it fulfills this function.[28] We know, however, that the greater part of the space in most newspapers in post-modern pluralistic societies is devoted to advertising. Much of the remaining space is used for what may be classified as tension-reduction purposes, including personal feature stories, crime and sex "news," etc. By providing escapist outlets for the tensions generated by the societal structure and by providing individualistic interpretations of them, this kind of journalism reduces the receptivity to fundamental criticism and the pressure for transformation. Only part of the remaining newspaper space is devoted to political and societal information, and only a fraction of this deals with interpretation and fundamental criticism. Furthermore, the norms upheld by most professional newspapermen seem to discourage a view of societal criticism as their proper function; "straight news" is encouraged instead.

The situation is different for a very small number of newspapers, the so-called elite newspapers[29] such as *The New York Times*, but even here the basic priorities with regard to space are as specified above. The major difference is that elite newspapers devote more space to information and less to tension-reduction; "crusading" is, nevertheless, rare and discouraged, and there is little fundamental criticism. Loyalty to the establishment curbs not so much the facts printed as the interpretation given to them.[30] The critical function is much more highly represented in such periodicals as *The New Republic* and *The Nation*, but their circulation is small even among the active publics and elites.[31] And many of the critical articles that are published in these journals are not written by professional journalists but by intellectuals whose structural base is not the press.

A second structural foundation for the critical function is national legislatures. While they undoubtedly have such a function, many have argued that it has been declining since the advent of the post-modern period.[32] Parliaments seem to exercise their critical function to a greater extent for domestic matters than for external ones in a period in which the importance of foreign affairs has greatly increased. The facilities of parliaments have grown little, while the societal and political activities—that is, the scope of what needs to be surveyed—have considerably increased.[33] While the units which need to be reviewed critically—governmental agencies and corporations, armed services, and school systems—have developed sizeable organs for the collection, synthesis, and promotion of knowledge, *legislatures have only very small knowledge-collecting-and-processing units and depend largely on knowledge provided and interpreted for them by either executive or partisan interests.*[34] Attempts at encompassing overviews are few and ineffectual.[35] Proposals to reform the fragmented budgetary processes of the United

States national government, for example, have been generally unsuccessful. The Legislative Reorganization Act of 1946 created a joint committee on the budget which was to report to each house a legislative budget which would include an estimate of all Federal receipts and expenditures for the coming fiscal year. In actual operation, however, the plan was generally viewed as unworkable.[36] We suggest that *unless legislatures are provided with greatly increased staffs and with large-scale and autonomous capacities to collect and process knowledge, their already low critical capacity will continue to diminish.*

While it is difficult to test statements about the relative roles of institutions in fulfilling a societal function, we suggest that in the post-modern, pluralistic societies the unattached intellectuals play a more important critical role than the press, the legislature, and probably both combined. By "unattached" intellectuals we mean those who have no institutional commitment to any elite; they are to be found in such societal enclaves as the bohemian quarters, autonomous policy-research centers, and the universities. Intellectuals, as opposed to experts, have two attributes: They are concerned with contextual matters, while experts are more bit-oriented, and they deal more with evaluative interpretations, while experts are more concerned with reality-testing and cognitive interpretation. Clearly, not everyone who works with symbols or his intellect is an intellectual; those who are not may be referred to as intellect-workers.[37] Intellectuals maintain a wholistic evaluative stance, and those who are unattached are more likely than others to maintain a critical one.[38]

Much of the criticism carried by the press or brought before the national legislatures originates in the autonomous centers which house these intellectuals. An important study would be to identify the main critical ideas of the last decades and to trace their origins and paths into the political system. University committees and individual scholars, for example, have dealt with the fundamental aspects of United States foreign policy; Michael Harrington has often been credited with calling elite and public attention to the realities of poverty in the United States.[39] The United States educational system was roundly criticized by a Harvard President and by a free-lance bohemian.[40] The university played the key role in introducing the notions of a rich economy and an impoverished public sector (the original conception of the Affluent Society),[41] of the American inability to guide the foreign world,[42] and of redefining the mentally ill and criminals as sick people.[43] Each of these deserves study in terms of the methods by which established assumptions were challenged, the extent to which the change was overdue, and other forces in favor of the transformation of the orientation.

The relative contributions of the three main loci of unattached intellectuals —bohemia, the unaffiliated policy-research center, and the university—have not been determined and may be changing. The structural–organizational conditions of each are of some interest.

The university provides, on the one hand, the necessary socio-political conditions for generating fundamental criticism; the tenure faculty has the necessary basic autonomy from undue economic and political pressures, at least in the leading universities. The rise of the government as a main source of funds, however, has generated numerous intra-university pressures against such criticism. Rather than direct pressures on the content of the intellectual's work or life, these pressures are often subtle, involving differences in the possibilities of obtaining a summer salary, secretarial and research assistance, or travel grants.[44]

University faculty members tend to have both the training and the tools, from libraries to computers, required for the production and interpretation of new knowledge. In pre-modern periods, it was easier to fulfill the critical function in less institutionalized settings, as fewer tools were necessary; coffee houses, patrons' homes, and small magazines served it well.[45] While these have not disappeared, fundamental criticism in post-modern societies may require training and facilities that are more available at universities than on the Left Bank, in Greenwich Village, in Munich's Schwabing, or in their sociological equivalents in other countries.[46] It also seems that post-modern societies find criticism more acceptable when it appears in the guise of science or information. There appears to be little place in post-modern society for the charismatic, purely normative, true prophet.[47]

Criticism emanating from bohemia or from unaffiliated policy-research centers is often more broad-scoped and radical than much of the criticism emanating from the universities. On the average, however, it is less "professional" in both appearance and substance.[48]

The products of these centers may, however, complement more empirical work by adding a stronger evaluative component and by appealing to segments of the active publics, even when such criticisms are less attuned to the elites. There seems also to be a tense but productive relationship between these centers and the universities, in that the centers act as the critics of the university in general and reinforce its critical function in particular.[49] In this sense, the unaffiliated critical centers serve as a third-order reviewing unit, with the universities as second-order and the government as first-order ones.

A common fallacy is the suggestion that the critics are ineffective because there is no consensus among them about what is faulty or what needs to be done to correct it. Further, it has been argued that consensus, when it does occur, is often based on a community-of-assumptions of the intellectuals which is no more tested and often no more testable than that of the political elites.[50] We suggest, on the contrary, first, that intellectuals' communities-of-assumptions are *relatively* more open to innovative interpretation and empirical testing than political ones or those of the public, because of the institutionalization of the value of truth and because the pressure of extrinsic interests and norms is relatively less. (There is, however, one factor which works in the opposite direction: Political elites are held accountable, in the long run, for the consequences of their positions, while this is much less true for the unaffiliated intellectuals.)

Secondly, consensus among intellectuals is not a prerequisite for the effective discharge of their critical function, which requires that the established communities-of-assumptions be challenged and that alternative ones be provided. It is not the function of the intellectuals to provide consensus, an agreed-upon line of action; *that* is the function of the political process. The intellectuals' role is to pry open the walls in which society tends to box itself and suggest various directions which the freed prisoner may take; which ones are preferred is to be decided by the community as a whole. To demand consensus from the intellectuals is to assume that the questions involved can be selected empirically and rationally while actually they are, in part, normative issues, and to assume that they can be settled by an elite while actually they must be worked out in societal consensus-building. The intellectuals enrich the debate, both on the elite and the public level, and often are needed to keep it alive, but this can be fully achieved, even better achieved, without consensus among the intellectuals.

The Societal Input of Criticism

The active orientation is most effectively sustained if societal decision-making, inevitably a political process, is subject to fundamental criticism *and* to empirical reality-testing. The degree to which the services of the political, critical, and empirical functions are articulated is considerably affected by the relations among three kinds of societal elites—political, intellectual, and expert. The service of any one function is not limited to any one kind of elite; political elites are somewhat concerned with empirical considerations, experts deal with fundamental criticisms to some extent, and intellectuals take empirical matters into account. Still, there is a tendency toward specialization, with each function being fulfilled largely by one of the three kinds of elites.

It seems productive to view the relations among the three elites as a three-filter screen through which new contextuating orientations are projected to guide societal efforts. The intellectual filter is the most open one; ideas are approved with comparative ease, especially if they are not in open conflict with a major body of known facts. Intellectual screening is more evaluative than empirical and more concerned with value-relevancy and "coverage" than with reality-testing. The expert filter is considerably less open and admits mainly ideas that withstand some kind of empirical test.[51] The political filter is the most narrow for it allows only one or two alternatives to pass through it—those which the elite will seek to implement.

The analytic schema whereby the three filters can be distinguished serves as only the first step in a morphological study of the input of fundamental criticism into societal decision making. This is the case because societal actors vary significantly in the degree to which (a) the filters are structurally segregated and their respective functional needs served; (b) the units which provide the major structural anchorages for the three filters are protected from interpenetration; and (c) a balance is kept among the three.

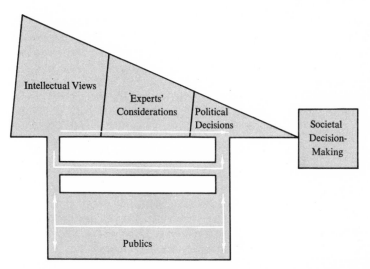

Limited structural segregation of the three filters is most evident in pre-modern societies in which the political elites attempted to carry out all three functions (though some delegation of the critical and expert functions to members of the courts' lay and clerical staff did occur).[52] In modern and post-modern societies, a lack of resources or other facilities so that the units in service of a given filter cannot function adequately poses greater difficulties than an insufficient segregation of the filters. Thus, as suggested above, the critical function cannot be carried out effectively if the unaffiliated intellectuals are not granted economic security, immunity from political and societal pressures, and access to the two other kinds of elites. Underdeveloped nations are often more deficient with respect to the second filter than with regard to the first or the third; ideas, thus, travel readily from the intellectual to the political elites without sufficient expert screening and, hence, empirical testing.

Even when the three kinds of units are segregated and resources are provided for them, some mixing of functions and interpenetration are to be expected. Thus, seeking to participate in or affect the societal evaluative trends, political elites penetrate into the intellectual realm; unaffiliated intellectuals become "co-opted" by or actually share in the margins of power; and experts get involved in intellectual criticism and anticipation of political considerations, pre-empting both roles and, to a degree, neglecting their own.[53] In comparison to earlier societies, which suffered from considerable political penetration into the expert realm, pluralistic post-modern societies often suffer from a *lack* of sufficient political guidance for experts (especially in the relations between civilian political elites and military experts). The active society requires the reassertion of the primacy of political guidance over the experts' view of the world.

The three filters' funnel significantly affects knowledge not only of society but also of other societal actors. The same basic structure and processes appear also on the sub-societal level, such as between the University and the state capital in Madison, Wisconsin; East Lansing, Michigan; and Austin, Texas; the body of a church; a labor movement, and so on. In all these situations, we suggest, a division of labor among the three kinds of elites is functional, and some conflict among them is inevitable and also functional. The critic, like the true prophet, cannot expect to be the court's favorite; the expert cannot have the intellectual's prerogatives; and the policy-maker cannot hope to please both.

The critical function is not hindered by inter-elite tensions and conflicts; instead such conflict may prevent the elites from losing their distinctive identities and the members from excessive interaction across elite boundaries rather than with members of their own elite. Tension and conflict become dysfunctional only when they rise to a level at which access is blocked and the conditions for work and for autonomy are undermined.

The Roles of the Publics

The interaction among the three kinds of elites does not take place in a societal vacuum; elites affect and are affected by the publics, especially the active ones. First, the deliberations of the political elites are inevitably affected by the publics' views of reality and their subsequent evaluations, and therefore by the degree to which the new expert findings and intellectual orientations (evaluations) are accepted.[54] Second, because the publics affect the structural relations among the three kinds of elites, the degrees to which there are tolerance for intellectuals, respect for experts, and support for the elites in power have a contextuating impact on both the actions and relations of the three kinds of elites.

Basically, there are two channels from the loci of societal criticism to the loci of political power. One is contact between intellectuals and political elites, either direct or mediated by experts[55]. Second, there is the more indirect route of appeals to the publics and to the political opposition—i.e., attempts to transform the communities-of-assumptions of the publics and to mobilize political support in order to force a change in the assumptions of the political elites.

The more institutionalized politics are, the more the first channel would be expected to be open, although we expect to find strong barriers en route in even the most effectively institutionalized political system because the political filter must be much more narrow than the intellectual one. Societies can be compared according to their relative reliance on the two channels; as a smaller amount of criticism travels through one channel, a greater burden is placed on the other. For instance, the United States may be seen as having moved toward a greater opening of the direct channel if the last generations of the modern age are compared with the first post-modern generation, though different national administrations can be ranked differently on this account.[56] But at the same time, the two channels should not be viewed as mutually exclusive alternatives; progress in one is often related to progress in the other. The public paid more attention to Michael Harrington's book about poverty in the United States after it became known that President Kennedy had read it with interest.[57]

The foregoing discussion of the interaction between the elites and the membership of societal units (both in this and in the preceding chapter) focused upon publics rather than collectivities and political organizations. The publics referred to here are often the members of one or more collectivities and their political organizations. "Active public," then, refers to the active members of a collectivity, and "passive public" refers to the other members. Active and passive publics are often bound together in one collectivity and/or political organization, with the more active members leading the more passive ones. The analysis of knowledge processes, though, can proceed, as we attempt here, without specifying at each step the morphological bases of each public and of the relations among them, because the knowledge held by the members, we suggest, is relatively more independent of structural position and organizational activation than their values and especially their interests. Therefore we have deferred analysis of the relations among elites, collectivities, and political organizations until the concepts of commitment and power are introduced.

Our purpose here is not to construct a full macro-sociology of knowledge but to illustrate the directions in which it may evolve if a societal guidance perspective is maintained. The three kinds of filters and the relations among the units that specialize in their services and between these units and the publics seem to be the most essential components to be considered. Two conclusions seem to emerge from this preliminary exploration: (a) The often-repeated emphasis on the need for pluralism in the production of societal knowledge points to only one (though major) functional prerequisite for an active society. The systematic provision for the three filters—intellectual, expert, and political—and for their articulation with each other and with the publics is essential. (b) A society that is free to test its ideas and to try out fundamentally new ones cannot be restricted to approaching the world and itself merely through the narrow political filter of the elites in power; such a society must provide for fundamental criticism and be open to it. Such a self-critical society—active in its use of societal knowledge—cannot be brought about unless the post-modern society is transformed by a fuller exercise of the critical function.

NOTES

1. Cf. Tom Burns who proceeds in the opposite direction, using the theory of the state to study corporations. "Micropolitics: Mechanisms of Institutional Change," *Administrative Science Quarterly*, Vol. 6 (1961), pp. 257–281.

2. Leonard Reissman, "A Study of Role Conceptions in Bureaucracy," *Social Forces*, Vol. 27 (1949), pp. 305–310. See also Etzioni, *Modern Organizations, op. cit.*, pp. 77 ff.

3. This is a central thesis of Don K. Price, *The Scientific Estate* (Cambridge, Mass.: Belknap Press of Harvard University Press, 1965).

4. Harold L. Wilensky, *Intellectuals in Labor Unions* (New York: Free Press, 1956).

5. Hilsman, *Strategic Intelligence and National Decisions, op. cit.*, Ch. VIII; Robert Dubin (ed.), *Human Relations in Administration* (Englewood Cliffs, N.J.: Prentice-Hall, 1951), pp. 121–123; and William Kornhauser with the assistance of Warren O. Hagstrom, *Scientists in Industry: Conflict and Accommodation* (Berkeley: University of California, 1962).

6. See Fred W. Riggs, *Administration in Developing Countries: The Theory of Prismatic Society* (Boston: Houghton Mifflin, 1964), pp. 21–23; and James R. Townsend, *Political Participation in Communist China* (Berkeley: University of California Press, 1967), p. 215.

7. "There is a division of labor between science, which seeks truth, and politics, which is concerned with power, purpose, and responsibility," Kenneth E. Boulding, summarizing Don K. Price, in a review of his book in *Scientific American*, Vol. 214 (April, 1966), pp. 131–134, quoted from p. 131.

8. See Sheldon S. Wolin, *Politics and Vision: Continuity and Innovation in Western Political Thought* (Boston: Little, Brown, 1960), pp. 352–434.

9. On the point of relations, see Riggs, *Administration in Developing Countries . . ., op. cit.*, pp. 63–67, and esp. pp. 436–441.

10. Data on federal obligations for basic research and applied research and development are for fiscal year 1965 and are taken from the National Science Foundation Report, *Federal Funds for Research, Development, and Other Scientific Activities: Fiscal Years 1965, 1966 and 1967*, Vol. 15 (Washington, D.C.: Government Printing Office, 1966), p. 77, Table C-1. The figure for applied research and development, excludes plant costs.

11. Leo A. Orleans, "Research and Development in Communist China," *Science*, Vol. 157 (July 28, 1967), pp. 392–400. See also P. H. Abelson et al., "Science in the U.S.S.R.", *Science*, Vol. 126 (Nov. 19, 1957), pp. 1095–1099.

12. See Bernard Barber, *Science and the Social Order* (New York: Collier, 1962), pp. 115–120.

13. For the main works on this subject, see Don K. Price, *Government and Science* (New York: New York University Press, 1954), pp. 134 ff; Ralph E. Lapp,

The New Priesthood (New York: Harper & Row, 1965), *passim*; and Wiesner, *Where Science and Politics Meet, op. cit.* See also C. P. Snow, *Science and Government* (Cambridge, Mass.: Harvard University Press, 1961) and Robert Gilpin and Christopher Wright (eds.), *Scientists and National Policy-Making* (New York: Columbia University Press, 1964), esp. essays by Bernard Brodie and Warner R. Schilling.

14. On the effects of fallout, for instance, compare Herman Kahn, *On Thermonuclear War* (Princeton, N.J.: Princeton University Press, 1961), pp. 3–116 with Robert A. Dentler and Phillips Cutright, *Hostage America* (Boston: Beacon Press, 1963), pp. 1–76. On the likelihood of nuclear war, C. P. Snow predicted in 1960 that "Within, at the most, ten years, some of these bombs are going off. I am saying this as responsibly as I can. That is the certainty . . . a certainty of disaster." *The New York Times*, December 14, 1960, p. 14. Kahn's estimate is much lower. See *On Thermonuclear War, op. cit.*, pp. 208–209.

15. For a fine study which reveals the inadequacy of the segregation model, see: Bruce L. R. Smith's description of the very active role which RAND plays in Air Force policy formation. "Strategic Expertise and National Security Policy: A Case Study," in John D. Montgomery and Arthur Smithies (eds.), *Public Policy*, Vol. 13 (1964), pp. 69–106. See also Albert Wohlstetter, "Scientists, Seers, and Strategy," *Foreign Affairs*, Vol. 41 (1963), pp. 466–478, and Edward S. Flash, Jr., "The Knowledge–Power Relationship," in his *Economic Advice and Presidential Leadership* (New York: Columbia University Press, 1965), pp. 308–325. Flash deals with the political advice the United States economists gave United States presidents. For additional elaboration of our position, see Amitai Etzioni, "Knowledge and Power," *The New York Times Book Review*, July 31, 1966.

16. On the need to promote new knowledge, even if valid, see discussion of the fluoridation fights and the failure to reduce smoking on a wide scale. For a study and references to other works, see Donald B. Rosenthal and Robert L. Crain, "Executive Leadership and Community Innovation: the Fluoridation Experience," *Urban Affairs Quarterly*, Vol. 1 (March, 1966), pp. 39–57. See also Stanley Joel Reiser, "Smoking and Health: The Congress and Causality," in Sanford A. Lakoff (ed.), *Knowledge and Power* (New York: Free Press, 1966), pp. 293–311.

17. "The sophisticated public servant knows not only that there is 'another' point of view on almost any scientific issue which bears on an important policy question, but he knows quite matter of factly to whom to turn to get it." Lawrence Cranberg, "Ethical Problems of Scientists," *The Educational Record*, Vol. 46 (1965), p. 289. Jerome B. Wiesner and Herbert F. York wrote an article on "National Security and the Nuclear Test Ban," *Scientific American*, Vol. 211 (Oct., 1964), pp. 27–31. In the article they characterized themselves as "scientists," and stated that they discussed "the matter from the point of view of our country's national interest." But a reporter, specializing in science affairs, suggested that "since 1964 was an election year, one must consider this article in another light. Drs. Wiesner and York wrote for the country's most influential, semipopular technical magazine one month before an election in which the role of nuclear arms was an issue." David Warren Burkett *Writing Science News for the Mass Media* (Houston, Texas: Gulf, 1965), pp. 3–4. He also pointed out that Wiesner was identified in the same magazine as one of two organizers of a bipartisan committee enlisting scientists and engineers in support of President Johnson. See also Nathan K.

Rickles, "The Battle of the Experts," *Corrective Psychiatry and Journal of Social Therapy*, Vol. 10 (1964), pp. 232–240 and Richard J. Barber, *The Politics of Research* (Washington, D.C.: Public Affairs Press, 1966).

18. H. L. Nieburg, *In the Name of Science* (Chicago: Quadrangle, 1966), esp. pp. 131–134.

19. For a detailed discussion of the difficulties attendant with measuring progress in many areas of societal efforts, see Albert D. Biderman, "Social Indicators and Goals," in Raymond A. Bauer (ed.), *Social Indicators* (Cambridge, Mass.: M. I. T. Press, 1966), pp. 68–153; see also Amitai Etzioni and Edward W. Lehman, "Some Dangers in 'Valid' Social Measurements," in Bertram Gross (ed.), *The Annals of Social and Political Sciences*, (September, 1967). Vol. 373, pp. 1–15.

20. Much material to support this statement is included in James L. Penick, Jr. et al. (eds.), *The Politics of American Science, 1939 to the Present* (Chicago: Rand McNally, 1965), see esp. pp. 34–48; 54–72; and 148–161.

21. Wallace S. Sayre, "Scientists and American Science Policy," in Gilpin and Wright, *Scientists and National Policy-making, op. cit.*, pp. 105–106.

22. Jacob Schmookler, *Invention and Economic Growth* (Cambridge, Mass.: Harvard University Press, 1966).

23. A moderate level of pressure rather than a high level, it has been suggested, is more conducive to learning. James G. March and Herbert A. Simon, *Organizations* (New York: Wiley & Sons, 1958), pp. 182–184.

24. Richard Neustadt, *Presidential Power, The Politics of Leadership* (New York: Wiley, 1960), pp. 157–158.

25. The danger of "tabu problems" is discussed by Klaus Knorr and Oskar Morgenstern, "Conjecturing about our Military and Political Future," *University*, No. 26 (Fall, 1965), pp. 33–34.

26. For a critique of C. Wright Mills' *The Power Elite*, see Daniel Bell, "Is There a Ruling Class in America? The Power Elite Reconsidered," in his *The End of Ideology* (New York: Free Press, 1960), pp. 43–67. See also Morris Janowitz, *The Professional Soldier* (New York: Free Press, 1960), pp. 233–255. Cf. J. Blondel, *Voters, Parties and Leaders: The Social Fabric of British Politics* (Baltimore: Penguin, rev. ed., 1965), pp. 234 ff.

27. Humor, especially satire, is, of course, a well-known instrument of criticism. On the one hand, it is relatively "safe," i.e., allows one to criticize and live, to see another occasion for criticism *and* to be heard ("he is just joking" or "one must be able to take it"). On the other hand, there is a danger that the humorous criticism may not be taken seriously. Criticism which becomes a form of entertainment, such as Hollywood movies about nuclear war, risks a generic danger. *Failsafe*, for instance, has much less critical value than *Dr. Strangelove* precisely because the former closely resembles conventional entertainment while the latter attempts to satirize—to shock the viewer into critical reflection. (The mad scientist and the infantile president, at the center of power, achieve this effect.)

28. For a discussion of the role of the press as "observer," "participant," and "catalyst," see Bernard C. Cohen, *The Press and Foreign Policy* (Princeton, N.J.: Princeton University Press, 1963). On the opportunities for and limitations on thoughtful criticism and comprehensive reporting by the press, see James Reston, *The Artillery of the Press: Its Influence on American Foreign Policy* (New York: Harper & Row, 1967).

29. For a discussion of elite newspapers in Great Britain, France, the United States, Russia, and Germany, see Ithiel de Sola Pool with the collaboration of Harold D. Lasswell, Daniel Lerner et al., *The "Prestige Papers", A Survey of Their Editorials* (Stanford, Calif.: Stanford University Press, 1952).

30. For a critique of American journalism in general and *The New York Times* in particular, see Irving Kristol, "The Underdeveloped Profession," *The Public Interest*, No. 6 (Winter, 1967), pp. 36–52. For *Times* Managing Editor Clifton Daniel's reply and Kristol's rejoinder, see *The Public Interest*, No. 7 (Spring, 1968), pp. 119–123. For additional discussion, see George Lichtheim, " 'All the News That's Fit to Print: Reflections on The New York Times," *Commentary*, Vol. 40 (September, 1965), pp. 33–46.

31. The average circulation of *The New Republic* for a six-month period in 1966 was 120,290 while that of *The Nation* was 29,470. *Ayer Directory of Newspapers and Periodicals* (Philadelphia: Ayer & Son, Inc., 1967), pp. 190, 757. For a discussion of the limitations of these publications, see Robert Lekachman, ". . . No, But I Read the Reviews," *Columbia University Forum*, Vol. 7 (Winter, 1964), pp. 4–9. See also Louis M. Lyons, "Chain-Store Journalism," *The Reporter* (Dec. 8, 1960), pp. 60–63.

32. For a discussion of this point and references, see Chapter 17, FNOQ, pp. 488–489, and Note 53.

33. Philip Donham and Robert Fahey, *Congress Needs Help* (New York: Random House, 1966). For specific suggestions to overcome this weakness, see Kenneth Janda, "Information Systems for Congress" in Cornelius P. Cotter, et al., *Twelve Studies of the Organization of Congress* (Washington, D.C.: The American Enterprise Institute for Public Policy Research, 1966), pp. 415–456, and Daniel P. Moynihan, "A Crisis of Confidence?", *The Public Interest*, No. 7 (Spring, 1967), pp. 3–10.

34. For reference, see below, Chapter 16, Footnote 54.

35. For discussion and some documentation of this point, see Chapter 11 below, pp. 268 ff.

36. "By 1949 it was obvious that the plan was not accomplishing its purpose, and the joint committee has not functioned since then." Joseph P. Harris, *Congressional Control of Administration* (Washington, D.C.: The Brookings Institution, 1964), p. 108.

37. For an elaboration of the distinction between intellectuals and intellect-workers, see Paul A. Baran, "The Commitment of the Intellectual," *Monthly Review*, Vol. 13 (May, 1961), pp. 8–18.

38. Raymond Aron reluctantly concurs that "there remains . . . a basis of truth in the hackneyed notion, which has been taken up in a more subtle form by certain sociologists (J. Schumpeter, for example), of the intellectuals as revolutionaries by profession." Raymond Aron, *The Opium of the Intellectuals* (Garden City, N.Y.: Doubleday, 1957), p. 209. On similar views of the intellectuals, see George Lichtheim, "The Role of the Intellectuals," *Commentary*, Vol. 29 (1960), pp. 295–307; Edward A. Shils, "The Intellectuals and the Powers: Some Perspectives for Comparative Analysis," *Comparative Studies in Society and History*, Vol. I (1958), pp. 5–22, and by the same author *The Intellectual Between Tradition and Modernity: The Indian Situation* (The Hague: Mouton, 1961), esp. pp. 17–21. See also Bennett M. Berger, "Sociology and the Intellectuals: An Analysis of a Stereotype," in Seymour Martin Lipset and Neal J. Smelser (eds.), *Sociology: The Progress of a Decade* (Englewood Cliffs, N.J.: Prentice-Hall, 1961), pp. 37–46.

39. Michael Harrington's influential book is *The Other America: Poverty in the United States* (New York: Macmillan, 1962). It is reported to have called the attention of President Kennedy to the issue and to have initiated the war on poverty. See footnote 57 below.

40. James B. Conant, *The American High School Today* (New York: McGraw-Hill, 1959). Paul Goodman, *Compulsory Mis-education* (New York: Horizon Press, 1964).

41. John Kenneth Galbraith, *The Affluent Society* (Boston: Houghton Mifflin, 1958).

42. William J. Lederer and Eugene Burdick, *The Ugly American* (New York: Norton, 1958).

43. Gregory Zilboorg, M.D., in collaboration with George W. Henry, M.D., *A History of Medical Psychology* (New York: Norton, 1941), pp. 175–244, 479–510. See also Michel Foucault, *Madness and Civilization: A History of Insanity in the Age of Reason,* translated from the French by Richard Howard (New York: Pantheon Books, 1965), which traces the attitude of Western European Society towards madness from the Middle Ages to the beginning of the nineteenth century.

44. Clark Kerr, *The Uses of the University* (Cambridge, Mass.: Harvard University Press, 1964), pp. 57 ff. In regard to Kerr's de-emphasis of the university's intellectual and moral identity, see Harold Taylor's review in *Commentary*, Vol. 38 (1964), pp. 68–73. For an analysis of the impact of federal financing of research on universities, see Charles V. Kidd, *American Universities and Federal Research* (Cambridge, Mass.: Belknap Press of Harvard University Press, 1959). For additional comment, see Joseph Ben-David and Awraham Zloczower, "Universities and Academic Systems in Modern Societies," *European Journal of Sociology*, Vol. 3 (1962), pp. 45–84; A. H. Halsey, "British Universities and Intellectual Life," *Universities Quarterly*, Vol. 12 (1958), pp. 141–152; A. H. Halsey, "The Changing Functions of Universities in Advanced Industrial Societies," *Harvard Educational Review*, Vol. XXX (Spring, 1960), pp. 119–127. See also Jason Epstein, "The CIA and the Intellectuals." *The New York Review of Books*, April 20, 1967, pp. 16–21.

45. See Lewis A. Coser, *Men of Ideas: A Sociologist's View* (New York: Free Press, 1965), pp. 11 ff.

46. For the sociological bases and limitations involved see Caroline F. Ware, *Greenwich Village, 1920–1930* (Boston: Houghton Mifflin, 1935): Malcolm Cowley, *Exile's Return* (New York: Viking, 1961); and Allen Churchill, *The Improper Bohemians: A Re-creation of Greenwich Village in its Heyday* (New York: Dutton, 1959).

47. Max Weber in *Ancient Judaism*, translated and edited by Hans H. Gerth and Don Martindale (New York: Free Press, 1952), analyzed the critical function of true prophets as distinct from the false, court-retained, ones. Weber's thesis of a disestablished, independent prophecy has been questioned by recent research. See Peter L. Berger, "Charisma and Religious Innovation: The Social Location of Israelite Prophecy," *American Sociological Review*, Vol. 28 (1963), pp. 940–950.

48. Paul Goodman of the Institute of Policy Studies has suggested that television networks be decentralized "as much as possible, on any plausible principle, to municipalities, colleges, local newspaper, ad hoc associations. With many hundreds of centers of responsibility and initiative, there will occur many opportunities for direct local audience demand and participation, and for the honest and inventive

to get a hearing and try to win their way." See Goodman's "The Continuing Disaster," *The New Republic*, Vol. 148 (January 26, 1963), pp. 24–26, quoted from p. 26. In a letter in reply, newscaster David Brinkley noted that with the exception of municipalities, the local groups of which Goodman spoke "are the very groups owning the television stations now—including some of the worst of them." Brinkley adds, "Does Mr. Goodman believe that, without networks, we could expect to see honest examinations of the civil rights story on stations controlled by Southern municipalities, which is to say Southern local politicians?" For Brinkley's letter, see *The New Republic*, Vol. 148 (March 23, 1963), p. 39.

Also see the exchange between Donald N. Michael of the Institute of Policy Studies, and Daniel Bell of Columbia University, over the factual basis of the alarmist approach to automation. *New York Review of Books* (Nov. 25, 1965), pp. 36–38, and *ibid*, August 26, 1965, pp. 23–25. See also Amitai Etzioni, "Speaking of Books: Protesting with Facts and Figures," *The New York Times Book Review*, March 14, 1965, and the following exchange with Paul Goodman (*ibid*, April 4, 1965). On the need for "reasoned criticism in the fullest sense," see Christopher Lasch's "The Banality of Liberalism," a review of Hans Morgenthau's *The Crossroad Papers* and Paul Goodman's (ed.), *Seeds of Liberation* in *The New York Review of Books* (September 30, 1965), pp. 4–6. For critiques of Lasch's review, see letters to the editor by Paul Seabury, John F. Withey, and E. Jeffrey Ludwig and Lasch's reply *ibid.*, November 11, 1965, pp. 36–37.

49. See Arthur A. Cohen (ed.), *Humanistic Education and Western Civilization: Essays for Robert M. Hutchins* (New York: Holt, Rinehart & Winston, 1964), esp. essays by David Riesman and Arthur A. Cohen. Robert M. Hutchins, *The University of Utopia* (Chicago: University of Chicago Press, 1953).

50. Barber, "Resistance by Scientists to Scientific Discovery," *op. cit.*, pp. 596–602.

51. Methodology is to a considerable extent also a part of a community-of-assumptions, as different communities of experts make divergent assumptions as to what constitutes validation. For instance, propositions which psychiatrists consider as well-tested, experimental psychologists hardly view as tested at all. See, for example, H. J. Eysenck, "The Effects of Psychotherapy: An Evaluation," *Journal of Consulting Psychology*, Vol. 16 (1952), pp. 319–324.

52. See, for example, T. F. Tout, "The Emergence of a Bureaucracy," in Robert K. Merton, Ailsa P. Gray, Barbara Hockey, and Hanan C. Selvin (eds.), *Reader in Bureaucracy* (New York: Free Press, 1952), pp. 68–79.

53. See Harold K. Jacobson and Eric Stein, *Diplomats, Scientists, and Politicians* (Ann Arbor, Mich.: University of Michigan Press, 1966). See Wiesner, *Where Science and Politics Meet, op. cit.*, and Barber, *The Politics of Research, op. cit.* On the mobilization of a group of scientists in an attempt to prevent the dropping of the first atomic bomb, see James R. Newman, "Big Science, Bad Science," *New York Review of Books*, August 5, 1965, pp. 10–12. See also footnote 55.

54. The dynamics of this process were discussed above in Chapter 7.

55. On this point, see Adam Yarmolinsky, "Shadow and Substance in Politics (2): Ideas Into Programs," *The Public Interest*, No. 2 (Winter, 1966), pp. 70–79. For an intellectual's interpretation of the problems of Negro family life and the ramifications of his report in both governmental and non-governmental circles alike, see Lee Rainwater and William L. Yancey, *The Moynihan Report and the Politics of*

Controversy (Cambridge, Mass.: Massachusetts Institute of Technology Press, 1967); for more discussion of the same point, see Cecil H. Uyehara, "Scientific Advice and the Nuclear Test Ban Treaty," in Lakoff, *Knowledge and Power: Essays on Science and Government, op. cit.*, pp. 112–161, and Francis L. Loewenheim (ed.), *The Historian and the Diplomat: The Role of History and Historians in American Foreign Policy* (New York: Harper & Row, 1967). Joan W. Moore and Burton M. Moore, "The Role of the Scientific Elite in the Decision to Use the Atomic Bomb," *Social Problems*, Vol. 6 (Summer, 1958), pp. 78–85. See also footnote 53.

56. Discussing the role of intellectuals, Seymour Martin Lipset cites *Harper's* Editor John Fischer's comment that "The Eisenhower administration employs more professors than the New Deal ever did." See Lipset's *Political Man: The Social Bases of Politics* (Garden City, N.Y.: Doubleday, 1960), p. 333.

57. Arthur M. Schlesinger, Jr., *A Thousand Days, op. cit.*, pp. 667 ff.

CHAPTER 9

Societal Knowledge:

Its Distribution and Reallocation

T HUS FAR, the knowledge of each actor or group of actors has been treated independently, and the intra-unit organization of knowledge has been explored. We now deal with the role of societal knowledge in affecting the relations *among* societal units. The major assumption on which the following discussion rests is that knowledge, both as a product and in terms of the facilities for its production, can be fruitfully viewed as a societal asset, and that the distribution of this asset among collectivities and societies significantly affects their position in this stratification structure and their political interaction. The macroscopic significance of knowledge-distribution, as we shall see, is an important factor in terms of which the modern and the post-modern periods differ.

Generally, when units interact, the most knowledgeable unit—all other things equal—will be the most effective. We say "generally" because an actor might overinvest in the production of knowledge, neglecting other functional needs and, thus, undermine his goals, the advancement of which depends on balancing the service of the various needs.[1]* Thus, there is an equivalent on the macro-level of the inactive scholar—ancient Athens, toward the end of the Golden Age, for instance—but such "reflective" societal units are not common. Underinvestment in the production of knowledge, especially in those aspects of knowledge more directly geared to reality-testing, is much more prevalent.

The Symbolization of Society: A Historical Trend

Growth of the Symbolic Sector

Historically, we suggest, there has been a secular trend in which symbols have become increasingly significant, while the relative importance of objects has declined.† This trend began in the modern period but seems to have accelerated since the advent of the post-modern era. Here we deal mainly with the sector of the symbolic realm in which the trend is most visible—societal knowledge. The increased symbolization of society is of twofold interest: Symbolic elements, as suggested above, are more malleable than objects, and therefore, the greater the role of symbolic elements in a society, the more readily, at least potentially, that society may be recast; and the controlling processes (as well as those processes which are controlled) are, as we have seen, more symbolic than uncontrolled societal processes. Consequently, an increased symbolization of societal processes in principle increases the societal capacity to actualize the potential inherent in the increased malleability of society.

Indications of the growth in the role of symbolic elements can be seen in the main sectors of post-modern societies. Beginning with the economic sector, the United States by 1958 became the first society in which more than half of the labor force was involved in the tertiary, service sector of the economy while less than half was employed in mining, agriculture, and manufacturing.[2] Services differ from primary and secondary productive activities in that they deal more with symbols and less with objects. The economies of other societies, as they progress further into the post-modern age, seem to be following a similar pattern.

---

* The reference notes for this chapter appear on page 214.

† On symbolic elements in society, see Albert Salomon, "Symbols and Images in the Constitution of Society," and Alfred Schutz, "Symbol, Reality and Society," in Lyman Bryson, Louis Finkelstein, Hudson Hoagland, R. M. MacIver, eds., *Symbols and Society* (New York: Conference on Science, Philosophy and Religion in Their Relation to the Democratic Way of Life, 1955, Distributed by Harper & Brothers, New York), pp. 103–133, and 135–203.

A proposition similar to ours was advanced by Daniel Bell, "Notes on the Post-Industrial Society (I)," *The Public Interest* No. 6 (Winter, 1967), pp. 27–28.

Among the service industries, one may distinguish a sub-sector—increasingly referred to as the knowledge industry—which includes research and development, education, and communications.[3] One author has estimated that total expenditure for knowledge in the United States in 1958 was almost 29 per cent of the GNP,[4] and the continued growth of the knowledge industry, absolute and relative, was widely expected.

This growth in the role of symbolic elements is not limited to the economic sector. The proportion of the total military expenditure spent on research and development has sharply risen since the advent of the post-modern period. It has been suggested that beginning with the early 1960s, the strategic arms race between the superpowers is to be measured less in quantitative terms, such as the numbers of missiles and nuclear weapons, and more in qualitative terms, such as the speed at which a country is able to shift from obsolescent models to newer ones (e.g., from fluid to solid propellant missiles). These qualitative developments are largely dependent on research and development.[5] The growing importance of research for health is well known. It is illustrated by the fact that since the beginning of the post-modern period, the number of research MDs has grown much more rapidly than the number of MDs engaged in medical treatment. The total expenditure of the United States on research and development has risen from $1.5 billion in 1945 to an estimated $17.3 billion in 1963.[6] The total expenditure on knowledge, both in absolute figures and as a percentage of GNP, has grown similarly[7]. While the increase is not expected to continue at the same rate, one characteristic which distinguishes post-modern from modern societies is a large, permanent—and probably growing—sector devoted to the production of knowledge.

Between 1960 and 1965, the United States government spent considerably more on research and development than on three other "permanent" sectors combined—subsidies to farmers, support to veterans of all previous wars, and foreign aid. Parallel statistics on the Soviet Union are not readily available, but trends in the USSR also indicate the increasing importance of research and development.[8] And even though their rate of increase is lower, other industrialized nations have moved in the same direction as they are entering the post-modern period.

Education as a Base of Stratification

A second reason that society is becoming more symbolic is that the foundations of stratification are becoming more symbolic and therefore more malleable as the importance of education as a stratification base increases while that of economic factors declines. While education does have an "objective" base, and while there are growing similarities between a university with large government contracts and an R & D corporation, education is still much more symbolic than even post-modern economic activities. This holds both for the differences in the products of the two kinds of societal activities and for their processes of production. The product of educational activities is a change in the state of the mind and character of those educated. Since the process through which this change is produced is based chiefly on interactions between the educators and those gaining an education, facilities and material are *relatively* unimportant.

The role of education is becoming even more important with the transition from the modern to the post-modern period. Formal higher education geared to specific industrial, technical, or professional needs (as distinct from "diffuse" religious or humanistic education)[9] is a typical feature of modern societies and is a component of modernization in developing countries. With the transition to the post-modern society, new and added emphasis is given to specialized education in terms of the proportion of the population that acquires a professional or graduate education,[10] the length of the median stay in educational institutions,[11] and the underemployment of less educated groups along with the overemployment of more educated ones.[12]

The increase in the portion of the population which has received higher education and the extension of the years of education are accompanied by changes both in the role of education in the stratification structure of society and in the relations between the economic and educational basis of status: As societies move deeper into the post-modern period, there seems to be a slow but definite shift from education as a reflection of economic relationships to education as a determinant of such relationships.[13] In modern pluralistic societies, the societal status of a person seems to have been more determined by the income and wealth of his parents and by his ethnic and racial origins than is the case in the post-modern period.[14] While educational achievements, even in the post-modern period, are still significantly affected by ascribed societal status,[15] the trend seems to be toward a *relative* freeing of education from such "background" factors. This has been attained, to a very limited degree, through societal guidance toward a less inegalitarian *allocation of educational resources* among units, be they nations, parts of nations, or neighborhoods in cities.[16] A more significant gain in this regard was effected by proceeding the other way around—by moving members from lower status groups to better educational institutions via special recruitment mechanisms, fellowships, and assistance in "catching up."

As the pattern of access to education has changed, the stratification effect of education has also increased: Although higher education is not becoming the only major basis of mobility (with the non-college educated constituting the lower class, the college educated the middle class, and holders of higher degrees the upper classes[17]), education still seems to be of increasing significance in determining economic status.[18] Also, the normative weight and prestige value of education have increased. Thus, education's role as a general basis of status, of stratification, has grown. And, in that sense, societal structure has become more symbolic and more malleable. (Statements about trends presented in this section ought to be viewed as propositions, like other statements included in this volume. We add this note here because the data seems particularly conflicting and cannot be discussed here.)

Knowledge as a Propellant of Transformation

The increasing role of knowledge as a transforming force has been recognized in studies of the development of new nations and of the economic growth of older ones. Economists formerly stressed the accumulation of capital or the development of specific industries as a "take-off" base for economic development. More recently, however, several leading economists have emphasized the significance of investment in "human" capital, in education and training.[19]

Similarly, there is a growing recognition of the role of investment in research and development in providing for the continued economic growth of developed nations. In the modern period, many economists, especially of the left, expected capitalism to die of overcapacity. They argued that the ability to produce would outgrow demand, and subsequent unemployment and further decline in demand would lead to the collapse of the economy. When capitalism did not collapse, increasing stress was placed on the role of innovation, of finding new products to create new demands.[20] For a while, it was held that "prosperity depends on investment, investment on technology, and technology on science. Ergo, prosperity depends on science."[21] More recently, it became evident that special conditions must be met for the knowledge industry to have the expected transforming power. Between 1958 and 1963, for example, Britain increased its expenditures on research and development by almost 60 per cent, but its economy grew at a much slower pace. This points to the fact that a mere increase in the size of the knowledge industry does not proportionally spur the economy. In the United States, federal expenditures on research and development grew from $3.1 billion in 1953 to $10.4 billion in 1962, but the economic growth rate was smaller than in the preceding ten years when the R & D investments were below $3 billion.[22]

Recent inquiries have devoted increased attention to the analysis of the conditions under which knowledge has a greater or smaller propellant force. This question has both substantive and analytic aspects. Substantively, the knowledge industry in pluralistic societies is more nationally guided than most other industries. In the United States, for instance, almost two-thirds of all R & D expenditures are financed by the federal government, *and* the government itself purchases most of the products.[23] That is, the government not only finances the activity, leaving the actual control to other authorities (as is largely the case with medical and educational activities), but also specifies the products ordered and checks the output.

The implications of this extensive national control of the knowledge industry for the societal effects of new knowledge are not clear. Some argue that it retards the innovative capacity of the knowledge industry and, thus, curtails its transforming effect. Others, noting that the main alternative to a nationally guided knowledge industry is private enterprise, argue that private knowledge-production would have even less transforming force. A third possibility is the public but non-governmental ownership and organization of the knowledge industry, as in "private" universities. While this may remove many of the constraints on the innovative orientation of knowledge production, there is little assurance that the knowledge thus produced will be encompassing and societally relevant. In short, the modes of the societal control of knowledge production—and not just the size of the sector—greatly affect the extent of the transforming effect of new knowledge and its role as a societal factor.

Analytically, the relationships between the differential distribution of investment in various knowledge sectors (governmental, other public, private) and the differential propelling force of various kinds of new knowledge are of major interest because they focus attention on the fact that societies differ greatly not only in the degrees to which their collectivities are integrated but also in the degrees to which their various functional sectors are linked. "Functional sector" refers to all the activities of a societal unit that are chiefly devoted to the service of one societal function, e.g., education. ("Institutions" refers to the normative principles applied in the societal regulation of such activities.) We shall refer to these links between functional sectors as *cross-sectoral links*. The weaker the links between any two sectors, the less likely is a change in one of them to cause a change in the other (referred to as secondary-priming, because the change is not originated in this other sector). Cross-sectoral links are a major factor in studies of development (to what degree can a modern occupational sector develop with a traditional or transitional socialization and procreation sector?), of political unification (can two or more societies merge their economies without merging their polities?), and of societal knowledge (which knowledge-sectors' expansions "spill over" to a greater extent into economic growth?).

One explanation for the relatively small secondary-priming effect of the United States and the British knowledge-industries is their heavy concentration on military and space R & D.[24] Of the more than $14.8 billion spent by the Federal government in the United States in fiscal year 1965 for research and development, more than 89 per cent was spent on space and defense. The suggestion that military and space research is particularly unproductive from this viewpoint—as compared to medical, social, and civilian research—calls attention to several generic inter-sectoral barriers: (a) For knowledge to have a large secondary-priming effect, relatively free communication between the knowledge sector and the other societal sectors is necessary; studies of military and space research suggest that secrecy may be a major inter-sector barrier.[25] (b) New knowledge seems to flow more readily among sectors that are similar in their functional requirements. Military and space research is reported to produce esoteric products and techniques—especially in its attempts to anticipate "hostile" environments—and this sets this research apart from the needs of most of the civilian economy,[26] which deals with "friendly" environments. For instance, products made for outer space or war conditions are overhardened and unnecessarily precise for the living room or swimming pool. (c) The question of property rights to new knowledge generates a set of new problems, from the question of copyright to the right to a finding made in military research that has civilian applications. The low capacity for legal innovation—e.g., formulating, gaining the legislation, and enforcing a new copyright law—has also been a barrier.[27]

Much more leverage is exercised, we suggest, by research and development sectors which are linked to a greater degree to the rest of society, such as medical, consumer, and social research. Western European societies, whose research and development expenditures in the 50s and early 60s were largely civilian, had a higher economic growth rate than the United States, whose investment in military and space R & D in the same period was 82 per cent of the total R & D budget.[28] Thus, it seems that if investments in knowledge are to propel a national economy and to generate related societal changes, for the *societal* role of knowledge to increase, investments must occur in those knowledge sectors most closely linked to the other societal sectors. It is, thus, not merely a question of more versus less investment in knowledge, but into which knowledge sectors new investments are channeled.

Symbolization and Inter-Actor Penetration

An unanticipated consequence of the growth of symbolization in post-modern societies is the macroscopic effect of differences in the technology of penetration (e.g., surveillance electronics) on interaction among societal units, a factor which had only marginal importance in earlier periods. *Penetration* refers to the capacity of one actor to learn the internal processes of another by linking one of his review overlays to the other actor's control processes. Guided societal units were often concerned with discovering the actual goals, policies, and internal relations of other societal units,[29] but in earlier periods such penetration was limited both in capacity and subject matter.[30]

The fact that the new technology of penetration has been the subject of popular treatments should not hinder serious analysis of its socio-political consequences for the post-modern period.[31] The significance of the new technology derives only in part from the fact that its instruments can be miniaturized and concealed or that their operative range and power has been greatly increased; another important factor is the change in societal processes. As the activities of a social unit become more symbolic and guided, penetration becomes more consequential. Thus, if the production plans of a factory which produces capital goods are discovered by a competitor who does not have the means of producing such goods, the plans themselves will not provide them. On the other hand, when the assets are largely symbolic, as in the post-modern drug industry where new research findings constitute the major value of a new product, their communication to a competitor may provide the opportunity for a major gain.[32] Similarly, if two producers, let us say, of tooth paste, turn out practically identical products whose differential value is based on image-differentiation, one company may make a major gain in obtaining the advertising plans of the other[33] by building its advertising on its competitor's plans. On the international level, the decoding of secret messages sent by a government to its diplomatic representatives in other countries is more consequential the more the world-wide guidance of foreign policy comes from the national capital.[34]

The exploration of the societal effects of the new technologies of penetration (and the related communications–knowledge technology) illustrates one unanticipated consequence of the increase in the symbolization of society—the increased potential not only for societal malleability but also for societal manipulability; other factors which increase the symbolization of society have the same basic effect.[35] The full effect of these factors, however, cannot be understood until we take into account that they do not affect all the actors involved to the same degree. The differential distribution of knowledge, its societal effects, and the capacity of societies to guide the distribution of this resource among their members are, consequently, our next subjects.

Distribution, Redistribution and Guidance

Skewed Distribution

We have already suggested that the amount and quality of societal knowledge significantly affect societal action; that the role of societal knowledge has grown historically; and that the large-scale use of knowledge requires investment of assets, development of new forms of societal organization (such as research organizations), and institutional patterns (such as freedom for fundamental criticism and contact between political and "knowledge" elites). We suggest, therefore, that (a) *these assets and techniques for the production, processing, and application of knowledge are unevenly distributed among societies and collectivities;* and that (b) *the inequality in the distribution of knowledge is greater than that of many other assets, especially utilitarian ones.*[36] The more significant knowledge becomes in affecting interaction, the greater will be the effect of this inequality. The developed countries annually invest more in their knowledge industry than developing nations invest in all their means of production combined.[37]

There is a significant emigration of highly trained men from "have-not" to "have" countries.[38] Moreover, inventions made in "have-not" countries are rapidly bought by "have" countries, but the opposite flow seems much smaller. As a consequence of all these factors, (c) *inequality in knowledge grows continually.*

Similar inequalities exist within societies. For instance, the most affluent states in the United States have almost twice times the income per capita of the poorest states, and many states have no high-quality institutions of higher learning, and their generally inadequate secondary schools make their use of the universities of other states problematic. Fifty per cent of R & D expenditures were concentrated in three states (California, New York, and Massachusetts).[39] Similar inequalities are common within other societies.

Some Illustrations

Since we have just discussed the effects of the new technology of penetration, let us consider the effects of its uneven distribution among societal actors. Similar illustrations could be provided for other knowledge-industries.[40] As long as manufacturers of drugs, toothpaste, or arms regularly inter-penetrate each other, the effects of such inter-penetration are likely to "cancel out" and some arrangement to limit inter-penetration may be developed. But when the advantage is unbalanced, the new penetration technology becomes a major source of power. It allows one actor to "read" the signals of the controlling overlayer of another without reciprocal capacities on the part of the other actor. Furniture salesmen, thus, gain a unilateral advantage by "reading" the intentions of their customers with listening devices in their showrooms;[41] corporations benefit from installing hidden microphones in places where their employees gather; authoritarian and totalitarian governments use the new technology of penetration to render indigenous opposition even more ineffective; and industrialized nations magnify their capacities to sway underdeveloped ones.[42]

In the early and mid-1960s, the Soviet Union and the United States based strategic defense increasingly on their missile technologies. The missiles with larger yields and longer ranges were land-based (as distinct from those carried by submarines which had comparatively smaller yields and shorter ranges). The United States protected its land-based missile force largely by "hardening" their emplacements; the USSR tried to conceal the placements. This meant that prevention of communication-penetration was much more important for the USSR's national security than for that of the United States. One may wish to reverse the statement to read that the USSR based its security on concealment because it was, or thought it was, more able to prevent communication-penetration, and the statement still holds true.

Gaining knowledge about other actors is only in part a question of "illegitimate" activities. Open sources are probably the most effective way of penetration. But in practice the two correlate; societal units which are more able to penetrate others illicitly tend also to be those which have a significantly greater capacity to obtain and process open information, from observation-satellites to sociological surveys.

Social science plays a role in both overt and covert inter-unit penetration, especially when the political attitudes of members of societal units other than the acting one are involved. The United States regularly surveys the attitudes of citizens of other countries toward its policy, which helps in its negotiations with these nations, in its information policy toward them, and in formulating its alliance policies.[43] In earlier generations, the ruling classes surveyed the attitudes of the poor.[44] Some such information gathering existed in ancient China, Egypt, and Greece. But these efforts were sporadic, almost completely qualitative, usually unreliable, and of limited sociopolitical importance. The systematic and regular use of relatively reliable social science techniques for such purposes significantly alters their scope and effect. The availability of these techniques for penetration purposes is stratified (among nations—in favor of the developed ones; among classes—in favor of the more affluent and more innovative ones; and among political units—in favor of those in office).[45] And, again, their macroscopic effects rest in their unequal distribution.[46]

Is Knowledge a Scarce Commodity?

One characteristic of knowledge somewhat mitigates the effect of its particularly skewed distribution: Unlike other products, the output of the knowledge sector is to some extent not subject to the laws of scarcity and of supply and demand. Knowledge is a pattern of symbols, and symbols can be transmitted without being lost. The teacher possesses no less knowledge after he has taught; nor does a book hold less information after it has been read. The American people are no less healthy if the findings of American medical research are made available to other countries. However, this characteristic of knowledge has fewer mitigating effects than might at first be expected. (a) There is *some* loss involved in the sharing of knowledge. The teacher who trains others is reducing, at least in some circumstances, the market for his skills. (b) Knowledge has carriers in the material world which are subject to the laws of scarcity—i.e., a book used by one student cannot be used at the same time by others. Moreover, both books and teachers have amortization rates.

While in some sectors of the knowledge industry, especially teaching and "arm chair" research, the role of material resources is *relatively* small, most societal investment is in applied research and development where the object components are *relatively* significant. Thus, the findings of American medical research may be made available to other nations, but often their application requires expensive medical technology and trained personnel. Engineers, unlike books, cannot be cheaply transported and reproduced. Hence, ultimately knowledge resources must be taken from some in order to be given to others, or—if the resources are new—some have to give up their claims to them if the less endowed are to gain.

The same holds for the distribution of resources among the goals of one societal actor. At any one time, knowledge resources are unevenly available for various societal goals. In the fiscal year 1965, the United States invested more than 55 per cent of the federal R & D budget (which accounted for about two-thirds of the national R & D expenditures) in military R & D and more than 34 per cent in space R & D (half of which was indirectly military). The rest, less than 11 per cent, was devoted to medical, social, international, and all other civilian research.[47] In part, this distribution reflected the strong emphasis on military goals; it roughly paralleled the percentage of the non-R & D federal budget that was spent on the military, although it was disproportionate on space (4.3 per cent of the non-R & D budget vs. 34 per cent of R & D). Aside from deliberate priorities, however, the distribution reflected other factors, such as the quality of the political leadership of various federal agencies and congressional committees, the public appeal of the respective activities of these agencies, and the relevance of these activities to international versus domestic values. NASA, for instance, led by a publicity-minded, politically astute elite and supported by two Congressional committees, related its lunar project to the cold war and gained much more support than the timid, domestic-minded, basic research of the National Science Foundation.[48] That is, the allocation of knowledge-investments among various national usages did not parallel national needs and purposes because of the impact of "irrelevant" considerations; there were not enough disposable* resources for all goals. And thus, here too, if some goals were to be more fully served, others would have to yield some of the R & D resources they previously commanded.

Societal Guidance of the Knowledge-Sector

To what degree does a societal unit, even a post-modern one, command the capacity for the internal reassignment of knowledge resources? Does the distribution of knowledge resources respond largely to other processes—e.g., the outcome of inter-agency rivalries—or can it be made to respond to national goals and needs?[49] A major need for the societal guidance of

---

* "Disposable" resources refer to the resources available for distribution to the unit under study. It is often argued that an affluent society can afford to satisfy both its military and civilian needs. But affluence here characterizes the total societal assets and not those available to the political overlayer. While the amount of disposable income may be increased, there are sharp limits to the degree to which this can be done, *and* at each point in time, whatever the amount of resources available, the pattern of their allocation constitutes an analytically independent question.

knowledge arises not from the incompatibility between societal priorities and the distribution of knowledge resources, but from the anti-social applications of some of these resources. This cybernetic issue is illustrated by the marketing of insufficiently tested drugs,[50] which suggested the need for some governmental regulation of the knowledge-industries. At the beginning of the post-modern period, there were almost no such regulations. Since then, they have evolved primarily in the highly industrialized societies but are still absent or ineffectual in most others. And even in the United States, the United Kingdom, and Western Germany, such regulations seem to lag far behind the societal needs.[51]

At the advent of the post-modern period, the conception of the *national* guidance of the production and use of knowledge was alien to the Western tradition. It was still believed that scientists are best left free to pursue whatever paths they wish.[52] While this was rarely explicitly stated, it was widely assumed that *the society has to adjust to the societal implications of new knowledge*.

This was part of the very ideology that supported the rise of industrial society. The Industrial Revolution was an encompassing societal change carried out largely by the accommodation of old institutions to newly invented machines and means of transportation, and by the evolution of new societal institutions, such as work segregated from family and the modern metropolis, geared to industrial needs. The changes entailed are widely viewed as desirable *on balance* because the resulting increase in utilitarian assets provided for greater realization of many values. While numerous social critics suggested that society would have done better without both the "benefits" and "costs" of industrialization, or that many of the benefits could have been achieved at a much lower societal cost, these criticisms had little effect on the evolution of industrial society. At least those in power accepted societal adjustment to rather than guidance of technological change.[53] (The fact that many of the gains were evident late in the transition, while the costs were apparent earlier, is a further indication of the at least implicit acceptance of the change.)

It is essential to observe, from our viewpoint, that no society has had any real choice in the matter. When the steam engine was invented in Britain, neither the government nor any other societal agency reviewed the consequences of its spread before mass production began. Actually, few could foresee the scope of mechanization, and Britain was neither aware of the consequences of mechanization nor in command of the instruments necessary to guide its development. Since the 1760s, British society largely has been accommodating to a technological revolution, a process that has not yet been completed. Societal guidance mechanisms of the United States, Germany, and other "late comers" do not seem to have greatly benefited from the British experience; they were too weak to be able to collect, analyze, absorb, and utilize this knowledge.

It may be said that while the society made no such decision, a prevailing sub-society did. But while the new industrial class probably on balance favored the transition, most of the members of the rural and aristocratic classes did not; the latter, however, did not have the capacities to block the transformation. Moreover, there is no evidence that the industrial class was aware of the societal world it was creating and the effects it would have on others and on the lives of its own members. After all, they were not exempted from the rising rates of suicide, crime, alcoholism, and mental disturbance. Possibly, if the members of the industrial class had met in a town hall in 1800 and been informed of all the desirable and undesirable outcomes of their efforts, they may still have opted for industrialization. However, no such meeting—or its socio-political equivalent—took place, and given the societal guidance capacities in 1800, the collective decision that would have been made probably could not have prevented industrialization. It perhaps was even more difficult for "late comers"; while they could see the effects of industrialization on other societies, they also faced the pressure of the new power that industrialization gave to these other societies.

Societal guidance capacities have increased since the Industrial Revolution which marked the advent of the modern age, but the major technological invention that led to the initiation of the post-modern period was still accommodated to rather than guided by societies; they barely estimated rather than systematically attempted to anticipate and affect the resultant societal changes. The American and British governments set out to develop atomic and thermonuclear weapons with only rather limited ideas of their international and societal implications[54] and without public knowledge or consent.

At present, scientists in various laboratories explore chemical means of controlling behavior; psychological research is being conducted that could lead to effective subliminal advertising; and drugs are being developed that will enable parents to choose the sex of their children.[55] The societal forces that will promote the introduction of these new technologies when they become available are already present. They include the military (e.g., use of chemical means of warfare),[56] private industry (e.g., subliminal advertising), and the universities, who tend to favor uninhibited and public research on almost everything (e.g., sex research). Thus, conceptions of national interest, financial profit, and truth all play a role. There is, however, no societal agency that systematically attempts to explore the implications of new technologies. While social critics occasionally discuss these implications (largely after the technology itself is available), they do not command the necessary resources and professional staff for comprehensive study and testing. Furthermore, their access to and capacity to communicate with the decision-makers are limited. Agencies in charge of overseeing segments of the knowledge–industry—the American Food and Drug Administration, for instance—are politically weak, understaffed, and underfinanced and have narrow jurisdiction.[57] Other agencies are controlled by the very forces which promote the use of the new technologies, and they are critical only about details. Thus, for example, the RAND Corporation, financed chiefly by the United States Air Force, was critical of some weapons systems[58] but is most unlikely to promote an inquiry into the validity of the basic community-of-assumptions of the Air Force itself: Potent and varied military technologies provide the mainstay of national security.

In short, we suggest that post-modern societies still have a basically passive, accommodating view of the relations between technology and society. This issue becomes more macroscopic as (a) more research is conducted, (b) its yields are more rapidly injected into the society, and (c) more research is oriented not toward realizing such consensual goals as health but toward class or nationalistic goals.

The adjustments that societies make to new technologies are themselves often a kind of societal cost; it is, however, spread among several sub-societies, and the total cost to any one sub-society may well not reach a "crisis" level. If all the costs of industrialization had been imposed on the workers, they might have rebelled or their productivity might have fallen so low as to make the system unworkable. But typically, other classes are also affected. Whatever the severity and distribution of the dislocations caused by industrialization, the basic question remains: Can society continually accommodate to whatever new technologies are thrust upon it by a growing knowledge industry and its commercial and political allies? In normative terms, does the value of unlimited freedom for researchers outweigh the possible consequences for billions of people, generation after generation? In morphological terms, can research be contextually guided without being stifled?

It may be argued that the sub-societies, which favor uninhibited research and promote the societal introduction of the findings—such as the managerial classes, the drug industry, or the armed services—have a higher anticipatory capacity than the rest of the society (including the government). It may be further argued that the issue is not a lack of societal investment in anticipation and control of the technological developments but rather a societal lack of will and power *vis-à-vis* these sub-societies. Our proposition is that while a lack of power over these sub-societies partially accounts for a society's inability to guide its technology, part of the deficiency is due to a lack of societal investment in the attempt to ascertain the consequences of new knowledge. From this viewpoint, the various partisans of technology are not much more effective than the representatives of society as a whole.

Second, because of the pluralistic nature of societal decision-making, the capacity of these sub-societies to *control* technological developments is even smaller than their ability to *anticipate* the societal consequences implicit in the new technologies. If, for instance, one industry decides to forego subliminal advertising, others may not follow suit; only a central societal guidance system could prevent the spread of such advertising.* Thus, our exploration of the guidance of knowledge returns us to the question of the *societal* capacity for such guidance.

It may be argued that it is irrelevant to focus on the production of knowledge because the uses to which society puts new knowledge are not determined by the nature of the knowledge but depend on the structure and organization of the society itself. For example, if and when subliminal advertising is available routinely and inexpensively, it will be used differently in Communist China than in the United States. While this is a valid observation, it does not follow that the nature of the new input is inconsequential. Actually, one of the surprising features of this problem is that societies which vary on many dimensions similarly "succumb" to basically the same technologies, such as unsafe cars, the mass production of cigarettes, or the mass use of water-polluting detergents. He who contends that these technologies are promoted chiefly by a power elite and its societal allies (e.g., automobile manufacturers) will have to recognize that the similar technologies (e.g., unsafe cars) have similar a-social effects in social-democratic *and* Communist nations. Of course, vested interests do have an effect, and occasionally the same basic distortion (e.g., neglect of safety) is caused by different factors. We seek to stress, however, that the capacity for the societal guidance of the use of knowledge is one central factor, and it is low in societies that differ significantly in their socio-political and economic structures.

Post-modern pluralistic societies seem to exhibit a historical tendency toward a slow increase in the societal guidance of knowledge. A much larger increase, however, is needed if a society is to be active in this area. A central element for the additional growth of the societal guidance of knowledge is more legitimation of such guidance. We may be able to learn about the conditions under which it will arise from the history of economic *laissez faire* as a conception of the societal organization of the production of goods and services. The decline in the legitimacy of economic *laissez faire* policies preceded the decline of *laissez faire* in the organization of the production of knowledge, just as the mass production of goods and its subsequent dislocations preceded the mass production of knowledge and its dislocations. By now, economic control is widely legitimated, for it is recognized that there is only little actual *laissez faire* production of goods, many societal values require some guidance of the economy, and prescriptive state control of the economy is only one, and probably not the most effective, form of societal guidance.

While all these statements apply to the production of knowledge as well, the ideology of *laissez faire* still has much potency with regard to this industry, not only among liberals but also among the Left. Few are aware of the fact

---

* This issue is explored later in the chapters dealing with decision-making.

that in post-modern pluralistic societies, the production of knowledge is already more nationally guided than the rest of the economy. Secondly, federal control is either direct (so-called "in-house" research) or involves a high degree of specification of the product, and only rarely is there the "finance without strings" prescribed by the ideological model.

One major reason, as we suggested above, that such a comparatively high degree of national guidance has few "stifling" effects on the production of knowledge is that most of the knowledge production is applied research or development which can be contextually guided with few dysfunctions. The consumer industry has many closely-supervised researchers working on specific problems. While engineers and technicians are not so closely controlled or controllable as unskilled labor, neither are they usually as free "to follow any lead" as, it is said, the scientist is in his laboratory. Moreover, in most pluralistic societies, a national guidance mechanism began to develop in the second decade of the post-modern period. Congressional committees that specialize in "science," the office of Science and Technology in the White House, and the Ministry for Science in Britain are part of this kind of mechanism.[59] National academies and professional and disciplinary associations also provide some societal control.

In short, the problem is not only a lack of guidance per se but also deficient legitimation of the societal guidance of knowledge; a paucity of means and resources; the over-pluralistic, under-centralized nature of guidance systems; and the lack of an anticipatory and therefore preventive guidance system—at present most such mechanisms defer review until after the technology has been introduced, thus making "recall" much more costly, if not impossible, and engendering accommodation rather than creative adaptation.*

While totalitarian polities may well have experienced a control of the knowledge industry that was too extensive and too prescriptive for the full development of this industry—especially as far as basic research is concerned—even they do not seem to have amassed the means by which the reallocation of knowledge resources may be accomplished. For example, the concentration of educational facilities in the major cities of the Soviet Union is not in accord with the societal goals, but attempts to redistribute them are at best partially successful.[60] Thus, overcontrol of some areas (e.g, basic research, especially in genetics) may be combined with a deficient control capacity in others.

Active societal guidance of the knowledge industry requires a differential rather than a total increase in existing guidance mechanisms: It should be relatively extensive when dealing with applied research—and, especially, with development—and minimal in basic research. Thus, scientists can be free to

---

* On various arguments for and against this proposition, see the later chapter dealing with societal decision-making.

study genetics (and there might be no way to curb them without curbing science altogether). But when it comes to an application of these basic insights—e.g., the development of a drug which allows parents to determine the sex of their future child—much more thorough societal examination of the consequences, policy formation, and regulation, through a combination of public supervision and professional self-discipline, seem possible without undermining the bases of the production of knowledge. *Thus, the guidance of knowledge in an active society may well focus on the use of knowledge rather than on its production.*

A Genetic and a Synchronic Aspect

Although several of these societal guidance problems are generic and are discussed below in the section on decision-making, the societal guidance of knowledge has some unique features that are reviewed here. First, knowledge production has a *much longer lead time* than most other goods and services. Therefore the systematic programming involved in the creation of new facilities and in the training of new professional manpower is more important than is the case for most other assets. New funds can be quickly generated by a legislature by raising the level of taxation or national debt or by ordering the printing of money, and resources and unskilled manpower can be drafted by administrative decree. But no national power can immediately create large numbers of highly skilled and trained personnel. Some ability to accommodate does exist in the short run because there is usually some "slack" in most systems. Increased salaries can bring some housewives back to teaching; highly trained personnel can be more "economically" used; and some professionals can be recruited from abroad. But when large numbers are involved, more manpower implies more training, and more training means more facilities and more recruitment into the particular disciplines involved. These adaptations have a lead-time of from five to twenty-five years.[61] The adaptation time is relatively short if only under-graduates have to be "re-channeled," longer if the number of undergraduates itself has to be increased, and very long indeed if the input into the total educational apparatus has to be enlarged (in terms of those who do not "drop out" of its lower rungs) and improved (in terms of the psychological preparation of recruits). It is here that the collective base and the cybernetic guidance of the mobilization of resources for societal guidance are most highly articulated.

Second, there is a relationship between length of lead-time (and, hence, the need for programming) and breadth of *system analysis*. If the shortage appears only in one or a few areas of specialization, *lateral accommodations in the same system are likely to substitute for longitudinal adjustment (over time)*. For instance, instead of simply getting more people to study, incentives may be offered to encourage shifts to the specific fields in which there are shortages. On the other hand, if system analysis indicates that the "slack" is being exhausted, longitudinal programming will become more necessary. Without system analysis, attempts are likely to be made first for lateral adjustment, before experience (rather than anticipatory analysis) shows that such accommodation is not adequate. Moreover, system analysis suggests that the redistribution of professional manpower is more difficult to achieve than that of most other assets. Unskilled labor can be comparatively easily transferred from mission to mission and from region to region, but highly trained manpower can be reconverted only within limits and shifted only with high economic and psychological costs and mainly in times of national crisis. The tendency toward the overemployment of professionals and the underemployment of unskilled manpower in post-modern societies further magnifies the organizational problems of societal knowledge. Therefore, societal guidance of the knowledge industry even more than guidance in general requires considerable longitudinal and lateral programming. And programming, probably more than any other cybernetic capacity, requires societal awareness or consciousness, the element of the societal guidance capacities of active units which we next explore.

NOTES

1. Homans reports a case study of an engineering company whose very survival was endangered because it was overcommitted to the increase of knowledge to the neglect of its marketing. George C. Homans, *The Human Group* (New York: Harcourt, Brace & World, 1950), pp. 369–414.

2. Victor R. Fuchs, "Some Implications of the Growing Importance of the Service Industries," in *The Task of Economics*, Forty-Fifth Annual Report of the National Bureau of Economic Research, June, 1965, pp. 5–16, see esp. p. 6. See also Table II-1, p. 7.

3. For a list of such companies, see Leonard S. Silk, *The Research Revolution* (New York: McGraw-Hill, 1960), p. 177. The concept of "knowledge industry" has been developed by Fritz Machlup, *The Production and Distribution of Knowledge in the U.S.* (Princeton: Princeton University Press, 1962).

4. Machlup, *ibid.*, pp. 360–362. Machlup calculates the amount spent on knowledge in 1958 as $136,436 million. Depending on the time periods used, he estimates GNP as $478,300 million or, alternatively, $475,600 million. This difference, however, does not significantly affect the ratio of knowledge production to GNP.

5. By private communication with Professor Samuel P. Huntington.

6. The 1945 figure is taken from United States Bureau of the Census, *Statistical Abstract of the United States: 1957* (Washington, D.C.: Government Printing Office, 1957), p. 495, Table 606. The 1963 figure is taken from *Reviews of Data on Science Resources*, Vol. 1, No. 4 (Washington, D.C.: National Science Foundation, May, 1965), p. 6, Table 2a. Since the government has changed its statistical methods of accounting, the latter figure excludes basic research expenditures. The 1963 estimate was the latest available when this book was sent to press.

7. Machlup, *Production and Distribution . . .*, *op. cit.*, pp. 366–374.

8. Alexander Korol, *Soviet Research and Development: Its Organization, Personnel, and Funds* (Cambridge, Mass.: MIT Press, 1965). Nicholas De Witt, *Education and Professional Employment in the U.S.S.R., op. cit.*, pp. 525–529. See also Albert Parry, *The New Class Divided: Science and Technology versus Communism* (New York: Macmillan, 1966).

9. On this comparison of kinds of education, see *From Max Weber: Essays in Sociology*, translated, edited, and with an introduction by H. H. Gerth and C. Wright Mills (New York: Oxford University Press, 1949), pp. 426 ff.

10. In 1940, the total number of higher degrees earned in the United States was 216,521; in 1950, 498,373; and in 1965, 667,592. The number of doctorates earned in 1940 was 3,290; in 1950, 6,420; and in 1965, 16,467. Data taken from United States Census Bureau, *Statistical Abstract of the United States: 1966* (Washington, D.C.: Government Printing Office, 1966), p. 137, Table 194.

11. The median number of school years completed by the civilian labor force eighteen years old and over in October 1952 was 10.9. By March, 1965, the median had risen to 12.2. Data taken from *Manpower Report of the President* and U.S. Department of Labor, *A Report on Manpower Requirements, Resources, Utilization and Training* (Washington, D.C.: Government Printing Office, 1966), Table B-9, p. 189.

12. This point has been repeatedly made with references to "dropouts" and racial minorities in the United States. Moonlighting is common among professionals, whereas part-time employment at unproductive jobs and low pay is often the case for the uneducated. On the relationship between educational attainment and employment, see Edmund deS. Brunner and Sloan Wayland, "Occupation and Education," in A. H. Halsey, Jean Floud, and C. Arnold Anderson (eds.), *Education, Economy, and Society* (New York: The Free Press, 1961), p. 56. (See also Note 14.)

13. While there are serious problems in determining causality, the kind of data cited below illustrate the relationship. In 1949, the median income for males 14 years and over, who completed eight years of school was $2,533; for those who completed four years of high school, $3,285; and for those who completed four years of college or more, $4,407. In 1963, the annual mean income for males 25 to 64 years old, who completed eight years of school was $4,921; for those who completed four years of high school, $6,693; and for those who completed four years of college or more, $10,062. If the 1949 median income of those completing eight years of school is taken as a base of 100, the index of income of those who had completed four years of college or more is 175. If the 1963 annual mean income of those completing eight years of school is taken as a base of 100, the index of income of those who had completed four years of college or more had risen to 205. While data from both years are not directly comparable, they do seem to indicate a trend of increasing significance of education.

Data for 1949 median income are taken from 1953 *Statistical Abstract of the United States*, p. 112, Table 122. Data for 1963 mean annual income are taken from United States Census Bureau, *Statistical Abstract of the United States: 1966* (Washington, D.C.: Government Printing Office, 1966) p. 116, Table 158. Jean Floud and A. H. Halsey have written that "the old elites were based on birth and wealth, which ensured to their members a distinctive education. The elites of a technological society, however, are based on education and wealth. . . ." See their

"Introduction" to Halsey, Floud, and Anderson, *Education, Economy, and Society*, *op. cit.*, pp. 1–12, quoted from p. 6. We expect the same trend to continue in post-modern society and not just for members of the elite. See also Bernard Barber, *Social Stratification* (New York: Harcourt, Brace & World, 1957), pp. 390–402. (See also footnote 18.)

14. For a description of the situation toward the end of the modern period, see Elbridge Sibley, "Some Demographic Clues to Stratification," *American Journal of Sociology*, Vol. 28 (1942), pp. 322–330. On the situation in the post-modern period, see Seymour M. Lipset and Reinhard Bendix, *Social Mobility in an Industrial Society* (Berkeley: University of California Press, 1960), p. 101. For the argument and data that socio-economic background still has a greater effect on academic achievement than the quality of the schools themselves, see James S. Coleman, Ernest Q. Campbell et al., *Equality of Educational Opportunity* (Washington, D.C.: Government Printing Office, 1966).

15. Patricia Cayo Sexton, Natalie Rogoff, and Harry S. Ashmore, *The Negro and the Schools* (Chapel Hill: University of North Carolina Press, 1954). Dael Wolfle, *America's Resources of Specialized Talent* (New York: Harper & Row, 1954). See also A. Girard, "Selection for Secondary Education in France," in A. H. Halsey et al., *Education, Economy, and Society, op. cit.*, pp. 183–194, esp. p. 187. St. Clair Drake, "The Social and Economic Status of the Negro in the United States," in Talcott Parsons and Kenneth B. Clark, *The Negro American* (Boston: Houghton Mifflin, 1966), pp. 11–46 and U.S. Commission on Civil Rights report, *Public Schools, Negro and White* (Washington, Government Printing Office, 1962).

16. A high proportion of federal and foundations support are still provided to a few established centers, e.g., Massachusetts Institute of Technology, California Institute of Technology, Chicago University, Johns Hopkins University, Harvard, Yale, Princeton. University of California, Harvard, University of Michigan, Stanford, University of Wisconsin, Chicago University and Columbia University all received more than $1,500,000 for social research in federal domestic programs in fiscal year 1965. All other universities received substantially less. A staff study of *The Federal Use of Social Research in Federal Domestic Programs* (Washington, D.C.: Government Printing Office, 1967), p. 65.

17. For a review of several studies, see Bernard Berelson and Gary A. Steiner, *Human Behavior: An Inventory of Scientific Findings* (New York: Harcourt, Brace & World, 1964), pp. 437–440, and Gabriel Kolko, *Wealth and Power in America: An Analysis of Social Class and Income Distribution* (New York: Praeger, 1962), pp. 113–117. See also Michael Young, *The Rise of Meritocracy, 1870–2033: The New Elite of Our Social Revolution* (New York: Random House, 1958), Ch. IV, V, and VII.

18. On the increasing significance of education in determining economic status, see Patricia Cayo Sexton, *Education and Income: Inequalities of Opportunity in Our Public Schools* (New York: Viking Press, Compass Books Edition, 1961), pp. 13–15. Some data to this effect have been represented, for businessmen—by Mabel Newcomer, *The Big Business Executive* (New York: Columbia University Press, 1955). More generally, Paul G. Glick and Herman P. Miller, "Educational Level and Potential Income," *American Sociological Review*, Vol. 21 (1956), pp. 307–312; Ernest Havemann and Patricia S. West, *They Went to College* (New York:

Harcourt, Brace & World, 1952). Newcomer has more in time depth, less in sample breadth than other studies. For a study and reference to other works, see Martin Trow, "The Second Transformation of American Secondary Education," *International Journal of Comparative Sociology*, Vol. 11 (1961), pp. 144–166. For Britain, see T. H. Marshall, "Social Selection in the Welfare State," in Halsey, Floud, and Anderson, *Education, Economy and Society, op. cit.*, pp. 148–163. See also *A Report of the Central Advisory Council for Education* (London: H.M.S.O., 1959).

19. "Education and Economic Growth," *Sixtieth Yearbook of the National Society for the Study of Education*, 1961; Gary S. Becker, Frederick Harbison, and Charles H. Myers, *Education, Manpower, and Economic Growth* (New York: McGraw-Hill, 1964). Among those who stressed the importance of education as opposed to material factors in developing nations is Eugene Staley, *The Future of Underdeveloped Countries* (New York: Harper & Row, 1954), pp. 232–234. See also Everett E. Hagen, *On the Theory of Social Change: How Economic Growth Begins* (Homewood, Ill.: Dorsey Press, 1962), pp. 36–49. He also noted that most theories dealing with economic barriers to growth "assume that the central problem in growth is capital formation, and . . . that sufficient technological creativity to carry forward economic growth is present in all societies." Cf. Machlup, *Production and Distribution of Knowledge, op. cit.*, pp. 58 ff.

20. Joseph A. Schumpeter, *Socialism, Capitalism and Democracy*, 2nd ed. (New York: Harper & Row, 1947), pp. 132 ff. Recently this argument has been advanced by John Kenneth Galbraith, *The New Industrial State* (Boston: Houghton Mifflin 1967).

21. London *Economist*, October 5, 1963.

22. Data on the amount of federal expenditures on research, development, and R & D plant in fiscal years 1953 and 1962 is taken from National Science Foundation, *Federal Funds for Research, Development, and Other Scientific Activities, Fiscal Years 1965, 1966, and 1967, op. cit.*, p. 4, Table 2. One economist, using output per man-hour as an indicator of economic growth, has written "Since the 1920's— when it first emerged as a significant element in the American economy—the rise in expenditures for R & D (absolutely, and as a proportion of the total) has been quite phenomenal. . . . After 1953, while expenditures for R & D skyrocket, the rate of increase in output per man-hour slumps. In any case, no positive correlation whatsoever is evidenced between the national rate of economic growth and the national level of R & D expenditures." See Robert A. Solo, "Gearing Military R & D to Economic Growth," *Harvard Business Review*, Vol. 40 (Nov.–Dec., 1962), pp. 49–60, quoted from p. 50.

23. Of the estimated total of funds used in fiscal year 1963 for research and development, 65 per cent came from the federal government. See *Review of Data on Science Resources, op. cit.*, p. 8, Table 4.

24. For the amount of expenditures on military and space R & D in the United States in fiscal year 1963, see Note 47, see also Note 28.

25. See Edward A. Shils, *The Torment of Secrecy: The Background and Consequences of American Security Policies* (New York: The Free Press, 1956). Half of the research reports processed by the Department of Defense are classified and, with few exceptions, not available to civilian industry. Committee on Government Operations, *Availability of Information From Federal Departments and Agencies*

(Scientific Information and National Defense), (Washington, D.C.: Government Printing Office, 1958), esp. p. 31.

26. Jerome B. Wiesner, science adviser to President Kennedy, stated: "There is not nearly as direct an application of an Atlas Booster to the civilian economy as there was of the B-52 to the 707 (airplane). All through the military and space developments you see this divergence. There are going to be such very important general developments as better materials, better understanding of computers . . . but in the future there will not be nearly the same direct impact of military and space research on the civilian economy." (Unpublished communication).

The segregation of the military R & D also works the other way around: there is little in civilian research of central use to military innovation. A large scale project which traces the sources of 20 important military innovations found 86 per cent came from research directly funded by the Department of Defense; 9 per cent— by defense-oriented industry, and only 3 per cent by commercially oriented industry. See Chalmers W. Sherwin and Raymond S. Isenson, "Project Hindsight," *Science*, Vol. 156 (June 23, 1967), p. 1575.

27. On proposed reforms of the patent system, see the "Report of the President's Commission on the Patent System" (Washington, D.C.: Government Printing Office, 1966). For a discussion of the report, see Bryce Nelson, "U.S. Patent System: Commission Recommends Reforms to President," *Science*, Vol. 154 (1966), pp. 1629–1630, 1632.

28. On the differences in growth rates see Bruce M. Russett et al., *World Handbook of Political and Social Indicators* (New Haven, Conn.: Yale University Press, 1964), p. 155. As far as the composition of R & D is concerned, for instance, in 1961–1962, of total government R & D funds, while the United States spent 71.4 per cent on defense and the United Kingdom, 63.8 per cent, France spent only 55.4 per cent of its R & D funds for the same purpose. (Figures for France are for 1961.) See Christopher Freeman et al., *Science, Economic Growth, and Government Policy* (Paris: Organization for Economic Cooperation and Development, 1963), pp. 91 and 92, Tables 14B, 14C, and 14D. See also footnote 47. Other factors affected this difference in growth rate as well. There seems to be no research which could prove that the difference is significantly affected by variations in the composition of the knowledge industry. Moreover, in 1966 and 1967 there was an increasing complaint in Western Europe that the United States, because of its greater investment in R & D could achieve an advantage even when the proportion invested in civilian R & D was smaller than in Europe.

29. For recent accounts of spying, see Oleg Penkovskiy, *The Penkovskiy Papers*, translated by Peter Deriabin (Garden City, N.Y.: Doubleday, 1965), and Gordon Lonsdale's memoirs, *Spy: Twenty Years in Soviet Secret Service* (New York: Hawthorn, 1965).

30. See Paul W. Blackstock, *The Strategy of Subversion: Manipulating the Politics of other Nations* (Chicago: Quadrangle, 1964), p. 321 and *passim*. Richard W. Rowan points out that no major act of World War I was significantly affected by espionage. "Espionage," *Encyclopedia of Social Science*, Vol. V (1937), p. 594. This, we expect, does not hold for the post-modern period. See the accounts cited in footnote 29 for "macroscopic" effects of spying.

31. For a discussion of the extent of wiretapping and eavesdropping and

proposals for controls, see Edward V. Long, *The Intruders: The Invasion of Privacy by Government and Industry* (New York: Praeger, 1967).

32. The same holds for fashion designs, a multi-billion dollar industry. See Robert A. Dallas, "The Fashion Pirates: Their Booty is the Treasure of Design," *The New York Times*, January 25, 1966.

33. On the effects on a sales campaign of Proctor and Gamble and on industrial spying in general, see Lawrence Stessin, " 'I Spy' Becomes Big Business," *New York Times Magazine*, Nov. 28, 1965, pp. 105–108. In the case of Time-O-Matic, two employees were brought to suit. One argued that he took nothing but "a mental picture." The company argued that this allowed those who retained him "to compete with Time-O-Matic on equal terms by sparing them the necessity of spending time and money in acquiring the knowledge." *Ibid.*

34. On the use of listening devices in diplomatic circles, James Reston reports that ". . . the F.B.I. has been bugging the telephones of foreign embassies, not merely to gather military information that could be vital during a major crisis, but to get diplomatic information that might be useful in some awkward diplomatic situation." See "Washington: The Kennedy–Hoover Controversy," *The New York Times*, December 11, 1966. On a specific case of eavesdropping, see "Officials Say F.B.I. Has Bugged Dominican Embassy Since 50's," *The New York Times*, December 3, 1966.

During the second Sinai Campaign in June, 1967, Israeli forces listened to exchanges between Nasser, UAR President, and Jordan's King Hussein. *The New York Times*, June 9, 1967, p. 17. It seems that these leaders did not have the same access to communications among the Israeli leaders. At the same time, a U.S. "communication" ship was hit when it neared the combat zone. It was implied that the ship was "eavesdropping." *Ibid.*, p. 19.

35. See Chapter 21 for additional discussion.

36. For developing nations, see Frederick Harbison and Charles A. Myers, *Education, Manpower, and Economic Growth* (New York: McGraw-Hill, 1964), p. 45. The figures by Harbison and Myers do not show the full measure of the gap in terms of quality of personnel, the use of professional employees for non-professional purposes (e.g., several of the few trained Tanzanians hold elective offices), and that Africanization further increases the gap. (Technical assistance from abroad does seem not to make up for the loss.)

37. Machlup reports that total expenditures for knowledge in the United States in 1958 were $136,436 million. *The Production and Distribution . . ., op. cit.*, p. 360. In 1960, the GNP of, for example, Ecuador, was only $759 million; of Pakistan, $7,489 million; and of Ethiopia, $812 million. William M. Sprecher, *World-Wide Defense Expenditures and Selected Economic Data, 1964* (Washington, D.C.: United States Arms Control and Disarmament Agency, January, 1966), p. 19.

38. For a discussion of the "human capital loss" suffered by countries whose students fail to return from study abroad, see Paul Ritterband, "Toward an Assessment of the Costs and Benefits of Study Abroad," *International Education and Cultural Exchange* (U.S. Advisory Commission on International Educational and Cultural Affairs, Fall, 1966), pp. 26–35. See also James A. Perkins, "Foreign Aid and the Brain Drain," *Foreign Affairs*, Vol. 44 (1966), pp. 608–619.

Senator Walter F. Mondale of Minnesota has stated that ". . . 12,077 Asian students admitted for 'temporary' study purposes adjusted their status to permanent

United States resident in the 1962–66 period—about 28 per cent of the total." Regarding Asian professionals, he says, "The 5,931 who came here in fiscal year 1966—the first year under the new immigration act—more than doubled the average of about 2,700 for the previous four years." Senator Mondale cites the brain drain in medicine as a "national disgrace." He writes that "more than 8,000—over 20 per cent—of the total of all the residents and interns now serving in American hospitals are graduates of medical schools in underdeveloped countries, countries with death and disease rates far exceeding our own. Most eventually return home. An estimated twenty-five per cent stay here." Senator Mondale asserts that "there is no doubt in my mind that the brain drain threatens the progress of a number of poor nations. If we are serious in saying that future world power and stability depend on this development, we are going to have to give the brain drain the same attention that we give to other major problems which keep the world's poor locked in poverty." *The New York Times*, May 28, 1967. For the view that the brain drain is less consequential, see *Some Facts and Figures on the Migration of Talent and Skills* (Washington, D.C.: Council on International Educational and Cultural Affairs, 1967).

39. In 1965, the three states with the highest per capita dollar income were: Connecticut, $3,390; Alaska, $3,375; and Delaware, $3,335. The three states with the lowest per capita dollar income were: Mississippi, $1,566; Arkansas, $1,781; and South Carolina, $1,838. Data taken from U.S. Census Bureau, *Statistical Abstract of the United States: 1966* (Washington, D.C.: Government Printing, Office, 1966), p. 330, Table 464. Data on states' receipt of federal funds for R & D from U.S. Census Bureau, *Statistical Abstract of the United States: 1966* (Washington, D.C.: Government Printing Office, 1966), p. 546, Table 779.

40. See preceding discussion of investment in civilian vs. military R & D, and higher United States investments as compared to European ones.

41. "Snooping Comes of Age," *The Monetary Times*, Vol. 134 (Feb., 1966), pp. 26–28. See also Austin Smith, "Business Espionage," *Fortune*, Vol. LIII (May, 1956), p. 118.

42. See Note 34, *Supra*.

43. See, for example, the report of the USIA survey which gauged reaction of the West European press to Multilateral Nuclear Force. Schlesinger, *A Thousand Days, op. cit.*, p. 874. For additional discussion, see Sorensen, *Kennedy, op. cit.*, pp. 360 and 654.

44. See Nathan Glazer, "The Rise of Social Research in Europe," in Daniel Lerner (ed.), *The Human Meaning of the Social Sciences* (New York: Meridian Books, 1959), pp. 43–69.

45. This holds not just for international or national politics. Mayor W. Harry Lister of Rockville Centre, Long Island, was reported to have acknowledged that village employees had hidden a microphone next to a telephone used by a critic of the mayor's administration. *The New York Times*, December 1, 1965.

46. This was illustrated in the 1966 British election, which Wilson called when the Labor Party enjoyed a "safe" though perhaps very temporary lead over the Conservatives in public opinion surveys.

47. In fiscal year 1965, federal expenditures on research, development, and R & D plant totaled $14,874.7 million. Of this amount, $6,727.6 million went to the Department of Defense and $1,520.0 million to the Atomic Energy Com-

mission. The National Aeronautics and Space Administration received $5,092.9 million. The total received by all other federal agencies combined was $1,534.2 million. Data taken from National Science Foundation, *Federal Funds for Research, Development, and Other Scientific Activities, Fiscal Years 1965, 1966, and 1967, op. cit.*, Appendix C, Table C-50, p. 152.

48. While NASA was able in 1963 to gain $25 million "extra" for its space-oriented fellowship program, NSF was not able to get an additional $9.6 million for its program to strengthen institutions that execute its basic research program. For an additional discussion see Amitai Etzioni, *The Moon-Doggle: Domestic and International Implications of the Space Race* (Garden City, N.Y.: Doubleday, 1964), pp. 58 ff. NASA, aware of the efficacy of public relations techniques, has tried to convince taxpayers that the spending of billions of dollars on the space program is beneficial to civilian needs. Norman O. Miller, Jr., reports in the September 12, 1962 issue of *The Wall Street Journal* that NASA has used a New York public relations agency report on the immediate "civilian dividends from space research."

49. On how these are set, see below, discussion of societal decision-making.

50. Richard Harris, *The Real Voice* (New York: Macmillan Company, 1964), *passim*. See also footnote 51.

51. Inadequacy of government regulation of the drug industry was illustrated by the premature marketing of thalidomide. In West Germany, Britain, Canada, Australia, and other countries, thousands of infants were born with deformities because their mothers had taken insufficiently tested thalidomide pills early in pregnancy. With regard to the United States, it was stated: "That thalidomide was not cleared for sale here was more luck than anything else. If it had been developed here instead of in Germany, it probably would have been cleared; pre-marketing safety tests considered adequate before the thalidomide incident probably would not have revealed the drug's dangers." See "Toward Safer Drugs," *Consumer Reports*, Vol. 27 (1962), pp. 509–511, quoted from p. 509.

52. Viscount Hailsham, Q.M., the first British Minister for Science, pays homage to this ideal before he advocates the planning of science. See his *Science and Politics* (London: Faber & Faber, 1963), pp. 12–13. See also p. 78.

53. Societal guidance of a scientific activity, in the applied realm, is well illustrated by the Salk vaccine. In 1934 the National Foundation for Infantile Paralysis was formed with the self-consciously predetermined goal of solving a specific problem. Twenty years, millions of dollars, and hundreds of research-years later it was solved. For details of the guidance involved, see Richard Carter, *Breakthrough: The Saga of Jonas Salk* (New York: Trident Press, 1966).

54. Warner R. Schilling, "The H-Bomb Decision: How to Decide Without Actually Choosing," *Political Science Quarterly*, Vol. LXXVI, 1961, pp. 24–46. For several case studies of technologies "forcing" themselves on societal units, see Elting E. Morison, *Men, Machines, and Modern Times* (Cambridge, Mass.: MIT Press, 1966).

55. Manuel J. Gordon, "Control of Sex," *Scientific American*, Vol. 199 (November, 1958), pp. 87 ff. Hermann Joseph Muller, "Human Evolution by Voluntary Choice of Germ Plasm," *Science*, Vol. 134 (September 8, 1961), pp. 643–649.

56. See Frank J. Granzeier, "Toxic Weapons," *Industrial Research*, Vol. 7 (August, 1965), pp. 69–72, 74; Elinor Langer, "Chemical and Biological Warfare

(I): The Research Program," *Science*, Vol. 155 (1967), pp. 174–176, 178–179; and, by the same author, "Chemical and Biological Warfare: The Weapons and the Policies," *Science*, Vol. 155 (1967), pp. 299–303. See also Hanson Baldwin, "The Pentagon States the Case for C.B. in Viet Nam," *The New York Times*, September 25, 1966.

57. Total Food and Drug Administration expenditures in fiscal year 1965, for example, were $40,649,000. Compare this amount with the $5,092,900,000 spent by NASA on research, development, and R & D plant in the same year. On FDA expenditures see *The Budget of the United States Government for the Fiscal Year Ending June 30, 1967* (Washington, D.C.: Government Printing Office, 1966). See also footnote 48.

58. Bruce L. R. Smith, *The RAND Corporation* (Cambridge, Mass.: Harvard University Press, 1966), pp. 195–240. See also Nick A. Komons, *Science and the Air Force: A History of the Air Force Office of Scientific Research* (Arlington, Va.: Office of Aerospace Research, 1966).

59. On the increased probing of the House of Commons in science affairs in the United Kingdom, see *The New York Times*, May 14, 1967. "The activist era in French science policy is usually dated from the beginning of the De Gaulle regime in 1958." See John Walsh, "Some New Targets Defined for French Science Policy," *Science*, Vol. 156 (1967), pp. 626–630, quoted from p. 627.

60. Nicholas De Witt, *Education and Professional Employment in the U.S.S.R.*, prepared for the National Science Foundation by the Office of Scientific Personnel, National Academy of Sciences, National Research Council (Washington, D.C.: National Science Foundation, 1961), pp. 352–360, esp. Table IV-57 on p. 352 and Table IV-60 on p. 359.

61. Hailsham suggests that it is thirty years. See *Science and Politics*, *op. cit.*, p. 20.

CHAPTER 10

Societal Consciousness and

Societal Action

I N THIS chapter, we will first discuss the reasons we consider consciousness an empirical concept and one which can be used productively not only for studies of personalities but also in theories of macro-action. The following questions are then asked: Under what conditions does societal consciousness develop? What are the dynamic relations among its components? And, how does societal consciousness affect societal action?

Our central proposition is that an actor who is conscious of his societal environment and of himself and his internal controls will be more active than an actor with otherwise similar characteristics who is not conscious. Consciousness, though, we shall see, can be a liability; it may accentuate the instrumental orientation of one actor toward another, thus undermining their expressive bonds, and it may drain energies that would otherwise sustain more activeness.

Consciousness Defined and Delineated

Before we explore the macro-aspects of consciousness, a brief digression is appropriate to discuss the position and foundations of this concept in universal theory.

Individual Consciousness: An Empirical Concept

To be conscious is to be aware, to pay attention. Here, we are primarily interested in the generalized capacity to be aware rather than in isolated instances of awareness. (Consciousness and awareness are used here as synonyms.) Individuals encounter awareness in themselves as an intuitive experience; this is no longer considered as inadmissible evidence.[1]* With the exception of a few positivistic, empiricist branches of psychology, concepts such as awareness are becoming more widely used.[2]

The concept of awareness can be given as much of an empirical referent as other standard concepts which are not directly observable, such as "values" or "charisma." To illustrate the empirical standing of this controversial concept, we list several attributes which we expect to be positively associated with consciousness. In other words, we expect that when a person is aware, he will behave differently from when he is not,† a difference that will be indicated by his acting more slowly and less rhythmically, making more errors, and being more able to change the pattern of his act. This is a proposition that can be tested in a routine activity—for instance, typing. Making a typist conscious of the positions of her fingers on the key board, we expect, will tend to retard the rate of speed at which she types, increase her errors, and make her typing less rhythmical, but it will also make it easier to teach the typist a new pattern.[3] A similar proposition has been advanced for a societal unit:

> The 'federal grant' universally has been emerging over the past twenty years, but until recently it has developed more by force of circumstances than by conscious design. The universities most affected have been making largely piecemeal adjustments to the new phenomena without any great effort at an overall view of what has been happening to them. Perhaps this was just as well—the transition probably was *smoother.* . . .[4]

---

* Reference notes for this chapter appear on page 244.

† A linguistic philosopher suggests to us that the question "do you know that . . ." is the same as "are you aware that . . .," but a record of the usages of the two questions would show a systematic difference. In the first case, one asks about the facts another person commands, while in the second case, one is concerned with how much attention is given to them. Compare, for instance, "Do you know that women are paid half as much as men for the same work?" to "Are you aware that women are paid half as much as men for the same work?" The second question means, "what do you make of this?"; "what kind of notice did you take of it?" rather than, "do you know this fact?" While verbal conventions need not be followed in formal analysis, this distinction seems worth explicating.

While this proposition about the empirical correlates of awareness may prove to be incorrect, we expect that others can be constructed and validated; we do not agree that " 'aware of' is something which cannot be defined or analyzed."[5] We will hold as a working proposition that awareness is a useful concept which can be empirically differentiated from non-awareness.

Awareness is a relational concept; it is always "of" something. It is best viewed as a beam of light which is cast on some objects and gives them a distinct status.[6] On the one hand, it can be deliberately shifted from some objects to others. On the other hand, it shies away from some objects and lingers on others; that is, it has a dynamic of its own.

The extent of an individual's awareness is always much more limited than the extent of his knowledge. One is never simultaneously aware of more than a fraction of the objects which tests would show one knows. Finally, still in accord with the light analogy, something is added to a person's knowledge of objects when he is aware of them as well. For instance, an actor is expected to be able to observe changes in objects he is aware of more quickly than changes in those he is not.

Consciousness may be characterized according to the objects of which the actor under study is aware with some degree of regularity (that is, those objects which come to his attention more frequently and/or for longer periods of time than others). Which classification of objects is used depends largely on the analytic questions under consideration. Consciousness of other actors, of self, and of guidance processes are our central concerns. Moreover, we are interested in the longitudinal and lateral scope of an actor's consciousness—that is, how deep and encompassing is his awareness.

Societal Consciousness

The concept of societal consciousness refers to the generalized capacity of a societal actor to be aware and not to an individual actor's awareness of societal processes. In part, societal consciousness is an aggregation of the members' consciousness, especially the active members; in part, it involves the institutionalization of awareness on the collective level—for instance, by the organization of sub-units charged with "paying attention" to an external set of "targets" (such as adding a country desk to one of the State Department's regional divisions) or to an internal set (e.g., collecting societal statistics on the ethnic composition of labor unions). British White Papers, for example, are a vehicle for creating and directing societal attention, and a similar function is served by Congressional hearings in the United States, as different in structure as the two mechanisms are.

While societal consciousness is analogous to a projector which highlights some targets while it neglects others, the total amount of the objects thus illuminated can be increased. By drawing simultaneously on the awareness of several men, a societal unit can be aware of more objects and relations than any individual, but, like an individual, no societal actor is ever fully aware of all the longitudinal and lateral links he knows about, not to mention those which exist.

A societal unit's distribution of awareness is reflected in its leaders' and members' distribution of awareness (e.g., do the leaders and members of a societal unit pay as much attention to domestic poverty as to China? To internal as to external affairs?). This distribution is also reflected in the structure of various societal organs (what proportion of the staff of the State Department is assigned to study Africa today as compared to 1945?).

Though increases in consciousness tend to be associated empirically with the search for more information, this is not a necessary correlation. To say that the United States in 1960 was more conscious of the Negro's plight than it was in 1950 does not imply more knowledge of the Negroes or more information about their problems. It may merely mean that the average citizen, the mass media, and the decision-making bodies paid more attention to the Negro problem for a longer time span and devoted more of their analytic capacities to it than they did ten years earlier.

Consciousness is not a prerequisite of action; individuals and societal units often act without awareness of their actions, of themselves, or of others. Consciousness is, however, a prerequisite of an active unit, one which is self-reviewing and self-correcting in order to realize more fully its values. In cybernetic terms, consciousness may be viewed as an attribute of a sub-layer of the controlling overlayer.[7] Among active units, we suggest, this overlayer is divided into two sub-layers; one sub-layer supervises and corrects the other one which, in turn, guides societal action "directly." Consciousness may be seen as an attribute of the "higher" sub-layer, one which determines the focus of the whole overlayer.

Consciousness, Context, and Synthesis

To be conscious of an object entails seeing it in a context, being aware of its place in a larger frame of reference. Consciousness may therefore be viewed not only as generalized awareness but also as a capacity to evoke a broader context. From this viewpoint, rules are aids to consciousness; they serve as reminders to evoke such contexts when predetermined benchmarks appear. A trivial example will suffice: The warning light built into many cars which flashes when the oil pressure falls too low or the generator malfunctions serves to alert the driver to check a set of processes to which he does not routinely pay attention. Thus, the warning light broadens his consciousness. In organized social systems, the "warning light" often signals the need to call in an expert or a supervisor, i.e., to bring in contextuating factors which are institutionalized in a higher authority of either knowledge or command.

To make a societal unit more conscious is to make it more aware of the societal context of isolated matters (or bits)—for example, the relationships between poverty and instances of racial discrimination or between the domestic socio-political structure and a particular foreign policy. Such an increase in the awareness of the interconnections among societal details should not be confused with the struggles among alternative contextuating orientations which we discussed above. The latter involve the question of *which* contextuating interpretation is to prevail, and therefore they assume an awareness of the contexts, a proper horizon of attention. To sustain consciousness, on the other hand, is an attempt to counter a tendency not to see things in *any* context. This tendency is in part due to a universal human predisposition towards entropy of consciousness; that is, to be conscious requires continual investment, while a loss of awareness requires no expenditure.

Consciousness is often kept at a low level by external elites who seek to limit the political action of an underprivileged collectivity. This may be accomplished, for example, by limiting the level of education, constricting contextuating information and interpretations, and promoting a world view that stresses the importance of bits over contexts. On the other hand, raising the level of consciousness entails promoting education (especially a social education and not merely an instrumental one), providing cognitive and evaluative contexts, and countering empiricism as an ideology.

The difference between synthesis and consciousness should be noted. Synthesis is an intellectual activity in that it is a process of finding places for bits in a context or building new contexts. Consciousness entails an awareness of the relationships of the bits to one or more contexts. Synthesis is completed once a relationship has been established; this requires such activities as data processing, analysis, and interpretation. But such a relationship may be forgotten or known only to the sub-unit which established it. In contrast, it requires processes such as information retrieval and communication for a societal unit to be conscious of a relationship. While a given synthesis may be relatively complete (though new bits may need to be related or relationships restructured), consciousness requires continual effort to counter erosion and to share the collective awareness with new members.

Societal Consciousness and Its Antecedents

The concept of societal consciousness is used here without its traditional metaphysical assumptions; no "group mind" is assumed to be hovering above the unit's members forcing their attention to this or that set of objects to any greater extent than the concept of shared values assumes a "group heart."[8]

It has been suggested that we use a more neutral and more technical term than "societal consciousness" because the term has many established and potentially misleading connotations, especially those associated with Durkheim's "collective consciousness" and Marx's "class consciousness." (Similar objections have been raised regarding our use of "normative" and "transcendental.") It seems necessary, therefore, to indicate briefly our position on terminology.

There are basically two procedures for the introduction of new terms: They are either invented or taken from a language and explicated for analytic usage. "Primary groups" is an example of the first and "consciousness" of the second procedure. (Most of the various usages of "consciousness" recorded by Webster are close to our definition of the term.) Both procedures are used in the natural sciences, and neither has logical superiority. The first kind of term may be difficult to remember and limits communication with those not familiar with a specific discipline or theory; the second may evoke the connotations of everyday speech, thereby eroding the explication. For the most part, we prefer the risks of explication over those of further extending the technical vocabulary, primarily because this vocabulary has been so extended that adding many more "invented" terms may limit communication to a dwindling few, and because the everyday connotations of the terms used here, while quite vague and imprecise from our viewpoint, are not basically wrong. This point holds also for the established connotations which the terms used here (including consciousness) derive from the history of the social sciences. While Durkheim's metaphysical and sociologistic assumptions about consciousness are wholly unnecessary for our purposes, his use of the term helps to remind us that collectivities have properties of their own and that consciousness is one of them.[9]

Our concept of consciousness is quite close to that of Marx,[10] although what he refers to as class consciousness is conceived by us as societal self-consciousness which a class or some other societal unit may possess. Moreover, while Marx limits his concept to socio-political consciousness, we see it as generalized awareness that may focus on other categories of objects, relations, or processes. Above all, Marx's use of this concept, as of others, is ideological. He views the consciousness of one class as "scientific" and that of another as false. To us, societal units differ in their degree of societal or self-consciousness, but no one unit has a priori a more valid consciousness than another, not even the intellectuals.[11] Finally, it should be noted that Marx as well as Mannheim often dealt with self-knowledge rather than self-consciousness. By our use of the term, *knowledge can be invalid; consciousness can be limited, misdirected, or unfocused but not false.* Societal consciousness is an expression of the level, extent, and "topics" of attention rather than information.[12] If "consciousness" is used in the traditional sense, it becomes indistinguishable from societal knowledge, and we have two terms for one concept and no term for the other. At the same time, consciousness and knowledge are obviously closely related; one is concerned with the focusing of the other.

In a Functional-Genetic Perspective

Making a societal unit more conscious of its societal environment, its structure, its identity, and its dynamics is part of the process of transforming a passive unit into an active one. Consciousness is an essential prerequisite for the active orientation: Although actors can act with limited or even no consciousness, we expect in this case that they will tend to realize fewer of their goals. On the other hand, an increase in consciousness *alone* implies mainly an increase in symbolic activity, and hence, if other elements such as commitment and power are lacking, the societal unit may not be more active. The Jewish community in Medieval Europe is an example of a collectivity that was highly self-conscious but weak and fairly passive.[13] From the viewpoint of an actor in whom the three components of the active orientation are balanced, it is possible to speak of an over-conscious actor, one whose investment in awareness outweighs his investments in the other components. Consciousness requires effort and imposes costs; it uses part of the actor's energies. It also reduces his spontaneity and tends to weaken his bonds to other actors by introducing a filter between them. It enables him to be more instrumental in his orientation toward others if he has been already so inclined. To the degree that the bonds he has formed with other actors are a source of support, this further reduces his capacity to act; to the degree that these bonds retard his activation, their weakening obviously increases his capacity to act. In either case, an increase in consciousness is expected to involve an expenditure of energy; however, the secondary effects, such as the potential increases in autonomy and in innovative behavior, may more than compensate for the loss.

Processes that build societal consciousness, as we shall see, include those which increase the consciousness of the members and those which change the "global attributes"[14] of the societal unit. For instance, the aggregate aspects of the consciousness of a societal unit are increased when the members' awareness of their differences *vis-à-vis* members of other societal units is increased and when the differences in levels of awareness among the members of the unit are decreased. The global aspects of consciousness are enhanced by increasing the amount of collective symbolic expression (and thus the unit's visibility) and by collective action. We will now explore briefly each of these mechanisms.

Decrease in Differential Awareness: Changing the Members

If the large numbers of attitudes and interests which the members of any societal unit hold at any point in time are compared, it is seen that the members differ in the attention they pay to various matters. An index could be built of the degree of their generalized awareness of any given set of "targets," including that of their own societal unit. The more *varied* the "targets" of awareness of the various members of a given societal unit and/or the lower their *average* awareness of any societal target, the lower the level of societal consciousness of the particular unit. Thus, the level of consciousness can be raised by increasing the awareness of those "targets" of which many members have a relatively low level of awareness *and* by making their "targets" more congruent. This can be achieved by de-emphasizing some "targets" and stressing others. If, for instance, members of the working class have varying religious and ethnic affiliations, working-class consciousness will tend to rise if shared economic interests are given attention while religious and ethnic concerns are "played down." This process may be referred to as a *decline in differential awareness*.

This reduction of differential awareness can be achieved at a relatively low societal cost under one condition: If the differentiation were largely the result of "pluralistic ignorance" (that is, the members were not aware that they actually held similar views and attitudes).[15] When the members are made aware of their *similar* views, these become *shared*; consequently, a societal bond is added, and the awareness of the boundaries between members and non-members grows. Such a process is likely to be relatively inexpensive because it entails no change of perspectives but merely adds the dimension of awareness; the social networks of the actors are unlikely to resist such a process because the members do hold similar perspectives. On the other hand, changing the perspectives of those members whose consciousness does not fit the societal unit's pattern tends to be slow and costly.

A major way to build societal consciousness in either situation is to reduce interaction, especially of the expressive variety, with non-members and increase contact with members.[16] This reduction makes the boundaries of the collectivity more visible, reduces the input of "alien" information and serves to reduce the "pluralistic ignorance" of the members while magnifying such ignorance between members and non-members, all of which enhances the self-consciousness of a societal unit.

The members of a societal unit may come to share awareness of practically anything, from cruelty to animals in Chicago slaughterhouses to the conditions in the German concentration camps. Of special interest for our purposes is the range of matters of which the members of a societal unit are aware—*their conceptual horizon*, especially their *societal map*. The modal map of the members of some societal units is limited mainly to their village; for others, it encompasses the national state; and for still others, it is worldwide.[17] Many studies report, quite atomistically, that the members of this or that unit do not have a given piece of information about the larger map—e.g., the name of the capital, the government of another state.[18] This is often somewhat misleading, as the question is rather one of context, because even persons whose horizon is world-wide do not have all the relevant information, and because specific bits can be readily provided *if* there is a context for them. What is important for the active orientation is whether or not the members' generalized awareness includes an awareness of a particular context (e.g., a national system). When such a context is absent, this seems to prevent the integration of information about items which belong in this context into the the conceptual map of the actors.[19] Further lines of investigation lead to studies of background factors which affect the range of the conceptual horizon (where the level of education seems to play a significant role),[20] of the processes of communication which may extend it, and of the consequences of extended horizons and societal maps. Of particular interest for our purposes is the finding that there is a close association between the unit (local, national) of which a person is aware and the unit in which he is politically active.[21]

Changing Global Attributes: Symbolizing a Societal Unit

The development or construction of *core institutions*, limited primarily to the members of a cohesive societal unit, serves to symbolize the unit and to make it more visible to itself and to others, express its identity, and increase interaction among its members to the exclusion of non-members. A major way in which consciousness can be "concretized" is to associate it with a place and a related set of activities.[22] The significant role played by places of worship in the formation and maintenance of the self-consciousness of religious and ethnic collectivities and sub-collectivities is not limited to their socialization function in the sense of introducing new members to the sub-culture's values and habits, nor to their social control capacity in the sense of reinforcing commitments to shared norms; these institutions also make the societal unit more visible and thus serve as anchoring points for self-consciousness. The national unity of several of the newly independent states, it has been said, is evident mainly when their cricket or football team plays against another country's team.

Societal Consciousness and Societal Action: Mutual Reinforcement Effect

One major way in which an increase in societal consciousness can be initiated is for a societal unit to act collectively. This statement is a reversal of the widely-held proposition that consciousness precedes collective action.[23] Once the process is initiated, there is a mutual-reinforcing effect with some collective action generating some consciousness, thus allowing for more collective action, which in turn makes for more self-consciousness, and so on, until the process is blocked by some external factor.

Sharing in a project, relating to a specific set of goals, and participating in a social movement are effective ways of enhancing collective self-consciousness. People are expected to be much more conscious of their membership in collectivities which have organizational arms than in those which do not. Often, working-class individuals seem to join labor unions and labor parties not because they have working-class consciousness, but they seem to develop working-class consciousness because they have joined labor unions and parties.

Among the collective actions which, it has been suggested, are conducive to the development of a high level of self-consciousness are confrontations, discussed first, and "intimate rejections," discussed subsequently. Confrontations (for example, with the community's police force) are more productive in this regard than peaceful negotiations (or bargaining), even when the latter yield major concessions for the collectivity involved. One reason for this difference in effect is that confrontations are much more likely to involve the membership as well as the elites. Confrontations are also more likely to prevent other collectivities or external elites from "co-opting" the elites of a collectivity. And they tend to provide intensive shared experiences which enhance the formation and maintenance of negative counter-symbols around which societal consciousness is often built,[24] such as the Boston Tea Party and the Haymarket riot.

In addition, confrontations tend to increase the number and activity of the "activation-agents" of the collectivity—that is, elements in a unit which, once activated themselves, are able to activate other segments of the unit. Elites and leadership[25] are typically such agents. Societal units, as we have seen, differ in the degree to which they have internal elites and active publics and in terms of the proportion of the members of the societal unit that is thus mobilized. It is expected that the score of a collectivity on this variable is positively associated with the collectivity's level of societal and self-consciousness. Modern and post-modern societies, we suggest, tend to provide for the upward mobility of members of lower-ranking collectivities who show leadership skills or to "co-opt" them. In either case, the lower collectivities are deprived of their internal leadership and thus lose a major source of their societal consciousness. Retaining the leadership and preventing its co-optation, we suggest, are two prerequisites for a high level of self-consciousness of a collectivity or a society.

Other conditions under which the consciousness of a collectivity increases to a point at which it will confront others (and begin the consciousness-building process discussed above) have been reviewed.[26] It is widely agreed that oppression and deprivation do not in themselves suffice; on the contrary, they are probably associated with a low level of self-consciousness. Self-consciousness, it has been suggested, increases when a relative improvement occurs and is then *discontinued*, or when a *stratification imbalance* is created by an increase in some kinds of collective assets without a parallel rise in others.[27] These two propositions do not necessarily contradict each other, in that both a discontinued but balanced increase in assets of all kinds and an unbalanced but continual increase could raise the level of self-consciousness. The latter situation seems to be more common because the reallocations of the various kinds of assets are often not synchronized. Lack of synchronization occurs, for instance, when the growth of participation in politics and an increase in utilitarian assets do not occur simultaneously. Examples may be found in the changing relations between the aristocracy and the rising bourgeoisie or between the bourgeoisie and the rising working-class,[28] as well as between world powers and newly independent states.[29] In all these cases, changes in the degree of participation in politics do not seem to have been synchronized with commensurate reallocations of wealth.

"Intimate rejection" is the second dimension of the analysis of the consciousness-building effects of collective action. Collectivities which are upwardly mobile often had been rejected by other collectivities for long periods with little resultant gain in self-consciousness. How, then, can a comparatively sudden increase in consciousness be explained? One possible answer is that changes in the stratification structure have brought about a status imbalance which did not exist previously, and such an imbalance is activating. (The induction of Negroes into the Armed Forces during World War II is often cited as such a development.[30])

While this may well be a relevant factor, another factor should be taken into account. In several instances, societal changes have increased the social contact between the underprivileged and the privileged collectivities, often within an atypical, relatively egalitarian sub-unit such as the university or other cultural groupings. Jewish students and intellectuals came to know non-Jews more intimately with the emancipation in the nineteenth century in Western Europe, Negroes came to know whites on a more equal footing in World War II, and students from African societies met British students in British universities. *When rejection is encountered in the context of intimate contact, after some measure of equality has been experienced, it is expected to have much greater alienating effects on those who are rejected because the host is now more of a "significant other" (even if the rejection is actually more limited than before)*. Thus, at the base of many counter-rejections is the hope of full acceptance, and *collective* leadership has often grown from the failure of individualistic "passing." Theodore Herzl, the leader of the Zionist movement, tried first to "assimilate" and was quite well accepted as a reporter in non-Jewish circles. During the Dreyfus trial,[31] he felt rejected, which led to his return to his collectivity in which he acquired a key role in building collective consciousness. Africans who studied in Britain and France tried to deal with intimate rejection by collectivizing their experiences, which resulted in a higher level of consciousness of membership in their native collectivities, a consciousness which they carried with them upon return to their countries.[32]

Relating Global and Aggregate Factors

Collectivities, we suggested, act and interact primarily in a representational manner; therefore some participants and some sub-units have greater effects on collective action than others. The same holds for societal consciousness; its structure, too, is "representational." While it is sometimes assumed that an increase in societal consciousness is really an increase in the consciousness of all or most of the members of a societal unit, this is rarely the case. As a rule, such an increase entails the growth of consciousness among the various elites of a collectivity, in particular political and intellectual elites, and some, though often much more limited, increase in the consciousness of the active publics. Often, there seems to be only a small increase in the consciousness of the rest of the collectivity.

It is only under relatively rare conditions, especially when inter-collectivity relations are hostile and one or more of the collectivities is considering (or engaged in) extensive conflict, that we expect the degree to which consciousness is shared by the rank-and-file to be a critical variable. Under many other conditions, such as non-hostile, cooperative relations among the elites and between them and their followers, the level of consciousness of the elites seems more important for societal action than the level of consciousness of the non-elites. This is not what is sometimes referred to as an "elitist" position, since we not only hold that there are conditions under which the consciousness of non-elites is essential for effective action but we also suggest that the elites must gain and maintain the support of the non-elites; i.e., the "delegation" of societal consciousness must be approved and reapproved if it is not to hinder the development of the active orientation.[33]

Societal Consciousness and the Active Orientation

What is the role of differences in the extent and level of societal consciousness in determining the degree to which a unit is active? To explore this question, we first examine variations in the extent to which an actor is conscious. We then discuss the relationship of consciousness to the actor's values and identity, and, finally, we explore the consequences of consciousness for transformability. That is, we ask first about the relationships among the internal components of consciousness, then about its external relationship to the actor's values (which indicate the direction of his commitment), and, finally, we relate consciousness to the highest level of activeness—the capacity for self-transformation.

The Extent of Consciousness and the Active Orientation

Consciousness, as we have seen, may encompass the environment, the acting self, and the controlling overlayers. We suggest that these three components tend to arrange themselves in a Guttman scale, in that consciousness of the environment is likely to be present when there is self-consciousness, but when there is consciousness of the environment, self-consciousness is not necessarily also present; and that both of these kinds of consciousness are likely to be present when there is consciousness of control processes, but their presence is not necessarily accompanied by this third kind of consciousness.

This "order" may be explained by a genetic–historical proposition which suggests that societies become malleable and aware in that "order," with the various sciences serving as major tools for expanding not only knowledge but also consciousness of whole fields. Natural science evolved first, social science later, and the systematic study of societal guidance is only gradually advancing in the contemporary, post-modern age. What we expect to hold for the sciences, seems also to be the case for the distribution of the attention of societal knowledge-units among the three components. It seems that most modern societies spend more time and assets on paying attention to "nature" and to other actors than on studying themselves (e.g., compare intelligence work about other nations to the study of one's own country), and least on the study of their guidance mechanisms.* In post-modern societies, there seems to be a trend toward a relative increase of investment in the second and, to a lesser extent, the third sector.

The expansion of the subjects to which attention is paid is expected to be associated with a separation of consciousness of self from that of a larger entity. Children are reported to be aware of the mother or of a child–mother unity before they are aware of a distinct identity of their own.[34] For classes, ethnic groups, and nations, the proposition would read that consciousness of their "mother" society precedes self-consciousness.[35] The American colonies, for instance, seem to have seen themselves first as part of "mother" Britain and to have gained self-consciousness only gradually.[36] Contemporary Canadian Jewry has been characterized as unaware of its differences from the Jews of the United States and as viewing the Canadian situation in terms of the United States (e.g., objecting to state support of religious schools).[37]

While there are many different kinds of societal self-awareness, the study of societal guidance is especially concerned with political consciousness, an awareness of the power relations and political organization of society—of where the political levers are, what the distribution of power is, and the ways and means by which change is possible. We expect, for instance, that collectivities which are equally poor in assets but differ in their political consciousness will differ in their capacity for societal action. For example, the income of students is on the average not much higher than that of people on relief, but

---

* The objective need for investment in the sectors seems not to be equal. Thus, there may well be no "place" to spend as much on the consciousness of controls as on that of nature. We are concerned here with comparing relative distribution patterns and their effects. We do not wish to imply that a 1:1:1 ratio is expected or preferable. Still, the ratio for post-modern societies may well indicate less investment in the second and third sectors than an active society may require.

their political consciousness (as well as their political knowledge and skills) is often much greater. This is especially true in developing nations[38] where the students' income is lower than that of students in modern societies. Their much higher level of consciousness is one reason for their much greater activeness. In seeking to determine the action potential of a collectivity, it is, therefore, useful to distinguish its command of utilitarian assets (and its power potential based on these assets) from its level of political consciousness. Obviously, if a societal unit is high on both dimensions, it is more effective than one which is low on both, but to some degree the two substitute for each other. For instance, efforts to organize the poor, to increase their self-confidence, and to build some collective political awareness are expected to increase the action capacity of the poor *before* they gain new resources.[39]

The inclusion of the extent of the awareness of control processes and of the capacity to restructure them encompasses a rather new "target" of societal consciousness. For instance, the United States Congress paid very little attention to the national guidance of scientific and technological activities until the late 1950s but has become much more aware of this problem and somewhat more active in dealing with it since then.[40]

The more encompassing the consciousness of an actor, the more active he can be, because consciousness that is more encompassing increases the actor's options and frees him to act more in accord with his values and less in terms of environmental pressures and structural constraints. An actor who is aware of the malleability of his environment but not of the malleability of his own internal make-up foregoes a major set of options and limits his creativity. Similarly, an actor that is aware of the transformability of his environment and his "body" but not that of his guidance mechanisms excludes a whole range of options.

The concept of consciousness relates knowledge to action in that it differentiates more active from less active knowledge. A central consideration here is that while an actor's knowledge may be extensive, much of it is stored and only part of it is recalled through various scanning devices (from assistant librarians to computers) for the purpose of guiding his action. The knowledge an actor can use in his conscious deliberations at any one time is, as a rule, much more limited. However, the knowledge which an actor does use can be extended; the staff of an organization or a decision-making body can be trained (or organized) to enlarge the span of its attention, and more knowledge can be telescoped so that the actor can take into account more of the knowledge he has. That is, more knowledge can be activated.

The attention of modern, pluralistic societies, we suggest, was focused more on non-social, environmental problems that on inter- and intra-societal concerns and, among the latter, more on the societal environment than on self-examination. In the post-modern period there seems to be a relative increase in the attention given to the international system and some rise in the investment in and use of domestic societal knowledge.* An active society will have to pay still greater attention to societal self-examination.

Similarly, for each collectivity and society, we can ask about the matters with which it is mainly concerned at a given time. We can suggest that the Republican Party pays more attention to the radical left than to the radical right, or that India, in the first decade of its independence, was concerned more with industrialization than with the modernization of agriculture, and we can test these statements empirically.

Societal actors can focus their attention on more than one area at a time,[41] drawing on such organizational devices as the division of labor among staff and the institutionalized shifting of attention of the highest-ranking decision-makers.[42] We suggest, however, that there is a limit to the number of topics which can receive high priority, in the sense of full examination by the top elites or detailed analysis by their staffs. While it is possible to expand the size of the staffs and the elites, studies of supervision have shown that the ability to extend the range of effective supervision of those lower in rank by those higher in rank is quite limited.[43] And while the supervision—and therefore societal attention—span can be increased by imposing supervisors on supervisors, the political consequences of an error at the lower levels are considerable, and hence top decision-makers tend to seek (and to have an objective need) to inform themselves of the details to some degree. Thus, we can propose that collectivities can be *greatly* aware of only a *few* topics at a time.[44]

Consciousness, Identity, and the Active Orientation

The identity of an actor is his position in a normative–cognitive pattern; it is to the evaluative structure what status is to stratification. Self-identity is the place an actor sees himself as occupying in this pattern. It is tantamount to the specification of his values and of his knowledge of himself, answering

---

* Three technical points should be added. (1) A comparison of statistics on investments in the three kinds of knowledge as an indicator of the attention devoted to them has to take into account the fact that some kinds of knowledge are more expensive per bit than others; for instance, on the average social science knowledge is less expensive than that of the natural sciences, and therefore changes in the respective investments do not fully reflect the change in awareness. It is probably best to compare relative growth within each field. (2) International knowledge does not include studies of armaments to the extent that these are studied in the natural sciences—for instance, studies of thermonuclear weapons. These are environmental. On the other hand, the study of deterrence as a political threat system or of bargaining is international knowledge. (3) The natural sciences might be used for domestic transformation (e.g., birth control), while some social science knowledge can be used for control of non-social environments (e.g., studies of the work flow in the primary sector). Roughly, though, the relative investments in the two disciplines reflect relative interests in the two environments, natural and social.

the question: Who am I? Actors differ significantly not only in the substance of their views of themselves (let us say, as "chosen" to be preferred, or as "picked" to be exploited) but also in the degree to which they have a clearly focused self-identity.

Self-consciousness increases the possibilities of a clear self-identity. The higher the level of self-awareness of an actor, the more likely he is to clarify his identity and focus it; the more he is aware of his boundaries, of his place *vis-à-vis* others, the more delineated we expect his self-identity to be.[45]

While the two concepts of self-consciousness and self-identity are closely related, they vary independently and affect each other. Self-identity seems to increase the more that positive values come to be associated with a collectivity (e.g., the Negro-Americans since the advent of the post-modern period), or to decline when more and more members of a collectivity come to view it in a negative light and attempt to reduce its visibility (e.g., assimilating groups). While we expect such trends to affect the self-consciousness of an actor and the consciousness others have of him, the relationship is obviously not one-to-one. For instance, a great effort to assimilate, to lose, or to conceal collective identity, may well be associated with a high degree of self-consciousness.

The clearer and more focused the self-identity of an actor, and/or the more self-conscious he is, the more active he may be. The self-identity of the actor is related to the values to which he is committed and to the goals he pursues. Within broad limits, we expect that the more specific this identity is, the more guidance for action it will provide. Similarly, self-consciousness will tend to make an actor take his basic commitments into account to a greater extent in his decision-making. To the degree that self-consciousness reveals a vague self-identity (while self-conscious attempts to focus and clarify the actor's identity, other factors may keep it blurred), self-consciousness cannot add as much to a sense of internal direction as it can when it is coupled with a clear self-identity. The more self-aware a faceless actor becomes, the more aware he grows of his lack of identity, and, hence, of autonomous direction.

Societal Consciousness and Detachment

We have already suggested that there is no necessary relationship between the levels of consciousness and activeness. This seems to be the case for two main reasons. First, the degree of activeness is affected by other factors which may hinder the growth of the active orientation at the same time that a rise in consciousness increases the potential for activeness. Second, even when no such factors are operative, an increase in consciousness may not lead to more activeness but rather encourage a more reflective, passive orientation. This may result from increasing the distance between the actor and his world or from making the actor more aware of the limitations of his capacities and of the constraining power of others. An increase in consciousness is therefore expected to generate activation only when either the other elements of the active orientation are also increasing or they were initially at higher levels, and consciousness was the lagging element. When consciousness is at a high level but commitment is low, we expect the societal equivalent of "I do not give a damn," sometimes found in what have been referred to as decadent societies (e.g., Rome in the third century or France in the pre-Revolution era).

When consciousness is at a high level but knowledge is low, the main effect of consciousness may be to heighten the actor's sense of being unable to cope with his problems. For instance, the United States 1966 Senate hearings about the ways and means of curbing the illicit use of LSD, which indicated an increase in the societal attention devoted to the problem, also revealed considerable uncertainty about how effectively to deal with the matter.[46] The hearings were concluded without any specific recommendations for legislation or provisions for any other effective course of action. When consciousness is at a high level but power is low, we expect a sense of frustration and helplessness, common among social movements which seek radical transformations in societies that can at best be gradually transformed. Thus, the levels of consciousness and of activeness may not be the same.

Actors whose self-consciousness has risen are also expected to be less well-integrated into their societal systems or communities. We expect more self-conscious actors to be more instrumental and more manipulative in their orientations toward other actors. The way in which this effect is evaluated depends on the initial relations between the actors in the system and on the frame of reference applied. If the members of the system previously constituted a community, and the frame of reference favors the community, the rise in the members' self-consciousness plays a negative, deunifying role. If the relationship among the members had been an exploitive one, and if one favors equality, an increase in the members' self-consciousness will play a positive role by increasing the likelihood of a transformation.

One pitfall to be avoided is the confusion of a slow reaction with a passive orientation. Even when consciousness is well-synchronized with the other elements necessary for a highly active orientation, we expect that actors with greater consciousness will be more "reflective," will spend more time and resources on considering alternatives, than less conscious actors.

Consciousness, Innovation, and Transformation

The reactions of the more conscious actors are expected to be more "creative" because these actors are more reflective and take more factors into account—i.e., are aware of more conditions and options. For the same reasons, we expect that more conscious actors will engage less in trial-and-error behavior when confronting a new problem and will attempt to a greater degree to design a solution; we therefore expect them to be both more transformable and more utopian.

There are two main links between the level of societal consciousness and the societal capacity for innovation and transformation. One concerns the building of new structures and systems; the other involves the "unlocking" of old ones. In terms of the first link, we stressed above that societal actors are, in principle, capable of transcending themselves which requires an ability to design new patterns and to direct efforts toward their realization. This capacity is in turn affected by consciousness of the environment, of self, and of the capacities to design and to transform. The less conscious an actor is and the more he is immersed in a broader societal unit or environment, the lower we expect his designing and transforming capacities to be.

While consciousness of the environment and of self is relevant, consciousness of the capacities to design and to transform is here the most significant factor, for if actors subscribe to views which conceal such options (a common feature of conservative ideologies[47]), they lack a necessary prerequisite for transformation.

The contribution which societal consciousness makes toward innovation and transformation can be provided by a relatively small sub-unit. It is, for instance, not necessary for all or even for most of a society's members to be aware of the internal make-up of their society in order for the intellectual or political elites to design a policy that takes such structural facts into account. On the other hand, the second contribution of societal consciousness—assistance in "unlocking"—requires a much more broadly based effort.

The widely held psychoanalytic proposition that increased consciousness enhances the ability to overcome inhibitions which block a "healthier" course of action finds here a macro-sociological analogy. Most societal units have some form of institutional, stratification, and power structures.* To change these (which transformation involves by definition) almost inevitably entails a power struggle between those who favor the existing structures and boundaries and those who favor new ones. We expect increased consciousness of the existing societal morphology by the members to be associated with a more effective unlocking of rigid patterns and easier transformation because: (a) increased societal consciousness entails, as we have seen, increased individual consciousness and this, it has been suggested, is associated with increased personal willingness to accept change; (b) elites that are more

---

* Social scientists have stressed over recent years that many underdeveloped countries do not have such an integrated society, and as a result many of the models constructed on the basis of the Western experience do not apply: There are no structures to transform. But it should be stressed that these statements refer to the national societies. Tribal, rural, or other local units are often rather well-integrated and structured. While their societal combination is often loose and does not make for a society sufficiently structured to be transformable, the units themselves can be transformed internally, and they may be changed to make more of a supra-unit, more of a society.

conscious of the societal patterns are more able to innovate and design alternate ones;[48] and (c) the societal patterns are themselves in part symbolic and therefore may be partly changed "directly" under the impact of increased consciousness (that is, without commensurate changes in the allocative structures of coercion or of utilitarian assets). We expect, for instance, that the prestige awarded to local units as compared to national ones will be reduced "directly" as the consciousness of a national society develops.

There also seems to be a societal analogy to the psychological proposition that new matters are first reviewed consciously and then routinized and delegated to non-conscious levels and again examined consciously only when deliberate and fundamental changes are attempted.* For instance, there were public debates, several Presidential messages, and Congressional deliberations, when American soldiers were first committed to be stationed in Europe in World War II and remained there in the first post-war years.[49] For the following two decades, such an American commitment, once inconceivable in time of peace, was out of the focus of societal attention and was routinely carried out until it again came under relatively more intensive review and attention in the 1966 and 1967 attempts to reorganize NATO.

How and to what degree does the focusing of societal attention on a heretofore latent structure—bringing it into the open, so to speak—allow for its transformation? We have already seen that there are systematic differences in the societal knowledge of the elites and the active and passive publics. There are related differences in the extent of their consciousness and in their attention span (the length of time of focus on the same topic). We suggest that while consciousness in general is mercurial in that its focus is quick to shift and hard to center on any target for a long time, there are systematic differences in this regard among the various societal members. The active publics' societal attention is highly mercurial, while that of elites and interest groups is relatively more stable. (The passive publics are relatively unaware of what is occurring at the societal level.) A typical cycle is for public attention to become focused on an issue but to shift quickly to some other issue unless organized.

Although the focusing of public attention alters the societal power constellations, its long-run effects depend on the degree to which the latent structure can be affected in the period in which it is at the center of public attention. If we take, for instance, the period between 1964 and 1967 in the United States, bringing into focus the role of the automobile industry in keeping cars unsafe (this was brought to attention by the industry's harassment of its main critic)[50] sufficed in 1966 to bring about legislation imposing some automobile safety standards. While the degree to which these will be actually imposed, diluted, or strengthened by further legislation depends, in

---

* This relates to a proposition advanced in Chapter 8, that individuals as well as societal units are more aware of bits of knowledge than of their contexts.

part, on the degree to which the problem of automobile safety is given public attention in the following years, a program was initiated. In the same period, the public attention devoted to proposed legislation for limiting the sale of guns, which reached an unusually high level following President Kennedy's assassination, shifted away before a law was passed. There are many reasons for the difference between these two issues, but the facts that the gun lobby has a more popular base than the automobile one[51] and that its activities were not opened to public scrutiny to the same degree as those of the automobile lobby were especially relevant. Clearly, a focusing of public attention does not change latent structures. Only a few such structures disintegrate after one exposure (usually only in part), some change only after repeated exposures, and some are altered only slightly. Finally, even in fairly responsive societies, bit reforms are much more likely to be "carried" than fundamental changes.

What the publics do focus on, for how long, and how often, are questions whose answers are affected by the political leaders, the intellectuals, legislative committees, "white papers," hearings, major trials, and the mass media, as well as by the activities of interest groups. More weight than is often granted is to be attributed to *public associations*, to organizations which make *continued* focusing of public attention on one or more targets their major concern. SANE (Committee for a Sane Nuclear Policy), for instance, devoted itself chiefly to mobilizing public support for a ban on testing nuclear weapons for several years; similarly, the Foundation for Infantile Paralysis kept public concern for the elimination of polio at a relatively high level for nearly two decades.

The concept of re-committing links the two activities of "unlocking" an old structure and of setting a new pattern and course. On the personality level, individuals seem to vary significantly in the rapidity with which they can "re-focus," i.e., turn their attention from one subject to another. Societal units vary on the same dimension: For instance, totalitarian societies, it has often been suggested, have a higher capacity to re-commit than pluralistic ones. One of the considerations raised when the United States decided to engage in a major space program in competition with the Soviet Union was that the Soviet Union could halt its part of the race to the moon fairly suddenly, while the United States, once it initiated a massive space program and interest groups and government agencies "jelled" around it, would find it much more difficult to re-focus its effort elsewhere. The United States, it was said, might find itself racing alone to the moon. In part because of such difficulties of re-committing, pluralistic societies seem frequently to continue obsolescent programs and to add new programs to existing ones rather than to eliminate old ones.

The relevant question for a theory of societal guidance is whether or not increased societal consciousness increases the capacity to re-commit. More generally, does increased awareness of the environmental and internal dynamics, especially of the "stiffness" of pluralistic societies' structures and controlling overlayers increase these societies' transformability? Or are the forces that make for a low degree of transformability, especially bureaucratization and institutionalization of the vested interests, greater than those generated by the organized focusing of the attention of critical publics, with or without the support of other transforming forces?[52] When the conserving forces concede, are their concessions only temporary and "token," or can public consciousness be focused for a sufficiently long period of time or refocused often enough to significantly increase recommitments? As the answer to these questions seems to be "sometimes yes," the next questions are: how frequently, to what net effect, and under what societal conditions?

It has been suggested, drawing on biological analogies, that the conditions under which the capacities for transformability are high are determined in part by the degree to which the environment is changing.[53] Rapidly changing environments provide opportunities to exercise and, thus, to develop these capacities, while stable environments encourage their degeneration. And when a stable environment does suddenly change, as in the instances in which white civilization penetrated into the stable worlds of preliterate tribes, there is a built-in incapacity to adapt because the static environment encourages the development of rigid structures and a lack of consciousness. In contrast, it is said, changing environments favor flexible orientations, including institutionalized reviewing and organization for re-committing, processes in which societal consciousness plays a key role.

The validity of this proposition is far from determined. While Japan's reaction to a sudden confrontation with the West was much more flexible than this proposition would lead one to expect, that of China was much more in accord with it.[54] Possibly, the difference lies in the fact that even though Japan had little experience in fundamental transformation, it was significantly more nationally organized than China; i.e., it did have a central, society-wide controlling overlayer including a measure of national consciousness and therefore a latent capacity for transformation.[55] The existence of a national control capacity and consciousness explains in part the earlier transformation of Britain from a pre-industrial to an industrial society as compared to France. The Soviet Revolution may be viewed as providing the industrialization of Russia with the needed national consciousness and controls.

The preceding discussion suggests the value of viewing some societal actors as having a *latent guidance capacity*, while others have little or none. Faced with a crisis, the first kind of actor would react creatively, activating his latent capacities, while the other would react routinely, which, under the circumstances, would mean rigidly.* Consciousness plays a key role in this

---

* Of course, this latent capacity must be assessed by indicators other than the response to a crisis.

situation both in reviewing various new societal designs and in exploring new identities which the actor is "trying out." It followed then that post-modern societies, whose malleability and guidance capacity are higher than that of modern societies, would benefit more from a rising level of conscious-ness and suffer more from its lack, because the more options available, the greater the possibility that the reviewing processes will ignore some viable ones.

In sum, societal consciousness may help societal units to become more the masters of their actions and to realize more of their own values and goals— i.e., to become more active. As consciousness, however, also reduces spontaneity and increases instrumentality, an increase of consciousness without a parallel increase in the other components of the active orientation may "dry up" the commitment of an actor and weaken rather than strengthen his activeness.

NOTES

1. See R. C. Oldfield, "Changing Views of Behavior Mechanisms," in A. G. Crombie (ed.), *Scientific Change, op. cit.*, pp. 576–589, esp. 584–589. See also essays in John C. Eccles (ed.), *The Brain and the Unity of Conscious Experience* (Cambridge, U.K.: University Press, 1965), esp. essays by D. M. MacKay and A. O. Gomes.

2. For an article which reviews various microscopic discussions of awareness, see Barney G. Glaser and Anselm L. Strauss, "Awareness Contexts and Social Interaction," *American Sociological Review*, Vol. 29 (1964), pp. 669–679.

3. For an empirical study of the consciousness of drivers, see Gunnar Johansson and Kore Rumar, "Drivers and Road Signs," *Ergonomics*, Vol. 9 (1966), pp. 57–62. Koestler, in *The Act of Creation, op. cit.*, pp. 44 ff., reviews several relevant studies. The transition process of newly acquired habits from consciousness to sub-consciousness and their re-emergence from subconsciousness to consciousness when one seeks to alter them is also reviewed.

4. Kerr, *The Uses of the University, op. cit.*, p. 49 (italics provided).

5. H. H. Price, "Some Objections to Behaviorism," in *Dimensions of Mind, op. cit.*, p. 79.

6. Mark Abrahamson, "Some Comments on Awareness," *American Sociological Review*, Vol. 30 (1965), p. 779.

7. On the two sub-layers, see above pp. 31–32.

8. On these assumptions, see Cohen, *Reason and Nature, op. cit.*, p. 302, and Nisbet, *Community and Power, op. cit.*, pp. 144–145.

9. Emile Durkheim's "collective conscience" was defined as "the totality of beliefs and sentiments common to average citizens of the same society," *The Division of Labor in Society* (New York: Macmillan, 1933), p. 79. This, of course, refers to shared values, not to knowledge or awareness. The fact that it is often translated as "collective consciousness" rather than "collective conscience" or "values" is what requires our explication. Conscience is a matter of values and commitment; values define its substance while commitment defines its intensity. Conscience might be

activated by new facts (e.g., the state of Soviet Jewry) but equally or more so by socialization and social control mechanisms—from Sunday preaching to a Presidential address. Its function is active moral concern, not attention to facts. On the use of conscience as defined here, see O. R. McGregor, "Social Facts and Social Conscience," *The Twentieth Century*, Vol. 167 (1960), pp. 389–396.

10. Karl Marx, *Economic and Philosophic Manuscripts of 1844* (New York: International Publishers, 1964), p. 113. See also Erich Fromm, *Beyond the Chains of Illusion: My Encounter with Marx and Freud* (New York: Simon & Schuster, 1962), especially pp. 91–94, 113–114.

11. Cf. Karl Mannheim, *Ideology and Utopia* (London: Routledge and Kegan Paul, 1954), pp. 138–146. Mannheim saw consciousness as a correct diagnosis of a situation, which we do not assume. See his *Diagnosis of Our Time* (London: Kegan Paul, Trench, Trubner, 1943), p. 61.

12. For another definition of consciousness without metaphysical connotations —"the feedback and simultaneous scanning of highly selected internal data"—see Karl W. Deutsch, *Nerves of Government, op. cit.*, p. 97. See also p. 130. For additional discussion, see Aron Gurwitsch, "On the Conceptual Consciousness," Kenneth M. Sayre and Frederick J. Crosson (eds.), *The Modeling of Mind: Computers and Intelligence* (Notre Dame, Indiana: University of Notre Dame Press, 1963), pp. 199–205.

13. For a fine sociological historical study, see Jacob Katz, *Exclusiveness and Tolerance* (London: Oxford University Press, 1961).

14. On this concept see Paul F. Lazarsfeld and Herbert Menzel, "On the Relation Between Individual and Collective Properties," *Complex Organizations: A Sociological Reader*, edited by Amitai Etzioni (New York: Holt, Rinehart & Winston, 1961), pp. 422–440.

15. On this concept, see David Krech and Richard S. Crutchfield, *Theory and Problems of Social Psychology* (New York: McGraw-Hill, 1948), pp. 388–389. See also Warren Breed and Thomas Ktsanes, "Pluralistic Ignorance in the Process of Opinion Formation," *Public Opinion Quarterly*, Vol. XXV (1961), pp. 382–392.

16. Seymour M. Lipset, Martin A. Trow, James S. Coleman, *Union Democracy*, (Garden City, N.Y.: Anchor Books, 1962), p. 277. See also Fernando Penalos, "Class Consciousness and Social Mobility in a Mexican–American Community," unpublished Ph.D. dissertation, University of Southern California, 1963.

17. Gabriel A. Almond and Sidney Verba, *The Civic Culture* (Princeton, N.J.: Princeton University Press, 1963), esp. pp. 79–100. See also Robert K. Merton's distinction between "cosmopolitan" and "local" in *Social Theory and Social Structure* (New York: Free Press, 1965), Rev. Ed., pp. 393–409, esp. 393. For a descriptive account see Susan Sheehan, *Ten Vietnamese* (New York: Knopf, 1967).

18. *American Behavioral Scientist*, Vol. 8 (March, 1965), p. 34. For additional documentation, see Chapter 15.

19. Daniel Lerner, "Communication Systems and Social Systems: A Statistical Exploration in History and Policy," *Behavior Science*, Vol. 2 (1957), pp. 266–275. For a discussion of "world view" as a prerequisite for consensus formation, see Douglas E. Ashford, "Patterns of Consensus in Developing Countries," *American Behavioral Scientist*, Vol. IV (April, 1961), pp. 7–10. See also Heinz Eulau and Peter Schneider, "Dimensions of Political Involvement," *Public Opinion Quarterly*, Vol. XX (1956), pp. 128–142.

20. Milbrath, *Political Participation, op. cit.*, pp. 110–128.

21. Almond and Verba, *Civic Culture, op. cit.*, pp. 230–257.

22. Solomon Sutker, "The Role of Social Clubs in the Atlanta Jewish Community," Marshal Sklare (ed.), *The Jews* (New York: Free Press, 1958), pp. 262–270.

23. See, for example, Albert O. Hirschman, "Obstacles to Development: A Classification and a Quasi-Vanishing Act," *Economic Development and Cultural Change*, Vol. 13 (1965), pp. 385–393.

24. See above, discussion on contextuating symbols, p. 167.

25. Leadership differs from mere elite membership in that the leader has also (or only) an element of personal and not just positional power. See Etzioni, *A Comparative Analysis of Complex Organizations, op. cit.*, pp. 89–91.

26. Karl Marx, *The Eighteenth Brumaire of Louis Bonaparte* (Moscow: Foreign Languages Publishing House, n.d.), pp. 123–126. For discussion and broad review of the literature, see Seymour M. Lipset, *Political Man* (Garden City, N.Y.: Anchor Books, 1963), p. 76 and *passim*. See also Seymour M. Lipset, Paul F. Lazarsfeld, Allen H. Barton, and Juan J. Linz, "The Psychology of Voting: An Analysis of Political Behavior," in Gardner Lindzey (ed.), *Handbook of Social Psychology*, II (Cambridge, Mass.: Addison-Wesley, 1954), pp. 1124–1175. See also Stanislaw Ossowski, *Class Structure in the Social Consciousness* (New York: Free Press, 1963).

27. For discussion and references to earlier works see Morris Zelditch, Jr. and Bo Anderson, "Rank Equilibration and Political Behavior," *European Journal of Sociology*, Vol. 5 (1964), pp. 112–125; and Zelditch and Anderson, "On the Balance of a Set of Ranks," in Joseph Berger, Morris Zelditch, Jr., and Bo Anderson, *Sociological Theories in Progress* (Boston: Houghton Mifflin, 1966), pp. 244–268.

28. David Thompson, *The Democratic Ideal in France and England* (Cambridge, England: Cambridge University Press, 1940), p. 48.

29. Bruce M. Russett, *Trends in World Politics* (New York: Macmillan Company, 1965), pp. 106–124.

30. Harvey Wish (ed.), in his introduction to *The Negro Since Emancipation* (Englewood Cliffs, N.J.: Prentice-Hall, 1964), p. 8.

31. Alex Bein, *Theodore Herzl: A Biography* (Philadelphia: The Jewish Publication Society of America, 1940), pp. 108–120, esp. 116.

32. Colin Legum, "Pan-Africanism and Nationalism," in Joseph C. Anene and Godfrey N. Brown (eds.), *Africa in the Nineteenth and Twentieth Centuries* (Ibadan, Nigeria: Ibadan University Press, 1966), pp. 528–540.

33. For further discussion of this point, see discussion of consensus-formation below.

34. O. J. Harvey, D. E. Hunt, and H. M. Schroder, *Conceptual Systems and Personality Organization* (New York: Wiley, 1961), pp. 24–49 and Robert E. Lane, "The Decline of Politics and Ideology in a Knowledgeable Society," *American Sociological Review*, Vol. 31 (1966), p. 654.

35. See Karl Marx, *The German Ideology* (New York: International Publishers, 1939), p. 19, for this proposition. See also pp. 13–14. For additional relevant discussion, see Karl Marx and Friedrich Engels, "Preface to 'A Contribution to the Critique of Political Economy'," *Selected Works* (Moscow: Foreign Languages Publishing House, 1955), Vol. I, p. 364.

36. Richard L. Merritt, *Symbols of American Community, 1735–1775* (New Haven, Conn.: Yale University Press, 1966).

37. E. Berger, "Un-American Jew," *Commentary*, Vol. 42 (1966), esp. p. 84.

38. Seymour M. Lipset, "University Students and Politics in Underdeveloped Countries," *Minerva*, Vol. III (Autumn 1964), pp. 15–56.

39. Saul D. Alinsky discusses some of the arguments in favor of this position in his "The War on Poverty—Political Pornography," *Journal of Social Issues*, Vol. 21 (1965), pp. 41–47, esp. 45–46.

40. In the modern period, Congress in effect did not oversee scientific activities. Little more supervision took place between 1945 and 1955. When the space program was initiated, two permanent and several ad hoc Congressional committees, devoted to this sector were established. See also footnote 33, Chapter 8.

41. The opposite notion has often been advanced. It was suggested, for instance, during the 1956 Sinai Campaign, that the Soviet Union would avoid involvement in the Middle East because it was "preoccupied" with the Hungarian uprising. A similar idea is expressed by Michael Polanyi. He distinguishes between focal and subsidiary awareness. The first we pay to a hammer, the other to a nail we hit. See his *Personal Knowledge* (Chicago: University of Chicago Press, 1958), p. 55.

42. For instance, the fact that the President customarily delivers a State of the Union message in January forces his attention to the matters covered in the preceding months and what will be taken up in the coming year.

43. Herbert A. Simon, Donald W. Smithburg, Victor A. Thompson, *Public Administration* (New York: Knopf, 1959), pp. 130–133.

44. Evidence in support of this proposition with regard to legislators is presented by Raymond A. Bauer, Ithiel de Sola Pool, and Lewis Anthony Dexter, *American Business and Public Policy: The Politics of Foreign Trade* (New York: Atherton Press, 1963), pp. 408–413.

45. Erik H. Erikson discusses the opposite process in which the identity is lost in his *Childhood and Society* (New York: Norton, 1963). He uses the concept as an attribute both of persons and collectivities (see especially p. 154). Note also that Erikson views identity as an experience (p. 42). A *sense* of identity would then involve varying degrees of awareness of identity, while identity itself would be more a matter of visibility. For our purposes, this additional subtlety is unnecessary; identity and the sense of it are treated jointly. See also Nelson N. Foote and Leonard S. Cottrell, Jr., *Identity and Interpersonal Competence* (Chicago: University of Chicago Press, 1955).

46. *The New York Times*, May 14, 1966 and May 20, 1966.

47. Mannheim, *Ideology and Utopia*, *op. cit.*, pp. 140–146.

48. For examples and a related line of analysis, see Peter F. Drucker, *Landmarks for Tomorrow* (New York: Harper & Row, 1957), pp. 26–49.

49. John W. Spanier, *American Foreign Policy Since World War II* (New York: Praeger, Inc., 1960), pp. 23–33. See also Lord Ismay, *NATO: The First Five Years, 1949–1954* (Paris: NATO, n.d.); William T. R. Fox and Annette B. Fox, *NATO and the Range of American Choice* (New York: Columbia University Press, 1967), pp. 13–16.

50. James Ridgeway, "The Dick," *The New Republic*, Vol. 154, pp. 11–13 (March 12, 1966); *The New York Times*, March 6, 1966, p. 94.

51. Carl Bakal, *The Right to Bear Arms* (New York: McGraw-Hill, 1966).

52. These other forces are discussed in Chapters 13–15.

53. Koestler, *The Act of Creation*, *op. cit.*, pp. 450–454; Gabriel A. Almond

and G. Bingham Powell, Jr., *Comparative Politics: A Developmental Approach* (Boston: Little, Brown & Co., 1966), p. 35. See also J. H. Milsum, *Biological Control Systems Analysis* (New York: McGraw-Hill, 1966).

54. Marion J. Levy, Jr., "Contrasting Factors in the Modernization of China and Japan," *Economic Development and Cultural Change*, Vol. 2 (1953–1954), pp. 161–197, esp. 188–194.

55. Levy, *ibid.*; See essays by William W. Lockwood and John Whitney Hall in Robert E. Ward and Dankwart A. Rustow (eds.), *Political Modernization in Japan and Turkey* (Princeton, N.J.: Princeton University Press, 1964).

CHAPTER 11

The Specification of Societal Commitments:

Rationalist and Incrementalist

Approaches

ACTIVE UNITS are more effective in realizing their goals and values than passive ones. Two major determinants of this difference in effectiveness are the level and intensity of the commitments of such units and the processes through which they are specified—in particular, the quality of societal consensus-building and decision-making. These two processes most directly determine the substance of the societal goals and values and the ways in which the actor will specifically attempt to implement them. Consensus-building is discussed below (Chapters 17 and 18); here, we deal with societal decision-making (Chapters 11 and 12).

Although both processes are concerned with the setting of commitments and with their specification, consensus-building deals relatively more with setting the context of that to which the actor is committed, while societal decision-making is more concerned with the specification of the context, of the efforts to realize the actor's values and implement his goals.[1]* *It is, thus,*

---

* Reference notes for this chapter appear on page 273.

mainly through the decision-making processes that vague and abstract societal commitments, whose directions are indicated by the values and goals to which the actor subscribes, are translated into specific commitments to one or more specific courses of action. As in the process the initial commitments may be either lost or reinforced, weakened or fulfilled, distorted or clarified, this continual specification—which is largely what decision-making entails—is of central interest to the theory of an active orientation. A vague, normative commitment—however intense—will not make a unit active; ways and means for translating the commitment into myriad regulating signals expressive of the basic commitment must be found if the societal unit is to be active.

From a morphological viewpoint, decision-making appears at the point of articulation of the cybernetic centers with the implementation processes (both are part of the controlling overlayer). Decision-making itself is a social process that deals in symbols; it is, however, just one step removed from implementation, the communication of controlling signals to the units and the application of power. Thus, the inputs into a decision (which, in this sense, "precede" implementation) include: the *knowledge* of the actor, used to chart alternative routes and to explore their expected consequences; the actor's *consciousness* of himself and of others, of the genetic and synchronic bonds and links which affect the degree to which he actively uses his knowledge in making decisions; and the actor's *general commitment*, the normative context of his decisions, the vague and general values and goals to be specified in the decision-making process. Implementation "follows" the decision-making process in that here decisions are communicated and power is applied to enforce them.

However, the distinction between the input and the output aspects, as is implied by the sequential notion of "before" and "after," is strictly analytic because *past decisions* affect present knowledge, consciousness, and normative commitments, and *present acts* of implementation affect future decisions. But for heuristic purposes, it seems productive to maintain an image of the factors that go into a single decision and those that follow it as if their relations did constitute a closed circle.

THE PLACE OF DECISION-MAKING IN THE PROCESS OF CONTROL

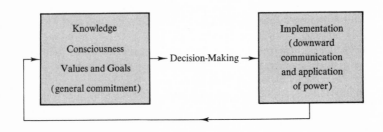

Decision-making, thus viewed, is a synthesizing process of the controlling centers in which knowledge and commitment are fused and related to *considerations* of implementation. It is also the point at which the element of choice (and, in that sense, of freedom) is most explicit; decision-making is the most deliberate and voluntaristic aspect of societal conduct. It is the attribute that most clearly distinguishes controlled from ongoing processes. Actors affect ongoing processes, too, through their actions or reactions, but it is only through the controlling overlayers and, ultimately, the decision-making units that they can deliberately project themselves into the ongoing processes and attempt to modify them in accord with what is preconceived and preferred by the actors.

This is the reason that the question of the rationality of societal action arises most clearly in the study of decision-making: To what degree can societal actors decide their course of action, and to what degree are they compelled to follow a course not chosen by them? We turn to this question after a brief discussion of a few definitional issues and the state of the art of studying decisions. We explore the extent to which a societal actor is able to make decisions that are effective in terms of his commitments. Our argument follows three dialectically related steps. First, we deal with intrinsic criticisms of the concept of rational decision-making—that is, with considerations that need to be taken into account in revising the concept if it is to be retained as central to societal analysis. We next review extrinsic criticisms, the major efforts to replace the concept with another—chiefly, incrementalism. Finally, we outline a third approach to societal decision-making which is less rationalistic in its assumptions than the first but more so than the second. Mixed-scanning (discussed in the next chapter) combines elements of both earlier approaches.

Decision-Making: A Delineation

Decision as a Conscious Act

By *decision* we mean a conscious choice between two or more alternatives. Not all choices are conscious, but those that are not are not decisions. A non-conscious choice made at one point in time might reflect a decision made at an earlier point; for instance, a labor union may authorize an employer to deduct $10 per month from each worker's salary for the Red Cross. A year later, the union leader may have forgotten the deduction; while he is still choosing to give to the Red Cross, he is no longer *deciding* to do so. The decision was made at the time of the initial conscious arrangement. In addition to non-conscious choices which were once conscious, there are other choices which were never decided upon; e.g., they were accepted "on authority" without any conscious examination. If the element of consciousness is removed from the definition of the concept of decision[2] and all choices are seen as decisions, a new term is needed for conscious choices which, we suggest, differ empirically from non-conscious ones. We expect, for example, that under most circumstances, conscious choices are relatively more rational in terms of the selection of appropriate means toward an end. As a consequence, we prefer to view decision-making as a conscious act, as implied in the common usage of the term.

The difference between conscious and non-conscious choices is important not only because non-conscious choices are made, but because even when an actor is conscious of some choices in a particular situation, there are some others in the same situation of which he is not aware but which are visible to trained observers. *For most societal actors, we suggest, the range of options is significantly greater than the number of alternatives of which they are aware.* The decision-making strategies actors follow differ in the degree to which they ignore as against recognize options which are available from the point of view of an observer.

Policy-making is a form of decision-making in which whole sets of decisions are considered and the contexts for decisions concerning bits are reviewed. It is not that contexts are never considered when a single, especially-important decision is made, but their critical examination is likely to be more extensive in the determination of policy. *Policy-making* is, hence, best viewed as more generalized and, in this sense, more abstract decision-making. In the following discussion, decision-making refers to both decision- and policy-making unless policy-making is explicitly mentioned for separate discussion.

The State of the Art

While many volumes have been written about decision-making, most of them do not deal with its societal form. To review these various studies would require a volume larger than the present one.[3] Here, we shall only mention the ways in which these studies differ from those needed for the analysis of societal guidance.

1. Guidance analysis has a theoretical foundation; i.e., it builds on a body of interrelated statements about reality that can be verified. The major purpose of many studies of decision-making, on the other hand, is normative —to present prescriptions.[4]

2. A theory of societal guidance inevitably deals with macro-actors, while the overwhelming majority of decision-making studies are concerned with individuals (voters, consumers, and so on).[5] Moreover, some of the relatively few studies that are concerned with macro-actors treat them as if they followed the same procedures as individual decision-makers.[6] In contrast, it seems to us that macro-decision-makers differ from individual ones on the following dimensions: They are internally more differentiated,

they can make use of larger amounts of knowledge and more sophisticated decision-making technology, and their process of decision-making is more institutionalized and organized.[7]

3. Of the few studies of decision-making that are macroscopic, several are deliberately descriptive.[8] They provide essential building-stones for a theory of macroscopic decision-making, but they themselves attempt no such analysis. The works of several political scientists approach a macroscopic theory of decision-making.[9] These works are pre-theoretical only in that they use paradigms—that is, a check-list of variables—without specifying, on the model level, the hypothetical scores of the variables and the relations among them. A typical study lists the conditions under which a decision was initiated, the actors that participated, the "setting for decisions," the "stages of decision-making," and the "organizational context in which the decision is set."[10] This is of value, as the same list is used for several studies and, thus, makes for uniformity in the collection of data. On the other hand, the study does not (nor does it pretend to) provide a theoretical framework.

Many studies of decisions deal with "atomized" actors, one at a time. A theory of societal guidance is concerned with actors who make decisions in situations in which there are other, partially related actors—that is, actors who also make decisions and who affect each other in the process. Societal decision-making must, hence, be studied as a multi-actor process.

4. Most decision-making studies are "universal" and non-structural. For instance, Simon's important distinction between optimizing and "satisficing," discussed below, is presented in abstraction, independent of any particular socio-political system.[11] It applies as much to a consumer in a supermarket as to the President of the United States. We seek to integrate such conceptions of decision-making with a theory of *societal* guidance; hence, macro-factors—for instance, the question of which societal forces encourage optimizing as against satisficing—are of primary interest. For this purpose, universal theories must be *specified* in a societal context and related to societal *structures and organizations*.

This is not to suggest that there are no macroscopic, morphological, and logico-empirical studies. The works of Banfield, Hirschman, Lindblom, Paige, Schilling, and Wildavsky closely approximate what is needed;[12] our major difference with these works is not with their level of analysis or methodology but is substantive, as the following discussion of incrementalism will attempt to specify.

Just as for our purposes decision-making is to be studied in a societal context, so studies of societal units that do not include decision-making are incomplete. The decision-making units are an integral part of the cybernetic centers of the controlling overlayers of societal actors; thus, theories of society which exclude them depict societies and collectivities as passive units which "interact" or "integrate" but have no control of themselves or of their interrelations. Control implies a capacity to select among alternatives, among the courses of action a unit seeks to follow—in short, a capacity to make decisions.

Rationality and Control

Instrumental Rationality and Its Limitations

Instrumental rationality is an open selection of means to serve a goal. Despite repeated, valid, and effectively presented criticisms of the notion of instrumental rationality, it still plays a central role in the social sciences in general as well as in popular conceptions of decision-making. In much of the work on administrative analysis and practice,[13] the prevailing image still seems to be that of an actor who becomes aware of a problem, carefully weighs alternative means to its solution, and chooses among them according to his estimates of their respective merits in terms of the state of affairs he prefers. Subjective instrumental rationality is said to prevail if the decision-maker is willing to consider alternatives other than the one he was first inclined to choose if these are shown to be superior. Objective instrumental rationality is defined as the scientifically determined best course. The more rational an actor, the more similar his choice will be to that made by scientifically trained observers. Thus, the relationship of subjective to objective rationality is like the relationship of the choices made to the options available.

The persistent use of the concept of instrumental rationality to the neglect of a more encompassing and balanced notion can be seen in the numerous works in which the associations of psychological attributes and sociological structures with behavior which is reported to be instrumentally rational (e.g., entrepreneurial conduct) are explored. The effects of these attributes and structures on the primacy of goals, on other goals of the same actors, and on the shared goals of these and other actors as well as on needs not expressed in terms of goals are not examined. These are often explored in a different category of studies (e.g., studies of interpersonal relations at work or of the alienating effects of organizational life), but, with that dubious capacity of scientists not to allow information in one "box" to disturb that in another, the implications of these other studies for instrumental rationality are frequently not taken into account when the psychological and socio-logical prerequisites of rationality are explored. Thus, we have, simul-taneously, studies which explore the conditions under which instrumental rationality can be promoted (and quite explicitly advocate the establishment of these conditions) *and* studies which specify the severe dysfunctions of instrumental rationality. This deserves some elaboration.

Psychologically, an actor who is wholly instrumentally rational must, in theory, suppress in his decision-making all "irrelevant" considerations. These considerations intrude because the actor is subject to various pressures to choose alternatives not because they best suit his goal but because he is emotionally affected (e.g., by fear) or related to the object of his decision (e.g., by kinship). Succumbing to such "irrelevant" intrusions is non-rational, by definition, so far as the instrumentalist position is concerned. While no one is completely immune to non-rationality, it is argued, the more alternatives an actor explores laterally and longitudinally before he is "distracted," the more rational is his decision. To be rational, it is proposed, the actor must be free from "particularistic" and "affective" commitments to the objects of his deliberations.[14] Detachment and rationality are, thus, viewed as intimately associated.

Arguments to the effect that attributes such as neutrality, a highly calculative orientation, and "coolness" are necessary for the effective administrator, entrepreneur, or researcher use this conception of rationality.[15] These qualities are seen as necessary for maintaining *detachment*. The attached, "affective," or "warm" personality is viewed as the opposite type, both in terms of psychological attributes and the capacity for rational decision-making. While it is no longer common to characterize ethnic groups, races, or nations as more or less capable of rational behavior, and it is common to emphasize that there are persons of all personality types in every societal unit, it is often argued that societal units differ in the frequency with which one psychological profile or another is found.[16] And while various terms are used—such as the Protestant Ethic, achievement motivation, entrepreneurship—it is often held, for instance, that Anglo-Saxons are more "detached" than Latins, and, hence, that economic development and effective administration are more common in the United States than in Latin America, more prevalent in Northern Europe than in Southern Italy, Greece, Spain, and so on.[17] The rational society is then viewed as the society that produces a relatively high proportion of detached men, and its family and educational systems are studied to establish the ways in which this is achieved.[18]

The limitations of this concept of rationality have often been recognized. David Riesman explicitly introduced the notion that the inner-directed man (his instrumental–rational type) is not *ipso facto* the more effective man.[19] Similarly, work in the Human Relations tradition contrasted the work-oriented, excessively instrumental, rigid supervisor, with the more flexible, worker-oriented one.[20] And Parsons and Bales use an instrumental–expressive dichotomy.[21]

Others put less emphasis on the genesis and psychological prerequisites and stress instead the morphology or phenomenology of rational society: Which societal structures encourage instrumental rationality? The answer is the highly differentiated structures.[22] Each societal unit has a variety of needs. Society must not only produce or introduce means to meet these needs but must also arrange for the allocation of means among member-units, educate members to their social duties, and "manage" tensions in and among members.[23] In simple societal units such as primitive tribes or traditional historical societies, the servicing of all these varying societal needs is fused together, and, hence, the internal "logic" of any one of them is not well developed. Moreover, such societal units are non-rational from the viewpoint of the servicing of any one need. Modern structures are said to provide a segregated unit for each sector of societal activities—economic, administrative, knowledge-producing and processing—relatively free from the pressures of such non-rational considerations as kinship ties, class, or caste.[24] The more differentiated a unit, it is argued, the more instrumental rationality is evident in the servicing of a particular societal need; this holds not only for production but also for public administration, research, and other societal needs. Similarly, it is argued that modern pluralistic polities are more rational than totalitarian ones in which units are differentiated but are not sufficiently protected from the penetration of "irrelevant" factors (e.g., the Party).[25] It is important to note that this conception of rationality underlies much of the contemporary writing in public administration,[26] Western studies of development,[27] and arguments about the merits of democratic polities and pluralistic societies.[28]

The validity of the conception that the more a society is differentiated the more it is rational is tested by determining whether or not the "dependent variable" is limited to instrumental rationality or takes into account the need for a more encompassing rationality as well. Does this approach encompass an analysis of the relations among the services of the various societal goals and needs, among the differentiated units? Are the decision-making criteria tied to unit-analysis or explored with a recognition of the need to relate the units to a more encompassing societal entity? Marx's basic sociological conception (though this varied from work to work and in *Capital* itself) was caught in this dichotomy. He contrasted a society of conflict and alienation with one of harmony and human integrity as if the classless society had no instrumental needs and no problems relating these to its expressive ones, while the conflict-ridden society was without expressive foundations. He, thus, avoided the crucial test of rationality by dividing the instrumental and expressive needs between two types of societies which he projected onto two historical periods, needs which must be related in one and the same society and period before the concept of rationality can be encompassing and serve as a satisfactory guide to effective decision-making.

Only a few studies deal systematically with both differentiation and the articulation of the differentiated sectors. Riggs compared two highly differentiated structures, one with high coordination which he called "fused" and one with low coordination which he called "diffracted."[29] Riesman adds to his study of the inner-directed and other-directed the conception of an autonomous man. Etzioni studied interstitial structures and higher-level decision-making structures that are neither instrumental nor expressive but attempt to relate these two orientations.[30]

A main function of the controlling overlayer of societal units is to mold sub-units into more encompassing entities with reference to the normative commitments of the units and the supra-units. This entails developing decision-making criteria in accord with a set of values; that is, the processes of control do not attempt to mold units into supra-units haphazardly but favor, from among the possible combinations, those more in accord with the normative commitments of the decision-makers and the various member-units. The relationship of the control processes to any one unit is like the relationship of comprehensive to instrumental rationality. The controlling overlayer need not be centralist or very powerful, but if there are *no* mechanisms for making decisions with regard to the allocation of means and for coordinating efforts among actors whose goals differ, or among units that specialize in serving different societal needs, there is no provision for comprehensive rationality. Typically, theories of society that deal with differentiation but not with the articulation of the units do not include concepts of a controlling overlayer or political organization.

Critical views on and amendments to the conception of instrumental rationality have been developed along three major lines which are quite well known and need only brief review here. They suggest that it is necessary to curb the open choice of means in order to sustain the actor's commitment to his goals; to take into account considerations other than service to the goal; and, above all, to note that the actor is committed to more than one goal at a time and, hence, that his decision-making must be based on compre-hensive rationality. We will now briefly discuss each of these three amendments.

Sustaining Commitment

Rationality is not a linear process in which the greater the detachment of the actor, the more rational is his decision-making. While some detach-ment may lead to greater rationality, further detachment may blur and eventually erase the goal for which the chain of calculation and means was composed. In psychological terms, the commitment to any given goal is emotional and, in that sense, non-rational; the greater the detachment (i.e., the more emotions are suppressed), the greater seems to be the danger that commitment to goals will be suppressed as well. A historical perspective is provided by Weber who pointed out that while initially the detached orientation was a means to a religious goal (the success of work in God's vineyard, austere living, and saving were signs of salvation), the religious value became lost while self-denial was maintained as a chain of means without a goal. Weber considered this the irrationality of rationality,[31] a situation which can be observed in administrative structures in which means have come to be "ritualized"—e.g., a bureaucrat imposes a rule (the means) even though suspension of that rule would better serve the goal in that particular instance.[32] The same phenomenon can be observed in those organizations which, though formed to serve a particular goal, continue to exist long after that goal has been realized, or the organization's elaboration and protection take priority over service to the goal.[33] In short, it cannot be held that the more an actor is instrumentally rational, the more rational is his decision-making. This is the case only to the extent that provisions are made to protect the goal toward which the decision-making is oriented, which, we suggest, as a rule *entails imposing some limitations on the open selection of means*—that is, on instrumental rationality.

Occasional "premature" gratifications and "irrational" asides must be permitted, even from a narrow mono-goal viewpoint. While instrumental rationality prescribes the deferment of gratification, maintaining goal commitments requires diverting some assets to provide rewards, even if these assets could have yielded more rewards at a later point had gratification been further deferred. The same holds for the introduction or tolerance of some other "non-rational" criteria for the selection of means—some bribery, political "kickbacks," and nepotism, or the diversion of a highway to avoid a shrine.

Morphologically, this requires a sub-layer in the controlling overlayer above the sub-layer which oversees the rational selection of means—a sub-layer which suspends (or otherwise limits) instrumental considerations before they erode the normative commitments of the societal actor. These limitations to instrumental rationality also, we suggest, reinforce the basic normative commitments. Thus, the presence of grades may distort the educational process, but they enforce the motivation to be educated; the imperfect enforcement of the law keeps the members of overmanaged societies from rebelling and blocking progress altogether.

Rationality—still viewed here in terms of the selection of means to realize one goal—is, thus, not the maximization of instrumental rationality but a proper balance between the selection of means according to their instrumental merits and sustaining the goal commitment. We say proper "balance" because once instrumentality has begun to be limited to maintain goal primacy, such limitations may go so far as to undermine instrumental rationality unnecessarily. Hence, both goal primacy and the curtailment of "irrelevant" criteria for the selection of means must be established in order to enhance rationality. There have to be both holidays and arrangements for their termination.[34]

"Secondary" Considerations

While the dangers of a loss of commitment have often been emphasized, the opposite dangers of overcommitment to a goal (or, the utopian approach) are recognized less often. Actually, as well as protecting the goal, which, so to speak, stands at the end of the means chain, a rational actor must also concern himself with protecting the "sides" of the decision-making process. When coal for a locomotive is scarce, there is some inclination to use planks from the sides of the train's cars to build up steam—that is, to undermine secondary unit-needs in order to maximize activities directly related to the goal. All societal units have a variety of needs; attempts to maximize the realization of the unit's goal tend to erode the servicing of other needs. The more instrumentally oriented a unit, the greater we expect will be the pressure to commit assets and efforts to activities directly related to the goal as against secondary activities—e.g., a greater emphasis on output than on the maintenance of tools, more stress on short rather than on long-run results, more emphasis on measureable versus less measureable outputs, more attention to quantity and less to quality. All these tendencies are distortions of instrumental rationality, since they violate its own logic. They occur not only in production but in all societal activities—in religion and in education, for example, when attendance, fund-raising, and building, being more measureable, are given more attention than the depth of the commitment achieved. National societies in periods of crisis tend to emphasize military rather than political considerations, even though the military ones are instrumental to the political goals.

The tendency to subordinate the societal unit's needs more and more to the service of a goal results in undermining the unit's capacity for goal-realization in the longer run. If there were clear measures of how much should be reserved for the maintenance of a factory or of the ways in which church attendance is related to salvation, the non-rationality of the distortion of overcommitment to a goal would be more visible. In fact, though, this is not the case, and when the pressure to realize the goal increases, one major accommodation—frequently made in the name of instrumental rationality—is to increase the allocation of assets and attention to the primary goal activities. Hence, maintaining rationality requires protecting the secondary needs against such encroachment.

One such protection mechanism is the establishment of a control-unit that specializes in looking after "secondary" considerations. In the corporate realm, units which specialize in quality-control, planning, or labor relations will, hopefully, have such a "protective" effect. On the national level, new agencies or ministries are often established to fortify a neglected activity. Such units are expected to be effective only if they are given some power and, especially, access to the centers of control so that they can affect decision-making.

But such a balancing of primary and secondary considerations in the activity of a unit or in the service of a goal still provides only a defective criterion to assess the effectiveness of societal decision-making. Actually, activity so fortified—in which a proper balance between commitment and instrumental rationality is maintained and secondary needs are taken into account—is especially likely to encourage the neglect of other goals of the same unit and similar goals of other units. Enhanced rationality in realizing any one goal of one actor invariably poses the potential threat of this goal's domination over other goals and other actors.

Comprehensive Rationality

Societal actors are committed to more than one goal at each point in time, and, in most situations, there is more than one actor. These two statements hold for other kinds of actors as well—that is, for microscopic social units and individuals; the mono-goal actors created in experimental laboratories or assumed in model-building by all too many students of decision-making alone are excluded. Those model-builders who do recognize a multitude of goals frequently postulate one superior value (or "utility") which provides a criterion for establishing the relative weights of the various goals; this allows for a repetition, on the inter-goal level, of the kind of relative merit examination that instrumental rationality implies is conducted among the means to one goal. In effect, this entails a selection of means and means-to-means, in a two-step process. Actually, this is rarely possible. Societal actors pursue several goals and values simultaneously, and there is neither a superior nor a common criteria. A typical list for the United States includes freedom, security, democracy, subjective equality, rationality, progress, and "appropriate inclusion."[35] Attempts at hierarchization of such lists seem doomed to failure, as there are no criteria that suggest the relative weights of the various values.

Since it is not possible to draw on an over-all value (or on an ordered set of values) to relate and assign priorities to the goals, an optimization calculus has been suggested as a means for relating a multitude of goals to each other. It is argued approximately as follows: The service of each goal has a declining marginal utility. Thus, while additional attention to the needs of a goal would advance it further, the relative amount of additional achievement would tend to decline. At this point, more can be achieved in terms of the total set of goals of the particular actor by diverting some means to other goals. The underlying assumptions are that (1) there is a scarcity of means; (2) as a rule, means assigned to one goal are not available for the service of other goals[36]; and (3) to some degree, maximizing the instrumental-rationality of one goal will tend to undermine the service of others.

A decision-maker who is *comprehensively rational*, it is suggested, is one whose decision-making approximates one version or another of such a calculus—i.e., an actor who takes not just one goal and the requirements of its servicing into account in his selection of a course of action but also considers the relations among the servicings of the various goals pursued. Non-rationality, here, involves not only undermining this or that goal-commitment by excessive means considerations, but also granting the servicing of one goal (or set of goals) more weight than is required for the optimization of the combined services of all of them.

In short, since the means assigned to one goal are, as a rule, not available to others, and the servicing of some goals conflicts with that of others, and, above all, because of the declining marginal utility of serving any one goal of the multiple goals to which an actor is committed, rationality is not to be conceived as maximizing the service of one goal but as the greatest combined servicing of all of the goals. Narrow, mono-goal rationality is instrumental, even when it takes into account the need to sustain commitments and "secondary" considerations, as it deals only with the articulation of means to a single goal. Working toward the greatest combined service to a set of goals is an attempt to evolve comprehensive rationality.[37] Instrumental rationality deals with the relations among means; comprehensive rationality is concerned with the relations among goals and their respective instrumental rationalities. What is rational from a comprehensive viewpoint is often non-rational from an instrumental viewpoint, though non-rationality appears also on the comprehensive level via the introduction of elements which prevent complete optimization.[38] To be fully comprehensive from the viewpoint of a societal actor, rationality must not merely combine considerations of several goals; it must also include a concern with the articulation of the instrumental and expressive needs of the societal unit in terms of its goals and values.

The differences between the secondary considerations of instrumental rationality and the calculus of comprehensive rationality need briefly to be indicated. The two conceptions overlap to the extent that instrumental rationality includes a concern for other goals that impinge as secondary considerations on the primary concern. Thus, for instance, the military, which is responsible for national security, may take into account the need for economy in its choice of weapons systems. A balanced budget, however, is not one of the military's goals. Hence, considerations which are secondary from the viewpoint of a member unit and are not the primary concern or goal of any other member unit will tend to be neglected unless they are taken into account on the comprehensive decision-making level.

Second, the status of a need as a secondary consideration of instrumental rationality and its status as a goal in the comprehensive matrix are quite different. In the first case, it has clearly a "means" status. For instance, a corporation may make some concessions in terms of the pace of production to maintain the workers' morale because it views such concessions as ultimately conducive to higher production, but if maintaining high morale requires undermining the opportunity for realizing the goal, then morale—so long as it is considered within the instrumentally rational context of production—will be allowed to decline. On the other hand, in principle, no goal is to be disregarded in the comprehensive matrix. Hence, while the secondary considerations of instrumental rationality and comprehensive rationality are related, they are not reducible; what is rational by one criterion is often not rational by the other.

It should be noted that "rational" as used in common parlance often refers to the narrow definition of the concept, to instrumental rationality, with limited concern for "secondary-considerations" and limited realization of the dilemma posed by comprehensive rationality (i.e., that the world is "inter-connected" and that advancing one goal may undermine others). This is important not only because instrumental rationality is the prevailing concept among the laity and, hence, among the subjects of social science research, but also because those disciplines which see the world in analytic slices rather than through the synthesizing eyes of systems metatheories often rely on this popular conception of rationality. And when they take a more comprehensive view, it tends to be segmental, as when economists take into account the relations and tensions between various economic values such as the stability of prices and economic growth but disregard other values which are directly affected by economic processes—for instance, political stability. It is not that every study can explore its subject with full comprehensive rationality, but there should be some evidence of an awareness of the limitations of the conclusions drawn from instrumental or segmental perspectives.

It might be said that these limitations are implicitly recognized even when not explicitly stated. But (a) it is often not clear whether it is being claimed that there are no effects on other values or whether these effects are deliberately left unexplored in a particular study, and (b) quite a few studies, especially those that lead to policy conclusions, would obviously reach different conclusions if they were more aware of their instrumental or segmental perspectives.[39]

A Societal, Comparative Perspective

From the viewpoint of comprehensive rationality, traditional societies give undue weight to expressive considerations to the neglect of instrumental ones. Early industrial societies suffer from the reverse imbalance—they stress economic, administrative, and technological considerations to the detriment of expressive ones. "Mature" capitalist societies and, especially, those societies under social democratic rule attempt to correct the industrial imbalance by introducing the welfare state, an expressive element. Left totalitarian party-states, in their attempts to develop more effective tools for correction than other industrial societies, seem to have done more damage to some values than they have advanced others, though their imbalance falls outside the traditional instrumental–expressive axis. It seems to be one of an imbalance between the control overlayer and the body of society, with both expressive and instrumental activities suffering from excessive attempts to control. We do not attempt to argue, in the limits of a paragraph, the relative merits of the various societal structures or decision-making approaches; we only wish to indicate the positions of these often mentioned societal types with regard to the conception of comprehensive rationality.

There is a close relationship between comprehensive rationality and the controlling overlayers, which may provide the necessary balancing. (Balancing does not imply giving equal weight to all goals and considerations but rather weights which conform to the actors' preferences.) It is here that the limitations of the traditional dichotomy between expressive and instrumental needs and activities become evident. While traditional societies stress expressive needs, the active verb is misleading; they rarely, if ever, review themselves from this viewpoint and have neither the idea that they can change their expressive–instrumental ratio nor the societal tools to do so. It would be, for instance, preposterous to suggest that eighteenth-century England decided to industrialize in order to enhance its deficient instrumentality. On the other hand, post-modern societies have a considerably higher level of self-consciousness and a much greater societal decision-making capacity as well as some tools for societal transformation. In comparing the levels of comprehensive rationality of various societal actors, then, it is necessary to take into account differences in their control capacities; otherwise, poor decisions (and, in this sense, non-rationality) might be attributed to passive actors, although only more active units have the option of making better decisions. To put it differently, to be rational (to make rational decisions and implement them), especially in the comprehensive sense, requires a high capacity for societal self-control. Passive societies, therefore, are not comprehensively rational by definition.

Finally, what is comprehensively rational for one sub-society may be non-rational (or instrumentally rational) from the viewpoint of the society as a whole. Statements about comprehensive rationality, hence, must always specify the actor to whose multiple goals they refer. The relationship to system analysis is evident: Optimization must take into account the effects pursuing one of the goals an actor has on the realization of his other goals, and his comprehensive rationality is increased if the sub-unit and unit criteria for decision-making are harmonized. The difference of perspective is that system analysis, in the socio-political tradition, tends to assume that the links between the units and the system are given or changing on-their-own; decision-making analysis views them as subject to guided change. In either case, comprehensive rationality must be viewed dynamically; what was comprehensive a generation ago is likely to be no longer so.

Impossibility of Rationality

Thus far, we have discussed criticisms of and amendments to the concept of rationality as a guide for societal decision-making which have been intrinsic to the concept. We turn now to an extrinsic criticism—that the model is not applicable because decision-makers neither do nor can meet its requirements. While this criticism applies to both kinds of rationality, it focuses upon comprehensive rationality on the grounds that the instrumental conception is inadequate even intrinsically.

Four questions are asked: What does rational decision-making require? What capacities are available to societal decision-makers? To what degree can these capacities be extended by the new knowledge-technology? Is the gap between the capacities and the requirements small enough to allow the use of the rationalistic model as a satisfactory simplification?

The Requirements

The requirements of rational decision-making have often been discussed:[40] (a) *information* about alternative courses of action and their consequences; (b) *calculation* of the alternative outcomes in terms of their meaning for the various values, and for various combinations of means;[41] (c) a set of *agreed-upon values* on the basis of which to select goals and to judge the consequences of alternative courses of action; and (d) an *exhaustive survey* of all relevant alternatives, since an unstudied alternative may be the optimal one. (The optimal alternative may not be a "good" one but only the best among a set of "bad" ones, and, hence, seemingly unappealing. Its relative merits may be established only if it is systematically compared to other alternatives.)

The Capacities

In most discussions of the actual capacities of decision-makers, the capacities of individual decision-makers are explored. It has been argued that, ultimately, all decisions are made by individuals.[42] We hold that decisions are also made by societal units—e.g., by Congress. For reasons discussed above, it is not correct to say, in terms of the language of societal analysis used here, that such units are aggregates of individuals. Nor are the decisions made by the occupants of the various roles (e.g., by Congressmen) acting autonomously or through an aggregation of such decisions (e.g., a majority vote) but rather via societal processes which are affected by the properties of the societal unit in which the decisions are made. If the members of any such unit were isolated from each other, they would reach decisions quite different in nature from those in which they share as members of a decision-making body. The decision-makers affect each other, and, in turn, this effect is in part determined by their positions in the structure of the societal unit which is deciding (i.e., has decision-making sub-units). Hence, societal decision-making is affected by the morphology of the societal unit.

In addition, capacities—from computers to a staff—which are usually unavailable to individuals are available for societal decision-making. While some members are likely to tend toward more innovative decisions than the societal decision-making units, the effectiveness of most decisions is determined by the capacity to collect and process information and to make computations; on this account, as we argued earlier, most societal actors are more effective than most individuals.

Being more effective, however, is certainly not synonymous with being very effective. In fact, our central proposition is that *societal decision-makers do not have the basic capacities for making rational decisions.*[43] Societal decision-making centers frequently do not have an agreed-upon set of values and goals; there may be dissensus within the decision-making centers themselves or in a higher-ranking unit that instructs the decision-makers, and/or the values and goals may be too vague to provide the necessary criteria. Values often become more specific only as decisions are implemented, as the actual consequences of a decision become visible. Moreover, member-units continually change their perspectives because of changes in their internal composition or in the environment. *Values are not given but are fluid* and affected by the decisions made as well as affecting them. The assumption that values and facts, means and ends, can be neatly (or even less neatly) separated by decision-makers seems to be invalid.[44]

Most societal decision-makers most of the time have only a part of the information they would need in order to examine all the relevant consequences of the various alternative courses. As a rule, they do not even know what information would be necessary and, hence, they do not know how much of this information they hold or its validity. Nor do they have the assets or time to collect more than an additional fraction of the needed information.

The necessary calculations cannot be carried out because, first, this capacity assumes that the two earlier prerequisites have been met—that criteria for evaluation (or weighing of utilities) have been provided, and that information about the consequences has been made available. Second, this assumes that there is a limited universe of relevant consequences that can be exhaustively surveyed; actually, the universe includes future consequences and these are "open."[45] That there is no adequate theory to account for cause and effect is well known.

Knowledge-Technology

While knowledge-technology, especially computers, is of some help in meeting some of these requirements, it does not allow for more than a narrowing of the gap between the requirements of the rationalistic model and the actors' capacities, even for the best-equipped actors. Knowledge-technology is most useful for the processing of information, especially from a "raw" to a semi-processed state; it also helps in the collection of information. It does make computation considerably less difficult, though even the most advanced computers either available or planned would find it difficult to carry out some of the computations required by the rationalistic model.[46] The machines are least useful in providing consensus or normative criteria where these are lacking. While the question of the range of the capacities of knowledge-technology, especially in its future development, has been a subject of considerable controversy, even the more optimistic assessors do not expect that the machines will be able to fulfill the needs of the model. And Simon has argued that even if they could meet these needs, the cost would be so high that human decision-makers would have to be used for most decisions.[47] In other words, comprehensive rationality would be either impossible or impractical.

The pattern of expectations initiated by the new advances in knowledge-technology is of some interest. Initially, the growth in knowledge-technology, especially the expectation that computers would be able to solve problems, led to the conclusions that decision-making would become more rationalized and that executive functions would be greatly curtailed, and the search for a science of politics—in the sense of making decisions on the basis of scientific criteria—was resurrected.[48] The underlying assumption of these projections followed what may be referred to as a straight-line fallacy. Such a fallacy was evident in earlier generations when declines in the power and functions of religion and in the size and functions of the family led to the expectation that these societal phenomena would continue to decline and, eventually, even disappear. Actually, what may be called "imperialistic" institutions released some of their "colonies" only to retain their "metropolitan" functions in both cases: Religion in modern societies left the attempt to provide an empirical characterization of the world to science, but science has rarely even attempted to penetrate into the metropolitan function of religion, the evaluation of the other-worldly.[49] Similarly, the family relinquished the functions of advanced education to the school and labor to a newly differentiated occupational sectors, but, instead of disintegrating, it has maintained without serious challenge its metropolitan functions of the initial "placement" and socialization of children.[50]

Now, similarly, expanded knowledge allows political elites to delegate some areas of decision-making to experts with the result that value and power decisions have "moved up" in the decision-making chain but have not been replaced. This retreat of political elites from some areas of decision-making is not without significance; it has increased the realm of "technical" competence and, thus, reduced the scope of normative and political conflict, but these trends should not be overly extrapolated. Modernization substitutes judgments on the basis of knowledge for "purer" political judgments mainly at the earlier (or lower) levels of the decision-making process; the higher levels are and, we expect, will remain greatly determined by normative and political factors.

A Tolerable Simplification?

A common defense of the rationalistic model is that it does not assume that decision-makers actually are rational but that it serves as a simplified model against which actual conduct can be measured. Rationalistic approaches, it is said, take into account that actors have "imperfect information." Were the rational actor to have complete information, he would be able to forecast the consequences of implementing various alternatives; decision-making models would then show him how to compute the utilities and choose among them or among various combinations of them. For actors who have "incomplete" information, the rationalistic models still apply, it is said, but they have to be used cautiously since they entail some degree of inaccuracy.[51] However, a model which more closely approximates reality is needed; otherwise, bridging the gap between observations and the model will remain highly uneconomical if not impossible.[52] One solution advocated is the other extreme—a concept of a non-rational man who is driven by urges, imprisoned by sentiments, constrained by values, manipulated by leaders; a man who occasionally may exercise some limited rationality but, for the most part, is not rational.[53] This seems to us to go too far in the opposite direction.

Using both models either simultaneously or alternately does not provide a solution, because the most central questions to be answered concern the articulation of the two elements, the rational and the non-rational. Our central concern is guidance, a process in which rational and non-rational elements are fused in varying degrees and ways. The concepts of rational and non-rational criteria for decision-making are highly abstract; societal analysis might more productively devote attention to processes in which these criteria are related and to the varying combinations that result. This fusing of the two kinds of considerations does not mean simply throwing them both into a vat and waiting at the spout for the mixture to flow. What is needed is a theory that will provide specific propositions about the processes and their outcomes.

The main utility of the concept of *fractional* information, which we prefer to "incomplete" information, is that while it does not assume that the actor has almost all the information he needs to be rational, it does recognize that the actor has *some* information. Were we to assume that he has almost no information, we would be using normative models that prescribe rational decision-making for "blind" situations—e.g., randomizing and equalizing one's bets.[54] If we are correct in suggesting that most actors most of the time have some valid information, such a random approach (as well as other purely prescriptive, a-empirical viewpoints) would encourage actors to perform less effectively than if they systematically took into account the information that is available to them.

What has been said about information holds also for the actor's capacity to calculate the utilities of the various courses of action and the results of various combinations of investments and efforts. The actor who is in command of relatively plentiful information is often "flooded"; i.e., he is unable to process this information. We would expect him to act confused in a manner not unlike that of an actor who has too little information. And even if he could digest all the available information, there are inherent limitations on his capacity to assign quantitative scores and weights to his values and to make the necessary computations. Knowledge-technology can markedly improve the initial processing of information and computations, once the relative weights of values are established and quantified, but it is much less useful for the higher levels of synthesis and for establishing criteria for computation. In short, the actor's capacity for calculation is also, at best, fractional. There are important differences in the size of this fraction, and we have seen above the importance of these differences in affecting relationships among actors. But the major societal decisions of even the best-equipped and most-informed societal actor cannot be understood—even "approximately" —within the framework of a rationalistic model.

Incrementalism—An Alternative Model

The Incrementalists

Gunnar Myrdal, John Dewey, and even David Hume have been credited with advancing the formulation of a model for decision-making that is less demanding than the rationalistic one. Among contemporary social scientists, Richard Snyder, Glenn D. Paige, Martin Meyerson, and Edward C. Banfield have disregarded the rationalistic assumption.[55] Karl Popper provided philosophical support for an alternative approach which is often referred to as the art of "muddling-through" or "incrementalism." He argued for piecemeal reforms rather than radical transformations, for attempting to avoid "evil" instead of actively seeking to introduce "good." Popper associates an active search for positive values with totalitarian societies and utopian efforts which, he argues, require a rationalistic model[56] and "may easily lead to an intolerable increase in human suffering."[57]

Scholars who recognize the rationalistic model's limitations have suggested several correctives or partial alternatives. Simon observes that most decision-makers do not even try to optimize but settle for "satisficing" solutions, those which provide a *relatively* satisfactory realization of their values.[58] Only if the realization of a value is frustrated is a search initiated for an alternative solution, but there is no attempt to find the maximum service of the value or the optimal combination of services which would require rationalistic analysis. Thus, a decision-maker can test a number of alternatives, either hypothetically or actually, and reject them one after the other until he finds one that "will do." This procedure is far less exacting than the rationalistic one.

Hirschman, in his studies of decision-making in developing nations, discusses and, indeed, advocates an "unbalanced" approach which is much less demanding than the rationalistic, "balanced" model in terms of the requirements it imposes on decision-making.[59] He points out that development requires both motivation and understanding, qualities which are not necessarily found simultaneously.[60] In the West, understanding often preceded motivation; in contemporary developing nations, motivation often precedes understanding. Hence, in the latter case, a decision-making strategy that has low knowledge requirements is needed, while the balanced model argues for well-coordinated progress that occurs in several areas at the same time.[61] This, Hirschman argues, overstrains the developing nations' decision-making capacities (and, we would add, the communication and power components of their controlling overlayers). The unbalanced approach envisages developing one sector even if other sectors are not "ready." Secondly, it expects that progress in one sector will "induce" development in related sectors, whereas the balanced approach would call for synchronized efforts.[62] Reactive ("induced") development must suffice until the higher, less common, more-difficult-to-achieve capacity for active ("autonomous") coordination grows. Thus, for example, while the balanced approach favors "spreading" investments among numerous industries, the unbalanced one is less reluctant to concentrate them in a few projects.* Further details of Hirschman's argument need not concern us here. For our purposes, his concept illustrates an effort to provide a guidance for decision-making which imposes almost none of the rationalistic requirements and allows actors who have extremely inadequate controlling overlayers to improve their decision-making as they seek to advance development.[63]

Among sociologists, the phenomenon of inter-institutional lag, especially in situations in which instrumental institutions "lag behind" expressive ones, is, in effect, an argument for synchronized progress.[64] It should be noted, however, that accepting unbalanced development still allows the recognition of the value of a balanced society and of future balancing.

---

* Hirschman does not favor simply going ahead with any project and hoping that the rest of the economy will fall into place; this would be a fatalistic, haphazard approach similar to the strategies advocated for situations in which there is *no* information. He offers some criteria for the selection of initiation points: (a) "Directly productive activities" are to be preferred over "social overhead capital" because the former provide an opportunity for a wide variety of solutions while the latter creates shortages which require specific solutions. *Ibid.*, p. 88. (b) Semiprocessed products are more effective for development than either raw materials or fully processed products because they generate pressure for development both "backward" (to produce raw materials) and "forward" (to complete the semi-processed materials). And (c) "high linkage" projects are preferable—that is, those which have many spill-over effects in directions other than the production process.

A state of balance can be achieved through unbalanced progress in one area and the subsequent "catching up" of the others, with the control mechanisms acting as a balancer and assisting those sectors left behind. Such a temporary lag may be preferred to synchronized progress, since the correction of such lags requires much less knowledge, a lower decision-making capacity, and a smaller power of control than balanced progress which may be so exacting that it is impossible. (That is, estimates of the costs of temporary imbalances may be weighed against the estimates of the "payoffs" of development.) On the other hand, it must be recognized that a correction is rarely complete and that the value of the unbalanced approach is greatly affected by the speed and scope of the corrections attained.

The Incrementalist Strategy

The fullest and most recent presentation of the "muddling-through" approach is found in the work of Charles E. Lindblom. "Disjointed incrementalism" is a decision-making strategy which Lindblom and others view as commonly followed; moreover, it is the strategy they seem to prescribe.[65] Using this strategy, decision-makers do not attempt a comprehensive survey and evaluation. They do not investigate all alternative policies but only those which differ incrementally (i.e., to a limited degree) from the existing policies. In addition, only a relatively small number of means is considered. This greatly reduces the scope and, therefore, the cost of the necessary information and computations. The incrementalist, Lindblom says, prefers the sin of omission to the sin of confusion which is the outcome of attempts to be rationalistic.*

Second, "one need not try to organize all possible values into a coherent scheme, but instead, can evaluate only what is relevant in actual policy choices."[66] Consensus is not a prerequisite and often develops only after the decision has been made. Since values cannot be ranked and weighed to allow for a comprehensive assessment of a policy's merits, and since trying to reach an agreement on values among the actors is difficult at best and is likely to delay if not prevent action, Lindblom argues that the measure of a good decision is the decision-makers' agreement about it. In incrementalist decision-making, rather than adjusting means to goals (as is called for by the rationalistic model), "ends are chosen that are appropriate to available or nearly available means."[67] If no consensus can be reached on even the immediate steps, the decision-maker might ignore the problem of consensus in groups other than his own.[68]

Decision-makers, the incrementalists stress, do not focus their attention

---

* The incrementalist procedure, Lindblom recognizes, entails not only omitting the exploration of fundamental alternatives but also incremental alternatives which fall outside the "familiar path of policy-making." *The Intelligence of Democracy, op. cit.*, p. 175.

on a clearly defined problem. There is no one decision, and problems are not "solved"; rather, there is a "never-ending series of attacks" on the issues at hand through successive or serial analyses and policy-making.[69] The incremental approach is deliberately exploratory. Rather than attempting to foresee all of the consequences of various alternate routes, one route is tried, and the unforeseen consequences are left to be discovered and treated by subsequent increments. Even the criteria by which increments are evaluated are developed and adapted in the course of action.

Morphological Implications

Beyond containing a strategy and a philosophy of decision-making, disjointed incrementalism also implies a structural model—it is presented as the typical decision-making process of pluralistic societies. In these societies, power is distributed among a large variety of actors such as interest groups, parties, executives, and factions of the national legislature. There is no one center of power but rather a continual give-and-take (or "mutual adjustment") among numerous centers of power. Formally, the President (with the "advice and consent" of Congress) serves as the major center of power, but, in actuality—the incrementalists argue—he must gain the support of the country, of interest groups, and of various agencies, and he has to adjust to their demands just as they adjust to his. The varying centers of power have varying interests and values, and one center can rarely impose its interests and values on the others. Policies are the outcomes of a give-and-take among numerous partisans; this is another reason for the disjointed and incremental nature of these policies.[70]

Disjointed incrementalism has as much in common with the politics of compromise and coalition as, historically, master planning has with centralist societies and socialism and rapid social change has with revolutionary politics.* The free-competition model strongly influences the incrementalist view of political life.[71] There are no intrinsically good or bad commodities; there are only those commodities which the consumers "vote" (with their

---

* "However much they may disagree over how policy should be made, however, almost all agree on how it actually is made in the United States. Policy is the product of muddling through: it is the result of incremental, ad hoc decisions, in which issues and values, ends and means are hopelessly confused. As a result, it lacks coherence, consistency, and rationality. . . .

"To what extent do they exist in the Soviet Union? If incremental, ad hoc, short-range policy-making also prevails there, this would be fairly conclusive evidence that it is a universal characteristic of complex decision-making structures. If it is much less prevalent in the Soviet system, this would suggest that the ad hoc method is typical of a particular type of political culture. On the whole, it can probably be said that Soviet history offers more examples of clear-cut selection, both domestically and in foreign policy. . . ."

From Zbigniew Brzezinski and Samuel P. Huntington, *Political Power: USA/USSR* (New York: The Viking Press, 1964). See also p. 51, quoted from pp. 224 and 225.

purchasing dollars) to buy. Similarly, Lindblom, who, like Hirschman, approaches political analysis with the background of an economist, questions the notion that policies can be guided in accord with normative preferences; this would require an agreement on values and the capacity to rank them.[72] Good policies are those that are accepted in the sense that agreements on them can be reached.[73] The notion of mutual adjustment is central to incremental politics, a notion presented as both a valid picture of the American polity (and, by implication, of other democratic polities) and the basis of the most effective approach to societal decision-making.

Most rationalistic decision-making models assume that the individual and, by extension, other member-units (firms, interest groups) know what their interests are and will pursue them.[74] There is little place for a societal decision-maker, collective interests, shared values, and non-rational bonds—elements which tie members into a cohesive societal unit and encourage them to support shared goals and societal decisions. In short, while incrementalists oppose collective rationalism and reject many of the assumptions of rationalistic decision-making in general (e.g., the capacity to know and to calculate and, thus, to optimize), they have a central conceptual similarity to individualistic rationalism and utilitarianism: atomism.[75]

Now, in our terms, decisions reached through the consent of partisans without a regulatory center and institutions reflect the interests and goals of the more powerful, as partisans almost invariably differ in their respective power. That is, decisions reached in this way would overrepresent the strong and under-represent the weak. (Actually, some sub-societies are likely to be completely excluded from decision-making, because their power is too small to affect the societal decisions reached through "partisan mutual accommodation.") In fairness to the incrementalists, it should be noted that they do not support such decision-making in a "raw" form. They point to several factors which "soften" the picture. The capacity of minorities intensively committed to their values to counter or even to supersede less-committed majorities is one such factor.[76] Also, shared values and the processes of political legitimation (factors which are introduced *ex machina*) are recognized as lending extra weight to some power-holders (public ones) over others (private ones).

While these considerations greatly refine the incrementalist position, they do not essentially change it. According to this approach, for decision-making to be democratic, it must occur through a process of partisan accommodation. Decisions are to be made by the actors who pursue their interests, and other actors whose interests have not been taken into account are free to protest after the decision has been made and to attempt to effect adjustments. The better decision-makers will take this into account to some degree in their initial decisions, thus making for an anticipatory rather than a *post hoc* accommodation. But this, we suggest, may well not include representation of the values and interests of the poor, ethnic minorities, untouchables, and so forth, since it is not the amount of protest or discontent which determines the adjustments made but rather the relative power of the actors, which is precisely what these groupings lack when decisions are made in the course of a political free-for-all. Other power groupings—those who are not without power but with proportionally less power—are also affected, although less drastically. Urban citizens, for instance, are under-considered in the United States rather than ignored. The incrementalists do not deny this implication of their strategy for societal decision-making. A good policy, it is stated, represents the existing differences of power; consent plus inequality is preferable to dissent and equality.[77] Any attempt to base the evaluation of policies on values rather than consensus, is it pointed out, returns to the rationalistic model and the problems of ranking and weighing values, and to centralized decision-making—the institutional opposite of pluralism—which, it is suggested, is undemocratic.

Finally, incrementalism tends to ignore not only the underprivileged and politically-weak collectivities but also overdue societal innovations. "Although Lindblom's thesis includes a number of reservations, these are insufficient to alter its main impact as an ideological reinforcement of the pro-, inertia and anti-innovation forces," and "the basic strategy of incremental change, as stated by Lindblom, is one of maximizing security in making changes. All reliable knowledge being based on the past, the only way to proceed without risk is by continuing in the same direction."[78] And, as another critic put it, according to this approach, "we do stagger through history like a drunk putting one disjointed incremental foot after another."[79]

There would be little interest in the incremental approach if it were merely the value-judgment of a few social scientists, however eminent they be. Its importance lies in that it is the only alternative to rationalistic decision-making which has a significant intellectual following *and* it does provide a characterization of the ways in which post-modern pluralistic societies, especially the United States, make decisions. What the incrementalists do not provide is a full representation of societal values and interests and a perspective that runs deeper than the next few increments. Incrementalism seems to us neither a description of nor a prescription for active decision-making. In the following chapter, we suggest a third approach that is less demanding than the rationalistic one but more demanding than the incrementalist one, one which is both feasible and comprehensive.

NOTES

1. For definitions and measurement see Clyde Kluckhohn et al., "Values and Value-Orientations in the Theory of Action," in Talcott Parsons and Edward A. Shils (eds.), *Toward a General Theory of Action* (Cambridge, Mass.: Harvard University Press, 1952), p. 390. Philip E. Jacob and James J. Flink, with the collaboration of Hedvah L. Shuchman, "Values and Their Function in Decision-Making: Toward an Operational Definition for Use in Public Affairs Research,"

Supplement to *The American Behavioral Scientist*, Vol. V, No. 9 (supplement, May 1962).

2. For one out of several such definitions see Kuhn, *The Study of Society*, *op. cit.*, p. 253. Once consciousness is omitted, the difference between the selection of a rat and the decision of a man disappears. On the relationship between consciousness and decision-making see Martin Shubik, "Studies and Theories of Decision Making," *Administrative Science Quarterly*, Vol. 3 (1958), pp. 290–291; Bertram M. Gross, *The Managing of Organizations* (New York: Free Press, 1964), p. 764.

3. Actually, several such reviews are available. Paul Wasserman with Fred S. Silander, *Decision-Making: An Annotated Bibliography* (Ithaca, New York: Cayuga Press, 1958). See a supplement by the same authors and publisher for 1958–1963 published in 1964. See also Richard C. Snyder and James A. Robinson, *National and International Decision-Making* (New York: The Institute for International Order, n.d.), and William J. Gore and J. W. Dyson (eds.), *The Making of Decisions* (New York: Free Press, 1964); Donald W. Taylor, "Decision Making and Problem Solving," in James G. March (ed.), *Handbook of Organizations* (Chicago: Rand McNally & Company, 1965), pp. 48–86. See also the special issue on decision-making of the *Administrative Science Quarterly*, Vol. 3 (December 1958), especially the article by Martin Shubik, "Studies and Theories of Decision Making," pp. 289–306. For another bibliography see Dwaine Marvick (ed.), *Political Decision-Makers* (New York: Free Press, 1961), pp. 334–343.

4. The suggestion that, if followed, the prescriptions would lead to desired results, is itself rarely supported by empirical evidence. On the normative and unempirical nature of these works, see Raymond A. Bauer, "Problem Solving in Organizations: A Functional Point of View," in Merwin M. Hargrove, Ike H. Harrison, Eugene L. Swearingen (eds.), *Business Policy Cases* (Homewood, Ill.: Richard D. Irwin, 1963), pp. 29–32. For a recent normative work, see Robert O. Schlaifer, *Probability and Statistics for Business Decisions* (New York: McGraw-Hill, 1958). For typical examples, see also Robert Duncan Luce and Howard Raiffa, *Games and Decisions* (New York: Wiley & Sons, 1957), esp. Ch. 14; Shubik, "Studies and Theories of Decision Making," *op. cit.*, pp. 289–306, especially p. 289.

5. See, for instance, the items listed by Paul Wasserman with Fred S. Silander, *Decision-Making: An Annotated Bibliography*, *op. cit.*, esp. pp. 1–43.

6. This point was made by Kenneth N. Waltz, *Man, the State, and War* (New York: Columbia University Press, 1959), esp. pp. 224–238.

7. Barry E. Collins and Harold Guetzkow, *A Social Psychology of Group Process for Decision-Making* (New York: Wiley, 1964), pp. 45–52. See also Peter M. Blau and W. Richard Scott, *Formal Organizations* (San Francisco: Chandler, 1962), p. 121.

8. Warner R. Schilling, "The H-Bomb Decision: How to Decide Without Actually Choosing," *Political Science Quarterly*, Vol. 76 (1961), pp. 24–46. Edwin A. Bock and Alan K. Campbell (eds.), *Case Studies in American Government: The Inter-University Case Program* (Englewood Cliffs, N.J.: Prentice-Hall, 1962). A brief discussion of the program is included. The emphasis is on the "clinical" approach. See also Richard C. Snyder, H. W. Bruck, and Burton M. Sapin, *Foreign Policy Decision-Making* (New York: Free Press, 1962), p. 18. "The Snyder–Bruck–Sapin conceptual framework is essentially an accounting system for taking note of processing effects, situations, and influences that bear on decision-making actions."

Charles A. McClelland, *Theory and the International System* (New York: Macmillan, 1966), p. 108.

9. See, for instance, Richard C. Snyder and Glenn D. Paige, "The United States Decision to Resist Aggression in Korea," *Administrative Science Quarterly*, Vol. 3 (1958), pp. 341–379. Allen S. Whiting, *China Crosses the Yalu: The Decision to Enter the Korean War* (New York: Macmillan, 1960). For a macroscopic aspect of decision-making, see Martin Patchen, "Decision Theory in the Study of National Action: Problems and a Proposal," *The Journal of Conflict Resolution*, Vol. 9 (1965), pp. 164–176.

10. Richard C. Snyder and Edgar S. Furniss, Jr., *American Foreign Policy* (New York: Holt, Rinehart & Winston, 1954), pp. 92–101.

11. Herbert A. Simon, "A Behavioral Model of Rational Choice," *Quarterly Journal of Economics*, Vol. 69 (1955), pp. 99–118.

12. For references and discussion, see below, pp. 268–270. For one of the best works in this category, see Warner R. Schilling, Paul Y. Hammond, Glenn H. Snyder, *Strategy, Politics and Defense Budgets* (New York: Columbia University Press, 1962).

13. Speaking for men of practice, who are critical of technical terms and abstract models, Roger W. Jones of the United States Bureau of the Budget provides a description of how he believes "the public administrator makes decisions and formulates policy." It is surprisingly close to the rationalist model. See his "The Model as a Decision-Maker's Dilemma," *Public Administration Review*, Vol. 24 (1964), pp. 158–160. See also John W. Dyckman, "The Scientific World of the City Planners," *American Behavioral Scientist*, Vol. 6 (1963), pp. 46–50. For another view of rationality see Richard M. Cyert, Herbert A. Simon, and Donald B. Trow, "Observation of a Business Decision," in Albert H. Rubinstein and Chadwick J. Haberstroh, (eds.), *Some Theories of Organization* (Homewood, Ill.: Dorsey Press, 1960), pp. 458–472.

14. See Harold Garfinkle, "The Rational Properties of Scientific and Common Sense Activities," *Behavioral Science*, Vol. 5 (1960), pp. 72–83.

15. Parsons defines "affective-neutrality" as the alternative in which an actor "renounced in favor of instrumental or moral" interest a relatively immediate gratification. *The Social System, op. cit.*, p. 60. Affective-neutrality is viewed as associated with division of labor and organization on pp. 158–159. On personality correlates of rationality, see Leo Srole et al., *Mental Health in the Metropolis: The Midtown Manhattan Study* (New York: McGraw-Hill, 1962). The concept of rationality here is somewhat different from the other studies referred to but the findings relate to the capacity to engage in an "open" means–end analysis.

16. David McClelland argues that there is a high association between the prevalence of the need for achievement in a population and its subsequent propensity to undergo development. *The Achieving Society* (Princeton, N.J.: Van Nostrand, 1961), pp. 46–50.

17. On some of these countries, see David McClelland, *The Achieving Society, op. cit.*, pp. 259–335. For some others, see Almond and Verba, *Civic Culture, op. cit.*, pp. 473–505; Robert A. Levine, with the assistance of Eugene Strangman and Leonard Unterberger, *Dreams and Deeds: Achievement Motivation in Nigeria* (Chicago: University of Chicago Press, 1966); Bernard C. Rosen, "The Achievement Syndrome and Economic Growth in Brazil," *Social Force*, Vol. 42 (1964),

pp. 341–354. For an Asian study see Amar Kumar Singh, "Hindu Culture and Economic Development in India," *Conspectus*, No. 1 (1967), pp. 9–32. For a study outlining general patterns of national differences, see Mason Haire, Edwin E. Ghiselli, and Lyman W. Porter, *Managerial Thinking: An International Study* (New York: Wiley & Sons, Inc., 1966).

18. McClelland, *The Achieving Society*, *op. cit.*, studies the effect of the family system on achievement, pp. 340–362, 373–376, and the effect of education on achievement, pp. 413–417.

19. David Riesman, Nathan Glazer, and Reuel Denney, *The Lonely Crowd* (New Haven: Yale University Press, 1950), pp. 275–349. The author expresses an indebtedness for this point to Erich Fromm. See *Man for Himself* (New York: Holt, Rinehart & Winston, 1957), p. 301. See also William J. Gore, *Administrative Decision-Making: A Heuristic Model* (New York: Wiley & Sons, Inc., 1964), pp. 8–12.

20. See for instance Rensis Likert, *New Patterns of Management* (New York: McGraw-Hill, 1961), esp. pp. 13–19.

21. Parsons, *The Social System*, *op. cit.*, pp. 79–88, 127, 334, 385, 401–403, 409–410. Parsons, Bales, and Shils, *Working Papers*, *op. cit.*, pp. 31 ff.

22. For references to works dealing with differentiation, see footnote 20, Chapter 4; footnote 30, Chapter 11.

23. Parsons, Bales, and Shils, *Working Papers*, *op. cit.*, pp. 180 ff.

24. On this concept of rationality, see Dahrendorf, *Class and Class Conflict in Industrial Society*, *op. cit.*, p. 68.

25. See Joseph S. Berliner, *Factory and Manager in the USSR* (Cambridge, Mass.: Harvard University Press, 1957), esp. pp. 231–300.

26. For a sophisticated recent review, see Gore, *Administrative Decision-Making*, *op. cit.*, esp. pp. 12–18. See also John M. Pfiffner, "Administrative Rationality," *Public Administration Review*, Vol. 20 (1960), pp. 125–132.

27. See Packenham's discussion of rational–legal studies in his "Approaches to the Study of Political Development," *op. cit.*

28. Robert A. Dahl, *A Preface to Democratic Theory* (Chicago: University of Chicago Press, 1956), pp. 124–151.

29. Fred W. Riggs, *Administration in Developing Countries: The Theory of Prismatic Society* (Boston, Mass.: Houghton Mifflin, 1964), pp. 19 ff. The term "fused" has been widely used by other authors to refer to undifferentiated systems.

30. This was the central theoretical concept of the author's doctoral dissertation, "The Organizational Structure of *Kibbutzim*," Berkeley: University of California Press, 1958. The main findings are reported in "The Functional Differentiation of Elites in the *Kibbutz*," *American Journal of Sociology*, Vol. 64 (1959), pp. 476–487, and reprinted in the author's *Studies in Social Change* (New York: Holt, Rinehart & Winston, 1966), pp. 4–29.

31. Max Weber, *The Protestant Ethic and the Spirit of Capitalism*, trans. by Talcott Parsons (New York: Scribner, 1964), pp. 180–182.

32. Merton, "Social Structure and Anomie," *Social Theory and Social Structure* (rev. ed.), *op. cit.*, pp. 149–153.

33. Robert Michels was one of the first to call attention to this tendency in his *Political Parties* (New York: Free Press, 1958). David Sills reviews a number of studies supporting and elaborating this proposition and adds one of his own:

The Volunteers: Means and Ends in a National Organization (New York: Free Press, 1957), pp. 253–270. The difference in the distortion of maintaining the instrumental orientation after the goal is realized and of investing in it instead of realizing the goal is often ignored.

34. The Carnival at Rio de Janeiro threatens to spill over into the rest of the year. The police, therefore, are expected not to tolerate mass street-dancing and free roaming bands from the *favellas* until the first of the year, after which such activities "in preparation of the Carnival" are tolerated but suppressed again after the third day of Carnival. This suppression has also a religious sanctioning as it marks Ash Wednesday and the initiation of solemn Lent.

35. Robert A. Dahl and Charles E. Lindblom, *Politics, Economics and Welfare* (New York: Harper Torch Books, 1953), pp. 28–54. Other lists for the United States are longer. Robin M. Williams, Jr., *American Society* (New York: Knopf, 1960), pp. 415–470. Report of the President's Commission on National Goals, *Goals for Americans* (Englewood Cliffs, N.J.: Prentice-Hall, 1960), pp. 3–23.

36. The fact that not all services of all goals are competitive—that some activities serve two or more goals, and to some degree the services of two or more goals may go hand in hand but then part company, as, for instance, teaching and research in graduate schools—further complicates the model but can be encompassed in it. For a sociological discussion of goals that are partially complementary and partially contradictory—e.g., therapy, research, and teaching in medical schools, see Etzioni, *Modern Organizations, op. cit.*, pp. 14–16.

37. There are numerous other concepts of rationality that cannot be reviewed here. Our concept of instrumental rationality is similar to Karl Mannheim's, "functional rationality," *Man and Society, op. cit.*, p. 53. We avoid the term "functional" because in the social sciences it has acquired the meaning of relating to a system, which Mannheim's concept does not imply. Mannheim seems to have been influenced by Weber's notion of "formal" rationality. (See *On Law in Economy and Society* (Cambridge, Mass.: Harvard University Press, 1954), pp. 63–64, and *The Theory of Social and Economic Organization* (New York: Free Press, 1957), pp. 185–186. Weber discusses relations to more abstract norms and measurability which are related but not essential to the notion of instrumental rationality.

Our concept of comprehensive rationality approaches Mannheim's of "substantive rationality," *op. cit.*, p. 53. He stresses the "insight into the inter-relations of events in a given situation"; we emphasize the inclusiveness or synthesizing nature of the perspective. Weber's concept of substantive rationality is more concerned with the opposition of normative to empirical elements, *op. cit.*, pp. 35, 185–186, 207. Cf. Gerth and Mills, *From Max Weber, op. cit.*, p. 331.

Another pair of concepts Weber used are relevant. *Wertrationlität* refers to a commitment to an "absolute value" and *Zwekrationalität* to a "rational orientation to a system of discrete individual ends." (*The Theory of Social and Economic Organization, loc. cit.*, p. 115 and Parsons' introduction, pp. 14–17.) This comes close to the distinction between instrumental and comprehensive rationality, though Weber does not fully recognize the role of optimization.

38. See Martin Meyerson, "Building the Middle Range Bridge for Comprehensive Planning," *Journal of the American Institute of Planners*, Vol. 22 (1956), pp. 58–64.

39. For an illustrative case, see below discussion of British Guiana, p. 295. See also p. 609, Note 11.

40. Various versions of the rationalistic model are advanced by Jan Tiņbergen, *Economic Policy, Principles and Design* (Amsterdam: North Holland, 1956), pp. 11 ff.; Marshall Dimock, *A Philosophy of Administration* (New York: Harper & Row, 1958), pp. 140 ff; Arthur Smithies, *The Budgetary Process in the U.S.* (New York: McGraw-Hill, 1955), pp. 192 ff.

41. A requirement that does not appear in all the versions of the model, but which is of special interest to the social scientist, is that a full-fledged inter-disciplinary theory is needed to carry out the calculations discussed above. Without such a theory, the effects of changes the decision-maker is considering could not be understood and safely forecasted.

42. "Decisions are the product of collaborative efforts of individuals," Gore and Dyson (eds.), *The Making of Decisions, op. cit.*, p. 1. Joseph Frankel, "Towards a Decision-Making Model in Foreign Policy," *Political Studies*, Vol. 7 (1959), pp. 1–11. See also Philip E. Jacob, "The Influence of Values in Political Inte-gration," in Jacob and Toscano (eds.), *The Integration of Political Communities, op. cit.*, p. 211.

43. An experiment by Jerome S. Bruner, Jacqueline J. Goodnow, and George A. Austin has shown that individual decision-makers cannot fulfill the requirements of the model. See their *A Study of Thinking* (New York: Wiley, 1956), Chs. 4–5. Braybrooke and Lindblom have argued societal decision-makers do not, cannot, and should not try. *Strategy of Decision, op. cit.*, pp. 48–50. See also pp. 111–143. See also *The Intelligence of Democracy, op. cit.*, pp. 137–139. Dahl, *A Preface to Democratic Theory, op. cit.*, pp. 145–146. The following discussion draws on these works.

44. For reasons for this statement, see above, Ch. 6, pp. 136–139.

45. Arrow pointed out that the rationalistic model requires "an impossible amount of calculation. (This impossibility, I may add, is not merely a question of the quality and quantity of calculating machines, though this consideration is by no means negligible. It is ultimately a difficulty in our ability to describe the world in a fixed finite linguistic structure.)" Review of *Strategy of Decision* by Kenneth J. Arrow in *Political Science Quarterly*, Vol. 79 (1964), p. 585. See also Herbert A. Simon, *Models of Man* (New York: Wiley, 1957), p. 198, and Aaron Wildavsky, *Politics of the Budgetary Process* (Boston: Little, Brown, 1964), pp. 147–152.

46. Hubert L. Dreyfus, "Alchemy and Artificial Intelligence," paper presented at the Rand Corporation in August, 1964, p. 65 and see also p. iii.

47. See Herbert A. Simon, *The Shape of Automation for Men and Management* (New York: Harper & Row, 1965), esp. pp. 31–32.

48. See Chapter 6, footnote 4.

49. On this functional definition of religion, see Parsons, *The Social System, op. cit.*, pp. 163–167, 304.

50. William J. Goode, *World Revolution and Family Patterns* (New York: Free Press, 1963), pp. 10–26. For additional discussion, see below, pp. 436–437.

51. Simon, *Administrative Behavior*, rev. ed., *op. cit.*, p. 77.

52. The same excess of exceptions, written off as "idiosyncrasies" afflicts the competition model and those of game theory. See Thomas C. Schelling,*The Strategy of Conflict* (New York: Oxford University Press, 1963), pp. 162–172.

53. The "irrational" position is not limited to the psycho-analytical traditions. On its place in the earlier writings of the "vitalist" tradition, see Ernst Cassirer,

The Myth of the State (New Haven, Conn.: Yale University Press, 1946), esp. pp. 176–185. For existentialist writings, see Barrett, *Irrational Man, op. cit.*, esp. pp. 269 ff. See also Henri Bergson, translated by Arthur Mitchell, *Creative Evolution* (New York: Modern Library, 1944) as well as his *Two Sources of Morality and Religion*, tr. by R. Ashley Audra and Cloudesley Brereton, with the assistance of W. Horsfall Carter (Garden City, N.Y.: Doubleday, 1954).

Recently there has been an increase in the interest in "post-rational" conceptions, which deny the superiority of rationality and see the rational civilization as one form, "next" to others, but not a higher stage of development. Unlike earlier anti-rationalistic positions, the frequent expressions are more intellectually developed, relatively less emotive. (I am indebted for this point to Daniel Bell.) See especially the recent work of Claude Lévi-Strauss, *The Savage Mind* (London: Weidenfeld & Nicolson, 1966) and Michel Foucault, *Madness and Civilization*, tr. Richard Howard (New York: Pantheon Books, 1965). Norman O. Brown's position, although in the same line, is more emotive.

54. See, for instance, Herman Chernoff, "Rational Selection of Decision Functions," *Econometrica*, Vol. 22 (1954), pp. 422–443.

55. *Strategy for Decision, op. cit.*, pp. 18–19, 250. See also Andrew Gunder Frank, "Goal Ambiguity and Conflicting Standards: An Approach to the Study of Organizations," *Human Organization*, Vol. 17 (1959), pp. 8–13. Donald T. Campbell provides an incrementalist model of knowledge processes in his "Blind Variation and Selective Retention in Creative Thought as in Other Knowledge Processes," *Psychological Review*, Vol. 67 (1960), pp. 380–400.

Empirical studies of incrementalism were conducted by Aaron Wildavsky, *The Politics of the Budgetary Process, op. cit.*; Richard F. Fenno Jr., *The Power of the Purse* (Boston: Little Brown, 1966); Otto Davis, M. A. H. Dempster, and Aaron Wildavsky, "On the Process of Budgeting: An Empirical Study on Congressional Appropriations," in Gordon Tullock (ed.), *Papers on Non-Market Decision-Making* (Charlottesville, Va.: Thomas Jefferson Center for Political Economy, University of Virginia, 1966), pp. 63–132.

56. Karl R. Popper, *The Open Society and Its Enemies*, Vol. 1 (Princeton, N.J.: Princeton University Press, 1963), p. 157. See also Michael Oakeshott, *Rationalism in Politics* (New York: Basic Books, 1962).

57. Popper, *Open Society, op. cit.*, p. 158.

58. Herbert A. Simon, "A Behavioral Model of Rational Choice," *Quarterly Journal of Economics*, Vol. 69 (1955), pp. 99–118.

59. Albert O. Hirschman, *The Strategy of Economic Development* (New Haven, Conn.: Yale University Press, 1958).

60. *Ibid.*, p. 19. The theme is much more advanced in Albert O. Hirschman's later book, *Journeys Toward Progress* (New York: Twentieth Century Fund, 1963), esp. pp. 309–313. See also his "The Principle of the Hiding Hand," *The Public Interest*, No. 6 (Winter, 1967), pp. 10–23.

61. Hirschman refers to the following as representations of the balanced approach: P. N. Rosenstein-Rodan, "Problems of Industrialization of Eastern and South-Eastern Europe," *Economic Journal*, Vol. 53 (1943), p. 205; Ragnar Nurkse, *Problems of Capital Formation in Underdeveloped Countries* (New York: Oxford University Press, 1953), Ch. 1; Tibor Scitovsky, "Two Concepts of External Economics," *Journal of Political Economy*, Vol. 62 (1954), pp. 143–152; William A.

Lewis, *The Theory of Economic Growth* (Homewood, Ill.: R. D. Irwin, 1955), pp. 274–283. See also Ragnar Nurkse, "Some International Aspects of the Problem of Economic Development," *American Economic Review* (Papers and Proceedings), Vol. 42 (1952), pp. 571–583 and Jan Tinbergen, *The Design of Development* (Baltimore: Johns Hopkins Press, 1958). Several studies of balanced and unbalanced approaches to development are reviewed in an outstanding essay by Warren F. Ilchman, "Rising Expectations and the Revolution in Development Administration," *Public Administration Review*, Vol. 25 (1965), pp. 314–328.

62. *The Strategy of Economic Development, op. cit.*, pp. 17 ff.

63. Actually, Hirschman argues that the West was also developed in an "unbalanced" way and by means of inducements; nor does he think that contemporary developments in the West are necessarily well-synchronized.

64. William F. Ogburn, *Social Change* (New York: Viking Press, 1928), esp. pp. 200–212. For a critique of this conception, see Horace Miner, "The Folk–Urban Continuum," *The American Sociological Review*, Vol. 17 (1952), pp. 529–537.

65. Charles E. Lindblom, "The Science of 'Muddling Through,'" *Public Administration Review*, Vol. 19 (1959), pp. 79–99; Robert A. Dahl and Charles E. Lindblom, *Politics, Economics and Welfare* (New York: Harper & Row, 1953); *Strategy of Decision, op. cit.*, co-authored with Braybrooke; Lindblom, *The Intelligence of Democracy, op. cit.*, is the most recent and advanced statement of the position.

Lindblom does not manifestly advocate a strategy which he calls somewhat disaffectionately "disjointed incrementalism." Three reviewers of *Strategy of Decision* point to this ambiguity. Morton A. Kaplan notes: "It is not clear throughout the book if the authors are more concerned with whether disjointed incrementalism is a description of how people do choose or a prescription as to how reasonably to choose," *The Annals of the American Academy of Political and Social Science*, Vol. 352 (1964), p. 189. "Whether the strategy is a description of a 'social process' or an alternative ideal of rationality is not clear," Victor A. Thompson, *American Journal of Sociology*, Vol. 70 (1964), p. 132. Lewis A. Froman Jr. concludes: "As Lindblom, the empirical theorist, and Braybrooke, the philosopher, try to suggest, it [the strategy] is really both," *American Political Science Review*, Vol. 58 (1964), p. 116.

66. Lindblom, *The Intelligence of Democracy, op. cit.*, p. 145. Another incrementalist describes this as the tendency of decision-makers to concentrate on certain "focus-elements." See G. L. S. Shackle, *Decision, Order, and Time in Human Affairs* (Cambridge, Mass.: Harvard University Press, 1961), esp. p. 122.

67. Albert O. Hirschman and Charles E. Lindblom, "Economic Development, Research and Development, Policy Making: Some Converging Views," *Behavioral Sciences*, Vol. 7 (1962), pp. 211–222, quoted from p. 215. Martin Shapiro speaks of the accommodation of ends to means in "Stability and Change in Judicial Decision-Making: Incrementalism or Stare Decisis?" *Law in Transition Quarterly*, Vol. 2 (1965), pp. 134–157.

68. Hirschman and Lindblom, *op. cit.*, p. 216.

69. For three examples of problems which were not solved but were repeatedly "attacked" over a period of time and thus treated, see David M. Potter, *People of Plenty* (Chicago: University of Chicago Press, 1954), p. 122.

70. Aaron Wildavsky and Arthur Hammond, "Comprehensive versus Incremental Budgeting in the Department of Agriculture," *Administrative Science Quarterly*, Vol. 10 (1965), pp. 321–346, esp. p. 323; and Lindblom, *The Intelligence of Democracy, op. cit.*, p. 28.

71. On the virtues of the market mechanism, see Charles E. Lindblom, "Economics and the Administration of National Planning," *Public Administration Review*, Vol. 25 (1965), pp. 274–283. On mutual adjustment among government agencies see Robert Jones Shafer, *Mexico: Mutual Adjustment Planning* (Syracuse, N.Y.: Syracuse University Press, 1966), esp. pp. 3, 127.

72. "The Science of 'Muddling Through,' " *op. cit.*, pp. 83–84; Lindblom, *The Intelligence of Democracy, passim*. See also Albert D. Biderman's discussion of "Obstacles to Consensual Evaluation" in his "Social Indicators and Goals," in Raymond A. Bauer (ed.), *Social Indicators* (Cambridge, Mass.: The M.I.T. Press, 1966), pp. 79–86.

73. As free market systems are purported to do, incrementalism "leaves an opening for the creative impulses of individuals; 'fluid themes invite, as settled rules do not, exploratory responses.' To this end, the social conflict of interests and desires acts as a vital prod in sharpening and deepening the quality of social argumentation; it is not the judgment of the impartial observer, using maximum information in accordance with a well-defined value system, but the conflict of partial, self-interested, and therefore highly motivated contestants from which the best social decisions will come." Arrow, review of *Intelligence of Democracy, op. cit.*, p. 586.

74. "Self-interest is an element embodied in most rational models," Gore and Dyson, *The Making of Decisions, op. cit.*, p. 4. See also Paul Diesing, "Socioeconomic Decisions," *Ethics*, Vol. 69 (1958), pp. 1–18. Olson, Jr., *The Logic of Collective Action, op. cit.*, uses as premises that "man is rational" and pursues his "self-interest."

75. See Braybrooke's part of *Strategy of Decision, op. cit.*, Chs. 7–10.

76. Dahl, *A Preface to Democratic Theory, op. cit.*, pp. 103 ff.

77. See *The Intelligence of Democracy, op. cit.*, Ch. 16, esp. p. 260 and Ch. 15, esp. pp. 239, 242. Lindblom is introducing various qualifications to the above statement, but these do not change his stand and need not concern us here. Economists frequently derive societal utilities from aggregates of personal preferences. For a good example see Kenneth Arrow, *Social Choice and Individual Values* (New York: John Wiley and Sons, 1951).

78. Yehezkel Dror, "Muddling Through—'Science' or Inertia?" *Public Administration Review*, Vol. 24 (1964), pp. 155, 154 respectively.

79. Kenneth Boulding in a review of *A Strategy of Decision, American Sociological Review*, Vol. 29 (1964), p. 931.

CHAPTER 12

Mixed-Scanning:

An Active Approach to Decision-Making

W E NOW explore a third approach to decision-making—
one we consider more activating than either of the two strategies discussed
above although it draws on elements of both of them. The first part of the
chapter introduces this third approach and explores its foundations; the
second part deals with the effects of other guidance factors on societal
decision-making, especially on the kind of decision-making needed for active
societies.

The Mixed-Scanning Strategy

Neither Rationalism nor Incrementalism

What is needed for active decision-making is a strategy that is less exacting
than the rationalistic one but not as constricting in its perspective as the
incremental approach, not as utopian as rationalism but not as conservative

as incrementalism, not so unrealistic a model that it cannot be followed but not one that legitimates myopic, self-oriented, non-innovative decision-making. The strategy of mixed-scanning, which we outline in the following pages, assumes that the criticisms of the rationalistic model are valid. While casters of well-balanced dice or tic-tac-toe players may be able to use a rationalistic model, an individual buying an everyday item in a local grocery store cannot, nor can a voter, not to mention an actor who makes decisions with macroscopic consequences.[1]* Referring to a rationalistic model, Charles Hitch states,

> The sort of simple explicit model which operation researchers are so proficient in using can certainly reflect most of the significant factors influencing traffic control on the George Washington Bridge, but the proportion of the relevant reality which we can represent by any such [rationalistic—AE] model or models in studying, say, a major foreign-policy decision, appears to be almost trivial.[2]

Rationalistic models do not provide an effective descriptive, normative, or analytic model for the conduct of macro-actors. Incrementalism, we suggest, is descriptive of a sub-set of decisions but not of the more effective decisions. In fact, if an empirical study were conducted, we would expect it to show that actors in a large variety of fields, when confronted with the impossibility of following a rationalistic model, use not an incrementalist but a mixed-scanning strategy. And more effective actors rely more on such a strategy than those who are less effective, as judged by the actual goals of the decision-makers.

Mixed-Scanning Defined

Actors whose decision-making is based on a mixed-scanning strategy differentiate contextuating (or fundamental) decisions from bit (or item) decisions. Contextuating decisions are made through an exploration of the main alternatives seen by the actor in view of his conception of his goals, but—unlike what comprehensive rationality would indicate—details and specifications are omitted so that overviews are feasible. Bit-decisions are made "incrementally" but within the contexts set by fundamental decisions (and *reviews*). Thus, each of the two elements in the mixed-scanning strategy helps to neutralize the peculiar shortcoming of the other: Bit-incrementalism overcomes the unrealistic aspects of comprehensive rationalism (by limiting it to contexuating decisions), and contextuating rationalism helps to right the conservative bias of incrementalism. Together, they make for a third approach which is more realistic *and* more transforming than each of its elements. We shall first examine the strategy in general and then its structural foundations. Initially, we illustrate the strategy by discussing situations which

---

* Reference notes for this chapter appear on page 305.

are limited in their societal importance but which allow us to outline the basic features of the strategy. We return shortly to macro-sociology.*

Mixed-Scanning Illustrated

Infantrymen taking positions in a new field in hostile territory scan it for hidden enemy troops. They are trained to scan a field. A rationalistic strategy is likely to be avoided because it would entail examining the whole field bit-by-bit, exhaustively, which would be dangerous and fatiguing and is likely not to be completed. Incrementalists would examine places in which enemy troops have been known to hide and some others near them or similar to them. Unlike the whole field, these places can be prodded by fire. Soldiers who are tired of marching and combat will sometimes follow this procedure. But armies known for their effectiveness train their soldiers in a different procedure. A major consideration in this regard is that accuracy of aim declines with distance. The infantrymen are taught first to scan the whole field in a rough, non-discriminating way for some obvious sign of danger (a movement, an unnatural shadow, and so on). If none is visible, they proceed with a bit-by-bit examination from the left to the right, beginning with the sub-fields closest to them and moving outward to more distant ones. The assumption is that scanning is going to become more superficial the longer it is carried out, which is made to coincide with the scanning of the more remote, less dangerous sub-fields.[3]

To take quite a different example, we find that weather satellites hold two cameras, one which takes broad-angle pictures covering large segments of the sky at one time in little detail and one which takes pictures of much smaller segments of the sky in much greater detail. Rather than covering all the sky in detail, bit-by-bit, thereby flooding the analyst with information that is likely to exhaust and frustrate him or make him non-discriminating, the dual scanning device is used first to take undetailed but encompassing pictures of the sky and then to scan for signs of trouble (e.g., cloud formations which might indicate a hurricane) which the second camera explores in detail.[4] It is more effective than merely examining the "familiar" hurricane cloud areas and a few others next to them, because even a rough scanning of the whole sky might show some obvious danger signs in other, unexpected areas. The same seems to hold for cameras on intelligence flights such as those of the U-2 and its latter-day versions and for reconnaissance satellites.

The relative investments active decision-making requires in the two kinds of scanning as well as in scanning in general depend on the cost of

---

* In terms of the languages of societal analysis, incrementalism is atomistic and rationalism is, voluntaristic (with instrumental rationalism solely voluntaristic and comprehensive rationalism containing collectivistic elements); no decision-making capacity is assumed in "pure" collectivistic language.

missing one hurricane, enemy, and so forth, and on the cost of additional scanning and the amount of time it takes. For instance, the scanning of Cuba was sharply increased after too little reconnaissance left the United States unaware of the positioning of Soviet missiles until they were almost fully erected.[5] Still, complete scanning was not possible.

Chess players are of interest for the study of decision-making strategy because the possibilities of combinations are much greater than those of infantrymen or cameras, and there is a clear measure of effectiveness in terms of the players' goals. A chess player cannot study all strategies at each move. Better players, we suggest, quickly review several strategies and then explore a sub-set of them in greater detail and an even smaller sub-set in still more detail. They reject all strategies of the first sub-set but one on the basis of some obvious disadvantages which make them undeserving of detailed examination. Were they able to examine all strategies in detail, they might discover that an alternative that had been rejected in this first round would have been the optimal one. But they cannot optimize. Still, we expect them to do better with this sequential combination of different kinds of scanning, going from vague but encompassing to detailed but exclusive examination, than players who only "increment" on the strategy with which they began or which have used successfully in the past.

Once the better player chooses a strategy, he will increment but only for a while. Sporadically, he will return to "higher" (or strategic) level of scanning, either because he sees outright signs of danger several moves ahead or because he wishes to explore whether or not the ever-changing situation allows for a still better strategy. The player who "increments" until trouble is only one or two moves ahead and engages in no strategic scanning even if there are no obvious dangers will, we expect, not do as well. Also, the better player attempts initially to establish a position in which several strategies can readily be adopted and often does not attempt to implement any one strategy immediately, because he is aware that such a procedure would reduce his capacity for *strategic* choices before the situation is relatively "developed"—i.e., specific.[6]

There is no reason that scanning has to be limited to two levels, one high in coverage and low in detail and the other high in detail and low in coverage; there can be more levels with varying degrees of detail and coverage, though it seems most effective to include one all-encompassing level (so that no major option will be left uncovered) and one level which is highly detailed (so that the option chosen can be explored as fully as feasible).

The decision to allocate the investments of assets and time among the levels is part of the strategy. The actual amount of assets and time spent depends on the total amount available and on testing various inter-level combinations. The amount spent also changes over time. At set intervals (or sporadically), an increase in the investment in encompassing (high-coverage) scanning is needed to survey the field for far-removed but "obvious" dangers, to re-ascertain fundamental assumptions, and to search for better lines of approach.* An increase in such investment is also effective when the environment radically changes or when the earlier increments lead to a crisis.[7]

Scanning (and, for that matter, almost all decision-making) combines the collection, processing, and evaluation of information with the process of making choices. As the actor "scans," he "takes in" information *and* explores alternative steps. Moreover, what information to collect, the extent to which to process it, etc., are also choices that need to be made in the decision-making process. While for some analytic purpose, knowledge-scanning and the making of choices are to be kept separate, in the following discussion—unless otherwise indicated—we explore them jointly.

Mixed-Scanning Specified

We now present the mixed-scanning strategy as an imaginary set of instructions written for an unimaginative decision-maker.[8] For heuristic purposes, we assume that at one point in time, the actor has no firm strategic commitments and faces a crisis that suggests that earlier policy lines ought to be reviewed fundamentally. United States foreign policy in the years after 1945, in which the containment strategy and the Truman doctrine emerged, would be a good example.[9]

Put into a program-like language, the strategy roughly reads:

a. *On strategic occasions* (for definition see d below) (i) list all relevant alternatives that come to mind, that the staff raises, and that advisers advocate (including alternatives not usually considered feasible).†

(ii) Examine briefly the alternatives under (i) (for definition of "briefly" see d below), and reject those that reveal a "crippling objection." These include: (a) utilitarian objections to alternatives which require means that are not available, (b) normative objections to alternatives which violate the basic values of the decision-makers,‡ and (c) political objections to alternatives

---

* More encompassing scanning may be undertaken either at set intervals (e.g., annual review occasions) or when there is a special reason to do so (e.g., a new difficulty is encountered). The first method is more "demanding" but also more activating. However, both assume a capacity for non-incremental reviews.

† This is a redundant rule because all "relevant alternatives" include ones which may not be feasible. It is not needed for a computer but for human decision-makers. Its purpose is to counteract somewhat the tendency to form and maintain communities-of-assumptions. Such an "instruction" in itself will, of course, not suffice, and a structural arrangement is needed to provide power in support of inclusiveness. This is discussed on pp. 182–190 above.

‡ The instruction reads "basic values" because we assume that a decision-maker has some normative integrity which should be encouraged, but that most decision-makers will deviate from a secondary value if other considerations support a strategy they favor, and the model will not dissuade them.

which violate the basic values or interests of other actors whose support seems essential for making the decision and/or implementing it.

(iii) For all alternatives not rejected under (ii), repeat (ii) in greater though not in full detail (for definition of scale see d).

(iv) For those alternatives remaining after (iii), repeat (ii) in still fuller detail (see d). Continue until only one alternative is left, or randomize the choice among those remaining (and ask the staff in the future to collect enough information to differentiate among all the alternatives to be reviewed).

b. *Before implementation** (i) when possible, fragment the implementation into several sequential steps (an administrative rule).

(ii) When possible, divide the commitment to implement into several serial steps (a political rule).

(iii) When possible, divide the commitment of assets into several serial steps and maintain a strategic reserve (a utilitarian rule).

(iv) Arrange implementation in such a way that, if possible, costly and less reversible decisions will appear later in the process than those which are more reversible and less costly.

(v) Provide a time schedule for the additional collection and processing of information so that information will become available at the key turning points of the subsequent decisions, but assume "unanticipated" delays in the availability of these inputs.† Return to more encompassing scanning when such information becomes available and before such turning points.

c. *Review while implementing.* (i) Scan on a semi-encompassing level after the first sub-set of increments is implemented. If they "work," continue to scan on a semi-encompassing level after longer intervals and in full, over-all review, still less frequently.

(ii) Scan more encompassingly whenever a series of increments, although each one seems a step in the right direction, results in deeper difficulties.

(iii) Be sure to scan at set intervals in full, over-all review even if everything seems all right, because: (a) a major danger that was not visible during earlier scanning but becomes observable now that it is closer might loom a few steps (or increments) ahead; (b) a better strategy might now be possible although it was ruled out in earlier rounds (see if one or more of the crippling objections was removed, but also look for new alternatives not previously examined); and (c) the goal may have been realized and, therefore, need no further incrementation. If this occurs, ask for new goal(s), and consider terminating the project.

---

* These rules are necessary, non-incremental preparations if later "incrementing" is to be possible.

† Rules (i) to (v) have been widely used in planning projects in which research and development play an important role. Reversibility declines (i.e., turning points are passed) with the transition (a) from research to the full-scale development of prototypes and (b) from prototypes to line production. (c) There are more such points, the more development is lateral rather than longitudinal. On the other hand, lateral development saves time.

d. *Formulate a rule for the allocation of assets and time among the various levels of scanning.* The rule is to assign "slices" of the available pie to (i) "normal" routines (when incrementing "works");* (ii) semi-encompassing reviews; (iii) over-all reviews; (iv) initial reviews when a whole new problem or strategy is considered; (v) a time "trigger," at set intervals, to initiate more encompassing reviews without waiting for a crisis to develop; and (vi) an occasional review of the allocation rule in the over-all review, and the establishment of the patterns of allocation in the initial strategic review.

Writing out all these instructions might make mixed-scanning seem unwieldy and complicated; actually, its main features are simple. It combines various levels of scanning, some more encompassing but less detailed and others less encompassing but more detailed. It also provides a set of criteria for situations in which a particular level of scanning is to be emphasized, with encompassing scanning (both lateral and longitudinal) appearing not only in a crisis situation but also at set intervals even when incrementing seems to lead toward the solution of the problem at hand. The annual Congressional debate over the budget, the President's State of the Union message, and meetings of the Council of Economic Advisers have some elements of such a strategy in United States' decision-making.

The Relations Between Fundamental and Incremental Decisions

The incrementalists do not deny the existence of fundamental decisions such as a declaration of war; they argue, however, that incremental decisions are much more common.[10] While incremental decisions do greatly outnumber fundamental ones, we suggest that the latter's significance for societal guidance is not commensurate with their number, and that it is a mistake to relegate non-incremental decisions to the category of exceptions. It is the fundamental decisions which set the contexts for the numerous, bit decisions. This observation can be elevated to the level of a proposition: We expect most fundamental decisions to be followed by incremental ones that tend toward the same general direction. Also, fundamental decisions are often "prepared for" by bit decisions. While this makes the fundamental ones—when finally made—less "fundamental," the fact that decisions—such as the declaration of war—are somewhat less drastic shifts in policy than is often maintained does not mean that they are not basically fundamental. The bit decisions which follow them cannot be understood without them, and the preceding bit decisions are often wasted unless they lead to fundamental decisions.

---

* If no objective measure is available, this is to be determined subjectively by the decision-makers.

Whether or not a series of incremental decisions is, by itself, less effective than a fundamental decision is an open question,* but the question is much less important than it appears if we take into account the relationship between fundamental and incremental decisions. The incrementalists say that the actor chooses between these two kinds of decision-making. We suggest that (a) *most incremental decisions specify or anticipate fundamental decisions, and (b) the cumulative value of the incremental decisions is greatly affected by the underlying fundamental decisions.*

Thus, it is not enough to show, as Richard Fenno did, that Congress makes primarily marginal changes in the federal budget (a comparison of one year's budget for a federal agency with that of the preceding year showed, on many occasions, only a 10 per cent or lower difference),[11] or that the defense budget does not change very much in terms of its percentage of the federal budget, or that the federal budget remains the same in terms of its percentage of the Gross National Product.[12] These bit changes are often indicative of trends which were initiated at critical turning points at which fundamental, contextuating decisions were made. The United States defense budget increased at the beginning of the Korean War in 1950 from 5.0 per cent of the GNP to 10.3 per cent in 1951. The fact that it stayed at about this level (between 9.0 and 11.3 per cent of the GNP) after the war (1954–1960) did reflect incremental decisions, but these were made within the contextual decision of engaging in the Korean War.[13] Fenno's own figures show almost as many changes of above 20 per cent as below this level (211 out of 444 budget changes, within one year, were 20 per cent or larger). Seven budget changes represented an increase of 100 per cent or more, and 24 budgets increased 50 per cent or more.[14] Once Congress set up a national space agency in 1958 and consented to support President Kennedy's space goals, it made "incremental," additional commitments for several years. But, first, a fundamental decision had been made. Actually, Congress, in 1958, drawing on previous experience and on an understanding of the dynamics of incremental processes, could not but have been aware that once a fundamental commitment is made, it is difficult to reverse. And while the initial space budget was relatively small, the acts of establishing a space agency and subscribing to the space goals were, in effect, supporting additional budget increments in future years. Of course, Congress and other societal decision-making bodies do make cumulative bit decisions without understanding the fundamental ones which underlie them, but, often, what appears to be a series of bit decisions is, in effect, the extension of a fundamental decision.

Incrementalists argue that incremental decisions tend to be small steps in the "right" direction, or, if and when it becomes evident that they are not,

---

* Of course, one incremental decision should not be compared to a fundamental one, as only a series of incremental decisions constitutes an attempt to treat the same problem that is dealt with by a fundamental decision.

the course can be altered. But if the decision-maker evaluates his incremental, bit decisions at all, which he must do if he is to decide whether or not they are "remedial," his judgment will be greatly affected by the evaluative contexts in which he views them. Here, again, we have to go outside the incrementalist model to ascertain the ways in which these criteria of evaluation are determined, which, we suggest, is very similar to the making of fundamental decisions.

Thus, while actors make both kinds of decisions, the number and role of fundamental decisions are greater than incrementalists hold, and when the fundamental decisions are absent, bit decision-making will amount to drifting, to action without direction. An active approach to societal decision-making requires two sets of mechanisms: (a) a high-order, fundamental policy-making process which sets basic directions, and (b) an incremental process which prepares for fundamental decisions and revises them after they have been reached. When rapid changes in the environment, in the societal unit, and in the step-structure nature of the problem, or prolonged mistaken treatment, lead to increasing difficulties, the higher order, fundamental review process must become operative.

Evaluating Decision-Making Strategies

The incrementalists argue that fundamental decisions tend to be poor decisions. Examples given are the Soviet decision to rapidly collectivize agriculture and French officers in Algeria deciding in 1961 to challenge the civil government's authority. It is asked, rhetorically, if it is possible to think of a single fundamental decision that was not poor? Remaining with these examples, the succeeding Soviet decision to decelerate collectivization and De Gaulle's decision to terminate the war in Algeria may be characterized as "good" fundamental decisions, as judged by the goals of the decision-maker at the time the decision was made, while it was carried out, and as it was implemented.*

The incrementalists further argue that without a comprehensive model for evaluation, "good" decisions cannot be defined, and that such a model cannot be generated. In contrast, we expect that the decisions actors make will be "better" (in terms of their goals), the more the actors adhere to a mixed-scanning strategy in their decision-making. While we recognize the serious difficulties in the evaluation of decision-making strategies, because factors other than these strategies affect both the decisions and their implementation

---

* This qualification must be added because there always may be later unanticipated consequences which may upset the balance and tip it against the original decision. But since these may have further consequences that may restore the balance in favor of the act, a cut-off point is a pragmatic need of evaluation. It also is suggested that the more important consequences will tend to be visible in the time period specified above.

and, hence, make comparisons of strategies difficult, we see no reason for this being a more difficult evaluation problem than most others.[15] Finally, while it is difficult to rank and weigh the values or goals of an actor, it is not so insurmountable a problem as the incrementalists argue. We can ask decision-makers to rank their values, at least in an ordinal scale, or we can derive a weight from examination of their actual decisions and accompanying discussions.

Many societal projects, unlike actors or units, have one primary goal such as reducing population growth, economically desalting sea-water, reducing price inflation, or increasing economic growth. Although there may be other goals which are also served, they are secondary from the viewpoint of the project (though not necessarily from the viewpoint of some or even all of the participants). We thus may deal with the degree to which the *primary* goal was realized and use this as the central evaluative measure of a "good" policy, while noting the policy's effects on secondary goals. Thus, we can state that the introduction of birth control pills provides for more contraception (a primary goal) but less opportunity for nursing training (a secondary goal) than the diaphragm. When we compare projects in these terms, we, in effect, weigh the primary goal as several times as important as all the secondary goals combined.[16] When there are two or even three primary goals (e.g., teaching, therapy, and research in a university hospital), we can still compare projects in terms of the extent to which they realize each primary goal, and we can state, for example, that project X is "good" for research but not for teaching while project Y is "good" for teaching but not particularly "good" for research, and so on, without having to deal with the additional difficulties of combining the measures of effectiveness into one numerical index.[17] While this relatively primitive method of evaluation is not without its own problems or limitations, it more closely reflects what successful decision-makers actually do than the incrementalist description and seems to us to provide a more active basis for societal decision-making.

Not all outcomes have the same saliency for an actor, a fact which makes encompassing decision-making less difficult to assess than the incrementalists argue. Most actors, for instance, seem to rank survival above most other values. They also tend to rank the prevention of major *losses* of assets as more desirable than *gains* of the same or even higher magnitude. (Actors who command very few assets, however, are often an exception and tend to accept courses of action which entail much greater risks than richer actors.) Many other propositions may be generated about the distributions of goals (or "utilities") and the ways in which they are related to decision-making strategies.[18] It suffices to say here that such relationships *among* values (or goals) seem to be highly relevant to theories of guidance but are rarely explored in macroscopic and sociological perspectives.

A Morphological Comparative Approach

The more we recognize that the bases of decisions neither are nor can be an ordered set of values and a full examination of reality, the more likely we are to take into account that decisions are made through interactions among actors which are affected by the structures in which they take place. For instance, the choice of less versus more encompassing scanning is not merely an intellectual issue, a matter of strategic reflection, but is influenced by the relationships between higher and lower organizational ranks. If the higher-ranking decision-makers do not favor encompassing scanning, specific dysfunctions are expected, in particular excessive stress on instrumental considerations. Similarly, the conflicts between experts, especially of the analytic type, and high-ranking decision-makers reflect the conflicts among various levels of scanning. This conflict may be functional so long as the distribution of power between the two units assures the ultimate primacy of encompassing scanning. However, when external pressures lead to the placement of experts in a decision-making center, the consequences are often highly dysfunctional from the viewpoint of the units involved. An extreme example of this was when, in response to British and International Monetary Fund pressures, the advice of a tax expert, who was concerned with little other than tax revision, was forced upon the government of British Guiana in 1962 and led to mass riots and general strikes.[19]

The structural profile used here differs considerably from the one often advanced in writings on administration according to which higher-ranking men make general decisions while lower-ranking ones work out specifications within the framework of these general decisions.[20] According to this view, the decisions made by men of various ranks differ only in their degree of specification, and there is a clear hierarchization. In our model, the decisions of those lower in rank differ substantively from those of higher rank in that the lower-ranking decision-maker (a) tends to have a more instrumental orientation; (b) tends to promote one goal (at least relatively) while the higher and, especially, the highest decision-making ranks are concerned with balancing several goals; and (c) tends more toward the incremental approach.

A measure of the extent to which a societal unit is active vis-à-vis its own structure is the extent to which the elites and active publics view the decision-making organization itself as subject to review and alteration. Relatively passive decision-makers are often unaware of the effects of the internal structures of the decision-making centers on the decisions made. More active actors might be aware of these effects, but their perceptions of the difficulties of changing the structures might constrain them to omit such revision from the range of alternatives considered. Finally, highly active, transforming actors include "constitutional" reforms in their range of options. This is fairly common in organizations but less common in states. Of course, we do not mean "constitutions" literally; these are rewritten with facility in some passive societies in which such rewriting does not involve changes in the decision-making organizations; actually, it may even serve to deflect attention from the fact that the organizations remain basically unchanged. Constitutional reforms, as understood here, entail changes in the institutional arrangements and procedures for making societal decisions. For instance, changes in the structure of representation are significant, to the degree that major decisions are made in and not outside of this structure.

The specific morphological approach taken here is a functional one—not one which assumes that all functions are always fulfilled, but one which suggests that if a decision-maker deviates markedly from the model, he will encounter specific dysfunctions whose nature can be derived from the elements of the mixed-scanning strategy he ignored. Scanning which is not sufficiently encompassing (which is the essence of the incrementalist approach) will tend to lead to relatively short-run, non-innovative, often costly decision-making. Such an approach may quite closely approximate what comprehensive rationality would dictate if the situation were stable and the actor's decisions (or policy) were initially effective, but it would be highly inappropriate if either the situation or the means available are rapidly changing—that is, if what were seen as crippling objections have disappeared rapidly, or new ones have risen quickly, or the policy that is being "incremented" was unrealistic when initiated.

In other words, there is no one effective strategy of decision-making in the abstract, apart from the societal context in which it is introduced and from the control capacities of the actors introducing it. The most effective strategy is the one that is most well-suited to the specific situation and to the actors' capacities. Rationalistic strategy is highly rigid; it provides the same basic prescriptions for all situations and all actors. The incrementalist strategy also claims general applicability, though it recognizes one minor sub-set of situations to which it does not apply—"large" decisions.[21] Mixed-scanning, too, claims universal applicability; its flexibility is achieved through changes in the relative investments in scanning in general (versus conduct not covered) and among the various levels of scanning. Thus, it calls for more encompassing scanning, the more transformable the environment and the actor.

Another major consideration here is the other capacities of the actor. An actor who is weak in the other elements of control—such as the capacity to mobilize power to implement or to communicate—may do better to rely on less encompassing scanning; even if remote outcomes are anticipated, he will be able to do little about them. On the other hand, there may be situations in which encompassing scanning may substitute for deficiencies in other control elements. Generally, we suggest, the greater a unit's control capacities, the more encompassing scanning it can undertake, and the more the unit undertakes such scanning, the more effective its decision-making.

This points to an interesting paradox: Developing nations, with much lower control capacities than modern nations, tend more to favor planning when they may well have to make do with a relatively high degree of incrementalism, while modern pluralistic societies—which are much more able to scan and, at least in some dimensions to control—plan less.*

Two factors highlight the differences in this regard among modern societies. While all modern societies have a higher capacity to scan because of their greater knowledge capacities, and while they all have some control advantages over non-modern societies, if only because they command better transportation and communication facilities, they differ sharply in their capacity to build consensus. Democracies must accept a relatively high degree of incrementalism (though not as high as that of developing nations) because of their greater need to gain support for new decisions from many and conflicting sub-societies, a need which reduces their capacity to follow a long-run plan. It is less difficult to reach a consensus, in non-crisis situations, on increments similar to existing policies than to gain support for a new policy. The role of crises, however, and their use in achieving major overdue reforms should not be excluded from the study of democracies. Crises are sufficiently important and frequent to merit systematic consideration. Specifically, we suggest, in relatively less passive democracies, crises serve to build consensus for major changes of direction which are overdue (e.g., the governmental guidance of economic stability, the welfare state, desegregation).

Totalitarian societies, which are more centralist and rely more on other kinds of power, which makes them less dependent on consensus, can undertake more planning, but they tend to overshoot their marks. Democracies tend first to build a consensus and then to proceed, often accomplishing less than was necessary later than was necessary. Their perennial problem is overdue change. Totalitarian societies, lacking the capacity to build consensus or even to assess the various resistances, usually try for too much too early and are forced to adjust their actions after the initiation of a plan because they only then discover its shortcomings and the lack of consensus. The revised policy is often less ambitious and involves more "consensus" than the original one. While totalitarian gross misplanning is a waste of human and capital resources, some initial overplanning and subsequent down-scaling is as much a decision-making strategy as disjointed incrementalism, and it is probably the strategy to which totalitarian societies, whose consensus-building machinery is ineffective, are best suited.

An active society will differ from earlier societies in its higher capacity for scanning (as a result of the development of knowledge-units), its higher

---

* The paradox is even more accentuated when modern pluralistic societies demand master plans or, at least, encompassing planning from underdeveloped nations as a condition for receiving foreign aid, while the donors themselves do not practice such planning.

capacity for consensus-building (because of mechanisms explored below), and, hence, its higher capacity for planning and guidance. It, thus, would be less incremental in its decision-making than modern democracies but not as rationalistic as totalitarian societies attempt to be.

The Correlates of Decision-Making

We have outlined three alternative approaches to decision-making which relate to each other dialectically in that the incrementalist approach is antithetical to the rationalistic one, and mixed-scanning attempts a synthesis. Much remains to be said about the factors which affect the degree to which an actor can develop a decision-making strategy. Without attempting to treat all these factors here, we briefly illustrate those which link the study of decision-making directly to the study of some of the other factors we explore. They include: (i) the concept of slack, which ties the study of decision-making to that of asset analysis (which is examined in Chapters 13 and 14); (ii) the concept of lead-time, which links decision-making analysis with the concept of control (as introduced in Chapter 3); (iii) the extent of the differences in perspective between the elites and the societal unit (introduced in Chapter 5), which affects the quality of societal decision-making; (iv) decision-making strategies as part of societal knowledge (discussed in Chapters 6 to 9); and (v) the role of power in decision-making, which serves as a transition to the next two chapters.

Slack

Several studies of decision-making point to the existence of a "slack," some assets and energies that are not committed to any specific use but are available. The concept appears in studies of development as one *ad hoc* reason that the lagging sectors of an economy or a society are able to respond to pressures placed on them by an unbalanced plan.[22] If there were no slack upon which to draw, these lagging sectors could not accommodate without external support. The concept is also used in studies of the decision-making of corporations, in which it is defined as those assets and energies that the management is free to recommit as distinct from those which are so committed that they are unavailable under normal conditions.[23]

It is important not to confuse subjective with objective slack. If a decision-maker believes that he has at his disposal a certain amount of assets only to find that he cannot utilize them without generating severe strains in the sectors he deprives, his decision-making will be faulty. We, consequently, need to know whether or not there is an objective slack—i.e., by an observer's standards—and to what degree the actor is aware of this slack and is able to distinguish committed from uncommitted assets. Within broad limits, the larger the objective slack, the more potentially active an actor. The actualization of this potential is significantly affected by the actor's awareness of its existence, location, and scope and by his capacity to mobilize his slack.

While the existence of a slack has many advantages, often discussed under the rubric of "strategic reserves," it tends to bias actors toward incremental decision-making because it conceals the contextual limits. For instance, it might be argued that a country in which the citizens are members of extended families and hold traditional values cannot be industrialized; there will not be the needed mobile labor force, and hiring labor and assigning jobs will be carried out on the basis of economically irrelevant considerations. But, it might be said, such countries often have efficient airlines. It might be concluded, therefore, that it is possible to proceed incrementally and introduce more modern industries, one by one. Actually, however, the successful airline may merely point up some slack in the system, atypical families in this case. The airline might be run by foreigners, by a minority, or by the few "modernized" families in the country.[24] Therefore, if an industrialist decides to establish other modern facilities, his plants will fail if the airline has exhausted the slack. This is more likely to happen, the less the actor is able to assess correctly the scope and kinds of slack in the system. More generally, slack tends to hide the lateral relationships because it allows one part of the system to be changed *without* adapting the others, leading the actor to neglect the treatment of the other parts only to be confronted with the reactivated system when the slack is exhausted. An incrementalist, we suggest, is more likely to neglect encompassing analysis and to ignore the initial signs of the exhaustion of the slack than is the mixed-scanner.

Lead-Time

The less encompassing the perspective of an actor, in terms of the links he takes into account, the less free to act he perceives himself. Some decisions have a genetic nature; that is, early ones create the conditions for later ones. The longer the series of decisions thus related, the longer the "lead time," the more important the anticipatory capacity of an actor for his active orientation. At each decision-making round, there are not only options among which the actor chooses but also conditions which—at this point—are, in effect, immutable. These, though, are in part the results of previous decisions, and, if their conditioning effect at this point had been taken into account earlier, they could have been partly shaped in accord with the actors' goals. Hence, the longer the lead-time, which is a dimension of the situation, the greater the need for the actor to scan in depth and to anticipate. For example, the management of monetary aspects of the economy, especially the attempt to anticipate the fluctuations of the business cycle and to act before depression or inflation has occurred, has been widely credited with reducing the mountains of inflation and filling in the valleys of depression in order to make the fluctuations much less extreme. In contrast, the less anticipatory approach, which characterized pre-Keynesian management, was to increment remedially only after the crisis had occurred; this entailed a costlier guidance system.

When the structure of the situation is such that options are related genetically in long sequences but decision-making is incremental, crisis-management is likely to result. That is, when the inadequacy of a policy finally becomes obvious, large efforts are made to overcome the barriers which have been allowed to accumulate.[25] As the major longitudinal and lateral links have not been recognized, "fixing" one spot with large investments will often accentuate the strain on other parts of the system.[26]

All this does not imply that a rationalistic plan must be developed ahead of time and that all major future needs are to be anticipated, at point one in time. The deliberate maintenance of a slack, for example, is a way of taking into account the need for later accommodations, *without* necessitating specific knowledge of what they will be. Thus, slack and depth scanning are functional substitutes. (A further gain in the active orientation is to be expected when both are available.) At the same time, decisions vary in their lead-time; those concerning professional manpower, for instance, have a much longer lead-time than those regarding taxation.[27] An anticipatory capacity enhances activation only if it is applied to decisions and activities which are genetically related and if there is a parallel power to act; otherwise, the added capacity is not particularly useful.

Societal Units and Elites: The Decision-Makers' Values

Just as survival seems to be paramount in the hierarchy of values of most societal units, most decision-makers seem to assign a very high priority to their continued "survival" as decision-makers—i.e., to maintaining their elite position. It is not that most elites would deliberately violate basic societal values to stay in office (although history is not without such occurrences); the choices they make do not, as a rule, entail such extreme challenges. The values which are sacrificed for "political" considerations are often less central, such as loyalty to friends, candor, and fiscal integrity.[28] Moreover, decision-makers often argue that their continued stay in office is essential for the propagation of the basic values, some of which the elite "must", temporarily it is said, disregard. While occasionally there is a one-to-one relationship between the position of one elite and the realization of societal values, these statements are much more often ideological rationalizations which attempt to conceal a conflict of interests, values, and viewpoints between an elite and its societal base.

Elites, even relatively responsive ones, seem routinely to reveal a double standard in their decision-making, taking into account both societal and elite needs. Unresponsive elites, found primarily in societies and sub-societies whose publics are relatively passive or have been inauthentically mobilized, are not those who have two sets of standards but, rather, those who take into account chiefly their own needs to the neglect of societal needs. The double-standard system entails screening out those alternatives which suit elite needs but not societal needs (e.g., the large-scale corruption of politicians), *and* those alternatives which serve the societal needs but undermine those of the elite (e.g., the introduction of necessary but "unpopular" programs such as an increase in taxation on the eve of an election). It is the elites who adhere chiefly to their own set of considerations that are known as the anti-social ones.

In stable societies, the double-standard perspective favors, under most conditions, an incremental strategy because it does not require the elites to undertake fundamental measures which are often politically dangerous (thus serving the elites' needs), while at the same time it seems to serve the societal needs.

Mixed-scanning, though, is a more effective strategy even from the viewpoint of a bifocal elite, because when incremental decisions are made in situations in which fundamental decisions are called for, the elite as well as the societal unit suffers. Actually, the elite's loss is often larger because the societal unit may accommodate by changing the elite, but the elite which is removed from office is often "fundamentally" powerless, at least for a period of time. President Truman, for instance, treated the cessation of the Korean War in a typically incremental fashion; General Eisenhower promised to terminate it at once, which was one reason for his election. The consequences of Truman's policy for his political career, friends, and advisers were non-incremental. Eight years later, President Eisenhower was charged with incrementing on the domestic front; Senator John F. Kennedy promised to get the country "moving again." Thus, in two instances, incremental administrations were replaced and the society initiated a basic change. Other examples include the Illia government in Argentina, 1963–1966, which was charged with incrementation before it was replaced; elite incrementation played a role in the replacement of Chamberlain by Churchill and in De Gaulle's replacement of the Fourth Republic. Effective decision-makers, thus, would seem to need a "rule" in their strategy: When necessary, stop incrementing and turn to more encompassing scanning and policies. (Of course, an elite cannot initiate a fundamental change just because it sees the need for one, but the elite's own decision-making strategy should not prevent it from seeing the need and attempting to act "fundamentally" when this seems in order.)

It has been argued that a well-functioning society moves back-and-forth between periods of accelerated change and consolidation (consolidation, in the terms used here, means incrementing within the context of fundamental themes that were established in the period of accelerated change). This entails either the same decision-makers' fluctuating between two "mixes" of decision-making strategies, one less and the other more incremental, or a change of the elites in control.

Unless specifically encouraged to do so by his "strategy," a typical decision-maker will tend to exclude the possibility of his own resignation from the alternatives he considers; this possibility is ruled out by most elites' communities-of-assumption.* Actually, as De Gaulle has shown—when his ability for effective leadership was blocked in 1946 and he was losing the prestige he had acquired as a result of his war-time leadership—resigning might be not only the most normatively but also the most politically practicable alternative. It is an alternative which Clark Kerr did not use when he was caught between the California right and the student left, a situation which cost him much of his national stature. (He was mentioned much more often as a candidate for national office before the Berkeley crisis of 1964 than after it.) Resignation is a costly fundamental alternative that an incremental decision-maker tends not even to consider, but those who do consider it at major review occasions and occasionally are willing to take it are more able, we suggest, to advance fundamentally different policies when they are societally needed.†

The Societal Role of Theory

Decision-making is more open to influence by treatises about decision-making than most other societal processes are open to influence by any symbolic-intellectual input. Hence, the effect of theories on the actors must be taken into account not only on the normative grounds that any intellectual who affects the subject he is studying must consider, but also because otherwise, the analysis of the system is not complete; the theory-makers are part of the process of decision-making.[29]

While there seems to be little empirical data, Dror argued that the incrementalist theory enforces inertia and agitates against innovation.[30] Boulding pointed out that "whereas the theoreticians have hitherto tried to make them [the decision-makers] ashamed of their failures to be 'synoptic,' the present authors turn the tables and try to make the theorists ashamed of not having noticed that the practical men were right all the time."[31] Incrementalism legitimates remaining on the familiar path, a lack of encompassing scanning,

---

* It would be difficult to test this statement because decision-makers occasionally threaten to resign but do not really consider doing so, or offer to resign but under conditions in which they expect their resignations not to be accepted. There is also a tendency to talk, usually in a light vein, about resigning: "I am sick and tired of it all." To test the proposition, a way would have to be found to distinguish an actual consideration of this alternative from a for-public-consumption one.

† Thomas B. Reed, the speaker of the House between 1889–1891 and 1895–1899, was a very effective leader. He is reported to have resigned in opposition to the Spanish–American War and United States imperialistic policies.

and adjusting goals to means—thus reinforcing the tendencies most decision-makers already have. This tendency to support the status quo and perceive it as needing, at most, amelioration is reflected in the incrementalists' use of basically the same set of statements to describe decision-making and to prescribe the strategy a decision-maker ought to follow. Thus, the incrementalists do not share in the critical function.

The incrementalists' counter-arguments are quite effective as far as they go. Implying that there are only two alternatives, incrementalist or rationalistic, they suggest that a decision-maker is in greater difficulty if he tries to be rationalistic because rationalistic conduct leads to frustration, paralysis, and, eventually, a rejection of the model. The model is too far removed from reality to have even a corrective effect.

While there is so far little evidence to test the following proposition, we expect that the mixed-scanning strategy is close enough to reality to be applicable but remote enough from it to provide a critical standard against which to measure differences among actors and changes in the decision-making of any one actor. The strategy of mixed-scanning generates demands for some scanning of the unfamiliar and for occasional reviews of alternatives excluded by the prevailing community-of-assumptions and refuses to sanction the adjustment of the ends to the means. The strategy also recognizes the function of leadership, of a decision-maker who is not merely a passive referee of existing pressures[32] but who mobilizes latent support for considerations that arise from his encompassing scanning.

There is a major tension in societal units between their normative commitments and the everyday pressures toward normative entropy; the decision-makers are in the center of this interplay, whatever strategy they follow. They may take no stand which, in effect, places them on the side of entropy. They may take a highly normative stand which, under many circumstances, will lead to their ceasing to be decision-makers. Or they may attempt to redress the balance in the direction of the societal unit's normative commitments, supporting and being supported by other anti-entropic forces. Active decision-makers seek such a balance; they never quite achieve it, but they have a net effect in favor of realization of the societal values.

The Role of Power

POWER AND KNOWLEDGE IN DECISION-MAKING

Societal decision-making is never a process in which means are allotted according to a systematic plan or policy; rather, it is a process in which a significant role is played by the relative power of the supporters of various societal goals and by the power of the decision-making elites and their goals.[33] Thus, the industrial management of a corporation—presumably more "rational" and less "political" than most elites—decides the relative weights of reinvestments, dividends, and wage increases not only on the basis of how many assets the respective goals of industrial growth, capital investment, and labor mobilization deserve in accord with some abstract economic model, but also on the basis of how much pressure the governmental tax agencies exert on those who do not reinvest, how many large stock-holders there are among the actual managers of the company, how well the workers are organized, etc. The same holds for the societal decision-makers, especially for the elites who guide the states, the political organizations of societies.

The role of power in societal decision-making can be empirically demonstrated when a change occurs in the relative power of the member-units; this tends to affect the decisions made by the system-elites.* Societal decision-making is, therefore, not merely a thought-process that balances goals and means but also a political process that balances various power vectors.[34] Each goal-and-means constellation has, in addition to its other relative merits, a different *political* weight.

The relative autonomy and power of the elites and the values to which they adhere also affect the societal decisions. Some elites are little more than "brokers" who register the relative power of the member-units and are instrumental in helping them to work out a joint policy.[35] Others have more power than all the member-units combined, although the members cannot, as a rule, be completely ignored. Many elites fall somewhere between these two extremes in terms of their power to affect societal decisions.

Second, decision-making centers, in the ways in which they are organized and function, often express value-commitments. In other words, certain alternatives are ruled out not because they are less rational or have less power "backing" than those which are chosen but because the decision-making centers consider them "unthinkable" or are so structured as to make them "unthinkable." While the relative power of the elites is indicated by the degree to which they can realize their preferences (as compared to following those of other units), their values are indicated by the content of their preferences. Decision-makers are rarely, if ever, completely neutral.

The struggles among agencies or services over their shares of the federal budget, among the various divisions of a corporation over the corporate "pie," and among the humanities, the social science, and the natural science faculties in a university are all parts of decision-making processes. In these processes, the various member-units use both arguments and power in terms of the next-level unit goals, whether they be the welfare of the nation, the corporation, or the university.

A member-unit which advances an alternative that is considered questionable in normative or knowledge terms will have to use much more of its power to gain the decision-makers' support than a unit which advances a

---

* We mention system-elites because a change of the members' power will affect member-elites by definition. For a discussion of the two kinds of elites, see pp. 114–115.

policy that is legitimate in terms of the system's values and goals and correct (or at least plausible) on the basis of available knowledge. On the other hand, it is quite clear that when a policy is illegitimate and when there are relatively valid arguments against it, elites will often implement the policy if enough power is exerted in its support. In short, values, knowledge, and power interact in the making of societal decisions and, to a degree, can be substituted for each other.

The relations between experts or knowledge-producing units and decision-making centers have a similar dynamic, although some interesting differences are to be noted. First of all, the knowledge unit's affiliation must be taken into account. Knowledge units themselves generally have little power and depend for allies on other participants in the political process. The allies may be one or more of the member-units that find the knowledge of political value to themselves. A decision-making center may use knowledge to reduce the counter-pressures exerted by member-units by showing them that experts believe their claims to be ill-founded. Any member-unit may have a knowledge-production sub-unit which may bias findings to suit the unit's needs or interpret the data in a way supportive of the unit. (For instance, public opinion polls are conducted not just "objectively" but also by candidates who wish to show that they have a reasonable chance of being elected.)* Decisions are, therefore, affected by the *relative* scope and skill of the use of knowledge units; the degree to which the decision-making centers command experts of their own to verify the arguments of member-units (e.g., Congress depends largely upon experts provided by the executive), and the degree to which the subject of the decision is given to reality-testing, affect the decision's relative "responsiveness" to knowledge, power, and normative commitments. Unaffiliated experts and intellectuals, as we have seen, become involved in the situation either through this "direct" political process or by gaining a following among one or more active publics.

It might be argued that power becomes important to decision-making in the form of an information input, and, hence, that the power analysis is reducible to an analysis of the knowledge processes.[36] The decision-makers take into account not only that unit X favors this course of action while unit Y favors another but also the units' power. Thus, changes in the relative power of a unit are registered as changes in the information input and, thus, are taken into account via the knowledge processes.

The influence of power on decision-making, however, is much more direct and intimate; its effects via channels other than the input of knowledge

---

* External conditions, circumstances, or events account for conflict only insofar as the choices or decisions of the conflicting parties are influenced by observation or knowledge of these facts. The loci of the study of such conflict are, therefore, the psychological, sociological, political, and legal processes by which choices or decisions are made—that is, the minds of the decision-makers.

are sufficiently important for us to consider it, in addition to knowledge and normative commitment, as a third major determinant of decisions.[37]

There are two reasons for our position. First, knowledge about the relative power of the members of a system is at least as fractional as knowledge in general and probably more so. Hence, the decision-maker is likely to misjudge the power distribution if he assesses it on the basis of knowledge alone. But the power of a unit is not less because a decision-maker underestimated it, and the exercise of that power will affect the decision despite the fact that it has been underestimated. And while knowledge, even when it is accurate, can be ignored, power cannot. A decision-maker may choose—because of normative commitments, psychological rigidity, or intra-unit politics—to ignore facts, but—by definition—he cannot ignore power. An elected government can ignore information about an imminent coup but not the tanks crushing the gates of the Presidential palace. A President might ignore the information that Congress will not pass a bill he favors, but this will not alter the fact that when the vote comes, the bill will not be approved; the decision will be shaped directly by power.[38]

DECISION, POWER, AND IMPLEMENTATION

Decision-making falls between policy-formation and implementation. While decisions theoretically can be made without devoting any attention to the question of whether or not the actor has or can marshal the power needed to implement them, the effectiveness of a decision will depend as much on its power-backing as on the validity of the knowledge and the decision-making strategy which were used. Again, it may be said that power appears here as one other item of knowledge—namely, whether or not the actor correctly judged the power available for the support of this or that course of action. While this is true, power "appears" again in guises other than as items of knowledge. An actor may underestimate the power he can marshal—and, as we assume that decisions are made with only fractional information, such misjudgment is not to be viewed as accidental but as a central feature of the process—but he still commands that power and he may apply it once implementation is initiated.

If the decision-making and implementation processes could be neatly separated, decision-making might be conceived as a passive, reflective, powerless process and implementation as the application of power. The two processes, however, are closely interwoven, with decisions affecting implementations and initial implementations affecting later stages of decision-making which, in turn, affect later implementations. Decision-making is hence not to be viewed as a passive process—as exploring alternatives and choosing from among them. There is a continual give-and-take between decision-making and implementation. If decision-making were a "one-shot" affair, this give-and-take would be less manifest; but, in fact, decisions are processes and early decisions are often only vague directional signals, initial proddings, or trial runs for later specifications and revisions. (Among other things, the actor is testing his power to gain his course before choosing which alternative he favors!)

Nor should the differences between the power which affects decisions and that which affects implementations be exaggerated. Early decisions shape the power which affects later decisions, and the more the initial decision took the relevant power into account, the more effective implementation is going to be. Thus, the pre-decision and post-decision environments are basically the same environment into which the controlling overlayers project themselves.

Finally, it should be noted that unless we add power analysis to that of decision-making, we do not know how decisions are related to the control of action. Let us take two actors who pursue the same decision-making strategy; one may be passive, reflective, and ineffectual, while the other is active, assertive, and effectual. The difference may be that one has less power than the other. Control is not just a process of information-collection, calculation, and the expression of commitments, but also a process of the mobilization and use of assets. Hence, all other things being equal, the more assets an actor has, the more effective will be his decisions. In addition, the nature of his decisions will change in terms of how relatively significant *additional* knowledge is, how careful he must be in making his initial decisions (which are those most likely to need revision or correction), how much "waste" he can afford, etc.

In Conclusion: Decision-Making and the Active Orientation

It might at first be expected that the more rationalistic an actor's decision-making, especially if his rationality is comprehensive, the more active he will be. The rationalistic strategy calls for adjusting means to a set of goals to bring about goal-realization, and its comprehensiveness would seem to assure that one goal will not be advanced to the neglect of the others or of the secondary needs of the actor. What, in theory, could be more active than that? The reason we expect more active actors not to adhere to more rationalistic decision-making strategies is that these strategies are not rational at all; as the incrementalists correctly stressed, the rationalistic approach does not provide a guidance mechanism for relating means to goals and realizing values. Moreover, rationalistic decision-making hinders effective action because, as we have seen, the prerequisites of the model cannot be met in the real world. A decision-maker who attempts to follow the model (as distinct from one who uses the model to legitimate the different procedures he actually follows) will either weaken his own commitments, as his resources and energies are spent trying to apply a model that he cannot satisfy, or will overact and initiate policies that he will assume are rational, only to discover that the policies do not withstand reality-testing and that he knows and controls less than he assumed. In both cases, the actor is expected to be frustrated and relatively inactive.

Incrementalism, we suggest, has effects that are surprisingly similar to those of rationalistic decision-making, though according to many viewpoints, it takes the opposite tack. For reasons discussed above, incrementalism encourages relative inactivity by its central tenet that the next decision-making situation will be like the last one, and by its assumption that the actor is unable to set a goal of any remoteness and generality and pursue it with any measure of effectiveness. An incrementalist actor responds and adjusts; he does not even try to transcend and transform.

Mixed-scanning allows for greater realization of goals than either the rationalistic or the incremental approach, and its requirements can be met. The combination of bit-incrementation with contextual decision-making provides both a short-run probing and a long-run criterion for evaluation, both a realization of the inability to take into account all alternatives *and* a "trigger" mechanism to recall broader considerations when necessary. Above all, it allows for linking the transcendental setting of goals to attempts to transform an existing societal unit, without which activation cannot reach its full measure.

When actors faced with the same situations and possessing the same societal assets and control capacities apply different decision-making strategies, we expect significantly different degrees of effectiveness; i.e., this variable is more powerful than more collectivistic theories imply.[39] While we suggest that most actors would do better by using mixed-scanning in most situations, there are differences in the degree of loss entailed in following other strategies and in the kind of mix of bit and contextual scanning which is most fruitful. In general, the less malleable the environment or the actor and the fewer the available resources, the less damage incrementalism will cause (and the less encompassing scanning is needed if a mixed-scanning strategy is followed). The more malleable the situation and the actor and the more resources available, the more dysfunctional is incrementalism and the more encompassing scanning is called for in the decision-making mix. The rationalistic approach, on the other hand, seems inappropriate in both circumstances, as in neither case can its requirements be even approximated. That both incremental and rationalistic strategies are frequently pursued is true, but this is also one reason that most societal actors are not highly active.

NOTES

1. While economists have used rationalistic models in giving macroscopic advice, it is not clear to what degree their advice is really derived from such a model, and it seems that the decision to follow, reject, or mix the advice with other considerations is not based on such models, and less rationalistic models are often used. Paul A. Samuelson, "What Economists Know," in Daniel Lerner (ed.),

The Human Meaning of the Social Sciences, op. cit., pp. 183–213. It should be noted that there are many assertions about the role of economic models in policy-making but much fewer empirical studies of their effects.

2. Quoted in Lindblom, *Public Administration Review,* Vol. 19, *op. cit.,* p. 80. Lindblom adds that the "claim that operations research is for low-level problems is widely accepted."

3. This procedure is used by the Israeli Army. Personal observation.

4. Personal communication with Professor Lloyd Motz, Professor of Astronomy at Columbia University. A similar camera system is employed in the Lunar Orbiter spacecraft. A "wide-angle" lens is used to produce overlapping pictures of large areas of the moon's surface. At the same time, a telephoto lens is used to reproduce small-scale surface features. This procedure is designed to yield the maximum of topographic information—general terrain and specific details—about possible lunar landing sites. See Press Release on Lunar Orbiter 3, *National Aeronautics and Space Administration* (January 31, 1967), p. 22.

5. Elie Abel, *The Missile Crisis* (Philadelphia: Lippincott, 1966), pp. 17–32, esp. p. 26.

6. For indirectly related works see A. D. deGroot, *Thought and Choice in Chess* (The Hague: Mouton & Co., 1965), pp. 271–274; Ernest Jones, "The Problem of Paul Morphy: A Contribution to the Psycho-analysis of Chess," *International Journal of Psycho-analysis,* No. 12 (1931), pp. 1–23.

7. This is by no means obvious or self-evident. Hirschman and Lindblom argue, that such scanning would make an actor ideologically rigid and would reduce his effectiveness. "Economic Development, Research and Development, Policy Making: Some Converging Views," *op. cit.,* p. 218.

8. I am indebted to Nelson W. Polsby for the suggestion to present the strategy in the form of a linear program and for some of the specific "instructions."

9. For our view of the context of this period, see Amitai Etzioni, *The Hard Way to Peace: A New Strategy* (New York: Collier, 1962), Ch. 1; for evaluation of the results, *Winning Without War* (Garden City: Doubleday, 1964), pp. ix–xiii, 1–27, and *passim.*

10. Braybrooke and Lindblom, *A Strategy of Decision, op. cit.,* pp. 62–65. The concern here is largely with the United States. Hirschman extends this position to developing nations. *Journeys Toward Progress, op. cit.*

11. Richard F. Fenno, Jr., *The Power of the Purse* (Boston: Little Brown, 1966), pp. 266 ff. See also Otto A. Davis, M. A. H. Dempster and Aaron Wildavsky, "A Theory of the Budgetary Process," *The American Political Science Review,* Vol. 60 (1966), esp. pp. 530–531; Wildavsky and Hammond, "Comprehensive versus Incremental Budgeting in the Department of Agriculture," *op. cit.*

12. Nelson W. Polsby, *Congress and the Presidency* (Englewood Cliffs, N.J.: Prentice-Hall, 1964), p. 86.

13. *Ibid.,* p. 86. While this decision itself had some "preparatory" bits and post-hoc specifying ones, a fundamental decision was made in 1950. For a discussion of a contextuating decision by the United States Supreme Court on desegregation which was then "spelled out" in a long series of incremental decisions, see Shapiro, "Stability and Change in Judicial Decision-Making," *op. cit.,* esp. pp. 145–146.

A decision-maker may make a fundamental decision when he intends to make an incremental one, for instance, if he wishes to keep his decision "minimal" and leave as many options open as possible. See Schilling's discussion of how President Truman's decision to "determine the technical feasibility of a thermonuclear weapon" led to Hiroshima. Schilling, "The H-Bomb Decision: How to Decide Without Actually Choosing," *op. cit.*, esp. pp. 36 ff. Bruce L. R. Smith pointed out that the distinction between incremental and fundamental decision-making was not completely clear. See his communication to *The American Political Science Review*, Vol. 61 (1967), esp. p. 151. See also rejoinder by Davis, Dempster and Wildavsky, *ibid.*, pp. 152–153.

14. Polsby, *loc. cit.*, p. 83.

15. For a discussion of evaluation techniques, see Herbert H. Hyman, Charles R. Wright and Terence K. Hopkins, *Applications of Methods of Evaluation* (Berkeley: University of California Press, 1962). See also Peter Rossi, "The Study of Man: Evaluating Social Action Programs," *Trans-action*, Vol. 4 (June, 1967), pp. 51–53.

16. David Osborn, Deputy Assistant Secretary of State for Education and Cultural Affairs is reported to have devised a method for such calculations with regard to the multiple purposes of cultural exchange programs. See Virginia Held, "PPBS Comes to Washington," *The Public Interest*, No. 4 (Summer, 1966), pp. 112–113. See also Elizabeth Drew, "HEW Grapples with PPBS," *The Public Interest*, No. 8 (Summer, 1967), pp. 9–29.

17. For additional discussion, see Amitai Etzioni and Edward W. Lehman, "Some Dangers in 'Valid' Social Measurement: Preliminary Notes," *The Annals of the American Academy of Political and Social Science*, Vol. 373 (Sept., 1967), pp. 1–15.

18. For studies on the computing of societal "utilities" see Ward Edwards, "The Theory of Decision Making," in Rubenstein and Haberstroh, *Some Theories of Organization, op. cit.*, esp. pp. 404–408. For surveys of quantitative developments, see Robert Schlaifer, *Probability and Statistics for Business Decisions* (New York: McGraw-Hill Book Company, 1959); Herman Chernoff and Lincoln E. Moses, *Elementary Decision Theory* (New York: Wiley & Sons, Inc., 1959); R. M. Thrall, C. H. Coombs, and R. L. Davis, *Decision Processes* (New York: John Wiley & Sons, Inc., 1954). See also, Marcus Alexis and Charles Z. Wilson, "Quantitative Decision Models," in their *Organizational Decision Making* (Englewood Cliffs, N.J.: Prentice-Hall, 1967), p. 222–255.

19. See *The Economist*, Vol. 202 (February 24, 1962), p. 693. For additional discussion see Bertrand de Jouvenel, "Political Science and Prevision," *American Political Science Review*, Vol. 59 (1965), p. 30.

20. Simon, *Administrative Behavior, op. cit.*, rev. ed., pp. 245–246.

21. Braybrooke and Lindblom, *A Strategy of Decision, op. cit.*, pp. 66–69.

22. Hirschman, "Unbalanced Growth: An Espousal," *The Strategy of Economic Development, op. cit.*, pp. 62–75.

23. Cyert and March, *A Behavioral Theory of the Firm, op. cit.*, p. 36 and *passim*. Other studies which use the notion include Roscoe C. Martin, Frank J. Munger et al., *Decisions in Syracuse* (Garden City, N.Y.: Doubleday, 1965), pp. 8–10.

24. This applies, for instance, to the airlines of Peru and of several Central American Republics. For another example, see David Corbett's discussion of Indian airlines in his *Politics and the Airlines* (London: George Allen & Unwin Ltd., 1965), pp. 303–323. The same point applies to Egypt's capacity to effectively run the Suez Canal but little else.

25. Anne Gibson Buis concludes a study in 1953 with the statement, "The

records reveal that the Congress has seriously considered federal aid to education bills only during periods of national stress. . . ." Quoted by Frank J. Munger and Richard F. Fenno, Jr., *National Politics and Federal Aid to Education* (Syracuse, N.Y.: Syracuse University Press, 1962), p. 181. The quotation is from "An Historical Study of the Role of the Federal Government in the Financial Support of Education, with Special Reference to Legislative Proposals and Action" (unpublished doctoral dissertation, Ohio State University, 1953), pp. 659–660. The Sputnik crisis is said to have produced such a momentum. Munger and Fenno, *op. cit.*, p. 182. See also Homer D. Babbidge, Jr. and Robert M. Rosenzweig, *The Federal Interest in Higher Education* (New York: McGraw-Hill, 1962), pp. 18–19.

26. Examples would include the attraction of students to study "space sciences" following the orbiting of the Sputnik in 1957, which generated a decline in the number of applicants to medical schools and, hence, in the quality of students in these schools, without significantly increasing the total number of students in graduate schools. Personal communications with deans of medical schools.

27. See *supra*, pp. 213–214, Ch. 9.

28. Alexander L. and Juliette L. George, *Woodrow Wilson and Colonel House, A Personality Study* (New York: Dover, 1964), pp. 166–167. See Robert Michels, *Political Parties, op. cit.*

29. There is much debate about the degree to which strategies affect the world of the decision-makers. Anatol Rapoport, for example, takes an extreme position. See Anatol Rapoport, *Strategy and Conscience* (New York: Harper & Row, 1964); Rapoport, "The Sources of Anguish," *Bulletin of the Atomic Scientists*, Vol. 21 (December, 1965), pp. 31–36. See also Donald G. Brennan, "Strategy and Conscience," *ibid.*, pp. 25–30.

30. Dror, "Muddling Through—'Science' or 'Inertia'?," *op. cit.*, p. 155. See also Richard A. Lester, "Economics Includes Politics," *The Yale Review*, Vol. 43 (Autumn, 1953), p. 147.

31. Kenneth E. Boulding, review of *A Strategy of Decision*, in the *American Sociological Review*, Vol. 29, *op. cit.*, p. 390.

32. Cf. Latham, *The Group Basis of Politics, op. cit.*, p. 390.

33. While within a person too there are different levels of support for various goals and for controlled versus ongoing behavior, the differentiation is much less articulated. The same holds for the average micro-unit.

34. Cyert and March, *A Behavioral Theory of the Firm, op. cit.*, pp. 27–32 and pp. 284–286.

35. Latham, *The Group Basis of Politics, op. cit.*, viewed all elites in this way.

36. "External conditions, circumstances, or events account for conflict only insofar as the choices or decisions of the conflicting parties are influenced by observation or knowledge of these facts. The center for the study of conflict is, therefore, the psychological, sociological, political, or legal processes by which choices or decisions are made—that is, in ordinary terms, the workings of the minds of the decision-makers." Quincy Wright, "International Conflict and the United Nations," *World Politics*, Vol. 10 (1957), p. 26. See Lewis F. Richardson, *Generalized Foreign Politics: A Study in Group Psychology* (Cambridge, England: The University Press, 1939); Charles Horton Cooley, *Human Nature and the Social Order* (New York: C. Scribner's Sons, 1902); Kurt Lewin, *A Dynamic Theory of Personality* (New York: McGraw-Hill, 1935); Frederick C. Barghoorn, *The Soviet*

Image of the United States: A Study in Distortion (New York: Harcourt, Brace, 1950). See also Peter Bachrach and Morton S. Baratz, "Decisions and Non-decisions: An Analytical Framework," *The American Political Science Review*, Vol. 57 (1963), esp. p. 633.

37. Simon, *Administrative Behavior, op. cit.*, includes only information and values.

38. Access to power has a particularly important effect on governmental decision-making. For an example see Everett E. Hagen and Stephanie F. T. White, *Great Britain: Quiet Revolution in Planning* (Syracuse, N.Y.: Syracuse University Press, 1966), esp. pp. 62–88.

39. Orville G. Brim, Jr. et al., *Personality and Decision Processes* (Stanford: Stanford University Press, 1962), pp. 233–235.

PART THREE

IMPLEMENTING

FACTORS

CHAPTER 13

Power as a Societal Force

WHILE IN the reality of societal action cybernetic factors and implementing factors are mixed, it is useful to treat the two kinds of factors separately for analytic purposes. If we imagine two actors who are committed to the same goals, whose cybernetic capacities are identical, and who operate in the same environment, the major difference in the degree to which their goals will be realized will be explained by their capacity to implement their decisions, which will be greatly affected by their relative power. In this chapter, we first briefly explore the question: Can power be defined as an operational concept? How important is power in the regulation of societal processes—is it a universal component of all societal organizations or found only in deficient ones? We then ask: What is the relationship between the distributive structure of society and the societal role of power? What is the relation of stratification to political processes? In the closing section of this chapter, we discuss the relationship between power and the other main implementing factor, communication. We ask: To what degree can communication substitute for power in an active society?

The Societal Scope of Power.

Power Defined

The realization of most societal goals, even in situations in which the actor's commitment and knowledge are considerable, requires the application of power. That is, under most circumstances, societal goals and decisions not supported by at least some degree of some kind of power will not be implemented. Hence, powerless actors are passive actors. The assumption which underlies these statements is that the realization of a societal goal requires introducing a change into societal relations, either in the societal environment or among the member units, and, as a rule, attempts to introduce changes (as distinct from changes that occur "anyhow," which do not constitute the realization of a goal), encounter some resistance. Unless this resistance is reduced, a course of action set will not be a course of action followed. *Power is a capacity to overcome part or all of the resistance, to introduce changes in the face of opposition* (this includes sustaining a course of action or preserving a status quo that would otherwise have been discontinued or altered).[1]*

Power is always relational and relative.[2] An actor by himself is not powerful or weak; he may be powerful in relation to some actors in regard to some matters and weak in relation to other actors on other matters. Here, we are interested chiefly in the macroscopic consequences of the application of power; hence, we are concerned with societal power and not with the power of individuals or small groups, although several of the following statements and propositions apply to these units as well.

Power as an Operational Concept

There has been considerable controversy about the definition of power for centuries.[3] Without attempting to review this controversy here or to deal with its many issues, let us briefly indicate our position on the question of whether or not the methodological difficulties involved in the use of the concept can be surmounted. The main methodological objection to the use of the concept of power is that power can be assessed only *post hoc*; we know that *x* has power only after he overcomes the resistance of *y*, and whether or not he can do so—it is said—is unknown until after he has done it.[4] Such *post hoc* analysis has no predictive value. To avoid this difficulty, let us use "power" not for a single exercise of it on a single issue over a single subject at one point in time, but rather to refer to a generalized capacity of an actor, in his relations with others, to reduce resistance to the course of action he

---

* Reference notes for this chapter appear on page 342.

prefers in a given field (i.e., in the "presence" of other actors) about a set of matters over a period of time.[5] This capacity can be anticipated with a certain degree of probability; on the basis of past instances of the exercise of power, the outcomes of future applications of power can be predicted.[6] Even before an instance of the exercise of power has occurred, we can make probabilistic statements about the expected outcome. These are based on our estimates of the relative assets and the uses made of them by the actors in a given field, which can be studied before power is applied.

All of this is possible once the distinction between assets and power is recognized. Assets are possessions of an actor which *may* be converted into power but are not necessarily so used; hence, there is a systematic difference between the assets of an actor, which may be viewed as a power base or potential, and his actual capacity to reduce the resistance of others, which is the power actually generated. ("Potential" refers to the latent energy "locked-into" the societal "material"; "actual" capacity refers to the energizing itself.*) If assets and power are viewed as analytically identical, it is impossible to use the one to formulate predictions about the other.

There are three reasons that the concept of power as a generalized capacity that draws on an asset base but is not identical with it, is particularly useful. First, analysis becomes more realistic. When, for a particular line of action, an affluent actor does not mobilize more than a small fraction of his assets and thus loses to a poorer but more mobilized actor, this, in itself, often leads to a greater mobilization of the affluent actor and, in the long-run, to his "victory." Atomistic power analysis, focusing on each instance of the exercise of power, would not be able to account systematically for the interplay between the loss of single campaigns and the winning of the whole drive.[7] Collectivistic power analysis, focusing on differences in assets, may expect the affluent actor to prevail initially.[8] Neither approach would alert the observer to the fact that in situations in which there are only a few rounds and the outcome is irreversible, the poor but highly mobilized actor who generated more power in the critical instance will tend to prevail. This applies, for instance, to movements of revolution or national independence (in systems which are poorly integrated) and to the passing of key legislation (in systems which are better integrated).

The second reason that the concept of power as a generalized capacity is particularly useful concerns the cross-sectoral application of power. Much has been said about the sectoral nature of power—that it cannot be deduced that an actor powerful in one area of societal activity will be powerful in other areas; again, the concept has been declared too fragmented to be fruitful. While we agree that power in one sector (e.g., in economic matters) does not necessarily imply power in others (e.g., in religion), there is none-theless some halo effect; that is, the very capacity to have one's way in one

---

* For discussion of the energy model, see pp. 35–36.

area generates a degree of superordination in another area.[9] An example used to illustrate the sectoral nature of power actually illustrates its inter-sectoral, generalized character as well. The United States, it is said, has a very large amount of economic assets and military power in comparison to small countries, but in terms of votes in the General Assembly of the United Nations, all this power is to no avail, since the United States has only one vote like the smallest, poorest, and militarily weakest country.* Actually, the fact that the United States has economic power over the Central American republics, for instance, greatly influences the votes of these republics in the General Assembly. Obviously, when one of them introduces a resolution that is incompatible with a major tenet of United States policy, that republic has a much more difficult task in making the United States vote in accord with it than the other way around. This is the case because power relations outside the General Assembly and in sectors of international relations which ostensibly are quite unrelated to it, such as the marketing of primary pro-ducts, greatly influence relations within the General Assembly. This, we suggest, is in part because power in one sector tends to invoke some power in other sectors (although, as a rule, not commensurate) and in part because power in one sector can be "cashed" in another sector, in the sense that votes in the United Nations can be "traded" for, let us say, an increase in the sugar quota. Thus, an actor whose generalized power is greater will enjoy an advantage over the less powerful actor even in sectors where there is formal equality. The concept of generalized power calls our attention to these power projections.

A third reason that this concept seems useful is that it explains submission even when there is no actual exercise of power. This is because the subjects' considerations—like the application of power—are probabilistic; a small nation or a group of workers refrains from resisting not because it is certain that it will be punished (or, not rewarded) if it were to block the power wielders' course, but because the probability of being treated punitively is higher than it is willing to accept. On the other hand, if the controlling agents cannot exercise sanctions at least occasionally, their power will erode and resistance will rise, as subjective probabilities are adjusted. For all these reasons, in the following discussion "power" means a *generalized* capacity to reduce resistance.

Like energy, power is directly observable only when used. The power of a unit can be predicted by studying its assets, its total structure, and its past performances in this regard. But like the world of physical energy, there is no gain-for-nothing, for power has a cost; assets used to generate it are no longer available to the particular actor. If the asset base is not replenished, the probability of compliance will decline.

---

* Leland M. Goodrich, *The United Nations* (New York: T. Y. Crowell, 1959), pp. 124–125.

Our concept of power is not tautological. While no power was exercised unless resistance was reduced, resistance may be reduced in other ways—for instance, by authentic consensus-formation. Secondly, while two actors may apply the same amount of power, we shall see in the next chapter that differences in the kinds of power used affect the conditions under which resistance is reduced, which, in turn, affects the active quality of the societal unit. All of this is not to suggest that the concept of power presents no difficulties, but that its merits for socio-political analysis outweigh its shortcomings.[10]

Is Power Universal?

The concept of power has provoked many debates concerning the socio-political stance it implies. As the concept is used here, the notion of resistance is central. The socio-political world implied is one composed of a plurality of societal actors, many of whom are committed to realizing one or more goals. Scarcity, we assume, prevails in the sense that the total amount of assets available is smaller than that needed to realize all of the goals of all of the actors. (Overcapacity or "affluence" might exist in this or that instrumental realm but is never universal.[11]) Nor are all or even most of the goals of the actors shared or complementary. Hence, while the realization of some goals does not distract from the realization of some others and may even advance them, there is a significant degree of incompatibility among goals (in that the realization of some goals limits the realization of some others) and among means (in that the use of most means for most goals makes these means unavailable for the advancement of any other goal).

From the facts that there is a plurality of actors and of goals and a scarcity of instruments, it follows that societal actors will tend to "resist" each other in the sense of hampering each other's actions. This is not to imply, as has been suggested, that conflict is the prevailing mode of societal relations. Actors often do share some goals and work out a set of priorities among some other goals and a pattern of allocation of scarce instruments. But even if such cooperation and mutual understanding were eventually to encompass the full range of societal action (a situation hard to imagine), the specific pattern of priorities and allocation would still reflect the relative power of the various actors. The agreements reached between an adolescent and his parents, a new nation and a superpower, the poor and City Hall are almost invariably a-symmetrical, as indicated both by the respective implementations of divisive (as distinct from complementary and shared) goals and by the respective shares of the scarce instruments and rewards obtained. (On the rare occasions that symmetrical arrangements are reached, they do not reflect a power vacuum but arise from the equally rare power situation in which the various actors command almost equal amounts of power.*) In cooperative relations, power appears in the ability to eliminate all arrangements which differ from those finally reached. It is true that some concessions are made because of non-rational commitments to shared values—for instance, national pride. Also, in part, the arrangements reached reflect the sides' *estimates* of the outcome of a more explicit use of power. But while the outcomes of negotiations or arbitration rarely reflect only the sides' actual relative power, they usually are significantly affected by it—if not in each round, as the rounds accumulate.

Another reason that power and cooperation are fundamentally related is that patterns of cooperation are not worked out on an *ad hoc* basis or completely voluntarily among the actors concerned; cooperation is often imposed by third parties or is institutionalized and enforced as the result of previous arrangements among the actors. For instance, the degree of cooperation among the republics in Central America in part reflects the power the United States has over them; the degree of cooperation between management and labor is affected by the power the national government has over them as well as by enforceable agreements between them. Power and cooperation are, thus, not a mutually exclusive pair of concepts; cooperation often has a power base, and power is exercised through cooperation.

The tendency to associate power with conflict rather than with cooperation is part of a more general tendency to view power negatively. Hence, it should be emphasized that at least in macroscopic social structures, the realization of many values depends on a "proper" power constellation rather than on the elimination of the role of power.[12] Thus, for instance, democratic processes presuppose a plurality of power centers, each strong enough to compete with the others but not so strong as to be able to undermine the societal framework in which the democratic competition takes place. And in societies in which the law prescribes civil and human rights for its members, the effective safeguard of these rights only in part rests with societal education and in the identification of various members with these values; they need also to be supported by at least a latent capacity for any group of citizens whose rights are denied to exert sufficient power to activate the societal mechanisms necessary to restore their rights. The same holds for "free enterprise" and "free" markets; they may exist between units similar in economic power but not between oil companies and gasoline stations or between automobile manufacturers and automobile dealers.[13] To put it differently, the power relations among the member-units of a society and between that society and other societies are a major determinant of the degree to which that societal structure will be consonant or in conflict with the values to which the members "individually" and as a collective unit are

---

* The only situation in which all the actors have *exactly* the same amount of power over each other is when none has any. Complete equality, a "limit" situation, is, hence, the only societal situation which is powerless.

committed. In short, effective universalism is not to be expected without an appropriate power distribution.

While power and conflict are not Siamese twins, they are intimately connected and frequently appear together. One reason that conflict is a common mode of societal relations rests in the poor societal knowledge most actors have of their potential power as compared to that of other relevant actors. The sources of societal power are many and varied and include such intangible elements as the capacity of a societal unit to mobilize the loyalties of the membership and the efficacy of its organization and elites. Therefore, it is usually difficult for even a detached observer to assess accurately the power of various actors, and when the assessor is himself an actor in the field, the reasons for misjudgment multiply. If the relative power of various societal units were completely measurable, and if there were a supreme judge who could adjust the patterns of priorities of shared projects and the allocation of assets not committed to shared projects—to the changing power assessments—societal conflict would be greatly reduced; a basic function of societal conflict is to substitute for the lack of such measurements and judges.[14] Societal conflict is, therefore, an inherent element of macroscopic processes. It is a major (although by no means the only) expression of power—of the discrepancy between the capacity of an actor to produce change and the readiness of other actors in the field to agree, between the actual distribution of societal power and that which the prevailing stratification structure and political organization of society assume.[15]

Power relations seem to be an inevitable feature of societal structure. It seems that there will always be a plurality of actors, each with a will of his own that is not completely complementary to, or shared, by all other actors, even if they all are members of one community. While the *intensity* of power —the extent to which societal relations are regulated by it—might well decline as the scope of shared values and authentic consensus broadens, so long as there is a scarcity of assets and societal actors have a degree of autonomy, some actors will meet with some resistance from some other actors and will use part of their assets to reduce it in order to further their own goals.[16] Although active societies may be less power-oriented than modern ones, they will not be without the application of power between members and by the controlling overlayer over the underlayer.

To make power a central element of societal analysis is not to assume that other elements—especially goals and values, knowledge and commitment— are less important. On the contrary, we view societal power as a form of the mobilization of societal energy in the service of societal goals. Political elites might seek power for power's sake or, perhaps more accurately, rank the gaining of the instruments of power higher than any other particular goal they seek[17]; but the societal consequences of power lie in the realization of societal goals, whether they be changes in the relations of the societal unit to its environment or the transformation of the societal self. To say that power is a universal feature of society is not to imply that power is omnipotent. A major limitation to power is the values to which actors are committed; actors restrain the use of power under certain circumstances because elites as well as followers *believe* they ought not to use whatever power they command in every situation.

Second, the power of any societal actor, however great, is limited by that of others. Writings in the "power-elite" tradition tend to overestimate the degree to which the power of business or the "military–industrial complex" is autonomous and unchecked.[18] The narrow range of the power of American Presidents is well known,[19] and the limitations on the power of even totalitarian leaders and parties are well documented.[20] Power can be exercised only because—and to the extent that—the power potentials are unevenly distributed among the actors.

Between Power and Coercion

To generate power is not necessarily to rely on force or to be coercive.[21] That there are other sources and means of power—for instance, economic assets—is too obvious to need comment. It is sometimes argued that all other kinds of power "ultimately" rely on force because it is used when economic or moral sanctions fail.[22] While there are cases in which this is true, there are others in which force is not applied even though economic or moral sanctions were not heeded as, for example, in numerous business and interpersonal transactions and relations. Second, even when there is force "in the background," the other sanctions clearly play an autonomous role, for instance, in the likelihood that force will need to be applied.

What is less evident is that although power, by definition, assumes a capacity to reduce resistance, it is not necessarily coercive in the sense of eliminating all or most alternatives to the course imposed on the actors who are subjected to the exercise of power. Of course, power may be coercive; more often, however, power takes effect indirectly by altering the situation. Rather than preventing those subjected to power from following a course of action, it makes the course less attractive (and, by implication, the other alternatives more attractive). Here, the actors still can—if they are willing to pay the higher costs—pursue their original courses. Since few if any acts are without costs (even when these are outweighed by gains), the more common effect of the injection of power into a situation is to alter the costs rather than to destroy the capacity to choose. That is, there is frequently a voluntary element in submission: the unwillingness to pay the cost of not submitting.

Complete coercion occurs when the subjects are, in effect, deprived of the opportunity to choose—e.g., when a parent carries a child away from his toys, or when United States forces physically prevented Cuban exile organizations from raiding Castro's Cuba in 1963 by arresting the leaders and impounding the boats. It has been argued that even in the most coercive situation, the actors have a choice; they can choose to die rather than submit. It is a fact, though, that coercive controls are typically used to foreclose this option, too—to force the subjects to live in jail. The same may be said of collectivities under extreme totalitarian conditions.

There are situations which approximate this extreme case in which, in effect, alternatives are eliminated and the available choices are very skewed— e.g., there are only two alternatives and the penalty of choosing one of them is very high. Therefore, it seems useful to treat the concepts of coercion and non-coercion not as a dichotomy but as points on a continuum. Accordingly, coercion is used to refer to compliance relations in which there is little or no effective choice. Non-coercive compliance includes utilitarian and normative relations. By this definition, some but by no means all or even most power is coercive, initially or "ultimately."

Another reflection of the liberal tendency to evaluate power negatively, apparent in the inclination to make all power seem coercive, is the focusing upon the illicit uses of power.[23] Actually, power might advance any societal goal, from conserving a status quo to altering it. The notion that evil is imposed by power while goodness flies on its own wings assumes an optimistic view of human nature and societal institutions that has little evidence to support it. The application of power is a principal way of getting things done. Its ethical standing depends in part on the kinds of things that get done and on the ways in which goals are set and attained; these factors, in turn, depend much more on the distribution of power (what proportion of the members of a unit to which power is applied shares in setting the goals?) and on the amounts and kinds of power used (e.g., the degree of coercion) than on the very fact that power was exercised. *Hence, most societal actors must choose not between getting things done voluntarily or through the exercise of power, or between exercising power or not getting things done, but rather among the varying degrees and kinds of power to apply.* A societal unit is more active the lower the intensity of the application of power, the more societal action is based on authentic consensus, and the less alienating the kinds of power used.

The Stratification Bases of Power

Theories of societal action can be characterized according to the degree to which they use a class or an elite approach. We refer to the first as a stratification approach to emphasize that societal units or sub-units which have similar status in terms of the allocation of assets may be regional or ethnic groupings as well as classes. We refer to the second as a political organizational approach to stress that there is not only a "head" unit or leadership involved but also such structures as cybernetic centers, organizational hierarchies, and communication networks as, for instance, those provided by modern political parties. Here, we draw on both the stratification and the political approaches and attempt to outline an analytic approach that combines them. In the following discussion, assets represent the distributive, stratification aspect and power the processual, political aspect. Assets represent latent energy; power refers to what is made out of the assets in the energizing of societal action. The two are closely linked both because the stratification structure sets limits, however broad, on the political organization and on societal action, and because the political organization and societal action have significant "feedback" effects on the structure of societal stratification.

Assets, Power, and Activation

An exploration of the complicated relations between the assets an actor commands and the power he wields is central for an understanding of the active orientation, because the capacity to act is greatly affected by the possessions of an actor *and* by what he does with these possessions. The common-sense view (and that of some political scientists) tends to estimate the power of an actor by an inventory of his assets. Nations with a large territory, a large population, high production of steel, oil, ship tonnage, or railroad miles are viewed as strong nations.[24] Or, among sub-societies, the rich are viewed as powerful and the poor as weak.

Actually, the amount of assets an actor has determines only the collectivistic context of his power, his power *potential* or base—that is, the amount of assets on which he can draw to support his action. The proportion of these assets he actually uses to generate power is a different, more organizational, more voluntaristic aspect of societal relations. Each actor constantly chooses, although often not consciously, how many of the assets he controls should be *consumed* (used to satisfy immediate needs), *preserved* for later consumption, *invested* to increase his assets, and *converted* into societal power.* Assets are, thus, a relatively "stable" (or structural) aspect of societal relations, while power is more dynamic (or processual).

The relation of power to assets is analogous to the relation of energy to material. The conversion of assets into power is not an abrupt "jump" but rather a process of transformation. Various steps may be taken to activate the assets and bring them closer to a power-yielding state without actually releasing the energy. Such activation occurs, for instance, when a collectivity

---

* It is essential not to change the time perspective when making assessments of the allocative pattern of a societal unit, as, for instance, consuming resources now may make the actor more powerful later (e.g., by enhancing the morale of the troops), or converting some assets into power now may increase the actor's ability to consume later. But an asset (or part of one) that is used for one purpose cannot be used *at one and the same time* for another. Assets remain potentially universal instruments so long as they are not used; when used, they become particularized.

or society is preparing for a conflict—whether it be a war, a strike, or a period of demonstrations. These preparations are modern analogies to the primitives' war dances. Again, as in thermodynamics or electronics, while societal assets or power potentials may be accumulated and stored or activated in anticipation of future use, there are some costs or "losses" involved since some of the potential energy is "dissipated" and increasingly so as time passes. Thus, arms or means of production grow obsolescent, and morale and leadership not actively engaged tend gradually to erode.*

Conversion Ratios and Patterns

The power of an actor is determined by an interplay between his controlling overlayer and his assets. On the one hand, his controlling overlayer greatly determines the degree to which he consumes his assets, accumulates assets, commits his assets to a specific course of action, and so forth. On the other hand, whatever the nature of the controlling overlayer, an actor's power is also affected by the asset base upon which he can draw. Obviously, if the base is narrow, the utmost curtailment of consumption and the highest commitment of assets to the generation of power may provide less power than a much smaller effort on the part of a more affluent actor; optimal control can substitute for affluence only to a degree. In addition, there is a declining marginal utility for both factors in the sense that once control is fairly effective, a small gain in assets will have a considerable effect while additional control improvements will have comparatively little effect. At the same time, additional resources will afford little gain to the fumbling affluent actor, while a relatively small improvement in his guidance mechanism may increase his action capacity considerably.

While both factors are operative, it seems that *in the short-run, the capacity to improve control is higher than the capacity to increase assets.* In crisis situations, for instance, many actors unveil "hidden" power; that is, they overcome resistance which previously they were believed unable to overcome, not because the societal unit suddenly possesses new assets but because the control of the assets is shifted from sub-societal to societal usages and from

---

* There is a difference here between the world of objects and societal processes, and it is here that a voluntaristic element is particularly evident: The continued accumulation of energy tends to generate high tension and a pressure to act. However, to respond to such a pressure is frequently not rational from any viewpoint other than the instrumental considerations of power storage. Hence, the controlling overlayers of an active unit require special provisions to deal with such pressures. This is achieved by the institutional and organizational segregation of the societal decision-making units from the organizational units in charge of societal power storage (especially of the coercive kind) and by a consciousness, preferably on the part of both elites and publics, of the need to contain these pressures. Otherwise, they become a major source of distortion of societal guidance mechanisms by mistriggering and pretriggering them and being generally hyperactive.

societal consumption to the generation of societal power. To the degree that such crises simply occur (i.e., are a result of processes in the environment or in the system), they are of limited interest for societal guidance. But many crises are produced by control centers or elites, frequently as part of their efforts to alter the allocation of assets in their societal units or to increase the proportion of assets converted into power.

In the long-run, the asset base itself, stratification, changes greatly and is to be conceived not merely as providing a base for generating societal power but also as reflecting the use to which such power has been put, for one of the major purposes toward which power can be applied is to gain possession of new assets. In comparing societal units from this viewpoint, differences in the conversion ratios and patterns are to be taken systematically into account. The conversion ratio specifies the proportion of an actor's assets which are used to generate power as compared to his total assets. The conversion pattern is the distribution of those assets earmarked to power usage among various kinds of utilization. A conversion pattern, for instance, may be narrow or broad in scope, encompass mainly external or also internal areas, and so on.

What are the historical trends with regard to the conversion ratios and patterns of societies? It at first seems that an increasingly higher ratio of assets is devoted to societal usages. But detailed statistical analysis is needed to establish whether, as the amount of assets possessed by the members of society has grown rapidly (as crudely indicated by the growth of the GNP), there has been a proportional increase in the amount of assets assigned to societal usages (roughly represented by the public expenditures of both governmental and non-governmental agencies), or whether the increase in the absolute expenditure (which has obviously occurred in the post-modern as compared to the late modern period) has been accompanied by a decline in this ratio.[25]

Regarding the conversion pattern, the extent of the discussions about the welfare state or welfare capitalism would lead to the expectation of an historical trend toward an increasingly internally-focused pattern. But the semi-war state which has existed in many societies since the advent of the post-modern period suggests that, if we take the post-war years as our base, defense expenditures have risen even more than domestic ones.[26]

The only trend which seems to be in accord with the common sense expectation is the breadth of societal control: More sectors of societal activity are guided collectively in the post-modern than in the modern period, though the main pattern had been established in the last modern century (1845–1945).

Bringing about an active society will require the assignment of a greater amount *and* ratio of societal assets to societal usages, since the realization of goals served collectively seems to lag behind the realization of those served directly by sub-units or by their unguided interaction. Similarly, more effort will be needed for internal than for external areas. Contemporary societies which are more active in other respects also have a more internally-oriented pattern. The scope of the sectors encompassed by collective guidance would

Country	GNP	Defense	Per cent	Education	Per cent	Health	Per cent
United States	628,700	51,323	8.2	30,400	4.8	10,000	1.6
Denmark	8,940	255	2.9	300	3.4	190	2.1
Norway	6,200	220	3.5	325	5.2	100	1.6
Sweden	17,200	826	4.8	800	4.7	400	2.3

Figures are in millions of United States dollar equivalents for 1964, and provided by Sprecher, *op. cit.*, pp. 7 and 8.

be expected to vary least because it is already quite broad.[27] The societal guidance of technology has been only initiated; the societal guidance of other areas—such as the reallocation of wealth and the restructuring of status-relations—has already begun, but it has not been sufficiently "energized," as judged by the actors' own goals. The most neglected area seems to be the development of societal guidance mechanisms, especially within the higher echelons of society-wide decision-making units, knowledge-units, and units devoted to the critical function.

In the conversion of assets into power, much of the potential energy is almost invariably lost, as when energy converted into light is wasted on generating heat. The higher the *quality* of a conversion process, the more societal energy is released. This is a question of the extent to which the conversion is well organized and politically responsive. For instance, the same amount of taxation will yield varying degrees of financing of societal action depending on the mode of taxation that is used. (Taxes vary significantly in terms of their administrative and psychological costs. Compare, for instance, sales taxes to income taxes and both kinds of taxes as collected in the United States to tax farming in ancient bureaucracies.) Other differences in mobilization and in cost result from the relative reliance on central as against local government agencies and on government as opposed to public authorities, such as the BBC or the Port of New York Authority. The higher the over-all quality of an actor's conversion processes, the more power he can derive from the same amount of assets—that is, the more societal action can be energized without an increase in the asset base and without additional commitment or mobilization of the actor's assets.

The dimensions of conversion—ratio, pattern, and quality—used in combination characterize a major aspect of the morphology of society. The term "societal character" is appropriate when the dimensions of conversion are largely set and are treated by the society as basically given. "Social character" is a collectivistic concept, used mainly by anthropologists and sociologists.[28] Another related term, used by political scientists, is "national

The Conversion Process

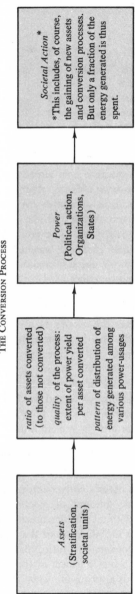

Assets
(Stratification, societal units)

ratio of assets converted (to those not converted)

quality of the process: extent of power yield per asset converted

pattern of distribution of energy generated among various power-usages

Power
(Political action, Organizations, States)

Societal Action *
*This includes, of course, the gaining of new assets and conversion processes. But only a fraction of the energy generated is thus spent.

style."[29] For instance, to say that a society or culture is "aggressive" often implies that the conversion ratio is high, its pattern is externally focused, its quality is poor, and, above all, it is unchangeable. Modern, post-modern to a greater extent, and, above all, active societies view the conversion of assets into societal power as changeable in accord with societal policy. It is considered possible to increase the ratio (or modify it upward and downward); to shift the investments (though mobilization for external usages still seems much easier than for internal ones, which limits the capacity to shift societal energy from exerting power over other factors toward self-transformation); and to find and implement more effective conversion methods (e.g., ways of selecting men for public office).

For relatively active societal units, the term "strategy" is appropriate, since these units deliberately decide the amount of the assets to be converted and in what way.[30] Strategy for economic mobilization is a case in point. While even these actors are not free to set their conversion ratios and processes as they wish (they, too, are subject to internal and environmental pressures), they are relatively aware of their capacity to reset the conversion ratio and pattern and, thus, are relatively voluntaristic and active.

It should be noted that while conversion is part of the societal guidance mechanism, it is affected by the values and the distribution of assets in the body of the societal unit or underlayer. However, these values and assets, in turn, are affected by the conversion processes. Thus, at each point in time, conversion, the societal asset structure, and the system of values should be taken as three independent variables and their relations to each other should be studied over time.

Power, Deviation, and Transformation

Societal structures, it is sometimes disregarded, are not composed only of internalized expectations, role-constellations, and institutionalized symbols and values.[31] All societies exhibit patterns of the distribution of assets.[32] While the patterns vary in different societies, they are always a-symmetrical in that some collectivities have a larger share of the assets than others.[33] While these assets include some symbolic ones (such as prestige) and while the patterns have symbolic aspects (e.g., some are viewed as more legitimate than others), relative access to assets has a "mechanical," objective base. Actors who command more assets, especially of the economic and coercive kinds, have more options to consume, save, invest, or generate power than other actors, irrespective of whether or not the actors are aware of the fact, legitimate it, or approve of it. Moreover, while the symbolic aspects of societal processes do affect the distributive patterns of assets, these, in turn, affect the symbolic aspects. The differences in prestige of such titles as lord or king when they commanded many utilitarian and coercive assets as opposed to their contemporary status illustrate this observation.

The neglect of the non-symbolic aspects of the societal structure and organization of power is particularly visible in much of the work on deviant behavior and its role as a source of societal transformation. In this section, we digress briefly to explore deviance from this viewpoint. Incomplete or distorted socialization, the successful internalization of deviant norms or of two or more sets of conflicting norms, or insufficient symbolic rewards by various mechanisms of social control have often been emphasized as the sources of deviant behavior.* While all of these factors, which rely considerably on symbolic processes, are significant, it is often not systematically taken into account that actors in many roles and situations, in order to conform, require, in addition to the motivation to do so and knowledge of the "proper" paths to follow, the appropriate means. If the societal distribution of assets fails to provide these means (or the bases from which they can be mobilized) to one or another societal grouping, this failure alone will tend to produce large-scale deviance,[34] both because the lack of available means is frustrating to those successfully socialized to the conforming norms and because the roles simply cannot be fulfilled without the means. When Pharaoh wanted the Jews in ancient Egypt to "deviate" so that he would have a pretext for punishing them, he demanded that they produce more bricks even though he provided them with less straw.[35]

In addition to the lack of assets needed to conform, a lack of assets allocated to control plays a major role in determining the scope of societal deviance and its macroscopic consequences. Once a deviant enclave has been founded, its future development and the chances that it will become a major societal force,[36] a transforming alternative, or perhaps even the basis of a new societal conformity, depend not only on the numbers of unsuccessfully socialized people or on the extent to which the society's "educational" efforts are encompassing and intensive but also on the distribution of the means between the societal units mobilized in support of the prevailing patterns and those which are deviating. Revolutions occur not so much because the deviant asset base in itself has been greatly extended but because the asset base of the supporters of the conforming patterns is collapsing. The weakness of the governments of Russia in 1917, China in 1949, and France in 1789 was a "final" cause of the transformations of these societies. The same seems to hold for less dramatic changes from one societal structure to another—e.g., the British transformation from an aristocratic to a bourgeois conformity.

The relations between the stratification structure and political organization of a society and the extent and intensity of deviation are twofold. On the one hand, the macroscopic outcome of the struggle between conforming and

---

* Most of the theories and studies reviewed in the encompassing essay by Albert K. Cohen fall in this category. See his *Deviance and Control* (Englewood Cliffs, N.J.: Prentice-Hall, 1966).

deviating forces depends on the asset bases of these forces and the quality of their power-generating mechanisms. In 1917, the Tsarist government's asset base, weakened by the war and economic anarchy, rapidly declined in its capacity to mobilize power, while the Bolshevik movement was much better able to mobilize its asset base and to focus its efforts. On the other hand, changes in relations between the conformers and the deviators register in changes in assets and power bases. One main result of the rise of a new societal alternative is a redefinition of the societal structure. A societal structure is, thus, to be viewed not as a given pattern of a system, but as a temporary form reflecting the past actions of conforming and deviating member-units and internal and external elites, and as a base line for future interaction among these actors within the environmental limits.[37] Societal structures are expected to be continually restructured or transformed; it is an exception rather than the rule when the relations among the units, supra-units, and elites are so balanced as to cause a forward and backward "swinging" of a pattern as if it were the focal point of a stable equilibrium. This concept of structure assumes that *the extent and intensity of deviance will be greater, the less the patterns of the distributive structure and the political organization parallel the patterns prescribed by the symbolic–normative system.* Moreover, even when this parallelism is maximal, a built-in strain is to be expected; differences between the symbolic–normative and asset facets of society are never completely resolved because the symbolic–normative systems tend to be relatively more integrated than the asset bases. This is the case because societal assets must provide for a multitude of partially incompatible functions, and because non-symbolic elements are more scarce than symbols. Additional societal strains are generated by differences in the distributive patterns of the various kinds of assets which create stratification imbalances.

Several concepts which are used later derive from this discussion and should be mentioned here. *Lower* and *higher collectivities* refer to their respective shares in the existing societal patterns of allocation. Higher collectivities have *vested interests* in existing structures, lower—in their change, whether or not their political action shows awareness of this. *Unbalanced collectivities* are high in some assets and low in others; the nature of their vested interests, as we shall see, depends on the specific nature of the imbalance.

Societal strains are collective experiences in that they are shared by large categories of members. The categories provide an objective base on which various associational and organizational processes operate to collectivize and mobilize shared experiences into political action attempting to change the societal structure, to reduce the strains for one collectivity or another, or to improve the "fit" between the symbolic–normative and asset–power aspects of the society. Hence, pressures toward change are built into the societal structure, and they are expected to be greater, the more complex the societal division of labor and the more widely distributed the associational, organizational, and mobilizing capacities among the members become.

It is, therefore, a "limit" situation when the society is integrated to such a degree that there is one dominant pattern of conformity in terms of which deviation can be simply defined. Aside from situations in which there is no prevailing pattern, there are many other situations in which, even though there is a prevailing pattern, other patterns have the status of what we refer to as *secondary alternatives*. Members who hold these secondary alternatives are tolerated and defined as conforming but are not considered in the "main stream." These patterns stand next to *semi-deviant* and *full deviant* ones.* The relative status of the various patterns continually changes; while there are a few "jumps" from full deviance to central conformity, smaller changes— from full to semi-deviance or from a secondary to a primary alternative—are more common. The accumulation of smaller changes may lead to the transformation from a full deviance to a central conformity pattern. At each point in time, however, rather than a conforming pattern and deviations from it, there are a variety of alternatives struggling over their relative status, with *the outcome of the struggle being greatly affected by the relative power mobilized by the various alternatives.*

It is necessary here to distinguish political from other deviant behavior. One of the major insights of social science was that common sociological and psychological attributes underlie such seemingly different deviant behaviors as alcoholism, extremist political activity, crime, and psychosomatic illness. But to label all these behaviors "deviant" conceals the fact that some deviant behaviors are *much* more likely to provide societal alternatives than others because they are able to evolve an alternative societal design and mobilize power to promote it. Non-political deviants tend to be "microscopic"; they exhibit personal, interpersonal, or, at most, sub-collectivity deviant behavior. Their deviations also tend to be narrow in scope; while deviating on some aspects, they may well conform on many others.[38] Above all, they usually do not promote an alternative design of society. Even when they are innovative,[39] their innovations tend to be limited to a freedom to choose among more sexual alternatives or to use drugs as a new escapist means. Political deviants are, first of all, usually of the innovative type, and their innovations tend to be broad in scope and macroscopic at least in intent and design, if not in consequence. They *may* provide the base of a new society (or the restoration of a fundamentally different "old" one), which cannot be said about the other types of deviants.

---

* This distinction is closely related to the difference between functional alternatives and functional equivalents. The above observations suggest that functional alternatives tend not to be functional equivalents, and one issue around which the difference can be expressed is the relative degree of deviation (or conformity) involved.

The degree to which the new designs are implemented is, again, to a large extent a question of the relative power of the deviant and conforming forces, with the outcome of the struggle often being a partial legitimation of the deviant alternative *or* a partial transformation of the prevailing conformity, and not necessarily complete suppression *or* full transformation. Changing the secondary alternatives, weakening the main one, and so on, are equally plausible and possibly much more common. While it is true that in some exceptional cases, non-political deviants will also form a macroscopic organization and collectivity—e.g., some sectarian religious movements or a nationally-organized crime syndicate which draws on an ethnic sub-collectivity—they still tend either to be narrow in scope seeking to neutralize or alter only a few aspects of societal control, rather than to engage in power mobilization and political action to change society at large (that is, become political innovators). Thus, the Mormons in their polygamist period were *religious deviants*; the New Left are macroscopic, *political innovators*. The Mafia is a *deviant* criminal organization; the Students for Democratic Society are macroscopic, *political innovators*. While for some purposes it may be useful to treat them all as deviants, for the student of societal change and guidance it is not.

The level of deviance and the societal pressure toward transformation are affected, we saw, by the relation between the symbolic–normative and asset–power facets of society. But, as the distributive patterns of assets and those of political organization are themselves not necessarily parallel, the degree to which they are articulated also affects the scope, frequency, and direction of deviance in general and political deviance in particular. The degree to which the stratification and political patterns of a societal unit are articulated is affected by several factors which we encountered before but which ought to be mentioned here; basically, they characterize the societal unit under study in terms of the degree to which the societal overlayers and underlayers are coextensive.

Political and stratification patterns are expected to be more articulated: (a) the more the activity of the unit as a unit—as distinct from an aggregation of sub-units—is controlled by members rather than by external elites; (b) the more such internal control is dispersed among the members and the less it is concentrated in one or a few *member* units (this defines the distribution of power as elitist versus egalitarian); and (c) the more control is distributed among the members of a system as against concentrated in the system's elites.

In the realm of power, members of units differ in the various *kinds* of power they can employ. For most societies and collectivities, the resulting profiles of the distributions of the three kinds of power are expected to be more similar to than different from each other, regardless of whether the profiles themselves are elitist or egalitarian.[40] However, we can always expect some discrepancy.

The next question concerns the relations among different power elites (which head the various power organizations). One of the common forms these relations take is for one kind of power elite to dominate and determine, in detail or at least in a highly specified context, the position, function, and direction of the others' efforts; this is the totalitarian pattern, with the Party or the Army constituting the dominant power elite and organization. In relatively pure pluralistic systems, which are approximated by some international systems, the relationship between the various kinds of power elites is more open, with no clear domination on the part of any elite and with a political elite acting as a broker among the various unit-elites. In less pure pluralistic systems, the political elite has a directive (though usually only broadly contextuating) as well as a mediating function. Other combinations, of course, are possible. Whatever they are and, more generally, whatever the various power profiles, the ways in which they are related to each other and to the societal underlayer and the way in which they change affect the capacity of the societal unit to marshal its energy for the promotion of its goals. That is, the internal power structure is a significant determinant of the external and internal uses of societal power, and the dimensions of this structure, briefly reviewed here, must be included in any theory of societal guidance and macro-sociology.

Exchange, Power, and Structure

The concept of power does not play so central a role in collectivisitic theories as it does in a theory of societal guidance.[41] One reason for this is that in the collectivistic perspective, system bonds are viewed as semi-organic, and, hence, there is no analytic place for a unit with a capacity to fundamentally restructure the system; as the scope of permissible societal action is limited, so is that of power. Collectivistic theories do not, so to speak, "need" the concept as much as a theory of societal guidance. More-over, collectivists tend to view the system bonds as primarily based on shared values, institutionalized symbols, collective sentiments, or converging interests emanating from the division of labor; power is rarely viewed as a basis of integration. The same theories tend to explore the distributive patterns of assets from the viewpoint of their contributions to the existing system and the prevailing structure and not as a potential base for the mobilization of power for transformation; they tend not to view the existing political organization as one—temporary—expression of a larger set of options the asset base could carry. And the role of power in limiting the bonds of a system or in transforming them to become more encompassing is not explored.[42]

More recently, the system role of power was recognized by various theoreticians, especially in their attempts to integrate exchange analysis with system theories.[43] For instance, it has been suggested that system bonds arise when sub-systems trade "legitimation of authority" for "moral responsibility for collective need" on the part of political elites.[44] The relationship is based on an exchange in that if one of the sides should not "deliver," the chain of reciprocity would be broken, and the relationship would be undermined. In further extending this approach, much may be gained by relating the exchange-in-a-system analysis to the study of stratification and political organization—i.e., to a morphological analysis.

Exchange, as we see it, is not random; it occurs within a structure, and the give-and-take are neatly balanced only in formal, technical terms and not in substantive or socio-political ones. Each societal unit has a power profile; that is, some of the members have greater effects on the course of the collective action than others. While this power profile is continually revised, at each point in time it affects not only the distribution of assets but also the rates of exchange—i.e., how many units of output must a collectivity or a society expend for each unit of input it obtains.[45] *These rates tend to be more favorable for a more affluent and powerful unit.* The rich in the United States, for example, can obtain credit at a much lower cost than the poor; women get paid less for the same work than men; the people of poor nations have to work more hours to obtain a unit of international exchange than those of rich ones—i.e., they have to work longer for the same inputs.

In short, exchange among equals is a "limit" situation; the terms of almost all exchanges are affected by the uneven power relations among the participants. To study the relationships among actors as if exchange were symmetrical (or balanced) is to conduct a faulty analysis and to be unaware of the normative implications of the extent to which power is used in exchange for unilateral advantage. The value of exchange analysis will be realized only if it is integrated into asset–power and morphological analysis.

Power and Communication

Power and communication are found in all societal relations: among member-units, between them and the supra-unit, and between the controlling overlayers and the action underlayers. Our prime concern is with the latter relationship; here, power and communication are the two main implementing factors which "transmit" the signals of the controlling centers to the performing units and carry their "feedbacks." Organizational networks and consensus-formation structures are, above all, institutionalized power and communication pathways. As these statements are certainly not universally accepted, we turn now to a brief discussion of the arguments raised by voluntarist and collectivist theoreticians in favor of a conception of societal guidance based on communication without the backing of power.[46]

Control Without Power?

There have been serious and repeated attempts in social and political science to do without the concept of power. It is not that the concept of power does not appear in the descriptive or *ad hoc* explanatory statements of those who attempt to avoid it, but that the concept is either explicitly excluded or simply omitted from the theoretical models used. For the most part, communication is stressed instead. The position is effectively telescoped in the following statement by Karl W. Deutsch, one of the most outstanding political scientists of this century. "Essentially, control involves the transmission of messages, and the understanding of control processes is a branch of communication engineering, not of power engineering."[47] Government is, accordingly, viewed as a communication network or a web of nerves. The network carries signals from various centers of control to the performing units and back from them to the control centers. Networks differ in the clarity of their signals, the degree of "noise" on the line, and the extent of the overloading of switchboards—all factors that affect the communication of the signals. But once appropriate signals reach the appropriate receiver and are clearly understood, they are expected to bring about the appropriate action, not by their power but by the change they produce in the actor's pattern of information. It is analogous to inserting the right key into the right keyhole; what is essential is not how much power is used to turn the key but that the appropriate key is inserted. The amount of resultant change is not relative to the power of the signal, which is often very weak, "much as the force of a gun shot need not be proportionate to the amount of pressure needed to set off the trigger."[48] Typically, communication and cybernetic systems are viewed as small energy redistributions which guide the work of large energy systems.[49]

In contrast, power analysis assumes that in order to act, power frequently has to be expended (to reduce resistance), and that the degree of action is greatly affected by the degree of the power mobilized and committed: Small expenditures of power can initiate only a little action unless resistance is low (which is rare when the scope of action is significant) or has already been overcome (which means that power analysis has to be applied to the previous situations). The analogy of the gun is cogent; while it is true that the power of the trigger is minute, this does not explain the power of the bullet to overcome the resistance of gravity and the friction of the air. The trigger is just a communication of a signal—"fire now!" The thrust of the bullet, however, is determined by the power that has been *previously* stored in the gun powder, which the trigger only releases.* If a government orders

---

* A relatively minuscule amount of power is involved, typically, even here—the power which set into motion the process of transforming the gunpowder into gas But in comparison to the energy released, it is negligible.

its troops into a particular region, a communication analyst explains what happens when the signal does not reach the commander, when he does not understand it, or when he is receiving conflicting signals. But his action is not wholly shaped by the signal, although this may seem to be the case if the act is studied with a short time-perspective. It is in part determined by the commander's "assets" (e.g., the number of troops he commands) and by his ability to convert them into power (e.g., the extent to which the troops are loyal to him). Without his troops, the commander's ability to respond to the signal would be no greater than the ability of a bullet to fly if there were no gunpowder in its shell. And central to the commander's response to the signal is his conception of the power that will be applied to him by the signalling center if he fails to comply.

Of course, communication does affect action, and the various factors determining the flow of communication must be studied if the dynamics of societal action are to be understood. It is also a valuable insight that the amount of energy used in transmitting communication is low in proportion to its results (although the investment in establishing and maintaining communication channels as well as in producing the message—i.e., knowledge—is to be included and increases the costs). But such communication analysis must be combined with power analysis and cannot replace it. To understand the different behaviors of various actors, we need to know the powers they command *and* the effectiveness of their communication networks. The controlling overlayer consists not only of signals but commands some power of its own; thus, if unit x does not respond to a signal, the controlling overlayer can make it act in accord with the signal not only by sending a clearer signal along a line with less "noise," but by dispatching another unit to force (or threaten) the recalcitrant unit x. (The unit sent might be a performing unit like the recalcitrant one or be attached to the center itself.)

This holds not only for the military but for other societal units and organizations as well. For instance, when the American aluminum and copper industries did not respond in 1965 to President Johnson's "signals" to refrain from raising their prices, he ordered the selling of aluminum and copper from the government stockpiles. Had the government not possessed such stockpiles or had they been substantially smaller, the power relations between the administration and the industries would have been quite different. In any case, it was not a matter of the industries' reading of the President's signal; what was not clear to them at first was how much power he was willing to use to make them follow his communication.

Controlling actors continually have to make two kinds of decisions: what communicative signals to issue and what power to use to support them. As, we suggest, the *assets from which power is generated are much more scarce than the symbols which are the main base of communication,* controlling overlayers typically issue many more communication signals than they can support by the use of power. Many of these signals do not require such support because they demand no action but, let us say, "emit" information. Furthermore, to the degree that an authentic consensus has been formed, communication will suffice. But if the signals are to control, they must be backed by a power potential. Actors can issue communication on power "credit," hoping not to have to cash it in, or "bluff"—communicate as if they had power when they do not.[50] But these are basically extrapolations and projections of the real power base; without it, the effect of controlling signals will decline and cannot be relied upon. Both bases of control have costs: Communication costs are incurred in getting the message from one unit to another; power incurs costs in making the recipient follow the message. The basic reason that students of communication have noted that the "transportation" of small energy can control the performance of high energy-consuming units is, we suggest, that the *higher* control costs under most circumstances are power costs, which they do not study.

To some degree, power and communication can be substituted for each other: If the message is less clear but more enforced or less enforced but more clear, similar results may be obtained. But such substitutions are limited in scope; when faced with resistance, the clearest communication will be useless unless it is backed with sufficient power, and a large application of power will yield little action if the control centers receive vague or conflicting information about what the performing units are doing and how the environment is changing. This may be illustrated by the relationship between military power and military intelligence, since in this context the relations between the two factors are particularly observable. If the "goal" is to rout an enemy from a sizeable jungle, extensive bombing will be of little use if no knowledge about the location of the enemy can be communicated to the pilots of the bombers. Similarly, full information and communication are to no avail if, because of weather conditions, the bombers cannot operate— i.e., both factors are needed for control. Within these limits, the more knowledge that is communicated, the fewer bombs that are necessary; and the less that is known, the more bombs that are needed for the same results.

Above all, *increasing both control elements offers the actors more options and, thus, the potential for more creative responses,* for a more active orientation. To illustrate: In a mid-western city, civil rights groups used to counter urban renewal drives which entailed destroying slums before adequate alternative housing was provided by lying in front of the bulldozers when they approached. This involved civil disobedience which is a "costly" operation. Over the years, the civil rights groups organized an "early warning" intelligence system to discover ahead of time which sites were designated by the city for urban renewal. This allowed the groups to protest in the press and to the legislature, to mobilize public support, to demonstrate, and still—if necessary—to block the bulldozers.

The same analytic issue appears in a context which is less macroscopic but of much interest to the theory of societal guidance—in the debate over the validity of the Human Relations approach to the study of industrial relations. The Human Relations approach has a variety of representatives and a development of its own, but all of its original advocates almost completely ignored power analysis.[51] The emphasis was typically on leadership *style*: Leadership that was more understanding, communicative, and sensitive to the subjects' needs was believed to be more effective in attaining high productivity, compliance, and morale. The underlying assumption was that the workers had identifiable psychological needs, such as those for affection and direction, which could no longer be satisfied outside of the corporations because of the disintegration of the societal fabric inherent in the industrial revolution.[52] If the industrial elites were to respond to these psychological needs by providing positive and authoritative leadership and communications, they could command the workers' efforts and loyalties. Such satisfaction of the workers' psychological needs, it was at least implied, could obviate increases in wages and unionization and the ensuing power struggle. Critics of the Human Relations School saw a degree of power struggle, conflict, and tension between workers and management as inevitable and not necessarily dysfunctional; differences in styles of leadership and communication were viewed as having comparatively little effect.[53]

Actually, it seems that when workers belong to unions which effectively express their sentiments and interests and when they are well paid, communication between workers and management plays a relatively important role; when the conflict between workers and management is latent and uninstitutionalized, either because unions have not been allowed or because they have been rendered ineffective, and when workers are underpaid, the effect of communication differences is small. Thus, again, power and communication analyses complement each other rather than one making the other superfluous.

Above and beyond the specific Human Relations writings, in general an emphasis on *leadership* tends to be associated with an emphasis on the manipulation of symbols and communication, while discussions of elites tend to be more oriented toward an analysis of power which includes non-symbolic ways of overcoming resistance as well as symbolic manipulations. While there is no one-to-one association between the use of these terms and an analytic position, the term used often provides an early indication of the author's position. (The use of "class" is similar to "elite" in this context, except that economic power is stressed more than military or political power.)

When two theoretical conceptions conflict, it is occasionally suggested that two parallel theories be developed and used alternately or that they be merged later. This has been suggested for the beam versus wave theories of light and for the integration versus conflict theories of social systems. But this procedure would be particularly harmful to macro-sociology if separate communication and power theories continue to be evolved, since several key issues require drawing on both conceptions and systematically articulating them. For example, controlling overlayers seem to differ significantly according to the degree to which power and communication networks are parallel and mutually supportive or their respective centers are segregated and in conflict. When the two networks are fairly well articulated, which of the two has priority affects the functioning of the controlling overlayer. The stronger the communication element in a control mix, the more the controlling overlayer approximates a pluralistic system in which actors synchronize their activities mainly voluntarily; where the power element is stronger, the controlling overlayer approximates a central administrative system in which synchronization tends to be higher but also less voluntary.* There are many additional ramifications for societal guidance of the various combinations of communication and power networks; our purpose here is not to ennumerate them but to highlight the need to explore these two major elements of guidance in one theoretical framework.

The Poker Face of Power

Once the fact that communication is only one component of control is accepted, the next question becomes the ways in which communication and power relate to and affect each other. We have already seen that the power actors wield is determined not only by the amounts and kinds of assets they command but also by the proportion of assets they convert into power and the effectiveness with which they convert and use them. A main factor here is the communication capacities and skills of the actors; this is so because the uses to which assets can be put (their power potential) are difficult to assess which, in turn, causes a permanent gap between the symbolic and objective facets of power and allows the actor the opportunity to magnify the impact of his power by skillful communications.

Actors use their power potential combined with various placings of messages in much the same way that poker players use their cards *and* their gestures; the effective player gains more from his cards than his hand actually "allows," and the poor player often loses even when he has a superior hand. Gestures, symbolic acts, play a central role in magnifying or deflating the impact of a hand. This does not mean that the gestures players make are unrelated to the "objective base"; he who regularly bluffs with poor cards will sooner or later lose his shirt. Thus, some degree of *credibility* in the relations between communication and power has to be maintained or the

---

* The "mix" defines the communication capacities and power available to *the controlling center*. If more power were available to *the member units* than to the control center, the opposite would hold unless consensus-formation structures substituted for the lack of central control. We return to this point below.

gestures become powerless. The maintenance of credibility itself, though, is in part affected by the players' communication strategies and not only by their assets. To explore this point further, in the balance of this section we concentrate on the poker face of power—i.e., on what actors are able to do with their assets, holding constant the amounts they control and the proportion of those they convert into power.

The macroscopic parallels of the poker players' gestures are *threats and promises* by societal actors, indications of intentions to withdraw or to grant support.[54] While these are related to the actual capacity to do so, the relationship is loose and the system of threats and promises has a set of norms, dynamics, and independent effects of its own. In the realm of economics, such a relationship exists between money and goods and services; in the realm of force—between threats to force (and promises to defend) and actual forcing; and in the realm of prestige—between the generalized status of a person and specific status-symbols.* In each of the three realms, there is no one-to-one relationship between symbols and assets. Governments often increase the money in circulation without a parallel increase in goods and services. They may threaten more without increasing their military forces. Thus, societal actors can promise and threaten more than they could afford to do if all the commitments had to be met at the same time and full cashing of the face value of the "notes" was demanded.

Second, while a degree of "bluffing" is a common strategy, the power of actors is affected by their reputation, which, in turn, is affected by how often they have been "called" and not "come through." In a monetary system, the value of the monetary unit declines as the number of units vis-à-vis the available goods and services is increased (inflation), and as the government reduces its rate of exchange for foreign currency (devaluation). Governments which devaluate often or allow prices to rise freely and rapidly lose the confidence of the users of the currency and, hence, the currency's action effect. In terms of prestige, the more symbols that are issued (e.g., titles of nobility), the less significant their consequences for action in terms of the respect they command and the smaller the efforts people are subsequently willing to make in order to gain them. In political relations, a labor union which promises to raise a given amount of campaign funds or to mobilize

---

* Prestige itself, unlike economic assets and force, is a standing in the minds of people and, in this sense, is symbolic. But, as it is a general standing in the minds of many people (a sub-society or society), it needs specific signs (status symbols) to communicate the standing of a person or collectivity. As in other relationships between symbols and assets, the relationship between these specific signs of prestige and prestige itself is loose in that some signs can be awarded or produced without having the prestige base, though if this is widely done, there is an "inflation" of the sign and it gradually loses its value. That is, status symbols need to be "cashable" in order to maintain their credibility. For a brilliant analysis of the prestige base, see Erving Goffman, "Symbols of Class Status," *British Journal of Sociology*, Vol. 2 (1951), pp. 294–304.

volunteers and voters but realizes only part of these promises will find it more difficult the next time to gain the legislation it favors or to block that which it opposes.

Third, in each of these cases, a change in the circulation of the symbols has some independent allocative effect of its own. The inflationary printing of money reduces the buying power of the government as well as of everyone else, but, meanwhile, it shifts some assets from non-government to government hands. Similarly, the diluting of prestige symbols is only gradually noticed, and, meanwhile, the symbols continue to buy support, favor, funds, or whatever else for which they are traded. The labor union which later will not be able fully to cash its political promissory notes may by then have won a major piece of legislation. And a declaration of support from the spokesmen of n collectivities may evoke a declaration of support from a wavering $n+1$, a declaration it might find difficult to reverse even if the other collectivities do not maintain theirs; even more likely, its declaration and others like it will either make "cashing" unnecessary or will transform the empty promises of the initial declarations into actual commitments.

Fourth, factors other than "cashing" determine the *credibility* of threats and promises. One is the conduct of other actors, as credibility is a relative virtue. For instance, the low credibility of a labor union might still be more reliable than the promises of most of the other actors and, hence, the union will continue to be effective. Another factor is the prevailing norms of the system. Domestic politics in Britain, for instance, seem to exhibit a much lower tolerance of a lack of *political solvency* than, let us say, politics in Greece. And in power plays, as in economic credit, the larger the total amount of assets of an actor, the easier it is for his temporary lapses to go unpunished and to be forgiven.

All of this is possible because neither promises nor threats nor what, in effect, is "delivered" can be measured with any degree of precision. Hence, actors' reputations for power credibility and solvency are, in themselves, open to manipulation. But ultimately, especially in showdowns, credibility has to be maintained or power is lost.

Several theoreticians addressing themselves to the similarities between economic and political dynamics did not take fully into account the importance of maintaining credibility and the difference between the symbolic face and objective base of power. Power is characterized as a "generalized symbolic medium"[55] which is to the polity what money is to the economy. And "it became increasingly clear that money was essentially a 'symbolic' phenomenon and hence that its analysis required a frame of reference closer to that of linguistics than of technology."[56] Elsewhere, Parsons has argued that "language is perhaps the prototype. ... Thus, a sign, 'Beware the dog,' may induce caution without the passer-by's actually seeing or hearing a dog."[57] While this is a valid observation, it seems incomplete without noting the relationship between such signs and real, barking and biting, dogs.

If there were no dogs behind the signs, the signs would soon lose their effect. The same holds for power: The relationship of threats or promises to the assets available for power purposes is like the relationship of money to the assets available for exchange; that is, while not every threat is "called" and while not every threat that is called must be "cashed," the action effect of threats is greatly affected by the frequency with which they are "cashed." Those that are not cashed at all have the same power as money that does not buy goods and services.*

A subsidiary point ought to be raised here. *Occasional* actual escalation of the degree to which threats are realized, whatever their initial intention, is not accidental but is inherent in the power-threat system; the more often that threats are not cashed, the lower the credibility tends to be, and the higher the gains that may be made by an occasional actualization. Thus, every use of a threat means that the pressure to actualize is mounting, as the stock of credibility is depleted.[58] Consequently, effective systems are not those that never actualize threats but those that have to actualize them less often than others. Contrast this with the view (advanced by Neustadt in his study of the Presidency and the federal use of force)[59] that any use of force is a sign of the failure of the system. As we see it, if Eisenhower had not sent federal troops to Little Rock, the federal government's capacity to achieve compliance with the Supreme Court's 1954 desegregation ruling and the 1964 Civil Rights Bill would have been seriously curtailed. In situations in which the actual use of force is to be avoided at any cost, it is necessary not to mount the first steps of the escalator. (This is, in essence, the position of those who favor complete disarmament.) Earlier balance-of-power systems typically allowed for an occasional war to restore the system by punishing but not annihilating actors that violated the rules of the game. That is, an occasional actualization of threats was part of the system. Most societal and inter-societal systems can still tolerate such an occasional "cashing in" of threats; but for a rising sub-set of international systems this use of the symbolic aspect of power entail great risks and, in this sense, is intolerable.

There are, thus, three different kinds of costs involved in the application of power: of the assets "consumed" as power is generated; of the power itself as it is spent; and of symbolic gestures which, the more often they are used, tends to bring closer the point of actual expenditure. The last may be viewed as a kind of credit established by the previous actual exercise of power. When gestures are made, the "credit" needs to be replenished or their effect is lost; thus, each gesture has a cost.

---

* In other places in the two presentations, Parsons himself draws on these basic notions, but in his definition of power as analogous to money, he seems to disregard the functions of the asset base. This can be explained by his attempt to view power as influence and by his stress on the symbolic aspects of power—legitimation, loyalties, and moral responsibilities —over the mechanical elements of power which rest to a greater extent upon the asset base.

An awareness of these costs further supports the point stated above—that language is a questionable analogy for power, in that teaching more people a language and, in this sense, extending the symbols to others usually does not reduce their effect or value and often even extends them. On the other hand, symbols that have an asset base cannot be multiplied without some dilution of their power. Parsons stressed that power is not a zero-sum property, for in giving to one you need not take from others—the power of all can be increased.[60] While this is a valid observation, the problems of allocation are still relevant because the distribution of power at any point in time is an important factor in determining which actors will gain a disproportionate share of the new assets as these become available and, thus, increase their power potential. In short, the patterns of distribution and of the dynamics of redistribution must be considered together; we are not dealing with the allocation of a finite set of assets but rather with the reallocation of a changing total.

We have suggested that the concept of power can be defined without its being tautological, a hindsight, or untestable. Societal power is viewed here as the generalized capacity of a societal unit to overcome the resistance of other units, sub-units, or supra-units. It seems useful to view societal power as the energy derived from assets. The amount of power a societal unit generates is determined by its asset base, by the proportion of that base which is being converted into power (as compared to those assets "kept" or otherwise used), and by the quality of the conversion processes. The power a unit commands can be "stretched" by various communications, but communications not backed by power do not provide societal control. Power is an inevitable component of societal control, guidance, and activeness. At the same time, the exercise of power has a societal cost, a distorting effect which curtails activation. Power may assure that "things get done" but often may not insure that the resulting world will be responsive to those who live in it, including the power wielders! The varying combinations of the energizing and distorting aspects of societal power and their macroscopic consequences are the subjects of the next chapter.

NOTES

1. "In general, we understand by 'power' the chance of a man or of a number of men to realize their own will in a communal action even against the resistance of others who are participating in the action." H. H. Gerth and C. Wright Mills, *From Max Weber: Essays in Sociology* (New York: Oxford University Press, 1958), p. 180. Cf. other discussions of the definitions of power: J. R. P. French, "A Formal Theory of Social Power," *Psychological Review*, Vol. 63 (1956), pp. 181–184; John R. P. French, Jr. and Bertram Raven, "The Bases of Social Power," in Dorwin Cartwright and Alvin Zander (eds.), *Group Dynamics, Research and Theory* (New York: Harper & Row, 1960), pp. 607–623; Dorwin Cartwright (ed.), *Studies in*

Social Power (Ann Arbor, Mich.: University of Michigan, 1959); Robert Dahl, "The Concept of Power," *Behavioral Science*, Vol. 2 (1957), pp. 201–215; Herbert Goldhamer and Edward A. Shils, "Types of Power and Status," *The American Journal of Sociology*, Vol. 45 (1939), pp. 171–182; Edmund Dahlström, "Exchange, Influence and Power," *Acta Sociologica*, Vol. 9 (1966), pp. 237–284; Herbert C. Kelman, "Processes of Opinion Change," *Public Opinion Quarterly*, Vol. 25 (1961), pp. 57–78; Adolf Sternberger, *Grund und Abgrund der Macht* (Frankfurt: Insel-Verlag, 1962). James G. March, "The Power of Power," in David Easton (ed.), *Varieties of Political Theory* (Englewood Cliffs, N.J.: Prentice-Hall, 1966), pp. 39–70. Richard A. Schermerhorn, *Society and Power* (New York: Random House, 1961).

2. William T. R. Fox, "In Defense of Talking About Power," in his *The Super-Powers* (New York: Harcourt, Brace & World, 1944), esp. p. 10. Truman, *The Governmental Process, op. cit.*, pp. 189–190.

3. "Like all data of the real world it [power] defies rigorous definition," Friedrich, *Man and His Government, op. cit.*, p. 159. For references and review of the large literature on the subject of power, see *ibid.*, Ch. 9, and Dahrendorf, *Class and Class Conflict in Industrial Society, op. cit.*, pp. 166 ff. For a less precise, more literary treatment, see the second epilogue of Tolstoy's *War and Peace* (New York: Modern Library, n.d.), esp. p. 1115.

4. Nicholas John Spykman, *America's Strategy in World Politics* (New York: Harcourt, Brace & Company, 1942), p. 22. Coser makes this point cautiously: "However, it would seem that without actual exercise, only some types of power can be measured with any degree of accuracy. Possibly in the economic order. . . ." *The Functions of Social Conflict, op. cit.*, p. 135. See also on the inability to generalize power relations, Dean G. Pruitt, "National Power and International Responsiveness," *Background*, Vol. 7 (1964), pp. 167–168.

5. Which time unit, range of matters, etc., are chosen depends on the problem studied.

6. The notion of probability has already been included in the definition of power. See Weber, *The Theory of Social and Economic Organization, op. cit.*, p. 152.

7. Annette Baker Fox shows how Turkey, weak on most accounts and scales, extracted a number of concessions from powerful Germany in 1941. See her *The Power of Small States* (Chicago: University of Chicago Press, 1959), pp. 10–42.

8. On the scholars who rely relatively heavily on asset analysis, see below, footnote 24.

9. Actually, this holds even for relations between economic and religious statuses. See, for instance, Liston Pope, *Millhands and Preachers* (New Haven: Yale University Press, 1942), pp. 141–203.

10. For additional discussion of the operationality of the concept, see Herbert A. Simon, "Notes on the Observation and Measurement of Power," *Journal of Politics*, Vol. 15 (1953), pp. 500–516.

11. In a curious twist, John Kenneth Galbraith's powerful lament over the scarcity of resources available for public purposes, in contrast to the abundance of assets available for private consumption, became known as the "affluent society"— i.e., one that suffers from general abundance. *The Affluent Society* (Boston: Houghton Mifflin, 1958). See also David Riesman, *Abundance for What?* (Garden City, N.Y.: Doubleday, 1964), pp. 103–368.

12. Cf. Lawrence K. Frank, "Psychology and Social Order," in Lerner, *The Human Meaning* . . . , *op. cit.*, pp. 214–241, especially 239.

13. Ivar E. Berg, Jr. and David Rogers, "Former Blue Collerites in Small Business," in Arthur B. Shostak and William Gomberg, *Blue Collar World: Studies of the American Worker*, (Englewood Cliffs, N.J.: Prentice-Hall, 1964), pp. 550–566; David Rogers and Ivar E. Berg, Jr., "Occupation and Ideology: The Case of the Small Businessman," *Human Organization*, Vol. 20 (1961), pp. 103–111. Max Weber pointed out that one of the main conditions for the rise of free markets was the leveling of societal differences. Gerth and Mills, *From Max Weber, op. cit.*, p. 215. See also Max Weber, *The Religion of China*, translated and edited by H. H. Gerth (New York: Free Press, 1951), pp. 84–107.

14. Coser, *The Functions of Social Conflict, op. cit.*, pp. 132–137. Harold D. Lasswell, "Compromise," *Encyclopedia of the Social Sciences*, IV (1931), pp. 147–149. See also E. T. Hiller, *The Strike: A Study in Collective Action* (Chicago, Ill.: University of Chicago Press, 1928), pp. 192–206.

15. On this concept and the dynamics involved, see Chapter 15.

16. Each generation seems to have to reargue this point. Thus, twenty years after Hans Morgenthau's classical writings on the subject, as well as the works of Peter H. Odegard, Elva Allen Helms, and V. O. Key, Jr., the search for a powerless world, in which the law of morality prevails without the support of any power but that of the values themselves, has not been given up. See, for instance, *Speak Truth to Power* (Philadelphia: American Friends Service Committee, 1955) for the Quaker position. See also Norman Cousins' suggestion to establish a new international order by no more than the "force" of a free debate of ideas, *In Place of Folly* (New York: Harper & Row, 1961), pp. 120–141. On the suspicion of power, see David Easton, *The Political System: An Inquiry into the State of Political Science* (New York: Knopf, 1953), p. 116 and Inis L. Claude, Jr., *Swords Into Plowshares* (New York: Random House, 1956), Chs. 18 and 19.

17. Ronald V. Sampson, *The Psychology of Power* (New York: Pantheon Books, 1966), p. 32. This is also a central assumption of Robert Michels' "Iron Law" of Oligarchy. And see Harold Lasswell and Abraham Kaplan, *Power and Society* (New Haven, Conn.: Yale University Press, 1950), p. 240.

18. This point was made by Andrew Hacker, "Power to Do What?" in Irving Louis Horowitz (ed.), *The New Sociology* (New York: Oxford University Press, 1964), p. 136.

19. Neustadt, *Presidential Power, op. cit.*, pp. 1–57. See also Theodore C. Sorenson, "The Outer Limits of Presidential Decisions," in Joseph R. Fiszman, *The American Political Arena*, 2nd edition (Boston: Little, Brown, 1966), pp. 180–188.

20. Brzezinski and Huntington, *Political Power: U.S.A./U.S.S.R., op. cit.*, pp. 191–232.

21. ". . . In that frame of thinking, power in international politics is essentially superior force, active or latent, with international political relationships determined in the long run by who coerces whom, or is presumably capable of doing so. . . . No matter how the word *power* is formally redefined, most people seem likely to go on talking about power as if it were largely a function of violence." In Harold and Margaret Sprout, *The Ecological Perspective on Human Affairs: With Special Reference to International Politics* (Princeton: Princeton University Press, 1965),

pp. 20–21. See also M. A. Ash, "An Analysis of Power, with Special Reference to International Politics," in *World Politics*, Vol. 3 (1951), pp. 218 ff. "Coercive *influence*, which is sometimes called *power*," states Robert Dahl in his *Modern Political Analysis*, *op. cit.*, p. 50. Coercion and power are treated as synonyms throughout Chalmers A. Johnson, *Revolutionary Change* (Boston: Little, Brown, 1966). See, for instance, pp. 17–18. Robert Bierstedt, "An Analysis of Social Power," *American Sociological Review*, Vol. 15 (1950), p. 731.

22. See Talcott Parsons, *The Social System* (New York: Free Press, 1951), p. 277.

23. Talcott Parsons criticizes C. Wright Mills for this association. "There is, second, the tendency to think of power as presumptively illegitimate; if people exercise considerable power, it must be because they have somehow usurped it where they had no right and they intend to use it to the detriment of others. This comes out most conspicuously in Mills' imputation of irresponsibility to his 'power elite' and the allegation, vaguely conceived and presented with very little evidence, that they are characterized by a 'higher immorality.'" *Structure and Process in Modern Societies* (New York: Free Press, 1960), p. 221. But a few years later, Parsons writes: "Money and influence may be conceived to operate as positive sanctions in the above sense. . . . The *negative* medium corresponding to money on the situational side is then power in the political sense." (Italics provided.) "On the Concept of Influence," *Public Opinion Quarterly*, Vol. 27 (1963), p. 44.

24. Stephen B. Jones, "The Power Inventory and National Strategy," *World Politics*, Vol. 6 (1954), pp. 421–452. Harold and Margaret Sprout, *Foundation of National Power* (Princeton, N.J.: Princeton University Press, 1945). More recently this position was advanced with much sophistication by A. F. K. Organski, *World Politics* (New York: Knopf, 1959), pp. 116–184, esp. 184. Cf. Blau, *Exchange and Power . . .* , *op. cit.*, pp. 116 ff.

25. Data relevant to the propositions advanced here will be found in Bruce M. Russett et al., *World Handbook of Political and Social Indicators* (New Haven, Conn.: Yale University Press, 1964); Bruce M. Russett, *Trends in World Politics* (New York: Macmillan, 1965); William M. Sprecher, *World-Wide Defense Expenditures and Selected Economic Data, 1964* (Washington, D.C.: United States Arms Control and Disarmament Agency, 1966). These works include the main references to other relevant sources. We expect to show that it supports the propositions advanced here in a future publication, to be devoted to testing of propositions. While the present one deals only with the advancement of propositions, we of course did not include propositions for which we found contradicting data.

26. Expenditures on defense are not all external, and some external expenditures are not defense items, but the defense expenditures provide a rough approximation for modernized societies.

27. It was atypically narrow in the United States, but the United States is catching up with expansion of the welfare state to be followed, we expect, by significantly more public guidance of education.

28. See, for example, Alex Inkeles and Daniel J. Levinson, "National Character: The Study of Modal Personality and Socio-cultural Systems," in Gardner Lindzey (ed.), *Handbook of Social Psychology* (Reading, Mass.: Addison-Wesley, 1954), p. 982.

29. Walt W. Rostow, "The National Style," in Elting E. Morison (ed.), *The American Style* (New York: Harper & Row, 1958), p. 247. For a discussion of the relations between the two concepts, see Daniel Bell, "National Character Revisited: A Proposal for Renegotiating the Concept," *Symposium of Personality*, to be published by Holt, Rinehart, & Winston, and Inkeles and Levinson, revised article (see Note 28), in the revised edition of the *Handbook of Social Psychology, op. cit.* (in press).

30. Stanley Hoffmann, "Restraint and Choices in American Foreign Policy," *Daedalus*, Vol. 91 (1962), pp. 680 ff.

31. "The structure of authority in science, *as it is in any institution*, is a symbolic structure." (Italics provided.) Duncan, summarizing Kenneth Burke, *Permanence and Change* (Los Altos, Calif.: Hermes Publications, 1954), in Duncan, *Communication and Social Order, op. cit.*, p. 130. See also Anthony Wallace, "The Psychic Unity of Human Groups," in Bert Kaplan (ed.), *Studying Personality Cross-Culturally* (New York: Harper & Row, 1961), pp. 129–163. Wolf, commenting on this approach, criticizes those who view "culture as a code for communication between individuals who must synchronize their separate and disparate lives." Such definitions, he says, are "literally ethereal." Wolf, *Anthropology, op. cit.*, p. 41.

32. Parsons discusses "reality factors" and adds, "But from the point of view of the central dynamics of the social system they are not the core of the problem. The core is to be found in the balance of forces which is involved in the building up and the counteraction of motivation to deviance, that is, of the alienative component of the need–disposition system." Parsons, *The Social System, op. cit.*, p. 278.

33. Harold Lasswell, *Politics: Who Gets What, When, How, op. cit.*, pp. 5–6, 9–14. Seymour M. Lipset and Reinhard Bendix, "Social Status and Social Structure: A Re-examination of Data and Interpretations, I," *British Journal of Sociology*, Vol. 2 (1951), pp. 150–168. Gerhard E. Lenski, *Power and Privilege: A Theory of Social Stratification* (New York: McGraw-Hill, 1966). On the relations between stratification and the polity, see, in addition to the preceding sources, the following: Raymond Aron, "Social Structure and the Ruling Class," *British Journal of Sociology*, Vol. 1 (1950), pp. 1–16, 126–143; Bottomore, *Elites and Society, op. cit.*, esp. pp. 18–41, and Lipset, *Political Man, op. cit.*, esp. Ch. II and Ch. VIII.

34. This point was made by Robert K. Merton's study of deviance under the concept of opportunity structure. *Social Theory and Social Structure* (New York: Free Press, 1957), pp. 145–146. See also Richard Cloward and Lloyd E. Ohlin, *Delinquency and Opportunity* (New York: Free Press, 1960), esp. 86–107; and Arthur L. Stinchcombe, *Rebellion in a High School* (Chicago: Quadrangle Books, 1964).

35. *Exodus*, 5:6–9.

36. On these conditions, see Ruth Leeds, "The Absorption of Protest," in W. W. Cooper, H. J. Leavitt, and M. W. Shelly II (eds.), *New Perspectives in Organization Research* (New York: Wiley & Sons, 1964), pp. 115–135.

37. For a similar view of structure, see Evon Z. Vogt, "On the Concepts of Structure and Process in Cultural Anthropology," *American Anthropologist*, N.S. 62 (1960), pp. 18–33, esp. 21. See also Walter Garrison Runciman, *Social Science and Political Theory* (Cambridge, England: Cambridge University Press, 1963), pp. 109–134.

38. Albert K. Cohen recognized that the delinquent was characterized by ambivalence in his book *Delinquent Boys: The Culture of Gangs* (New York: Free Press, 1955), pp. 136–138; Gresham M. Sykes and David Matza, "Techniques of Neutralization: A Theory of Delinquency," *American Sociological Review*, Vol. 22 (1957), pp. 664–670; David Matza, *Delinquency and Drift* (New York: Wiley & Sons, 1964), pp. 27, 36, 60–62, 101.

39. On the place of innovation in a typology of deviance, see Merton, *Social Theory and Social Structure, op. cit.*, pp. 141–149.

40. For empirical indicators, albeit in a micro unit, see L. S. Shapley and Martin Shubik, "A Method for Evaluating the Distribution of Power in a Committee System," *American Political Science Review*, Vol. 48 (1954), pp. 787–792.

41. On the role of power in collectivistic theories, see Talcott Parsons et al., *Toward a General Theory of Action, op. cit.*, p. 200. Roland Robertson, "The Analysis of Social and Political Systems," *British Journal of Sociology*, Vol. 16 (1965), pp. 256–257.

42. For discussion of this point in the context of a theory of societal guidance, see Chapter 20.

43. David Easton, *A Framework for Political Analysis* (Englewood Cliffs, N.J.: Prentice-Hall, 1965), pp. 119–124; Homans, *Social Behavior: Its Elementary Forms, op. cit.*, p. 78; Blau, *Exchange and Power . . . , op. cit.*, pp. 115–142.

44. Talcott Parsons, "On the Concept of Political Power," in Reinhard Bendix and Seymour M. Lipset (eds.), *Class, Status and Power* (New York: Free Press, 1966), 2nd edition, pp. 240–265.

45. On this concept and its sociological applications, see Etzioni, *Political Unification, op. cit.*, pp. 77, 315–317.

46. "Communication is the main process of *inter*action, by which processes of 'action' and behavior of units of the system are 'controlled.' " Parsons, *Structure and Process in Modern Societies, op. cit.*, p. 273. Parsons includes the concept of power but sees it as a mode of communication, as a language. Lasswell, discussing in detail the "act of decision," includes implementation, without a concept of power, in what has been referred to as "cybernetic ancestry of much recent thinking about the political process." The reference is by Richard R. Fagen, *Politics and Communication* (Boston: Little, Brown, 1966), p. 11. The work by Harold D. Lasswell referred to is *The Future of Political Science* (New York: Atherton Press, 1963), pp. 15–16. "According to cybernetics, society is a communication network for the transmitting, exchanging, and pooling of information, and it is this that holds it together. No emptier notion of society has ever been propounded." Hans Jonas, *The Phenomenon of Life* (New York: Harper & Row, 1966), p. 126. "Communication is the web of human society. . . . The flow of communication determines the direction and pace of dynamic social development." Lucian W. Pye, in the introduction to his edited *Communications and Political Development* (Princeton, N.J.: Princeton University Press, 1963), p. 4. See also p. 6. According to Kenneth Boulding, "an organization might almost be defined as a structure of roles tied together with lines of communication." Kenneth E. Boulding, *The Image, Knowledge in Life and Society* (Ann Arbor: University of Michigan Press, 1961), p. 27. Rieger, "The Mechanics of Bureaucracy . . . , " *op. cit.*, sees bureaucracy as an "information processing system" p. 176.

For a typical cybernetic statement, see Charles R. Dechert, "The Development of Cybernetics," *The American Behavioral Scientist*, Vol. VIII (June, 1965), esp. 19. See also Richard H. McCleery, *Policy Change in Prison Management* (East Lansing, Mich.: Government Research Bureau, Michigan State University, 1957); and Richard L. Meier, *A Communication Theory of Urban Growth* (Cambridge, Mass.: M.I.T. Press, 1962); H. A. Innis, *Empire and Communications* (Oxford, England: Clarendon Press, 1950). For another theory which focuses on transmission of the signals, lacking much of Deutsch's sophistication, see Thomas H. Crowley et al., *Modern Communications* (New York: Columbia University Press, 1962). See also Colin Cherry, *On Human Communication* (New York: Wiley & Sons, 1957), and Robert C. North, "Communication as an Approach to Politics," *The American Behavioral Scientist*, Volume X (April, 1967), pp. 12–23.

47. Deutsch, "Communication Theory and Political Integration," in Jacob and Toscano, *The Integration of Political Communities, op. cit.*, p. 49. See also his *Nationalism and Social Communication* (New York: Wiley & Sons, 1953), and especially his *The Nerves of Government, op. cit.* Deutsch's position on this matter is somewhat ambiguous. The following statement, taken from the jacket, represents the general tenor of his book:

"The theory that government is more a problem of steering than of power politics provides the basis for this new analytical framework for political study. It represents a significant contemporary shift in emphasis from the study of 'muscles'—arms, manpower, money—to the study of 'nerves,' the channels of communication by which the exercise of power is controlled."

"Shift in emphasis" would imply full recognition of both sets of factors and a systematic attempt to relate the two. Actually, most of the book implies that nerves are important and muscles are not, and there is no systematic study of "muscles" and their relations to "nerves." On the other hand, Deutsch avoids an outright renunciation of power as an analytic tool.

"There are those who suggest that all of political science be reconceptualized in terms of communication, and of the factors which generate messages and determine their impact." (Reference is to Deutsch, *The Nerves of Government*.) Gabriel A. Almond and G. Bingham Powell, Jr., *Comparative Politics: A Developmental Approach* (Boston: Little, Brown, 1966), p. 165.

48. Deutsch, *Nerves of Government, op. cit.*, p. 146. See also pp. 82–84.

49. Charles Ackerman and Talcott Parsons, "The Concept of 'Social System' as a Theoretical Device," in Gordon J. Direnzo (ed.), *Concepts, Theory, and Explanation in the Behavioral Sciences* (New York: Random House, 1966), pp. 24–40, esp. pp. 31, 33. Aaron V. Cicourel, *Method and Measurement in Sociology* (New York: Free Press, 1964), pp. 149, 212–218.

50. For an example, see Wilson, *Negro Politics, op. cit.*, p. 111.

51. For one of the more sophisticated representatives, see William F. Whyte, "Human Relations—A Progress Report," *Harvard Business Review*, Vol. 34 (1956), pp. 125–132.

52. See Elton Mayo, *The Human Problems of an Industrial Civilization* (Boston: Division of Research, Graduate School of Business Administration, Harvard University, 1946), Ch. 8; and his *The Social Problems of an Industrial Civilization* (Boston: Division of Research, Graduate School of Business Administration, Harvard University, 1945), Chs. 1 and 6.

53. Reinhard Bendix and Lloyd H. Fisher, "The Perspectives of Elton Mayo," *Review of Economics and Statistics*, Vol. 31 (1949), pp. 312–319.

54. This subject has been the central attention of the work of Thomas Schelling. Schelling focuses almost exclusively on threats and avoids the subject of promises, as his main concern is conflict and not cooperation. Analytically, both have the same status and hence are treated here jointly. Thomas C. Schelling, *The Strategy of Conflict* (New York: Oxford University Press, 1963), esp. Part I. See also his *Arms and Influence* (New Haven, Conn.: Yale University Press, 1966).

55. Parsons, "On the Concept of Political Power," *op. cit.*, p. 261. Parsons turned to examination of power mainly after his main works were published. On the absence of power in Parsons' earlier work see David Lockwood, "Some Remarks on 'The Social System,'" *British Journal of Sociology*, Vol. 7 (1956), pp. 134–146.

56. Parsons, "On the Concept of Political Power," *op. cit.*, p. 258. See also Parsons, *Structure and Process in Modern Societies*, *op. cit.*, pp. 273–274.

57. Talcott Parsons, "On the Concept of Influence," *Public Opinion Quarterly*, Vol. 27 (1963), p. 38.

58. Nowhere is the fact that threats make systems of their own more evident than in the relations between nuclear powers, in which the balancing of threats and counter-threats is the basis of a strategic stalemate between the sides. The need to build up occasionally the credibility of these threats has been discussed effectively by Kenneth Boulding.

"Such a system may be fairly stable for short periods. But it has a fatal instability. Its stability depends on the mutual credibility of the threats. . . . Credibility, as it were, is a commodity which depreciates with the mere passage of time . . . the time eventually comes when threats are no longer credible enough to keep the system stable. One party or the other decides that it believes so little in the threats of its potential opponent that it can defy them. When this happens the system experiences crisis. . . . The cyclic character of war is clearly a product of a system of deterrence which, as we have seen, will be stable for a while but will eventually break down into war."

See his *The Meaning of the Twentieth Century* (New York: Harper & Row, 1964), pp. 80–82.

59. Neustadt, *Presidential Power*, *op. cit.*, pp. 9–32, esp. 27–28.

60. *Structure and Process* . . . , *loc. cit.*, pp. 219–220.

CHAPTER 14

Power, Alienation,

and Societal Goals

W HAT IS the place of power in an active society? Can a society use power to bring about its transformation and the realization of its values without undermining the bases of authentic commitment, participation, and legitimation? This dilemma is highlighted by the following comparison: If another actor uses power against ego, violating values central to ego, and the power he uses is physical coercion—the exercise of power and the active quality seem diametrically opposed. On the other hand, if ego uses power to advance one of his central values in the face of reluctant but not opposing others, and the power he uses is based on appeals to values— let us say, in an educational campaign to convince white southerners to extend civil rights to Negro-Americans—the use of power seems to advance the active quality. It is not only that the ethical status of power varies with different goals, if the perspective of the subject is substituted for that of a power wielder, and when wrong is imposed rather than corrected, but also that the kind of power that is used makes a difference. While all kinds of power in any context have distorting effects on those subject to it *and* on those who wield it, when the commitment to a goal is high and the distortions introduced by the particular kind of power used are comparatively low, most actors most of the time prefer this combination to neglecting their normative goal-commitments and not resorting to power at all.

The problem of societal guidance is, hence, not *whether* to use power but *which uses* of power minimize its distorting effects. The actors have already made the basic ethical choice—they use power, and even if every social scientist were to subscribe to a theory without a conception of power, this would not alter the basic disposition of societal actors to exercise power. The contributions social science may make in this area are to reduce the scope and intensity of the use of power and to moderate and mitigate its distorting effects by determining which usages, under what conditions, are less distorting than others, rather than to seek vainly for a design of a societal system free from power relationships in which societal action will have the support of a freely formed, authentic consensus of all concerned.* To limit societal action to that which is fully acceptable to all involved is utopian because the very existence of societies implies a division of labor, a differential distribution of assets and commitments, and, hence, power relations. Moreover, even if society were as integrated as one monolithic actor who has one set of needs and one will, he would still subject himself to some constraints, to some institutions. He still would seek to control himself, to enforce the choices made in more normative situations—in other situations he is less so inclined. Thus, the societal use of laws entails not only the control of deviancy but also the enforcement of the morality of the members so that they will not have to rely upon the strength of their voluntary commitments at all times. Traffic and social security legislation are familiar examples, but the same point applies to the constitutional and legal frameworks of responsive societies.†

To explore the relative merits of varying kinds of power, we, for the most part, compare them with each other; only in passing are we concerned with powerless relations, those among actors who have authentically reached a consensus regarding the goals which are to be pursued, the means to be applied, and the pace to be followed. While action based on such authentic consensus rarely appears in a pure form, it is useful as a standard against which various kinds of power relations can be assessed: The closer the relations among actors approach this ideal type, the more limited and the less distorting the application of power.

Distorting effects register (*a*) in the commitments of those subjected to the exercise of power, who involuntarily participate in the realization of a goal and, thus, are not authentically active; (*b*) in power wielders who are not authentically related to those they control, because to apply power is to

---

* Authenticity is defined and its operational indicators discussed in Chapter 21.

† Responsiveness is defined and responsive societies are explored in Chapter 18.

treat others as objects or means and not as goals; and (c) in the societal structures in which the power wielders and subjects share—that is, the application of power affects relations other than the ones in which it occurred. For instance, it prevents the development of an authentic community and sharing of goals between the power wielders and the subjects.

Our effort here is largely analytic. We deal with the basic kinds of power relations in the abstract, dissociated from the concrete societal contexts in which they are found primarily in various mixed combinations. In the following discussion, we first examine the elements from which alternative modes of societal organization are developed. We then ask: Under what conditions may the societal reliance on authentic consensus and on the less alienating modes of power be increased; i.e., societal control may be not only more intensive and encompassing but also may have fewer distorting effects, a combination which effective societal guidance and activeness require.

Power and Alienation in a Comparative Perspective

The Dilemma of Power

To use power, to overcome resistance, entails the generation of some resistance. The dilemma of power is how to increase the capacity to act without generating counter-currents so that the very movement forward will not reduce the capacity to move on this and future occasions. As this dilemma can never be fully resolved, the realistic question becomes one of which kind of power produces relatively weak counter-currents? The resistance generated by the use of power takes many forms and has many expressions. The term which most inclusively describes the various kinds of resistance is "alienation." It increases when power is exercised, adding to alienation which has other sources.

The term "alienation" serves to emphasize that the issue is not only one of the overt hostility of those subject to power, for their reactions may also express themselves in the victimization of others, neurosis, alcoholism, and so on. Secondly, the term reminds us that varying applications and kinds of power create different kinds of subject-and-power-wielder relationships and affect the totality of social* organization. Thus, if one kind of social organization relies to a greater extent on force to advance its goals than another, this will affect not only the psychic states of those subjected to the exercise of power but also the pattern of the relevant social structure and most social relations within it. For instance, the application of power is expected to increase the distance between the members of the social unit and

---

* "Social" rather than "societal" because the point applies to micro- as well as macro-units.

the fruits of their labor, render their social world less meaningful, and make the social structure less responsive. Thus, alienation has both subjective and objective facets—the psychic states of the subjects and power-wielders and the patterns of the societal unit.*

The exercise of power can be observed without manifest signs of alienation. However, we still would hold that some new resistance is an inevitable outcome of the use of power, even though the focus of the alienation thus generated might be deflected from the sources of power. Actually, when alienation is very high, especially in situations in which the power applied is brute force and there is little hope of neutralizing it, the subjects are quite likely to deflect their psychic responses. Inmates in concentration camps, for instance, seem more often to have attacked each other than their guards.[1][†] To demonstrate the validity of our proposition, we would have to demonstrate either that the brutal exercise of power is the cause of the victimization orientation which the subjects exhibit toward each other and/or that a significant weakening of the power-wielders will lead to the focusing of alienation on them; i.e., alienation is latent and becomes manifest when circumstances allow. In less extreme and more common power relations, we expect that at least part of the alienation will tend to be directed manifestly toward the wielders of the power.

While all actors face the dilemma of power, the need to minimize its self-contradictory consequences (or costs) is particularly evident on the macroscopic level. On the personal level, the application of the more alienating forms of power may satisfy sadism, vanity, or exhibitionism—i.e., fulfill a "need." The same phenomenon may occur on the microscopic level in which personalities play a relatively large role. But on the macroscopic level, this seems less common; while some leaders may harbor such tendencies, the control of macro-units is usually mediated through other personalities, organizational arrangements, and structural constraints, each of which tends to dissociate power to a great extent from personality traits and to rationalize it in the sense of making it *relatively* more goal-oriented. (The less a societal structure is responsive to the personality of one leader, the less the macro-unit is like a micro-actor from this viewpoint.) Finally, most macro-actors seem to be consciously concerned with applying the kinds of power that will gain the desired results while generating little new resistance. Therefore, this is the key problem in the *societal* application of power: On the one hand, there is often the fear of alienating, which slants the societal unit toward inaction; on the other hand, there is often the unnecessary use of power or use of the "wrong" kinds of power, which generates unnecessary alienation. The level of activeness attained depends on the balance which is achieved between these tendencies.

---

* For additional discussion of the concept of alienation see Chapter 20.

† Reference notes for this chapter appear on page 381.

Alternative Modes of Social Organization

We now review briefly the major sociological responses to the question of the bases of social organization, in order to place our endeavor in relation to these responses. Past efforts pointed chiefly to two bases of social organization. According to the first, men are related to each other through emotional and moral bonds which form natural social groupings subject to natural leadership. These traditional social units, it is widely agreed, were being undermined by the impact of industrialization, and the second principle of social organization was increasing in importance. According to this principle, actors are related by shared interests and the interdependence emanating from the division of labor, specialization, and exchange. Since this mode of social organization is based on self-interest, no need for leadership was recognized. In short, man was not predatory to man either because he believed in a value that supported social organization (including the value of the other) or because it was profitable to be sociable and organized.

Despite the fact that this opposition between the normative and the utilitarian bases of social organization appears in many guises, a common element is found in almost all of its expressions: An analytic preference for normative bonds over utilitarian ones. Weber viewed traditional authority as inherently more stable than the rationalist, bureaucratic type. Durkheim suggested that every contract has a pre-contractual foundation; that is, the containment of the centrifugal forces which utilitarian relations generate depends on their normative underpinnings.[2] Weber made the same point in his study of stock exchanges.[3] De Tocqueville, Maine, Tönnies, Redfield, Mayo, Schmalenbach and numerous others saw the transition from a normatively-based social organization to a more utilitarian one as a decline in social organization if not an outright disintegration of the social fabric.

Even Marx, who in many ways is outside this tradition, shared in this basic perspective in that he saw history as a series of conflicts of interest to which man was subject from the time he was expelled from the harmonious, normative garden of the primitive commune until his eventual return to the conflictless, normative life of the classless society. Marx's disapproval of the utilitarian principle is evident in that he saw in it a foundation for the organization of a transforming conflict but not a basis of a stable society; it was not to be a basis of the classless one. Actually, the main difference between his and other socio-political theories on this point is that while Marx separated the two modes of societal relations into different periods and assumed a sharp transition from one to the other, most of the other theorists viewed modern society as a mixture of the two modes with only gradual changes in the mix.

For the Parsonian theory of action, the foundation of social organization is still the internalization and institutionalization of normative symbols which bind the actors into social groupings.[4] Utilitarian interests might support the normative order, but they cannot be relied upon because at any point, actors who seek to maximize short-run interests at the cost of long-run ones or actors whose long-run interests differ might undermine the social order. Stability, continuity, and order rest on normative foundations.

If the normative principle took precedence almost unanimously in Western social philosophy over the utilitarian one as a basis of social organization, coercive relations were widely treated as chiefly destructive. As early as Plato, force was relegated to the relations of a polity to non-members, to barbarians and foreigners, and to the anarchy of interstate relations. The internal life of the *polis*, in which order reigned, was to be based on education and persuasion.

Hobbes' social philosophy is often represented as one in which violence plays a key role; this is true, but it is not as a foundation of social organization. It is the *escape* from the anarchy of violent life which Hobbes views as so desirable that it takes priority over all other values and leads man to bind himself into the protection of an absolute state. But the order of this state is based on a contract, or an understanding of the value of the institutions, and on a political formula—i.e., on legitimacy. In short, it is a part utilitarian, part normative order.

In Marxist theory, force has a more ambiguous status but, in balance, a destructive one. So far as the state is concerned, force is used for subjugation, an instrument of the propertied classes which contains the seeds of its own destruction: It is not an order but a preparation for and an element of warfare. Insofar as force is used by the proletariat, "violence is the midwife of history," the birth cry of the new society but not part of it. It destroys the old regime, the world of conflict, in a violent showdown, but—as the state withers away—force has no place in the new world, the truly ordered one.[5]

A small group of Italian writers, among which Mosca and Pareto are the best known, saw in the use of force an organizing principle similar in status to the normative and utilitarian principles found in other theories (as well as in their own). Mosca saw in the protective function a foundation of a social order (though, again, the relations between the knights and the peasants were of mutual interests, an exchange of protection for services and goods, with the force aimed toward outsiders). Pareto's circulating elites used force not only for unseating an elite whose removal was overdue but also as a source of the power of the "lions" who rigidly enforced their rule.[6] He came close to recognizing force as a permanent foundation of social organization.

The main lines of sociological thought, however, continued either not to treat force at all or to view it as largely destructive, generating a need for social organization rather than as a source of such organization.[7] Authority, Weber stressed, is the legitimate use of power, and force is one source of power. But it is the legitimacy that makes for the order; naked power leads to disorder. In Parsons' writings, force without legitimacy has a destructive status similar to that of sex without love.[8] It is a sign of anomie, of unsocialized or desocialized behavior, of the animal in man emerging from under the social super-structure. It is a threat to the social fabric and needs to be channeled into legitimate outlets: Just as sex is channeled into love, so force is channeled into authority. In political science, one of the most widely held propositions is that governments that rely on force are not firmly established (or "stabilized"). "You can do everything with bayonets but sit on them."

We suggest that the three organizational principles—the normative, the utilitarian, and the coercive—are equal in theoretical status.[9] There are no a priori or empirical grounds on which to hold that one of these serves as a more general principle of social organization than the others. The relative distortive effects of the three principles of social organization cannot be examined without relating the kind of power used to the goals served.

In the following discussion, our treatment of power is analytic: We ask about the effects of changes in the kind of power used if all other factors remained unchanged.* The actor who is deciding which of the alternative kinds of power to use is faced with a problem which is analogous to the analytic model; he might attempt to affect other elements of the situation outside the power matrix, but he will be likely also to consider the differential consequences of forcing his way, of ensuring pay-offs to those who might otherwise hinder his action, of trying to convince others of the justice and wisdom of his course, or various combinations thereof.

We first classify the kinds of power, and we then examine their relationship to other abstract factors (or variables). We first relate the kind of power used to the level of alienation generated, then relate these two factors to the kinds of goals advanced, and then relate these three factors to various features of the social organization, such as the social distance (and the distribution of the access to power) among the member status-groups. When these factors are considered altogether, toward the end of the chapter, ideal types of societal organization emerge. *We find that the kind of power used tends to be associated with different kinds of societal organization.* Where force prevails, a terror regime is likely to prevail, with its concomitant factors—fear, hate, and a sharp differentiation between those in power and those subject to it. Where exchange is the prevailing mode of gaining one's way, where each person is a means to the other and the

---

* Analytic in two senses: (1) concrete power might be a combination of two or more kinds of power as seen from the viewpoint of the analytic classification. (Which kinds are combined and which kind prevails in the combination, if any, can be empirically determined.) (2) Variables used for classification belong to an analytic scheme—in this case, a theory of compliance.

accounting and calculative orientations dominate, market relations prevail. Finally, where appeals to values, consensus, education, and debate are prevalent, members are more committed to each other and to the shared societal goals.

Even these three principles of organization are highly "ideal–typical" (or, analytic) in that any actual societal control mixes, to varying degrees, these types. In later chapters, these are treated more synthetically, in relationship to actual societal structures such as modern democracies and totalitarian states. This approach allows for considerable economy. By using three ideal types and varying degrees of approximation to and mixing of them, we can characterize by the use of a few concepts the large variety of regimes which we encounter and their continual changes. It also serves to stress that societies are not simply totalitarian or democratic but use varying "mixes" of power, and that each regime may and frequently does change its mix.

Finally, it should be emphasized that while we begin our exploration of the relationships among the various factors by comparing the effects of the use of various kinds of power, we do not wish to suggest that power is the determining factor and that the level of alienation and the kinds of societal goals to which the actors are committed are determined by it. As we see it, these three factors interact and tend toward "typical" constellations; none of them has a clear primacy.

A Classification of Power

The conversion of assets into power generates a variety of sanctions, rewards, and instruments to penalize those who resist, to reward those who assist, to remove those who block, and to provide facilities for those who implement a collectively-set course of action. These sanctions, rewards, and instruments differ in their substance: They are either physical, material, or symbolic.[10] This makes for a threefold classification of assets and power: Power is either coercive (e.g., military forces), utilitarian (e.g., economic sanctions), or persuasive (e.g., propaganda). The classification is exhaustive. Each concrete application of the use of power is either one of the three or is composed of their various combinations.[11] The classification covers both "real" and "ideal" elements, mechanical and symbolic elements, and elements representing the three sociological orientations reviewed above. Threats and promises are classified in terms of their asset base, though they are all symbolic and, in this sense, similar to persuasive power. Thus, a threat to bomb is coercive, a promise to provide foreign aid is utilitarian, and a threat to excommunicate is persuasive. In general, threats and promises are "milder" in their effects than the actual exercise of the same kind and amount of power.[12]

Utilitarian assets include economic possessions, technical and administrative capabilities, manpower, etc. Utilitarian power is generated when these assets are applied or exchanged in such a fashion as to allow the unit which possesses them to bring other units to support its line of action.*

Coercive assets are the weapons, installations, and manpower which the military, the police, or similar agencies use. There is a thin line between utilitarian and coercive assets; civilians may be inducted into the military and factories might be converted to military use. But so long as such a conversion has not occurred, these means will not be viewed as coercive assets. Coercive power (or force) results when one unit uses coercive assets to impose its preferred course of action on others. Note that coercion refers here to the employment of violent means and not to pressure in a more generic sense. Or, to put it differently, coercive power refers to the use of force and not to other means of enforcement.

Persuasive power† is exercised through the manipulation of symbols, such as appeals to the values and sentiments of the citizens, in order to mobilize support and to penalize those who deviate (e.g., by excommunicating them). Unlike utilitarian and coercive power, two concepts which are frequently applied, the concept of persuasive power is not widely used and raises several analytic problems which need to be discussed briefly, especially since the relations between assets and power are less evident in regard to persuasion than with respect to the other two categories.

The normative bonds of societal units, the bases of persuasive power, are often perceived as either resting on personal attitudes and interpersonal relations or as having no structural and organizational base at all. Actually, the capacity to persuade is not randomly distributed in social systems. For instance, in societies in which the church is a main source of persuasive power, the power-holders themselves constitute a hierarchy with a variety of goals, in the pursuit of which the hierarchy brings its power to bear. And the secular authorities which have the church's blessing possess access to a source of power that other secular authorities do not. In the Spanish civil war, for example, Franco was granted such support and the Republicans were undermined. Similarly, in democratic societies, access to the mass media is a source of persuasive power that is more available to political incumbents than to the opposition; in totalitarian societies, this source of persuasive power is largely monopolized by the establishment. In short, persuasive power is structured and organized, allocated and applied, in much the same ways as other kinds of power.

The capacity to persuade is a power; like other kinds of power, it enables those who have it to reduce the resistance to the course of action they prefer—that is, initially the actors subjected to persuasive power were not supportive

---

* *Utilitarian power* is preferred over "economic power" because administrative and technical assets as well as economic ones are included.

† We used "normative" or "identative" power in previous publications. Our reason for this change of terminology will become evident in the following pages.

of the action advanced by the power-wielder, but they suspended their preferences in the face of the power. Had they been fully convinced that the course of action to be followed was in accord with their preferences but that they did not have sufficient information to be aware of this or had their preferences been altered without residue rather than suspended, information would have been given or influence would have been exercised but no application of power would have occurred. The indication that power has been exercised is the remaining latent resistance of the actors who suspended their preferences. Persuasive power differs from information and influence in much the same way that suppression differs from specification (or re-specification) and full substitution.

The socialization of a people, the values to which they subscribe and the intensity with which they hold them, largely determines the scope and limits of persuasive "assets." At each point in time, we suggest, the values to which actors are committed cannot quickly be changed because these commitments are the result of slow processes.* These commitments are assets to those who can appeal to the values and to a power potential not available to those who seek to promote a course of action outside the context of the possible courses of action which these values approve. While commitment to a new value can be developed and then used to support a line of action, this is a much more costly process than appealing to a value that has already been internalized. Hence, the existing distribution of values almost invariably provides an advantage for some lines of action—and of persuasion—over others. The amount of these assets can be measured either in terms of the costs and efforts that were necessary to create and reinforce the relevant commitments (or those which would be required to alter them) or in terms of the scope and amount of action that can be generated by drawing upon them.

The greater the potential appeal of these values and symbols, the larger will be the amount of the persuasive assets of the unit under examination. Persuasive assets are transformed into persuasive power when a member unit or a system-elite succeeds in demonstrating that a particular course of action which it seeks other units or all member-units to follow is consistent with or an expression of those values and symbols to which the other units are committed.

Power, Influence, and Authority

Influence and power are often used synonymously. We suggest, however, that it is useful to keep these two terms separate in order to express a significant conceptual distinction. An application of *power* changes the actor's situation and/or his conception of his situation—but not his preferences. Resistance is overcome not because the actor subjected to the use of power

---

* For references to relevant studies and discussion, see below, Chapter 21, pp. 624ff.

changes his "will" but because resistance has been made more expensive, prohibitive, or impossible. The exercise of *influence* entails an authentic change in the actor's preferences; given the same situation, he would not choose the same course of action he favored before influence was exercised.[13] While from the power-wielders' viewpoint, the difference between the two might be relatively small (the exercise of influence also consumes assets though it produces fewer or no counter-currents), from the subjects' viewpoint, it is more significant in that influence involves not suspension or suppression of their preferences but a respecification of their commitments.

Of the three kinds of power, persuasive power is the most similar to influence, since both are symbolic and draw on values and sentiments. The difference between them rest in the depth of their effects; persuasion suppresses the actor's preferences without changing them; it, hence, resembles influence on the surface, but there is really an exercise of power beneath. The difference between persuasion and influence is analogous to the difference between propaganda and education.[14] When persuasive power is very effective and influence is superficial, the two are very similar, but, in general, it is not difficult to distinguish one from the other. Persuasive power works more quickly and is less costly in assets than influence,* but is more alienating and less commitment-inducing and has an impact that is more superficial and temporary.

Many individuals and collectivities do not have a fully developed "will" or position in regard to many issues. When they consent to a course of action, is this influence or persuasion? Assisting them to specify their positions—by helping them to articulate what they earlier only diffusely sensed they wanted—is an exercise of influence and not of power, so long as the subjects view the course of action finally followed as consonant with their needs, interests, and values. When this is the case, no resistance is overcome. When, on the other hand, people are "talked into" a course of action and have an unarticulated uneasiness about having been pressured or cheated, persuasive power has been exercised, resistance is being overcome, and alienation is being generated. The fact that the borderline between a weak exercise of influence and the competent exercise of persuasive power is blurred does not mean that the two categories are indistinguishable.

Both concepts are related to the concepts of authority and legitimation. *Authority* is defined as legitimate power—that is, power that is used in accord with the subject's values and under conditions he views as proper. But even power that is completely legitimate may still support a course of action that is not desired by the subject and is therefore alienating. This is because the course of action, legitimate or not, is still not an expression of the subject's preferences.[15] Army officers who take their men into battle have the right

---

* When we seek to deal with influence and persuasive power together, we refer to *normative control.*

to do so, a right which the subjects may acknowledge, but this does not necessarily make combat a course of action preferred by the subjects. Illegitimate power is doubly alienating, because the action is both un-desirable *and* violates the sense of right and wrong. But if an authorized individual orders the same act, this still would not make the act desirable. Paying taxes to a rejected government, such as a colonial one, after the peoples' consciousness has been aroused by a national independence move-ment as compared to paying taxes to one's own government when identifica-tion with it is high illustrates the difference. Legitimation and satisfaction are not to be confused.[16] On the other hand, when influence is exercised, the act does become *desirable* even if the influence were illegitimate (although, as a rule, a full measure of influence would require that it be legitimate in terms of the subject's values).[17]

Kinds of Power and Levels of Alienation

Actors applying power have a degree of choice among the various kinds of power which differ in their alienating effects. We suggest that the applica-tion of persuasive power tends to be the least alienating (e.g., when the United States succeeds in persuading a country that not trading with Cuba is in line with values the particular country and the United States share). The application of force is the most alienating (when, for example, American military forces assume control of a foreign country). The exercise of utilitarian power, such as reducing the sugar quota or foreign aid, is less alienating than the use of force but more alienating than persuasive power.

Since societies are highly complex social systems which rely in various areas on all three kinds of power in intricate combinations, it is useful to consider the relations between the kinds of power and the corresponding levels of alienation and the social organizations associated with them first in a context less intricate (but far from trivial) than that of a total society— that is, in complex organizations. The instruments which the elites of complex organizations use to control the lower participants (e.g., students in schools, workers in factories, inmates in prisons) differ greatly in terms of their power composition.[18] Elites which rely heavily on force to control their lower participants tend to have highly alienated lower participants; prisons are the archetype of the resulting mode of social organization. Elites which rely heavily on persuasive power and other normative controls* tend to have the least alienated or even committed lower participants; progressive schools are the archetype of this mode of organization. Elites which rely heavily on utilitarian power tend to have lower participants who are "in the middle"— less alienated than those subject to force but more alienated than those

---

* We examine these points in more detail in *A Comparative Analysis ...*, *op. cit.*, pp. 14–16.

subject to normative control; factories are the archetype of this kind of organization. While organizations tend to mix two or three kinds of power, most "specialize" in their reliance on one kind. There is some empirical evidence to support the proposition that the varying mixes of the three kinds of power used are associated with varying degrees of alienation, as the preceding discussion implied.[19] For instance, when the elites of an organization rely on a mix of power that is less coercive and more utilitarian than that which is found in prisons—e.g., in company towns—the alienation of those subject to control is lower and the social structure is less "distorted" by the uses of power than in prisons.*

Attempts to apply these and other findings on compliance structures in complex organizations to the exploration of the foundations of societal control and organization have often proceeded by treating kinds of complex organizations as direct analogies to types of societies. Societies have been loosely characterized as prisons (for instance, totalitarian ones), as factories and market places (in particular, capitalist societies), or as giant bureaucracies. Comparisons to normative organizations are used when utopian societies are depicted.

The analogies are not without value. Some general and some specific points learned about compliance relations on one level can be transferred to the other and found to be valid. Thus, for instance, if the elites of one society rely on coercion to a greater extent than the elites of another society, or more so than the elites of the same society in an earlier period, or more to control one sub-society than others, this is expected to generate more subjective and objective alienation in the relevant societal units; we expect other specific propositions to hold as well. In prisons, it was found that the guards, themselves unable to control coercively the large numbers of inmates, grant a small number of inmates privileged positions and, thus, gain their cooperation in imposing a particular regime on the rest.[20] In South Africa, the white police are reported to be lenient, even encouraging, toward African gangs who victimize and keep in a state of terror and suppression African neighborhoods.[21] In concentration camps, a few Jewish "councilmen" played a role in preventing the uprising of the Jews.[22] Similar analogies have been drawn concerning the relations between the workers and the management in industry and among the classes in the industrial society, and for other kinds of organizations and societies as well.

The direct analogy of one organizational type to one societal structure, however, is limited in the sense that societies are more complex and varied if for no other reason than that they contain organizations of all the three main types. Hence, there is a need to draw on organizational analogies other than a direct, isomorphic one; societal controlling overlayers differ in their relative

---

* The dimensions which may be used to characterize social structures from this viewpoint are discussed below.

reliance on coercive, utilitarian, and normative organizations, which, in turn, is expected to affect the societal level of alienation in accord with what we know about relations in these organizations.

In this context, it is fruitful to view alienation as a continuum ranging from high to low and not to assume a sharp dichotomy between alienating and non-alienating societal structures. Some modes of control are more oppressive than those of the most capitalistic industry—i.e., control by force; on the other hand, there may be a considerable degree of alienation even when there are few market relations and the role of the state is minimal, as when a societal order relies on persuasion. A guidance mechanism which is not alienating can be theoretically depicted; it is one in which action will be limited to that which is approved in a process of authentic consensus-formation in which nothing closer to power than influence is used to promote consensus among actors who differ in their needs, viewpoints, interests, and values. This, however, is likely to be a very passive society. In such a society, the lack of societal action and realization of societal goals may be more alienating than more intensive societal controls.

Alienation, it is here assumed, is generated by all users of power and not only by economic ones. Coercive power is not merely an instrument to protect property relations but a general base of power which appears more extensively in societies in which the principal means of production have been nationalized by the state than in market economies. Similarly, persuasion has alienating effects. In the sociological literature, much has been written about the directly alienating effect of work relations and the indirectly alienating effects of the societal structures based on such a work world—about the alienating impact of bureaucratic societies. Much less attention has been devoted to force and terror as modes of societal organization and the resulting distortions. Of course, the role of force in totalitarian societies is widely discussed, but there has been much less analysis of its scope in other societies.[23] Some scant data and personal observation lead us to suggest that in developing and undeveloped nations, the fear of the use of force by the police, a gang, or the local power elite constitutes a major mode of societal control. It is easy to imagine that when hundreds of thousands of men are killed in a country in a relatively short period of time, as they were in Colombia between 1948–1962[24] and in Indonesia in 1966,[25] millions of others live in great fear, and this greatly affects their relations to each other and to the power-wielders. The role of force in "undeveloped" sectors of post-modern societies has been given even less attention. Whenever the subject is raised—Spanish Harlem,[26] Negroes in Mississippi, working-class neighborhoods, the Mafia in New York[27]—the roles of the fear of force and the actual use of force stand out as major components of societal control. Consequently, the question of the conditions under which force is curbed and milder forms of power are used is a central rather than a marginal subject for a theory of societal guidance.

We refer to *compliance* structures as the typical patterns of relations between power-wielders and their subjects; these are affected to a considerable extent by the kinds of power used and the orientations of the subjects. The main compliance structures are based on force and high alienation (coercive compliance), remuneration and comparatively lower alienation (utilitarian compliance), and normative control and commitment or low alienation (normative compliance).

Before we proceed with our main argument, it seems worth noting that, insofar as the largely qualitative and secondary data we have used allow the drawing of a conclusion, the data suggest that the same associations between the kinds of power used and the levels of alienation generated seem to hold for relations within societal units (e.g., among ranks within complex organizations), among parts of the societies (e.g., upper and lower classes), and among societies.[28] For instance, to the degree that the United Kingdom succeeded in persuading the West Indian elites that a federation was an expression of their values, its pressure to federate the islands was least alienating; to the degree that Britain used the allocation of development funds to promote support for the federation, resistance was intensified. No force was used in the case of the West Indies, but it was used elsewhere— for example, in attempts to keep the federation of Nyasaland and Northern and Southern Rhodesia intact and, for a short while, in attempts to keep Syria as a part of the United Arab Republic. In both instances, force was found to be highly alienating.

Congruent and Non-Congruent Types of Compliance Structures

The association between the kinds of power employed and the amount of alienation generated can be explained in part by self-enforcing processes built into the relationship: When force is used, those subject to it tend to become highly alienated (with the exception of extreme force, as discussed above), and those who are highly alienated can hardly be controlled except by the use of force. Or, those who are highly committed can readily be guided by normative means, and the reliance on normative guidance tends to build up commitment (or, at worst, to generate comparatively mild alienation). Of the nine possible combinations of the three kinds of power and the three levels of subject involvement (high alienation, high commitment, middle to low in both), only three types of compliance structure seem to be congruent: force and high alienation, normative control and commitment (or low alienation), and utilitarian power and middle to low alienation. We expect that the other six combinations are inherently unstable in that when they do occur, pressure is generated to move toward one of the three congruent combinations. When corporal punishment is introduced into a school system which has committed students, because, let us say, a new generation of teachers is not sure that it can maintain discipline in any other way, the system's compliance structure will soon shift from a coercive-committed combination to a coercive-alienated one. When a change of personnel in a prison system brings about an attempt to move from a custodial to a thera-peutic orientation and, thus, to rely on normative controls rather than on force, this initially makes for a normative-alienated non-congruent com-pliance structure. But either the inmates will alter their orientations, leading to a congruent normative-committed pattern (as in some rehabilitation centers), or the staff will tend toward more coercive forms of control, thus restoring the coercive-alienated balance. This seems to hold on the societal level as well, with reference to the relative reliance on police forces, full employment and welfare policies, and normative leadership or opportunities for authentic participation—and the level of citizens' alienation. (There are, of course, significant differences in the ways in which various groups of participants in organizations and citizens are controlled and in the expected levels of their alienation.)

Non-congruent types occur because the orientations of those subjected to power and the kinds of power that elites employ are only partly determined by each other. The subjects' orientations toward the power-wielding elites are partly determined by the socialization, association, and mobilization of the subjects themselves. These factors might, for instance, keep a prison's inmates highly alienated even if the prison increases its reliance on normative guidance.

Similarly, the power which the elites of a societal unit employ is de-termined in part by such factors as the unit's market position which affects the elites' ability to rely on utilitarian power, the elites' societal license to use force, and their normative standing (e.g., endorsement by the church) which affects the elites' ability to appeal to the values of the subjects. In other words, supra- and inter-unit system factors affect both sides of the intra-unit com-pliance relationship: The orientation of those subject to power toward those who wield it, and the ability of the elites who wield power to exercise the various kinds of power.

The interplay between collectivistic system factors and the controlling overlayer is evident here. On the one hand, both power and the subjects' orientations, as we have seen, are affected by various system relationships (e.g., the members' affiliations with collectivities other than the one under study or the collectivity's position in the society's stratification structure). On the other hand, each societal unit has a degree of freedom—for instance, in terms of the ways in which it internally allocates whatever assets it com-mands. Does the unit, for example, allocate a high proportion of its utilitarian assets to the higher ranks and rely on coercion for the control of the lower ranks, or does it allocate its utilitarian assets more evenly among the ranks? Similarly, although the subjects' orientations to the elites in power are in part determined by factors external to the relationship (which, let us assume, make their predisposition a hostile one), they still are in part affected by the kinds of power used in the relationship itself. This is not to suggest that the power composition of the controlling overlayers is not affected by system factors—e.g., by what the overlayers of other units are drawing upon and by what is culturally acceptable—but to suggest that the system, in turn, is also affected by the controlling overlayers of the various member-units in that their actions help to stabilize or transform it. Hence, at each point in time, it is best to view separately the compliance (power and alienation) relationship and other relationships in the same system, and to study their reciprocal effects over a period of time.

Non-congruent types of compliance structures may persist despite internal strains for two major reasons: (1) system constraints (e.g., the lower the GNP level of a society, the more difficult it is for the society to rely on utilitarian rewards), and (2) limitations of the controlling overlayer—for instance, in its knowledge of the system (e.g., those higher in rank often have erroneous conceptions of the values, interests, and outlooks of those lower in rank). The proposition that these are non-congruent types can be tested, in that we expect the compliance structures to move in a congruent direction when the system constraints "untighten" or when a controlling overlayer's effectiveness is increased.

Neutralization, Mixing, and Dual Structures

So far, we have analytically explored the patterns of compliance; we have illustrated them by pointing to those concrete units which approximate the compliance ideal-types, for in these units, one pattern of compliance is unusually predominant (e.g., coercion in prison systems). It should be noted, however, that even in those units in which one pattern is predominant, other patterns are operative (e.g., in prison systems, some inmates cooperate with the guards in exchange for goods and services).[29] Second, several important units combine patterns of compliance much more evenly. We refer to these as dual-compliance structures.

It might at first seem that the ability of an elite to draw simultaneously on two or even three kinds of power would simply increase its capacity to control its subjects. If the subjects can be influenced *and* paid *and* forced, would the power-wielders not establish maximum control? The problem here is that each kind of power tends to slant compliance in its own direction which is partially incompatible with that of the others, and that, hence, the various kinds of power tend to have neutralization effects on each other. In particular, force and influence seem to be incompatible if relied upon 'n *the same control relation*; the combining of other means of control, we suggest, will also generate neutralizing effects. To illustrate, a study of mass persuasion showed that when utilitarian and normative appeals were combined to urge that the purchase of federal bonds during World War II was both a good investment and a patriotic act, this combination was less effective than when the campaign stressed normative themes alone.[30]

However, the controlling overlayers of several societal units do mix various kinds of power without giving clear priority to one kind. In part, this is because they are unaware of the neutralization effect, and, thus, some of their power is lost. In part, the neutralization effect is minimized by segregating the application of different kinds of power, in the sense that initial attempts rely on one kind of power (usually one of the less alienating kinds), and only when they fail is the other, more alienating kind of power exercised. Thus, during a war, the population is first exhorted to increase its productive efforts before more coercive measures are introduced. And those who violate laws for the first time are more likely to be reprimanded or to have their sentences suspended (normative controls) or to be fined, and only repeated offenders are likely to be jailed (including those who did not pay their fines or heed the conditions of their suspended sentences). In addition, societal units shift controls from predominantly one pattern to another; e.g., peacetime armies change their compliance patterns as they go to war, and labor unions shift as they move from nonstrike to strike periods. Thus, various divisions—through time, between ranks, between groups of participants of the same rank—allow a dual compliance structure to be maintained with more effectiveness than when the patterns are "mixed" in the same control relation.

At the lower alienation end of the compliance continuum, utilitarian and normative controls seem to be "dissonant" when mixed, which is one reason that educators object to parents paying their children for doing their homework. Similarly, in societies, voluntary and paid services are segregated: When workers are asked to work for a cause and are given low pay, this tends to be ineffective except for limited, usually crisis, situations. (This proposition could be studied in situations in which labor unions were urged to hold down wages in time of war, to prevent inflation, or to help a labor government.)

Moving further toward commitment, we expect a strain between pure normative control and social power. Social power rests in the interpersonal ties which bind the members of a unit to each other, in terms of symbolic sanctions against leaving the unit (or secession) and against violating its norms (or changing its structure). Thus, social power rests in horizontal, associational relations and, as such, is not available for downward, hierarchical control. Normative control, on the other hand, tends to be hierarchical, to work down a rank structure, however informal it is. While social power is not hierarchical, it can be mobilized for downward control purposes, as, for instance, when leaders (who elicit normative commitments) appeal to their sub-collectivities or collectivities rather than directly to the subjects. Thus, the President, like a teacher appealing to a class not to support disorderly students, may ask the nation not to support the inflationary wage demands of labor unions. In this way, normative controls are linked to horizontal networks and make the power built into these networks available for control purposes. (This is approximated by the colonial method of indirect rule using the tribes and tribal chiefs, as opposed to the more direct control of the subjects.)[31]

While social power supports normative control under the circumstances just depicted, it tends to neutralize normative control when those circumstances are not present, despite its similarity to normative control in that they are both symbolic and relatively committing. This occurs macroscopically when a collectivity or a sub-collectivity is mobilized against societal leadership (or elites). Actually, this often entails a conflict between two normative elites of which one mobilizes the social power of the unit. A purer form of this normative versus social power conflict appears when those who seek to mobilize an unmobilized unit (or its unmobilized segments) are confronted not by a counter-elite but with apathy institutionalized in social bonds and reinforced by expressive associational activities.

The strain between normative and social power has been observed in religious movements, in which, in recent decades, increased emphasis has been placed on associational–social activities to induce people who otherwise would not do so to participate in normative activities. These social activities have grown in scope and have, thus, created a serious conflict over the amount of time which is to be devoted to religious (normative) activities as opposed to recreational (social) ones.[32] Similarly, nuns are warned not to become too friendly toward each other lest their prime commitment to the service of God be diluted.[33] And members of radical movements are expected to maintain their primary normative commitments to the movements rather than to other members.[34] In addition to conflicts concerning time and the primacy of commitments, strains arise from those normative activities which, like producing activities, have an instrumental aspect (though the instrumental aspects of activities tend more often to be collectivistic than individualistic). When the instrumental aspect is stressed, man is viewed as a utensil; this is as true of totalitarian social movements as it is of the ideal–typical capitalistic corporations. It is only in egalitarian social relationships that alienation is reduced to its lowest level and man is treated as a goal unto himself. In these relationships, however, the capacity for directed collective action, for the realization of goals, is low.

The Correlates of Compliance

Many socio-political factors tend to co-vary with changes in the prevailing compliance pattern. It is not our purpose to review all or even the most important of these factors but rather to highlight the significance of compliance patterns for the understanding of the complex relationships among societal factors and their dynamics. For instance, the *internal divisions* of societal units and the *relationships among them* (both in the stratification structure and in the level of system-integration) are greatly affected by the prevailing compliance pattern. Where coercion is the rule, a caste system with sharp and rigid divisions between those in power and those subject to it tends to evolve. The divisions are sharp because there tends to be very marked social distance between the associational networks of those who are in control and those who are not (though there are always some power differences among those in control and among those who are not in control but command some power by virtue of their contact with those in control or their influence over the powerless caste). The divisions are rigid because there are little upward or downward mobility between the castes and few opportunities for gradual change in the stratification structure or polity. Such caste relations are approximated in the relations between inmates and guards in prisons, occupation forces and native populations, and racially divided societies.[35]

Where normative controls prevail, stratification is likely to be flat—that is, there are few ranks, ranking is informal, mobility is common, and associational gradations are mild and continuous. The "ideal type" is approximated to varying degrees in therapeutic mental hospitals, in progressive schools (in the original *Kibbutzim*), and, above all, in social and political movements. Utilitarian compliance tends to be associated with a "middle" score on most of these dimensions—sub-units are less sharply segregated than they are in coercive units but more so than in normative ones; mobility is of an intermediary range, etc. Many established corporations in contemporary Western societies approximate this ideal-type.

Societal units that differ in the ways and means by which they maintain discipline also differ in their *leadership patterns*. In relatively pure coercive units, the ruling caste in its control of the subjugated caste cannot rely on leadership, for the subjugated caste tends to follow its own leaders. Inmate communities and "harsh" colonial situations, as in Algeria during the war between the French and the National Liberation Front, are cases in point. (This societal pattern is not to be confused with the pattern of control which draws on a combination of coercion and persuasion; in the latter case, the caste in power is more likely to provide some leadership to the subjugated caste. Also, early colonial situations, in which the subjugated caste does not act as a collectivity, should be kept separate.) In units that use relatively exclusive normative compliance, much of the leadership comes from the higher ranks, not only because it is accepted by the lower ranks but also because there are relatively few barriers to the promotion of informal leaders from lower to higher ranks. Social movements are a case in point. Units in which compliance is largely based on an exchange of remunerative rewards by the elites for the work of the subjects show little leadership on either level; they either never had an internal expressive life, or, so to speak, it ran "dry." To the degree that these units maintain associational–social bonds among the members, leadership emerges, but compliance also tends to move from the highly utilitarian pattern toward the normative (or normative-social) direction.

Other features of societal units are related to their respective compliance patterns, including the shapes of the intra-unit communication networks, the degree to which there is consensus among the various sub-units, and the degree to which the unit encompasses the life of the members ("scope" and "pervasiveness"). These and other related factors need not be discussed here; our purpose was only to illustrate the importance of differences in compliance patterns for societal structure.[36] The main point is evident: The more alienating usages of power tend to split the societal units, increase the distances among the divisions, increase the instrumental or manipulative orientation, and lessen the opportunity for authentic leadership and participation—in short, decrease the possibility of an active society.

Societal Goals and Compliance Patterns

Goals, Power, and Alienation

Assuming that our basic proposition is valid—that normative controls incur the least costs (in terms of the alienation and resistance generated), and influence is even less costly than persuasive power—the question arises: What prevents societal units from limiting their projects to those on which there is a consensus or to those which can be guided by normative controls? If existing societies, distorted in various ways, are unable (or perhaps not committed) to do so, could an active society be thus designed and guided?

The study of complex organizations casts some light on both the limits and the possibilities of moving toward more normative and less coercive societal control. The limits are inherent in the variety of goals served, since the goals differ in the services which their realization requires—that is, in their ability to rely on the three major kinds of power. *Cultural* (or symbolic) *goals*, it seems, are, in general, most readily implemented by normative controls. That is, if the goal is education, socialization, rehabilitation, the reinforcement of normative commitments, or tension release (as in entertainment), little other power is needed and the alienation generated is comparatively low. When other kinds of power are employed to advance cultural goals, alienation is increased and effectiveness is reduced. Paying subjects to be socialized tends to generate a calculative orientation which undermines identification with the agents of socialization, an identification which is a prerequisite for the effective implementation of cultural goals.* Force

---

* This statement should be viewed as a proposition that needs to be supported; we shall assume that it is valid for the sake of our analysis.

undermines even further the conditions under which socialization succeeds; this is one of the principal reasons that rehabilitation efforts in custodial prison systems tend to be unsuccessful, or, when they are successful, they follow or are accompanied by a reduction of the prisons' use of force. This also partially accounts for the fact that totalitarian regimes, with an abundance of force at their command, invest a good deal in persuasive controls.

Production goals, including not only the manufacture of goods but also the provision of services, white collar work, and monetary activities, are served more effectively by utilitarian power as compared to both coercive and normative controls. Production is a "rational" activity in that it requires a systematic division of labor and responsibilities, a considerable amount of comparatively precise coordination, and a relatively detailed and close control (schools, churches, and prisons, it is widely agreed, can be run much more loosely than a bank or an assembly line and can still function quite effectively, probably even more effectively than if they were more "orderly"). Therefore, production requires sanctions and rewards that can be readily measured and allocated in relatively close association to performance, and utilitarian assets can be precisely applied as compared to prestige, force, or other sources of rewards and sanctions. Coercion will not suffice because most kinds of work require some degree of initiative, responsibility, and commitment on the part of even the lower participants. Only work which is routine and easily supervised, such as carrying loads or rowing in the galleys, can be controlled effectively by a reliance on coercion. Studies of forced labor camps and of societies similarly organized show that if any other kind of work is to be accomplished, either coercion is reduced or effectiveness is low.[37]

Symbolic rewards and sanctions are quite adequate for limited, intermittent work, especially when the effort is dramatic and the relation of the project to societal goals and values is highly observable; thus, fire and flood control brigades can rely quite effectively on normative controls so long as the demands for service are infrequent and only insofar as the effort itself is concerned, as distinct from the less rewarding requirements of long alerts. The more routine, continual, and instrumental a project, the less it is able to rely on symbolic rewards and the greater the need for utilitarian ones. Nursing was a voluntary, highly normative mission when it was limited and sporadic, as in its early, Florence Nightingale days; when it became a profession, the utilitarian element in its control was greatly increased.[38] A comparison of peacetime armies with combat troops further highlights this point: Utilitarian power is much more necessary and normative control is much less effective in the routine situation.

Order goals involve the control of deviants by segregating them from the body of society, by punishing as well as segregating them, or by eliminating them. For all of these goals, the task involved is one of protecting the society as a system and the particular societal mold that the elites in power favor. Organizations that implement the order aims of a society tend to see the maintenance of control as their major task since the confinement of deviants, as a rule, is involuntary and punitive. Thus, it is not accidental that most prison systems are not very effective agents of resocialization, for the re-socialization goal is secondary and partially incompatible with the primary goal of keeping the inmates confined. This makes reliance on controls other than coercive ones highly ineffective in terms of these organizations' primary societal goal.

The kind of power used and the nature of the compliance maintained are closely associated with the kinds of societal goals pursued as well as with the degree to which these goals are shared by elites and subjects. If the purpose of those in power is to educate and if those subject to control wish to be educated, normative control can be quite effective. If the purpose of those in power is to render ineffective those subject to power, as the subjects seek to escape, rebel, or subvert the power-wielders, violence is to be expected from both sides. If production is the goal of those in power and if those subject to power seek to exchange their labor for income, utilitarian power will serve.

This relationship also holds for more subtle differences between power-wielders' and subject-populations' goals, in terms of the kinds of power used, the alienation incurred, and the extent to which the goals are implemented. Thus, if the administration of a prison is less concerned with suppressing all deviance and more concerned with output, less force will be employed and less alienation incurred than when the prevention of escapes is the only goal and whatever the inmates produce is considered a bonus.

The same can be said for the relationship between governments and the population at large. Compare, for instance, three periods of Soviet control: The NEP (New Economic Policy) period, in which output was relatively emphasized; the Stalinist purges, in which the suppression of deviation was stressed; and the Khrushchev liberalization years, in which the mobilization of consensus increased in importance. In regard to Communist China, Skinner shows that the means of control of the peasantry by the political elites changed as a modification of goals occurred; the response of the countryside changed as well (and in the direction that would be expected from the preceding analysis).[39] For instance,

> In each case the campaign began at a time when the prevailing compliance structure was essentially utilitarian and was inaugurated by an increase in normative appeals. While the goals of the campaign might appear to be of somewhat less import than the issues at stake in war time, the efforts of the elite could hardly have been more energetic had they been leading the peasants into battle against foreign invaders. Seemingly no limits were placed on the massiveness of the injection of normative power. At the beginning of the campaign an intense effort at resocialization sought to bring peasant norms closer to the socialist content of those employed in normative appeals.[40]

Later, Skinner shows, the power used again became less normative, the peasants exhibited greater alienation, and goals were adjusted accordingly.

In exploring the relationships among power, alienation, and goals, it must be taken into account that: (1) We are dealing with relative weights; that is, no society or government ever gives up completely the use of any of the three instruments of power. Rather the differences and trends are in the mode of compliance and the related societal organization which are relatively emphasized. (2) In the same society or collectivity, the mode of compliance varies from one sub-unit to another; for instance, the "purging" of one collectivity (i.e., increased coercion and alienation) might be accompanied by "liberalization" for another, although there seems to be some pressure to follow unit-wide patterns (a) to change the controls of various sub-units in the same general direction, and (b) to treat higher strata less coercively than lower ones (note, for example, stratified law enforcement in the Western societies, in which offenders from higher classes are more likely to be controlled with a reprimand or a suspended sentence or are committed into the custody of the family, while offenders from lower classes are more likely to be incarcerated).

A Comparative Perspective on Compliance

The final answer to the question of how much counter-current a particular mode of societal organization generates rests in the goals pursued, because these differ in their intrinsic requirements in terms of the kinds of power their effective service demands. And in turn, these kinds of power differ in terms of the relative amounts of alienation they generate. The significance of the relative emphasis a society places on order, production, or cultural goals is further magnified in that such differences in commitment affect not only the compliance relationship between the elites and the non-elites, but also the whole societal structure and organization, from the degree to which collectivities are segregated from each other to the level of conflict among them.

Our position differs from those who see the main source of alienation in the economic or political structure (expecting capitalist societies to be and socialist ones not to be alienating), as well as from those who view "modernization" as generating alienation because of the rise of large-scale societal organizations or bureaucratization. We do recognize that the shape of the distributive patterns and the level of political responsiveness of a society are affected by the ownership of the means of production and by the size and complexity of the societal organization, and, these factors, in turn, affect the level of alienation and the power relations. We suggest, however, that although societies do differ considerably in the general levels of alienation which they generate, there are also significant differences *within* each society with respect to the goals which the particular societal sector serves and the control mix employed in that particular sector. And since all societies devote portions of their activities to cultural, production, and order goals, all societies—whatever their stratification structure and political organization—are expected to have respectively a relatively less alienating and a relatively more alienating sector. Thus, inmates of American and Soviet prison systems are expected to be more subjectively and objectively alienated from their respective societies than children in the more successful school systems in these societies, despite the important differences between the stratification structures, polities, and cultures of the two countries. Similarly, we expect factory workers in both societies to be less alienated than inmates and more alienated than students in successful schools.

To shift to another comparative dimension, we expect some important similarities in the reactions of factory workers to their role in the organization of production in developed, developing, and undeveloped societies, despite large differences in the size and complexities of their societies[41] as well as in their stratification and political structures and cultures. The same would hold for inmates of the respective prison systems and for members of normatively controlled organizations—let us say, non-violent ideological political parties. To put it differently, against the backdrop of *differing societal structures*, there are *sectoral similarities* due to similarities in the goals served, in their intrinsic needs, and in the "typical" means of control used. Actually, there is repeated suprise expressed in some social science literature about the similar ways in which organizations that are similar in their societal goals are managed, since the societies in which they are located differ considerably in their cultural, societal, and political life—e.g., similarities in factories in Poland, India, West Germany, the United States, and Britain.[42] The theoretical framework presented here may help to account for this similarity.

Secondly, the cross-societal differences themselves are due, in part, to differences in the relative emphases given to goals and means of control and in the scopes of the respective sectors rather than to differences in overall societal structures. Thus, if society X is less alienating than society Y, this is in part because society X produces less and is more supportive of associational–social activities (which are classified here as "cultural") as well as because of differences in the ownership of the means of production or in societal complexity. Thus, for instance, if inmates of Norwegian prisons are less alienated than inmates of American ones, this is not because Norway's means of production are more nationalized or Norway is a less complex or modernized society, but because there is a *relatively* greater emphasis placed on rehabilitation and on normative means of control in Norwegian prisons than in American prisons.[43] The fact that those prisons in the United States in which the compliance mix is similar to that in Norwegian prisons seem to have less alienated inmates supports this statement.[44]

Societal structures are relevant in that they affect the degrees to which the various goals are emphasized and the various means of control are favored. For instance, modernization tends to entail an increased emphasis on production and a greater reliance on utilitarian controls; market economies are more tolerant of utilitarian controls than centrally regulated economies. But there are limits, all too often ignored, to the degree to which (a) the services to the same basic goal can be differently controlled in terms of the kind of power employed; and (b) societies can reduce their emphasis on order and production goals and increase their emphasis on cultural ones, which is the primary way of reducing alienation resulting from the means of control. (The secondary way of reducing such alienation is to use less alienating means of control within each category—e.g., to control prison systems with as little coercion as possible.) The active society, hence, will be neither without power nor without alienation. Their scope will depend on the extension and acceleration of the various historical trends we briefly review in the next section.

In a Historical Perspective: Post-Modern Trends and Options

To begin with the secondary considerations, modernization and to an even greater extent the beginning of the post-modern period seem to be associated with an increased understanding of the differential effects of various means of control and with an increased reliance on the less alienating means within the limits of the constraints set by the goal requirements and the societal context. For instance, industrial management in the late-modern period, while still basically alienating in its reliance on utilitarian control, was less coercive and less alienating than industrial management in the early-modern period; occasionally, normative control, which was always operative to a very limited extent, was even somewhat increased in amount.[45] Prison management has become relatively less coercive and school management more normative without changes in their basic societal goals.[46] In our exploration of the new options which post-modern historical trends seem to offer, we can only provide some highly tentative speculations; our purpose is to illustrate a line of analysis rather than to attempt to predict the future.

PRODUCTION AND UTILITARIAN COMPLIANCE

As industrialized societies move more into the post-modern world, the technological and organizational prerequisites of work seem to be changing. To the degree that, on the average, they make work less routine and needing more skill, initiative, and responsibility, and as more routine work and even supervision are conducted by machines through the process of what is referred to as cybernation,[47] the more the objective need for utilitarian control will decline, and the option of a relatively more normative guidance of work will be available. Not all of the effects of cybernation reduce routine labor; for instance, cybernation produces temporarily an increased need for card punchers.[48] It has also increased centralization, at least in some instances, and decreased the responsiveness of the work process to the participants.[49]

Moreover, cybernation may cause some chronic unemployment among lower skilled groups. Some even argue that the net effect of cybernation will be to make work more alienating.[50] But, in general, we agree with those who expect that the long-run and net effects of cybernation will tend to make work, on the average, less routine and thus more open to relatively less alienating guidance,[51] especially as the composition of work changes with a declining blue collar as compared to a white collar segment and a declining white collar as compared to professional segment. Each of these shifts (which have been quite well documented and are expected to continue) suggests that more work will be conducted within the less alienating organizational forms and compliance relationships. Another trend which leads to a reduction of the role of production in society and, with this, to a decrease in the reliance on utilitarian compliance is the increase in productivity. While a once widely-expected decline in the length of the working day of men has occurred only to a limited degree in post-modern societies, the working day of the average post-modern woman has been shortened (although this has been negated, to a degree, by the increased employment of woman), making her more available for non-work goals. The rise in the average age of first employment, the increase in education (a cultural goal), and the growth in the number of old people who are not working are other indicators of the decreased reliance on utilitarian compliance. Before these trends of changes in compliance can significantly alter the society's compliance structure and reduce alienation, the legitimacy of non-work and the value of cultural activities must continue to be more widely and deeply recognized.*

In assessing this compliance trend, the simplistic model which implies that all workers have the same basic need for autonomous, self-directive, creative work ought not to be used. Actually, there are significant differences in workers' "tastes," with some workers preferring work that is routine and psychologically non-demanding.[52] Also, some workers are reported to prefer directive to non-directive supervision.[53] (This, though, might be due to the fact that the workers are so self-estranged they cannot, unless so educated, fully "accept" meaningful and participatory work.) This would suggest that to reduce alienation, the distribution of the demands for various kinds of work needs to approximate more closely the distribution of workers' preferences (though the conditions need to be provided under which the workers can discover their authentic preferences). Work in the post-modern society could be more alienating than in the modern one, despite the fact that an increasing segment of the work may well be highly autonomous and creative. This could occur if this increased segment were to become larger than the segment of the labor force that is able, willing, or prepared to under-take such work. The matter is further complicated in that workers' capacities and preferences themselves are changing and changeable. The extent to which

---

* See below for a discussion of "societal usefulness."

normative guidance can be relied upon is, therefore, partly affected by the extent of the societal effort to make work and the work-force's capacities and preferences more congruent. This seems to require an approach to the organization of production (and other work) which aims not toward the maximization of profits but toward a decrease in alienation without significantly reducing (or perhaps even increasing) productivity. This, in turn, seems to require an intensification of the societal guidance of the organization of work.*

There are other sources of alienation which can be reduced as utilitarian controls decline and normative ones increase (which the changing nature of work allows), but there is no assurance that this reduction of alienation will occur. For instance, the control of post-modern work could be, on the average, less bureaucratic and more self-guided. This can already be observed in the growing R & D units in comparison to most other production units, or in professional work in organizations as compared to blue and white collar work; this kind of control allows for more communication across the ranks and for greater participation of the workers in decision-making.[54] But all of these correlates of compliance do not change automatically with changes in the objective possibilities. Corporate and societal management will have to support the necessary organizational and institutional reforms, and the political organizations of the employees must provide political support for the transformation. So far, most labor unions—a major potential source of such mobilization—have shown little understanding of the post-modern world, as indicated by their almost exclusive focus (even in the most affluent societies) on utilitarian rather than normative matters; expectedly, their appeal is declining, especially among those segments of the labor force which are increasingly in a mixed utilitarian–normative control structure.[55] The perspectives of the few labor unions and labor parties which have sustained a broader political concern tend to be similarly obsolescent in that they seek a solution to alienation either by substituting the bureaucracy of the state for that of the corporations or by promoting more national welfare legislation, both of which are chiefly utilitarian alternatives.

ORDER AND FORCE

The most significant factor in determining the intensity with which force is used in the post-modern period is the state of inter- rather than intra-societal relations. Modern societies have tended to suppress the use of mass violence among their members and have externalized it, raising the "we" feeling and community organization to the national level and projecting the negative "they" on other national societies. In the modern period, the extent

---

* We outline below the reasons that such an intensification of control may well require only a small increase in quantity and more of an increase in sophistication and in the scope of guidance.

of international integration increased much less than that of intra-national bonds. The scope and frequency of the mass violence applied to societal non-members increased sharply with the rise of national, modern societies, and this trend has continued in the post-modern period. The reduction of this violence, we suggest, requires the evolution of integrative bonds among societies just as they were previously evolved among what are now integral parts of the same society (e.g., between the German states).* Such containment of the inter-nation violence is obviously a central problem of the post-modern age, especially for industrialized societies. Societies currently in the process of industrialization and of the development of a national community often have yet to curb internal mass violence and are expected to do so only to the degree that their levels of utilitarian assets and normative integration rise.

Regarding the intra-societal management of violence in developed post-modern societies, we expect a continuation of the transformation of the control of deviants from custodial (coercive) toward more therapeutic (normative) patterns, a trend which began in the modern period. Post-modern societies will probably treat more kinds of deviants as members whose socialization has not been sufficiently advanced or has been distorted or who have not been given the opportunity to conform and, therefore, are to be socialized rather than segregated and punished.† Other deviations are likely to be redefined so as to be included in what the society regards as tolerable behavior—behavior which it does not advocate or reward but which it does not see a need to control and suppress (i.e., as "secondary alternatives").‡ Tolerances of some forms of drug addiction and homosexuality as practiced by consenting adults seem typical cases in point, with the Scandinavian countries and Britain leading other post-modern societies. These trends could greatly reduce the scope of the use of coercion for societal order goals. To mention an often cited statistic: About half of the crimes in New York City are committed by drug addicts who are forced to obtain their drugs illegally and at high prices. If and when drugs become available under the supervision of medical and public authorities (as is the case in Britain), much of this crime may disappear.[56] The transformation has already begun with regard to mental patients and inmates; it is much more advanced on the ideological

---

* This proposition has been contested both theoretically and by the use of evidence. We discuss the reasons we support it, p. 564ff.

† Murray Schumach, "On the Third Sex," quotes the District Attorney's office of New York County as stating: "The tendency in recent years here has been to be less severe in dealing with homosexuals," *The New York Times*, May 7, 1967. *The New York Times* of May 21, 1967, reports on a similar change of attitude toward prostitution in New York ("Leary Changes the Rules").

‡ Milton Greenblatt, R. H. York, and Esther L. Brown with R. W. Hyde, *From Custodial to Therapeutic Patient Care in Mental Hospitals* (New York: Russell Sage Foundation, 1955).

than on the action level, a gap which is expected to shrink.[57] Some societies in the pre-industrial and pre-national phase were more advanced in this regard than some so-called developed societies (e.g., the treatment of some mental patients in late 18th century France and Britain was more therapeutically sound than in many modern societies), while developing societies are moving in a direction similar to that taken by the industrial nation-states: from more to less custodial care.[58]

The levels of intra-societal deviance and alienation are related in still another way. One major source of deviance is believed to be the alienating or inauthentic nature of society; the more responsive and active society becomes, the more deviance is expected to decline. Thus, for instance, certain kinds of deviant behavior occur primarily among the poor and underprivileged; the more society treats these societal sources of anti-social behavior, the smaller will be the need for coercion and the less will be the added alienation generated by it.

In addition to using force to deal with deviants or other societies, societies use force to suppress political innovation, and political innovators employ it to attempt to transform or actually to transform societies. We deal with this subject in the next chapters; it suffices to say here that the use of force is associated with such factors as the timing and pace of change. All other things being equal, the less overdue and the more rapid the transformation of a societal structure, the less need there is for order-enforcing organization; the more premature *or* slow a transformation, the greater the need for such organization.*

As we have said, in principle, the three kinds of power have the same theoretical status; none is viewed as more "basic" than the others. Force, however, in more integrated and responsive societal structures, is used primarily when the two other kinds of power (and various combinations thereof) fail. For example, when the unrest of the lower collectivities increases, to the extent that they are considered part of the society and that its structure is generally responsive, there will be an increase in utilitarian and normative efforts rather than continued, increased mass oppression. The history of labor movements in modern pluralistic societies is a well-known case in point. Recent race riots in American cities is another. And when force is employed—e.g., when the United States used force to prevent the secession of the South, or when the USSR halted Hungary's attempt to withdraw from the Communist camp—its use is terminated after a short period of time, and economic reconstruction and ideological efforts are expected to carry the load again. In this sense, force is a residual power, a retreat line, for effective controlling overlayers, and its activation indicates the temporary lack of

---

* The extent to which a change is overdue or premature is measured in terms of the relationship between the time the demand for the specific change gained support and when it was implemented.

the other kinds of power.[59] On the other hand, when no significant utilitarian and normative societal efforts follow the use of force, this suggests that the societal cybernetic and implementing capacities are deficient, and the probability of a breakdown in the prevailing societal pattern (if there is one) is high.

GENERAL COMPLIANCE TRENDS

The historical, "secular" trends seem to be toward less coercion and toward more utilitarian and especially more normative compliance, with an increase in the utilitarian controls of "have-not" countries to the degree that they develop economically and a relative increase in the options for normative guidance in developed societies as they enter the post-modern period.[60] The more active a society—the greater the number of citizens whom it involves and is responsive to—the more it is expected to rely on normative guidance, for the lower level of resulting alienation makes it more effective, and normative guidance, in turn, further reduces the level of alienation.

Many of these broad statements can be questioned and, especially, can be made more specific. For instance, rather than discussing delinquents and mental patients together (both kinds of deviants are expected, on the average, to be treated less coercively in post-modern than in modern societies), one could state that this trend is and, for a while, will continue to be further advanced for mental patients than for delinquents. Similarly, different categories of developing nations could be treated separately. Our purpose here, however, is neither to detail and specify these trends and projections nor to present data in support of the statements made, but (a) to highlight the relationships among the kinds of power employed, the levels of alienation produced, and the goals served, and (b) to suggest that the relationships among these societal elements seem to be changing in the general direction of providing new options for a less alienating society. These options will be actualized if international mass violence is contained, if the organizational context of work is made more compatible with the options of new production and control techniques, and so forth, as discussed above.

On the other hand, if the new technologies are abused rather than used, international violence will reach unprecedented levels,* societal policing will

---

* In a statement before the House Armed Services Committee in 1965, Secretary of Defense McNamara stated that *if* the United States spent an additional 25 billion dollars in the next five years on fallout shelters and antimissile defenses, and *if* the attacker waited an hour after launching his initial nuclear attack on our military targets before striking the cities (in McNamara's words, "an unlikely contingency") "only" 41 million Americans would be killed. If the attack on the cities came at the same time as the attack on military targets, 78 millions, or every third American would die; without the additional expenditure of 25 billion dollars, 71 out of every 100 Americans would die. *The New York Times*, February 19, 1965, p. 10.

replace welfare and education, and instead of a deeper restructuring and authentication, the new means of work and guidance will be the tools of subjugation and alienation. Which outcome will occur depends to a significant degree on the scope of social mobilization, responsiveness, community-building, and the reduction of inauthenticity—factors to which we turn next.

NOTES

1. Bruno Bettelheim, "Individual and Mass Behavior in Extreme Situations," *Journal of Abnormal Social Psychology*, Vol. 38 (1943), pp. 417–452. See also Eugen Kogon, *The Theory and Practice of Hell* (New York: Farrar, Strauss & Giroux, 1950), pp. 279, 284–285; and Elie A. Cohen, *Human Behavior in the Concentration Camp* (New York: Grosset & Dunlap, 1953), pp. 177–179. On the deflection of aggression of the oppressed Negro in the American South, see John Dollard, *Caste and Class in a Southern Town*, 3rd. ed. (Garden City, New York: Doubleday, 1957).

2. Emile Durkheim, *The Division of Labor in Society* (New York: Macmillan, 1933), pp. 206–219. See also Hermann Schmalenbach, "Die soziologische Kategorien des Bundes," *Die Dioskuren*, Vol. I (1922), pp. 35–105.

3. Max Weber, "Die Börse," *Gesammelte Aufsätze Zur Soziologie und Sozialpolitik* (Tübingen: J. C. B. Mohr, 1924), pp. 256–322.

4. Talcott Parsons, *Societies: Evolutionary and Comparative Perspectives* (Englewood Cliffs, N.J.: Prentice-Hall, 1966), pp. 16–17.

5. Marx' view of force as destructive is revealed in his reluctance to sanction it even for the revolution of the proletariat and in his preference for mature revolution over premature one. On Marx disdain of violence see Joseph A. Schumpeter, *Capitalism, Socialism and Democracy* (New York: Harper & Row, 1950), pp. 57–58. According to Engels, to reject violence is the "parsons' mode of thought—lifeless, insipid, and impotent. . . ." Friedrich Engels (trans. Emile Burns), *Herr Eugen Dühring's Revolution in Science* (New York: International Publishers, 1966), pp. 209–210. Lenin expressed himself against reactionary violence but in favor of revolutionary violence. See *Selected Works* (New York: International Publishers, 1935–1938), Vol. VII, p. 175.

6. Vilfredo Pareto, *The Mind and Society* (New York: Harcourt, Brace & World, 1935), Vol. 4, 1513–1519.

7. Lewis A. Coser, "Some Social Functions of Violence," *The Annals of the American Academy of Political and Social Science*, Vol. 364 (1966), p. 8. See also Dahl, *Modern Political Analysis, op. cit.*, p. 76.

8. On sex, see Parsons, *The Structure of Social Action, op. cit.*, p. 692. On force, see Parsons, *The Social System, op. cit.*, pp. 162–163.

9. See *supra*, Chapter 5, pp. 96–97. Marx deals with all three, under the terms of state, church (or religion), and technological and economic forces but, of course, gives analytic priority to utilitarian factors. Weber deals in a similar trinity: social economic, and political power. *From Max Weber: Essays in Sociology*, H. H. Gerth and C. Wright Mills, translators (New York: Oxford University Press, Galaxy Book, 1958), p. 78.

10. Boulding, Neumann, and Commons have suggested similar classifications. Boulding has developed a classification of "willingness" of persons to serve organizational ends which includes identification, economic means, and coercion. He suggests, however, that identification should be seen as an "economic" way of inducing willingness, a position which we believe is unacceptable to most sociologists. See Kenneth E. Boulding, *The Organizational Revolution* (New York: Harper & Row, 1953), p. xxxi; and R. Niebuhr, "Coercion, Self-Interest, and Love," in Boulding, *ibid.*, pp. 228–244. F. L. Neumann has suggested that "three basic methods are at the disposal of the power group: persuasion, material benefits, violence." "Approaches to the Study of Political Power," *Political Science Quarterly*, Vol. 65 (1950), pp. 161–180, quote from p. 168. John R. Commons distinguishes among physical, economic, and moral power in his *Legal Foundation of Capitalism* (Madison, Wis.: University of Wisconsin, 1957), pp. 47–64. Morris Janowitz analyzes international relations using the concepts of "economic resources, violence, and persuasion" in his *The Professional Soldier* (New York: Free Press, 1960), p. 258. See also Deutsch, *Nationalism and Social Communication, op. cit.*, pp. 218 ff., and David L. Westby, "A Typology of Authority in Complex Organizations," *Social Forces*, Vol. 44 (1966), pp. 484–491.

11. This classification is extensively discussed and applied in the author's *A Comparative Analysis of Complex Organizations* (New York: Free Press, 1961), especially Chapter 1, and *Political Unification, op. cit.*, pp. 38 ff. It is part of a more general classification of three kinds of social relations, discussed in Chapter 5, pp. 95–97.

12. See Blau, "broadly defined, power refers to all kinds of influence between persons or groups," *Exchange and Power . . ., op. cit.*, p. 115. Kelman, *International Behavior, op. cit.*, ". . . power can be defined as the capacity to influence," p. 399. James G. March, "An Introduction to the Theory and Measurement of Influence," in Heinz Eulau, Samuel J. Eldersveld, and Morris Janowitz (eds.), *Political Behavior: A Reader in Theory and Research* (New York: Free Press, 1956), pp. 385–396. Dahl, *Modern Political Analysis, op. cit.*, p. 50.

13. We draw here on a point made by Simon, *Administrative Behavior, op. cit.*, pp. 126–128.

14. The difference between education and persuasion involved important and complicated aspects of personality dynamics which need not concern us here. See William J. McGuire's discussion of "Education vs. Propaganda" in his "Personality and Susceptibility to Social Influence," in Edgar F. Borgatta and William W. Lambert (eds.), *Handbook of Personality Theory and Research* (forthcoming). See also Carl I. Hovland and Irving L. Janis, "Postscript: Theoretical Categories for Analyzing Individual Differences," in their *Personality and Persuasibility* (New Haven: Yale University Press, 1959), pp. 255–279.

15. Geiger points out that John Dewey did not see value and desire as two distinct dimensions. *John Dewey in Perspective, op. cit.*, p. 113. Blau does not distinguish between what is legitimate and what is desirable in his analysis of power. *Exchange and Power, op. cit.*, esp. 221–222.

16. Weber focused on the legitimation question: the Michigan studies on satisfaction. See, for example, Nancy C. Morse, *Satisfactions in the White Collar Job* (Ann Arbor, Michigan: University of Michigan, 1953). Daniel Katz et al., *Productivity, Supervision and Morale Among Railroad Workers* (Ann Arbor:

University of Michigan, 1951). Daniel Katz et al., *Productivity, Supervision and Morale in An Office Situation* (Ann Arbor: University of Michigan, 1950).

17. Otherwise a residue of guilt is to be expected.

18. For a detailed account, see the author's *A Comparative Analysis . . . , op. cit.,* pp. 23 ff.

19. *Ibid.* The material presented deals chiefly with data on complex organizations in the United States. G. William Skinner presented some striking data to show that the same relations hold in a very different context, that of Communist China. See his "Compliance and Leadership in Rural Communist China," presented to the 1965 annual meeting of the American Political Science Association, Washington, D.C. See also Garth N. Jones and Aslam Niaz, "Strategies and Tactics of Planned Organizational Change: A Scheme of Working Concepts," *Philippine Journal of Public Administration,* Vol. 7 (1963), pp. 275–285; Joseph Julian, "Compliance Patterns and Communication Blocks in Complex Organizations," *American Sociological Review,* Vol. 31 (1966), pp. 382–389; Zelda F. Gamson, "Utilitarian and Normative Orientations Toward Education," *Sociology of Education,* Vol. 39 (1966), pp. 46–73.

20. McCleery, *Policy Change . . . , op. cit.,* pp. 11–20.

21. Private communication with Immanuel Wallerstein.

22. The extent of this collaboration with the Nazis and its impact is much contested, but not the fact itself. Hannah Arendt, *Eichmann in Jerusalem* (New York: Viking Press, 1963), pp. 107–111; and Gideon Hausner, *Justice in Jerusalem* (New York: Harper & Row, 1966), pp. 156 ff.

23. For one of the few exceptions, see Marvin E. Wolfgang (ed.), special editor of issue on patterns of violence, *The Annals of the American Academy of Political and Social Science,* Vol. 364 (1966). On the neglect in the study of social violence, see *ibid.,* Lewis A. Coser, "Some Social Functions of Violence," *ibid.,* p. 8. See also Samuel P. Huntington, "Patterns of Violence in World Politics," in Huntington (ed.), *Changing Patterns of Military Politics* (New York: Free Press, 1962), pp. 44–47; Pierre Hassner, "Violence, Rationalité, Incertitude: Tendances Apocalyptiques et Iréniques Dans l'Étude des Conflits Internationaux," *Revue Française de Science Politique,* Vol. 14 (1964), pp. 1155–1178; and Vernon Fox, "Sociological and Political Aspects of Police Administration," *Sociology and Social Research,* Vol. 51, (1966), pp. 39–48.

24. Monseñor German Campos, Eduardo Unaña Lana, Orlando Fals-Borda, *La Violencia en Colombia* (Bogota: Ediciones Tercer Mundo, 1964). Especially Vol. II, for a detailed description of this period.

25. *The New York Times,* April 13, 1966; "Blood Bath with Reds on Receiving End," *U.S. News and World Report,* Vol. 60 (January 31, 1966), p. 34. Over 100,000 were executed without trial in France following liberation. Paul Sérant, *Les Vaincus de la Libération* (Paris: Robert Laffont, 1966).

26. Patricia Sexton, *Spanish Harlem* (New York: Harper & Row, 1965), pp. 109–116.

27. Daniel Bell, *The End of Ideology* (New York: Free Press, 1960), esp. 126, pp. 155–159.

28. For additional discussion and documentation of the following statements, see Etzioni, *Political Unification, op. cit.*

29. For instance, to use the kitchen for illicit whiskey brewing if they "behave."

Richard A. Cloward, "Social Control and Anomie: A Study of a Prison Community," (unpublished Ph.D. dissertation, Columbia University, 1959), pp. 148–149.

30. Robert K. Merton, *Mass Persuasion: The Social Psychology of a War Bond Drive* (New York: Harper & Row, 1946), pp. 45–47.

31. Immanuel Wallerstein, *Africa: Politics of Independence* (New York: Vintage Books, 1961), pp. 40–43, 64–65. "German administration, in contrast to the British, was 'direct' and was established in many instances on the ruins of indigenous tribal governing systems, not unlike those employed with great effectiveness in the implementation of indirect rule by the British in Uganda." Fred G. Burke, *Tanganyika: Preplanning* (Syracuse: Syracuse University Press, 1965), p. 93, Note 3.

32. Will Herberg, *Protestant–Catholic–Jew* (Garden City, New York: Doubleday, 1956), esp. pp. 256–272.

33. Monica Baldwin, *I Leap Over the Wall* (London: Hamilton, 1960).

34. For literary illustration based on a world the author knows well, see Jean-Paul Sartre, *Dirty Hands* in his *Three Plays* (New York: Knopf, 1949), pp. 1–152; translated by Lionel Abel. See also John Steinbeck, *In Dubious Battle* (New York: Modern Library, 1936).

35. See Dollard, *Caste and Class in a Southern Town, op. cit.*

36. A detailed analysis and some evidence are presented in Etzioni's *A Comparative Analysis . . . , op. cit.*; Chapter V of this previous publication deals with leadership, Chapter VI with communication and consensus, Chapter VII with scope and pervasiveness.

37. Stefan Rosada and Jozef Gwozdz, *Forced Labor and Confinement Without Trial in Poland* (Washington, D.C.: Mid-European Studies Center, 1952). See also Jerome N. Blum, *Noble Landowner and Agriculture in Austria, 1815–1848* (Baltimore: Johns Hopkins University Press, 1948), esp. pp. 142–202.

38. William A. Glaser, "Nursing Leadership and Policy: Some Cross-National Comparisons," in Fred Davis (ed.), *The Nursing Profession* (New York: Wiley & Sons, 1966), pp. 1–25, 43–45.

39. Skinner, *Compliance and Leaderships in Rural China, op. cit.*

40. *Ibid.*, p. 8.

41. Some data to this effect are now being made available by a comparative study of modernization in six countries by the Harvard Project on Social and Cultural Aspects of Development, directed by Alex Inkeles and to be published under the title "Being Modern."

42. On the organization of factories in various cultures see A. K. Rice, "Productivity and Social Organization in an Indian Weaving Shed," *Human Relations*, Vol. 4 (1953), pp. 399–428. Jiri Kolaja, *A Polish Factory: A Case Study of Workers' Participation in Decision-Making* (Lexington: University of Kentucky Press, 1960). Elliot Jacques, *The Changing Culture of a Factory* (London: Tavistock Publications, 1951). Arthur Niehoff, *Factory Workers in India* (Milwaukee: Public Museum, 1959). J. C. Abegglen, *The Japanese Factory: Aspects of its Social Organization* (New York: Free Press, 1958).

43. On Norwegian prisons see Thomas Mathiesen, *The Defences of the Weak* (London: Tavistock Publications, 1965), pp. 29–30, 40. Johan Galtung, "The Social Functions of a Prison," *Social Problems*, Vol. 6 (1958), pp. 127–140.

44. Stanton Wheeler, "Role Conflict in Correctional Communities," in Donald R.

Cressey (ed.), *The Prison: Studies in Institutional Organization and Change* (New York: Holt, Rinehart & Winston, 1961), pp. 243, 256–259.

45. Sidney Pollard, *The Genesis of Modern Management: A Study of the Industrial Revolution in Great Britain* (Cambridge, Mass.: Harvard University Press, 1965). Reinhard Bendix, *Work and Authority in Industry* (New York: Wiley & Sons, 1956), pp. 281–340.

46. Lloyd E. Ohlin, "The Reduction of Role Conflict in Institutional Staff," *Children*, Vol. 5 (1958), p. 65. See also H. E. Barnes, *The Evolution of Penology in Pennsylvania* (Indianapolis: Bobbs-Merrill, 1927). And his "Some Leading Phases of the Evolution of the Modern Penology," *Political Science Quarterly*, Vol. 37 (1922), pp. 251–280. J. H. S. Bossard, *The Sociology of Child Development* (New York: Harper & Row, rev. ed., 1954), pp. 593–657. D. R. Miller and G. E. Swanson, *The Changing American Parent* (New York: Wiley & Sons, 1958), p. 8.

47. Donald N. Michael is credited with coining the term. See his *Cybernation: The Silent Conquest* (Santa Barbara, Calif.: Center for the Study of Democratic Institutions, 1962).

48. Ida R. Hoos, *Automation in the Office* (Washington, D.C.: Public Affairs Press, 1961), pp. 45, 120.

49. Floyd C. Mann and L. Richard Hoffman, *Automation and the Worker: A Study of Social Change in Power Plants* (New York: Holt, 1960), pp. 60–64.

50. John Diebold, *Beyond Automation: Managerial Problems of An Exploding Technology* (New York: McGraw-Hill, 1964). Michael, *Cybernation, op. cit.* Ben B. Seligman, *Most Notorious Victory* (New York: Free Press, 1966).

51. Daniel Bell, "The Bogey of Automation," *The New York Review of Books*, Vol. 5 (August 26, 1965), p. 23.

52. Charles R. Walker and Robert H. Guest, *The Man on the Assembly Line* (Cambridge, Mass.: Harvard University Press, 1952), pp. 52–56, 62, 145. See also Chinoy, *Automobile Workers and the American Dream, op. cit.*

53. A large number and variety of studies reviewed by Likert show a minority which prefers close supervision, "harsh" supervisors, and so on, although his discussion naturally focuses on the large majorities which prefer less tight supervision, etc. See Rensis Likert, *New Patterns of Management* (New York: McGraw-Hill, 1961), esp. pp. 5–60.

54. Donald C. Pelz, "Some Social Factors Related to Performance in a Research Organization," *Administrative Science Quarterly*, Vol. 1 (1956), pp. 313–325. D. C. Pelz and F. M. Andrews, *Scientists in Organizations: Productive Climates for Research and Development* (New York: John Wiley & Sons, 1966), cf. these findings to those of other Michigan studies, of blue and white collar workers cited in footnote 16.

55. There are many other factors at work. It ought to be noted though that the size of the welfare state may well be less prominent than has often been argued, as the appeal of the unions is weaker among white collar and semi-professionals than it is to blue collar workers, while these benefit more from the welfare state, especially unemployed benefits and relief.

56. For British approach to drugs, see Edwin M. Schur, *Narcotic Addiction in Britain and America* (Bloomington, Ind.: Indiana University Press, 1962). See also Bernard Barber, *Drugs and Society* (New York: Russell Sage Foundation, 1967), *passim.*

57. J. Sanbourne Bockoven, "Some Relationships Between Cultural Attitudes Toward Individuality and Care of the Mentally Ill: An Historical Study," in Milton Greenblatt, Daniel J. Levinson, Richard H. Williams (eds.), *The Patient and the Mental Hospital* (New York: Free Press, 1957), pp. 517–526. See also Albert Deutsch, *The Mentally Ill in America* (New York: Columbia University Press, 1949).

58. See, for instance, reports on reforms in Bicetre in France (beginning with 1793) and York Asylum in Britain (after 1792). George W. Henry, "Mental Hospitals," in Gregory Zilboorg, *A History of Medical Psychology* (New York: W. W. Norton, 1941), pp. 571–572. On the Japanese treatment of mental patients, which dates from pre-modern days, see William A. Caudill, "Similarities and Differences in Psychiatric Illness and Its Treatment in the U.S. and Japan," *Mental Hygiene*, Vols. 61–62 (1954), pp. 15–26. Hutterite communities take care of the mental patients at home rather than in a hospital. See Joseph W. Eaton and Robert J. Weil, *Culture and Mental Disorders*, (New York: Free Press, 1955.) See also Paul K. Benedict and Irving Jacks, "Mental Illness in Primitive Societies," *Psychiatry*, Vol. 17 (1954), pp. 377–389.

59. The signalling role of violence is stressed by Hirschman, *Journey Toward Progress, op. cit.*, esp. pp. 155, 212, 229–230. For a fine discussion of the steps leading toward outbreaks of violence, see Neil J. Smelser, *Theory of Collective Behavior* (New York: Free Press, 1963), esp. pp. 247–270.

60. In *Ideology and Power in Soviet Politics* (New York: Praeger, 1962), Brzezinski observes that in recent years the Soviet leaders have attempted to increase indoctrination and decrease terror as a means of societal control, pp. 71–82.

CHAPTER 15

Societal Mobilization

and Societal Change

I N OUR attempt to explain why some societal actors realize more of their goals than others—even though these others command similar knowledge and assets and act in basically the same environments—the higher commitment of the actors who realize more of their goals seems to be a major factor. Most societal units most of the time commit only a small fraction of their assets, constituents, and attention to the pursuit of their collective goals. The size of this fraction is a measure of their societal commitment. Under what conditions this commitment is high instead of low and increases instead of declines are the basic questions for the study of societal mobilization. The same statement, put into terms of societal control, reads: the degree to which a particular controlling overlayer is able to implement the designs its cybernetic centers outline is significantly affected by the amount of energy it is able to mobilize.*

---

* This, of course, may be the overlayer of a social movement rather than of an establishment and the intellectual and political elites rather than a computer center.

Mobilization is the process by which energy that is latent from the viewpoint of the acting unit is made available for collective action. A more mobilized unit can get more done collectively either by increasing the number of goals it realizes or by increasing the intensity with which it pursues those goals it is already realizing. The concept of societal commitment was briefly encountered in our discussion of the relations of assets to power, especially when we dealt with conversion ratios and patterns. Here, we examine, in much more detail, the question: How are societal guidance and societal change "energized?" And, rather than treating the level of commitment as given, we view it as a dynamic quality and explore the conditions under which it is altered and the effects of changes in it on societal change.

It is essential in this discussion to maintain the differences among sub-units, units, and supra-units, because mobilization of one entity often entails the de-mobilization of some others. The first and second sections of this chapter deal with the basic concept of mobilization as it applies to all three kinds of entities. The third and fourth sections are concerned with the mobilization of a unit, be it a collectivity or a society, and with the implications of this process for its sub-units. The fifth and sixth sections deal with the relation of the mobilization of one unit to that of others—inter-unit mobilizations—and with supra-unit mobilization. In short, after a "universal" introduction, we deal first with mobilization as an internal process and then with its "external", interactional and system, aspects.

The Concept and Its Measurements

Mobilization Defined

We refer to the process by which a unit gains significantly in the control of assets it previously did not control as *mobilization*.* By definition, it entails a decline in the assets controlled by sub-units, the supra-unit of which the unit is a member, or external units, unless the assets whose control the unit gained are newly-produced ones. (New assets may also be studied in the same framework: Who would have gained control of them had no mobilization occurred? That is, mobilization may entail the loss of potential control for some actors and a gain of potential control for the mobilizing one.) A mere increase in the assets of members, of sub-units, or even of the unit itself

---

* The term "mobilization" has recently been used by a variety of writers in a number of different ways which are not wholly consistent with each other. The term has also been used more to develop other concepts, such as modernization, mobility, and integration, than in its own right. Also, the concept has been frequently used to refer both to the process of mobilization and to the degree to which a unit is mobilized. We suggest that the above definition is analytically independent of other concepts and limited to mobilization as a process. It is compared to other definitions below.

does not mean that mobilization has occurred, though it increases the mobilization potential. The change in the capacity to control and to use assets is what is significant.

Depending on the kinds of assets involved, mobilization is coercive (as when feudal lords turn their armies over to the control of the king), utilitarian (as when a state raises the level of taxation), or normative (as when loyalties to the nation are increased, while those to local communities decline).*

While the mobilization of a unit tends to increase the power of its controlling overlayer, mobilization itself is affected by this overlayer and is often initiated and directed by it. When mobilization occurs, the controlling overlayer, as a rule, invests part of the assets it already controls in an effort to increase its power.

Mobilization, thus, has a cost. Even when it is normative support or consensus that is mobilized, mobilization still is a "downward" process— from a controlling overlayer to the controlled member units. The relations of the mobilization of consensus to consensus-formation, an upward process, are explored below. The main point is that when the *direction* of mobilization (the unit(s) which gain in control), its *scope* (the sectors encompassed), and its *intensity* (the extent of the change within each sector) do not coincide with what is legitimate for and supported by the evolving consensus, mobilization generates alienation in the same ways as other exercises of power. That is, the cost of mobilization depends upon the kind and intensity of the power used to accomplish it.

The minor and non-accumulative fluctuations in the level of control which, in effect, are continually occurring are excluded from the concept to restrict the concept of mobilization to the study of relatively encompassing or intensive changes in the control structure (i.e., in the pattern of the distribution of control among units, sub-units and supra-units). Thus, mobilization is, by definition, both a process of change (in the control structure) and a changing process (of societal structures and, as we shall see, of boundaries).

Mobilization as a Process of Change

To state that mobilization is a process of change is to place the concept in the analytic classification of societal processes; the latter are characterized in terms of which of two broad categories of functions they for the most part serve. Processes of *maintenance* support an existing system and/or its structure. (This may include some changes "within the system.") The underlying assumption is that all societal systems tend toward entropy—i.e., toward atomization and anarchy—unless continual investments are made in

---

* This classification is not concerned with the means used to bring about the particular mobilization, but with what has been mobilized.

maintaining their levels of integration and organization. Processes of *change* entail a more-or-less permanent modification of the boundaries of the system or its structure—its patterns of integration and organization. While maintenance processes are continually operative, processes of change are more sporadic and probably vary more in their intensity. Any concrete societal process may serve either function or varying degrees of both functions; e.g., the production of new means of control might merely replenish used means, alter the allocative pattern, or accomplish varying degrees of both of these. That mobilization is a process of change rather than of maintenance is evident in that if it were continued ad infinitum, it would exhaust itself; either all the assets would come under unit control and no further increase in asset control would be possible, or, in the case of unit demobilization, the control of all the assets would be assumed by or delegated to other units, sub-units, or supra-units.

We shall refer to the *level* of unit-mobilization when we seek to refer to the degree to which a unit is mobilized—i.e., the fraction of the assets that are controlled by the unit as compared to those controlled by its sub-units or supra-unit; the process of change, of altering this control ratio, is referred to as mobilization.*

Some social scientists have used "mobilization" to refer to a sub-set of maintenance processes—in particular, to the continual socialization and social control processes which maintain a particular societal or political structure.[1]† They cite as examples of these processes the efforts of ideological political parties to maintain the commitment of their members and followers and the attempts of totalitarian states to sustain legitimation of their political organization. It seems to us more useful to reserve the term for changes in the controlling overlayers or guidance mechanisms.

The concept of mobilization was first used to refer to the shifting of the control of resources from private–civilian to public–military purposes.[2] More recently, it has been applied to a society's (or collectivity's) deliberate increase in the control of a variety of assets, such as new nations' mobilization of economic resources for development or a civil rights movement's mobilization of the attention of previously less attentive and inattentive citizens. The characteristic which these processes share with military mobilization is that they all entail an increase in the assets the unit under study controls collectively, which increases the unit's ability to act in unison within the limits explored below.

---

* The level of mobilization and the conversion ratio are identical concepts with different perspectives. The level of mobilization calls attention to the processes which created the particular conversion ratio we find. The conversion ratio is a static and comparative concept.

† Reference notes for this chapter appear on page 422.

The Measurement of Mobilization

The measurement of mobilization requires specification of: (a) the unit whose mobilization is being measured; (b) the time period under study; (c) the ratio of assets under unit control as against those controlled by sub-units, supra-units, or external units at the beginning as compared to the end of the period; and (d) the kinds of assets studied. The assets that are included depend on the kind of mobilization—utilitarian, normative, coercive, or general societal mobilization which encompasses all three kinds.[3]

It is relatively easy to measure *utilitarian* mobilization. For instance, one aspect which can be measured quite readily is changes in the control of manpower—e.g., the ratio of people employed by the mobilizing unit as against the sub-units. A relative increase in the ratio of those employed by a federal government as against state and local governments is a measure of the centralization of the system and the power of unit-controls as compared to sub-unit ones.* The same holds for the percentage of the GNP taxed by all levels of government and the distribution of these funds among them.[4]

Coercive mobilization, reflected in changes in the control of troops, arms, and so on, is also relatively easy to measure. On the other hand, it is more difficult to develop reliable measurements of *normative* mobilization, e.g., changes of loyalties. Changes of attitudes expressed in sequential public opinion polls provide one indicator. Changes in the frequency of the use of various symbols in the press have been used to study historical changes of loyalties.[5]

An interesting measure of the relative and changing level of mobilization of a collectivity into a polity is the extent of its "bloc" voting—i.e., the degree to which its members vote as one unit, "suppressing" other dimensions of potential political mobilization. This is a potentially deceptive indicator because factors other than the level of mobilization affect the extent of bloc-voting—for instance, changes in the amount of education and alienation of the membership over time. But a comparison of the extent of bloc voting in different collectivities—for instance, ethnic ones—seems to provide quite meaningful measures of mobilization, and other factors may be controlled to enable genetic comparisons.[6]

The *mobilization potential* of a unit is probably the most difficult aspect to measure. Not all the assets the sub-units control at one point in time are available (even potentially) for unit-mobilization at later points; some assets are, in effect, "unmobilizable" under most conditions and for almost

---

* This is only a partial measure, as the changing relationships between the unit and the sub-units must also be taken into account. If the ratio of employees of the federal government over those of local and state governments were to decline but the control of the sub-units by the unit's controlling overlayer were to increase, there may have occurred no net loss in the power of the unit.

any goal. The mobilization potential of a unit is, hence, best defined as that portion of the assets which can, in effect, be mobilized under given conditions for a given goal.

The Main Theoretical Considerations

Mobilization as a Societal Energizer

The concept of mobilization answers the analytic question: What is the source of the energy for *societal* action? As the libido is "mobilized" by the various mechanisms of the personality to energize its actions *and* the work of these mechanisms, so are the assets of member sub-units, unused from the unit's viewpoint, made available—through the processes of mobilization—to "energize" (or cover the "costs") of the actions *and* controls of the unit.

Maximum unit-mobilization, however, does not assure maximum realization of the goals of the mobilizing unit because some of these goals tend best to be served by activities of the sub-units; hence, these sub-units must retain some of the assets and manpower. To some degree, these statements about the relations between unit and sub-unit actions (or performances) also hold for the controlling processes: The activities in the service of some *unit*-goals are controlled by *sub*-units' overlayers. But, we suggest, if a unit's goals are to be realized to a high degree, the ratio of unit-*controls* over sub-units' controls needs to be higher than the ratio of unit-*activities* over sub-units' activities, because unit-goals are realized to a greater extent if some of the *sub*-units' activities are controlled by the unit rather than by the sub-units. The realization of unit-goals is expected to be greater if, in addition, the relations *among* the sub-units are in part regulated by the unit and not determined only by the existing bonds among the sub-units, their relative power, their unregulated interaction, or other "ongoing" processes. Thus, the high realization of unit-goals requires that unit-mobilization provide assets for both unit-activities and for unit-controls, but especially for the latter.

To Mobilize Is to Collectivize

The transformation that mobilization entails is collectivization—not necessarily of ownership but of effective control. The assets themselves may remain in their original locations and need not necessarily be directly transferred to or used by a controlling elite or organization. It is, rather, the unit's capacity to control the use of the assets—including those held by the sub-units—that is increased. For example, to the degree that corporations can be instructed to follow government-set "guidelines," a gain in the national level of mobilization is achieved. Or, more indirectly, by issuing large sums of money (i.e., by generating an inflation), a state can gain control of the assets of some member-collectivities (e.g., those collectivities whose assets are in the form of savings and whose incomes are fairly "fixed") without orders being issued to or even requests being made of the collectivities.

Whatever the form of mobilization, whether it be direct or indirect, the process entails a shift of control and/or a shift of the usage of assets, except when the newly-available assets come from external sources. Since the ratio of the assets used by a societal unit over the assets used by the sub-units increases, *mobilization makes the societal unit* in toto *less private, more public, and, hence, more politically intensive.**

Mobilization Is a Control Concept

Mobilization, like decision-making, social planning, and other related concepts, implies a collective actor who is capable of controlling societal processes, at least to some degree, and is not merely subject to them. Thus, mobilization is viewed as a drive which is, at least in part, deliberately initiated, directed, and terminated, and not as a by-product or an outgrowth of the "interaction" among macro-units or as a compilation of the decisions of myriad micro-units. This is not to imply that mobilization has no unanticipated consequences or that the actor's controlling overlayer is in full or even in considerable command of the fluctuations of the process; however, there is the assumption of a voluntary element, represented by one or more sub-units—such as a government, an organizational leadership, or a regional council—which are steering the process. That is, the societal change involved is, in part, intended.

Mobilization as a Changing Force

The theory of societal guidance differs most from other theories in contemporary social science in that it sees the mobilization drives of collectivities and societies as a major source of their own transformations and of the transformations of their relations to other societal units. As a societal unit mobilizes, we shall see in some detail below, it tends to change its own structure and boundaries *and* the structure of the supra-unit of which it is a member. For instance, the drive of West European societies to overcome the disintegrative and depleting effects of World War II entailed both internal transformation (in favor of those collectivities represented by "center" parties) and the initiation of a trans-national community. De-Stalinization, a process of de-mobilization, not only altered the internal structures of East European communist societies but also de-unified the bloc and made it less

---

* The level of political intensity refers to the ratio of societal activities which are politically controlled as compared to those which are not.

like an empire and somewhat more like a commonwealth.[7] To stress the importance of mobilization as a transforming force is not to underplay the roles of new ideas, of changes in the means of production, or of forces in the societal environment as sources of societal change.[8] But these are, to varying degrees, extra-societal (especially for any given society as distinct from societies in general). The most central *intra*-societal source of change, as we see it, is the successful drive on the part of one or more collectivities or of the society at large to mobilize new internal or external sources of energy. Most other intra-societal changes in this direction tend to establish the conditions which provide the *pre*requisites for increases in the unit's activities. Mobilization is the process by which potentials are brought closer to actualization; the raw material is processed to provide the societal energy to fuel the pursuit of societal goals, and energy locked in other entities is made available.

Marx argued that history is propelled by inter-class struggle;[9] we hold that the acting units are often collectivities whose primary base is not shared economic interests but shared values and statuses, especially ethnic ones, and that the relationships among collectivities are various mixes of conflict and cooperation and not only "struggles." Even more importantly, *the struggle that is most significant for the explanation of societal change, of history, is one which is internal to each collectivity (and society). This is the struggle to mobilize under the given conditions and for the purpose of changing them; it occurs between the mobilizers and the unmobilized* in one and the same collectivity (or society). Were all the members of a collectivity (or a society) to mobilize all of their assets and themselves in support of a line of collective action, it would be as if all the latent energy locked in a pound of material were released and transformed into power; it would propel the collectivity into the highest levels of activeness and alter the societal map.

Of course, mobilization drives are themselves affected by external conditions. Lower collectivities find it more difficult to mobilize than collectivities which rank higher in the societal structure. And environmental conditions affect the mobilization process—for instance, the United States' penetration of Japan in 1853 triggered the internal mobilization of the society under state guidance.[10] But these external conditions, it should be emphasized, do not determine the level of mobilization; rather, they provide new options that may or may not be exercised. Western powers penetrated into Japan and China at about the same time, for example, but Japan mobilized to a much greater extent than China.[11] Although every mobilization drive (or lack thereof) can in part be explained by factors outside and beyond the control of the societal unit under study, the drives are also greatly affected by the internal makeup of the collectivity or the society and by changes within it; among these factors, the initial level of mobilization ranks high in importance. And while this level of mobilization might be partly determined by environmental forces that operated earlier to shape the "character," to set the conversion ratio and pattern of the societal unit, the effects of these earlier forces and the degree to which the societal unit submits to them are significantly affected by the unit's collective decisions and efforts. And, to a degree, the unit participated and participates in shaping the environment that, in turn, "shapes" its internal makeup; it is not merely passively subject to that environment.

In the next two sections, we explore the common levels of mobilization and the ways in which they can be altered to make for more mobilized and more active societal units. A further step must be taken, however, for the mobilization of one unit may be neutralized by that of others or blocked by the supra-unit. The last two sections, therefore, explore the relations among unit, inter-unit, and supra-unit mobilization. It suffices to say here, by way of introduction, that the mobilization of units (e.g., collectivities) does significantly change the supra-unit (e.g., societies), though the scope and quality of this change depend on the specific inter-unit and inter-level relationships.

Before the discussion can be advanced, two points related to the differences between the internal (unit: sub-unit) and the external (inter-unit and unit: supra-unit) aspects of the process must be noted. First, the mobilization of a unit—as a process of change—may be solely internal (limited to the mobilization of sub-unit assets to unit controls), or it may also be external, drawing on the assets of other units or supra-units. Second, while mobilization may be aimed at a variety of goals, viewed as a changing process the most relevant distinctions are between changing structure and changing boundaries and between changing the structure or boundaries of the mobilizing unit (self-change), of other units, or of the relations of the actors to each other. We shall see that there are systematic differences from this viewpoint, the most significant of which is that mobilization for self-change is politically much more costly than mobilization for changing others. Compare, for example, the mobilization for social welfare goals to the mobilization for war. But it is precisely such mobilization for self-change which is the most necessary for activating a society, and, hence, it provides the focus for the following discussion.

The Levels of Internal Mobilization: A Comparative Dimension

Typically, the Level of Mobilization is Low

The levels of mobilization of pluralistic-modern societies and of most member-collectivities tend to be low. Most of the assets are controlled by individuals and micro-social units (such as families, friendship and peer groups) and not by society at large, society-wide organizations (such as armies and churches), or collectivities and their organizational arms. The average level of·mobilization seems to have increased only slightly since the advent of the post-modern period.

These statements about the typical levels of mobilization are a major way in which social science perceptions of society differ from those of common sense; the latter often (a) see the level of societal mobilization as high, and (b) tend to view a low level of mobilization as a sign of weakness if not of degeneration. The expression of the notion that societal mobilization is at a high level is found most clearly in conservative views of the welfare state. But even liberals (in the American sense of the term), who tend to favor a somewhat higher level of societal mobilization, tend to believe that the existing level—e.g., about 15 to 20 per cent taxation of the GNP—is fairly high and that additional mobilization has to be limited in scope and cautious in pace lest the economic, social, or political foundations of pluralistic societies be endangered. In a typical statement, the National Board of Americans for Democratic Action, the only nation-wide liberal political organization in the United States, called, in December of 1966, for a $5 to $10 billion increase in federal spending on poverty, urban affairs, unemployment, and all other social welfare programs combined.[12] (The 1965 GNP was $676.3 billion, and the 1965 Federal expenditures were $96.5 billion.)[13]

The tendency to associate a low level of mobilization with weakness or degeneration is well illustrated by the prevailing view of public opinion and information. It is frequently assumed that the public ought to be well informed on public matters (i.e., its attention ought to be highly mobilized), and public opinion surveys which show that between a quarter and a half of the population lacks basic political information (e.g., 28 per cent of American adults did not know in 1965 that there was a communist government in China)[14] are viewed with alarm and a sense of loss and decline. Actually, so many polls have shown that the extent to which the public is informed about many public matters is limited, that this is to be viewed as "typical." In June, 1952, two months before he was nominated as the Democratic Presidential candidate, Adlai Stevenson was unknown to 66 per cent of the American public; 67 per cent of the adult Americans in 1955 could not identify Karl Marx. While only 45 per cent did not know the number of United States senators from their states, only 19 per cent could name the three branches of the Federal government, few more than a third knew the names of their Congressmen, and less than half knew which party controlled Congress.[15]

We favor treating a given percentage of correct answers as a "typical" base for information concerning most matters in which a public of a given country in a given historical period—particularly, developed societies in the post-modern period—is not personally and directly involved. (Different "bases" may be used for various sectors—e.g., 35–50 per cent as "normal" for public health matters as compared to 10–25 per cent for foreign affairs.) An information level that is higher than the base would be characterized as "high" and an information level below it as "low." Forty-five per cent correct answers, then, would seem unusually high for most matters and would need to be explained.[16] Twenty-five per cent correct answers on many kinds of questions would not seem at all a sign of social decay.

Again, it is seen as a weakness that many American labor unions cannot "deliver" more than approximately a third of their members' votes for the presidential candidate they endorse.[17] We suggest that a highly mobilized union is rare, and that it is more fruitful to compare actual levels of mobilization to each other than to compare them to the abstract notion of a fully mobilized union. Thus, American labor unions which can "deliver" a third of their members' votes might well have a higher capacity for mobilizing their members than most other voluntary associations.*

On most matters in most modern pluralistic societies (and, for the most part, in post-modern ones) most of the time, more assets are spent by the individual, his family, and his peer units than by any larger unit.[18] The percentage of the GNP that is taxed is a rough indicator of this ratio. In the United States, toward the end of the modern period (1938), it was 13 per cent. In the post-modern period, it was only slightly higher—about 19 per cent (in 1962). The ratios were about the same in "social democratic" countries, such as in the Scandinavian ones: In Sweden they were 14 per cent in 1938 and 18 per cent in 1962 (in Denmark, respectively, 13 per cent and 21 per cent). In short, most assets most of the time are not mobilized for collective usages, and, while this is a sign of passivity, it is by itself not a sign of social disintegration or entropy.

Crisis Mobilization and the "Permanent Revolution"

This section discusses the "surprising" increase in the capacity for societal action when the level of mobilization is sharply increased, which occurs in crisis situations. Thus, when natural disasters occur, many communities show a capacity to rapidly construct large networks of public assistance. Typically, they use the mechanism of the redistribution of resource control, particularly in utilizing time which the citizens usually spend in private pursuits for public service.[19] In the pre-mobilization days of the mid-1950s, the civil rights movement in Chicago, a city of 750,000 Negroes, could not raise $10,000 for the Urban League. NAACP meetings were attended by less than fifty people, and usually no more than three or four of the three hundred Negro lawyers were willing to volunteer to work for the legal defense of

---

* The extent to which an organization mobilizes has to be explored in "typical" years, and the vote that would in any case be cast in favor of the candidate because of socioeconomic, ethnic, and other such "background" factors, must be discounted. Or the rates of mobilization when an organization supported and opposed candidates of the same party may be compared—ideally, the same candidate in different elections, "deducting" the differences in his general appeal to a collectivity of the kind the organization he is mobilizing.

victims of racial persecution.[20] In the crisis period of 1966–1967, much larger amounts of money and manpower were available.[21] Social movements are relatively highly mobilized collectivities, war induces relatively highly mobilized societies,[22] but both are atypical, crisis mobilizations.

It should be emphasized that while crisis-mobilization is considerable in comparison to the "normal" mobilization level of the average collectivity in a pluralistic society or to the mobilization of these kinds of societies themselves, the level of mobilization tends not to be high in an absolute sense.[23] Thus, even if mobilization in a crisis triples the amount of societal energy, no more than a third of the potential assets, manpower, and attention of the members may actually be mobilized. Quite often, the fraction is smaller. From 1960 to 1965, the American civil rights movement was greatly aided by a student movement in the North, but actually not more than 5,000 students out of more than 5,000,000—less than one in one thousand—were involved. Although the estimates of the number of students involved in the New Left—which gained increasing attention in the same period and affected university structure and organization—4 per cent, was considered high.[24]

Uprisings of "the people" or "the masses" to bring about changes in regimes have, as a rule, involved fewer than 5 per cent of the population, usually mainly residents of the capital and a few other cities (e.g., Cairo, 1952; La Paz, 1952). To the degree that other indicators of the extents of such mobilizations are available, such as the budgets of revolutionary or independence movements, their expenditures seem quite low in comparison to the average annual expenditures of the populations involved. The three major full-time armed units of the Israeli independence movement, the *Palmach*, *Irgun*, and *Stern* groups, together had not more than 10,000 men, even at the height of the anti-British drive, in a community of 600,000. The Viet Cong was estimated, in 1964, to have had a hard core of about 35,000 people who carried the major part of the Vietnam war before North Vietnam units intervened.[25] (The population of South Vietnam was about fourteen million at the time.) The French Revolution was launched by as many as 80,000 persons (the second invasion of the Tuilleries; the march on Versailles); only about 800 or 900 stormed the Bastille.[26]

The image of the popular uprising as involving "the" peasants, workers, Negroes, or colonial people is almost invariably inaccurate. The mass membership of the collectivities involved is usually only marginally active; while the level of mobilization of this mass might double and triple during a crisis, the mobilization is generally limited to some economic support and sympathy for the movement. Thus, the societal assets mobilized—those that energize such transformations as revolutions, de-colonization, and wars of independence—are often only a small fraction of those potentially available. That is, major societal changes are propelled by small changes in the absolute level of mobilization because they constitute sharp increases in the *relative* level of energy available. Thus, without approaching a level even approximating full mobilization, there seems to be considerable leeway for a higher level of societal action.

The main questions for the transformation toward an active society are whether or not societies can mobilize themselves and their member collectivities to high, crisis-like if not higher, levels in *non*-crisis situations, and whether or not they can generate power for internal, self-transformations instead of exerting their wills on other societies. Further, can this level and kind of mobilization be attained without generating so many counter-currents and so much alienation that the consensual base of society and values related to it will be undermined as the realization of the values expressed in the goals advanced is enhanced? In short, is a "permanent revolution," a continual and authentic social-movement society, possible?

From this viewpoint, post-modern societies are further from the level of mobilization required by active societies than modern societies were from post-modern ones prior to the introduction of income taxes, social security systems, and large-scale governmental staffs. All of these post-modern measures entail a level of mobilization that would have seemed inconceivably high to most of the members of earlier generations. The active society requires the same (or a higher) level of mobilization for self-transformation that post-modern pluralistic societies can maintain for external purposes. But an active society must be more authentically consensual, so that a high level of mobilization will not produce a society that is as distorted as those which are war oriented or geared to the maximization of production.

Finally, mobilization in an active society will have to be broad in scope as well as at a high level, i.e., it should not be focused around a few societal projects. In conversion terms, while non-active, pluralistic societies tend to mobilize partly by increasing their conversion ratios, they also focus their conversion patterns, i.e., they take energy away from other goals and shift it toward the prevailing one. The neglect of societal welfare in times of war is a typical example. (This mobilization procedure is typical to instrumental rationality.) An active society will require a comprehensively higher realization of all its major goals, and this cannot be achieved by focusing the conversion pattern but rather by greatly increasing the general amount of assets available and the over-all conversion ratio. In this way, societal energy can be increased rather than increasing that available to one societal goal at the cost of others, especially at the cost of self-transformation.* The additional tools that would be necessary for a *permanently* significantly higher level of mobilization will be explored below.[27]

Activists in social movements decry the low levels of mobilization of their movements and the apathy of groups of their followers. Bakunin at the end

---

* The budget of self-oriented programs may rise somewhat in war years, but the neglect will express itself in the decline of that budget in terms of its proportion of the GNP, and the total governmental budget, and, above all, that devoted to the particular societal need.

of his life was disillusioned by the apathy of the masses, and Lassalle railed at "the damned wantlessness of the poor."[28] To a degree, these disillusionments are in themselves a means of mobilization rather than attempts at sociological analysis. When they are accepted as valid sociological perspectives, however, it should be stressed that apathy and a low level of mobilization are as universal features of collectivities and societies as are the internal struggles between the mobilizers and the unmobilized. These characteristics are less visible in charismatic movements, crises or confrontations, and are more visible in other, more common situations, but they are present in both. They are more evident in some social movements than in others (e.g., more in moderate movements than in militant ones, more in "open" churches than in selective sects, and more in movements in their decline than in those at their apex), but the basic features are universal. Hence, the focus of social analysis ought to be the *relative* and *changing* differences in mobilization levels rather than the search for the utopia of a full, egalitarian, leaderless, consensual mobilization.

Structural Differentiations

At any given point in time, the collectivities of a society can be compared (as can the societies which compose a trans-societal system) in terms of both their relative assets and their relative levels of mobilization. Such a comparison leads to the concept of a *mobilization-structure* which, it is well-established, is highly inegalitarian. Evidence in support of this statement is available although mainly in atomistic, individualistic terms. Milbrath, summarizing a large number of studies about pluralistic societies, especially the United States, at the onset of the post-modern period, stated that only about 4 or 5 per cent of the American adult population is active politically (holds office, solicits funds for a political purpose, contributes time to a campaign, and so forth). "About 10 per cent make monetary contributions, about 13 per cent contact public officials, and about 15 per cent display a button or sticker. Around 25 to 30 per cent try to proselyte others to vote a certain way, and from 40 to 70 per cent perceive political messages and vote in any given election."[29] "About one-third of the American adult population can be characterized as politically apathetic or passive; in most cases, they are unaware, literally, of the political part of the world around them."[30]

For macro-sociological analysis, it is essential to take into account that the passive, semi-active, and active members of a society are very unevenly distributed among the member collectivities and among the sub-collectivities which constitute a collectivity. Studies for practically all pluralistic societies show that collectivities whose members are more affluent, prestigious, and educated also have a higher ratio of active and semi-active members and seem to be more active collectively.[31] Data for differences among sub-collectivities within collectivities, such as upper-working class versus working class *in toto* or urban workers versus workers *in toto*, are somewhat less abundant but almost equally unanimous.

As the mobilization of a societal unit encompasses not only its economic resources but also its membership—both as manpower and in terms of their psychological assets (e.g., loyalties, attention), we can say that the extent to which a collectivity or society marshals itself, or commits itself, is at stake. This capacity is *in part* determined by the unit's position in the societal stratification structure. Units which are low in assets *tend* to be less in command of themselves than those which have more assets, because the power of the higher units is used not only to counteract the power of the lower units but also to constrain their levels of mobilization and, hence, their capacity to generate additional power as well. That is, there is a degree of parallelism between the mobilization and the stratification structures. This parallelism seems to exist because (1) societal units higher in stratification position (i.e., access to assets) tend to be more mobilized, since being high in this structure seems to facilitate mobilization *and* (2) because those less mobilized tend to be kept low in the stratification structure.

There is a tendency to view the stratification position as a cause and the level of mobilization (or capacity to mobilize) as resulting from it.[32] In contrast, we wish to stress the interaction effect of the two factors. This effect is particularly evident when new collectivity or society-wide movements rise. These often entail the mobilization of heretofore less mobilized or unmobilized collectivities or societies, which are often relatively low in the stratification structure. As there then are both mobilized and unmobilized units which are low in the structure, *being low in stratification in itself explains only in part the level of mobilization.* Further, the level of mobilization can be increased before a significant change in stratification position occurs.

Mobilization is more likely to be initiated if one or more of the following conditions is met: (a) if a stratification imbalance has been created due to an increase in one kind of assets but not in other kinds—e.g., an increase in utilitarian but not in normative assets (*nouveau riche*); (b) if a decrease in one or more kinds of assets has occurred, whether it is balanced or not (downward mobility); and (c) when external elites—either from a more mobilized collectivity of the same society (e.g., the middle-class leaders of early labor movements) or from a different society (Cubans in Bolivia)— help to launch the process.[33] We turn now from the exploration of the level of mobilization and the structural conditions related to it to the study of the process itself.

Mobilization as an Intra-Unit Process

In what ways does an internal mobilization process start, evolve, and mature? An important factor in answering this question is the unit's level of mobilization at the point at which a new mobilization drive is initiated. For highly mobilized units, "ceiling effects" are to be expected and retard the extent of additional mobilization. Most units most of the time, though, are only slightly affected by this factor, because their levels of mobilization are far from high. So far as these units are concerned, the main difference is between those which are mobilized in part and those which are largely unmobilized. The drive to increase the mobilization of the first kind of unit is of little analytic interest, as previous mobilizations tend to provide the instruments, procedures, and experience upon which to build later drives. A new set of decrees or taxes or an increase in the draft quota are cases in point. Of much more interest is the mobilization of collectivities or societies which are largely unmobilized.

A part of the study of such units concerns the pre-disposing conditions which usually change in favor of mobilization in the period preceding its initiation. The average levels of income and education tend to rise in the preceding decades (though not necessarily in the very last years before a mobilization drive is launched; actually, interruptions of such trends often trigger mobilization). It is these predisposing factors which are usually stressed in the collectivistic approach. We seek to emphasize that while such changes in the pre-conditions do enhance the possibility that a mobilization drive will be launched, they do not determine whether or not it will be initiated; they are auxiliary but not sufficient conditions.

A factor which often does spark the drive is the presence of an external elite (or elites); intellectuals, students, clergy, and foreign elites are especially likely catalytic agents. But, again, the spark must ignite an internal force before the process takes off. What can be said about this internal process? Here, we stress the role of personal and collective projects as providing the internal stimulus, followed by a slow chain-reaction from one sub-collectivity to additional and more encompassing ones, guided by internal leadership and organizations.

The following discussion of these factors draws on an accumulation or "value-added" model.[34] That is, we first discuss the factor which initiates a large number of processes. Only a sub-set takes-off from every such initiation. For those processes which do take-off, we ask: What is added? Of all Y processes that both were initiated and have taken-off, only a sub-set expands to encompass a *relatively* large sub-section of the unmobilized assets of a societal unit. We then ask: What is added at this round to those processes? As a full model must also explore the causes of the failures,[35] the processes which did not take-off or expand, we turn to those following our discussion of the factors involved in successful mobilizations. (See "limits of mobilization" and Part V.)

The factors which make for a successful mobilization drive are treated as if they relate to each other both in a Guttman-scale manner—in that if the latter factors are present, the earlier ones are expected to be present too, and in an ever-narrowing cone-shaped sequence of filters—in that there are more processes which pass through the first filter than through the second, and more that pass through the second than through the third.

Projects and Mobilization Take-off

The take-off stage of an internal mobilization is often marked by increasing numbers of collective projects. A *project* is a concerted effort which entails the focusing of energy and a comparatively intensive and guided activity oriented toward specific tasks. A village may make its project the building of a school or the provision of illiterates with basic literacy skills within a year. But to maintain a school system or to educate is not a project; it is a set of activities. In principle, a project may be personal, microscopic, or macroscopic; it may use energy which was already mobilized or serve as a mobilization effort. Here, we are interested in projects which typically indicate the take-off stage of the mobilization of a heretofore largely unmobilized societal unit.

Projects tend to entail mobilization (at least in terms of a focusing of the conversion pattern) because they involve a higher expenditure of energy than the ongoing activities. The Montgomery bus boycott and the Boston Tea Party were typical projects. Hence, the double interest in projects: As a form of mobilization and as preparing a unit for further mobilization.

While projects have a cost, they are primarily a means of tapping new, heretofore latent, assets; their importance lies in that they, like other catalytic agents, may release much more energy than they themselves can use or command. This is more than a mere analogy. There are two reasons that a project may act as a societal catalyst. First, the "walls" which kept the members and elites of a low collectivity from mobilizing may be "psychological," and the projects—which test them—show that they are "unreal" and thus dispel them, releasing the blocked energy. For example, the members of the elites of a low collectivity may hesitate to challenge the elites of a higher one because of the severe deprivations they experienced in the past when they engaged in such a challenge. If a project shows that these past experiences are no longer predictive of the future or were misinterpreted, considerable mobilization may follow. Or, the constraints may be "real" but their power may be overestimated; a project may suffice to remove them. Sometimes, the walls of Jericho do tumble at the sound of a trumpet. Finally, in those cases in which the constraints do prove too powerful and unyielding, projects may build collective consciousness of these constraints and, thus, launch—although, in themselves, not provide for—a macroscopic effort to overcome them. Of course, not all projects succeed in any of these terms; structural factors do set limits. Our discussion seeks to explain that which occurs when projects do have a mobilizing effect.

Historians of social movements or of societal mobilizations often begin their stories in an earlier time in which the ideas that later served a particular mobilization drive or project were formed or the first cells that later formed the nucleus of a movement were organized; they start the story of the movements at their initiation rather than at their take-off stage.[36] But there are *many* more ideas in the social air in any one period and *many* more cells are formed than mobilization drives launched which have a societal consequence. However, the launching of a project, especially an accumulative and expanding sequence of projects, often indicates that the stage has been reached at which ideas and small elites begin to gain a social base on which more encompassing mobilization drives may be built.[37] Although encompassing mobilization is still far from inevitable, after such projects, it is more likely to occur.

The projects which lead to mobilization take-offs are often more readily identifiable in the history of collectivities than of societies; the former, being less institutionalized, have to rely more on the formation of new organizations. But major mobilization drives of societies—that is, drives that transform the levels of mobilization—are often marked by a mobilizing event (or set of events), whether it be the Pearl Harbor attack on the United States in 1941 for the American war effort or the Communist coup in Czechoslovakia in 1948 for the mobilization of several West European societies into the subsequent NATO effort.[38] While at first it might seem that projects are planned by social movements whereas mobilizing events "occur" in societies, the difference is one of degree rather than dichotomous. Thus, the civil rights movement was, at most, only partially aware, at the initiation of the Montgomery bus boycott, of the take-off nature of this project, and the United States government over-dramatized the expansionist tendencies of the Soviet Union in 1948 to enhance American mobilization.

Projects entail an internal change in the mobilizing units because they generate new personal and collective commitments. There is growing evidence that the most effective way to commit a person is for him to act, to participate, in a "sample" of the intended line of action. Under conditions which are far from specified, that which is at first a minor commitment may gradually expand in scope and intensity (from signing a petition to carrying a sign; from boycotting a shop to participation in a sit-in).[39] Other personal changes than an increase in emotional commitment are involved: Consciousness of the political map and news grows; some resources are shifted from personal to collective use; the pattern of the consumption of time is altered—e.g., from the pool room and the neighborhood bar to participation in a social movement. It is our impression that not only do very few of the student activists who participate in political projects take part in panty raids, goldfish swallowing, and telephone booth stuffing, but also that in the months and years in which political projects are more common, the incidence of a-political, expressive, tension-releasing activities is lower than when political projects are less common.

This would suggest that some shifting from one kind of activity to another occurs. This shifting seems not to mean that the leaders of tension-releasing activities become the leaders of political projects, but that they do become participants in these projects, which suffices, we suggest, to reduce the frequency of the so-called "rowdy" activities. The same may hold for deviant activities.[40]

Closely related are the changes in interaction patterns; since not all members are mobilized to the same degree at the same time, we expect that the more mobilized members will tend toward higher interaction with other more mobilized people and avoid interaction with less activated ones.

Chain Reaction

Although projects may be necessary for moving the mobilization process of a previously unmobilized societal unit from the initiation to the take-off stage, they are not expected to suffice, under most circumstances, to mobilize broadly even a collectivity and certainly not a society. Many mobilization processes have taken off for a short time, lost momentum, and been extinguished after a period of heightened activities; mobilization then returns toward the old level.

In those sub-sets of processes from which a more encompassing, macro-scopic, and permanent mobilization results, the process follows the pattern of a slow chain reaction. When a passive collectivity or society is activated through a mobilization process, the process resembles the conversion (or transformation) of a poorly combustible material rather than of a highly volatile one. In other words, the process is relatively slow and there is almost never the simultaneous activation of all or even of the majority of the sub-units of any societal unit. Or, to put it differently, collectivities on the move do not move frontally, with all or most of their members in roughly the same position like an attacking platoon; rather, the members differ in the extents of their activation with some sub-units more activated than others. Mobilization, as we see it, is usually not a mass situation in which a charismatic leader activates a large body of men (or a societal movement) more or less simultaneously, like a match set to gasoline. Rather, the process is similar to lighting heavy, damp, wooden logs. If the projects are the societal matches, they will ignite the conversion process only in a few limited sub-units, and only if some relatively more volatile (i.e., more given to activation) twigs are available. That is, some elites or some relatively more educated or self-conscious or unbalanced sub-units are the first to be activated. Even when these are highly mobilized—i.e., yield a relatively high amount of energy for the collective action—other sub-units of the same societal unit are merely beginning to "warm up" and to be mobilized to a lower degree, while many others are still largely passive. On those occasions in which the process of conversion is continued, the ratio of the sub-units activated to those left relatively or completely passive slowly increases. Descriptive· accounts of such processes are available even in the daily press. For instance, of the approximately 2,000 colleges and universities in the United States, the student bodies of only a few followed the 1964 Berkeley Free Speech Movement with similar movements; another few engaged in smaller projects, a somewhat larger sub-set actively re-examined student-faculty and student-administration relations without engaging in any projects, a still larger sub-set devoted increased attention to the issue, and the remaining ones were barely affected.

The sequences which this process of gradual and uneven mobilization follows are as yet unspecified: Which elites and sub-collectivities are mobilized earlier and which later? In which situations does the process advance rather than exhaust itself? Under what conditions does a backlash ensue? In short, the details of societal chain reactions are yet to be explored.

Another main point for which the thermodynamic analogy holds is that the activation of some sub-units has a similar—though usually, at least, initially, a smaller—effect on a sub-set of the other sub-units; that is, activated sub-units have a catalytic role. A full study of the relative efficacy of various catalytic agents under various environmental conditions for the mobilization of different kinds of societal units should be as much a part of societal analysis as it is of thermodynamics.

It follows from the above discussion that we expect *mobilization to be an elitist process*. There is not one elite and a mass of followers but rather several elites, semi-elites, and various sub-collectivities activated to varying degrees, some of whom are more mobilized than others but not as mobilized as the elites, as well as various groups of more passive sympathizers, onlookers, and occasional contributors.

The Mobilization Struggle

The capacity of a societal unit to act and its historical impact depend considerably on the outcome of the internal struggle between the mobilizers and the unmobilized members of a unit, a struggle which is evident in practically all major mobilization processes.[41] The Cecil B. De Mille version of history has the slaves (or occupied nations, or colonized peoples) "rise." Actually, if and when such an uprising occurs, it usually follows many years of mobilization efforts, during which an internal leadership is slowly built up and expanded and the mobilizing sub-units gain in members and sympathizers; even at the end of such a process, the attention, loyalties, and utilitarian assets of the members are unevenly tapped. Mobilization is, thus, a process which slowly penetrates from one societal layer to another but rarely encompasses all of them or progresses very rapidly precisely because of this internal struggle.

The struggle takes place because, in principle, some if not all of the sub-units and their members are opposed to releasing assets at their command to other goals and to the mobilizing unit, and even when goals are shared, there are differences in the views of the means to be applied and the pace at which mobilization is to proceed, and so on. While in part these differences are resolved through various consensus-formation mechanisms, in part their resolution almost invariably involves the exercise of power of one kind or another by the mobilizers against those members who impede the expansion of the process.[42]

In a period of crisis, the societal unit gains an additional action capacity, as each sub-unit moves up several notches on the mobilization scale; supporters of the action augment their contributions, volunteers work harder and longer, the elites increase their efforts, and usually passive sub-units are partially activated. But these factors reduce the extent of the internal differentiation of the mobilization structure only to a limited degree, and even in crises, the struggle between those who seek higher levels of mobilization and those who are relatively passive continues. Thus, for instance, even at the height of a struggle for national independence, many sub-collectivities wish to proceed more slowly and take fewer risks. The differentiation may be in the other direction—with some sub-collectivities seeking more activation than those in control of the collectivity-wide organizations—but the differences remain in any case.

The Role of Organizations in the Mobilizations of Collectivities

Internal mobilization can proceed under the control of external elites, but the more external the control, the lower the level of mobilization reached, the less encompassing the process in terms of the sub-collectivities and the facets of their activities mobilized, and the higher the cost of mobilization. These disadvantages occur because external elites tend to be less responsive than internal elites.[43] Moreover, mobilization take-off is often associated with the internalization of control—that is, the shifting of control from external elites to internal ones. This holds for such mobilizations as the European labor movement in which control shifted from middle-class leaders to workers, colonial independence movements in which native elites superseded foreign ones, the Zionist movement in which control shifted from Jews in the Diaspora to Jews in Palestine, and many other processes.

Another relevant subject (which need not be studied here) is the change from one kind of elite to another with the mobilization take-off. Theoretically, the same elite may control both a pre-mobilization and a post-mobilization unit as well as the mobilization processes. In practice, however, few elites seem to show sufficient flexibility in their steering capacities, communities-of-assumptions, and personalities; a change of elites is commonly associated with the mobilization take-off.[44] Since in some cases this entails a radicalization of the mobilization while in others it leads to its moderation, the causes, patterns, and consequences of these changes of elites need yet to be explored.

Elites are often the heads of organizations, or, conversely, organizations are the arms of elites. Organizations are a major tool of the *process* of mobilization and a major instrument through which collectivities "fix" the higher *levels* of control obtained in the process. Organizations—their elites, staffs, power hierarchies, and communication networks—usually constitute the most mobilized sub-unit of a collectivity (the main exceptions are mass situations and social movements). Viewed dynamically, this means that the act of organizing a previously unorganized collectivity or sub-collectivity tends to entail an increase in its level of mobilization, even though organizations rarely encompass more than a small fraction of the collectivities they "represent."[45] The launching of new political parties or new labor unions are typical examples of such organizational mobilizations.

Rarely is the mobilization of a collectivity controlled by one organization, even though a society is frequently mobilized by one state. On the collectivity level, as a rule, the initial mobilization is carried out by two or more organizations. While this may seem redundant and wasteful, especially as these organizations tend to be in conflict with each other, it should be noted that these organizations tend to differ in their recruitment bases in terms of the sub-units of the same collectivity on which they draw. Frequently, some appeal more to lower sub-collectivities and some to higher ones in the same broad stratification layer, in terms of the average education of the membership, the members' psychological orientations (e.g., as established by the authoritarianism F-scale), etc.[46] There is much reason to believe that if there were only one organization, the mobilization would be lower and less encompassing.

Relations between the various organizations which mobilize the same collectivity, aim for the same basic transformation, and face the same external opposition are frequently marked by strain and conflict as well as by a low level of and a difficult coordination. This holds for labor movements (e.g., the struggle between Social Democrats and Communists), peace movements (e.g., the conflict between religious and left pacifists), independence movements, and religious movements.

The considerable analytic similarities in the strains between the militant and the moderate organizations (or sub-organizations) in these varying movements and historical, societal, and cultural contexts are rarely observed by the participants and often ignored by observers. The lack of coordination, the energy consumed by conflicts "within the movement," and the charges of passivity and timidity on the one hand and of irresponsibility and a lack of appeal to a broad base on the other are frequently presented as problems idiosyncratic to particular movements.[47] From the viewpoint of sociological analysis, such strains and conflicts among the organizational arms of any mobilizing collectivity should be "routine" and expected. What is of interest and in need of study are the differences in the extent of this conflict. Secondly, efforts to eliminate these strains and conflicts are futile, and, at least to a degree, from the viewpoint of the actors involved, these strains are "functional." On balance, they seem to enhance mobilization and to reduce counter-mobilization. The squabbles between "left" (pro-China) Communists and "right" (pro-Soviet) Communist Parties in Kerala, India, did not prevent both parties from increasing their share of the vote and from gaining jointly a majority of the State Assembly, in 1967.*

The disparate organizations which activate any one collectivity also tend to differ in the degrees of commitment they require—that is, in the levels of mobilization they require the sub-units they mobilize to reach. Some organizations are more demanding than others—for instance, a religious order as compared to the Church, or a political movement as against a political party. The divergent organizations provide legitimation for different levels of mobilization, thus allowing individuals who seek higher levels of commitment to be recruited without imposing the same standards on those who are only willing to participate less intensively and whose support would be lost if every member who wanted to participate in the mobilization had to do so at a high level of intensity.

Some members are interested primarily in political action (labor parties, NAACP), while others are concerned with economic action (most trade unions, the Urban League); some members seek to join moderate organizations and would not join a radical one and *vice versa*; still other members belong to both radical and moderate organizations, some of which are political while others are economic. As the commitments of the members in each organization are frequently ideological, too great an extent of inter-organizational coordination and cooperation would antagonize some of the members of each of the organizations.[48] Under these conditions, two or more organizations which are in some conflict with each other may mobilize more members than one "united" organization or two well-coordinated organizations. Furthermore, a measure of conflict among organizations tends to enhance the members' loyalty and engagement.[49] It does not follow, however, that the greater the number of organizations, the higher the level of mobilization; there is a sharply declining marginal utility once there are more than two organizations. But two disparate organizations seem to mobilize a collectivity more effectively than one, and three are probably more effective than two, though in the latter case, the marginal gain is probably considerably smaller.

The multi-organizational character of mobilizing collectivities also seems functional for the limiting of counter-mobilization. Here, the key variables seem to be the scope and intensity of the internecine conflict. The less total

---

* Joseph Lelyveld, "Communism, Kerala Style," *New York Times Magazine*, (April 30, 1967), p. 30.

the conflict, the fewer the losses entailed and the higher the gains which are often attained. The following historical instance illustrates this point; scores of others could be provided. In the 1940s, the British, as the colonial power in Palestine, faced two major underground organizations, one broadly based and moderate (*Hagana*) and the other much more narrowly based and militant (*Irgun*). The two organizations were in conflict. They criticized each other venomously; in some instances, the *Hagana* informed the British police of activities of the *Irgun*, and the *Irgun* provoked the British in ways and situations opposed to *Hagana* policy. It was widely believed by members of both organizations that they would have been much more effective had there been no such inter-organizational conflict, and various attempts were made at reconciliation and unification. In retrospect, however, it seems that the British were considerably hampered by these two facets of the Israeli independence movement. Liberal public opinion throughout the world and in Britain itself supported the moderates (though the militant *Irgun* was not without a following). When the *Irgun* engaged in an "extremist" act which otherwise might have brought massive British retaliation, the *Irgun* members hid in the community at large, which had basically moderate *Hagana* sympathies. With few exceptions, British forces found it difficult and politically unwise (because of external public opinion and the fear of encouraging the moderates to become more militant) to constitute harsher police measures against the community at large. Thus, *Irgun* and *Hagana* could both function, with one increasing the costs and casualties of the colonial regime, and the other—while, of course, also participating in the anti-colonial strife—maintaining the all-important support of "third" parties ("world" public opinion) and deterring harsher counter-measures. (The situation is somewhat analogous to a guerrilla movement's having a sanctuary across the border). The harsher the opponent and the less reluctant he is to treat the moderates that shield the militants as if they were militants themselves, the smaller the advantages of inter-organizational diversity and conflict for the mobilization of a collectivity. However, even the Nazis in their occupation of Europe, could not completely escape the negative (from their viewpoint) effects of the division between local moderates and militants in the occupied communities.[50]

The Limits of Mobilization

In short, the generally low level of mobilization, its slow and uneven (or elitist) nature, and the functional aspects of inter-organizational diversity, strain, and conflict seem to be three universal features of the mobilization of social movements.

Mobilization itself has a cost; that is, some energy is expended in increasing the level of mobilization to bring about the entailed changes in the structure of the unit. Moreover, under most conditions, mobilization has a *rising* marginal cost. We expect that the transfer of each additional segment of sub-unit assets to unit control costs significantly more than the transfer of the preceding segment. And, a societal unit's ability to mobilize is limited by the fact that, after mobilization reaches a given level (to be determined empirically), any additional increase will cost more than the gains in assets that may be achieved and, hence, will curtail rather than increase the unit's action capacity. This is the so to speak absolute limit of mobilization; beyond this level, it become self-contradictory. Many barriers are encountered, though, well before the absolute limit is approached.

Mobilization barriers affect many societal situations. For instance, they limit the amount of taxes a government can levy by entailing rising administrative costs and, more importantly, rising citizens' resistance. Similarly, the extent of the psychological mobilization of members of totalitarian regimes is limited by the fatigue, boredom, and resistance generated by excessive attempts to indoctrinate. The fruitfulness of the concept of mobilization barriers is illustrated in that when it is projected onto processes not previously explored in these terms, it alerts us to analytically parallel phenomena. For instance, there seems to be a barrier to the mobilization of political support in election campaigns. As new and "floating" votes are or seem to be exhausted, the mobilization of additional voters entails an appeal to members of the opposition by a campaigning party, which, in turn, often leads to the dilution of the party's program and image. If this is continued, a point is reached at which more voters of the mobilizing party are lost than voters of the opposition are gained. Even before this point is reached, parties encounter the rising "costs" of appealing to the voters of other parties.

While every societal unit encounters mobilization barriers, these barriers differ among cultures and historical periods. In general, totalitarian societies can mobilize more easily and can remain relatively more mobilized for a longer period of time than pluralistic ones. Modern societies are more mobilized than were most previous societies and developed nations are more mobilized than developing ones. These differences can be roughly measured by the percentage of the GNP the governments use, the percentage of the manpower employed or drafted by the governments, and the intensity of the identification with the nation or with national bodies (such as the Party) as against the identification with sub-units (such as tribes, local leaders, and regions). For these comparisons to be more accurate, differences in costs as well as in the amount of energy mobilized must be taken into account. To state that a barrier is different in two kinds of societies or in two periods in the same society is to suggest that the levels of mobilization attained are significantly different though the costs vary to the same degree.

External Mobilization: Inter- and Supra-Unit Relations

We have explored the ways in which a societal unit, under a given set of conditions, raises its level of mobilization. But the analysis of the degree to which such internal mobilization leads to an increased capacity to act must take into account the mobilizing unit's relations to other units in the same situation and to the supra-units of which it is a member. While there are common types of societal situations in which the relatively limited mobilization of one societal unit resulted in a major transformation—many instances of decolonization, for example—there is another category of situation in which the opposite relationship prevails: A relatively high level of mobilization of one societal unit yields little societal change. The question becomes: Under what conditions does the mobilization of a unit lead toward an increased capacity to change other units and itself?

We have stressed the macroscopic significance for societal action of intense mobilization as compared to the significance of other, particularly external, factors. This is most evident in an analytically pure situation in which the actor and the system under study are the same—i.e., there are no supra-unit constraints. The United States in the last generation of the modern period approximated this analytic situation. Many societal actors, though, are members of systems in which they are bound, to a much larger degree, to other units and into supra-units. A study of the effects of the mobilization of such units is incomplete without taking into account their relations to other units and to the supra-units.

This is the case for two related reasons: (a) The mobilization of a unit increases its power and, thus, by definition, changes the power of some other units. To understand the new relations created by mobilization, it is necessary to understand the preceding relations. For example, the rising role of the right and the center in France under De Gaulle's regime must be viewed against the background of their pre-1958 relative weakness vis-à-vis the left. (b) At the same time, the mobilization of a unit tends, by itself, to have effects on the mobilization of other units and supra-units, and, thus, in order to analyze the results of the efforts of any one unit, not only must the unit's relations to other units be studied, but also the effects of the changes in the *internal* state of one unit on the *internal* states of the others.

Inter-Unit Effects: Counter-Mobilization

First, the action effects of the mobilization drive of one unit depend considerably on the degree to which this drive triggers *counter-mobilizations* in other units in the same system or situation, which seek to neutralize the new power of the mobilizing unit or to block its intended self-changes. Of course, other processes are simultaneously operative which affect both the relations among and the relative power of the various units. But there is no reason to believe that these other factors—which are unrelated to the drive in question —will suddenly change in the direction of increasing the resistance to a line of action only because unit X is pursuing it more actively. However, this is the case with mobilization; the mobilization of a unit frequently does trigger the mobilization of opponents either of the unit or of the line of action that the new mobilization is expected to energize. The United States and Russia, in the period between 1947 and the mid-1960s, continually counter-mobilized each other, which generated an upward-spiralling arms race. A California poll reported that 92 per cent of the adult public had heard or read something about student demonstrations at Berkeley; while this was a very high mobilization of attention, it was not quite the mobilization the students favored, since most of the attention amounted to counter-mobilization— 74 per cent of those asked expressed disapproval of the demonstrations.[51]

Increases in the action capacity of a unit are determined by the net amount of its mobilization—that is, by the results of its mobilization minus the results of the counter-mobilization(s) it triggered. A universal strategic problem of mobilizing units is finding modes of mobilization that will trigger as little counter-mobilization as possible or at least less "static" than the unit itself can gain in "dynamics." This is by no means always accomplished. For instance, the Soviet Union's production of new intercontinental missiles in the late 1950s was perceived by influential groups in the United States as creating a "missile gap," which, in turn, helped to bring about an American counter-mobilization much larger than the initial Soviet effort. The student burning of draft cards in 1965 to draw the public's attention to their objections to United States policy in Vietnam motivated demonstrations in support of the policy and adamant rejection of the students' critique of the war. In the following weeks, the percentage of Americans supporting greater involvement in Vietnam significantly increased. Gallup asked a national sample of Americans: "If a candidate for Congress in your district advocated sending a great many more men to Vietnam, would you be more inclined or less inclined to vote for him?" In September, 1965, before the demonstrations, 33 per cent said they would be more inclined. By mid-November, this had risen to 46 per cent.[52] Other answers to similar questions showed the same basic response.

Counter-mobilization also encompasses organizational aspects; when labor organized itself nationally, the manufacturers responded by forming nation-wide manufacturers' associations.[53] Independence movements often paralleled colonial administrations, and the boundaries of many new African nations remain the arbitrary boundaries initially drawn by the colonial powers.[54]

Inter-Unit Mobilization

There are almost always more than two actors in a system. Often, the actors are not only, at least initially, advocates and proponents but include "third parties," uncommitted units who are potential allies of the mobilizing sides. As a rule, the outcome of the mobilization drive of any one unit cannot be determined or explained unless the actions and reactions of these other units are studied. In surprisingly many cases, *the units least involved in a conflict have the greatest amount of power over its outcome*, because they are more powerful than any of the actors directly involved (e.g., the United States and the USSR in the conflicts between Israel and the Arab states and between India and Pakistan); they exert a major make-weight effect (e.g., the balancers in several traditional balance-of-power systems); or, while weak, they consitute the main "floating" vote which the sides can hope to gain (e.g., in many democratic national elections). Quite often, when we explore the reasons that a particular mobilization drive was much more successful than others (in terms of the goals of the actor), the unit which prevailed was not the actor who mobilized more of his own assets or kept his opponent(s) least mobilized but was the one who mobilized the most help from other units—i.e., in effect, made the greatest use of other units' assets to energize a course of action he favored.

Israel's successful anti-colonial effort in 1948 cannot be understood without taking into account the support of American Jewry; India's independence must be studied in relation to the support of the British Labour Party; the initiation of a southern civil rights movement probably would have been much weaker without the support of northern liberals; and a study of the Puerto Rican "boot strap" development must include the role of North American capital, New York City relief laws, and United States tax concessions. Historical accounts, especially those written by members of the acting units, tend to underplay the allies' role and to exaggerate that of the actor. The significance of allies often rests in the fact that they command many more assets than the mobilizing actors, and, hence, even a small amount of mobilization on their part might suffice to tip the scale.[55] This is especially dramatic when the ally is a sub-unit of the opponent of the acting unit, as was the case, for instance, in Gandhi's independence movement. Without the support of the Labour Party, his non-violent techniques would have been much less effective.

Supra-Unit Mobilization

When the units are members of a supra-unit—for instance, when the actors are collectivities and the supra-unit is a society, especially one that is organized by a state—the side(s) which mobilizes the supra-unit is much more likely to prevail than those which do not, especially in the post-modern period. The state commands an increasingly larger amount of coercive, utilitarian, and even normative assets and power, both legitimate and illegitimate, than most other units. The significance of the changing support of the federal government in the civil rights movement in the South illustrates this point. It is true that, in part, the direction the government took reflects that of the various member units of the American society; as the civil rights movement lost societal support in 1966, its Federal support also declined. But, to a degree, the state has an autonomous and mobilizing effect of its own, reflecting *its* institutionalized values, *its* leadership, and *its* interest groups. And the very large amount of power it has provides a focus for the struggle among the member collectivities: Mobilizing its "alliance" becomes increasingly important in these kinds of systems. In contrast, unit, ally, and counter-mobilization increase in relative significance when the supra-unit is weak, as is illustrated by the 1966 tribal warfare in Nigeria.

Transforming the Supra-Unit Structure

So far, we have explored the process of mobilization from the viewpoint of a mobilizing unit—its internal efforts, its mobilization of allies, the counter-currents it generates, and the role a supra-unit may play. We now take the viewpoint of a supra-unit whose member units are mobilizing to change not so much themselves as the structure of the supra-unit of which they are members. To avoid an excessively abstract discussion, we assume for the balance of this section that the units are collectivities which are organized in varying degrees, while the supra-unit is a society that is sufficiently integrated to constitute a viable entity. The mobilization of the other kind of supra-units (i.e., those which are poorly integrated) is explored in the next section.

The mobilization of one or more collectivities, it seems, must often precede the introduction of significant changes either in their inter-relations or in the society's structure. The reason seems to be that existing societal structures have a stratification and a political, an ideological and a power base. The actor who seeks to initiate change usually must support his action with power that is *greater than his share in the existing structure*. Hence, mobilization usually must precede transformation (or fundamental change).

Excluded from this generalization are (a) changes in factors which are trivial from a societal viewpoint, such as in the fashions of the consumption of cultural items (these changes are often large in quantity and in scope, which gives them a macroscopic appearance without, in effect, having a societal significance);[56] (b) institutionalized changes (e.g., of the party in office, following elections); and (c) mature changes, especially if they are overdue. That is, the demand for the change has been built up—i.e., was mobilized in earlier periods—and the factors which were retarding it have disappeared or have been weakened. But, we suggest, transformations of societies are not of these kinds and are often "premature." Given the plurality of collectivities, the diversity of interests and viewpoints among them, and, above all, the tendency of those high in power to favor the existing structure (at least its basic features)—transformation requires considerable mobilization among those who favor it.

Attempts at transformations of societies do occur without sufficient unit or inter-unit mobilization. Many collectivities are often poorly organized, have poor societal knowledge, and are likely to misjudge the power needed to bring about societal transformations. (This holds especially for lower collectivities whose command of knowledge facilities is poor and whose access to state facilities is slight, but who are most likely to be interested in such transformations.) This leads to premature attempts at transformation, to change without adequate mobilization. From this viewpoint, most successful societal transformations can be seen as the final attempt at change, following a series of futile or partially unsuccessful efforts in which the level of mobilization was insufficient. Thus, 1905 may be viewed as a "trial run" for 1917 in the history of the Russian Revolution, and 1776 as a "trial run" for 1789 in the history of American federation. Often, the "trial runs" are less intensive and encompassing than the subsequent actions and serve both to weaken the opponent and to increase the level of mobilization of the transforming collectivities and their allies.

Still, it may be asked, will not the mobilization of one or even of a coalition of collectivities be neutralized by others', with the society's placing its extra weight on the side of those who seek to preserve the existing societal structure? Three answers might be given: First, the collectivities which constitute a society are in a "mixed" conflict–cooperation relationship, and when some of the society's goals are served, this increases the "payoffs" to all or most of the member units. The mobilization of a collectivity may, hence, occur simultaneously with the mobilization of a society. This took place in Britain in 1940, after Dunkirk.

Secondly, even when the relationship among the collectivities is one of conflict, the increased mobilization of all of the collectivities transforms the society in that it increases participation, reduces alienation, and builds up commitment. A society whose members are more mobilized is more active, even if this entails a reduction in the level of consensus and a rise in the amount of conflict.* Democratization—the introduction of previously excluded members into a democratically constituted polity or the development of such a polity—entails such a mobilization and seems to have the expected effects though, of course, only for those collectivities which the democratization encompasses and only to the degree that it is broad in scope

---

* We deal here with well-integrated societies. This point does not hold for supra-units that are poorly integrated, because, here, the additional mobilization of the members may destroy the system.

and not only formal–political. For instance, though the mobilization of Negro-Americans generated conflict, to the extent that the civil rights movement increased its democratization, it did increase the activation of the American society.

Moreover, even if the societal structure and polity do not become less rigid and more democratic, there is, in every society, some leeway, some slack, some options for even the lowest actors. If these are exercised in the direction of mobilization, the objective situation is changed and the distribution of power is altered. This, in turn, often allows an additional increase in the assets of the lower collectivities and, hence, improvement in their mobilization potential. Moreover, often the first actors to mobilize are not the lower collectivities but the unbalanced ones which then involve the lower ones in the process, though usually not the lowest ones.

Finally, as the various collectivities that constitute a society are unevenly mobilized at any point in time, changes in the levels of mobilization of the various member collectivities invariably alter the relative mobilization levels of the collectivities and, hence, their respective power and the society's structure. For instance, a greater mobilization of the lower collectivities— often the least mobilized ones, other things being equal—tends to make for a more egalitarian society.

Thus, from the viewpoint of each collectivity, its mobilization efforts and the external constraints upon them (which include the society's structure) affect each other. Mobilization uses whatever options the structure allows for changing it, and changing the structure can expand these options. Thus, the mobilization of Negro-Americans in the early nineteen-sixties led to some reallocation of utilitarian assets, increased political representation, and so on, which, in turn, improved the conditions for the additional mobilization of this collectivity.

Such mutual reinforcing processes frequently exhaust themselves before a tipping point in favor of transformation is reached.[57] But after such a process, the members remain more committed and active, and—to the degree that the objective situation has changed to allow for more activation—the collectivity is more in line with its socio-political context, and future mobilizations will be less difficult. Of course not every actor can be mobilized to do everything; the objective situation does set constraints, often narrow ones, which hold in check even the most mobilized actors. The question is one of relative emphasis. Our thesis is that (a) much can be gained by the self-mobilization of an actor and by the mobilization of others' support for the actor's goal or for joint and shared goals, and that (b) the actor's capacity to be mobilized and to mobilize others is determined by external factors to a lesser extent than is often assumed. Under conditions which have been in part explored above and which in part need specification in future research, projects trigger a chain reaction which leads a societal unit to exercise the relatively more active options within the range available under the given structural constraints, which, in turn, loosens these constraints. This may lead to societal transformation. And even when it does not, the stratification structure and polity of a mobilized collectivity and of a society whose collectivities have been mobilized are rarely the same as those of passive, pre-mobilized ones.

The theory of societal guidance outlined here differs from the main functionalist theories not only in its greater concern with transformation as a *process* but also in its systematic concern with the *sources* of change—with societal energy, assets, and power. It does not suffice to specify the norms which characterize a new societal pattern and to say, for instance, that industrialization requires an "achievement" orientation (or a universalistic, specific, or neutral one), even if the socialization and institutional patterns necessary for such an orientation are spelled out. We need to know the ways in which the "achievement"-oriented (e.g., commercial) classes did or may gain in power over the ascribed classes (e.g., the landed aristocracy) or achieve their cooperation, changes which—assuming the initial weakness of the new classes—require a study of the sources of their new power. This leads, in part, to a study of changes in technology and in the societal environment; it also leads to the study of changes in the internal makeup of the achievement-oriented classes—above all, in their capacity for mobilizing themselves and others. The concept of mobilization, thus, ties asset and power analysis to the study of the sources and patterns of societal change and transformation.

Supra-Unit Building

When there is no supra-unit or when it is weak, unit-mobilization drives may be aimed not at triggering the power of the supra-unit on the side of the unit or at transforming the supra-unit's structure, but at initiating or strengthening the supra-unit; i.e., new energy will be invested to build up the supra-unit bonds. Modernization and unification are two processes which involve such mobilization. Our purpose here is not to explore these important processes in their own right but to relate them briefly to the general process of mobilization.

Mobilization and Modernization

The concept of mobilization is often encountered in discussions of modernization,[58] in which it is widely associated with the transfer of the control of assets from collectivities (tribes, rural communities) to societies (often, national ones). The term is used to refer to the increased exposure to national mass media (such exposure increases the receptivity of the members of the society to the messages of a national government), to the shifting of the labor force from traditional to modern pursuits, to an increased level of education, to a loss of traditional religious orientations, and to a rise in the extent of secular political identification.[59]

The relation of modernization to mobilization is obviously very close; it seems, however, fruitful not to use mobilization as a synonym for modernization because we then have two terms for one process and none for the process referred to here as mobilization. Also, many of the aspects of modernization do not involve mobilization—for instance, the processes entailed in determining the usages of the assets made available by mobilization. (To put it technically, while conversion ratios and patterns do affect each other, they vary independently.) There are mobilization processes that do not lead to modernization, as, for instance, when the assets built up are used for war or to finance territorial–political ambitions. Finally, some forms of mobilization block rather than advance modernization; for instance, the increased mobilization of traditional collectivities is often a major source of the resistance to modernization.

One reason that the two concepts are occasionally treated as synonyms is that the same concrete process *may* serve both mobilization and modernization. An increase in literacy, for example, may enhance the ability of a society to draw its population into national service *and* simplify the introduction of modern administrative or production techniques. But analytically, the two processes—an increase in the ratio of assets under an actor's control and the use of assets for modernization—are best kept separate.

Several authorities seem to assume that mobilization barriers are lower— i.e., the capacity to mobilize at a given cost is higher—the more disintegrated a traditional society. Dissolving traditional villages and weakening the bonds of extended families are viewed as prerequisites for the mobilization of a population into a modern societal framework. Deutsch, for instance, first defines mobilization as modernization: "Social mobilization is a name given to an overall process of change, which happens to substantial parts of the population in countries which are moving from traditional to modern ways of life."[60] He then sees mobilization as following an integration–disintegration–reintegration sequence: "... social mobilization can be defined, therefore, as the process in which major clusters of old social, economic and psychological commitments are eroded or broken and people become available for new patterns of socialization and behavior."[61] The hypothesis that mobilization or modernization requires the disintegration of traditional social units deserves to be tested, but it should not be part of the definitions of the concepts. Moreover, it seems to us that the hypothesis is at most partially valid—that is, true under some circumstances.

Some weakening of traditional ties and identifications probably enhances the mobilization for modernization. A high level of integration consumes many assets and members' energies and, thus, competes with the service of other goals. Second, and more important, it makes transformation more difficult, as a high degree of cohesion is likely to obstruct the reconstruction which modernization requires. But by no means is the ability to modernize greater the more disintegrated and, hence, anomic the old structures have become.[62] First, highly disintegrated collectivities or sub-collectivities have their own particular barriers to mobilization. Their membership is hard to organize (e.g., farm hands, slum dwellers), lacks social discipline, and tends to be psychologically rigid and socially deviant, which makes the learning of new behavior patterns difficult and social control costly. For national projects, the mobilization barriers of such units may be as considerable, if not higher, than those of traditional units. Second, traditional units can serve as effective foundations of mobilization for modernization if they are trans-formed rather than disintegrated.[63] Associational processes are a base on which to build mobilization; if they are deficient, mobilization—both in opposition to and in favor of change—is more difficult than when they are stronger.

An example might illustrate this point. Shortly after the state of Israel was founded, there was a wave of mass immigration from a large number of countries. The immigrants differed considerably in terms of their cultural backgrounds, levels of education, languages, and other such variables. The most effective way in which to integrate these immigrants rapidly into Israeli society, it was believed by Israeli authorities, was to dissolve the traditional groups and to "mix" the immigrants into such modern units as classrooms, army platoons, and new settlements. Unable to communicate with each other in their respective languages and to reinforce each other's immigrant culture, they would have to speak Hebrew and absorb the Israeli culture. Disintegration of the old groups would open the way to new integration. Actually, this approach seems to have generated a ritualistic adherence on the part of the immigrants to their old norms and groupings. It became increasingly evident that effective acculturation required gaining the support of the existing leadership of the immigrant groups and maintaining the groups or providing them with new "Israeli" leadership, attempting to *transform* their cultures and structures rather than attempting to "erode" or "disintegrate" them.[64]

In some cases, modernization may entail demobilization rather than mobilization, at least in the sense that fewer commitments to the collectivity are demanded and more leeway is allowed for private initiative. The rise of Western industrial societies, especially those which grew from absolutist states, and the political liberalization of the economies of communist totalitarian societies have such demobilization aspects. For currently developing countries, various levels of mobilization and demobilization might be combined, such as the mobilization of the extended families and the demobilization of castes.

It is important to bear in mind that the concept of mobilization ought always to refer to a particular unit or set of units, and that the mobilization of one unit often constitutes the demobilization of another. For example, at each point in time, an increase in the national control of utilitarian assets requires a decrease in the control of these assets by some other unit(s). It, therefore, is essential to keep the reference unit fixed for any single study.

The relationship between the rise of modern society and mobilization further illustrates this point: A society may show many of the symptoms usually associated with the concept of "mass society," either because the micro-social units are disintegrating *or* because their ties to the society at large have been undermined. In the first situation, if mobilization occurs, it is much more likely to be totalitarian; in the second, it is much more likely to be associated with a revival of some mode of democratic or authoritarian institutions.

Mobilization and Political Unification

A basic feature of mobilization should be restated here because of its particular significance for the study of unification—the bonding of units into supra-units. This bonding requires a shift of control from the units to the supra-unit. It also needs energy to support the effort and, often, power to overcome the resistance to unification often encountered. Mobilization entails a change of control and a re-channeling of energy. A poor unit may contribute more energy to "fuel" supra-unit actions than an affluent unit if a larger fraction of the former's assets is mobilized. An increase in the possessions or output of the member units only potentially increases the supra-unit's capacity to act, because the new assets may not be mobilized for the particular line of action in question or for any action by the supra-unit but rather be used for the activities of units or sub-units. It, therefore, is of interest to note that historical processes of political unification were preceded not by a general increase in the assets of the member units of the unifying systems but by improvements in the administrative and communication capacities and assets of one or, at most, a few member-units, which provided for the unification process. That is, these increases were not in just any unit but in those units which led the process of unification and were willing to mobilize part of their increased organizational capacities and new assets for unification. Prussia served as such a unit in the unification of Germany and Piedmont in the unification of Italy.[65]

While both unification and mobilization entail a change in the control of assets, the processes differ from each other in two ways: (a) Unification entails many other changes as well—for instance, in the scope of the associational bonds, the substance of the values, and so forth. That is, unification has a mobilization aspect but it is a more inclusive concept. (b) On the other hand, the mobilization included in a process of unification is only one kind of mobilization—that in which the supra-unit control of unit-assets increases. As we have seen, many other mobilization processes are possible, including the unit mobilization of supra-unit assets. The two concepts, thus, relate like two cross-cutting circles.

Finally, unification may proceed without unit or supra-unit mobilization when an external elite covers the costs. This, however, tends to have distorting effects on the developing political structure of the rising supra-unit. In the West Indies, for instance, Britain provided funds and administrative skills to assist in the federation of ten islands. This permitted the federation to be initiated with a very limited degree of indigenous mobilization. But Britain also provided for the disproportionately high representation of the smaller islands in the federal institutions, which ultimately was one of the reasons for the secession of the larger islands.[66] The price of a low level of mobilization was not only a lack of support but also a political structure that did not fit or adjust sufficiently to the indigenous societal reality and soon collapsed. For a societal unit or supra-unit to be active, its political structure must "fit" its societal base, at least within broad limits. This concept of socio-political "fit" or responsiveness is a subject of the next part of this volume. Thus, while societal mobilization—like the other elements of societal control explored so far—constitutes an essential element of activation, it does not suffice to provide for an active society; consensus-formation must be added to transform societal control into societal guidance. This is the main difference, as we shall see, between the applications of societal and physical energy.

NOTES

1. Neil J. Smelser, *Theory of Collective Behavior* (New York: Free Press, 1963), pp. 17 ff.; William C. Mitchell, *The American Polity* (New York: Free Press, 1962), p. 238.

2. For some recent studies which use it in the traditional sense, see Klaus Knorr, *The War Potential of Nations* (Princeton, N.J.: Princeton University Press, 1956), pp. 19–28, 119–160; James Schlesinger, *The Political Economy of National Security* (New York: Praeger, 1960), pp. 74–75, 78–103; and Charles Hitch and Roland N. McKean, *The Economics of Defense in the Nuclear Age* (Cambridge, Mass.: Harvard University Press, 1960), pp. 218–239.

3. A detailed attempt to measure mobilization along seven different dimensions in nineteen countries is provided by Karl W. Deutsch, "Social Mobilization and Political Development," *American Political Science Review*, Vol. 55 (1961), pp. 493–514. The sources used would serve many other studies of mobilization. They include the *United Nations Report on World Social Situation* and *United Nations Compendium of Social Statistics*. Most useful is Bruce M. Russett, Hayward R. Alker, Jr., Karl W. Deutsch, and Harold D. Lasswell, *World Handbook of Political and Social Indicators* (New Haven, Conn.: Yale University Press, 1967).

4. Carlton J. H. Hayes, *The Historical Evolution of Modern Nationalism* (New York: Macmillan, 1950), pp. 164–231.

5. Russett, *Community and Contention: Britain and America in the Twentieth Century, op. cit.*, pp. 121–127. See Quincy Wright, *A Study of War* (Chicago: University of Chicago Press, 1965), pp. 1448–1453, for studies of language used in the press as indicative of the degree of hostility toward national "enemies."

6. Angus Campbell et al., *The American Voter* (New York: Wiley & Sons, 1960),

pp. 301–327; Roma Lipsky, "Electioneering Among the Minorities," *Commentary*, Vol. 31 (1961), pp. 428–432. See also Samuel Lubell, "The Negro and the Democratic Coalition," *Commentary*, Vol. 38 (1964), pp. 19–27.

7. Zbigniew K. Brzezinski, *The Soviet Bloc: Unity and Conflict*, rev. ed. (New York: Praeger, 1961), pp. 157–181. Andrzej Korbonski, "COMECON: The Evolution of COMECON," in *International Political Communities* (Garden City, N.Y.: Doubleday, 1966), pp. 351–403.

8. Cf. Dahrendorf, *Class and Class Conflict in Industrial Society*, *op. cit.*, p. 127.

9. Max Eastman (ed.), *Capital, the Communist Manifesto, and Other Writings by Karl Marx* (New York: Modern Library, 1932), p. 321.

10. Edwin O. Reischauer, *Japan: Past and Present* (New York: Knopf, 1946), pp. 108–112.

11. Marion J. Levy, Jr., *Modernization and the Structure of Societies: A Setting for International Affairs* (Princeton, N.J.: Princeton University Press, 1966), Vol. I, p. 106, Vol. II, p. 396.

12. Press release of the ADA, December 11, 1966. See also Marjorie Hunter, "ADA for Tax Rise to Pay for Gains," *The New York Times*, January 5, 1967.

13. United States Bureau of the Census, *Statistical Abstract of the United States: 1966*, 87th ed. (Washington, D.C.: Government Printing Office 1966), pp. 320, 390.

14. "Facts of Social Life (Updated,)" *American Behavioral Scientist*, Vol. 8 (March 1965), p. 34.

15. The last figure is affected by the fact that there are only two choices. Figures are from various studies quoted by Lane and Sears, *Public Opinion*, *op. cit.*, pp. 58–61. See also Arthur Kornhauser, Harold L. Sheppard, Albert J. Mayer, *When Labor Votes: A Study of Auto Workers* (New York: University Books, 1956), pp. 122–145, 212–213; Alfred O. Hero, Jr., "The American Public and the UN, 1954–1966," *The Journal of Conflict Resolution*, Vol. 10 (1966), pp. 436–475. Hero takes into account the differences in activity score and the influence people have on public opinion.

16. See discussion of goal versus system models applied in such evaluations. Amitai Etzioni, "Two Approaches to Organizational Analysis: A Critique and a Suggestion," *Administrative Science Quarterly*, Vol. 5 (1960), pp. 257–278.

17. Kornhauser et al., *When Labor Votes*, *op. cit.*, pp. 146–155.

18. It is often argued that a national program X, e.g., race to the moon, is not costly because it amounts to less than the citizens spend on cigarettes or liquor, which amounted to $7 billion and $10.4 billion respectively in the USA in 1960. Actually, the comparison should be made in terms of the proportion of the public income spent on the public program versus the proportion of the personal income spent on cigarettes or liquor. As the public sector is much poorer, $5 billion "waste" here equals in significance about $25 to $37 billion in the personal consumption.

19. For a survey of relevant studies and of conditions under which mobilization occurs as against those under which it does not, see Allen H. Barton, *Social Organization Under Stress: A Sociological Review of Disaster Studies* (Washington, D.C.: National Academy of Sciences, Publication 1032, 1963).

20. James Q. Wilson, *Negro Politics: The Search for Leadership* (New York: Free Press, 1960), pp. 4–5.

21. The crisis followed the retreat of many white liberals from active support of the movement. In 1967 it was reported that the "initial response to a drive to enlist the support of wealthy Negroes for civil rights movement indicates 'easy achievement' of the million-dollar-a-year goal—$100,000 had already been pledged in Chicago alone." *The New York Times*, April 30, 1961.

22. For a discussion of revolutionary wars as breaking down the "unmobilized gap," see David Wilson, "Nation-Building and Revolutionary War," in Karl W. Deutsch and William J. Foltz (eds.), *Nation-Building* (New York: Atherton Press, 1963), pp. 84–94.

23. For some evidence, see below, pp. 475ff.

24. Seymour M. Lipset, "Student Opposition in the United States," *Government and Opposition*, Vol. 1 (1966), pp. 351–374. The International Brigade, which played a key role in the Spanish Civil War, is estimated to have had about 40,000 men. Vincent Brome, *The International Brigades* (London: Heinemann, 1965). Captain Jose Larios Fernández de Lerma, *Combat Over Spain* (New York: Macmillan, 1966) argues that the number was 125,000, but this is considered Franco's figure.

25. Jean Lacouture, *Le Viet Nam entre deux paix* (Paris: Éditions du Seuil, 1965), p. 179. A U.S. Senate report put the figure of the Viet Cong "main force" in 1965 at 59,000. *The New York Times*, January 19, 1966.

26. George Rudé, *The Crowd in the French Revolution* (Oxford: Oxford University Press, 1959), pp. 56, 76, 89, 153–154. "The actual Madero revolution of 1910 was scarcely the mass uprising of a downtrodden people.... Many of the details about its critical episodes are still controversial; no thoroughgoing investigation has yet appeared. But the available published materials point unmistakably to the conclusion that less than 20,000 men, and less than $1.5 million (raised in Mexico) killed an era. Even by Mexican standards it was a small affair, but its repercussions were great." Howard F. Cline, *The United States and Mexico* (Cambridge, Mass.: Harvard University Press, 1965), p. 121.

27. For additional elaboration of this point, see below, especially Chapters 16–18, and the last sections of this chapter.

28. Tuchman, *The Proud Tower, op. cit.*, p. 413.

29. Milbrath, *Political Participation, op. cit.*, p. 19. Data based on studies by Campbell et al., *The American Voter, op. cit.*, pp. 90–96, 473–498. Robert E. Lane, *Political Life: Why People Get Involved in Politics* (New York: Free Press, 1959). Julian L. Woodward and Elmo Roper, "Political Activity of American Citizens," *American Political Science Review*, Vol. 44 (1950), pp. 872–885.

30. Milbrath, *loc. cit.*, p. 21. For additional discussions along similar lines, see Dahl, *Modern Political Analysis, op. cit.*, especially pp. 60 ff.; Mitchell, *The American Polity, op. cit.*, pp. 175–178.

31. Seymour M. Lipset, *Political Man: The Social Bases of Politics* (Garden City, N.Y.: Doubleday, 1960), p. 67; Juan J. Linz, *The Social Bases of West German Politics*, Ph.D. dissertation, Department of Sociology, Columbia University, 1959, pp. 804–805; Milbrath, *op. cit.*, pp. 16–17; Almond and Verba, *The Civic Culture, op. cit.*, pp. 246–265; Berelson and Steiner, *Human Behavior, op. cit.*, p. 422.

32. See, for example, Clark, *Dark Ghetto, op. cit.*, p. 27.

33. We only mention these propositions briefly as they have often been discussed. For references, see below, Ch. 17, footnote 18, and Ch. 16, footnotes 62, 63, 67.

34. Such a model was developed and applied by Neil J. Smelser in his analysis of

industrial development. See his *Social Change in the Industrial Revolution* (London: Routledge and Kegan Paul, 1959), esp. pp. 402–409, and his *Theory of Collective Behavior, op. cit.,* p. 80 and *passim.*

35. The reasons for this statement are indicated *supra,* pp. 80–82.

36. On the difference between take-off and initiation points, see Etzioni, *Studies in Social Change, op. cit.,* pp. 38–41.

37. Arthur I. Waskow, *From Race Riot to Sit-In, 1919 and the 1960's: A Study in the Connections between Conflict and Violence* (Garden City, N.Y.: Doubleday, 1966).

38. Frantz Wendt, *The Nordic Council and Co-operation in Scandinavia* (Copenhagen: Munksgaard, 1959), p. 234; Neustadt, *Presidential Power, op. cit.,* p. 58; see also Harry S. Truman, *Memoirs* (Garden City, N.Y.: Doubleday, 1956), Vol. II, pp. 277–279; Hugh Seton-Watson's *Neither War Nor Peace* (New York: Praeger, 1960), pp. 19–45, especially p. 42.

39. Social psychologists have studied the steps by which people become committed. On the personal mobilization process involved, see also Robert Coles and Joseph Brenner, "American Youth in a Social Struggle: The Mississippi Summer Project," *American Journal of Orthopsychiatry,* Vol. 35 (1965), pp. 909–926. Dorwin Cartwright, "Some Principles of Mass Persuasion: Selected Findings of Research on the Sale of United States War Bonds," in Daniel Katz et al., *Public Opinion and Propaganda* (New York: Holt, Rinehart & Winston, 1954), pp. 382–393.

40. For additional discussion and some evidence, see below, Chapter 21, note 29.

41. For two typical accounts, see George Brager, "Organizing the Unaffiliated in a Low-Income Area," in a volume edited by Mayer N. Zald, *Social Welfare Institutions* (New York: Wiley & Sons, 1965), pp. 646–648, and Donald Janson, "Dr. King Plagued by Resistance and Apathy in Chicago Slums," *The New York Times,* January 16, 1967.

42. On the tense and changing relations between upper-class progressives and working-class trade unionists in New York in the pre-World War I period, see Irwin Yellowitz, *Labor and the Progressive Movement in New York State, 1897–1916* (Ithaca, N.Y.: Cornell University Press, 1965). On the relationship between "labor aristocracy" and the working class, see Rayden Harrison, *Before the Socialists: Studies in Labour and Politics, 1861–1881* (London: Routledge & Kegan Paul, 1965).

According to Michels, 28 of the 33 parliamentary representatives of the Italian Social Democrats in 1903 were of bourgeois or aristocratic origin. The percentage was much lower among the German Social Democrats in that year, only 13 out of 81, but this seems to us due to the fact that the German Social Democrats were in a more advanced "evolutionary" state. Robert Michels, "Proletariat und Bourgeoisie in der socialistichen Bewegung Italiens," *Archiv fuer Socialwissenschaft,* Vol. 21 (1905), pp. 379–380.

43. For detailed argument, see below, pp. 580–586.

44. On the changes of leadership in the civil rights movements, see Wilson, *Negro Politics, op. cit.,* pp. 295–313; Lewis Killian and Charles Grigg, *Racial Crisis in America: Leadership in Conflict* (Englewood Cliffs, N.J.: Prentice-Hall, 1964), pp. 84–90. On change of leadership in revolutionary movements, see Crane Brinton, *The Anatomy of Revolution* (New York: Vintage Books, 1959), pp. 148 ff.

45. Truman, *The Governmental Process, op. cit.*, pp. 111–155.

46. The more militant *Irgun* members were, on the average, lower in SES and education and, above all, were of "oriental" origin, when compared to the active *Hagana* or *Pal-mach*, members. See also Catherine V. Richards and Norman A. Polansky, "Reaching Working-Class Youth Leaders," *Social Work*, Vol. 4 (1959), p. 38. On the difference of the political activity of middle-class Negroes and other Negroes in the United States, the middle-class members being more passive, see Wilson, *Negro Politics, op. cit.*, pp. 90, 99–100. Brent M. Rutherford, "Psychopathology, Decision-Making, and Political Involvement," *The Journal of Conflict Resolution*, Vol. 10 (1966), pp. 387–407. The author provides an activity score including correlation with SES; see pp. 396–401.

47. For a discussion of such a mistaken perspective, see Philip Selznick, *The Organizational Weapon* (New York: Free Press, 1960), pp. 56–65, 276–291.

48. For some illustrative material, see Jacquelyne J. Clarke, *These Rights They Seek: A Comparison of the Goals and Techniques of Local Civil Rights Organizations* (Washington, D.C.: Public Affairs Press, 1962).

49. For the "anti-coalitionist" tendencies of many members of the New Left, see Jack Newfield, *A Prophetic Minority* (New York: New American Library, 1966).

50. Robert Aron, *Histoire de la libération de la France, juin 1944–mai 1945* (Paris: Fayard, 1959).

51. Colin Miller, "The Press and the Student Revolt," in Michael V. Miller and Susan Gilmore, (eds.), *Revolution at Berkeley* (New York: Dial Press, 1965), p. 347.

52. *The Los Angeles Times*, November 21, 1965. Other factors were at work at the same time, and it is impossible to prove conclusively a cause-and-effect relation. But analyses of letters to the editor, editorials, and so forth, seem to support our conclusion.

53. Bendix, *Work and Authority in Industry, op. cit.*, p. 270.

54. Emerson, *From Empire to Nation, op. cit.*, pp. 105–131. On a similar development between Negro political organizations and city machines, see Wilson, *Negro Politics, op. cit.*, pp. 22–24.

55. Winston Churchill's personal physician, Lord Moran, wrote: "He is a different man since America came into the war. The Winston I knew in London frightened me. . . . And now—in a night, it seems—a younger man has taken his place. . . . And at night he is gay and voluble, sometimes even playful."

"The P.M., I suppose, must have known that, if America stayed out, there could only be one ending to this business. And now suddenly the war is as good as won and England is safe." "Aboard battleship Duke of York, En route to America, Dec. 20, 1941." Charles McMoran Wilson Moran, *Churchill: The Struggle for Survival, 1940–1965* (Boston: Houghton Mifflin, 1966), pp. 9–10.

56. Cf. Mary Ellen Roach and Joanne Bubolz Eicher, *Dress, Adornment, and the Social Order* (New York: Wiley, 1965).

57. For additional discussion, see Mayer N. Zald and Roberta Ash, "Social Movement Organizations: Growth, Decay and Change," *Social Forces*, Vol. 44 (1966), pp. 327–341; Sheldon Messinger, "Organizational Transformation: A Case Study of a Declining Social Movement," *American Sociological Review*, Vol. 20 (1955), pp. 3–10. C. Wendell King uses a combination of a natural history approach and organizational analysis in accounting for the transformations of movement

organization. *Social Movements in the United States* (New York: Random House, 1956), pp. 39–57. Herbert Blumer, "Social Movements," in A. M. Lee (ed.), *Principles of Sociology* (New York: Barnes & Noble, 1955), pp. 99–220; Joseph Gusfield, *Symbolic Crusade: Status Politics and the American Temperance Movement* (Urbana, Ill.: University of Illinois Press, 1963); and Brian Crozier, *The Rebels: A Study of Post-War Insurrection* (London: Chatto & Windus, 1960).

58. See, for instance, N. A. Khan, "Resource Mobilization from Agriculture and Economic Development in India," *Economic Development and Cultural Change*, Vol. 12 (1963), pp. 42–54; Moshe Lissak, "Social Change, Mobilization and Exchange of Services between the Military Establishment and the Civil Society: The Burmese Case," *op. cit.*, Vol. 13 (1964), pp. 1–19.

59. This approach is most explicitly and systematically represented in a much-quoted article by Karl W. Deutsch, "Social Mobilization and Political Development," *American Political Science Review*, Vol. 55 (1961), pp. 493–514. Cf. Gino Germani, *Politica y sociedad en una época de transicion: De la sociedad tradiciónal a la sociedad de masas* (Buenos Aires: Ed. Paidos, 1962), p. 151, and Gino Germani, "Social Change and Intergroup Conflicts," in Irving Louis Horowitz (ed.), *The New Sociology* (New York: Oxford University Press, 1964), p. 396. Since this book was written, a thoughtful and comprehensive book on the subject has been published which we could not have taken into account here: J. P. Nettl, *Political Mobilization: A Sociological Analysis of Methods and Concepts* (London: Faber & Faber, 1967).

60. Deutsch, "Social Mobilization and Political Development," *op. cit.*, p. 493.

61. *Ibid.*, p. 494.

62. Gino Germani argues: "It may be said as a general rule that the faster the process of 'disposability' and mobilization, the greater the proportion of the population which becomes mobilized in a given period of time." See his "Social Change and Intergroup Conflict," in Horowitz, *The New Sociology, op. cit.*, p. 403. Disposability is the effect of disintegration. See p. 395. See also Deutsch, "Social Mobilization . . . ," *op. cit.*, p. 494.

63. On the mixture of traditional and modern in contemporary democratic industrial societies, see Lucian W. Pye and Sidney Verba, "Introduction" to their (eds.), *Political Culture and Political Development* (Princeton, N.J.: Princeton University Press, 1965), pp. 19–21. That "traditional" characteristics might be conducive to modernization was shown by Robert E. Ward and Dankwart A. Rustow in the conclusion to the volume which they edited, *Political Modernization in Japan and Turkey* (Princeton, N.J.: Princeton University Press, 1964), pp. 434–468, esp. pp. 441–447, and by Simon Ottenberg's "Ibo Receptivity to Change," in William R. Bascom and Melville J. Herskovits (eds.), *Continuity and Change in Africans Culture* (Chicago: University of Chicago Press, 1958), pp. 130–143.

64. S. N. Eisenstadt, "Patterns of Leadership and Social Homogeneity in Israel," *International Social Science Bulletin*, Vol. 8 (1956), pp. 36–53.

65. Karl W. Deutsch et al., *Political Community and the North Atlantic Area* (Princeton, N.J.: Princeton University Press, 1957), p. 50. This book is out of print. The main body of its findings are reprinted in a Doubleday anthology *International Political Communities* (Garden City, N.Y.: Anchor, 1966).

66. Etzioni, *Political Unification, op. cit.*, pp. 138 ff.

PART FOUR

SOCIETAL CONSENSUS

AND RESPONSIVENESS

ACTIVE—FOR WHAT?

"Active for what?" is a central question of this study. If this question were to be answered in terms of the personal values of the various observers, the social sciences would be divided into as many ideologies as there are sets of personal values. On the other hand, the answer may evolve from the societal directives reached through a process of authentic consensus-building among the actors under study. Such an assumption allows the social scientist to maintain both a scientific stand and a transcendental and critical viewpoint, as he seeks to explore the different degrees of activeness of various societies and, above all, the reasons that a society is not more responsive to the demands of *its* members. But are not the demands of various members in conflict or incompatible? The answer to this question is that (a) to the degree that a society is able to act in unison at all, it has *some mechanisms for converting the aggregate demands of its members into collective directives*, and it is its responsiveness to these directives that can be assessed. (b) Societal values may be realized in situations in which various members have conflicting, even incompatible, demands so long as the society is responsive to the needs of the membership at large and not merely to those of a minority.

Two central substantive questions for the study of societal guidance, therefore, are (a) under what conditions do societies realize their values, and (b) in what ways are these values determined? Most societies, most of the time, are unable to achieve the goals they pursue or to solve the problems they seek to solve. The generally low capacity to guide societal processes, especially societal change, can be traced analytically to two major kinds of limitations—to deficiencies in control processes, which have been the focus of much of the previous discussion, and to the lack of consensus, especially an authentic one, to which we turn our attention now.

The concept of consensus, Marxists have argued, conceals the fact that conflict is the basis of society. There is no general will which is expressed by the existing societal pattern; rather, this pattern reflects the imposition of the will of the powerful on the weak, and consensus is one of the tools used by the powerful to ease their domination. While we concur that conflict is a basic fact of societal life, and that societal consensus does often reflect the will of some members of society more than others, many societal systems do evolve a shared pattern; conflict may continue to occur within and around this pattern, but it is a shared pattern nevertheless. While there exists no general societal will that operates as a force above and beyond the members, viable societies have mechanisms which produce, from the disparate wills of their members, a shared will which—under conditions to be specified—does reflect, if to varying degrees, the will of all the members.

To explore the quality of the consensus of a particular kind of society we must first specify the societal members—i.e., the actors who participate in shaping the societal directives. Are they individuals whose preferences are aggregated by the market and voting mechanisms to provide a societal consensus? Are they elites which produce consensus among the masses as well as the policies which this consensus endorses? Or is the society composed of a complex web of collective bonds and organizational links which constitute both the "upward" means of expression of the collectivities and the "downward" means of control of the societal elites? In Chapter 16, we explore this morphological question. This discussion of the composition of society provides a "static," structural backdrop for the study of societal dynamics that is the subject of Chapter 17. The interrelations between consensus and power and the conditions under which consensus is relatively responsive to the changing needs of the members of a society are explored in Chapter 18.

We cannot over-emphasize that the following discussion provides neither a theory of modern society and democratic and totalitarian politics, nor an analysis of American, Soviet, Chinese, and Israeli societies. We are concerned with the development of a theory of societal guidance and with the specification of its various components and mechanisms. These are illustrated with examples taken from the political and societal processes of various types of societies; while this theory may aid in the analysis of various societies, such an analysis is not attempted here.

The fact that all the chapters of a book cannot be read simultaneously with "later" arguments supporting "earlier" ones is more regrettable in this part of the book than in others. Here, we deal with one component of consensus-building; in contrast to the "mass society" theory, we stress that consensus-building does occur in post-modern societies—its structural foundations have not been eroded. It is not until Chapter 21, however, following the discussion of the boundaries of systems (in Chapters 19 and 20), that we explore the other major element of consensus: As we see it, although there is consensus-building in post-modern societies, a significant part of it is inauthentic.* Our position is, thus, an intermediary one between those who see the post-modern society pessimistically as a "mass" society and those who optimistically see it as a pluralistic society and recognize only one main modern aberration, totalitarianism. (The reasons for our differences from the first position are discussed in this part; we deal with the second position in the Epilogue.)

---

* The concept of inauthenticity is defined and discussed later, pp. 616ff.

CHAPTER 16

The Morphology of Modern

and Post-Modern Societies

W HAT ARE the structure and organization of modern and post-modern societies?* Do these societies provide the morphological conditions which enable the building of consensus? To answer these questions, we first specify the members of a modern (or post-modern) society and explore the ways in which these members relate to each other (in the first section of this chapter); we then seek to delineate the differences in the morphological bases of consensus-building between democratic and totalitarian politics (in the second section of this chapter).

---

* Here, we treat late-modern and post-modern societies together; they are not significantly different in terms of the dimension discussed in this part. Early-modern societies are used as a base for comparison.

432

Collectivities and Societies

Consensus in "Mass Societies"?[1]*

One popular model of the morphology of modern and post-modern society depicts a mass society in which the leaders who initiate a policy gain its endorsement by relying on their charismatic appeal and on the mass media which they control. The leaders are viewed as appealing directly to the individual members of society who, in turn, respond directly to the leaders. The model posits direct interaction between the leaders of the state and the atomized masses; it, thus, assumes that the structures "in between" have been eroded.

> Looking at the individual and his government, one is tempted to see him as lonely, powerless, and somewhat frightened by the immensity of the powers he faces. This is in fact one of the most frequent descriptions of the average man in modern political societies. In the theory of the "mass society" the individual is described as related directly as individual to the state. He has no other social resources to support him in this relationship and naturally feels ineffective and anxious.[2]

The study of the morphology of the modern societies and of their political organization is, therefore, irrelevant.

In contrast, we hold that while there is some direct interaction between the national elites and the citizenry, a high proportion of the socio-political articulation in modern society occurs in other, less direct, relationships. Moreover, much of the direct interaction which does occur is greatly affected by the membership of the citizens in a variety of collectivities, sub-collectivities, and their respective organizations. The national elites devote most of their time and energy to dealing with organized collectivities and their elites and only a small part of their resources to direct appeals to "the people." And the effect of these appeals on the individual citizens is largely determined not by their specific nature or by the particular elites involved but by the multiple membership of the citizens in micro- and macro-cohesive groupings and in the organizations of these groupings.[3] (While the role of direct interaction seems to increase in importance in situations of societal disorganization and crisis,[4] these situations are highly atypical and cannot be used to study typical societal morphology.) In short, we hold that an understanding of the composition and dynamics of the collective units and organizations is essential for an understanding of the morphological bases of modern and post-modern consensus-building.

While the process of modernization did entail some disintegration of the cohesive collective units, we suggest that a much more important effect of

---

* Reference notes for this chapter appear on page 456.

modernization is the transformation of the sub-collectivities', and collectivities' structures, functions, and links to the society and state. While most members of modern and post-modern societies seem to have reduced the scope and intensity of their commitments to these collective (or "intermediary") units and to the units' elites, those societal sub-units still constitute a major if not primary basis of membership and action. Although the modern and post-modern state and society are superimposed upon and, to a degree, even penetrate these collective units, they do not replace them. The finding that many citizens are "nationalistic" does not weaken our proposition so long as the sub-national units themselves support and identify with the national unit; there is no necessary conflict between the two levels of commitment.[5] When these levels do come into conflict—as between ethnic and national loyalties— the potency of the sub-national units becomes evident in societies as different from each other as Canada, the Soviet Union, Belgium, and Israel. We hold that all modern and post-modern societies have such sub-units of one variety or another; these are often ethnic and occasionally religious, regional, or economic.* In a sense, they constitute national overlayers, which vary in their scope and degree of penetration, superimposed upon feudal, federal, or tribalistic underlayers.[6]

A society with viable collective units may still constitute a "mass society" if the units have no autonomy—i.e., if they are controlled by the supra-unit elites. Hence, once it is established that societal units have not disintegrated, we need to determine the direction of the flow of consensus—is it upward, an approval which the "grass roots" grant to the political elites if their actions are satisfactory? Or is the flow downward, manufactured by the political elites? For the most part, we suggest, the process of consensus-building constitutes a multi-level interplay between individual members and their collectivities and between these collectivities and the various political elites; i.e., the process flows both upward and downward.[7] The societal elites' capacity to produce consensus through manipulation (rather than through responsiveness to the perspectives of the individual members and the collectivities) decreases as the competition among the elites increases and becomes more public. While there are significant differences from this viewpoint among societies, some competition exists within all societies, as well as some external penetration in which the elites of one society reduce the capacity of the elites of another society to manipulate its membership (e.g., the British Broadcasting Corporation may constrain to some degree the Soviet elites). The elites of each society are also constrained by the commitments around which they or their predecessors have built societal consensus in the past; as we have seen, it is difficult and costly to change contextuating orientations, and unless contexts are changed, the new bits which can be introduced are limited to those which fit existing contexts.[8] Finally, the

---

* Some evidence in support of this proposition is cited below.

members of societies—the collectivities and sub-collectivities—have their own organizations and elites, policies and power, including some capacity to change the elites in charge of the society-wide organizations and the state— i.e., the national political elites.

From the viewpoint of the national political elites, the collectivities act as constraints; they must be taken into account and can be manipulated only to a degree, and organized collectivities offer greater resistance to manipulation than unorganized ones. From the viewpoint of any collectivity and its elites, the national political elites act as constraints in that they respond to other collectivities as well and have perspectives of their own.* The study of consensus-building is, therefore, largely a study of the details of the structured interaction between collectivities (and coalitions of collectivities) and the national political elites rather than a study of the responses of the masses to national charismatic leaders.

The structure of consensus-building has been analyzed as an exchange between society-wide elites and collectivities. For example, the elites grant legitimacy to some policies and goals, and the collectivities, in turn, provide political support (e.g., votes).[9] On a highly analytic level, this model suffices; for the purposes of a more concrete morphological analysis, we must add that the consensus-building exchange between society-wide elites and collectivities is itself not direct but mediated and affected by various organizational structures. These include private and public interest groups, political parties, voluntary associations, labor unions, and social movements.†

For similar reasons, the analysis of consensus-building can use only indirectly the findings of public opinion studies which divide the public by analytic rather than action categories. The analytic approach has greatly improved public opinion studies by its recognition that the public is to be treated not as one monolithic unit but as a set of sub-publics. For many purposes, it has proven productive to characterize these sub-publics according to their individual members' attributes.[10] However, the consensus-building structure, especially for domestic policies, is composed not of educated, semi-educated, and illiterate publics or attentive and inattentive ones, but of societal units that cut across these categories—namely, collectivities and organizations. While the membership of these units does vary in terms of education, attention, and activation, we suggest that in significant societal matters, the heterogeneous membership of any unit acts more in unison than in accord with the members of other units. Thus, for instance,

---

* A similar relationship, as we shall see, exists between collectivities and the sub-collectivities.

† Here a difference is to be observed between the initiation of a policy or a line of action and the mobilization of support for it. Initiation in Washington, for instance, is largely in the hands of middle-level officials. Support must be won more widely and on both higher and lower levels. See, for example, Brzezinski and Huntington, *Political Power: USA/ USSR, op. cit.*, p. 203.

we expect that the passive members of the American Medical Association (AMA) will tend to act in terms of the medicare issue more like the active members of the AMA than like the passive members of, let us say, the AFL–CIO.[11] A characteristic of organized collectivities is that active and passive members are "packed" together and act together. The active members to a degree mobilize the passive ones in a direction that is in accord with the active members' perspectives. That is, the passive members would be even more passive if they were not somewhat activated by the active members. (There are some individuals who are not members of any collectivity, but they seem to be a minority, are usually not mobilizers, and are often difficult to mobilize.)[12] We will now explore in some detail the proposition that the main societal units have been transformed rather than have disintegrated and specify the ways in which this fundamental change affects societal consensus-building.

Modernization of Collectivities

An important approach to societal analysis, as we have seen, has accepted the proposition that the historical transition to modernity has entailed the destruction of the collectivities, both as cohesive units and as bases of autonomous political action.[13] The "mass society" proposition was stated with reference to the basic societal unit, the family; to ecological sub-collectivities such as the village community; to religious, ethnic, and racial collectivities; to classes; and to voluntary associations. In short, the complete societal matrix between the state and the individual was expected to disintegrate. This prognosis projected on-going processes in a straight line into the future, expecting them to continue in the same direction until they reached their logical conclusions. However, this has not occurred. *The family, the community, and the intermediary bodies did decline in significance*, but we suggest, *the process was not one of continued disintegration but of "decolonization" and transformation*. In other words, the cohesive units* shed some of their "colonies," but the "metropolitan" (or core) unit was transformed rather than destroyed.†

As the metamorphoses of all these cohesive units were similar in nature, it is of interest to specify briefly the ways in which modern cohesive units emerged from traditional ones. In general, "decolonization" occurred

---

* This term is used to refer to collectivities and sub-collectivities as well as to cohesive units which are microscopic, especially the family.

† This process is similar to the often-discussed differentiation process—only, as we see it, the social units under study did not differentiate and continue to serve some of their earlier functions in a more differentiated structure but "lost" some functions to other, new units. The *total system* may be differentiating (though, to a larger degree, it did not exist at all in the past), but the *units* are not. Rather, they have decolonized.

through the delegation of functions to new, specialized units. The family, for example, lost most of its functions as an organizational unit of labor to the corporations. More generally, traditional collectivities have to a great extent surrendered their instrumental functions to rising organizational units but have retained their expressive ones and, thus, have become specialized units themselves. This growing expressive specialization has been referred to, in regard to the modern family, as the rise of companionship,[14] but it seems also to have occurred in ecological units (compare the modern suburb to the rural community),[15] in ethnic groups (which lost many of their instrumental functions to the welfare state but have maintained some of their social and normative importance),[16] and in religious groups (often criticized for their increased "social" nature).[17]

In the process of transformation, the internal structure of the "metropolitan" units has changed to become less hierarchical and less authoritarian, and membership has become less ascribed. These two trends seem to lead to a greater responsiveness of these units to their members. This, in turn, is functional for their new expressive specialization. Viewed in this light, the higher divorce rate in the modernized family finds a parallel in the higher tolerance for the turnover of membership in religious groups (through increased conversion), ethnic groups (through increased inter-marriage), and ecological groups (through an extension of the "open door" policy). For all of these units, a smaller stress on ascription is an accommodation both to the increased vertical and horizontal (ecological) mobility which modernization requires and fosters and to the greater capacity for members to change their affiliations to those with more compatible units.*

In addition to the adaptation of the traditional cohesive units, new cohesive units have emerged whose main functions are expressive. Unlike the old units which have acquired only elements of achievement, the new ones tend to be highly achievement-oriented. These include some occupational and professional associations[18] and social clubs which are either purely or primarily expressive.[19] (Even political clubs may be highly expressive.)[20]

A major difference between traditional and modern collectivities lies in their scope and pervasiveness.[21] Rather than being composed of a few collectivities which contain most of the members of society and which impose similar sets of norms, modern and post-modern societies are composed of numerous sub-collectivities whose memberships are only partially overlapping. Thus, a typical person will be a member of several sub-collectivities, no one of which can fully determine his membership in others

---

* This line of analysis ties functional to a genetic analysis, that of change, by the use of future-system models. We seek to specify the functions of a structure in an old system, its functions in the new system, and the structural alterations which the functional changes entailed.

(which is what we refer to as narrow scope). The capacity of modern and post-modern collectivities to set norms for their members, especially for behavior in other than their own internal affairs (their pervasiveness) is limited, and their normative guidance tends to be less "harmonized" than that of the traditional collectivities. Hence, the relative influence of these collectivities on their members—especially on their political behavior—is comparatively limited, and this accounts for the inability of organizations that are based on such collectivities to "deliver" more than a fraction of their members' votes. Typical members of modern and post-modern societies, therefore, do lead lives that are fragmented among several not fully coordinated collectivities. While these multiple and partially incompatible affiliations produce some conflicts, these affiliations also increase the autonomy of the members.[22]

The fact that these late and post-modern collectivities are less pervasive and narrower in scope than the earlier ones does not imply that their members are isolated atoms. There is no lack of membership in micro-cohesive units (such as families, friendship groups, and peer work groups)[23] which, in turn, are encompassed by sub-collectivities, collectivities, and societies. Furthermore, these units are involved in the political process. For instance, suburban neighborhoods provide an expressive base for political clubs, friendship groups—for political cells or cliques in political organizations, and the family—for societal knowledge and consciousness, elements of normative and political education.[24] We explore below the conditions under which such activation of the cohesive units is meaningful and the extent to which their societal and political links to the societal supra-units are effective. It suffices to say here that, in general, the extent to which the political efficacy and societal relevancy of the cohesive units are insufficient is primarily due not to the transformations of these units but to deficiencies on the next level— especially, the society-wide consensus-building mechanisms, the allocation of assets, and the opportunities for political participation.

The Stratification Base of Collectivities

We have argued that the major member-units of modernized societies are collectivities and organizations rather than masses of individuals. We now explore the ways in which these collectivities and organizations are bound into societies and states, which, in turn, will provide us with the morpho-logical background for the analysis of the ways in which society-wide consensus is built. The combination of societal sub-units into larger entities is affected by the fact that each collectivity and its sub-units has a position in a stratification structure—that is, in the societal distribution of assets. The associational and symbolic bases of a collectivity may be many, varied, and not parallel, but we still can rank each collectivity as compared to others in the same society in the same period.* Some collectivities are "horizontal" (i.e., most of their members have a similar stratification position), some are vertical (which tends to be the case for regional units), and some are diagonal (which often occurs in regard to semi-assimilated immigrant groupings, because mobility tends to spread the members among the stratification layers). The position of some collectivities is unbalanced; they are high in terms of some allocations of societal assets and low in terms of others. In each case, however, a collectivity's position relative to other such units in a stratification structure can be established and compared to the positions of other units or to its own position in earlier time periods.

Thus, while the possible stratification positions are much more varied and complex than the class theory assumes, collectivities are meaningful stratification units. Their members tend to have shared positions and, hence, shared objective interests (e.g., to change or conserve the existing allocations), similar vantage points (society looks different from the bottom of the scale than it does from the top), and, usually, a shared consciousness as collectivities superimpose a subjective superstructure of associational and organizational processes on the shared stratification positions.† These propositions may at first seem contrary to the considerable amount of data which indicates both the existence of divergent perspectives among the members of any one stratification unit and the multiple memberships of each person. We present below the reasons that we hold that collectivities are a significant (though, of course, not the exclusive) basis for determining a person's societal perspectives, and, hence, act as a constraint on the extent to which he can be manipulated by the supra-units of the state and the society. It suffices to say here that we are dealing with cohesive and organized units; they are more integrated and autonomous than mere stratification categories and, therefore, also more homogeneous and better able to act in unison.‡ Macro-analysis can avoid the errors of atomistic analysis by using

---

* The difficulties of such ranking have often been discussed and the methods reviewed. For an overview, see Bernard Barber, *Social Stratification: A Comparative Analysis of Structure and Process* (New York: Harcourt, Brace & Co., 1957), esp. pp. 176–185. See also Louis Guttman, "A Revision of Chapin's Social Status Scale," *American Sociological Review*, Vol. 7 (1942), pp. 362–369.

† These are the processes which accentuate the similarities and minimize the differences among the members of a collectivity. For additional discussion, see *supra*, Chapter 10, pp. 231–234.

‡ When the associational and organizational processes of a collectivity are externally controlled, its consciousness may be misdirected and its authentic identity concealed, but, nevertheless, the collectivity still tends to have a distinct character. The so-called false consciousness of the working class is not identical to the self-consciousness of the middle class even when the direction of consciousness of the working class is slanted toward middle-class perspectives.[25] There are, of course, diverse perspectives within each collectivity and even sub-collectivity, but—as has often been shown—to a lesser extent than exist among them.

the collectivities as meaningful societal units and exploring the consensus-formation among them; collectivities are the starting point rather than the individual members of society. Moreover, it should be noted that the relations among the collectivities are not completely given; thus, more encompassing units can be formed through society-wide consensus-building processes. The collectivities are, by virtue of their positions in a stratification structure, related to each other, and this structure limits both the need and the capacity to build consensus. We now explore these more encompassing relations, shifting our frame of reference from that of a collectivity (and its sub-units) to that of a society (and its components).

Societies: Collectivities and Mass Sectors

Although all societies are combinations of collectivities and sub-collectivities, they differ in the extent to which they have an unaffiliated "mass" sector (even in a post-modern society, however, this sector contains only a minority of the members). Societies also vary in the degree to which their supra-organizations, particularly their states and society-wide economic systems, draw on non-collective elements, but even in systems in which this degree is relatively high, the units that are being related—which exchange in the market and which are being administered by the state—are to a great extent collectivities and sub-collectivities and not individuals.* Societies also differ in the degree to which their collective units are integrated into supra-units by shared values and symbols and interaction processes, and in terms of the ways in which such integration is accomplished. However, again, the units which compose these varying combinations are primarily collectivities.

Several primitive societies have been shown to be combinations of a few sub-collectivities with minimal market and state supra-organizations.[26] This was also true for feudal societies with the difference that the latter tended to have a collectivity, such as the knights and barons,[27] which cut across the local sub-collectivities. Ancient bureaucratic societies such as China, Egypt, and Byzantium[28] as well as early nation-states imposed an expanding state on the underlying collectivities and somewhat weakened their power, thus providing a relatively centralized political shell for the multi-center societal base.[29] From this viewpoint, the modern and post-modern societies are not a new kind of society but exhibit an extension of this earlier trend. The "mass" sector has grown and the role of the state and the market has increased; collectivities have become less strong, less

---

* The particular commodities that are bought, for instance, are partly determined by the individuals' purchasing power and tastes, the kind of shops available, and the range of choices, but all of these factors are affected by the collectivities to which the individuals belong—e.g., pawn shops are found in lower-class neighborhoods; high-quality clothing stores are found in affluent suburbs.

encompassing, less pervasive, and, as we shall see, less authentic. But the pluralistic (or "feudal") underlayer remains.

In late modern and post-modern societies, there are, in addition to the state, numerous organizations which either combine sub-collectivities into collectivities (as in many ethnic and labor organizations) or serve as the core of a "new," achievement-based collectivity (as do some professional and occupational organizations).[30] Those organizations which are not of these two kinds, but which cut into various collectivities, directly organizing individuals—tend to have limited societal significance. Thus, stamp collectors of all ethnic groupings and classes may unite within an organization, but churches tend to draw on local sub-collectivities;[31] radio hams typically seem to be isolated individuals, but farm associations rest on local sub-collectivities.[32] We suggest that *the state and, more generally, the society-wide political processes deal much more with organizations that represent sub-collectivities and their combinations than with organizations which have no collective base.*

The degree to which the state and organizations deal with individuals directly rather than as members of collective units increases in limited historical periods of sharp transition in which there often is a relative increase in the "mass" element; even in these situations, however, only a fraction of a society has the attributes of a mass. Actually, such periods often entail a regression of the polity to a point of greater reliance on the member units (such as local communities or tribes) and less reliance on the society at large.

Only when the political overlayer collapses and society-wide associations and organizations cease to function—a situation approximated by the combination of national defeat with uncontrolled inflation or depression for a sustained period (as in Germany in the early 1930s or in Russia in 1916–1917)—does the mass sector significantly increase. And even under these rare and highly adverse conditions, most parts of the society continue to function as sub-collectivities and collectivities. However, under these circumstances, the mass sector may become sufficiently large to create the societal base for a political transformation, and the collectivities' lack of effective society-wide articulation with the national polity may lead to the formation of a new society and, thus, also to structural transformation—unless, of course, the old political organization quickly rights itself.

It should also be noted that these relatively "mass" situations of political and societal anarchy tend to generate that which, on most dimensions, is their opposite—social movements, in which mobilization and commitments are great, cohesive bonds are intimate and authentic, and the level of political macroscopic action is high. In turn, these movements, often lead to the formation of a new polity and societal structure. Thus, society seems to "abhor" the "mass" situation—to avoid it most of the time and leave it rapidly when it arises.

In a Comparative Perspective

The basic macroscopic building-stones are similar in all modern and post-modern societies. The ways in which they are combined into supra-units, however, differ considerably and greatly affect the degrees to which collectivities and their organizations are viable and autonomous, authentic society-wide consensus can be produced, and the society is able to transform itself. Having focused in the first section of this chapter on the common features of late modern and post-modern societies, we now explore the differences among them. The comparison is deliberately schematic and focuses on the morphological dimensions (introduced in the preceding section) largely in terms of ideal-types.

The Societal Context of Collectivities: The Degree of Specification

Societies and states differ in the degree to which they merely provide a context for their member units as against the extent to which they also specifically control their conduct. Contextuating control sets the limits within which those who are subject to control are free to alter their conduct and make their own decisions.[33] Prescriptive control is the opposite term; here, the subjects' conduct is specifically directed. As controlling overlayers differ in their degrees of prescription or contextuation, we use *prescriptive control* to refer to a high degree of specification and *contextuating control* to refer to a low degree of specification; we refer to a "medium degree of specification" when a control mechanism falls between prescriptive and contextuating controls.

Democratic societies and states fall on the contextuating side of this continuum of the specification; they provide, respectively, supra-collective and supra-organization of control contexts for their member collectivities and organizations. Democracies have often been characterized as pluralistic societies, which is a valid observation in that they contain pluralities of collective actors whose interactions greatly affect their political processes. However, the plurality of actors in a democratic society is not to be viewed as interacting in an atomistic fashion, without a context. The various member units are tied both by integrative bonds and organizational links into supra-units, though these supra-units tend not to be prescriptive. In fact, these society-wide supra-units tend to exercise control which is less prescriptive than the units' control of their sub-units. This can be seen in the fact that rights to dissent and to conflict are more highly institutionalized in the relations between democratic societies and their collectivity-members than in the relations between these collectivities and their member sub-collectivities and between the sub-collectivities and their individual members.

To state that member-collectivities are not prescriptively controlled in democratic societies is to state that they are autonomous within the limits of the prevailing contexts. The extent to which and the purposes for which the collectivities use their autonomy are explored below. It suffices to say here that they do have a potential capacity to affect the society and the state rather than merely being affected by them.

Totalitarian societies fall on the prescriptive side of the continuum. The more prescriptive character of their control processes is evident both in the more encompassing and more intensive relations between the state (and the society) and the individual citizen *and* in the more specific control of the collectivities and organizations by the society-wide political overlayer. Still, the totalitarian societies are not mass societies; the Party–State does not atomize but rather penetrates and controls, transforms and adapts, the collectivities and their organizations.

There are significant differences in terms of this control dimension within each type of society. The Soviet Union, for instance, tends toward more prescriptive control than Poland; in the control of most societal sectors, the United States is less contextuating than New Zealand.[34] There are also differences within each society over time; e.g., Khrushchev's Russia was, in general, less prescriptively controlled than Stalin's.

Despite these differences within each type of society, however, the typology is useful as a first approximation. So far as the guidance of most societal sectors is concerned, the less specifically controlled totalitarian societies (e.g., Tito's Yugoslavia) are still more prescriptive than the more specifically controlled democracies (e.g., De Gaulle's France). For reasons discussed below, we expect the control of democracies to become much more encompassing but not much more prescriptive, while we expect the control of totalitarian societies to become less prescriptive without necessarily reducing its scope.

Before we can discuss—for the limited purposes of the theory advanced here—the differences among totalitarian societies (especially Hitler's Germany, Mao's China, and the post-Stalin Soviet Union), another dimension must be added to our analysis: Political penetration.

Political Penetration, Disintegration, and Transformation

One major way in which a mass society is said to be generated is through the deliberate mobilization of the individual members by the state (or by other society-wide political organizations). This kind of mobilization can be accomplished either by the deliberate disintegration of the existing macro- and micro-cohesive units to afford the state *direct* access to the individual members, or by the state's control of the elites of the cohesive units from above, thus controlling the individual members *indirectly*. The Chinese attempts to dissolve the traditional families and villages and to replace them with communes illustrates the first approach to political penetration. Subsequent Chinese attempts to use the traditional villages and extended families for mobilization is an example of the second approach.[35]

While direct penetration does not always accompany highly prescriptive control and indirect penetration is not always evident with less prescriptive control, these factors do tend to correlate. Thus, to the degree that our assumption of the necessity of restricting the penetration of cohesive units to the indirect type for long-run societal policies is correct, this sets a limit to the degree to which political control can be prescriptive—i.e., the units which are viable from the viewpoint of the political overlayer are also, at least to some extent, autonomous.

In other words, we suggest that a society's political overlayer cannot maintain an intensive, direct-penetration, control organization. Nazi Germany made an extensive effort in this direction, especially during World War II, but its polity collapsed before the stability of the system was tested. (The fact that direct-penetration was used primarily to mobilize the citizens for war limits the applicability of the German experiment because crises, temporary by definition, facilitate the use of intensive direct penetration.)* The attempts of Mao's China at intensive direct penetration of the villages and extended families were so costly economically that, despite the control assumption of the regime that political considerations should take priority over all others, the regime was forced to shift to an indirect penetration organization.[36] The same seems to hold, though to a lesser degree, for the organization of Chinese urban workers, even though their cohesive units were less viable initially than those of the Chinese peasants. Moreover, the extent to which China was able to maintain direct political penetration of the cohesive units for a fairly extended period of time might be in part explained by the external pressures to which it was subject; this may have encouraged a relatively longer and more intensive crisis-mobilization. (This factor seems to have been relevant in the case of the Soviet Union as well.)

The Cultural Revolution in China has been viewed as an effort to strengthen the direct relations between the leadership and the "masses," and to reduce oligarchization and institutionalization—i.e., to restore intensive direct penetration. But even if this be the case, the very fact that a revolutionary restoration was needed shows that the societal processes were tending toward the opposite, particularistic direction. While it may be said that a direct penetration organization can be maintained by sporadic Cultural Revolutions, such a "fits and starts" organization is very costly, almost impossible to stabilize, and itself denotes long periods of particularism that are "interrupted" by short periods of more intensive—though not necessarily very intensive—direct penetration. In short, the morphological conditions

---

* For the reasons for this statement, see Chapter 15, pp. 397–400, above (discussion of crisis-mobilization). Other reasons are discussed below.

for a "permanent revolution," for high activeness, seem to lie in a more continual and more "indirect" organization than the Chinese model offers.

On the other hand, society-wide mobilization may be greatly enhanced by intensified indirect penetration, especially if this helps to transform the particularistic units in the direction of becoming more committed to the societal goals, more modern, and more supra-unit oriented. (Communist revolutions in underdeveloped countries, it has been suggested, often entail a degree of modernization and nation-building as well as the introduction of specific societal patterns.)

Hence, the alternatives are not between political mobilization (often depicted as direct penetration, as the disintegration of the traditional units and the avoidance of new particularisms) *or* institutionalization,[37] but between varying degrees of control and transformation of the cohesive units— i.e., between varying modes of institutionalization. These may allow for more indirect penetration and, thus, for increased mobilization.

Therefore, we view the contemporary Soviet Union rather than more revolutionary or "radical" societies such as Stalin's Russia, Mao's China, and Hitler's Germany as the typical totalitarian society, and it is this society which we compare to the typical democratic society. In other words, if two types of societies are to be compared, the comparison ought to be either of their formative or their "mature" (and relatively stable) stages but not of the formative stage of one type of society to the mature stage of another. Nazi Germany never matured beyond the social-movement, crisis-mobilization phase. Mao's China deliberately seeks to extend this phase, but we expect that it, too, will move in the "mature" direction. (Unlike the USSR, China has yet to weather a succession crisis, the test of the stability of totalitarian polities.) It is the Soviet Union and several East European societies which reveal the features of a mature totalitarian society—a society which can sustain its societal organization over a long period of time without fundamental transformation.

The question of whether or not more than one type of "mature" totalitarian society could evolve is relevant here. Thus, it could be argued that there are important permanent differences between the Soviet Union and Communist China. Especially relevant to these considerations are China's greater reliance on normative controls and social power (involved in the "mass line" use of study, discussion, and critique groups) and relatively smaller reliance on coercion as compared to Stalin's Russia, and China's lesser emphasis on utilitarian controls as compared to either Stalin's or post-Stalin Russia. China's interest in de-centralization seems to have longer and stronger roots than the Soviet experience. If this particular control mix continues to be applied in China, it may allow for relatively more direct penetration in the long run. But these are variations within the basic limits of the totalitarian type of society. Extensive atomization to serve direct totalitarian penetration, we hold, cannot be stabilized.

Thus, as we see it, it is only the early, "immature" totalitarian society that seeks to disintegrate the micro- and macro-cohesive units. While some such tendencies still exist in the contemporary USSR, they are neither effective nor pursued with much vigor. The family, for example—little challenged initially is now both adapted to and highly legitimated by the regime.[38] Traditional villages and other ecological communities seem to have been replaced only in part, and the new ecological units (especially collective farms) which have been organized seem to be cohesive.[39] Ethnic groupings (or "nationalities") were recognized from the beginning; the extent of their legitimation has increased, and they have regained some of their original functions.[40]

While the old (though adapted) and new cohesive societal units seem viable and controlled mainly through indirect penetration, the totalitarian aspect is evident in the specificity with which they are controlled: These units are organized largely through the use of downward control mechanisms; only to a limited degree do these units serve as a basis for viable upward consensus-formation mechanisms. Thus, totalitarianism is much more manifest on the level of political control than in the structure of the societal underlayer. But even on the political level, there is a degree of pluralism and of contextuating control. There are nation-wide collectivities with values, symbols, interests and leadership hierarchies of their own which participate in the political processes. The military, the scientific establishment, and the industrial administration all seem to have some such attributes within the context of the Party–State.[41] Elites of organizations and of collectivities deal, to some extent, directly with each other about joint policies. These imply a less than complete separation of the polity from the society and some politization of societal interaction. However, the framework within which the interaction among the elites of cohesive units occurs is much more prescriptive, both ideologically and structurally, than in a democracy. The Party–State, the supra-organization, rules out a large number of options and agitates for a specific option in terms of which the participants (e.g., unions and management) are allowed to work out only minor variations.[42]

In summary, we have explored some differences among societies in terms of the ways in which the society-wide political overlayers control and penetrate the member units and, thus, provide the framework within which the societies attempt to build consensus. In discussing these differences, we have focused on society-wide organizations—in particular, the state and the totalitarian party on the one hand and on collectivities on the other hand. We now introduce the additional element of the organizations which are based on the collectivities and provide either an instrument for the autonomous action of collectivities, or another method for controlling and indirectly penetrating them. To explore this question, the relations of the sub-collectivities to the collectivities must also be studied.

Collectivities and Organizations

In the late modern and post-modern societies, sub-collectivities seem to be bound into collectivities by associations, integrative communication networks, collectivity-leadership, and collectivity-based organizations; they are also combined into action units through organizations that are not coextensive with any collectivity. Some collectivities are mobilized by two or more organizations, with only partial overlap of membership and leadership. Some organizations, even though they appeal to different collectivities, have interlocking directorships. Thus, in one way or another and often in several intricate combinations, sub-collectivities are built into larger societal units.

Attempts to explore further these societal bonds and links must take into account that the organizations tend to be much narrower in scope than the sub-collectivities which they mobilize. Actually, the organizations that are not themselves core-organizations of collectivities tend to be "mono-sectoral" (professional, religious, *or* social), while sub-collectivities tend to be multi-sectoral and multi-faceted. Typical sub-collectivities are: Lower class, Italian, and Catholic in South Boston;[43] lower class, Puerto Rican, and Catholic in East Harlem;[44] middle class, Reform Jewish, and third-generation American on the upper east side of Manhattan.[45] (The ethnic character of sub-collectivities has often been viewed as a special quality of American society in which class lines are "blurred" or superseded by ethnic ones. In fact, many societies evidence strong and powerful ethnic groupings which cut across other potential bases of collectivity-building, while economic status seems only infrequently to provide such a powerful base.)[46]

The mobilization of collectivities by organizations seems to occur to a lesser extent in democratic societies than in totalitarian ones; in turn, the role of the collectivity-associations seems to be greater in democratic societies. That is, collectivity-organizations tend to be significantly more autonomous from societal and state control and the relations among organizations that mobilize the same as well as different collectivities are less specifically determined in democratic than in totalitarian societies.

The range of political alternatives and societal mobilization and action cannot be derived from the number of organizations to which a citizen belongs. The number and variety of political options that are available to most of the citizens of a democracy are considerably smaller than the number of organizations they join, and they join fewer organizations than has often been suggested. Americans, for example, are widely believed to be greater "joiners" than the citizens of other democracies,[47] though even in the United States such affiliations are much less frequent than is often supposed. Thus, while various travelers and commentators have referred to the forty or fifty organizations to which an average American belongs and historians have talked about a "general mania"[48] of affiliation, data show that the overwhelming majority of American citizens seem to belong to two or fewer organizations.[49] The number is higher for the middle than for the lower class, but even the majority of middle-class citizens do not belong to more than four organizations, many of which are "specialized"—either educational, or religious, or political.[50] Some of these organizations are of little societal consequence, while others have much greater societal significance but largely in nonpolitical matters; it, thus, seems correct to expect that *most citizens have no or only one political affiliation, and most of those who have more than one tend to "harmonize" them.* Only a minority are caught in cross-pressures and remain caught.

The number of political alternatives of the citizens of totalitarian societies is obviously smaller than that available in democracies, but it is not necessarily as small as the number of organizations with which they are affiliated. Informal and semi-formal factions (or sub-organizations) are tolerated and provide a base for political action.[51] Moreover, a wider range of organizations is fused with political functions in totalitarian societies than in democracies. For instance, membership in the armed services seems to provide a base not only for influencing foreign policy but also for participating in the domestic political processes. More generally, the various nation-wide executive agencies seem to provide political bases which constitute a "functional alternative" (though not a functional-equivalent) to the multi-party system common in Western European societies.

In studying the relations between sub-collectivities and "their" organizations, as we argued above, it is necessary to take into account that sub-collectivities usually are multi-faceted, while their organizations differ greatly in the number of facets they mobilize. While each sub-collectivity is itself ecologically concentrated, their combination into society-wide units builds on one or more of their other facets (e.g., economic, ethnic, religious, or prestige positions). The sub-collectivity is an expressive and not a geographic or formal-administrative unit;[52] that is, it is a pattern of associational activities, symbolization, and integration.* A sub-collectivity is rarely coextensive with an ecological unit such as a county or a district. Frequently its boundaries even cut across a city block, defining part of it as "in" and part as "out." Middle-class sub-collectivities tend to be more dispersed and less ecologically concentrated than lower-class ones; that is, families which belong to a middle-class sub-collectivity often live among families of other sub-collectivities, with automobiles and core-institutions sustaining the interaction among members of the middle-class group. Although the best known examples for our proposition are derived from urban areas, the propositions are expected to hold also for other communities,[53] though the latter tend to be more homogeneous. In short, a country may be viewed as a complicated mosaic of sub-collectivities combined into larger entities.

---

* For a discussion of these mechanisms, see Chapters 5 and 10, *supra*, pp. 100–102, and 231–234.

In democratic societies, superimposed on these ecologically based sub-collectivities are national associations, leadership, and organizations, collective symbols, and specialized newspapers;[54] these mobilize the multi-faceted sub-collectivities into nation-wide units—often in terms of one "facet" at a time. The sub-unit that is mobilized, however, is often the same *core sub-collectivity*. For example, upper east side New York Reform Jews form a core sub-collectivity; it is partially mobilized by the civil rights movement, various peace organizations, and the Americans for Democratic Action (together with other sub-collectivities), but the same core sub-collectivity "appears" in all these activities. Another Jewish sub-collectivity is the Orthodox one; being of lower class, different ethnic origin, and different ecological areas, it is much less favorably disposed to the above-mentioned activities and is mobilized to a much lesser extent by them. Other examples could readily be provided.

When two or more sub-collectivities act jointly, they provide a base for organizations that can be characterized according to which of their facets is being mobilized—religious, ethnic, economic, and so forth—but the core sub-units remain the same. Thus, the Irish of South Boston march together with the Irish from other parts of Boston on St. Patrick's Day, raise funds for a Catholic charity along with the Italians, or join with Protestants in a labor union for a strike, *but these are often organizational actions of the same sub-collectivity and, thus, draw on the same set of associational bonds and stratification bases.* This is evident in that the "joining" in an activity tends to occur not on an individual but on a sub-collectivity basis and, hence, will be affected by that sub-unit's mechanism.[55] To put it differently, we expect that in democracies, the action units often are *sub-collectivities* that are at least in part *under the guidance of their own elites*, and not merely groupings of individuals.

We cannot provide a detailed description of this process in totalitarian societies, for much less is known about their local sub-collectivities and their relations to each other and to organizations. It seems, though, that the sub-collectivities in these societies are the units which are most similar to their counterparts in democratic societies. In comparison, there seem to be fewer opportunities in totalitarian societies for lateral, associational collectivity-building and organization on a national level. The society-wide organizations that do exist are to a greater extent downward control mechanisms—from the supra-unit to the members—than bases for autonomous and upward action, though these organizations do seem to have some such capacities. If the democratic organizational network is viewed as an *arena* whose boundaries are set by the state and society which provide a *structure* within which the member organizations interact, the totalitarian network is to be seen as an *organization* whose member organizations, the sub-units, command some measure of autonomy. In general, the totalitarian network is more malleable than the democratic one; it can be re-cast relatively more rapidly (e.g., de-centralized). However, it is not responsive to the membership. As in democracies, each organization mobilizes one or a few of the facets of the sub-collectivities, but all the organizations are prescriptively controlled by the Party–State, and, thus, together with it, are in effect a multi-faceted organization.

The differences between these two morphologies are often stated in the Weberian terms of a charismatic as opposed to a bureaucratic (legal–rational) authority. "The Chinese style emphasizes the quality and morality of political leaders, rather than legal and institutionalized popular controls, as the guarantee of good government. The democratic style exalts its legal and institutional framework and aims at 'a government of laws and not of men.' "* While this characterization has validity, it must be taken into account that (a) these are differences only in the political overlayers which are superimposed on more similar "feudal" underlayers. In both types of societies, sub-collectivities exist and affect their governments to varying degrees; or, in Weber's terms, there are traditional elements in both. (b) There are charismatic elements in democratic societies, and not just at the top of the organizational structure (e.g., Senator Joseph McCarthy) and China (or any other complex society) cannot be governed entirely by charismatic leadership; it does have a body of laws, regulations, and rules. The conditions under which national and local leaders can set themselves apart from these laws, regulations, and rules need to be explored but—even ideal-typically— they must be assumed to be operative.

Many aspects of this subject still require further study. In particular, organizations in the "pre-mature" totalitarian societies need to be compared to more "mature" ones from this viewpoint, and the organizations of any one totalitarian society need to be studied with a genetic perspective. Thus, there may be a lesser degree of Party–State prescription of associational and organizational activities in contemporary USSR than in Stalin's Russia, but the process of the despecification of control may cease before it reaches the level common in the West.

The morphology of an active society can be expected to resemble that of post-modern societies in that its basic units will consist of sub-collectivities, collectivities, and organizations. In terms of the dimensions on which democratic and totalitarian societies differ, it is tempting to suggest that the active society will fall somewhere "in between"; it seems more likely, however, that it will combine several features of both types and other features not found in either to form a third type. For instance, the mobilization of collectivities is expected to be higher than in both democracies and mature totalitarian societies (probably, near the high level found in premature totalitarian societies). The role of the state is expected to be more encompassing than in democracies but not as prescriptive or penetrative as in

---

* Townsend, *Political Participation in Communist China, op. cit.,* p. 3.

mature or premature totalitarian societies. There may even be a lesser specification of control than is found in democracies and, hence, a greater reliance on contextuation. The most important difference, however, will be the extent of the active society's capacity to build authentic consensus, an aspect which is subsequently explored and for which the preceding discussion provides a morphological base.

A Methodological Note

When the multi-faceted sub-collectivities are studied one facet at a time (e.g., in terms of their religious or their economic status), these highly potent bases of societal action[56] appear to correlate relatively weakly with attitudes and behavior. The fact that the correlations improve when cross tabulations are made[57] supports our contention that the core bases of varying societal activities are the multi-faceted sub-collectivities and their combinations. Statistical categories, especially mono-faceted ones, cannot express these sub-collectivities because the categories—Jews, middle class, and so on— include many individuals who are not integrated into the particular sub-collectivity (just as there are members of each sub-collectivity who are not mobilized by its various organizations). Thus, it is the methodology that is atomizing rather than there being an atomized societal reality.

A number of studies have shown that political behavior, especially voting, is greatly affected by an individual's party identification, orientation toward the issues, and candidate preference in this order of saliency.[58] However, it may be argued that these individual attributes are themselves greatly affected by associational processes and collectivity-based organizations.[59] The greater similarity in the attributes of those individuals who are members of the same sub-collectivity and who are mobilized by the same organization (as compared to those who are not) would tend to support this interpretation.[60] While such similarity of perspectives is often explained only by similarity in "background" statuses—e.g., in stratification terms—we seek to stress that the same set of statuses can be mobilized by a variety of associations and organizations; hence, the collectivization and politization of these personal attributes must be studied as well as the psychological and stratification aspects.

The concept of "cross pressures" has also had an atomizing effect on societal analysis.[61] Individuals are depicted as having allegiance to two cohesive units—let us say, friends who are Democrats and a Republican family. The explanation of such resulting conduct as withdrawal from controversy or delay in taking a stance is atomistic–psychological. For example, the individual is seen as experiencing conflicting loyalties which lead him to curtail his involvement.

It should be noted, first, that even according to this line of analysis, the majority of the persons studied are *not* subject to cross-pressures.[62] For reasons discussed above, the individual's various societal statuses and affiliations usually promote a similarity in attitudes, beliefs, and opinions.* That is, the various stratification positions of most individuals support the same sub-collectivity and the same direction of political organization—e.g., they are Catholics *and* poor *and* Democrats. Those with "unbalanced" statuses who are subject to cross-pressures seem to be in the minority, even though they may be critical for tipping an election or for explaining the "do not know" responses.

Second, many of the members of this atypical minority seem to belong to atypical sub-collectivities rather than to be subject to cross-pressures. The well-to-do Negroes and the Tory workers are often cited as typical examples of persons caught in cross-pressures. But there is some evidence that these two groupings are ecologically, associationally, and organizationally segregated from the collectivities that are said to pressure them—poor Negroes and well-to-do whites, labor workers and the Tory middle class.[63] When a person is exposed to cross-pressures, the experience is tension-producing and painful; hence, he is to be expected to attempt to reduce his exposure to such pressures by moving toward one of the sources of pressure and away from the other(s), by changing his interaction patterns and their saliency. On the group level, a parallel solution lies in the tendency of a sub-collectivity to provide the predominant affiliation. And its orientation will affect to a great extent the direction in which the cross-pressures are resolved. That members of these groupings adhere to different norms may well be explained by the fact that they "normally" conform to the standards of a different sub-collectivity.† Thus, manual workers who vote Republican or Conservative and are less liberal on economic issues than workers who vote for the Democratic or Labor parties but are more liberal than middle-class supporters of their own party[64] are a separate sub-collectivity that, in terms of its stratification position, is "in between the other groupings."[65] There are, of

---

* Werner S. Landecker, "Class Crystallization and Class Consciousness," *American Sociological Review*, Vol. 28 (1963), pp. 219–229. Irwin Goffman, "Status Consistency and Preference for Change in Power Distribution," *American Sociological Review*, Vol. 22 (1957), pp. 275–281. Lenski, *Power and Privilege, op. cit.*, p. 81 and *passim.*

‡ That such behavior as vacillation or uncertainty can be conforming rather than deviating has been noted in Goffman's study of embarrassment as a behavior that is socially defined as conforming (and tension-releasing). For a gentleman who enters a bathroom and finds a disrobed lady, it is proper and functional to act embarrassed. Erving Goffman, "Embarrassment and Social Organization," *American Journal of Sociology*, Vol. LXII (1956), pp. 264–271. Similarly, political vacillation might be a highly functional and socially prescribed behavior for some sub-collectivities, just as hyper-activism is for others.

Merton pointed to another functional solution in the following terms: "To the extent that there is a *prior* consensus on the relative 'importance' of conflicting status-obligations, this reduces the internal conflict of decision by those occupying these statuses and eases the accommodation on the part of those involved in their role-sets." *Social Theory and Social Structure, rev. ed., op. cit.*, p. 382.

course, individuals whose personal ties conflict, but we suggest that this is much less common than has often been assumed and that much of the behavior frequently explained by such personal disequilibrium can be accounted for by macroscopic factors.

A concept closely related to that of cross-pressures is the "unbalanced statuses" of persons or social units whose status in one stratification ranking is significantly lower or higher than their status in other rankings.[66] Two widely cited examples are the high prestige and low utilitarian positions of declining aristocracies and the low prestige and high utilitarian positions of the rising middle class. Although the members of these groupings have been shown to be associated to a greater extent than members of more balanced group-ings with radical (right or left) political behavior, this is still a low correlation. A recent study found only a 4 per cent difference between the extents of the right-wing extremism of the "consistency" and the "inconsistency" groups.[67] And, whatever difference there may be might be explained by the fact that the majority of the members of these unbalanced groupings are not engaged in the same or similar political behavior; the nature of that behavior—for instance, the mild conservatism or radical right views of small businessmen—seems to be affected to a significant degree, by the alternative sub-collectivities which members of these groupings join and the organizations that mobilize them.

It should be noted that the political organizations that draw from these "unbalanced" sub-collectivities are often reported to be more intensively committed in their conduct than their positions in the stratification structure would suggest (e.g., small business is more radical than big business). This is in opposition to the proposition which suggests that cross-pressures (which unbalanced statuses tend to generate on a personal or a collective level) tend to cause apathy, withdrawal of commitment, and so on. On the other hand, this finding is not surprising in terms of the macro-action approach which argues that a stratification position provides only a potential that cohesive units can collectivize and organizations can mobilize in different ways, sometimes toward greater activism and sometimes toward norms which prescribe low commitment. It is the reasons that some sub-collectivities and organizations mobilize in one direction and some in others that need to be explored. Again, the explanation seems to rest only in part on stratification characteristics; the direction chosen might well depend to a significant degree on such often ignored factors as the control structure (e.g., the back-grounds of the leadership) and the historical situation (that is, the societal context and phase in which the grouping evolved).[68]

The macro-action units, whether they be sub-collectivities permanently combined into a collectivity and mobilized by collectivity-organizations (e.g., labor parties and unions for the British labor class), or combinations of sub-collectivities mobilized for political action by cross-collectivity organizations (e.g., the civil rights movement), are rarely if ever homogeneous in terms of

stratification positions.[69] Many of the core organizations of social movements, for instance, draw on "unbalanced" middle-class as well as on
lower-class sub-collectivities. When encountered in an individual case (e.g.,
Tory workers), this heterogeneity is viewed as an exception that requires
explanation. In contrast, we suggest that as a rule, sub-collectivities are
multi-faceted; they tend to be combined for action in terms of one facet and,
hence, the resulting action-unit tends to be dissimilar in terms of the other
facets. The exception that does need explanation is the situation in which the
membership of a political organization is homogeneous in terms of several
stratification dimensions. Homogeneity may register if a social scientist
uses gross categories (e.g., only three classes), but such categorization tends
to conceal the considerable heterogeneity that would appear if more subtle
categories were used. In short, we suggest that the core building stones for
the study of societal action and consensus-building in democracies are multi-
faceted, local sub-collectivities that are combined into collectivities and
mobilized by intra- and cross-collectivity organizations.

We have already noted the lack of information on this subject for totalitarian societies. To the degree that relevant data are available, they seem to
repeat the "Western" methodological focus on atomistic analysis and on
psychological and stratification attributes to the neglect of associational and
control processes. We have argued above that the sub-collectivities in these
societies have not been disintegrated and that the degree to which they can
be penetrated—and, hence, their consensus produced rather than won—is
limited. Thus, all late-modern and post-modern societies must build
consensus, for their control mechanisms alone cannot be relied upon even
for effective societal action and especially for societal activeness.

Appendix: Further Implications

The preceding argument has implications for the study of the societal
action of collectivities which cannot be explored here. An interesting question
concerns the different internal rearrangements and reallocations that result
as the same sub-collectivity is mobilized toward different lines of societal
action, and consequently, the different appearances of one and the same
societal unit as it acts on various fronts. A societal unit, we suggest, is not
weak or strong, integrated or fragmented, passive or active but is rather
active, integrated, and powerful for some lines of action and less so for
others. A general index may be constructed for a unit, but while it indicates a
base, the unit's action characteristics on any specific front cannot be derived
from it (or from its score on any one front).

Differences in action on various fronts, we suggest, are due in part to the
fact that the unit tends to have several sets of leaders, each of which
specializes in action on a particular front. These leadership sub-sets may be

in open or latent conflict with each other (a strictly inter-unit relation); all of them may be "lieutenants" of the same "boss" (supra-unit control which may vary in its degree of specification); they may be in various mixes of conflict, hierarchization, and cooperation; or there may be no clear pattern at all.[70]

Similarly, there are different kinds of commitments within the membership. Women may be more mobilized by religious organizations, while political mobilization might reach a higher level among men.[71] Similar differences occur among age groups, generations, clans, cliques, and other member groupings.[72] The sub-collectivity acts in unison on most fronts, but differences in the ways in which leaders and members are activated and in the degrees to which they are activated will lead to different levels and kinds of societal action (for example, the size of the financial contributions to one cause as compared to another and a greater number of volunteers for one activity than for another).*

These factors are affected by the fact that no sub-collectivity is ever fully or nearly fully mobilized; hence, different organizations can mobilize it with different results. Thus, if two organizations were each to mobilize all the members of a sub-collectivity, the results might still be quite different, because one organization might have more appeal than the other, be more expressive, have more effective leadership, and so on. But if each organization mobilizes, let us say, only 10 per cent of the members of a collectivity, there may be no (or only very little) membership overlap. It is still the same entity because the organizations draw on a membership which is tied together by a set of integrative bonds and a structure and dynamics of its own.

If the "flexible" relationship between statistical categories, the multi-faceted nature of collective units, and the mono-faceted quality of organizations are not taken into account, partial mobilization is likely to be interpreted as weakness when actually it is either normal or even comparatively high. In addition, heterogeneity is likely to register in situations in which there is really a typical multi-faceted and perhaps quite homogeneous sub-collectivity. Above all, organizations that are actually varying forms of mobilization of the same set of collective units are likely to be treated as distinct action units. Thus, we have a picture that is more fragmented and atomized than the socio-political reality. As we see it, modern societies are highly intricate webs of collective units; these units are knit somewhat loosely

---

* The explanatory principles are different in terms of this approach; thus, if we see sub-collectivity X donating more to the NAACP than to the church while Y is giving more to the church than to the NAACP, we might conclude that this is due to differences in the orientations of the sub-collectivities, when actually it is related to the different compositions of the sub-collectivities (e.g., a higher percentage of women in Y). In other words, the differences in the sub-collectivities can be most adequately explained by the fact that the women in one sub-collectivity and the men in the other are more likely to determine to which causes the larger contributions are made.

together in democracies, more tightly in mature totalitarian societies, and still more tightly in premature totalitarian societies, but collective units are the bases of societal consensus-building and action in all of them.

NOTES

1. For a critical discussion of various concepts of "mass" society, see Daniel Bell, *The End of Ideology* (New York: Free Press, 1960), esp. pp. 22–24 and William Kornhauser, *The Politics of Mass Society* (New York: Free Press, 1959), pp. 21–38. For a typical popular treatment, see Michael Reagan, "America as a 'Mass Society,' " *Dissent*, Vol. 3 (1956), pp. 346–356. Kenneth Keniston, *The Uncommitted: Alienated Youth in American Society* (New York: Harcourt, Brace & World, 1965). The author refers to the "shattering of community" (p. 248). "We live as members of organizations and not of a community" (p. 249).

Both totalitarian and democratic societies have been seen as "mass societies." See Robert A. Nisbet's discussion of de Tocqueville, Durkheim, and others in his *The Sociological Tradition, op. cit.* The mass society view is far from defunct. Giovanni Sartori sees the "loss of community" as an essential feature and suggests we update the etymology of democracy by referring to it as "masso-crazia." *Democratic Theory* (Detroit: Wayne State University Press, 1962), p. 21. William Kornhauser provides a full review of the political theory of "mass society" in his *The Politics of Mass Society, op. cit.*

Key provides an unusually moderate version of the basic political proposition: "The party organization remains, with workers in almost every precinct who seek to build up person-to-person relationships with the electorate in their baili-wicks; but the radio, the newspaper, and the mass meeting are more important channels for the dissemination of appeals calculated to manipulate the attitudes of the electorate. . . . Political power has been based on a stable network of the party machine, around each member of which was clustered a little group loyal through thick and thin. For this there seems to be in the process of substitution a power structure broadly based on mass consent and support." V. O. Key, Jr., *Politics, Parties, and Pressure Groups* (New York: T. Y. Crowell, 1942), pp. 570–571.

2. Almond and Verba, *The Civic Culture, op. cit.*, p. 146.

3. For overviews of numerous studies, Berelson and Steiner, *Human Behavior, op. cit.*, pp. 546–555, esp. p. 550. See also Matilda White Riley and John W. Riley, Jr., "A Sociological Approach to Communications Research," *Public Opinion Quarterly*, Vol. 15 (1951), pp. 445–460, and "Mass Communication and the Social System," in Merton, Broom, and Cottrell (eds.), *Sociology Today, op. cit.*, pp. 537–578; Lazarsfeld and Katz, *Personal Influence, op. cit.*, pp. 329–330.

4. Even here there is some reason to hold that "mass" tendencies are less likely than is often suggested. When natural disasters strike modern cities, people, rather than engaging in mass behavior, seem to retreat to their families and friends. A sum-mary report of disaster studies states: "(1) Mass panic is a phenomenon that occurs rarely and only under certain circumstances; (2) Few actual cases of looting can be discovered; (3) Stricken populations are not a 'dazed, helpless mass' . . ." National Research Council, quoted by Berelson and Steiner, *Human Behavior, op. cit.*, p. 625. Moreover, "the first reaction is typically concern for the safety of one's family and

other intimates and then for the larger community." *Ibid.*, p. 624. See also Lewis M. Killian, "The Significance of Multiple-Group Membership in Disaster," *American Journal of Sociology*, Vol. 57 (1952), pp. 309–314; *The Effects of Strategic Bombing on German Morale*, The United States Strategic Bombing Survey, Morale Division (Washington, D.C.: Government Printing Office, 1947).

5. For a study that provides a review of the literature and a theoretical model for analysis of upward transfer of political loyalties, see Harold Guetzkow, *Multiple Loyalties* (Princeton, N.J.: Princeton University Press, 1955), esp. pp. 39–43. An instrument is discussed which allowed two researchers to distinguish empirically between "patriots" and "multiplists" who have—in addition to a national commitment—also a commitment to a more encompassing community (though they do not necessarily grant it superiority in case of conflict). The study referred to is by William Buchanan and Hadley Cantril, *How Nations See Each Other: A Study in Public Opinion* (Urbana: University of Illinois Press, 1953). See also p. 13 for an instrument used by N. C. Morse and F. H. Allport, "The Causation of Anti-Semitism: An Investigation of Seven Hypotheses," *Journal of Psychology*, Vol. 34 (1952), pp. 197–233. There seem to be relatively few difficulties in exploring this dimension empirically.

6. In Communist China, in which probably the most extensive and lasting attempt was made to secure party penetration, still the extended family and village remain as powerful local units. See James R. Townsend, *Political Participation in Communist China* (Berkeley: University of California Press, 1967), *passim*. For a major study on the importance of local units in contemporary democracies, see Almond and Verba, *The Civic Culture, op. cit.*, pp. 79–100.

7. On "upward" and "downward" positions regarding consensus-building, see Bernard Berelson, "Democratic Theory and Public Opinion," *Public Opinion Quarterly*, Vol. 16 (1952), pp. 313–330; Walter Lippmann, *Public Opinion* (New York: Harcourt, Brace & World, 1922), esp. pp. 234–249; Bernard C. Hennessy, "Democracy and the Opinion-Policy Process," in his *Public Opinion* (Belmont, Calif.: Wadsworth, 1965), pp. 104–129.

That government is dominated by mass opinion is the position of Walter Lippmann. See his *Essays in the Public Philosophy* (Boston: Little, Brown, 1955); C. Wright Mills, especially in his *The Power Elite* (New York: Oxford University Press, 1956) and *The Causes of World War III* (New York: Simon & Shuster, 1958), is representative of the opposing position: The power elite largely determines the opinions of the masses. David B. Truman reviews both positions and takes an intermediary, "interaction," stand. See his "The American System in Crisis," *Political Science Quarterly*, Vol. 74 (1959), pp. 481–497. See also excerpts of the works of James Bryce, A. Lawrence Lowell, and John C. Calhoun in Katz et al., *Public Opinion and Propaganda, op. cit.*, pp. 3–23, and William C. Olson. "The Public Ingredient in Statecraft," *World Politics*, Vol. 10 (1958), pp. 318–326.

8. See *supra*, pp. 157 ff.

9. Talcott Parsons, " 'Voting' and the Equilibrium of the American Political System," in Eugene Burdick and Arthur J. Brodbeck, *American Voting Behavior* (New York: Free Press, 1959), pp. 80–120; Seymour M. Lipset, "Party Systems and the Representation of Social Groups," *European Journal of Sociology*, Vol. 1, No. 1 (1960), pp. 3–4; Easton, *A Framework of Political Analysis, op. cit.*, pp. 108–117.

10. On this approach, see footnote 58 below.

11. This, of course, is a relative statement; not all the passive members of AMA will act alike but more so with each other than with those of the AFL–CIO. Stouffer's often-quoted study which is said to show that leaders of various associations are more liberal than members actually does not allow for such a comparison because figures are not given by organization, and the leadership sample was not drawn from the same population. Samuel A. Stouffer, *Communism, Conformity and Civil Liberties* (New York: Doubleday, 1955), pp. 244–249. James W. Prothro and C. M. Grigg, "Fundamental Principles of Democracy: Bases of Agreement and Disagreement," *Journal of Politics*, Vol. 22 (Spring 1960), pp. 276–294, showed acceptance of democratic procedure and values to be higher among those who are politically aware and active. See also Herbert McClosky, "Consensus and Ideology in American Politics," in Joseph R. Fiszman, *The American Political Arena* (Boston: Little, Brown, 1966), 2nd edition, p. 46.

12. On the association between isolation and political sense of powerlessness, and passivity, see Kornhauser et al., *When Labor Votes: A Study of Auto Workers, op. cit.*, p. 194. Kornhauser shows that individuals who feel socially alienated, indicated by a lack of confidence in other people and in the future, are likely to feel personally impotent in political matters. While 60 per cent of those high on political futility were also high on alienation, only 9 per cent of those high on alienation were low on political futility, and only 12 per cent of those high on political futility were low on alienation, p. 194. See also Melvin Seeman, "Alienation, Membership and Political Knowledge: A Comparative Study," *Public Opinion Quarterly*, Vol. 30 (1966), pp. 353–367.

13. For an effective overview of the societal and political assumptions of this model, including a discussion of Park, Durkheim, Weber, and de Tocqueville, see Reinhard Bendix, "Social Stratification and the Political Community," *European Journal of Sociology*, Vol. 1, No. 2 (1960), pp. 3–32. See also references *supra*, Ch. 16, footnote 1.

14. Ernest W. Burgess, "The Family in a Changing Society," *American Journal of Sociology*, Vol. 53 (1948), pp. 417–422. On the viability of the modern family, see Goode, *World Revolution and Family Patterns, op. cit.*, esp. pp. 27–86, and Arnold M. Rose, *The Power Structure: Political Process in American Society* (New York: Oxford University Press, 1967), pp. 202–203. See also Eugene Litwak, "The Use of Extended Family Groups in the Achievement of Social Goals," *Social Problems*, Vol. 7 (1959–1960), p. 179; Marvin B. Sussman, "The Isolated Nuclear Family: Fact or Fiction?" *Social Problems*, Vol. 6 (1959), pp. 333–340. See also Michael Young and Peter Willmott, *Family and Kinship in East London* (London: Routledge & Kegan Paul, 1957).

15. See Morris Axelrod, "Urban Structure and Social Participation," *American Sociological Review*, Vol. 21 (1956), pp. 13–18; Wendell Bell and Marion D. Boat, "Urban Neighborhoods and Informal Social Relations," *American Journal of Sociology*, Vol. 62 (1957), pp. 391–398; Joel Smith, William H. Form, and Gregory P. Stone, "Local Intimacy in a Middle-Sized City," *American Journal of Sociology*, Vol. 60 (1954), pp. 276–284; David Riesman et al., *The Lonely Crowd: A Study of the Changing American Character* (New York: Doubleday, 1953), p. 331.

16. D. W. Brogan, *Politics in America* (Garden City, N.Y.: Doubleday, 1960), pp. 85–95.

17. Will Herberg, *Protestant, Catholic, Jew* (New York: Doubleday, 1956), pp. 45–53, 256–272.

18. Seymour M. Lipset, Martin A. Trow, and James S. Coleman, *Union Democracy* (New York: Free Press, 1956), p. 69; Elizabeth Bott, *Family and Social Network* (London: Tavistock, 1957), p. 86.

19. Sills, *The Volunteers, op. cit.*, pp. 233–252.

20. Samuel J. Eldersveld, *Political Parties: A Behavioral Analysis* (Chicago: Rand McNally, 1964), pp. 295–303, esp. p. 303; Seyom Brown, "Fun can be Politics," *The Reporter*, Vol. 21 (November 12, 1959), pp. 27–28; Currin V. Shields, "A Note on Party Organization: The Democrats in California," *Western Political Quarterly*, Vol. 7 (1954), pp. 673–683; Francis Carney, *The Rise of Democratic Clubs in California* (New York: Holt, Rinehart, and Winston, 1958).

21. For a fuller discussion of these concepts as used here, see Etzioni, *A Comparative Analysis of Complex Organizations, op. cit.*, pp. 160 ff.

22. For elaboration of this point, see Amitai Etzioni and William R. Taber, "Scope, Pervasiveness, and Tension Management in Complex Organizations," *Social Research*, Vol. 30 (1963), pp. 220–238.

23. Dubin's study of 1,200 industrial workers in the United States found that only 9 per cent were interested in "informal group life that is centered in the job" as most had effective primary relations off the job. Robert Dubin, "Industrial Workers' Worlds: A Study of the 'Central Life Interests' of Industrial Workers," *Social Problems*, Vol. 4 (1956), p. 136. On the job and off the job social relations, see Lipset, Trow, and Coleman, *Union Democracy, op. cit.*, pp. 72 ff.; Charles R. Walker and Robert H. Guest, *The Man on the Assembly Line* (Cambridge, Mass.: Harvard University Press, 1952), pp. 66–80.

24. On suburbs, see below, FN 53. On organizations, see Tom Burns, "The Reference of Conduct in Small Groups: Cliques and Cabals in Occupational Milieux," *Human Relations*, Vol. 8 (1955), pp. 467–486. See also Robert T. Golembiewski's discussion of "The Small Group in a Macro-System," in James G. March (ed.), *Handbook of Organizations* (Chicago: Rand McNally, 1965), pp. 101–113. On the family, Herbert H. Hyman, *Political Socialization: A Study in the Psychology of Political Behavior* (New York: Free Press, 1959), esp. pp. 69–91.

25. Bennett M. Berger, *Working-Class Suburb: A Study of Auto Workers in Suburbia* (Berkeley: University of California Press, 1960), pp. 84–89, esp. p. 85.

26. See discussion of "Segmentary tribes," in M. Fortes and E. E. Evans-Pritchard (eds.), *African Political Systems* (London: Oxford University Press, 1950), pp. 5 ff.

27. Marc Bloch, "Feudalism, European," *The Encyclopedia of the Social Sciences* (New York: Macmillan, 1931), Vol. 6, pp. 203–210.

28. S. N. Eisenstadt, *The Political Systems of Empires* (New York: Free Press, 1963), pp. 273–299, esp. 297–299.

29. John H. Herz, *International Politics in the Atomic Age* (New York: Columbia University Press, 1960), pp. 43–48.

30. For one of the first and still best studies, see Edward A. Shils and Morris Janowitz, "Cohesion and Disintegration in the Wehrmacht in World War II," *Public Opinion Quarterly*, Vol. 12 (1948), pp. 280–315.

31. Robert S. Lynd and Helen M. Lynd, *Middletown* (New York: Harcourt, Brace & World, 1959), pp. 332–337 and Liston Pope, *Millhands and Preachers, op.*

cit., pp. 70–140. For studies of other organizations that have a collective base see Jacques Van Doorn, "The Officer Corps: A Fusion of Profession and Organization," *Archives Europeennes de Sociologie*, Vol. 6 (1965), pp. 262–282; Ralph C. James and Estelle D. James, *Hoffa and the Teamsters* (Princeton, N.J.: D. Van Nostrand, 1965), esp. pp. 81–84; Oliver Garceau, *The Political Life of the American Medical Association* (Cambridge, Mass.: Harvard University Press, 1941), esp. pp. 30–61, 103–108. William A. Glaser, "Doctors and Politics," *The American Journal of Sociology*, Vol. 66 (1960), pp. 230–245.

32. Ethnic sub-collectivities are often the base of an organization which itself does not deal with ethnic issues. The American Ethical Union in New York (where it is called the New York Society for Ethical Culture) is said to be mostly "dissident Jews." Elsewhere in the United States Ethical Culturists are mostly ex-Protestants. *Time* (May 20, 1966), p. 96. Few Roman Catholics reach the top at G.M., where most of the hierarchy belong to the same Masonic Lodge. *Ibid.*, p. 100. On Mexican farm hands organization, see Edgar Z. Friedenberg, "The Grape Workers Strike," *The New York Review of Books*, Vol. 6 (March 3, 1966), pp. 10–13. Marvin Alisky, "The Mexican-Americans Make Themselves Heard," *The Reporter*, Vol. 36 (February 9, 1967), pp. 45–48.

33. It is the opposite of Barnard's concept of the realm of indifference or discretion; it is the realm of non-indifference. Cf. Chester I. Barnard, *The Functions of the Executive* (Cambridge, Mass.: Harvard University Press, 1956), pp. 167–171, 185–199.

34. On societal controls in New Zealand, see John B. Condliffe, *New Zealand in the Making: A Study of Economic and Social Development* (London: Allen & Unwin, 1959), rev. ed., pp. 186 ff.; and John A. Lee, *Socialism in New Zealand* (London: T. W. Laurie Ltd., 1938), pp. 146–186.

35. Townsend, *Political Participation . . . , op. cit.*, pp. 111–115, 169–172.

36. Townsend, *ibid.*, pp. 207–209, 216 and Schurmann, *Ideology and Organization . . . , op. cit.*, pp. 483–500. Ezra Vogel, "From Friendship to Comradeship: The Change in Personal Relationships in China," *China Quarterly*, No. 21 (January–March, 1965), pp. 46–60.

The "costs" of the Cultural Revolution are illustrated by the weakening of the educational system which it caused. See Tillman Durdin, "China's Schools Reported in Chaos," *The New York Times*, June 1, 1967.

37. Cf. Samuel P. Huntington, "Political Development and Political Decay," *World Politics*, Vol. 17 (1965), pp. 386–430, esp. pp. 393–394. See also David E. Apter's contrast between "reconciliation" and "mobilization" systems in his *The Politics of Modernization* (Chicago: University of Chicago Press, 1965).

38. Peter H. Juviler, "Soviet Families," *Survey*, No. 60 (1966), pp. 51–61, and his "Marriage and Divorce," *Survey*, No. 48 (1963), pp. 104–117. See also, by the same author, "Family Reforms on the Road to Communism," in Peter H. Juviler and Henry W. Morton (eds.), *Soviet Policy-Making.* (New York: Praeger, 1967), pp. 29–60.

39. Merle Fainsod, *Smolensk under Soviet Rule* (Cambridge, Mass.: Harvard University Press, 1958), p. 185; Fedor Belov, *The History of a Soviet Collective Farm* (New York: Praeger, 1955), esp. pp. 53–81; Steven P. Dunn and Ethel Dunn, "The Great Russian Peasant Cultural Change or Cultural Development," *Ethnology*,

Vol. II (1963), pp. 320–338. See also Robert G. Wesson, *Soviet Communes* (New Brunswick, N.J.: Rutgers University Press, 1963).

40. John S. Curtiss, *The Russian Church and the Soviet State, 1917–1950* (Boston: Little, Brown, 1953); Walter Kolarz, *Religion in the Soviet Union* (New York: St. Martin's Press, 1961). Both studies show differences in Soviet policies, one over time, the other in comparison of various religious groupings.

41. Joseph S. Berliner, *Factory and Manager in the USSR* (Cambridge, Mass.: Harvard University Press, 1957), esp. pp. 248–263; David Granick, *Management of the Industrial Firm in the USSR* (New York: Columbia University Press, 1954), esp. pp. 203 ff. on relations among the managers of Soviet heavy industry, the government and the Party. Cf. Jeremy R. Azrael, *Managerial Power and Soviet Politics* (Cambridge, Mass.: Harvard University Press, 1966), esp. pp. 167–172, who finds little new power or innovative capacity in the relations between the Soviet managers, the Party, and the government. On limited "play" for lower echelons, see Brzezinski and Huntington, *Political Power: USA/USSR, op. cit.*, p. 52. See also 79, 97, 111–112, 122. See also Arvid Brodersen, *The Soviet Worker: Labor and Government in Soviet Society* (New York: Random House, 1966), esp. pp. 202–236. Sidney I. Ploss, *Conflict and Decision-Making in Soviet Russia: A Case Study of Agricultural Policy, 1953–1963* (Princeton, N.J.: Princeton University Press, 1965).

42. Alec Nove, "The Constitution, Governmental Organization and Political Practice," in Alex Inkeles and Kent Geiger (eds.), *Soviet Society* (Boston: Houghton Mifflin, 1961), pp. 166–182; Cyril Black, "Soviet Political Life after Stalin," *ibid.*, pp. 182–189.

43. Herbert J. Gans, *The Urban Villagers* (New York: Free Press, 1962), esp. pp. 17–41.

44. Sexton, *Spanish Harlem, op. cit.* See also Dan Wakefield, *Island in the City* (Boston: Houghton Mifflin, 1959); Gilbert Osofsky, *Harlem: The Making of a Ghetto* (New York: Harper & Row, 1966). For a study of eight American cities from this viewpoint, see Richard E. Engler, Jr., *The Challenge of Diversity* (New York: Harper & Row, 1964).

45. Nathan Glazer and Daniel P. Moynihan, *Beyond the Melting Pot* (Cambridge, Mass.: M.I.T. Press, 1963), pp. 139 ff.

46. For studies of other multi-facet collectivities, see Seeley et al., *Crestwood Heights: A Study of the Culture of Suburban Life, op. cit.*, on a Canadian suburb. For a study of Canada, Porter, *The Vertical Mosaic, op. cit.*, esp. pp. 60–103. See also Everett C. Hughes, *French Canada in Transition* (London: Routledge & Kegan Paul, 1946), pp. 74 ff. In Israel, see Alex Weingrod, *Israel—Group Relations in a New Society* (New York: Praeger, 1965); Judith T. Shuval, *Immigrants on the Threshold* (New York: Atherton Press, 1963). On Britain, see John Rex and Robert Moore, *Race, Community and Conflict* (New York: Oxford University Press, 1967). See also George De Vos and Hiroshi Wagatsuma, *Japan's Invisible Race: Caste in Culture and Personality* (Berkeley: University of California Press, 1966). The political role of this "race" is completely passive. For a more general treatment, see Tamotsu Shibutani and Kian M. Kwan, *Ethnic Stratification: A Comparative Approach* (New York: Macmillan, 1965). George E. Simpson and J. Milton Yinger, *Racial and Cultural Minorities* (New York: Harper & Row, 1965), 3rd ed., esp. pp. 152–154.

47. Almond and Verba, *The Civic Culture, op. cit.*, esp. p. 246.

48. Charles and Mary Beard, *The Rise of American Civilization* (New York: Macmillan, 1927), Vol. 2, pp. 730–731.

49. Mirra Komarovsky, "The Voluntary Associations of Urban Dwellers," *American Sociological Review*, Vol. 11 (1946), pp. 686–698, esp. p. 689; Charles R. Wright and Herbert H. Hyman, "Voluntary Association Memberships of American Adults," *American Sociological Review*, Vol. 23 (1958), pp. 284–294. Hyman and Wright find in their study of two national cross-sections of American adults that 64 per cent belong to none, 20 per cent to one and 9 per cent to two; thus 93 per cent of Americans belong to two or fewer. For a review of several relevant studies as well as his own, see Bernard Barber, "Participation and Mass Apathy in Associations," in Alvin W. Gouldner (ed.), *Studies in Leadership* (New York: Harper & Row, 1950), pp. 479–484.

50. On class differentiation in participation in voluntary associations, see John C. Scott, Jr., "Membership and Participation in Voluntary Associations," *American Sociological Review*, Vol. 22 (1957), pp. 315–326; Thomas B. Bottomore, "Social Stratification in Voluntary Organizations," in David V. Glass (ed.), *Social Mobility in Britain* (London: Routledge & Kegan Paul, 1954), pp. 381–382; Detroit Area Study of the University of Michigan, *A Social Profile of Detroit* (Ann Arbor: University of Michigan, 1952), pp. 13–16. For additional references and discussion on voluntary associations, see Rose, *The Power Structure: Political Process in American Society*, *op. cit.*, pp. 313, 252.

51. See studies cited in footnote 38 *supra*, especially Berliner, *Factory and Manager . . ., op. cit.*, pp. 224–230, and Azrael, *Managerial Power, op. cit.*, pp. 177–179. See also Roger Pethybridge, *A Key to Soviet Politics: The Crisis of the Anti-Party Group* (New York: Praeger, 1962), and Robert Conquest, *Power and Policy in the U.S.S.R.* (New York: St. Martin's Press, 1961).

52. For an example of use of formal units for sociological analysis, see Walter T. Martin, "Structuring of Social Relationships Engendered by Suburban Residence," *American Sociological Review*, Vol. 21 (1956), pp. 446–453.

53. Frederick M. Wirt, "The Political Sociology of American Suburbia: A Reinterpretation," *The Journal of Politics*, Vol. 27 (1965), pp. 647–666, esp. pp. 656–658; William Dobriner (ed.), *The Suburban Community* (New York: Putnam, 1958), p. xxii; Berger, *Working-class Suburb, op. cit.*, pp. 15–27; Robert C. Wood, *Suburbia: Its People and Their Politics* (Boston: Houghton Mifflin, 1959), Ch. 5; Leo F. Schnore, "The Functions of Metropolitan Suburbs," *American Journal of Sociology*, Vol. 61 (1956), pp. 453–458. For a recent study of communities in another modern democracy, see Ronald Frankenberg, *Communities in Britain* (Baltimore: Penguin, 1966), esp. 266.

54. On collectivity press see Abbott J. Liebling, *The Wayward Pressman* (New York: Doubleday, 1947). On the high percent (84 to 97 per cent) of readers of local press within an ecological unit, see Morris Janowitz, *The Community Press in an Urban Setting* (New York: Free Press, 1952), Ch. 7.

55. Like other such statements in this volume, this one is a proposition. Some qualitative evidence in its support is included in the studies cited, *supra*, footnotes 43 and 44.

56. The importance of the local sub-collectivities is explained in part by the expressive intensity of the interaction and leadership patterns, and in part by the fact that the members of these sub-collectivities tend to share the same position in

the stratification structure, more so than do members of any nationwide collectivity or organization.

57. Werner S. Landecker, "Class Boundaries," *American Sociological Review*, Vol. 25 (1960), pp. 868–877. See this work also for a bibliography.

58. Angus Campbell, Gerald Gurin, and Warren E. Miller, *The Voter Decides* (New York: Harper & Row, 1954), pp. 157–184; Campbell et al., *The American Voter, op. cit.*, pp. 179–187, 245–248, 524–530; Heinz Eulau, "Perceptions of Class and Party in Voting Behavior: 1952," *The American Political Science Review*, Vol. 49 (1955), pp. 364–384. See also Philip E. Converse, "The Nature of Belief Systems in Mass Publics," in David E. Apter (ed.), *Ideology and Discontent* (New York: Free Press, 1964), pp. 206–261. See Ch. 8 *supra*, pp. 188–189 for additional discussion.

59. This point was made by Herbert Blumer with his macro-action approach, "Public Opinion and Public Opinion Polling," *American Sociological Review*, Vol. 13 (1948), pp. 542–549, and Bernard R. Berelson, Paul F. Lazarsfeld, William N. McPhee, *Voting* (Chicago: University of Chicago Press, 1954), pp. 277–309. Herbert H. Hyman and Paul B. Sheatsley, "Some Reasons Why Information Campaigns Fail," *Public Opinion Quarterly*, Vol. 11 (1947), pp. 412–423. Cf. Floyd H. Allport, "Toward a Science of Public Opinion," *Public Opinion Quarterly*, Vol. 1 (1937), pp. 7–23, whose approach is atomistic. Aaron V. Cicourel approaches this question from a general methodological perspective, when he asks about the differences between measurements of structural attributes and those of social action. See his *Method and Measurement in Sociology* (New York: Free Press, 1964), pp. 29–38. See also John Rex, *Key Problems of Sociological Theory* (London: Routledge & Kegan Paul, 1961), pp. 115–135.

60. Members of labor unions vote more in a "liberal" way than non-members. Berelson and Steiner, *Human Behavior, op. cit.*, p. 432. Stark shows the differences in church attendance hold between white collar and blue collar American workers, as he compares those mobilized by two or more, one, and no organizations. Rodney Stark, "Class, Radicalism, and Religious Involvement in Great Britain," *American Sociological Review*, Vol. 29 (1964), pp. 698–706. Table I, p. 700. To fully test the proposition, additional information would be needed concerning the degree the workers studied form a collectivity and two sub-collectivities, and the degree of mobilization of each organization.

61. Paul F. Lazarsfeld et al., in *The People's Choice* (New York: Columbia University Press, 1948), pp. 60–64. Gerhart H. Saenger, "Social Status and Political Behavior," *American Journal of Sociology*, Vol. 51 (1945), pp. 103–113.

62. The Elmira study reports that 269 respondents experienced no cross-pressure or "one," and 128 "more than one." Lazarsfeld, et al., *The People's Choice, op. cit.*, p. 62. Cf. Richard Centers, *The Psychology of Social Classes* (New York: Russell & Russell, 1949), esp. p. 204. See also Truman, *The Governmental Process, op. cit.*, p. 165.

63. Cross-cleavages disappear upon closer examination. Liston Pope, "Religion and the Class Structure," *Annals of the American Academy of Political and Social Science*, Vol. 256 (1948), pp. 84–91. See also Vattel E. Daniel, "Ritual and Stratification in Chicago Negro Churches," *American Sociological Review*, Vol. 7 (1942), pp. 352–361, and Robert Alford, *Party and Society: the Anglo-American Democracies* (Chicago: Rand McNally, 1963), esp. pp. 54–58 and pp. 287–292,

Mark Abrams, "Social Class and British Politics," *Public Opinion Quarterly*, Vol. 25 (1961), pp. 342–350.

64. Berelson, Lazarsfeld and McPhee, *Voting, op. cit.*, p. 27; Mark Benney et al., *How People Vote* (London: Routledge & Kegan Paul, 1956), p. 194; Seymour M. Lipset and Reinhard Bendix, *Social Mobility in Industrial Society* (Berkeley: University of California Press, 1960), pp. 94–95.

65. For data, discussion, and references to other works see Lipset, *Political Man, op. cit.*, pp. 220–236. See also David L. Westby and Richard G. Braungart, "Class and Politics in the Family Backgrounds of Student Political Activists," *American Sociological Review*, Vol. 31 (1966), pp. 690–692.

66. For references, see *supra*, Ch. 10, footnote 27.

67. Gary B. Rush, "Status Consistency and Right-Wing Extremism," *American Sociological Review*, Vol. 32 (1967), pp. 86–92, esp. p. 90. See also Seymour M. Lipset, "The Sources of the Radical Right (1955)" in Daniel Bell (ed.), *The Radical Right* (New York: Doubleday, 1963), pp. 259–312; Richard Hofstadter, "Pseudo-Conservatism Revisited: A Postscript (1962)," *ibid.*, pp. 81–86; Gilbert Abcarian and Sherman M. Stanage, "Alienation and the Radical Right," *The Journal of Politics*, Vol. 27 (1965), pp. 776–796. For a recent work and references to earlier ones, see Richard G. Braungart, "SDS and YAF: Backgrounds of Student Political Activists," paper presented at the annual meeting of the American Sociological Association, August 31, 1966, Miami, Florida, esp. p. 12. Hoffer pointed to several atypical sub-collectivities, which are at both ends of each collectivity and take a similar stand:

". . . The least and most successful among the Italian Americans were the most ardent admirers of Mussolini's revolution; the least and most successful among the Irish Americans were the most responsive to De Valera's call; the least and most successful among the Jews are the most responsive to Zionism; the least and most successful among the Negroes are the most race conscious."

Eric Hoffer, *The True Believer* (New York: Harper & Row, 1966), p. 53.

68. Scott A. Greer, "The Social Structure in Political Process of Suburbia," *op. cit.*, illustrates this approach in the study of suburbs.

69. George Rudé, *The Crowd in History 1730–1848* (New York: Wiley, 1964), pp. 178–190. Even a comparatively monolithic organization such as the Communist Party combines sub-collectivities of considerable diversity, such as intellectuals and workers, or—as Allardt suggested for Finland—those who find in political activities a more expressive element, and who are more prevalent in the north and east of Finland, and those who treat it more instrumentally, as in the south and west of the country. Erik Allardt, "Institutionalized Versus Diffuse Support of Radical Political Movements," *Transactions of the Fifth World Congress*, September, 1962 (International Sociological Association, 1964), Vol. 4, p. 369.

70. All these patterns have been reported for community decision-making structures but only rarely studied on the collectivity level. On community decision-making studies and reference to other works, see William L. C. Weaton, "Integration at the Urban Level: Political Influences and the Decision Process," Jacob and Toscano (eds.), *The Integration of Political Communities, op. cit.*, pp. 120–142, and Nelson W. Polsby, *Community Power and Political Theory* (New Haven, Conn.: Yale University Press, 1963). See also Wallace S. Sayre and Herbert Kaufman, *Governing New York City* (New York: Russell Sage Foundation, 1960).

71. Gerhard Lenski, "Social Correlates of Religious Interest," *American Sociological Review*, Vol. 18 (1953), pp. 535–536. Milbrath, *Political Participation, op. cit.*, pp. 54, 133, 135–137.

72. *Ibid.*, p. 53 and *passim*; Lipset, *Political Man, op. cit.*, pp. 264–275.

CHAPTER 17

The Mechanisms

of Consensus

THE CAPACITY of any one societal unit to act is determined only in part by its ability to control the other units or by the extent to which it is controlled by them; this capacity is also affected by the degree to which the goals the unit chooses to pursue and the means it employs are compatible with those chosen and employed by the other units—i.e., the degree of societal consensus.

The capacities of societies to control their members and to build consensus among them tend to be low. While societies differ in their over-all guidance capacities, the more productive analytic approach seems to lie not in ranking them in terms of their relative capacities but rather in establishing the sources of their respective deficiencies. Low guidance scores of two societies may be explained by quite different deficiencies.

To start with an elementary classification derived from the basic components of societal guidance, four types of societies suggest themselves: (1) those low in both control and consensus-building, *passive* societies, a type approximated by many underdeveloped nations; (2) those whose control capacities are less deficient than their consensus-building mechanisms, *overmanaged* societies, a type approximated by totalitarian states; (3) those whose consensus-building is less deficient than their control capacities, *drifting* societies, a type approximated by capitalistic democratic societies; (4) and societies effective in both realms, *active* societies, a type which is a "future system" or societal design.

In the first post-modern decade, the capacity to develop a backward country was considered high, and master plans were formulated for many underdeveloped nations. Most of these programs failed.[1]* More recently, it has become widely recognized that the societal guidance of underdeveloped societies is an extremely difficult task.

Democracies have endeavored to reallocate wealth, to alter the relations among races, and to integrate nations into larger communities, but there have been only minor changes in the allocation of wealth, race relations may have been improved but have not been transformed, and mountains of international efforts have yielded only a few molehills of supranational unification.

Revolutionary regimes have shown, on balance, no more effective a capacity for societal guidance than the other types. Soviet efforts to abolish the state, religion, and stratification have largely failed.[2] Following the 1952 revolution, the government of Bolivia decided to attempt radical agrarian reform, but the Bolivian pattern of land distribution has yet to be significantly altered.[3] Mexico's 1910 left-oriented revolution spawned a sizeable middle class rather than advancing the cause of the peasants.[4]

Some societal actors, it may be argued, either project goals to which they are not actually committed or are not in high agreement about the goals they do pursue so ineffectually. But, it seems, even when there are fairly high levels of consensus and commitment, the level of implementation is not high. For example, the *kibbutz* movement was once the favorite of those who desire guided societal change; now, its advocates are largely disillusioned, not only because the *kibbutz* movement has not equalled their expectations but also because it is turning from the goals it set for itself.[5] The actors' initial goals are to be disregarded, it may be said, because these change as realization is attempted. But the reasons that societal actors are so often forced to abandon their initial goals and to choose new ones must be studied further. Finally, in those instances in which societal actors do realize their goals, this is in part due to "unintended" consequences (i.e., to factors beyond the actors' awareness), which, in turn, is another indicator of the generally low capacity to guide.

The conditions under which the control component of guidance may become more effective were discussed above; here, consensus-building is explored in general and societal and political consensus in particular. This

* Reference notes to this chapter appear on page 495.

leads to the specification of the comparative dimensions of various kinds of consensus-building structures. The chapter closes with a brief review of societal attempts to articulate more closely societal control and consensus, in order to improve societal guidance.

Consensus and Societal Action

Societal Structure and Consensus-Building

The level of societal activeness affects the extent to which consensus-building is required: The more a society "gets done," the more the differences in the values, interests, and viewpoints of the members "need" to be resolved. This "need" can be viewed in two ways: (a) if the extent of the differences among the members is not reduced, the level of societal resistance will tend to rise, ultimately blocking action; and (b) if consensus-building is neglected, the values that are based on consensus are undermined, even if other values are realized by the increased societal activeness.

There is a close relationship between a society's structure and its capacity to build consensus; the societal structure provides the background for consensus-building. The fewer the societal bonds and links, the greater the "load" consensus-building must carry (for the same level of activeness). Second, differences in structure are related to the kinds of consensus-building upon which the society can draw. For instance, when the specification of societal control is high, the tendency seems to be toward a greater reliance on downward mechanisms of consensus-mobilization, while upward mechanisms of consensus-formation are more prevalent when specification is low. At the same time, the amount, quality, and substance of consensus affect both the stability and the shape of the societal structure. Hence, the relationship between morphology (discussed in the preceding chapter) and consensus-building (discussed here) resembles the relationship between a static and a dynamic aspect of the same phenomenon.

So far as consensus is concerned, societal actors are to be viewed not as "given" but as changeable. The capacity of two or more actors to realize their values is significantly affected not only by the congruence of their commitments but also by their ability to establish the degree to which their goals are complementary or shared and the extent to which their paths toward goal-realization are affected by the degree to which, in the process of such interaction, the goals of the actors are re-specified in the direction of reciprocal or shared projects. Often, the initial positions of various sub-collectivities or collectivities (expressed through their various organizations) are relatively vague and fluid, and—if consensus-building is effective—they become specified in a congruent direction. Or, when their positions have been previously specified, they are altered in the process of consensus-building for such reasons as the actors' realizations that they cannot pursue their original courses and that they prefer a change of course over a deadlock or being "left out," or because expressive processes such as leadership (let us say, of the system's elite) affect their preferences. This flexibility of societal actors means that consensus-building is available in a much larger variety of situations than would be the case if all the participants had fixed positions; it is not merely a question of agreement or of splitting the difference, but also of the generation of new *shared* goals, leadership, and other related factors.*

The capacity of two or more actors to build consensus is reflected in the degree to which they can both determine their reciprocal and shared needs and formulate new needs. The lower this capacity is—either because of divergence of "background" factors or because of ineffective consensus-building mechanisms—the lower is their capacity for societal guidance.[6]

Consensus—A State and a Process

Consensus is a congruence in the perspectives of two or more actors.[7] Since consensus-building is often only in part a conscious, deliberate process, the term "consensus" is preferred to "agreement." Similarities in perspectives are often mistaken for consensus, and homogeneous groups are expected to be in consensus.[8] But many actors whose goals are similar are in dissensus and bitter conflict, as is illustrated by the famous statement of the king of Austria about himself and the ruler of Spain: "We both want the same thing; we both want Milan." While we expect that actors who are committed to identical or similar *values* are more likely to reach an agreement about *goals* and *means* than those who have divergent—and, especially, opposing—value commitments, it cannot be assumed that consensus about goals, means, and priorities will automatically result from consensus about values. Such consensus needs to be constructed, and unless there are effective mechanisms to build consensus, it may remain only a potential.

Consensus is viewed by typical collectivistic theories as largely given (or as changing under the impact of ongoing processes); voluntaristic theories

---

* Several thorough studies have shown that there is little consensus among the American electorate; that there is more consensus among the leaders of divergent parties than among the members; that the concept of democracy is endorsed by the voters but not understood, and so on. These studies claim to show that democracy is operative without the fulfillment of the prerequisites which consensus-models have stipulated.[6] This conclusion is valid to the degree that the studies challenge those models which assume that most members of a society must be in agreement most of the time on most issues. On the other hand, their criticism does not apply to such models as the one used here which—for reasons discussed above—assumes that some consensus among the relatively active members is needed. Second, we apply a revised functional model. That is, we expect that if some of the required consensus is lacking, democracy will function less effectively but will not necessarily collapse. The studies neglect to relate the particular consensus deficiencies they unveil to other deficiencies of the democracies they study.

tend to view it as open to manipulation by charismatic leadership and/or the mass media. From the viewpoint of a theory of societal guidance, consensus is the result of a process in which existing perspectives *and* guided efforts affect the outcome, which is a changing consensus. Many studies have applied such an approach; here, it finds a theoretical base.

Dissensus is the entropic state of societal nature; consensus is not found but must be produced.[9] "Normal," ongoing socialization processes prepare the background for it but not the actual consensus that societal guidance requires. Once established, consensus does not act in accord with the laws of inertia; if the efforts to sustain it decrease significantly, society moves toward the entropic state of dissensus.* When dissensus is high, the capacity of the societal units to act tends to be low. We use *consensus-formation* to refer to the upward processes (from member-unit to controlling overlayer) which increase the congruence in perspectives; *consensus-mobilization* refers to the downward processes which increase the congruence; and *consensus-building* encompasses both the upward and the downward processes.

The Level of Consensus Needed

Some social scientists stress the fact that consensus is not a prerequisite of societal action. This seems a valid observation, but we would like to add that some degree of consensus is a prerequisite of *effective* action. We, thus, assume neither that consensus needs to be high nor that ineffectual action cannot be carried out in the face of dissensus. We do assume that high dissensus has a cost. Since we are interested in the conditions under which goals are realized, we are concerned with the factors which reduce rather than increase this cost.† At each point in time, the bonds among the member collectivities in a society both reduce the options the collectivities will consider and emphasize some preferred option, thereby providing a context for consensus-building on specific policies.

There are shared values that make some options "unthinkable," others legitimate, and still others desirable. A set of shared symbols provides an additional basis for concurrence—one that might be stronger than that of shared values, for the same symbol can be accepted by actors whose values differ. Not all the societal bonds that provide a foundation for consensus are normative; they are in part cognitive in that shared definitions of the world affect the options of the various collectivities. Second, all societies, particularly modern ones, constantly allocate a variety of assets. When a

---

* High dissensus encompasses not merely ultimate purposes but also immediate goals and means. This should be noted because high dissensus on ultimate goals may be coupled with consensus on immediate goals, and this suffices for fairly effective societal action.

† This does not mean that the less costly option is always preferable either normatively or pragmatically. We still need to know the nature and extent of these costs.

particular allocative pattern is taken for granted, it constitutes another foundation of consensus. Social security in the United States in the 1960s, for instance, was widely accepted. Although its boundaries were contested, the option of abolishing it was not a viable political alternative. The importance of these allocations for consensus-building is often overlooked. Like shared values, they expand the area of concurrence, they also provide a "pay-off" which limits the extent of the dissent of various members of society. The welfare state, for instance, developed from the recognition by the more affluent collectivities that *some* reallocation of assets in favor of the weaker members of society must be conceded if the consensus is to be maintained. This consensus becomes an inauthentic one if the reallocations are insignificant in absolute terms or in terms of the respective needs of the members, and especially, if they prevent rather than lead to the needed societal transformation.* On the other hand, if these reallocations do satisfy the requirements, they may constitute a mechanism of change which improves the bases of authentic consensus-building.

In addition to these normative and utilitarian bases of consensus, ongoing processes of consensus-building are also required. The optimal relationships between these bases and the ongoing processes, we suggest, are roughly as follows: Ongoing processes use the consensual bases to narrow the range of alternatives considered, as reference points for settlements of differences, and to indicate preferred solutions. The specific consensus reached on "live" issues tends to fall within the context set by these bases, thus adding to it and reinforcing it. When this is not the case, ongoing consensus at first becomes more difficult to achieve, then the bases are questioned, and finally, the potential for transformation grows, which tends to entail a period of dissensus on basic issues. In *stable* systems which have no capacity to transform, the old consensual bases must collapse before new ones can be formed. On the other hand, *transformable* systems fundamentally revise their consensus during the course of their activities. An interesting mechanism by which this revision is accomplished is the broadening of a system by the legitimation of a new alternative and then a gradual shifting of the weight from earlier alternatives to the new one until the center of gravity of the whole system is altered.

In exploring the level of consensus of a given society and the ways in which it is generated and maintained, several pitfalls are to be avoided. First, the level of consensus differs from one societal sector to another. We deal here, for instance, with societal consensus in regard to the role and scope of the political overlayer. Consensus regarding other sectors of societal activity affects the political consensus, but there is no one-to-one relationship

---

* See Chapter 21 below on the transformation referred to. An example of this process is the introduction of the Labour Party in Britain at the beginning of the twentieth century and the shift from aristocratic–bourgeois to bourgeois–labor politics.

among the sectors. In fact, there are several conditions under which dissensus in non-political values may have relatively little effect on political consensus: (a) If the other values are defined as belonging explicitly to an area unrelated to politics; (b) if the same political policy can be shown to advance divergent or even conflicting non-political values; and (c) when the actors who are politically committed are less committed to non-political values, and those who are more concerned with non-political values have few political commitments to matters which do not affect their extra-political concerns.*

Second, the building of political consensus should not be confused with the democratic mode of government. Political consensus may evolve among those who have power, often including only a small fraction of the population. And the consensus reached reflects the relative power of those who do share in it, without the extent of their power being determined only (and, often, not even mainly) by the number of votes they can mobilize. Political power also results from the capacity to make campaign contributions, to gain the church's blessing, to gain the favor of external forces, and so on. In all societies, there are significant differences in the political power of different collectivities. The need to win their support to assure effective societal action varies directly with their capacity to contribute to or undermine a specific line of action, other activities of the same societal unit, the tenure of the elites in control positions, and the structure of control itself. Democratic government is, therefore, one of a variety of modes of building political consensus.

Third, although high dissensus must be avoided if concerted, effective action is to occur, consensus is not needed for every single activity; most actors have some consensus "slack" upon which they can draw. Nor is it necessary to gain support before the action occurs. A new activity that initially generates hostility or indifference but later wins the support of the relevant actors commands a more effective over-all consensus than an activity that is initially supported but increasingly opposed as it is implemented.

In short, consensus need not be present before an action, on all matters, or among all actors, but some consensus, in the long run, is a prerequisite of a high degree of realization of the actors' goals. There cannot be an active society without a comparatively high capacity to build consensus, for otherwise the increased activeness would entail a highly imposing and, hence, distorting controlling overlayer.

---

* It is almost impossible to understand the Israeli political consensus in the period between 1948 and 1966 without taking into account the differences in the intensity of commitment of the religious parties and Mapai. Most Israeli coalition governments were based on a "trade": Mapai made concessions on religious matters in exchange for an almost completely free hand in matters of economics and foreign policy. For details, see Amitai Etzioni, "Kulturkampf ou coalition, le cas d'Israel," *Revue Française de Science Politique*, Vol. 8 (1958), pp. 311–331.

Societal and Political Consensus

The Post-Modern State: The Focus of Societal Consensus

The major action agency of modern and, especially, of post-modern societies is the state. The state is to society what organizations are to collectivities;[10] i.e., it is the tool of societal mobilization and action. Societal consensus-building in post-modern societies, therefore, is focused around the use to be made of the state and the way it is to be molded and remolded. Of course, societal consensus also affects other relations among members (e.g., relations among classes or ethnic collectivities), but the patterns of the state must be changed before the majority of the changes in an inter-collectivity consensus can affect the society's action. Some of the patterns which must be changed are: the extent of political centralization (e.g., less states' rights), the distribution of access to the state's control centers (e.g., more access for Negroes), and the state's effect on societal processes (e.g., increased regulation of the economy). There are, of course, socio-political processes apart from the state and societal action via other agencies—for instance, public corporations such as the BBC and the Port of New York Authority. But the post-modern state provides the context in which such action occurs. This context includes legislation, enforcement agencies, and economic power. Furthermore, it is via the state that consensus is most readily formulated, since the mechanisms for consensus-building, as we shall see, are most explicitly structured around it, especially in institutionalized political leadership, legislative bodies, political parties, and interest groups.[11]

The state, as we have seen, can best be understood as society's organizational tool. Like other organizations, it tends to have a written charter, explicit criteria for "membership," and specification of various member roles. There is a division of labor among levels of government and between agencies, hierarchization, lines of communication, authority, and decision-making. As a supra-organization, the state contains many organizations either as its own sub-units or as members allowed to act within its context.

The state also resembles other organizations in that it has a procedure for determining the highest-ranking elites, from elections to various forms of appointment or succession. But even when all the members select these elites in open elections, the state exhibits oligarchic tendencies similar to those Michels observed in other organizations. While the change of the elites of democratic states is much more institutionalized than, let us say, the change of the elites of labor unions, this is not the case for other kinds of states, and even democratic states tend to favor incumbents and to choose candidates who are similar in political and social background to those previously elected. And, when an elite is elected which does not "mesh" with the orientations institutionalized in the state machinery—a rare occurrence—

there is a tendency to bring about a change in or of the elite rather than to alter the state.[12]

Finally, the post-modern state does exhibit some features which the organizations of collectivities do not. While other organizations usually mobilize only a fraction of their membership, the state creates at least a minimal role for most members, that of "citizen." To attain such encompassing mobilization, at least some reliance on coercion is expected on the theoretical grounds discussed above and is, of course, found in all states. Another difference is that while most organizations are in at least limited competition and conflict with some others which attempt to mobilize the same collectivity, the post-modern state claims and maintains a comparatively effective monopoly in *some* areas of societal activity and is highly intolerant of competition.

Society and State: Societal and Political Power

While the state is the organizational tool of society, it has a power of its own; it does not merely execute the lines of action which the members jointly or collectively favor but also itself affects their relations and consensus. Hence, no analysis of consensus-building is complete without some discussion of the relations between the society and the state. The relative autonomy of the state depends on its relations to its society.[13] The power of the state is relatively great when it or other forces have weakened the various member collectivities and the bonds among them, and/or when the state elites and their staffs (the officialdom) have acquired their own status as a collectivity (as in the Third Republic of France) or have been fused with a non-state organization (such as the Party or the military) or collectivity (e.g., the gentry in traditional China). The state has relatively little autonomy when it acts largely as a referee among the societal members or is under the control of a few of them and serves as their tool against the others.

In all these variations (including the latter), the state never merely reflects societal consensus or the preferences of those who use it; it always has an orientation and a power of its own. Like all organizational tools, the state not only serves a master but also affects that which he can and wishes to do.[14] For each collectivity-member, this means that its *societal power* (as reflected in its power vis-à-vis other member collectivities) and its *political power* (expressed in its share of the control of the state and of other downward political processes) are unlikely to be parallel. In the political processes, societal power is converted into power to guide the state, but *en route*, fortunes at least to a degree are altered; some members gain and some lose, depending upon the side toward which the state casts its net power and whom the slant of its mold favors. Differences among the political processes of various types of societies lie in the degree and direction of the state's slant and not in the presence or absence of this slant.

The distribution of political power is reflected in the composition of the representative structure, the leadership of executive branches, the constitutional and effective freedom of each collectivity to organize itself and to gain political positions, and the slant of the values and administrative patterns embodied in the state machinery and upheld by its staff. All of these affect the extent to which a given collectivity, under a given level of organization and mobilization (holding constant the other factors), can guide the directions in which the society's controlling overlayer is turned. That is, all of these are filter-like factors which magnify the societal power of some collectivities and reduce that of others. While these filters can be restructured under the impact of changing distributions of societal power, they tend to be rigid: Constitutions are difficult to amend; the administrative patterns of the state are difficult to alter; it is difficult to resocialize the staff, and so on.

The relationship of societal power to consensus-formation is so close that the consensus reached reflects the distribution of societal power: A major use of societal power is to affect that which is *societally* agreed upon. Consensus, it should be repeated, is not merely a normative or cognitive concurrence; it also involves the satisfaction of the interests of the participants. And the relative power of the participants affects all three elements: the values they endorse, the facts they recognize, and the interests they seek to realize.*

Once it is recognized that the morphologies of the state and the society are not co-extensive even in situations in which this is true of their boundaries, the extent of the discrepancy between political power and societal power and, above all, the conditions under which societal changes are converted into political ones must be determined. If these questions are not answered, the conditions under which the activation of the members will register in changes in the society's actions will remain unknown. Thus, we now explore the various mechanisms for conversion and, hence, political consensus-building; we seek to ascertain the relative efficacy of these mechanisms.

Alternative Consensus-Building Structures

Our exploration of the various patterns and processes of consensus-building involves questions of the extent to which consensus-building is "specialized"; if so, the number of tiers among which it is divided; and the degree to which the consensus-building structure relies on lower as opposed to higher tiers. All of these factors affect the amount and quality of the consensus produced and, thus, the levels of both activation and alienation.

---

* For additional discussion of this point, see below, the discussion of equality and responsiveness.

Degree of Specialization

When consensus-building is *interwoven*, it is "carried" by processes aimed primarily at fulfilling some other function. Holidays, national education, and welfare services tend to have "interwoven" consequences for consensus. Thus, holidays tend to release tensions and reinforce shared values; these have the consequence of enhancing consensus-building, though their primary intended purpose is not to build consensus. In an interwoven structure, consensus-building is largely a result of the ongoing interactions among the societal units rather than produced in specialized structures. For instance, consensus-formation in smaller and less complex preliterate tribes seems to rely primarily on such interaction among the member-families. The relatively little consensus-mobilization which occurs is often also interwoven —for instance, in tribal religious rituals which precede hunting or warfare.[15]

When consensus-building is *segregated*, it takes place in specialized structures—in political units (e.g., parties and legislatures) which are distinct from "regular" societal units. In these political units, societal differences are converted into political differences before society-wide consensus is built. Segregated consensus-formation seems more effective than the interwoven kind, though for reasons discussed below segregated structures seem able to produce only enough consensus to support a comparatively low level of activeness. They are like a sophisticated machine that cannot be used for heavy duty.

In segregated structures, political units which are not coextensive with any collectivity serve to "semi-process" the divergent perspectives of the large variety of collectivities; they act as intermediaries between the perspectives of the collectivities (or sub-collectivities) and their combinations and the perspectives of the society-state.[16] As these perspectives are transferred upward in the conversion process, they are altered; the tendency is to bring them closer together and to reduce their number. As they are transferred downward, the tendency is to relate the general societal perspectives to the specific ones of the member units. In this way, the polity's consensus is related to the perspectives of the member societal units through intermediary units that are greater in number and divergence than the polity, but are fewer and less divergent than the societal units.

To give a simple example, in the United States, coalitions of organizations, which in themselves are based on collectivities, enter the political process with at least a score of contenders for presidential candidacy; in the intermediary stage, this number is reduced usually to two agreed-upon party candidates, one of whom becomes the president who is supported most of the time by the majority of the people.[17] Whether this is the result of authentic consensus-formation or of mass manipulation is a question to which we turn below (Ch. 21). We should mention here that an upward flow is not assumed; the parties may first pick their candidates and run them against others in primaries, or the President may give his support to one candidate and help him win the election. The layers of the conversion process, though, remain the same, whatever the order in which they are activated.

The more interwoven the consensus-building, the less societal and political processes are differentiated from each other in that there is no or only one "specialized" political unit, and the more interaction among collectivities and their respective organizations constitutes both the societal and the political give-and-take. "Settlements" are reached through the guidance of one collectivity or organization (often the Party–State or the military in conjunction with a collectivity) that penetrates the other units and limits the options from which they choose.

Most of the consensus-formation processes of societies fall somewhere between these two ideal-types. Capitalistic democracies, as we shall see, are closer to the segregated type, while mature totalitarian societies are more similar to the interwoven one.

Partial Autonomy and Multi-Tier Structures

In a society in which the consensus-building is of the segregated type, the political units (e.g., parties) are not instruments or arms either of the polity or of the stratification units but are partially autonomous from both. Segregation is more effective if the political units cut across collectivities (e.g., if parties are not the representatives of one collectivity, and if a collectivity is not represented by one party). The political autonomy of collectivities is measured by shifts in their political commitments. It is not that all businessmen who voted Republican suddenly vote for the Democrats, but so long as the percentage of businessmen voting Democrat increases or decreases with the degree to which they are satisfied with their political representation by the Republicans, this mode of convergence is enhanced.

When there is a one-to-one association between a stratification unit and a political unit, segregation is not operative. Many arguments, not mutually exclusive, have been advanced to explain the necessity of the partial autonomy of political units. One of these involves a theory of representation which argues that negotiations are unproductive if the representatives are instructed in detail rather than given "space" in which to be able to maneuver.[18] Others stress the importance of cross-cutting status-sets for the reduction of the intensity of societal conflict, which, in turn, facilitates the development of political consensus.[19] Some emphasize the importance of the "floating vote" for rewarding the continuation of peaceful political competition and the political units that are more responsive to a wide range of collectivities.[20] Others believe that the political units must be bound in part by the perspectives of the society rather than only by those of the collectivities, so that societal needs (e.g., defense) will not be neglected in favor of particularistic ones, and so that a base for determining the criteria for the allocation of assets among the collectivities will be provided.[21] All of these arguments help to explain the ways in which the segregation model of consensus-formation operates. We add a morphological explanation.

Division Among Tiers

All other things equal, *the larger the number and the greater the diversity of the perspectives of a group of units, the more difficult it is to achieve a consensus.** Under the same conditions of initial divergence, consensus is formed more easily, we suggest, if a two or more tier structure is employed. On the first and lowest tier, the participant units are combined into sub-groups according to the relative affinity of their perspectives. Each of these subgroups forms consensus among its members and sends a representative to the next tier, which is composed only of representatives. Their number is smaller than the number of the units on the lower level, and the diversity of their perspectives is likely to be of a lesser degree, because they tend to represent an "average" view of their constituency rather than an extreme one. These representatives then may work out a consensus for the whole unit.

If the diversity is still too great, consensus is expected to increase if another tier is added—one composed of representatives of the subgroups of representatives—in which the "averaging" effect is expected to repeat itself. The proposition as advanced so far applies to any social unit. We expect it to hold for individuals in experimental groups in social science laboratories; it is reported to be in accord with the experience of organizing "buzz" sections in some human relations conferences and training courses.[22] Societal structures, in their differentiation of collectivities from political units, provide an *institutionalized* multi-tier structure. A lower level is composed of the sub-collectivities; the higher ones are the political parties, the local governments, and the national agencies. The lower levels, in general, are less institutionalized than the higher ones (e.g., pre-primary deals in comparison to primary votes, and the latter as opposed to votes in the Senate). The final consensus is occasionally brought for ratification—which may be authentic or merely formalistic—to the full membership (e.g., national elections). Usually, only a few alternatives—those that have been processed through the structure —are presented. (When the membership is presented with the full range of alternatives, the consensus-formation processes have failed.)

If representatives at higher levels do not act within the context of the consensus reached at lower levels—either by representing one of the units

---

* For many other considerations, the heterogeneity is the important variable rather than the number of units involved; here, both are relevant, for it seems that if the same degree of diversity is spread among a larger number of units, consensus-formation is more difficult.

to the partial or complete neglect of the others (e.g., a business representative looks after the interests of big businesses to the neglect of small
ones), or by frequently returning to their collectivities for renewed instructions*—the effectiveness of the process is reduced.

Multi-tier structures differ in the ways in which they distribute the consensus-building among the levels. Anglo-Saxon countries (the United States,
the United Kingdom, Canada, Australia, New Zealand) rely heavily on the
lower levels, usually leaving only two alternatives for the last round which
are often focused around change as opposed to consolidation on domestic
issues and militancy as opposed to moderation in foreign affairs.[23] When
some of the formal elements of a multi-tier structure are lacking such as in
Mexico or the Southern United States, various accommodations—such as a
semi-institutionalized struggle among the factions of a party—emerge and
act as partial functional alternatives.[24] Several European multi-party
systems and coalition governments, such as those of Italy, Holland, and
Austria, retain much more consensus-formation for the higher and more
formal levels.[25]

The "pure" versions of the two major kinds of multi-tier structures have
different weaknesses but lead to similar results. The consensus generated by
the top-heavy structure tends to be insufficient—as indicated, for instance,
by the relative inability to form coalition governments within these structures,
the instability of these governments once they are formed, and the relative
passivity of the national polities. These are all signs of insufficient semi-
processing on the lower levels and of not allowing sufficient leeway in which
to exercise choice and innovation on the higher ones. In the bottom-heavy
structure, an alternative tends to be widely supported once it reaches the
highest levels, but too many alternatives never pass through the lower tiers,
as too much processing—and, hence, elimination—occurs within them. There
seems to be no optimal structure; both structures are workable, both allow
for the conversion of societal differences into political consensus, and both are
ineffective in their extreme forms.

Thus, a consensus-formation structure will be better able to convert the
diverse perspectives of the collectivities into an agreed-upon policy—or to
produce inter-collectivity arrangements which draw on, elaborate, reinforce,
and specify the existing context of consensus—the greater the extent to which
it fulfills the following prerequisites: (a) that it be partially segregated,
(b) that the political units be less numerous than the societal units, (c) that
they function as intermediaries, partially autonomous from both the societal
units and the supra-unit polity, (d) that there be a multi-tier structure whose

---

* That is, they "reopen" the consensus that was already reached, which is a procedure
that is favored by representatives who disagree with the consensus they are expected to
represent but were unable, in an earlier round, to gain approval for a line of action they
favored.

higher and lower tiers are balanced, (e) that the process of consensus-formation encompasses all of the member collectivities, and (f) that a considerable degree of equality exists.*

While no particular collectivity will usually gain its way as it initially conceived it within such a structure, the perspectives of the various members are more likely to be taken into account in determining societal action than in other structures, and a more authentic alteration of the perspectives of the members toward a shared perspective may occur. (Some alienation is still likely to exist, as the alteration of the collectivities' perspectives is never complete, and, hence, some aspects of the policy pursued will tend to be supported but not preferred by one or more of the member collectivities. Alienation, though, is expected to be lower than in any other structure.) No society has ever fully evolved such a consensus-building structure, but societies differ significantly in the extent to which they are able to meet its prerequisites, especially the prerequisite of substantial equality. In the next chapter, we explore the ways in which consensus-building is affected by the differential distributions of assets and power and the consequences of this effect for the study of the active society. Now, we discuss the ways in which the relationship of consensus-building to our second key variable, societal control, affects the level and quality of societal guidance.

The Control-Consensus "Mix"

A Substitution Curve

The quality of societal guidance is greatly affected both by the quality of its components—societal control and consensus-building—*and* by the relative degree to which it relies on one component as opposed to the other. The distinction between control and consensus-building is analytic; the same unit or act may serve both functions, and both components include upward and downward elements. Control draws on the upward flow of information—have the signals that flow from the members to the control centers been received, understood, and followed? Have there been new developments that require a change of signals? But the application of power and the specification of decisions are downward: Those of higher ranks control those of lower ones. On the other hand, while consensus-building is in part a downward flow of influence from the leaders and the application of symbols—since the purpose of consensus-building is to win the support of the member collectivities, their leadership and their membership—basically, consensus-formation is an upward process. As we have seen, this is particularly true because the collectivities are viable societal units with some degree of political

---

* The reasons for this last prerequisite are discussed in the next chapter.

autonomy, and they cannot be readily manipulated both because they have become committed to particular lines of action as a result of consensus-building and because they have capacities and perspectives of their own.[26]

It is comparatively easy to increase one of the two elements of guidance by "trading" it for the other. More control and less consensus or more consensus and less control are "easy" solutions, roughly approximated by mature totalitarian and capitalistic democratic polities. In effect, totalitarian societies are not only stronger in control than capitalistic democratic societies but are also overprescriptive and deficient in their consensus-building capacities, even though they have greater consensus-building capacities than the "ideal-type" of the overmanaged society. Similarly, while capitalistic democratic societies have increased to some extent their control capacities and, hence, are more directed than an ideal-type drifting society, they can be quite effectively characterized as high on consensus and low on control.*

It has been argued that the two main types of post-modern societies—of which the United States and the Soviet Union are often considered typical representatives—are moving closer to each other, though there has been much controversy about the scope and the specific nature of this convergence.[27] Such convergence, so far as societal guidance is concerned, would suggest a reduction of control and an increase in consensus-building for totalitarian societies and an increase in control (even if this requires some reduction of consensus) for democracies. First, it should be noted that the level of societal action that a political organization can effectively handle depends on its combination of the two components of societal guidance. While there is no simple, straight-line substitution, by and large, increasing one element reduces the other and produces little net gain in societal action. A gain is achieved if the alteration in the "mix" increases the *balance* of the two components rather than undermines it, a rule on which is based the law of declining marginal utility. A balanced guidance mechanism can handle more societal action in the long run than one that is high on one component and low on the other, even though the "sum" may be the same. But the most effective combination is achieved not by improving the balance of the "mix" but by increasing both components. To gain active societal guidance for a democracy requires an increase in control or political intensity while maintaining as much of the *relatively* high consensus as possible and expanding its bases by mobilizing the excluded collectivities into the political processes. For a totalitarian society, an increase in active guidance requires a sub-

---

* While, in general, the scope of control is much greater in totalitarian than in democratic societies, it does not follow that every single issue controlled by democracies is also controlled by totalitarian societies. Thus, an important segment of the societal management problems of democracies concerns civil rights, a segment that is much smaller in totalitarian societies.

stantial increase in the capacity to form consensus; at the same time, the control must be improved in quality so as to become much less prescriptive rather than curtailed. In both types of societies, consensus must be made more authentic by increasing the extent to which it is based on education as opposed to persuasion. (Other mechanisms for the reduction of inauthenticity are explored below.) The two main types of modern societies, therefore, might not be moving toward each other but rather toward a third meeting point—toward an active society which is high (and not "middling") in both control and consensus (i.e., in societal guidance).

Simmel noted that freedom is not the absence of societal guidance but rather guidance that allows a man to be free.[28] Mannheim stressed that freedom is to be planned.[29] Drawing on these ideas, we emphasized that it is not more control that is needed but rather a qualitative change of control toward a more encompassing but not prescriptive, more closely related to consensus-building and less coercive and alienating control. That this is important not merely in the economic realm should be stressed; professional ethics is a case in point. The subtle interplay between professional self-control and governmental contextuating control serves not to introduce prescriptive control but to apply pressure on the professions to increase their self-control. The correct balance is difficult to specify and may be reached only via the political processes. But it might be noted that the democracies, especially the United States, tend to err in the opposite direction: They are underplanned and undercontrolled and they often allow the narrow freedom of a few to impose rigid constraints on the freedom of the many. The freedom of advertisers, gun manufacturers, and pharmaceutical industries is much more effectively protected than that of the public and the consumers. "Natural" processes are unlikely to provide effective correctives; when new power relations—under conditions of increased equality—permit, societal planning for *more* freedom will have to be introduced if societal activeness is to be increased.

The relations between the kind of guidance "mix" that predominates in a society and its power "mix" (explored in Chs. 13 and 14) ought to be indicated. (a) If control is increased without increasing consensus-building, we expect a greater reliance on force. (This occurs to a greater extent, the more prescriptive the added control.) (b) If consensus is increased without increasing control, a relatively greater reliance on normative means is possible. This occurs to a greater extent, the higher the existing level of societal guidance, because well-balanced but low-level guidance is likely to generate considerable alienation and to lead to the use of more coercive means of control. (c) Utilitarian means of control are most likely to be relied upon heavily in guidance systems that are intensive but narrow in scope—limited mainly to production and administrative activities and exclusive of status-relations, stratification, and education.

A Genetic Perspective: The Time Sequence

The three ideal-types of societies which differ in their societal-guidance "mix" also differ in the sequential relations between the two elements of guidance. In capitalistic democractic societies, there is a tendency to build up consensus first and then to implement a policy. Some policies, especially those which affect only bit changes, are carried out with little or only *post-hoc* consensus-building. Others are initiated before consensus is greatly advanced. But in comparison to mature totalitarian societies, consensus-building tends to come "early" in the action-policy sequence. Policies that are not favored by the more powerful societal members often are not implemented until an internal crisis (e.g., widespread rioting) or an environmental one (e.g., war) demonstrate the overdue need for them. This impetus may also be provided by a rise in the power of new or previously weak collectivities. Keynesian controls of the economy were introduced in the United States largely after the great depression.[30] And contemporary desegregation began when the Negroes were mobilized during World War II.[31]

The tendency in democracies is to delay actions that entail societal changes and to proceed slowly when they are initiated; thus, changes often lag behind societal needs. In Britain, pressure groups are officially and unofficially brought into the process of legislation and administration. This is true for such groups as producer and consumer associations—from automobile manufacturers to the Cake and Biscuit Alliance—welfare organizations, and labor unions. They all have the capacity to affect and, particularly, to limit political action.[32]

> The interests are so faithfully represented and bring such pressure to bear indicating how far each is prepared to move—which is usually little distance at all—that the degree of movement is negligible. The reports of the committees go up, they are again submitted to democratic scrutiny in public debate, the debate is resubmitted to the committees for their comments, and by the time a decision is taken the problem under discussion has frequently changed its character. To make large-scale changes, for instance, in the field of transportation or town planning, is exceptionally difficult.[33]

The United States has been discussed in similar terms.[34]

The resulting lag can be measured in that the same needs are often more societally and economically costly to serve at a later stage than would have been the case had they been served earlier. This holds not only for such complex matters as slum clearance and desegregation, but also for more trivial matters such as changes in the direction of the flow of traffic. Swedes used to drive on the left side of the road, but with the increase in road transportation to other countries—most of which require driving on the right side—the desirability of changing the direction became quite obvious. When such a change was advocated in 1945, it was expected to cost about 37 million kroners. By the time it was introduced in 1967, the number of cars had increased enormously and the cost was estimated at 600 million.[35]

Totalitarian societies tend to act *first* and to seek consensus *later*. There are some campaigns to marshal public acceptance before a plan is launched, and there is some consulting of the collectivities before a major decision is made. But, by and large, the scope of the action that is planned and initiated greatly exceeds the consensus that is marshaled before initiation. Most of the efforts to marshal support are undertaken during the course of the implementation of a plan. This is necessary, in part, because the deficient consensus-formation structure does not allow the highest-ranking elites—even if and when they wish—to gain a realistic picture of the divergent perspectives of the member collectivities, especially of those of the weaker ones. Second, the elites, especially in those societies' hyper-active periods, tend to overestimate their capacity to control and to mobilize consensus. The result is often aiming too high at first, followed by the curtailment of goals and the planning to bring them closer to those which the society will "take" or which can in effect be imposed. The Soviet NEP and the Chinese curtailment of the "Great Leap" are among the best known examples of such *post-hoc* down-scaling.

Initial "overshooting" may be said to be an effective procedure for maximizing societal change; if the initial goals had been more "realistic," less change would have been achieved. While this may be a valid proposition to a degree, there is obviously a limit beyond which aiming still *higher* provides *fewer* results, more frustration, greater resistance, and higher alienation. Much of totalitarian planning, we suggest, is of such a hyper-active nature.

It should be noted, however, that it is rather difficult to determine which of the two strategies is less effective—first overshooting and then down-scaling, or first resisting change until it is overdue and then underchanging. This is, in part, an academic question, since each society seems to have the guidance mechanism it "deserves," in the sense that it seems as difficult for a totalitarian government to gain high consensus before action as for a capitalistic democracy to act with a high degree of anticipation and acceleration. With changes in the society and in the polity in the active direction, as discussed above, the prerequisites of a more balanced approach to societal guidance are likely to develop.

Mechanisms for the Articulation of Control and Consensus

In an effort to strengthen societal guidance, all modern societies have experimented, often quite deliberately, with a variety of mechanisms whose function is to improve the articulation of control and consensus without undermining either element. The results of these experiments are far from clear and the experimentation has not yet been completed. We now explore three mechanisms for the linking of the segregated control units with the consensus-building units: (i) the combination of societal knowledge-production and decision-making units with consensus-building units (which was used in the new approaches to planning following the decline in the significance of legislatures); (ii) the change of ownership to bring control and consensus closer together; and (iii) the evolution of normative criteria which reduce the distance between the two kinds of units.* Each of the topics mentioned here is the subject of a large body of literature; our concern is only with their role as a mechanism for the closer articulation of the two components of societal guidance.

Interwoven Planning

Much of the late-modern and early post-modern intellectual debate about societal experimentation has been concerned with the discovery of mechanisms which would allow for more control *and* more consensus-building. The search for such mechanisms becomes more critical as the societal awareness of the need for guidance seems historically to grow, and as new post-modern technologies seem to offer options for new kinds of planning. Encompassing and intensive societal guidance requires both high communication capacities and advanced knowledge-technology. Earlier attempts at macroscopic planning often failed not only because of the internally imbalanced consensus and control elements or the low level of investment in both components, but because the required facilities were not available.[36] Attempts to introduce a high level of societal guidance into underdeveloped countries often led to prescriptive control because, among other reasons, the subtle art of contextuating control requires technologies that were not available in 1917 in Russia or in most underdeveloped nations in the modern period.[37] The more developed nations, as they move deeper into the post-modern age, for the first time in history command the necessary means for the broad—but not overly specific—contextuating control that is more conducive to consensus-formation than prescriptive control and, hence, can achieve a higher total guidance level and greater societal activeness with a much lower level of alienation.

---

* Only mechanisms with which democratic societies have experimented are discussed. Even in these polities, there are numerous other mechanisms including: civilian review boards to increase the responsiveness of the police to civil and human rights; various ombudsmen to act as macroscopic complaint-and-suggestion boxes; decentralization—a multi-level approach in which federal and state authorities collaborate; expert commissions; the participation of the clients of government agencies—such as welfare departments and the Office of Economic Opportunity—in the supervision of programs catering to their needs; co-determination in industry; and consumer representation in political bodies.

Modern planning tended to be remote, utopian, or overmanaging. The post-modern societies experiment with *new organizations and societal techniques of contextuating control so as to link control more closely to consensus-formation.* This is closely related to changes in the organization of societal decision-making.

The rationalistic planner, the prevailing species in earlier generations, tried to produce a master design that optimized the values presented to him by the political decision-makers. He formulated a plan which he then hoped to submit to the decision-makers for approval and to the administrative agencies for implementation.[38] Aside from the facts that political decision-makers are unable to provide the planners with a neat set of ranked values and that even if such a scale were available, it would not allow optimization,[39] such segregated and "a-political" planning is likely to be an ineffectual base for societal guidance. *Its products are likely to be rejected, ignored, or radically altered by the political decision-makers,* and an attempt to implement plans produced in this way requires a large application of power and, thus, generates considerable resistance and alienation, because such planning is very remote from consensus-building as well as from control.

More "interwoven" approaches to planning can be ranked according to their degree of integration into the processes of societal guidance: (a) relatively more "political" planners attempt to learn about the perspectives of the decision-makers and to take these perspectives into account in their planning. These perspectives are not taken as "given," but attempts are made not to require their change if at all possible.

(b) Still more "political" planners also explore the perspectives of those who are likely to be affected by the plan. For example, in a study of a plan to stagger the working hours in downtown Manhattan to reduce the congestion in the subways, a sample of workers as well as leaders of labor unions and industry were asked if they would accept the plan if it were advanced.[40] This is a fairly rare occurrence. There are, of course, other ways in which to estimate the responses to a plan, but such exploration is rarely considered the duty of the planners as rigid separation of control, consensus-formation, and planning tends to prevail.

(c) A much higher level of articulation of planning and societal guidance is achieved when decision-making units and planning units are less segregated, as, for instance, in the executive authority of the European Economic Community, the French General Planning Commissariat, and the British National Economic Development Council,[41] all of which are agencies of the post-modern period.*

The plans produced by these West European interwoven planning units

---

* John and Anne-Marie Hackett explore in detail the ways in which the planning commissions and various related bodies, while including representatives of interest groups, are "contextuated" by the civil servants who act as the chairmen, vice-chairmen, and

are in part a result of a give-and-take between the planners and the elites of the collectivities that will be affected by the plans. The British NEDC, for instance, includes equal numbers of representatives of labor and business and a "leavening of public and governmental representatives."[42] Next to the executive body of the EEC, there is a Social and Economic Committee which includes representatives of the major interest groups. It is too large to serve as an effective consensus-formation body (having 101 members in 1960), but its work is supplemented both by a good deal of informal contact between the EEC experts and those attached to the national delegations to the temporary capital of *Europa*, Brussels, and by the frequent visits of EEC planners to the capitals of member countries where they consult with interest-group representatives about plans they are developing.

In the consultations between the planners and the collectivities' representatives, both the plan and the perspectives of the units are altered to allow for more consensus and for less alienating and more effective control (thus increasing the likelihood that the units will comply and will do so voluntarily). Second, the plan almost never assumes a capacity for detailed forecasting or prescriptive control; it aims only at keeping the guided processes within a context.

The Means and Scope of Planning

Planning agencies—where they do exist—differ greatly in the assets available to them for use in the political give-and-take, and the means which planning commands affect significantly the "distance" between the planning units and other guidance processes. Segregated planning requires no such assets; the planners do not need them, since they are not empowered to give-and-take. "Interwoven" planning units differ in the kinds of means available to them, in accord with our general classification; e.g., some have only normative power, appealing to the social and national responsibilities of labor leaders, businessmen, and so on. The information the planners make available also has a symbolic effect; for instance, when they report that there is expected to be a shortage in area X and an overabundance in area Y (based on their national surveys of producers and consumers), this tends to lead some marginal producers to shift, which is a self-correcting mechanism.[43] (It should be noted that such information is usually not available in any detail and scope unless it is provided by a national body.)[44]

Other planning agencies command utilitarian assets as well as normative ones; the former take the forms of low interest credits, tax concessions, outright subsidies, priorities in export or import licences, and so on.[45] Finally

---

rapporteurs of most of these bodies as well as constitute a significant proportion of their members. *Economic Planning in France* (Cambridge, Mass.: Harvard University Press, 1963), pp. 397–400.

(and this is rarely the case for agencies of contextuating planning), some coercion is available in the forms of fines and outright government decrees (e.g., the closing of obsolescent coal mines).[46] In general, though, the new planning is voluntary and based on consensus. It is designed to operate on the basis of "average" compliance rather than complete compliance (the expectation of which tends to encourage systems to use coercion, which has a high "delivery" capacity but also generates considerable resistance and alienation).

So far, contextuating, interwoven planning has been largely in this sector, its scope increased from the curbing of gross depressions and inflations to include the avoidance of mass unemployment and the stimulation of economic growth. A transition toward an active society will require that planning encompass other sectors as well, including the guidance of professional services, of education, and of changes in status relations (such as desegregation in the United States and the absorption of immigrants in Australia). Democracies differ markedly in the degree of activeness with which they approach these non-economic sectors. The United States entered the post-modern period with a highly passive approach; other democracies demonstrated varying degrees of activation. Thus, for instance, education in Britain is partially guided, while in the United States, its trends are viewed as "ongoing."[47] The United States government gradually came to assess educational developments (though even this generated considerable resistance, precisely because it was perceived as a step toward national guidance) but has almost no control of this sector.[48] France moved quite deliberately in the direction of more encompassing planning with the Fourth Plan insisting that its goal was "a more complete view of man" rather than merely the planning of economic processes, a "civilization of gadgets."[49] The Scandinavian and Israeli planning of non-economic sectors is well-established, though there are few systematic studies of its effectiveness.[50] Other democracies have accepted more planning in more areas than has the United States.[51] But even the United States has been entering new sectors. In a country in which societal planning was considered unacceptable only a few years earlier—and, ideologically, is still widely questioned—the government began the control of population by supporting birth control programs.[52]

Declining Legislatures

The need for a greater articulation of planning (in which societal knowledge is used for macro-decisions), control, and consensus-building arises not only from the difficulty of producing plans that are sufficiently realistic to meet the administrative and political requirements of societal guidance in segregated structures, but also because the agencies traditionally engaged in consensus-building (and, to a lesser degree, in control) are weakening. The decline in the power of the national legislatures of democracies—the modern, society-wide consensus-building units—as opposed to their executives has been frequently noted.[53] We expect this trend to continue, and we see a growing tendency for the task of consensus-building to be assumed by other agents. The executive branches further reduce the power of the legislatures by monopolizing much of the state-collected information and analysis, which they present selectively to the legislatures.[54] First, the legislators have only very small knowledge-producing units of their own and few funds for the purchase of information from independent sources.* And the knowledge they obtain free-of-charge from non-executive sources is often highly partisan. Second, within the executive itself, the role and power of experts as opposed to those of the lay administrators seem to be increasing. The experts, hence, ought to be "woven" more directly and effectively into the control and consensus processes.

Another reason that legislatures are losing some of their capacity to participate effectively in societal guidance is that the units which their members represent are often regional while the action and planning units are functional or national; in either case, they are trans-regional. Sub-collectivities are usually ecological and, in that sense, sub-regional, but in the society's political processes, the sub-collectivities are combined into regional or national units. The regional combination is older and was found in relatively "pure" form in feudal societies. The representative structure of the United States still has strong regional elements while that of Britain is less regionally based. The Scandinavian representative structures are semi-regional,[55] while the Israeli one is national. Thus, there is a close association between the relative degree of activeness of a society and its national structure of consensus-building. Where the regionality of a society is considerable and is to be reduced, the tier of consensus-building below the political parties must be trans-regional and the relevant sub-units must be "functional"—for example, labor unions or intellectuals—and not regional. Thus, legislatures have lost much of their consensus-building capacity; unless representation is restructured, they are unlikely to be the centers which will provide the increased consensus-formation and mobilizing capacity which activation requires.

Public Ownership and Management

In the last century of the modern period, there was much ideological controversy about whether or not societal control would be more closely linked to consensus-building if property were publicly rather than privately owned and/or managed. Much societal experimentation along these lines followed. Left-oriented totalitarian societies rejected private enterprise

---

* Philip Donham and Robert J. Fahey, *Congress Needs Help* (New York: Random House, 1966).

as non-consensual and adopted societal (in effect, state) control which they perceived as consensual, while capitalist societies assumed the opposite ideological stance. Both types of societies have moderated their positions—one toward the acceptance of an increased role for the profit motive, interest rates ("capital charges"), and other market mechanisms,[56] and the other in the direction of considerable societal (largely state) control. In both types of societies, the ideological recognition of these changes is lagging behind their structural counterparts. Each of these kinds of societies has been said to be becoming more like the other kind, but they both seem to be moving toward a third type—one in which no one mode of societal guidance prevails but there are rather various combinations of ownership, management, and utility (the right to benefit from the assets, to use them) in the economic sector as well as in those of welfare, education, health, and other activities.

"Mixed" guidance societies have an important state-owned and state-managed economic sector, public authorities, producer and consumer cooperatives, private enterprises, regulatory agencies, and varying combinations of these elements—in particular, many combinations of state and private enterprises. These include the state's provision of contextuating control for privately managed and owned enterprises (many utilities), the state's financing of part of the costs of privately managed enterprises (e.g., schools), complementary projects (such as state-built highways for privately-produced automobiles), and many other forms.[57]

Often, such "mixing" is viewed as a transition toward a purer type, but "mixing" is to be expected as a permanent feature of the post-modern society. Hence, the central question is not one of whether or not there will be more state control in the United States or more private control in the Soviet Union, but which combinations are likely to emerge, and what are the ways in which their relative efficacy, quantity, and quality of output, suitability to different societal sectors, and responsiveness to the members' needs can be determined.

Producing cooperatives, for instance, tend to link control and consensus more closely than most other modes of organization but are highly unresponsive to non-members and to general societal needs; they seem to provide, at best, a microscopic solution. Other arrangements that are quite suitable for economic production, are not adequate for non-economic activities. For example, proprietary hospitals (owned by the doctors) tend to be substantially lower in quality than publicly-owned ones.[58] Regulatory commissions—which set the contexts without owning, managing, or benefiting from the supervised industries—proved quite effective in situations in which two organized groupings, such as labor and business, countervail each other, which is the case for the United States National Labor Relations Board. But such commissions as the Civil Aeronautics Board and the Federal Communication Commission are much less effective, as they deal with situations in which unorganized consumers face an organized industry—i.e., the airlines or the television networks.[59] In still other areas, some public enterprises have affected the conduct of private ones. For instance, the introduction of educational television in some American cities increased the investment of private networks in public affairs programs. Finally, in some sectors, the potential of state intervention led to increased "house cleaning."

Little is known about the most conducive "mix" for an active society at this stage of experimentation and study. In principle, we expect that a guidance system which relies heavily on inter-unit adjustment—whether it be of private enterprises or among cooperatives—will tend grossly to neglect one or more societal values and needs, such as the rights of weaker collectivities and anticipatory societal management. On the other hand, prescriptive supra-unit control tends toward over-management. Hence, we expect the societies that combine contextuating state control with the "delegation" of bit control to a plurality of member organizations to be most "active," so long as the society's ultimate superiority is established administratively and accepted normatively. This specific "mix" seems superior to a system that has a mixed management but no clearly-established superiority of the society if all the major values and not merely productivity are to be taken into account.

To illustrate the numerous specific questions that have not been conclusively answered in this area and the reasons that we favor a "superior" societal control, we now explore briefly a problem in "managing" unemployment. Economists debate two approaches to unemployment. One approach advocates mainly a general increase in demand—stimulated by the government, if necessary—which will indirectly result in corporations hiring more workers, training or retraining them, and so forth. The second approach, known as the "structuralist" one, calls for the direct treatment of unemployment—e.g., by a government-financed retraining program. Many economists are "eclectic" in that they favor programs which have some elements of both approaches. (This is especially the case for the structuralists because they recognize that if unemployment is at a high level, structural programs cannot significantly improve the situation.) But there are important differences of emphasis among the various programs. United States "management" of unemployment between 1961 and 1966, for instance, was largely of the non-structuralist type.[60] This difference in programs illustrates varying assumptions about the intensity and specificity of state control. It is greater and more prescriptive for the structuralist approach than for the aggregate-demand one. The more contextuating the state control, all other things equal, the smaller the danger of over-management and alienation, and thus, the aggregate-demand approach would seem advantageous. But not all things are equal: Stimulation by general demand seems to require an "over-heating" of the economy before unemployment is significantly reduced. This stimulation tends to undermine exports and to retard economic growth, which, in turn, generates pressure to reduce the government stimulation. Hence, if the structuralist approach can achieve the same reduction of unemployment with less "over-heating" than the aggregate-demand treatment, the increased state control involved in the structuralist approach will be more effective.

We specified elsewhere the reasons that we accept the proposition that structuralist treatment is needed.[61] Briefly, the reasons point to sources of rigidity within the economy and society that curb secondary-priming (the activation of one sector by changes in another), which the non-structuralist approach assumes. An increase in the general level of demand seems to increase the trade among the more modernized sectors of the economy (which often have initially high rates of employment) with relatively little carry-over to the less modernized sectors.* Typically, the number and percentage of the long-term unemployed increase in both slump *and* boom periods. At midyear in 1953, this grouping in the United States numbered 58,000 or 3.7 per cent of all of those who were unemployed; in 1957, they numbered 260,000 or 9.6 per cent; in 1960—411,000 (9.6 per cent); and in 1963—643,000 (15.8 per cent). In the national economy, there seem to be relationships roughly similar to those which appear in international trade: Increases in transactions tend to concentrate among the "have" countries while the "have nots," weaker initially, continue to lag behind.

Second, leaving the ultimate decisions and actions in private hands may as readily lead to more automation (as labor shortages rise) as to increased investment in the retraining of employees. In addition to continuing unemployment, this generates increased featherbedding, wildcat strikes, resistance to technological innovations, and political tensions due to the concentration of unemployment and underemployment in some collectivities —e.g., Negro-Americans. Hence, it seems that a more direct guidance of societal efforts, which the structuralist approach advocates, is required. That which has been illustrated here for the management of unemployment, we suggest, holds also for the management of numerous other societal problems.[62]

"Societal Usefulness"

Values have an independent role in the transformation of societies. We can productively compare various normative developments from the general viewpoint of the transformation of post-modern into active societies, or, specifically, we seek to establish the degree to which these developments support the necessary societal guidance systems. Much attention has already

---

* A similar rigidity appears when common markets are formed. Unless special measures are taken, the weaker areas continue to lag—e.g., South Italy following Italy's unification, and the South in the United States following federation.

been paid to the changing legitimation of welfare, the reallocation of wealth, public ownership, and state control. The rise in the weight of "societal usefulness" as a normative criterion is a related but more abstract and encompassing development which has gained much less attention. A brief discussion of this development serves to illustrate the normative changes which—to the degree that they do occur—support the transformation to an active society.

The transition from one societal system to another as a rule does not take the form of the abolition of the old system and the establishment of a new one. Typically, a new system gradually replaces the old one, and often this replacement is carried out by first superimposing new elements on the old ones, both of which co-exist for long periods in which some of the old elements acquire new functions and become permanent features of the new society.* The relatively increasing weight of "societal usefulness" as a basis for consensus-building in post-modern democratic societies is a case in point. This involves not only the addition of another shared value on which to build consensus, but also a new criterion on which to base the conception of the legitimate proportion of societal energy to be invested in public as opposed to private pursuits.

The degree to which the values of a particular society have shifted in this direction must be determined by empirical research. Here, we can mention briefly the indicators that may be employed in this measurement. The most direct indication is an increased acceptance of the idea that a member, in making his decision, ought to take into account the extent of the usefulness of the projected activity for the society at large (or, for "others"). This implies that the pursuit of self (or unit) goals is not automatically societally useful. In popular terms, it suggests that not all that is good for General Motors is good for the United States, and that G.M. *ought to be* concerned with its effects on the United States' welfare.[63]

Since business activity is traditionally associated in the West with self as contrasted to societal (public or governmental) services (such as teaching, social work, and civil service), the changing rankings of the various occupations involved is relevant.[64] An analysis of cultural heroes is similarly of interest: To what degree have the intellectuals, scientists, and astronauts replaced the entrepreneurs?[65]

Finally, an increased interest in activities that deal with symbols (cultural and political activities) as compared to those that are concerned with objects (especially, materialistic acquisitions and consumption) is a corollary develop-

---

* For instance, the bureaucratic nation–state was superimposed on the early feudal society, but the underlying feudal arrangement continued to function for hundreds of years on the village and local levels and to some degree on the national one. And in the bureaucratic state, foreign policy was in part conducted by the aristocracy; the special skills of this grouping found a new use in this area.

ment to an increase in the emphasis on societal usefulness.* Such a change facilitates consensus-building because material scarcity is inevitable while there is no such limit to the participation in cultural and political activities. While an increase in the commitment to symbolic activities prolongs the development of a specific consensus—as more actors seek to participate— such consensus, when it is finally reached, is more mobilizing, for the same reason. The sociological conditions under which such a change may occur are likely to become more available in post-modern societies, following a long-term increase in material affluence and the extension of liberal arts education. (For both reasons, Western Europe and the Soviet Union may be entering an age of conspicuous consumption at the same time that the United States begins to outgrow it, but they may later follow suit.)

When the weight of societal usefulness as a normative criterion for action increases, this allows for an increase in the symbolic gratifications of the power elites and the privileged collectivities, thus making politically more feasible a significant reallocation of economic resources in favor of the under- privileged collectivities (and "have-not" societies). It also aids in the legitima- tion of the shifting of assets from the private to the public sector, since there is a growing consensus to the effect that consumption is less valuable than the improvement of the public sectors and the resolution of major societal problems.

The mechanisms of consensus, when they are operative and effective, assure that those who command power will endorse the lines of societal action followed, even if they have to adapt their perspectives because of other actors who also command power, including the power invested in the societal overlayer. The state mechanisms, as we have seen, vary in their relative reliance on consensus as opposed to control, in their articulation of the two elements, and in the total amount of societal guidance they are able to pro- vide. The picture, though, is incomplete. Those who have little or no active voice in the councils of consensus also affect societal action, if only by their passive resistance or disaffection. And their needs command the same ethical status as those of the more powerful members of society. The concepts of responsiveness and equality serve to extend this particular line of analysis so that it encompasses the societal positions and roles of those whom consensus tends to exclude.

---

* The increased emphasis on service jobs such as the Peace Corps, VISTA, the Job Corps in the anti-poverty program, encourages the association of high status and societal usefulness with non-business roles.

NOTES

1. Albert Waterston, *Development Planning: Lessons of Experience* (Baltimore: Johns Hopkins University Press, 1965); A. H. Hanson, *The Process of Planning: A Study of India's Five-year Plans, 1950–1964* (London: Oxford University Press, 1966), esp. pp. 525–538. See also various reports in Bertram M. Gross (ed.), *Action Under Planning: the Guidance of Economic Development* (New York: McGraw-Hill, 1967); Fred G. Burke, *Tanganyika: Preplanning* (Syracuse, N.Y.: Syracuse University Press, 1965), pp. 53–57.

2. Barrington Moore, Jr., *Soviet Politics: The Dilemma of Power* (New York: Harper & Row, 1965). For recent reports from Russia, see Peter Grose, "Soviet Propagandists Denounce Anti-religious Campaign as Inept," *The New York Times*, March 27, 1966; Raymond H. Anderson, "Russians Abandoning Plans to Reform Spelling," *The New York Times*, April 23, 1966; and Walter Sullivan, "How the Russians Deal with Birth Control," *The New York Times*, June 4, 1967. On the difficulties in dealing with religion and magic in Communist China, see David Oancia, "Red China Fights Venerable Ways," *The New York Times*, May 15, 1966, p. 16. On the persistence of status differentiations, see A. Doak Barnett, "Social Stratification and Aspects of Personnel Management in the Chinese Communist Bureaucracy," *The China Quarterly*, No. 28 (1966), pp. 8–39. See also Adam B. Ulam, *The Unfinished Revolution* (New York: Random House, 1960).

3. On the initial hopes, see Robert J. Alexander, *The Bolivian National Revolution* (New Brunswick, N.J.: Rutgers University Press, 1958); Richard W. Patch, "Bolivia: U.S. Assistance in a Revolutionary Setting," in Richard N. Adams et al., *Social Change in Latin America Today* (New York: Random House, 1960), pp. 108–176.

4. "Mexico's rural areas, however, still constitute its greatest problem. After thirty-five years of reform rural Mexico, where about 70 per cent of the people live and slightly over half of the total population carry on agricultural pursuits, has barely been brought into contact with the stimuli of the modern world. The islands of progressive agriculture created by a small new landowning class of entrepreneurs are still engulfed in a sea of rural backwardness and unproductiveness. The ideal of the *ejido*—communal ownership of land by the village—has not proved a great success. Though Mexican governments have built thousands of schools in rural villages there are more illiterates than a quarter of a century ago and more children out of school than ever. The great majority of peasants, whether on community farms or private holdings, still work their land by primitive traditional methods. . . ." I. Robert Sinai, *In Search of the Modern World* (New York: The New American Library, 1967), pp. 160–161. See also Pablo González Casanova, *La Democracia en México* (Mexico: Ediciónes ERA S.A., 1965), pp. 69 ff.; and Frank Brandenburg, *The Making of Modern Mexico* (Englewood Cliffs, N.J.: Prentice-Hall, 1964), on the revolution, see pp. 47–118, on the farmers, pp. 252 ff.

5. Eva Rosenfeld, "Social Stratification in a 'Classless' Society," *American Sociological Review*, Vol. 16 (1951), pp. 766–774; Richard D. Schwartz, "Democracy and Collectivism in the Kibbutz," *Social Problems*, Vol. 5 (1957), pp. 137–147; and Melford E. Spiro, *Kibbutz: Venture in Utopia* (Cambridge: Harvard University Press, 1956), esp. pp. 201–239.

6. James W. Prothro and C. M. Grigg, "Fundamental Principles of Democracy:

Bases of Agreement and Disagreement," *Journal of Politics*, Vol. 22 (1960), pp. 276–294, present evidence that agreement on "fundamentals" does not exist in the US, on many issues. See also Herbert McClosky, "Consensus and Ideology in American Politics," in Joseph R. Fiszman, *The American Political Arena*, 2nd ed. (Boston: Little, Brown, 1966), pp. 39–70, and Herbert McClosky, Paul J. Hoffmann, and Rosemary O'Hara, "Issue Conflict and Consensus Among Party Leaders and Followers," *American Political Science Review*, Vol. 54 (1960), pp. 406–427. For data on the homogeneity of social characteristics and values among American elite groups, see James N. Rosenau, "Consensus-Building in the American National Community: Hypotheses and Supporting Data," *Journal of Politics*, Vol. 24 (1962), pp. 639–661.

7. For a review of definitions and approaches to this subject, see Theodore M. Newcomb, "The Study of Consensus," in Merton, Broom, Cottrell (eds.), *Sociology Today, op. cit.*, pp. 277–292; Orrin E. Klapp, "The Concept of Consensus and Its Importance," *Sociology and Social Research*, Vol. 41 (1957), pp. 336–342; Thomas J. Scheff, "Toward a Sociological Model of Consensus," *American Sociological Review*, Vol. 32 (1967), pp. 32–46; Irving Louis Horowitz, *Three Worlds of Development* (New York: Oxford University Press, 1966), pp. 367–369. For measurements of this concept, see Matilda W. Riley, John W. Riley, and Marcia L. Toby, "The Measurement of Consensus," *Social Forces*, Vol. 31 (1952), pp. 97–106, and N. R. Luttbeg and H. Zeigler, "Attitude Consensus and Conflict in An Interest Group: an Assessment of Cohesion," *American Political Science Review* (1966), pp. 655–666.

8. On the difference between "like" and "common" values, see Robert M. MacIver and Charles H. Page, *Society* (New York: Holt, Rinehart & Winston, 1949), p. 440.

9. Hopkins, *The Exercise of Influence in Small Groups, op. cit.*, p. 11.

10. See Ch. 5 above for elaboration.

11. For a definition of politics as focused around the state, see Max Weber, "Politics as a Vocation," in Gerth and Mills, *From Max Weber, op. cit.*, p. 78; and Truman, *The Governmental Process, op. cit.*, p. 263. These definitions concern macro-politics; Dahl provides a more inclusive definition that also covers micro-politics. See his *Modern Political Analysis, op. cit.*, pp. 1–7. Unless otherwise specified, we are concerned with macro-politics.

12. Seymour M. Lipset, *Agrarian Socialism* (Berkeley: University of California Press, 1950), esp. pp. 255–275. On the varying degrees of lack of neutrality of the state (as an administrative body) in Russia, France, and Britain, see Eric H. Strauss, *The Ruling Servants* (New York: Praeger, 1961).

Noel Annan argued that in Britain the "Civil Service tradition is indeed so strong that one can almost speak of it as a political force moulding legislation and administrative decisions." "This Unhappy Breed," *The New York Review of Books*, November 11, 1965, pp. 25–28, quoted from p. 27. Annan is discussing Samuel H. Beer's book, *British Politics in the Collectivist Age* (New York: Knopf, 1965), but is reporting his own view of Britain.

13. We deal here only with societies and states which are more or less coextensive. On others, see below, Chs. 19 and 20, esp. pp. 580–586.

14. Cf. Marx' view of the state. Marx saw it as the coercive tool of the ruling class. And "political power, properly so called, is merely the organized power of one

class oppressing the other." The democratic state is merely the latest (though more stable tool) and "the executive of the modern state is but a committee for managing the common affairs of the whole bourgeoisie." For discussion and references, see Henry B. Mayo, *Introduction to Marxist Theory* (New York: Oxford University Press, 1960), p. 157.

15. See, for example, Harry Holbert Turney-High, *Primitive War: Its Practice and Concepts* (Columbia, S.C.: University of South Carolina Press, 1949), pp. 215–220, and pp. 233–234.

16. In this ideal type, these two are coextensive, an assumption we remove later.

17. Public opinion polls show that very rarely less than 40 per cent, and often more than 50 per cent of the Americans approve of the over-all policy of the president, whatever policy he follows.

18. Edmund Burke, *The Works of Edmund Burke*, Bohn edition, (London: G. Bell & Sons, 1890–1897), "Thoughts on the Cause of the Present Discontents," Vol. I, p. 356; "Speech to the Electors of Bristol," Nov. 3, 1774, Vol. I, p. 447.

19. Gerhard Lenski, "Status Inconsistency and the Vote: A Four Nation Test," *American Sociological Review*, Vol. 32 (1967), pp. 298–301.

20. On the "floating vote," see Jean Blondel, *Voters, Parties, and Leaders* (London: Penguin Books, 1965), pp. 69–73.

21. For a recent work and references to earlier ones which take a similar position, see F. A. Hermens, *The Representative Republic* (Notre Dame, Ind.: University of Notre Dame Press, 1958), esp. pp. 201 ff.

22. "Buzz" refers to the noise which results when numerous small discussion groups take place simultaneously in a big hall. On the reports, see Halbert E. Gulley, *Discussion, Conference and Group Process* (New York: Henry Holt & Co., 1960), pp. 42, 309–310 and J. Donald Phillips, in "Report on Discussion 66," *Adult Education Journal*, Vol. 7 (1948), pp. 181–182.

23. There are various arrangements which somewhat increase the role of the higher level in the consensus-formation process, such as the internal splits in the two parties and different regional affiliations of the president and the vice president in the United States. For details see Etzioni, "Consensus Formation in Heterogeneous Systems," *Studies in Social Change*, *op. cit.*, pp. 136–151.

24. On Mexico, see González Casanova, *Democracia en Mexico*, *op. cit.* On Southern United States, see V. O. Key, Jr., *Southern Politics: In State and Nation* (New York: Knopf, 1950). A state by state account is provided in Part I. See also Etzioni, *Studies in Social Change*, *op. cit.*, pp. 157–179.

25. Maurice Duverger, *Political Parties: Their Organization and Activity in the Modern State* (London: Methuen, 1955). See index, by countries.

26. The arguments in support of this position are presented in Ch. 16 *supra* and Ch. 21 below.

27. Almond, *The American People and Foreign Policy*, *op. cit.*, p. xvi and Moore, *Social Origins of Dictatorship and Democracy*, *op. cit.*, stress the similarities. Philip E. Mosely, "Soviet Foreign Policy Since the 22nd Party Congress," *Modern Age*, Vol. 41 (Fall, 1962), pp. 343–352; and Brzezinski and Huntington, *Political Power: USA/USSR*, *op. cit.*, stress the differences. See also Amitai Etzioni, *Winning Without War* (New York: Doubleday, 1964), pp. 1–26. Raymond Aron, *Eighteen Lectures on Industrial Society* (London: Weidenfeld and Nicolson, 1967).

28. Kurt H. Wolff, *The Sociology of Georg Simmel* (New York: Free Press, 1950), p. 122.

29. Karl Mannheim, *Freedom, Power, and Democratic Planning* (New York: Oxford University Press, 1950), pp. 29–31, 111–112. This point is illustrated by Berle who states: ". . . To restore the conditions thought to have been endemic in the free market, the state was forced to intervene. Thence came the Sherman Antitrust Act, later the Clayton Acts, the Federal Trade Commission, the Patman Act, and the continuous and close supervision of the Department of Justice. Paradoxically, it came to this: If there was a government powerful enough and willing to intervene, it could maintain a variety of free market." Adolf A. Berle, Jr., "Concentrations of Private Power," in Edward Reed (ed.), *Challenges to Democracy: The Next Ten Years* (New York: Praeger, 1963), p. 132.

30. Others have put the date as late as 1961, and view John F. Kennedy as the first "Keynesian" president.

31. See *supra*, Ch. 15, Note 44.

32. Samuel H. Beer, *Modern British Politics: A Study of Parties and Pressure Groups* (London: Faber & Faber, 1965), pp. 109–113, 388–389.

33. Annan, "This Unhappy Breed," *op. cit.* p. 27

34. See discussions of the "veto groups" theory by Riesman et al., *The Lonely Crowd, op. cit.*, pp. 257 ff.; cf. C. Wright Mills, *The Power Elite* (New York: Oxford University Press, 1959), pp. 242–268; and William Kornhauser, " 'Power elite' or 'Veto groups'?" in Seymour M. Lipset and Leo Lowenthal (eds.), *Culture and Social Character* (New York: Free Press, 1961), pp. 252–267.

35. Private communication with Professor T. Husén. The value of the kroner about halved in the period; the cost difference would still be in the order of 1 to 10.

36. Shonfield illustrates this point in regard to Britain in his *Modern Capitalism, op. cit., passim.*

37. Holt and Turner studied the political conditions for economic take-off. They suggest that in the laggard countries, France and China, government regulation and intervention was larger than in more successful Japan and England. Robert T. Holt and John E. Turner, *The Political Basis of Economic Development* (Princeton, N.J.: Van Nostrand, 1966). Note though that they deal with states which had poor knowledge, communication and control capacities.

38. It should be noted that many planners and experts, even in post-modern societies, see their tasks more or less in these terms. Waterston, *Development Planning, op. cit.*, pp. 333–339.

39. See *supra*, Ch. 11, pp. 263–268.

40. Based on participant observation by the author.

41. After the Labour Party took office in 1964, a new Ministry of Economic Affairs took over most of the functions of the NEDC (National Economic Development Council).

42. Neil W. Chamberlain, *Private and Public Planning* (New York: McGraw-Hill, 1965), p. 153.

"By law all plans which the *Commissariat au Plan* formulates must be submitted for examination to the Economic and Social Council (formerly, the Economic Council), a body of more than 160 members all but a few of whom represent economic interest groups.

"The Conseil Supérieur or High Planning Commission is a much smaller superior body. Many of its members participate in the planning process described below, and therefore in general approve the plan as it is drawn up. This is one main reason why it has not seemed necessary to refer the completed plan to the Conseil Supérieur."

Everett E. Hagen and Stephanie F. T. White, *Great Britain: Quiet Revolution in Planning* (Syracuse, N.Y.: Syracuse University Press, 1966), p. 102 and footnote 2. Werner Feld, "National Economic Interest Groups and Policy Formation in the EEC," *Political Science Quarterly*, Vol. LXXXI (1966), pp. 392–411.

43. Pierre Bauchet, *L'Expérience Française de Planification* (Paris: Éditions du Seuil, 1958); John Hackett and Anne-Marie Hackett, *Economic Planning in France* (Cambridge, Mass.: Harvard University Press, 1963), pp. 119–130; Michael Crozier, *The Bureaucratic Phenomenon* (Chicago: University of Chicago Press, 1964), pp. 213–314.

44. A systematic effort to provide information about societal as well as economic conditions in the United States and a model for their analysis, was urged and initiated by Bertram M. Gross. See his *The State of the Nation: Social System Accounting* (London: Tavistock Publications, 1966). See also Raymond A. Bauer (ed.), *Social Indicators* (Cambridge, Mass.: The M.I.T. Press, 1966); Wilbert E. Moore and Eleanor Bernert Sheldon, "Monitoring Social Change: A Conceptual and Programmatic Statement," *Proceedings of the Social Statistics Section, 1965* (Washington, D.C.: American Statistical Association, 1966), pp. 144–149; and the May and September, 1967 issues of *The Annals of the American Academy of Political and Social Science*.

45. See, for instance, Petter J. Bjerve, *Planning in Norway, 1947–1956* (Amsterdam: North-Holland Publishing Co., 1959), pp. 250–257. See Hagen and White, *Great Britain, op. cit.*, pp. 105–110, on economic incentives in the French plan.

46. This was available to European Coal and Steel Community. See Haas, *The Uniting of Europe, op. cit.*, pp. 47–48.

47. Trow illustrates this difference by pointing out that Britain was planning a degree of expansion of its higher education system while the United States was guessing at the future demand. Martin Trow, "A Question of Size and Shape," *Universities Quarterly* (G.B.), Vol. 18 (1964), pp. 136–137.

48. On the difficulties in educational assessment, see Luther J. Carter, "Educational Testing: National Program Enters Critical Phase," *Science*, Vol. 156 May 5, 1967), pp. 622–626.

49. Shonfield, *Modern Capitalism, op. cit.*, p. 227.

50. Benjamin Akzin and Yehezkel Dror, *Israel: High-Pressure Planning* (Syracuse, N.Y.: Syracuse University Press, 1966). David Kochav, *Les Aspects Administratifs de la Planification de Developpement en Israël* (Jerusalem: Prime Minister's Office, Economic Planning Authority, 1964).

51. Hagen and White, *Great Britain, op. cit.*, pp. 127–128. Yehezkel Dror, *The Netherlands: Mutual Adjustment Planning* (forthcoming).

52. Howard A. Rusk, M.D., "Birth Control as Policy: U.S. Position, a Reversal Since 1959, is to make information available to all." *The New York Times*, May 15, 1966, p. 74.

53. John P. Mackintosh, *The British Cabinet* (London: Stevens, 1962); R. H. S. Crossman's introduction to Walter Bagehot, *The English Constitution* (London: Watts, 1964); Otto Kirchheimer, "The Waning of Opposition in Parliamentary

Regimes," *Social Research*, Vol. 24 (1957), pp. 127–156; Axel Vulpius, *Die Allparteienregierung* (Frankfurt a/M, Metzner, 1957); cf. Joseph P. Harris, *Congressional Control of Administration* (Washington, D.C.: The Brookings Institution, 1964), especially pp. 15–45. "The House of Commons has become so powerless now, so incapable of disputing what the Government decides, that demands for reform have become insistent." Anthony Lewis, "Panel of M.P.'s Questions a Minister," *The New York Times*, May 14, 1967. For an earlier work, see Lawrence H. Chamberlain, *The President, Congress, and Legislation* (New York: Columbia University Press, 1947), pp. 11 ff. This work covers the period between 1880 and 1945 and finds a decline in Congressional power since the beginning of the 20th century. In foreign policy, the role of the U.S. Congress is chiefly to legitimate and amend and seems on the decline. James A. Robinson, *Congress and Foreign Policy-Making: A Study in Legislative Influence and Initiative* (Homewood, Ill.: The Dorsey Press, 1962), esp. pp. 1–116. Gerhard Loewenberg, *Parliament in the German Political System* (Ithaca, N.Y.: Cornell University Press, 1967).

54. See Peter Woll's discussion of "Information and Policy Making" in "Administrative Domination of Legislative Process" in his *American Bureaucracy* (New York: Norton, 1963), pp. 130–133. Pointing to the difference between the American system, of Cabinet members subject to questioning by Committees, and the British one—of questioning on the floor of the House of Commons, Anthony Lewis adds: "And, most important, he has no staff to help him and little chance to become an expert in any field." In his "Panel of M.P.'s Questions a Minister," *The New York Times, op. cit.*

55. Each region is represented by several legislators. The votes are allocated among the national parties, within each region.

56. Marshall I. Goldman, "Economic Growth and Institutional Change in the Soviet Union," in Peter H. Juviler and Henry W. Morton (eds.), *Soviet Policy-making: Studies of Communism in Transition* (New York: Praeger, 1967), pp. 61–81.

57. For a study of the American economy as mixed and the various combinations, Eli Ginzberg, Dale L. Hiestad, and Beatrice G. Reubens, *The Pluralistic Economy* (New York: McGraw-Hill, 1965). With the United States in mind, Michael Reagan speaks of the "merger of public and private," which manifests itself in several forms: in the Communication Satellite Corporation which is, in part, government-owned; in the insertion in government contracts of terms giving effect to public policy, for example, fair employment practices; in interrelationships between federal regulatory agencies and the industries that they are supposed to regulate. Michael D. Reagan, *The Managed Economy* (New York: Oxford University Press, 1963), pp. 190–210. For France, see A. Chazel and H. Poyet, *L'Economie Mixte* (Paris: Presses Universitaires, 1963). For Britain, see J. W. Grove, *Government and Industry in Britain* (London: Longmans, 1962).

Having studied situations in which a relatively strong publicly owned airline competes with a relatively strong privately owned airline in the same country, Corbett concludes that "what appears to be needed is a theory of the mixed economy, a theory which presents the mixed economy not as a half-way house to something else but as a system having its own virtues, a system worth deliberately creating." David Corbett, *Politics and the Airlines* (London: George Allen & Unwin, 1965), p. 331.

58. Ray E. Trussell et al., "Prepayment for Medical and Dental Care in New

York State" (New York: School of Public Health and Administrative Medicine, Columbia University, 1962). Also by Trussell et. al., "A Study of the Quality of Hospital Care Secured by a Sample of Teamster Family Members in New York City," (*loc. cit.*, 1964). Alice Lake, "Patients for Profit," *The Saturday Evening Post*, (September 20, 1962,) pp. 19–23.

59. Merle Fainsod, "Some Reflections on the Nature of the Regulatory Process," in Carl J. Friedrich and Edward S. Mason (eds.), *Public Policy*, Vol. 1 (1940), pp. 297–323, esp. 308. For an early study, see Robert E. Cushman, *The Independent Regulatory Commissions* (New York: Oxford University Press, 1941). See also Robert Bendiner, "The FCC—Who Will Regulate the Regulators?" *The Reporter* (September 19, 1957), pp. 26–30. See Marver H. Bernstein, *Regulating Business by Independent Commission* (Princeton, N.J.: Princeton University Press, 1955). For a critical look at the commissions, see United States Senate, Subcommittee on Administrative Practice and Procedure of the Committee of the Judiciary, *The Landis Report* (Washington, D.C.: Government Printing Office, 1960). See also Victor Rosenblum, "How to Get into TV," in Alan F. Westin (ed.), *The Uses of Power* (New York: Harcourt, Brace & World, 1962), pp. 193–194, 196–197.

60. Gilpatrick, *Structural Unemployment and Aggregate Demand, op. cit.* Two leading structuralists are Charles C. Killingsworth and Robert Theobald. The aggregate-demand policy was advocated, in these years, by the Council of Economic Advisers.

61. Amitai Etzioni, "Getting R & D out of Orbit," *The American Behavioral Scientist*, Vol. 8 (Oct., 1964), pp. 6–10.

62. We hope to support this statement in a future publication. See Amitai Etzioni and Sarajane Heidt, "Toward a Theory of Social Problems," in Erwin O. Smigel, *Handbook in Social Problems* (Chicago: Rand McNally, forthcoming).

63. A survey showed that more than 80 per cent of the Americans sampled expected business to help find cures for disease, aid college education, eliminate racial prejudice, and so on. *Newsweek*, May 2, 1966, p. 85. The findings of this survey cannot be used as indicative of the said change. It seems very likely that the respondents referred to business contributions and application of business management methods and not that business decisions per se should take societal needs into account. On the sense of social responsibility that some great corporations have developed and about the philanthropy in which they engage, see Reagan, *The Managed Economy, op. cit.*, pp. 121–156. See also Peter F. Drucker, "Big Business and the National Purpose," *Harvard Business Review*, Vol. 40 (March–April, 1962), pp. 49–59 and John W. Riley, Jr., in association with Marguerite F. Levy (eds.), *The Corporation and Its Publics: Essays on the Corporate Image* (New York: Wiley & Sons, 1963).

64. Asked which career they would like best, a sample of 1966 United States college seniors ranked business far down the list; professions, 55 per cent; teaching, 24 per cent; business, 9 per cent; government, 9 per cent. (*Newsweek, ibid.* reporting a Harris poll). For a *New York Times* (July 3, 1966) survey of the views of 52 leading executives on the social responsibility of their corporations, see Robert A. Wright, "Effort is Seen Designed to Avoid a Collision Course." While all executives subscribed to the norm of societal responsibility, their interpretations of what it implied varied sharply. See also Bernard Barber, "Is American Business Becoming Professionalized? Analysis of a Social Ideology," in E. A. Tiryakian (ed.),

Sociological Theory, Values, and Sociocultural Change: Essays in Honor of Pitirim A. Sorokin (New York: Free Press, 1963), pp. 121–145, and Robert W. Austin, "Who has the Responsibility for Social Change—Business or Government?" *Harvard Business Review*, Vol. 43 (July–August, 1965), pp. 45–52.

65. "Science *is* the burning idea of the 20th century . . . the altruism of science, its 'purity,' the awesome vistas it opens . . . have won from all groups . . . passionate interest and conviction." Heilbroner, "The Future of Capitalism," *op. cit.*, p. 34.

CHAPTER 18

Unresponsive Societies

and Their Transformation

Responsiveness, Transformation, and Equality

Consensus may not provide a basis for an active society because it may be limited largely to an expression of a coalition of the powerful. Such an excluding consensus can serve as a base for a society's action, but those not included will constitute a barrier both to more effective action from the elites' viewpoint and to the fuller realization of most societal values. Consequently, a society's degree of responsiveness to the changing needs of all of its members significantly affects its capacity to realize most societal values and to reduce alienation in the process. However flexible the polity of a society may be, this flexibility in itself does not suffice to assure responsiveness. In this chapter, we first explore the concept of responsiveness and its relation to the notion of political flexibility. We then discuss the conditions under which responsiveness is limited. We close by exploring the sources of un-responsiveness in totalitarian and democratic societies and the conditions under which they may be overcome.

Responsiveness and Flexibility Defined

The core image of responsiveness is taken from cybernetic systems which have decision-making centers that issue responses to incoming messages. The level of responsiveness of a guidance system is determined by the "appropriateness" of the responses issued to the messages received and, in that sense, by their appropriateness to the needs of the member units (and, although this is frequently ignored, to the needs of the system). The level of responsiveness is particularly affected by the effectiveness of the control centers.[1]* Cognitive factors are usually stressed in this regard, such as the capacities to "read" and "digest" correctly incoming messages and to "learn" from past experience. When used in connection with electronics, the concept tends to assume no resistance by the member units to the signals of their control center. There is neither a political nor an ethical issue involved in "rigging" the controlling overlayer in such a way that the center will always prevail. And responsiveness can be increased by ordering the reassignment, remodeling, or "sacrifice" of a "stubborn" unit.

In the guidance of societal processes, such an approach to the building of responsiveness is neither feasible nor ethical. A societal controlling overlayer must both act for a supra-unit (otherwise there will be no societal actor), and respond to the needs of the member units.† Complete disregard of the members' needs would require that the overlayer have sufficient power to recast the member units in its own image, so to speak, if responsiveness is to be maintained; but no societal overlayer commands such power. *Under*-responsiveness to the members' needs will result in a system's being either too rigid (conservative) or too creative (radical); if under-responsiveness is considerable or accumulative, it will generate more resistance or alienation than can be "tolerated" by the elites involved, the particular societal structure, or even the integrative bonds of the system.

On the other hand, a complete adaptation of the overlayer to the incoming messages from the system's members would negate the system's capacity to follow a collective policy or course of action and would thereby render the system passive and drifting, merely reflecting the fluctuating changes in the preferences of the members and fluctuations in the environment. Creative responses are unlikely under such conditions of *over*-responsiveness, because creative responses entail delays in reactions while alternative courses of action are explored. Similarly, under these conditions, anticipatory guidance is unlikely, and crisis management will tend to prevail. Optimal responsiveness, hence, entails the capacity to react *creatively*—that is, the capacity to discover new modes of action that will take into account the changing needs

---

* Reference notes for this chapter appear on page 541.

† The concept of needs of the members of a society is explored below, Ch. 21, pp. 619–629.

both of the membership at large and of the supra-unit which the controlling overlayer helps constitute and aids in realizing its goals. Similarly, an optimal system balances the attention devoted to immediate needs with the attention extended to longer-run and non-pressing lateral and contextual needs.

For example, when a member unit is reporting to the center strain due to the acceleration of its efforts, it would be unresponsive to the member if the center were merely to signal back—"keep up the acceleration"; deceleration on the part of the member unit would disregard the supra-unit's needs and policy. But the commitment of some reserve assets which the supra-unit commands to alleviate the unit's acceleration costs would be responsive *and* creative (or innovative), because a new pattern of allocation is being developed.

There is, thus, an intimate link between societal creativity (and, hence, transformability) and less-than-full responsiveness. Complete responsiveness, we saw, is destructive to the supra-unit's active orientation and holds the seeds of its own destruction. Another reason that complete responsiveness is self-contradictory is that, because of differences in functional specialization and in position in the stratification structure, the various members of a societal unit tend to have at least some non-complementary needs; hence, responsiveness to the needs of one member often entails some unresponsiveness to those of another member. Even in an active society, consensus-building will help only to achieve a relatively high degree of *averaging* responsiveness and cannot bring about a maximal level of responsiveness.

Consensus, it should be stressed, is produced in systems which vary considerably in their degrees of responsiveness. When responsiveness is inadequate, consensus-building will be inauthentic because the members to whom it is not responsive will not be committed to it.* While such consensus can and does serve as the basis of societal action, the latent resistance and the untapped energy of the excluded members limit the activation of the societal unit. When responsiveness is adequate (and other conditions to be discussed below are met), consensus is authentic.* The difference between inauthentic and authentic consensus is a matter of degree; a particular mode of consensus may be relatively more responsive than another but less than optimally responsive. The numerous preceding statements on societal guidance (of which consensus-building is a main component) must be applied with this qualification in mind: The less authentic the consensus, the less likely societal guidance is to activate.

By linking the analysis of consensus-building with that of transformation, the concept of responsiveness renders dynamic the study of societal guidance. Many discussions of consensus-building assume that the actors have set interests or values and "work out" a shared policy or course of action through mechanisms such as compromise, "splitting the difference," or arbitration.[2] Actually, though, the actors—their preferences and internal

---

* The concept of authenticity and related propositions are discussed in Chapter 21.

makeups as well as their relations to each other—are constantly changing; consensus-building, therefore, can be much more creative than merely offering a solution to differences among given positions, since it affects these very positions. A key factor in determining the creativity of consensus-building is the degree to which a society's structure and political organization—including the consensus-building mechanisms—are themselves changeable in response to changes in the actors' needs, including those of their relations to each other. The more rigid these structures and organizations, the less creative consensus-building will tend to be. Moreover, structural rigidity will decrease the extent of the realization of the society's values and increase alienation.

There are significant differences among societal structures and polities in terms of their relative rigidity (or lack of malleability) which is indicated by the extent to which they do not accommodate to changes in the power relations among the members. Political rigidity occurs where there is no (or only inadequate) reallocation of political power as the distribution of societal power changes (e.g., no reallocation of seats in the legislature following the rise of the cities).[3] Societal rigidity is illustrated by the failure of the societal allocative system to increase the share of the wealth available to under-privileged collectivities which have become more powerful. Societal rigidity may not be all-encompassing but may appear only in some societal sectors (e.g., ethnic relations) or institutions (e.g., educational ones).

Political and societal flexibility are not co-extensive with responsiveness, as they indicate a capacity only to adapt to changing power relations and not necessarily to members' needs. On the other hand, responsiveness assumes flexibility, for reasons which will become evident below.

It is essential to keep the reference points fixed for any specific comparison, as that which is responsive from one viewpoint may be unresponsive from another. We use the society and its total membership as our frame of reference. The distribution of assets among collectivities is part of the society's *structure*. Administrative patterns of the state, the constitution, and the representational organization form the *political shell*. Political processes convert societal power into political power; this is carried out in specialized units and processes such as parties and elections, interest groups and legislation.

Both kinds of rigidity, especially the political kind, lead to revolutions. Flexibility coupled with under-responsiveness leads to a variety of societal "pathologies," since those who are weak but excluded cannot rebel. Only flexibility coupled with responsiveness (and, hence, authentic consensus-building) makes for an active society.

Political Shells and the Concept of Rigidity

The democratic mode of government is an obvious answer to the question of which kind of political shell is most likely to provide more political flexibility. However, societal power may be converted into political power through processes other than free elections, parliamentary representation, and multi-party systems. An authoritarian ruler who measures the changing societal winds carefully and who regularly samples the views of leaders of key organizations and collectivities can be quite flexible. Occasionally, such a ruler is even better able to assess the changes in the powers of the member collectivities and is more innovative in his policy than an elected government. While the comparison is not completely fair because of the considerable changes in circumstances, Bismarck seems to have been less rigid (for instance, in his treatment of the rising working classes) than the Weimar government (e.g., in its treatment of the conservative forces). A government that disenfranchises most of its citizens (as was the case for the French citizens following the Bourbon restoration in 1815 or the Negroes in the Deep South following Reconstruction) can hardly be considered democratic, but if the disenfranchised citizens are passive, the government may well be quite flexible from the viewpoint of those who have power.

Democracy is a concept that implies a form of government, a pattern of political institutions, a shell. Its conceptual counterparts are totalitarian, authoritarian, and monarchic governments. Political flexibility refers to the relationship *between* the political shell and the societal substance, to the degree of parallelism (and synchronized change) between the political shell (and the distribution of political power within it) and the distribution of societal power. It is a concept that can be applied to any regime; for instance, we might say that Stalin's government was less flexible than Khrushchev's. We can make the same comparison between monarchs or within the same regime—e.g., compare the early to the late Victorian period. Developing nations, it has been proposed, need not start with a democratic government, but a measure of flexibility is essential.

The concepts of flexibility (and, we shall see, of responsiveness), allow us to avoid formal, constitutional classifications of democratic versus non-democratic countries; instead, we refer to changes in the degree of political flexibility (or responsiveness) in governments of the same form. We can then compare the levels of flexibility of various democracies (e.g., Danish vs. American), of the same country under different administrations (e.g., Eisenhower vs. Kennedy), and of societies to different collectivities (e.g., the Soviet government has so far been more adaptive to the demands of the heavy than the light industries). Without these concepts, we are led to state that one democracy is more "democratic" than another, thus using the same word with two meanings in one statement; flexibility (or responsiveness) often seems to be the implied meaning of the second use.

The Political Flexibility of Democracies

While political flexibility is sometimes high in a non-democracy and low in a democracy, we suggest that *on the average, political democracy is the* *least rigid existing form of government.* We hold this proposition for two main reasons. First, the factors which make for high flexibility in non-democratic governments are often not institutionalized and, hence, are unstable. Thus, while one monarch is open-minded, willing to listen to community leaders, and so on, his successor (or the same monarch as he grows older or as one of his prejudices affects the matter under consideration) may be far less flexible. In democracies, on the other hand, a significant and continued loss of flexibility would be likely to lead to a change of the party in office, if the situation is not corrected by such intra-party mechanisms as changing the premier or the composition of the cabinet. (The British Conservatives used all of these mechanisms in rapid sucession. They unseated Eden after the Suez crisis because the majority of Britons did not favor their country's involvement in the affair; the new prime minister, however, did not build up his leadership or change his party sufficiently;[4] nor did a reshuffling of the cabinet lead to a sufficient increase in political support. Thus, so in 1964 the Labour Party won the elections.)* The institutionalized change of the party in office following and in line with changes in the societal power of various collectivities and in their preferences seems to us much more essential to democracy than the holding of free elections, multi-party systems, and above all, the non-morphological definition of the rule of the majority.[5] It is not only that the majority may be tyrannical toward a minority, but there tend to be not majorities but only minorities (or, as we would see them, collectivities).[6] The democratic process is not one in which a larger group prevails over a smaller one, with the groups' relative sizes being assessed once every few years, at election time. Rather, many of the continual outputs of the democratic process, such as legislations and executive rules and decisions, are being negotiated continually with organized "minorities."[7] Elections reflect the degrees of success of inter-election consensus-building, as much as they set a context for them. And, the votes cast during elections are not those of myriad individuals but, to a large degree, those of members of collectivities, and as such, they reflect the various attributes of the collectivities, including the degree to which they are included in the consensus-building processes.

Our second reason for suggesting that democratic polities tend to be less rigid than others lies in the way in which they articulate knowledge and power. For their revisions of policy, all control centers must draw on incoming knowledge about the changing power relations among the member collectivities and environmental changes which the society confronts. Non-democracies rely mainly on upward communication links such as various

---

* Of course, changes of the ruling elite can also occur in non-democracies, and such changes are not automatically forthcoming as a result of significant decline in political support in a democratic regime. They are, however, more likely to occur with less costs and following a smaller loss of support in democracies because of the institutionalization of change of the party in office.

intelligence networks, upward reporting by the state bureaucracy, and so on. These tend to slant their reports, and the greater the extent of this slanting, the greater the rigidity of the elites.[8] This leads to a situation in which more correctives come to be needed at the same time that these consensus-building mechanisms are less able to provide them. Moreover, these communications, which are not backed by power, can be ignored. Democracy—in its representative structure—provides the only political organization in which there is an institutionalized combination of upward communication *and* power.[9]

To illustrate: Egypt and Syria were unified in 1958 into the United Arab Republic. Initially, there was a fairly sizeable Syrian representation in the joint government and in two regional ones, and elections in Syria affected the composition of these representative bodies. They served to bring to Nasser's attention the changing perspectives and power relations *in* Syria. But, gradually, Nasser replaced the Syrians with Egyptians, and the parties as well as elections with the National Union, a downward organization set up by Cairo. Regional governments were abolished. Consequently, the Cairo government increasingly lost contact with Syrian representatives. At the same time, dissatisfaction with the union mounted in Syria following a drought, unemployment, flight of capital, and the introduction of a nationalization scheme. Nasser relied increasingly on a secret police machine (the *Deuxieme Bureau*) for his information about Syria. When reports reached him that Syria was about to rebel, the president of the United Arab Republic is said to have ignored them.[10] Had there been free elections in Syria, Nasser would have been aware of the gradual loss of support for the union and the inadequacy of the measures he introduced in reaction to incoming signals. If his legislation for Syria had had to be approved by Syrian representatives, many of the acts introduced would not have been approved. Had he himself been subject to reelection, he would have found it more difficult to ignore signs of mounting dissatisfaction; and, if he had continued to ignore these signs, the result might have been his replacement by a more flexible leader rather than dissolution of the Union.

The relationship of our concepts to the voluminous discussions of democratic theory deserves a brief elaboration. According to one major traditional view, democracy is the rule of the people whose will is determined by representatives which the majority elects. Modern criticism has stressed that this conception is unrealistic. It has focused instead on a "competitive" concept, on democracy as a plurality of groupings (or, "minorities"), which reach a shared societal course of action via electoral institutions. Private interest groups, public interest groups, and political parties have been seen as the key actors. This approach views the state primarily as another set of public interest groups rather than as an organizational expression of society, a controlling overlayer which commands a degree of unity. For instance, it has been stressed that the American federal agencies act vis-à-vis each other in much the same way that private interest groups act toward each other and toward these agencies. Federal agencies have been shown to have close ties to private interest groups—e.g., the Labor Department's relationship to labor unions and the Commerce Department's links with business circles. Consensus is said to be worked out in the interaction among private and public interest groups. Even the President has been characterized as a "public interest group"—and not as the head of the State administration—because of his limited ability to control the federal agencies. Political parties are treated as a third kind of interest group.

To put it in traditional terms, if the first approach relies on the concept of a general will (a voluntaristic view), the second one sees no such will but only a variety of sub-societal wills (an atomistic view of democracy). As we see it, there are both a general will and a plurality of sub-societal wills.

The carriers of both "wills" are the same basic units: the citizens, their cohesive units and organizations, and the society and state. That is, the continual struggle—as well as mutual support—between the two "wills" occurs in all these units. For example, the citizens, through socialization, acquire commitments to society-wide values and learn to view the world with the help of cognitive maps provided by society (these have been recently discussed as "civic culture"). They *also* acquire partisan commitments to sub-societal perspectives. Similarly, there are society-wide organizations, of which the state (or at least elements of it) is the most important one, *and* there are a plurality of sub-societal organizations (private and public interest groups). Totalitarian political parties are part of the society's political supra-organization, i.e., on the side of the general will; democratic political parties serve as an intermediary tier between the plurality of sub-societal wills and the general will.*

Societies differ in the extent to which their cultures are "civic" versus "partisan" and in the degree to which their government agencies are part of the societies' supra-organizations or are merely another set of interest groups. Moreover, interest groups themselves may be more or less partisan. For instance, small business associations tend to be less "socially responsible" (i.e., to the society at large) than several of the larger business corporations. This same distinction applies to public interest groups (for instance, the radical right in comparison to the conservative groups).

---

* Throughout this volume, the term "collectivity-based organizations" is used rather than public and private "interest groups," because we seek to stress the societal bases of these units and because we seek a concept which covers both the democratic and totalitarian varieties of sub-societal organized groupings. We use here the traditional terms of public and private interest groups to tie our discussion to the literature of contemporary political science. We deal with political parties as a different level unit and not as just another kind of interest group for reasons discussed above. For an important discussion of the public interest concept, see Glendon A. Schubert, *The Public Interest* (New York: Free Press, 1960). A key concept involved in the notion of "the public interest" is the "latent pressure group." This is discussed in Truman, *The Governmental Process, op. cit.*

Democracy depends on the balance between the autonomous sub-societies (and their organizational expressions) and the society (and its political organization). If the sub-societies are more powerful than the society's political organization, anarchy, tribalism, or feudalism will prevail. If the society's political organization is sufficiently powerful to neutralize or narrow sharply the partisan expressions, totalitarianism will occur. In active societies, the balance between the sub-units and the society falls "in between": It is more "societal" than in democracies but less so than in totalitarian societies. Only anarchic systems are without societal integration and a supra-political overlayer.

It should also be noted that the particular democratic theory that is held has normative implications. For instance, the atomistic view of post-modern democracies (or, the view of them as "competitive" systems) legitimates, however unwittingly, tribalism and partisanship and undermines universal values. Such a view supports the powerful members of a society because one of the ways in which the self-oriented interests of these members are checked is by their society-wide commitments and another such mechanism is the society-wide organizations. If the general will is stressed to the neglect of the sub-societal ones, the effect is totalitarianism. The search for balance is the essence of the democratic position, and the debate about the specific nature of this balance constitutes a major debate among various democratic theories.*

A democratic government, we have seen, may be flexible but not responsive. The main differences between a highly flexible polity and one that is also responsive are (a) in the ratio of members included in the political processes as opposed to those who are excluded; (b) in the degree to which political power is equally distributed among the members; and (c) in the degree to which societal power (and assets) is equally distributed among the members. We examine these factors and the conditions under which the political base—and, thus, responsiveness—can be extended in the following pages.

A Dynamic Perspective: Expanding the Base

Most polities have one or more collectivities that have little societal and political power; polities differ greatly, however, in the ratio of such excluded (or passive) collectivities to those that do participate. This ratio can be further specified by determining the scope and depth of the participation of the members in their collectivities. High participation is necessarily indirect;

---

* See Nicholas Wahl, "The French Political System," in Samuel H. Beer et al. (eds.), *Patterns of Government* (New York: Random House, 1962), esp. p. 409. Note that here, as in many other cases, foreign policy decisions seem to be made in a more prescriptive manner than the average domestic decision.

it is obtained by a two- or three-step process through a chain of sub-collectivities, collectivities, and cross-collectivity organizations, with a parallel hierarchy of elite and member commitments. That a person who is not a leader is much more interested in, informed about, and politically effective in his own sub-collectivity than he is in relation to the national polity is, hence, not a sign of alienation or passivity so long as the elite of the sub-collectivity is informed about and effective on the next level.[11]

What characterizes most (though not all) nearly modern democracies, those of the eighteenth and nineteenth centuries, is a high degree of exclusion of large segments of their populations from the political processes. As has often been recorded, with increased modernization, most of these countries also experienced an increased participation by collectivities that were previously passive.[12] Actually, the political sociology of western countries can to a considerable extent be written in terms of a gain in the societal and political power of new collectivities (such as the middle class, the workers, ethnic and racial minorities) following technological, cultural, educational, stratificational, and political–institutional changes.[13]

It is not so much that the relative fortunes of collectivities that are included in the political system change (e.g., the Whigs gain more votes than the Tories) but that (a) new collectivities are formed (as Marx put it, the workers are brought "under one roof"); (b) they pass from an immobilizable stage—in which their action coefficient is so low that almost no external or internal elite can mobilize them into sustained political action—into a pre-mobilization stage; (c) priming by external elites occurs; and (d) this is followed by internalization of control. Flexible political systems alter their political organizations (or "shells") and the distributions of power within them to allow the gradual entrance of the new collectivities into the political processes as they pass through these stages. Less flexible systems resist longer and to a greater extent before they "open up"; rigid systems do not alter their shells sufficiently and "break" when their centers of gravity (or society) move outside their political base. One and the same society may pass through less and more rigid organizational phases, although an over-all score can often be given. Britain, for instance, is considered generally more flexible than France and Italy; in turn, they are considered more flexible than Spain.* And the broader the political base becomes, in terms of the participation of the membership of a society in the political processes, the more responsive the polity becomes. Flexibility here is indicative of the capacity to transform; responsiveness is a result of the particular transformation—the expansion of the political base.

---

* Lenski ranks the main democracies on a similar dimension. See *Power and Privilege, op. cit.*, pp. 323–324.

Political and Societal Rigidities

When political flexibility is high, there is a close "fit" between the distributions of political and societal power. Societal power is distributed among the member collectivities; political power (in the macro context) is control over the state and other society-wide political organizations. When the distributions of the two kinds of power are parallel, the state—as a supra-organization—relates to its "units" (such as ministries or agencies) and to the political parties and interest groups in the same way that the society relates to its member collectivities. And, there are relatively few "rigidities" which prevent the reorganization of the state and of the society's allocative patterns. A close "fit" (or, high degree of parallelism) is by no means automatic. First, the societal and political units are not parallel; in a society sufficiently integrated to act as an entity, the political units, we suggest, tend to be fewer in number and less diverse in perspective than the collectivities they "represent." Secondly, the conversion of societal into political power is never perfect; a collectivity's capacity to affect others in direct give-and-take or conflict situations (e.g., that of labor in its relations with management) and its capacity to affect the direction of the political action via the state are rarely identical. But societies differ significantly in the extent of this lack of "fit" or political rigidity.

An important expression of political rigidity is the political over-representation of societally powerful collectivities and the under-representation of weaker collectivities; that is, the political conversion process further magnifies differences in societal power, adding some of the autonomous power of the state to already powerful collectivities. Dynamically, political rigidity often rises when changes in the distribution of societal power fail to lead to a redistribution of political power. "Rotten boroughs" in British history and the over-representation of rural sectors in the United States are well-known examples.* As some lag is common, what is of interest is the degree of over-representation, the duration of the lag, and the ways in which it is corrected when adjustment does take place.

---

* Disproportional representation in mass democracies is not a matter of a few percentage points and is not limited to the modern period. Dahl computed an index of advantage, in which the index would be 1 if actual and proportional representation were equal. His figures, based on votes cast in the 1952 election, show a score of 14.8 for Nevada as compared to 0.17 for New York. *A Preface to Democratic Theory, op. cit.,* pp. 114–114. At that time, a majority of the votes in the U.S. Senate could be cast by Senators representing less than 15 per cent of the American voters. (*Ibid.*, p. 116.) Under-represented societal groupings included not only Negroes but also sharecroppers, migrant workers, wage earners, and coal miners.

The median age of present-day Americans is twenty-eight, but among the House and Senate chairmen it is 67. Congressional leadership does not reflect modern America even in terms of religion. In the House, seventeen of the twenty committee chairmen are white, Anglo-Saxon Protestants. In the Senate, Allen Ellender from Catholic Louisiana is the only

How can a collectivity's gain in societal power be determined if this gain is not reflected in new political power? One approach is to show an increase in the societal bases of power (especially assets) or an increase in the mobilization and organization of a collectivity as compared to those of other members in the same system. Another is to explore increased incidences of "direct" expressions of societal power such as demonstrations, strikes, and attempts at revolution as indicators that the new societal power of a collectivity is not being converted into political power and, thus, is not absorbed into the political process.*

Besides seeking to determine the conditions under which the distortions politics introduce can be minimized, a critical question for consensus-building concerns the degree to which political power can be adapted or reallocated following changes in the societal power distribution and consensus. Societal power and consensus are in continual flux with changes in the relative degree of mobilization of member collectivities, the education of the members, external influences, and so on.

The discrepancy between political and societal power tends to increase over time; to the degree that this does not lead to political reforms, the capacity of the state to serve as a framework which contains the conflict between those collectivities favoring the existing shell and those seeking its alteration is weakened. When tension mounts, and if accommodations are still not forthcoming, a revolution is likely to occur, after which the state's mold is recast towards those whom it "favors." Revolutions are commonly depicted as direct changes in societal structures, especially in class relations. As we see it, revolutions often are initially changes in members' access to the control of the state, or, more generally, to the political overlayer of society; after a revolution, the state is more representative of the collectivities that have previously gained in societal power and now use the state's extra power as well as their own to introduce *societal* changes, including those which previously neither these collectivities nor the state could introduce.

The other avenue of transformation involves the reorganization of the state so as to grant more political power to collectivities whose societal power is rising and to curtail that of those whose societal power (and ability to marshal consensus for goals they favor) is declining. We are not referring to the familiar dichotomy between revolution and reform, for such "reforms" provide an alternative route for the required transformation only so long as

---

non-WASP who chairs a committee. Geographically, the former Confederate States of America, with one-fifth of the United States' population, provides nine out of sixteen chairmen in the Senate and eleven out of twenty in the House. This distribution would be even more skewed were the border states included. News release from Joseph S. Clark, U.S. Senator, Pennsylvania, March 31, 1967, p. 3.

* Both indicators are being used jointly because "direct" expressions may also occur when power is declining, though in this case they tend to be in favor of the existing or past system rather than transformation toward a future one.

their pace and scope are sufficiently encompassing to keep the changing distribution of societal relationships and political power relatively parallel. "Smaller" reforms may serve only to give momentum to a revolutionary movement or to appease and deflect it. Reforms alone are no assurance of a close and continuous "fit" between society and state; their extent, pace, and effects on the revolutionary forces are the factors which determine their macroscopic consequences. The demarcation line is thus not between revolution and reforms but between revolutions and transforming reforms on the one hand and bit reforms on the other.

Secondly, we do not accept the opposition between violent revolutions and peaceful reforms. Some revolutions ("ripe" ones) are quite peaceful (e.g., the Nasserite one in 1952), while some reforms follow or entail considerable violence (Mao's "cultural revolution" in 1966–1967). And there are numerous instances of societal violence (coups, riots) which are not revolutionary. To extend our earlier point, we see, on the one hand, transforming revolutions and reforms (which differ in pace and scope) and, on the other hand, bit reforms, coups, and riots which are not transforming.

Active societies are those which transform gradually. Even here full "parallelism" between societal and political power cannot be expected, but such parallelism can exist to a relatively high degree, even to a greater extent than is the case in such semi-active societies as Scandinavia and Israel.[14]

The grand attack on the state and on administration in general (in which Marxists, Fabian and Utopian social democrats, liberals, and laissez-faire conservatives participated),[15] fails to recognize the necessity for organizational expressions of both collectivities and societies if most goals of post-modern actors are to be realized, whether they be high standards of public health or the goals of science and production. Furthermore, many of these critics do not differentiate sufficiently between the sins of states and the evils of political rigidity (and unresponsiveness). A transition toward an active society requires a closer "parallelism" between society and state, a more flexible (and responsive) polity, which, in turn, allows societal guidance to be less centralized and to decrease greatly the reliance on coercion as compared to the situation in post-modern states. In short, the state can be made much less alienating, but it is not feasible to abolish it altogether. Nor would this be desirable, for, besides being a major tool of societal transformation and of the societally approved reallocation of wealth and status, the state has a permanent role in the protection of civil and human rights and in the curbing of intra-societal armed conflict.* While the state has been abused in both of these areas, it is precisely to the degree that its political base is expanded that its legitimate use can be increased.

---

* T. H. Marshall, *Citizenship and Social Class* (London: Cambridge University Press, 1950), pp. 1–85.

The source of the state's special power is its capacity to penetrate collectivities more readily than other organizations. It is not merely one organization countervailing the others from the outside; it also can impose peace from above and provide individuals *within* a collectivity with power against intra-collectivity tyranny. No other arrangement provides a *comparatively* more effective and universalistic safeguard, just as when it becomes the tool of one collectivity over others, the state is the most intensive and penetrating instrument of subjugation. Also, the state, so long as it is not overpowering and is countervailed by society, provides one more foundation of pluralism, another basis for collective action. While it may be true that it is potentially more powerful than other societal organizations—hence, the need to check it is greater than the need to check other organizations—it does not necessarily follow that the state is overpowering, rigid, or unresponsive. Moreover, a flexible and responsive state is a way of reducing part of the alienation whose source is societal.

The state, thus, is neither the source of all societal evil—as much of Western tradition has viewed it—nor the great hope of universalistic citizenship and justice.[16] It is, rather, the great option for fundamental societal change. Hence, the transition to an active society does not involve abolishing the state but rather making it more flexible and, above all, more responsive. Societies that absorb the state by almost eliminating its autonomy (a situation approximated at the height of feudalism) and societies which have never evolved more than a weak state (and, often, weak society-wide links and bonds in general)—i.e., politically underdeveloped countries—tend to drift. States that absorb the society are totalitarian. A separate but mutually responsive existence for both the state and the society constitutes the basis for the most active combination.

Responsiveness, Consensus, and Inequality

Societal consensus is usually worked out among actors that differ in their societal power. Thus, even when consensus is high, it still reflects the existing inequality: By and large, the compromises made, the assumptions built upon, and the values implemented are closer to the preferences of the powerful than the weak. From a dynamic viewpoint, effective consensus-building mechanisms are those which allow a variety of actors to concur on a course of action without much delay, cost, or violence, but mechanisms which meet these conditions do not eliminate the differences in power among the actors. On the contrary, if an attempt is made to use the consensus-building mechanisms as a lever for equalization (if such equalization is not supported by the existing distribution of societal power—as when labor in a capitalist society promotes wealth-equalization legislation)—this is likely to generate neither much equalization nor high consensus. The privileged groups in control of the state can hardly be expected to consent to a policy that would significantly curtail their privileges and power.* The substantial increase in equality required for an active society will have to be produced through some process other than consensus-building.

Equality exists if any randomly drawn sample of the membership of a society receives the same share of the assets as any other random sample of the same size drawn from the same membership.[17] Substantial equality of the main distributive assets seems to be the most a society is able to achieve without grossly violating other values. The question of whether or not complete equality is feasible or desirable is a highly abstract one. The real question confronting theories of societal guidance is the specification of the conditions under which gross inequality can be substantially reduced.

Here lies the key point: Consensus per se—even broad participation in its formation—provides no assurance that the resulting policy, action, or societal structure will not be alienating, because differences in power lead to inauthentic consensus in support of patterns which are not responsive (or at least relatively less so) to the needs of the weak. Substantial equality is a prerequisite for the relative neutralization of power and for the building of authentic, non-coerced consensus and, hence, for responsiveness.

The less egalitarian the distribution of power in a society, the larger the number of collectivities that are being alienated and to which the policies followed and the patterns maintained are not responsive. An increase in the action coefficient of the weaker collectivities—whether it is brought about through an increase in their share of assets or in their mobilization—may not increase or decrease the consensus, but rather alter its substance to reflect more equally the members' perspectives and make it less alienating.

One central difference between democratic (especially capitalist) societies and active societies is that the first type stresses consensus but is inegalitarian; it includes many passive and alienated collectivities. Democratic societies are much less responsive than they are flexible. Active societies emphasize the egalitarian distribution of power; they have no passive or alienated collectivities and are responsive (and, hence, also flexible) societies. The peculiar power constellation which enables the approximation of optimal responsiveness is explored in the following section.

Sources of Unresponsiveness

Control Deficiencies

Cybernetic analysis suggests two sets of factors that account for unresponsiveness on the part of the control centers: deficiencies in the centers

---

* We say "significantly" because the granting of token concessions to forestall substantial reallocation is a common strategy and is not without its own logic; it often "fools" the other groupings, or these concessions are the most they can bargain for under the circumstances.

themselves and deficiencies in the incoming and outgoing communication lines. Many of these factors have already been explored and are only briefly listed here.

(a) *Expressive factors* include *psychological rigidities* of the decision-makers, their staffs, and their gatekeepers that prevent them from realistically assessing incoming messages about changes in the needs and powers of the member units and about the effects of signals issued earlier by the centers. *Ideological rigidities* have similar effects. Actually, it is often rather difficult to distinguish them from psychological rigidities. Fanaticism and dogmatism are used to refer to both, and the symptoms and effects of the two kinds (both block reality-testing) are quite similar.

(b) *Instrumental factors* include those knowledge-limitations which exist because of a shortage of assets, limited experience, poor learning, poor theories, deficient processing of information, inappropriate strategies, and decision-making that is either overly incremental or rationalistic.

Besides these intra-center factors that limit responsiveness, there are (c) *communication deficiencies* that distort the incoming and outgoing messages which the center receives and emits. Even if the center is highly responsive, it cannot react appropriately if there are communication gaps, "noise" on the line, or deliberate or unwitting overloading of the center. Communication blocks can arise not only because of deficiencies in the communication lines themselves—such as poor technology and low investment—but also because of sociological factors such as cultural differences between the elite and the collectivities with which it tries to communicate and status differences which would make an elite more accessible to some groupings (e.g., businessmen) than others (old-type labor leaders).[18]

Means for reducing these sources of unresponsiveness have been discussed above—for instance, mixed scanning as a decision-making strategy; a critical knowledge-producing unit that is related to, but not dominated by, the decision-makers to ensure "openness"; and "balanced" investment in processing information and in its collection. Such measures not only increase the effectiveness of societal control (an aspect which we attempted to illustrate in previous chapters) but also specifically allow for this effectiveness to be increased by making the control centers more responsive. To these must be added factors outside the control mechanisms, especially the effects of the *distribution* of societal power.

The Effect of Power Distributions

To characterize the distribution of power under which the controlling overlayers will be most responsive to the members' needs, both the distribution of power among the member collectivities *and* between them and the controlling overlayer must be specified. So far as the members are concerned, *the more egalitarian the distribution of power among them, the more responsive the overlayer will tend to be to their needs.*[19] The more power is concentrated in the hands of one or a few member units, the larger the number of those to whose needs the overlayer does not respond. So far as the autonomy of the overlayer (its relative power versus that of the members) is concerned, *a "medium" amount, we suggest, would make it more responsive than either a low or a high degree.* If the overlayer's power is low, the system will *drift*, reacting to changes in the environment and the members with little "creative" or anticipatory capacity and, therefore, at the mercy of the more powerful members. If the overlayer's power is great (not only greater than that of any one collectivity or subset of collectivities but greater than that of all of them together), it will *overmanage*, imposing policies that run counter to the members' needs.

A high concentration of political power in the hands of one or a few collectivities may not hinder the system's flexibility, but—as we saw—such a system will be unresponsive, as the members without power (in this situation, most of them) still have needs which are not being taken into account. High concentration has two consequences: (a) the realization of many societal values which entail a broad base—such as distributive justice, equality, and political freedom—is ruled out by definition; and (b) the members whose needs are ignored impose on the societal management some costs which would not be incurred were the policy advanced more responsive to them.* The Chinese peasants probably had little effect on Mao's policy formation via established consensus-building mechanisms, but this does not mean they can be ignored. They blocked, for example, several farm policies he advanced which were unresponsive to their needs.[20]

The Main Types

These two dimensions of power distribution—among members, and between them and the overlayer—define the main types of power structures which make for unresponsive guidance mechanisms. Their degree of unresponsiveness depends on the extent to which they approximate one of these "pure" types.

When the controlling overlayer is weak and one or a few of the members has most of the power, the guidance mechanism will be unresponsive to most members *and* will not carry much of a load, as most societal transactions will occur as a result of direct interaction among the collectivities and the organizations based on them. Early capitalist societies approximated this model. The political organization of the society was controlled by the commercial and industrial classes (sometimes in conjunction with some other, small "have" class, especially the aristocracy), and the state provided largely a

---

* As responsiveness is not a zero-sum property, it is a mistake to assume that taking into account more of the needs of these members would necessarily entail a loss to those in control; it is rather a question of a more creative and a more anticipatory policy.

negative context to rule out alternatives and block transformation when less coercive measures failed. The Haymarket affair symbolizes this period for the United States. Much of the societal control is directly in the hands of industrial and other collectivity-based organizations.[21]

Modern capitalism was marked by a similar distribution of power among the members (though there was some increase in the power of the working classes, and the earlier non-capitalistic "have" classes almost disappeared), but the power of the state had been greatly increased. Considerable unresponsiveness was found here in the power distribution which favored the capitalistic classes, though the relative rise in the power of other classes and the democratic legitimation—on which the political system drew— had somewhat increased the responsiveness to these classes. The United States in the first generation of the twentieth century, after industrialization and before the initiation of social security, approximated this model.

Welfare capitalism is mainly a post-modern extension of modern capitalism; it involves some additional increase in the power of the state and in the concessions to non-capitalistic classes, but without a basic change of structure. Post-modern America illustrates these trends.

When the power of the state approximates the "medium" level but the distribution of power among the members is much more egalitarian than that found in even the most egalitarian capitalistic society, we move toward the optimum responsive society. Societies which were for long periods under the rule of Social Democratic Parties are the closest existing approximations. A continued increase in egalitarianism, if it does not entail much additional increase in the power of the state (though a rise in the efficacy of its use is, we saw, both possible and necessary), would lead to the power constellation most conducive to optimal responsiveness. And, if other factors are favorable, to an active society.

The types of societies we have considered so far have had strong members and a relatively weak state; we turn now to those societies in which the state is powerful and the member collectivities are weak. This makes for a highly unresponsive constellation, approximated by the post-revolutionary regimes in Russia and China. Here, the collectivities which held most of the power were largely neutralized by a revolutionary movement which used as its main tool the Party in conjunction with the State.* Little power is allotted to

---

* Most writings on left Party–States stress the role of the civilian bureaucracies, assuming a priority of these and the Party over the military forces. A left Party–Military State, though, is no less possible, and Mao's China seems to have increasingly relied on the military, especially as of the mid-Sixties. The significance of the support of the Army was acknowledged in the May 13, 1967 issue of *Jenmin Jih Pao*, the official Maoist organ, published in Peking, in the context of stressing the significance of Army support for carrying out the Cultural Revolution. See also John Gittings, "Military Control and Leadership, 1949–64," *China Quarterly*, No. 26 (April–June, 1966), pp. 82–101. J. C. Cheng (ed.), *The Politics of the Chinese Red Army* (Stanford, Calif.: Hoover Institution on War, Revolution, and Peace, 1966).

societal units; their autonomy is not legitimated ideologically and is tolerated only to a limited degree. The lack of responsiveness of the Party–State is revealed in the high number of new programs which the members (especially significant segments of the peasantry, ethnic minorities, religious groupings and the intelligentsia) do not support and in the high reliance on coercion against those who do not share in the revolutionary movement.

Nazi Germany started with some recognition of pluralism but moved, especially in the war years, toward a fuller approximation of the Party–State and the gradual elimination of the autonomy of capitalistic and aristocratic collectivities.[22] At the same time, its program became even less responsive and it relied even more on coercion.

The Soviet Union seems to be moving in the opposite direction, toward some reduction of the power of the Party–State and some increase in the autonomy of the member collectivities. An indication of this trend is some increase in direct societal interaction (e.g., by labor-management, the intellectuals), though this still occurs largely within a fairly tight Party–State context. There is also some increase in responsiveness and some decrease in the reliance on coercion. These trends fluctuate, but their long-run direction seems clear. East European Socialist Republics varied in the degree to which they allowed the Party–State to neutralize the power of the collectivities and their organizations. For instance, the church (and probably the peasantry) in Poland was never as weak as it was in the Soviet Union.[23] The same general trend seems to be operating in these republics. China seems not to have reached this stage yet, or had entered it (between 1949 and 1956) but left it again, drawing on sweeping drives to maintain "the superiority of politics," i.e., the Party–State.[24] The decrease in the overbearing power of the state and the limited increase in the autonomy of the members move these societies in the direction of a responsive society.*

Between Totalitarian and Authoritarian Societies

A key question for this line of analysis is difficult to answer because the data are incomplete or contested: To what degree do the controlling over-layers of non-democratic societies constitute a *fusion* of some member collectivities and state organizations, and to what degree do they constitute the overpowering of the society by the political overlayer itself? Relatively pure cases of overpowering are probably encountered only in inter-society relations, especially in conquest situations in which an external elite attempts

---

* A comment on the approach followed here is necessary. The proposition that is explored is that changes in the two dimensions of power distribution we discuss co-vary with changes in the responsiveness of the societal guidance mechanism. It is not suggested that the concrete changes in the societies to which we refer or their analytic attributes can be exhausted by this two-variable sub-model.

to control a conquered society. Where the Party–State is the internal supra-organization (even if it develops some collectivity characteristics), we have a case of a political overlayer that has overpowered the society to a significant degree, and overmanagement is likely to occur. This seems to be what is often considered totalitarian. Where a collectivity and a state organization become closely interwoven but the collectivity has an autonomous existence—such as an aristocracy that controls an army which controls the society—we have a case of member-monopolization (of the controlling overlayer, *not* necessarily of staff recruitment). Such a society is likely to suffer less from political overmanagement and more from societal exclusiveness—from over-responsiveness toward some member collectivities (which, thus, become the privileged ones) and underresponsiveness to others (the underprivileged). This seems to be one of the main attributes of societies referred to as authoritarian.[25]

Looked upon from a modern vantage point, the problem of authoritarian societies is a dual one: both nation-building, i.e., the creation of a society-wide structure and political organization *and* a decrease in inequality to a level that modernization might be possible.* The role of both democratic political development and Communist parties, as well as national insurrectionist movements, have often been viewed as providing for these societal changes. As authoritarian regimes attempt to develop without democratization, over-management is more likely to occur; as left totalitarian governments stabilize and liberalize, privileged collectivities and exclusiveness seem more likely to rise.

No society is completely totalitarian or completely authoritarian, by this characterization. Even in the most totalitarian state, some member collectivities tend to have more influence over the Party–State than others, e.g., the German industrialists as compared to the intelligentsia (and probably to the working classes and labor leaders) in Hitler's Germany. And even in the most authoritarian country, the state has some *autonomous* power of its own. Thus, member-monopolization and state-control should hence be considered as two extreme points on a continuum.

The positions of various countries on such a continuum are not clear. It has been argued, for instance, that in the Soviet Union, a privileged class of managers and officers has been formed that has acquired many of the characteristics of a collectivity.[26] Others have argued that this collectivity is the Party itself.[27] Still others say that the group of those who have special influence over the state is "open" and members are recruited according to merit. There is a high turnover of membership, and the party includes

---

* Lenski showed that inequality in non-modern societies is much greater than that found in even the most inegalitarian modern ones. While, he figured, about 15.5 per cent of the personal income of American people went to the top 2.3 per cent, it was and is about 50 per cent for an agrarian society. *Power and Privilege, op. cit.*, p. 310.

members of most, if not all, collectivities and, hence, does not form a collectivity in itself.[28] There are similar differences in interpretation of the data on authoritarian states. Do one or a few collectivities control the authoritarian state? Or is a wider range of collectivities included? While the answers to these questions will have to await more macro-research and analysis, we can state on a high level of generalization that, by and large, totalitarian societies are "closer" to the overmanaged ideal type than authoritarian societies are to the member-monopolized ideal type.*

In comparison, democracies—especially capitalistic ones—tend to have weak controlling overlayers and disproportionate member control but not monopolization of the controlling overlayer by one collectivity or even high concentration, as compared to authoritarian governments (out of which most of them grew, historically). Actually, the transition from an authoritarian to a democratic government often entails some redistribution of political and societal power in favor of the weaker collectivities—i.e., some decrease in inequality. The transition to an active society requires the extension of this trend. Early capitalistic societies are more exclusive from this viewpoint than later ones, and "social-democratic" societies are relatively closer to the egalitarian end of the continuum.

The Over-Managed Society and Its Transformation

Collectivities and Consensus-Formation

Compared to the active society, totalitarian regimes are not particularly ambitious in their aims of accelerated and encompassing societal engineering but rather overmanage in their heavy reliance on the Party–State as the lever of change. This is reflected in two main ways: (1) highly (and often unnecessarily) prescriptive management and (2) deficient consensus-formation. Without attempting to form here another theory of totalitarianism, its place in our scheme should be briefly indicated.

Mature totalitarian societies, of which the post-Stalin Soviet Union and Eastern European societies provide the main examples, are not without consensus-formation structures, but they seem quite different from those of capitalist-democratic societies. If democratic governments were to pursue domestic policies as lacking in societal support as collectivization of the farms

---

* Another dimension of the difference between these two types of societies is the degree of political intensity, or penetration of the controlling overlayer into the collectivities, which is higher in totalitarian than in authoritarian societies. Also, totalitarian polities tend to be ideologically on the left, while authoritarian governments tend to be conservative, though there are obvious exceptions: Nazi Germany was not "left," and Ben Bella's Algeria and Nkrumah's Ghana were authoritarian but hardly conservative. Both dimensions are obviously related to the basic difference in power profiles discussed above.

(in the USSR) or elimination of the church (in Poland), they would be ousted in the next election. Totalitarian guidance mechanisms are like jeeps built to drive on rough roads; they are constructed to carry heavier loads with less support. The system relies more on a mixture of normative and coercive power and less on utilitarian power than the capitalist-democratic one. It is basically less responsive to the needs of its members but probably more responsive to those of the system, at least under adverse social and non-social environmental conditions. The decision-making processes involve only a very limited segment of the membership and have only a very limited capacity to determine the needs and performances of the membership at large, even if—or when—the determination of such indications are the prevailing norm. In that sense, the member collectivities' participation in the political processes is much more limited than in the democratic model, and the capacity of the system to respond to the members is much smaller.

Toward an Active Society

The movement of a totalitarian society toward an active one is not the same as democratization or "liberalization." These concepts are often associated with the increased role of societal consensus-formation (e.g., more upward representation) and a reduction of state control (e.g., less power for security police, an increase in human and civil rights). In comparison, the movement toward an active society requires such an increase in consensus-formation; a transformation of control from the prescriptive to the contextuating type but only a limited reduction in the scope of control; and a great increase in the societal responsiveness.

While a central problem of the "steering" of totalitarian societies is the large imbalance between control and consensus, equilibrium may be reached at a considerably higher level of collective (as compared to private) action than is common in capitalist, and even in semi-active, democracies. Hence, if an active society is the goal, the emphasis must be on increasing consensus-formation and responsiveness rather than on the reduction of control and on changes in the nature of control rather than on the reduction of its scope. Bases on which "medium" powerful control could be evolved include: (1) first, the levelling of major power differences among the member collectivities and then the generation of new differences in perspective and power in various specialized sections; and (2) first, the formation of a shared ideological base and then the allowance of some differentiation. The effectiveness of both of these bases, however, requires responsiveness to the needs of the member collectivities. This requires an increase in their autonomy which, in turn, requires an increased capacity to form consensus. To increase only the collectivities' autonomy, without providing for more consensus-formation, would entail a reduction of societal action.

The Social Movement Aspect

The transformation of the totalitarian state in the direction of the active society entails a return to some of the features of the social movement "society" out of which Soviet and Chinese Communist polities emerged (as well as that of Nazi Germany).[29] The social movement is characterized by a high level of activation of the members. While there is no elaborate machinery of control, the effective chain of leadership as well as the deep normative commitments of the membership allow the movement to "run" more on influence than on power.* The low level of internal bureaucratization, the broad participation, the close relationship between means and widely shared goals, and the drama of success and rapid change encourage high mobilization and a high rate of collective action.

But the social movement "organization" is inherently unstable, short-lived, and soon becomes more bureaucratized, first imposing itself on others (non-members) and soon on its own membership. Influence turns into persuasion, and frequently persuasion is increasingly backed by force. The question, hence, is not how to maintain a social movement organization permanently (which seems a utopian effort), but how to maintain some of its features, in particular the high level of commitment and participation. Mature totalitarian societies, by despecifying their over-prescriptive controlling overlayer and by segregating their consensus-formation processes, may increase the normative and non-bureaucratic elements of their political organization; this allows for a more social-movement-like society. In such a transition, these totalitarian states can invoke the legitimation of earlier "founding" periods, in which the movement elements were stronger.

The concept of "permanent revolution" has been applied to the idea of a continual social-movement society. The basic concept is valid. Societies tend to bureaucratize, decline in responsiveness, weaken their commitments, and give rise to oligarchies and privileged collectivities; if the active orientation is to be maintained, continued effort, investment, and attention are necessary. This raises the question of which specific structural conditions such continuous effort requires. It is on this dimension that the concept is open to divergent interpretations. On the one hand, permanent revolution literally means continued violent purges such as those China knew late in 1966 and early in 1967—the Cultural Revolution of Mao's Red Guards against bureaucratization and ideological impurity.[30] But this kind of permanent revolution entails (a) considerable de-activation interspersed between spurts of mobilization and (b) costly purges to sustain it. The active society will have to seek a less violent and more constant base of high-level activation. Some of the factors involved in this kind of activation are discussed in preceding

---

* The differences between influence and power are explored *supra*, pp. 359–361.

chapters and below; much research is yet to be done. However, the task is clearly different from the totalitarian interpretation.

The active society is, to a degree, a social-movement society, but there are three major differences between the totalitarian social-movement period and active societies. The most obvious one is historical; totalitarian governments —to the degree that they were conceived indigenously—were born in revolutions and hostile environments; active societies are likely to emerge more gradually and in less hostile environments. The two other differences concern direct versus indirect mobilization and the relative reliance on persuasion versus education in consensus-building. Totalitarian movements attempted, initially, to accentuate rather than alleviate the "mass" elements of the societies in which they arose by a heavy reliance on mass propaganda, national leadership cults, and direct access of the state to the individuals. This was marked by an attempt to downgrade all cohesive units other than Party membership.

Active societies stand near the opposite end of the continuum on all of these dimensions. The active society seeks to sustain and strengthen the plurality of micro- and macro-cohesive units which constitute the body of society. Its activeness is based on increasing the mobilization of societal units rather than on direct appeals to the membership. And, its mobilization must be based on political education and consensus-formation to assure a more effective commitment than persuasion can provide.[31]

Finally, it should be noted that whether the route leads to democracies or to active societies, the necessary increase in responsiveness requires much more than the expansion of civil liberties and human rights, often considered a sign of this transition. Assuming that the preceding analysis is valid, it would entail a relatively high degree of de-politization and a decline of ideology, the rise of cross-cutting political units (the middle tier of the structure), and some formalization of the rules of the game not only for the members of a small body such as the Praesidium but also for societal collectivities and political units (a development that occurred in the West with the expansion from an aristocratic democracy to a popular one). Thus, while the totalitarian societies may move directly to active societies, "skipping" the democratic "stage," and while they may already have some elements of an active society (their levelling of dominant collectivities and their strong controlling overlayers)—on other dimensions they have hardly begun to transform.*

---

* A discussion of the road to be covered if such transformation is to be achieved is found in Communist literature in the contrast between the "socialist" and the "communist" society. Education as a means of transition based on higher consensus and the reduction of the state as a coercive instrument are most often stressed. Other changes, especially the increased recognition of pluralism and the development of the needed machinery for consensus-formation, are much less often recognized. The stress is on a conflictless society rather than on the machinery necessary to work out peacefully and effectively inevitable differences of perspective.

The Monopolized Polity and Its Transformation

The "Vulgar" Power-Elite Proposition

The concentration of political power in one or a few member collectivities is always a matter of degree. Not even the most dominated polity is ever "run" by a military-industrial complex, as is portrayed in some radical descriptions of capitalist democracies.[32] First, internal divisions within the military and within the industrial organizations and sub-collectivities are usually too great to allow for effective monopolization. Inter-service rivalries and conflict *among* industrial groupings allow for at least a measure of legislative and executive autonomy and for other political units to "play" the industrial and military ones against each other.[33] Around what issues and to what degree military and business groups join together vary a great deal over time and among capitalist societies, but it does not follow from the fact that these groups act jointly on some matters that they have a broad and prescriptive monopoly of the state; this is especially erroneous in regard to domestic guidance as distinct from foreign policy.

The United States is the most "militarized" capitalist society.[34] But even here, the per cent of the GNP devoted to military activities was only about 10 per cent between 1955 and 1965. The other 90 per cent cannot simply be ignored, especially if the government policies are seen as determined by the economic interests. Suggestions that the economic impact of the military–industrial complex is actually larger than these figures show, because of the multiplier effect, ignore the fact that other sectors of the economy also have a multiplier effect.* Nor is the industry that specializes in serving the military more monolithic and more able to act in unison than several other industries —e.g., the automotive industry.

To suggest, as Lenin did, that the entire business structure is pushing the capitalist society into war and armed preparations to protect overseas investments and to maintain or gain raw materials and markets,[35] will explain United States foreign policy in some areas for some periods (e.g., oil in the Middle East during the last decades of the modern period, or the United Fruit Company in Central America in the first decades of the twentieth century). But more important in explaining the causes of the last two world wars, especially the aggressive policies of Germany and Japan, are lingering pre-capitalist, feudal collectivities and conceptions, as compared to the largely passive, even reluctant, role played by most capitalist groups. United States military interventions in Vietnam, the Dominican Republic, and Lebanon cannot be accounted for by the hold of dominant collectivities

---

* The military multiplier seems to be lower than that of most other sectors because of the esoteric nature of its production, the segregation of its personnel from the rest of the economy, and its secrecy. For references and additional discussion, see *supra*, pp. 201–203.

on political decision-making; they were in part the result of deficiencies in this process itself, which was "boxed in" by a context the public learned to accept in earlier periods.[36] The fear of psychological loss resulting from conduct unfitting this context and related political, domestic losses were at least as important a factor, as were also poor knowledge input and analysis.[37]

If there is a trend in the post-modern period as compared to the late modern one and in the latter as compared to the earlier modern period, it is for business influence to decline. Business interests overseas are now protected by government insurance rather than by reliance on military intervention. There are more corporations penalized by the arms race than benefit from it.[38] And disarmament would not be profitless either, as it requires, at least initially, considerable investments in inspection instruments and staff, and the transition—which would inevitably be gradual—could be absorbed by the American economy without major dislocations.[39] Rapid disarmament in 1945 did not generate the depression which many expected.[40] While there was, at that stage, an accumulation of demands not satisfied during the war years, there is considerable reason to believe that the necessary demands could be produced for another disarmament, especially as it is likely to be more gradual. The military and the industry do have disproportionate political power; but they do not come even close to monopolizing control of the society. They must coalesce with other forces if they are to prevail, and, hence, they may also be politically countervailed by other members of the system.

Furthermore, so long as the members of the dominant elites and collectivities subscribe to democratic values and procedures—either because they were socialized to believe in them or because of expediency—this commitment requires the making of some concessions to and the allowance of some participation for the other collectivities. These collectivities—religious, labor, ethnic, and various social movements—have, especially when in coalition, prevailed on a large variety of domestic matters and on some foreign ones. In the United States, often viewed as the country most controlled by a military-industrial complex, their support played a pivotal role in the Senate ratification of the 1963 nuclear test ban treaty and in the enactment of the 1964 civil rights bill, the 1965 federal aid to education act, and the 1966 medicare law. More generally, these groups have spurred the evolution of welfare capitalism.* All of these measures were opposed by some industrial and/or military groups.

---

* In a fine case study of one of these bills, the authors show that while both parties and interest groups came to favor federal aid to education, and more innovative and powerful presidential leadership was exercised in its support than in previous years, the shift in public opinion in favor of the bill *preceded* the other shifts. Note also that the authors deal mainly with what may be referred to as public opinion. Changes in party and presidential politics are also to be attributed in part to changes in public opinion. See Munger and Fenno, *National Politics and Federal Aid to Education, op. cit.*

A "Sophisticated" Power-Elite Proposition

While there is no monopolization of political power, political power is concentrated in the hands of some collectivities and their organizations while others are excluded. The extent of this concentration differs, of course, from country to country and over time. The central question for the study of transformation toward an active society is not the degree of concentration but whether or not the *aggregation of power by some members is sufficiently great to prevent the accumulation of societal and political power by weaker collectivities whereby they could transform an unresponsive society.* On the one hand, power concentration is of limited importance if it is not sufficiently great to prevent a transformation which includes abolishing the specific privileges prevalent in democratic societies and the concentration pattern itself. On the other hand, varying degrees of participation for and concessions to underprivileged collectivities have little transforming value if they are limited to those tolerated by the powerful and allow their continued disproportionate control of the polity.*

The evidence is by no means clear. On the one hand, capitalistic polities have been changed in the direction of an active society in countries governed by Social Democratic parties and, to a lesser degree, in Britain. Even in the United States, the rise of the welfare state and the ability to mobilize first a labor movement and then a civil rights movement—and the societal effects they had—suggest that transformation may be possible. On the other hand, the "gradualist" transformation of these societies, especially the larger ones (i.e., Britain and the United States), did not greatly advance. For long periods, these societies were "frozen," and when they moved, as the United States did with multiple welfare bills in 1964 and Britain did under the Wilson labor government in improving planning—the motion was slow, narrow in scope, and much overdue. A generation of efforts to redistribute the wealth in a less inegalitarian form yielded little change.[41] Since the 1930s in the United States, the political intent—as expressed in legislation and taxation—has been to increase the egalitarian distribution—e.g., the introduction of estate taxes that levy imposts of about one third on net estates of $1 million and one-half on net estates of $5 million, supported by other legislation limiting tax free gifts, and so on. Still, the share held by the top families has only decreased from 33 per cent of all personal wealth in 1922 to 29 per cent in 1954.[42] It might be suggested that social democracies have been more active and more effective in this direction, but at best their record is only marginally superior.[43]

---

* Traditionally, the same question has been asked in other terms: Could capitalist societies be transformed into social-democratic ones without a revolution, by parliamentary procedures and social reform? We prefer the societal guidance formulation because the traditional formulation is less accurate, its terminology is not part of an analytic scheme, and it is ethnocentric.

A study of the concentration of control in the hands of the two hundred largest American corporations showed they controlled nearly half the corporate wealth in 1929.[44] A generation later—despite numerous new laws, a decline in the legitimation of big business, and some governmental efforts—the concentration did not decline significantly.[45] A thorough United States Senate hearing and investigation found public utilities to be disguised monopolies; repeated after a generation, it found only few alterations in monopolistic practices.[46] The influence of business groupings on state legislatures in the United States is greater—much greater, it seems—than on the federal level.[47] Hence, it can be argued that no change "of the system" has been achieved. Second, radicals may still hold that concessions were tolerated only because they were minor in scope, that if continued accumulation of incremental changes were to exceed the limits of the fundamental context, the need for a showdown between the forces of transformation and the monopolizing ones would be necessary. More generally, it seems correct to state that no society so far has significantly levelled its power base and stratification structure without a revolution. (Even after revolutions, substantial and lasting equality tends to be highly elusive.)

The counter argument (and we choose this term deliberately, as much of the exchange is argumentative) is that Western societies did transform gradually at least once and are moving toward transformation again. The transition in Britain and the United States from agricultural to industrial societies entailed the transformation of all the major institutions of these two societies, including peaceful change of the state and its control and a shift of the concentration of political power from the aristocracy (in Britain) and rural collectivities (in the United States) to capitalist, urban collectivities. Now, a second transformation is in process—an expanding welfare state, government guidance of the economy and other societal processes, and mobilization of weaker collectivities. Labor governments in the United Kingdom and the participation of labor in the political processes in the United States have already transformed an "early" capitalism into "mature" (or "welfare") capitalism, and the process is still unfolding.

We are not aware of the data or arguments which would allow this issue to be settled. The central observation for us is that the ability to advance the transformation of democracies by mobilization of the underprivileged and weak collectivities has not been exhausted, and whatever "apathizers"—mass media, foreign distractions, and token domestic concessions—the powerful groups are using, have not sufficed to prevent its extension. Whether mobilization will eventually tip the balance in favor of a transformation to an active society without a showdown, or will lead to a showdown, remains to be seen.

The traditional argument, it should be noted, centered around the transition to state socialism; nationalization of the means of production was often viewed as the key measure of how far the transition had advanced. More broadly, state regulation is considered essential for transformation.

We are concerned with the transition toward an active society, which can be much advanced with quite limited nationalization and might be blocked by a high degree of state regulation. The economy of the active society, we saw, may well be a "mixed" one—of private, cooperative, and governmental sectors. The key changes as far as control of the economy is concerned are some expansion of the power of the state *and* the participation of all collectivities in this control; much reduction in private regulation; and a considerable increase in public, cooperative, and various "mixed" forms of regulation. In addition, the active society requires a considerable expansion of the societal guidance of non-economic processes such as knowledge-production and education. For all of these reasons, a society that seems "tolerant" of only a rather limited transformation toward state socialism may be open to considerable movement toward an active society, and a society quite favorable to state-socialism may be antagonistic to the kind of societal activation that the move toward an active society entails.

Three secondary considerations should be mentioned. The question of a showdown is less dichotomous than is often implied and may well not be a matter of revolution or reform but of various degrees of the use of force. For instance, if transformation requires a brief use of force mainly for signalling purposes (as occurred in Britain in the mid-nineteenth century[48] and again at the eve of World War I), this is quite a different matter from building a revolutionary army large enough to overwhelm the armed forces of a post-modern regime.

Barrington Moore conducted a monumental study of this question and provides as close to a definitive answer as can be expected.* He showed that all the instances of industrialization (the core of the transformation to modern societies) he studied entailed revolutions from above, "the work of a ruthless minority." His case studies include the Puritan revolution in England, the French Revolution, the American Civil War (which he sees as "the last capitalist revolution"), the decline of imperial China, the rise of modern India and Japan, and briefer examinations of Germany and Russia. While he sees a major violent upheaval in each case, the level of violence (which he classifies as revolution, rebellion, or "violence") differed significantly from society to society as did the societal resistance to change. China is at the "revolutionary" end; Britain and the United States—at the "violent" but gradualist transforming end; France, India, and Japan lie in-between. Of special interest to a theory of societal guidance is that Moore shows that a central factor affecting the levels of violence and flexibility of the polity in each case was whether the agricultural economies (i.e., the pre-modern society) operated under "segmented," bureaucratic, or feudal authority, which, in turn, significantly affected the quality of the political overlayer. (A second factor was the

---

* Barrington Moore, Jr., *Social Origins of Dictatorship and Democracy* (Boston: Beacon Press, 1967).

degree to which the ruling classes opened their ranks to the rising classes and the rulers themselves transformed.)

Just as a measure of violence by the transforming forces does not preclude a gradualist transformation, so some harassment of radicals (or other political innovators) by a regime cannot be seen as "proof" that transformation cannot be advanced within the context of a given society. Actually, certain low levels of harassment tend to build up the consciousness, commitment, and mobilization of the underprivileged collectivities. The alternatives seem to be between less and more violence at tipping points rather than "reform" or "revolution." And the question of which it will be—a gradualist or abrupt transformation—depends at least as much on the flexibility and responsiveness of the powerful elites and polity as on the ideology and organization of the mobilizing collectivities.

Secondly, it should be recognized that the more active the weaker collectivities become, the more "neutral" the state tends to become. And the more neutral the state becomes, the less the powerful collectivities can add the state's power to their own in controlling the weak collectivities, and the more freely can the latter mobilize. When we compare the worker–management–government relations in the United States in the middle of the nineteenth century to those of the 1950s, we see that labor became much more mobilized and politically effective, and, in the same period, the state became relatively less partisan in its regulation of labor–management conflicts. Strikebreakers are no longer deputized as federal marshals and armed; police and state troops are much more reluctant to shoot into groups of peaceful pickets; and judges hesitate to issue openly biased, anti-labor injunctions.[49] Similar developments have taken place in other democratic, industrialized countries. Another illustration of the same "law" at work can be seen in northern American cities in the 1960s. Following the mobilization of Puerto Ricans and Negroes by the civil rights movement, the police became relatively more careful not to violate the rights of these groups; in earlier periods, the police took such care only with members of other, more powerful, collectivities.[50] In the Deep South, this change has yet largely to take place.

In neither of these cases was the neutralization of the state complete, since the mobilization of the weak collectivities was far from high and the redistribution of societal and political power was still rather limited. But the trends and their correlaries seem evident: They support the proposition that the responsiveness of the state depends on a specific power constellation— on a relatively egalitarian distribution of societal power, and that it can be increased through the mobilization of the underprivileged.

The State as a Transforming Agent

The rise in the responsiveness of the state explains, in part, a contradiction intrinsic to democratic societies: The decrease in the inegalitarian use of legitimate force, brought about by the increase in the responsiveness of the state, has not been paralleled by the redistribution of utilitarian assets. While the enforcement of the law, at the end of the modern period, still varied inversely with the stratification position of the law-breaker, the law itself was largely uniform. The importance of this can be seen when democratic polities are compared to pre-modern ones in which the law itself was differentiated by estates. Reallocation of utilitarian assets, though, we saw, was slow and netted only a comparatively limited increase in equality. It may be said that there is a time lag between decreases in political and in economic inequality, but at least three-to-four decades did not significantly narrow the gap, and the trend shows no acceleration or significant accumulation.

The difference in the pace of reallocation seems to be due in part to the differences in and relations between political and societal power. The regulation of electoral rights and law enforcement is *relatively* more independent of the collectivities than is reallocation of their wealth. An act of parliament can give members of a new or rising collectivity the right to vote and the state administration can move comparatively far and quickly in making those rights effective; similarly, police reforms, while not dissociated from societal changes, are relatively easier for the state to institute, it seems, than reallocation of wealth, which requires changes in the societal structure rather than in the political shell. Also, increasing the neutralization of the state is a matter of upgrading, of giving to the "have-nots" something the "haves" have already achieved. Reallocation, on the other hand, takes part of what the "haves" possess and gives it to the "have-nots." Upgrading is generally easier than reallocation.[51]

Thus, political anchoring of mobilization is not sufficient; there must be societal restructuring if transformation is to take place. This poses a dilemma for both Marxist and liberal analysis: If the state is in the control of the powerful collectivities, why does it allow a greater reallocation of political power than of societal assets? If the state reflects the society, how can it change without commensurate change in the society?

The answer lies, in part, in the political formula, in the democratic legitimacy which garbs the capitalist society and to which it is willing to make some concessions, especially political ones—e.g., to increase the representation of the weaker collectivities. But the powerful collectivities are much more reluctant to make any but token concessions in terms of the essence of the inegalitarian distribution—the societal assets. To put it differently, the powerful are willing to allow underprivileged collectivities to gain in *participation in political decision-making in the hope that such participation will drain rather than build up their drive to change fundamentally the societal structure.* Since the state has some autonomy,* so long as changes are

---

* The autonomy of the democratic state is reflected, among other things, in the fact that the weaker collectivities gain some leverage and the powerful lose some leverage in the conversion of societal into political power.

"internal"—as, for instance, representational changes—they can be relatively more easily introduced than when stratification and status-relations are to be restructured. A typical example is the 1962 reapportionment decision of the U.S. Supreme Court, which was believed, at the time, would significantly curtail the overrepresentation (political power) of the rural collectivities and their conservative urban allies. There is little doubt that had the matter been settled "directly" among the collectivities, on the societal level, there would have been no such adjustment (as there was none in most of the state legislatures which are less under the influence of the society and the federal government and are more controlled by the powerful collectivities).[52] In 1966, conservative groups mounted a campaign for a constitutional amendment that would largely block the egalitarian effect of the Supreme Court ruling. This was defeated because of a Senate rule—which has no parallel in the societal structure—that two-thirds of the votes are needed for ratification (the actual vote was 55 in favor, 38 against).[53] Had the conservatives not been committed to the democratic rules of the game, reapportionment—i.e., a change in the political conversion rules—would not have been possible. The achievements of the civil rights movement have followed the same pattern. When it comes to desegregation, for instance—not in a formal but in a societal sense, not of voting but of jobs, not of the right to use public facilities but of the right to share in the community's life—no "two-thirds" rule applies; the conservative forces have much more power, and greater inequality prevails longer.

No less important is the relative power of the state itself. Countries which have experienced revolutions which more or less neutralized the political power of capitalistic or feudal collectivities differ in the extent to which the state has acquired power. Where it is relatively weak, as in Mexico and in Bolivia, no significant restructuring of society, in terms of reallocation of wealth, has taken place. The peasants are still, after a generation and a half in Mexico and half a generation after the 1952 revolution in Bolivia, the weakest and most underprivileged collectivity.[54] In comparison, the state in left totalitarian societies acquired too much power vis-à-vis the society. This is indicated not only by violation of human and civil rights, but also in the incapacity to build authentic consensus and responsiveness. These require an upward expression which cannot be effectively assured without granting greater autonomy to societal units.

The optimal level of societal responsiveness to members' needs is hence expected to be more closely approximated (a) the smaller the power differences among the members, and (b) the more the situation is one in which the state is powerful enough to bring about agreed upon societal changes but not sufficiently powerful to act against the consensus of the members. This entails, as we see it, an increase in the power of the democratic state and of the states of most underdeveloped countries, and a decline in the power of mature and especially "early" totalitarian states.

The Reallocation of Normative Assets

In general, changes in the distribution of normative assets are much more difficult to assess than changes in the distributions of other societal and political assets. The access to education, though, provides an opportunity to study this aspect of societal transformation. It is of additional interest because education is a major mechanism for the acquisition of status symbols, one whose societal importance increased in the post-modern period; it helps to determine the utilitarian bases of "life-chances," and it lays foundations on which societal consensus may be built.

The distribution of normative assets seems in general to be intermediary, in its inequality and changeability, between those of other societal and political assets; there seems to be a significant decrease in the inequality of access to education, but, at the same time, considerable inequality in the quality of education is maintained, and this, in turn, is a main source of status and income differences.[55] While the data are far from clear, it seems that the distribution of access to education is somewhat more egalitarian than that of income and is changing *relatively* more quickly than the latter, precisely because the impact of the state is greater (the schools are, by and large, part of the state organization). But even in semi-active societies, it does not approximate even a roughly egalitarian structure.[56]

Equality, again, is relatively more closely and increasingly approximated to the degree that the state can provide for access, especially through financial aid. But the state commands much less power to reduce the differences in the quality of education available, which have deep societal roots and are highly resistant to changes. Education seems less unequally distributed in those sub-sectors in which the state has greater power—primary education in Israel, and higher education in the United States.* Finally, in this societal sector, as in others discussed above, upgrading encounters less resistance than reallocation.

The Role of Mobilization

The key role of the mobilization of the weaker collectivities and of society stands out in this analysis of transformation.† Various changes in "background conditions" increase the possibility of transformation, but they must be accelerated and their potential actualized, and this is what requires mobilization. In addition, improvement in the capacity to build society-wide consensus can exact additional ounces of tolerance to change from the

---

* Reference here is to the federal government and not to those of the fifty states.

† We discussed the role of mobilization in some detail in Ch. 15. We return to this subject here, to relate the discussion of mobilization to that of the fundamental change of monopolized societies.

powerful members, but, in part, this in itself is affected by the changing power relations (if the weaker collectivities rise, then prudent power-elites may consent to more reallocation), and, alternately, the reallocation of societal power toward more equality is a change necessary for an increase in responsiveness and transformation toward an active society.

To advance this transformation, not only weaker collectivities but also society itself must be mobilized. Why is this so? Does not society, by being on the side of the privileged, neutralize the mobilization of the underprivileged collectivities? The answer is that for transformation to be politically feasible within the confines of the democratic state and consensus-building, it will have to rely to a great extent on "upgrading," which in turn depends on the availability of new societal assets. These will become available either because the total "pie" has increased, or because more of it is being made available for non-private usages; both alternatives require some society-wide effort. If kept at a high level of employment of men and resources, the GNP of the United States was expected to almost double by 1975 as compared to its 1965 size.[57] Thus, the United States could provide for a large variety of societal goals, out of the *new* product, even without an increase in the taxed portion of the GNP.

We do not expect that mobilization in itself, of either collectivities or of the society, can be sufficient to bring about transformation. Mobilization of the collectivities provides new energy for their action by drawing on assets which the collectivities command, by making them more available for societal action, by changing the conversion rules, and by increasing the action coefficient of the members. But the inequities in societal power are only in part due to the unevenness of the mobilization rates of different collectivities; in part, they are due to the uneven distribution of assets. Now, once mobilization advances, gains in societal power must be converted into an increased share of the political control of the state, and reallocation of assets in favor of the underprivileged collectivities must take place in order to lead to transformation—i.e., mobilization must lead to structural changes. This occurs to some extent as a result of direct action among collectivities, but, to an important degree, it requires that the state reallocate assets it controls and use its power to affect intercollectivity relations.

In this context, it is useful to refer to the political and societal "anchoring" of the results of mobilization. Mobilization of a collectivity may have some lasting internal effects; it may transform a collectivity as it internalizes leadership, as the members gain in political experience, etc. But mobilization tends to be cyclical, advancing in spurts but rarely stabilizing. Hence, before it has a lasting societal effect, part of the newly mobilized energy must be converted into changes in the political and societal structure. Such conversions, in turn, provide a base for later mobilization drives. Moreover, if mobilization drives are converted only into "token" political and societal alterations, they will not accumulate toward a gradual transformation. They will be either below "take off" or under the threshold of this or that "tipping" point. More often than not, mutual reinforcing effects, between increased mobilization of the underprivileged and reallocation of societal assets, run out of steam before a transformation is achieved, and the efforts to bring it about are, at least temporarily, halted.

The need to "anchor" the gains of mobilization, to convert them into structural changes, has not always been understood by the mobilizers themselves. The anarchists' conception that once the blocking oppression of the powerful collectivities is removed, the heretofore oppressed will rise and never allow such oppression to be re-established, played a major role in the failure of the 1905 revolution in Russia; the belief that the powerful collectivities, temporarily defeated, will limit their attempts at a comeback to a fight according to the rules of the game (legitimate mainly to the mobilizers) was one of the several weaknesses of the Weimar Social-Democrats.

Finally, the role of the political shell in transformation deserves a brief comment. On the one hand, its formal pattern is an expression of the distribution of political and societal power, and, hence, changes in it will have little effect if no parallel changes in political and societal power have taken place. On the other hand, the elements of the shell—laws, institutional arrangements, electoral procedures—have some power of their own, and, hence, if changes in societal and political power are not registered in changes in the political shell, they are likely to be eroded later and not to accumulate. The Prohibition experience has shown that the law cannot change society when it is too remote from societal reality. But the law can (a) record the new power relations and (b) affect them to some degree, as the desegregation laws illustrate. Many social scientists, in a reaction to the earlier emphasis on formal and legal factors, have tended to over-emphasize the "informal" factors to the neglect of the formal ones. With the renewed interest in the state as a transforming agent, a revision of the view of law as an instrument of societal guidance is to be expected.[58]

The Rise in Mobilizers

The preceding analysis suggests that a key to the transformation of monopolized societies lies in the mobilization of weaker collectivities and of society in general. This analysis is not complete unless the bases of new or additional mobilization, and its historical sources, can be shown.

Based on analysis of the stratification structure alone, it would seem that the powerful collectivities could hardly be expected to provide the mobilizers for the weaker ones. The weak are difficult to mobilize, and are unlikely to experience a sudden increase in the number and skills of mobilizers if only because the powerful collectivities, as part of their dominance, tend to curtail the capacity of the weaker collectivities to acquire such elites.

The identity of the collectivities that are poor in assets, undermobilized and underrepresented, and weak in societal and political power is evident. What marks their status in the late modern and earlier post-modern period is a low level of societal consciousness, since they tend to accept the prevailing view of society and share in its consumption obsession, mass culture, and a-political deflection. If there were no evidence that under their surface participation remains a strong streak of alienation (to which we turn below), we would have to conclude that their societal problems have been resolved. Actually though, the inauthentic involvement of these collectivities only serves to magnify the task for mobilization because their objective condition is even more hidden than it was during the first period of industrialization. In short, the relative weight of mobilization versus background conditions seems higher in post-modern society than in the modern one, because alienation is more concealed.

At the same time, the weaker collectivities are more mobilizable and their potential for societal action increases as the middle-class norms which keep down their political self-consciousness also prepare them for mobilization. This is especially indicated by the growth of interest in education, achievement, and organizational experience. While each of these may be deflecting rather than mobilizing (e.g., education may be narrow in scope, technological and bureaucratic), they nevertheless help to make these collectivities more "reachable" (e.g., the semi-educated are more reachable than the uneducated). Although the processes involved are slow, the long-run trends seem unmistakable: Post-modern societal processes are producing the conditions which make the transformation of monopolized societies more likely.

In addition to these historical trends for the mobilization potential of underprivileged collectivities to rise, the potential base of mobilizers seems also to be broadening. Mobilizers are recruited largely from two kinds of stratification bases; each of these yields only a small fraction of its members to this transformation leadership, but as the bases expand, so does the absolute size of the fraction. First, there are those who *deal in symbols*, especially professionals, college faculties, and other "intellect workers." The mobilizers are more likely to come from a sub-grouping—from among those who are employed in synthesizing rather than analytic work (e.g., more from liberal arts schools than from professional ones), those who are relatively immune to economic and political pressures (faculty members), and those who are not yet fully exposed to them (students). The second most important recruitment source are the unbalanced collectivities, especially those whose utilitarian status is higher than their prestige (normative) ranking. They have the capacity to move (as they are already "up" on one or a few dimensions) and the motivation to do so (to transform the structure so that their own statuses can be balanced).

The growth of the first grouping results from the knowledge revolution; the second is a product of economic mobility. There is some overlap between the two groupings; a disproportionate number of intellect workers comes from these unbalanced collectivities, and among the intellect workers, those that come from these unbalanced collectivities are more likely to be mobilized.[59] But it cannot be stressed enough that these "background" categories explain only part of the mobilization for transformation, for only a small fraction of these groupings actually becomes politically active and serves as mobilizers for other, underprivileged, collectivities.

Next in the political "processing" and closer to the "output" end are organizations of the mobilizers which, like religious orders in earlier ages, tend to be core-organizations of *service-collectivities*, in which service to others and to a societal cause is a central value. Even the details of life in such a modern grouping as the British CND (Committee for Nuclear Defence) or American SNCC (Student Non-Violent Coordinating Committee) and SDS (Students for Democratic Society), are like those in the early religious orders: Personal and organizational austerity; funds used for purposes of collective action; a high percentage of one's time collectivized and mobilized; the members' special clothing and hair style mark the vows of poverty and distinguish members from non-members; a combination of tight organization with much informality and anarchy; much wandering from place to place, no formal and little informal social distance between leaders and followers; a suspicion of and from the outside world; and guilt on the part of those who believe in the standards of the service but do not themselves lead a life of service. These norms and patterns tend to make for a very high conversion ratio; willingness to sacrifice almost all time and energy to the service of a societal cause allows a small grouping to act more effectively than much larger organizations whose members are not willing to devote more than a small fraction of their time and energy to political action.

Transforming movements are generated out of a combination of service-collectivities (or organizations of mobilizers which have a cohesive base) and one (or more) underprivileged collectivity that has a comparatively high mobilization potential. But not all service-collectivities initiate a transforming movement. For such a grouping to act as a mobilizer it has to (a) be sufficiently alienated to be fundamentally critical; (b) be educated enough to be able to create counter-symbols and ideologies; (c) command enough organizational skills to serve as part of the controlling overlayer of the transforming movement; (d) accumulate sufficient societal knowledge and analysis to be able to evolve an appropriate theory of society and political strategy, and (e) be able to prevent personal, a-political, deflections from prevailing. In general, student groupings are particularly likely to meet these conditions; groups in bohemia, professionals, clergy, and "unbalanced" ethnic minorities in the middle class tend to meet them less fully. Coalitions of such groupings have played a critical role in the mobilization of transforming movements, from the suffragettes to Castro's revolution.[60]

The resulting mobilization tends to be limited by the subjugating forces of the society and by the low action coefficient of the weaker collectivities (which, in turn, may be the result of earlier oppressions or intra-collectivity factors—e.g., divisions among member sub-collectivities). It should, however, be noted, in line with our general approach, that *in addition* to these "objective" limitations, deficiencies in "control" factors—that is, in the mobilizers themselves—often limit their capacity to activate. Typical of these are shortcomings in societal knowledge and analysis, of which the early anarchists provide a prime example. For ideological and psychological reasons, the movement renounced all organization, not just of the state but also of themselves.[61] Soon, they lost most of their capacity to act in unison, and they were driven from the control of the labor movement they helped to initiate by Marx and his followers who had no qualms about organizing themselves.[62] Later-day anarchists recognized the mistake of their predecessors, and once they embraced (quite reluctantly) an organizational strategy, they were much more successful—for instance, in the French syndicalist movement.

Similarly, one of the weaknesses of the new and old left radical mobilizers in post-modern United States is their deficient societal analysis and political strategy. For instance, there is a tendency to romanticize ideologically the weakest collectivities and to *focus mobilization efforts on the groupings lowest in the stratification structure which tend also to be those lowest in mobilization potential*, i.e., where mobilization yields per investment are smallest. The Communist Party's concentration on mobilizing Negro-Americans in the 1930s and 1940s because they were the most "alienated" grouping is a case in point.[63] This strategy is more ineffectual the more the collectivity is suppressed and not merely the victim of inauthentic commitments—e.g., more ineffective in the South than in the North of the United States. (The Party's efforts focused on the South.) Contrast this with a "chain-reaction" strategy, in which efforts are first focused on expanding the mobilizers' base, then on expanding into semi-mobilized groups and groups with a high mobilization potential, and finally on mobilizing allies, all before an attempt is made to activate the largest and most decisive but also the most difficult base for transformation.

"Background" factors which increase the mobilization potential of the underprivileged collectivities often also create new barriers to mobilization. The very expansion of the functions and control of the post-modern state tends to bring more and more intellect-workers, professionals, and universities to work for and with the state, and many become increasingly "coopted." Similarly, the treatment of political innovators in mature capitalist societies is typically one of "secondary" reward,[64] which makes sustained innovation (an initiation base for transformation) more difficult than when such political action is met by counter-hostility. To illustrate, when Fred W. Friendly resigned from CBS in 1966 because the network refused to carry critical views of the Johnson Administration's Vietnam policy (and following an intra-organizational power struggle), he barely had a chance to develop his position into a critique before he was retained by a major foundation and was once again in a role that required considerable conformity.[65] In many ways, this incident is similar to the story of many (though not all) political innovators.[66] Such "cooptations," which symbolize many other societal forces which are suppressing the expression of alienation, are not authentically committing. Opportunities for authentic commitment will be available only following radical transformations or the accumulation of accelerated reforms of post-modern societies.

.   .   .

As long and involved as this part of our discussion—the exploration of the relations between control and consensus-building; societal guidance and power relations; responsiveness, equality, mobilization, and transformation —has been, we have covered only part of the factors involved. We studied the societal units and their political organization and testified to their viability and changeability, but we did not yet face the proposition that both the units and their relations have lost their meaning and content, their authenticity; that while all of these units and relations exist and function, they are without foundation, presenting elaborate facades behind which uncommitted forces rage. We shall attempt to explore this aspect, to look behind the facade—if indeed it is a facade—in our epilogue (Ch. 21), after another complicating set of factors is introduced: External factors, the relations among societies, the international foundation of both alienation and transformation.

NOTES

1. Deutsch, *The Nerves of Government, op. cit.*, pp. 98–100 and *passim*; and his *Nationalism and Social Communication, op. cit.*, p. 96. Cf. Etzioni, *Political Unification, op. cit.*, pp. 43–44 and *passim*.

2. For a good discussion of these mechanisms at work, see Leon Lindberg, *The Political Dynamics of European Economic Integration* (Stanford, Calif.: Stanford University Press, 1963) esp. pp. 4–13 and pp. 60–63.

3. For a discussion of what is referred to here as political rigidity, see Almond and Powell, *Comparative Politics, op. cit.*, pp. 201–203.

4. Macmillan was quite successful; his government's reign, which lasted from 1957 until late 1964, was quite long but still his efforts did not suffice, in terms of reference used here.

5. For a definition of democracy as an orderly change of the party in office, see Joseph A. Schumpeter, *Capitalism, Socialism and Democracy* (New York: Harper & Row, 1950), p. 269. Seymour M. Lipset, "Some Social Requisites of Democracy: Economic Development and Political Legitimacy," *American Political Science Review*, Vol. 53 (1959), p. 71. Etzioni used it in his study of Israeli democracy, *Studies in Social Change, op. cit.*, pp. 157–197.

6. That the basis of democracy is a "selective system of competing elected minorities" was stated by Sartori, *Democratic Theory, op. cit.*, p. 126. See also Edward Pendleton Herring, *Politics of Democracy* (New York: Norton, 1940),

pp. 93, 313. On the other hand, the conception that democracy is the rule of the people or the majority is still held. See, for example, Francis W. Coker, *Recent Political Thought* (New York: Appleton-Century-Croft, 1934), p. 291; Robert K. Carr, Donald H. Morrison, Marver H. Bernstein, and Richard C. Snyder, *American Democracy in Theory and Practice* (New York: Holt, Rinehart & Winston, 1951) p. 24; and Dahl, *A Preface to Democratic Theory, op. cit.*, pp. 30, 128–132, and, *passim.*

7. To the degree the political alternatives (or parties) are limited to the representation of only a constricted sub-set of the societal variations and powers, the value of the democratic process as building responsiveness is much curtailed, and the process becomes inauthentic. For a discussion of this point, see Ch. 21, pp. 632–638.

8. See Gilles Perrault, *The Secret of D-Day* (Boston: Little, Brown, 1965), esp. pp. 166–167. The author shows that Hitler was provided by his officers with information slanted to suit his preconceptions, including his misconceptions.

9. Hence, it is not fully correct to state the representatives in a democracy represent an "image." "We talk frequently of a Representative or Senator 'representing' or 'failing to represent' his constituents. This is shorthand. The fact is the congressman represents his image of the district or of his constituents." Lewis A. Dexter, "The Representative and his District," in Theodore J. Lowi (ed.), *Legislative Politics U.S.A.* (Boston: Little, Brown, 1962), p. 159. If a Congressman allows his image to drift too far from the power realities of his district, forces will be activated to correct him. And if these are to no avail, there is an institutionalized, legitimate mechanism for removing him from office, thus giving reality to the image. (To the degree these mechanisms are not operative as in parts of the South of the United States of America, the political structure is of course not democratic.)

10. For details, see Etzioni, *Political Unification, op. cit.*, pp. 123–129.

11. Hence, the fact that the majority of the citizens of a society are not directly informed or active vis-à-vis the political center is not by itself a sign that they are politically excluded or passive. Cf. Miller and Stokes, "Constituency Influence in Congress," *op. cit.* and Campbell et. al., *The American Voter, op. cit.* For additional discussion of our position on this point, see *supra* Ch. 8, pp. 188–189. Almond and Verba present data which show that most active members of democracies are active in a local unit. *The Civic Culture, op. cit.*, pp. 79–100.

12. See David Thomson, *The Democratic Ideal in France and England* (Cambridge: The University Press, 1940), pp. 42–49; Richard Rose, *Politics in England* (Boston: Little, Brown, 1964), pp. 38–44. See also Samuel H. Beer, *Modern British Politics* (London: Faber & Faber, 1965), pp. 83 ff.

13. On the dates various extensions of votes granted in various European countries see Stein Rokkan, "Mass Suffrage, Secret Voting and Political Participation," *European Journal of Sociology*, Vol. 2 (1961), pp. 132–152. For United States see Chilton Williamson, *American Suffrage: From Property to Democracy, 1760–1860* (Princeton, N.J.: Princeton University Press, 1960). Lipset, "Some Social Requisites of Democracy: Economic Development and Political Legitimacy," *op. cit.*, pp. 69–105, esp. 93 f.

14. While these societies are more active than other ones, passive elements in their self-conduct have been pointed out. For instance, see especially Dankwart A. Rustow, *The Politics of Compromise: A Study of Parties and Cabinet Government*

in Sweden (Princeton, N.J.: Princeton University Press, 1955), esp. Ch. 3. See also Nils Andren, *Modern Swedish Government* (Stockholm: Almquist & Wiksell, 1961), esp. pp. 219–225. J. A. Lauwerys (ed.), *Scandinavian Democracy* (Copenhagen: Danish Institute et al., 1958), esp. Chs. 1 and 5; and Göran Tegner, *Social Security in Sweden* (Tiden: Swedish Institute, 1956). For another example, see Judah Matras, *Social Change in Israel* (Chicago: Aldine Publishers, 1965).

15. Usually the state and other forms of complex organization are jointly attacked, often under the generic term "bureaucracy." For a sociologist's review of the grand attack, see Nisbet, *Community and Power, op. cit.,* Chs. 5 and 6, and Wolin, *Politics and Vision, op. cit.,* esp. pp. 414–419.

16. Among the modern sociologies which glorified the state, none surpasses the efforts of Lorenz von Stein, in his long introduction to his three-volume *Geschichte der Sozialen Bewegung in Frankreich von 1789 bis auf unsere Tage,* edited by G. Salomon (Munich: Drei Masken Verlag, 1921). Stein saw the society as conflict-ridden and the state "the community of all individuals wills elevated to a personal union." Vol. I, p. 42 ff. Cf. Harold Laski, *The State in Theory and Practice* (New York: Viking, 1935).

17. We draw here on the Lorenz curve. For discussions of equality as a sociological concept see Bottomore, *Elites and Society, op. cit.,* pp. 122–143; R. H. Tawney, *Equality* (New York: Barnes & Noble, 1952), revised edition, esp. pp. 193–197. See also John Wilson, *Equality* (New York: Harcourt, Brace & World, 1966). The ethic dimensions of this problem are often discussed. For a representative sample as well as discussion of other works, see Nat Hentoff, *The New Equality* (New York: Viking Press, 1964). On the problems involved in operationalizing this concept, see "Measuring Inequality," Hayward R. Alker, Jr., *Mathematics and Politics* (Englewood Cliffs, N.J.: Prentice-Hall, 1965), pp. 29–53. See also J. Roland Pennock (ed.), *Equality: Nomox IX* (New York: Atherton, 1967).

18. Truman, *The Governmental Process, op. cit.,* p. 265.

19. The concept of needs is explored in some detail below, Ch. 21, pp. 619 ff.

20. For discussion and evidence, see Skinner, *Compliance and Leadership in Rural Communist China, op. cit.,* pp. 12 ff.; Franz Schurmann, *Ideology and Organization in Communist China* (Berkeley, Calif.: University of California Press, 1966), pp. 431–447, and Townsend, *Political Participation in Communist China, op. cit.,* pp. 207–209.

21. R. F. Hoxie, *Trade Unionism in the United States* (New York: Appleton-Century-Croft, 1923), 2nd ed., p. 166. See also Henry David, *The History of the Haymarket Affair* (New York: Farrar, Strauss & Giroux, 1936) and Bendix, *Work and Authority, op. cit.,* pp. 254–267.

22. Louis P. Lochner, *Tycoons and Tyrant: German Industry from Hitler to Adenauer* (Chicago: Regnery, 1954), pp. 2–5. Gerard Braunthal, *The Federation of German Industry in Politics* (Ithaca, N.Y.: Cornell University Press, 1965), pp. 18–22. See also Franz Neumann, *Behemoth* (New York: Octagon Books, 1963), pp. 202–210. For an empirical study in an industrial context, see W. Read, "Factors Affecting Upward Communication at Middle Management Levels in Industrial Organizations," Unpublished Ph.D. dissertation, University of Michigan, 1959.

23. On the failure of collectivization in Poland, see Stanley J. Zyzniewski, "Soviet Tutelage and the Polish Economy from 1945 to 1956," *The Polish Review,* Vol. IV (Summer, 1959), pp. 21–31, esp. pp. 28–29; Jan H. Wszelaki, "The Polish

Economy Since 1956," *ibid.*, pp. 32–47, esp. pp. 32–35; and Adam Bromke, "Poland's Rough Road to Socialism: Mr. Gomulka's Dilemma," *Queens Quarterly*, Vol. LXV (1958), pp. 615–30, esp. p. 619. See also Frank Gibney, *The Frozen Revolution: Poland, A Study in Communist Decay* (New York: Farrar, Strauss & Giroux, 1959).

24. Mark Gayn, "China Convulsed," *Foreign Affairs*, Vol. 45 (1967), pp. 246–259; Franz Schurmann, "What is Happening in China," *The New York Review of Books* (October 20, 1966), pp. 18–25; Joseph R. Levenson and Franz Schurmann, "An Exchange on China," *The New York Review of Books* (January 12, 1967), pp. 31–34; Roderick MacFarquhar, "Mao's Last Revolution," *Foreign Affairs*, Vol. 45 (1966), pp. 112–124; Harry Gelman, "Mao and the Permanent Purge," *Problems of Communism*, Vol. 15 (Nov.–Dec,, 1966), pp. 2–14; Ross Terrill, "The Seige Mentality," *Problems of Communism*, Vol. 16 (March–April, 1967), pp. 1–10; Yuri Ra'anan, "Rooting for Mao," *The New Leader*, Vol. 50 (March 13 1967), pp. 6–10; Roger Howard, " 'Red Guards are Always Right,' " *New Society*, No. 227 (February 2, 1967), pp. 169–170.

25. For one of the best discussions, see Juan J. Linz, "An Authoritarian Regime: Spain," in Erik Allardt and Yrjö Littunen (eds.), *Cleavages, Ideologies and Party Systems: Contributions to Comparative Political Sociology* (Helsinki: Transactions of the Westermarck Society, 1964), Vol. 10, pp. 291–341. See also Lewis A. Coser, "Prospects for the New Nations: Totalitarianism, Authoritarianism or Democracy?" *Dissent*, Vol. 10 (1963), pp. 43–58.

26. Alex Inkeles, "Social Stratification and Mobility in the Soviet Union: 1940–1950," *American Sociological Review*, Vol. 15 (1950), pp. 465–479; Merle Fainsod, *How Russia Is Ruled*, rev. ed. (Cambridge, Mass.: Harvard University Press, 1965), pp. 206–207; and Milovan Djilas, *The New Class: An Analysis of the Communist System* (New York: Praeger, 1960), esp. pp. 37–69. Albert Parry, *The New Class Divided* (New York: Macmillan, 1966), pp. 159–177.

27. Leonard B. Schapiro, *The Communist Party of the Soviet Union* (New York: Random House, 1960), pp. 322–324; see also pp. 312–313. On the relatively "achieved" and not ascribed nature of Communist party membership in the USSR and its broadening social composition, see T. H. Rigby, "Social Orientation of Recruitment and Distribution of Membership in the Communist Party of the Soviet Union," *American Slavic and East European Review*, Vol. 16 (1957), pp. 275–290. See also Fainsod, *How Russia is Ruled, op. cit.*, pp. 209–252.

28. Robert A. Feldmesser, "Social Classes and Political Structure," in Cyril E. Black (ed.), *The Transformation of Russian Society: Aspects of Social Change Since 1861* (Cambridge, Mass.: Harvard University Press, 1960), pp. 235–252, esp. pp. 248–252. He argues that differentiation exists but not classes.

29. Mussolini's Italy, Nasser's Egypt and Chiang Kai-Shek's Formosa have elements of a party–state that emerged out of a revolutionary movement. See Robert C. Tucker, "Towards a Comparative Politics of Movement-Regimes," *American Political Science Review*, Vol. 55 (1961), pp. 281–289; Peter Wiles, "Comment on Tucker's 'Movement-Regimes,' " *ibid.*, pp. 290–293.

30. According to at least one authoritative source, this was a key element in this uprising. Schurmann, "What is Happening in China," *op. cit.* For additional references to this and other viewpoints, see *supra*, footnote 24.

31. Almond and Verba go further than most studies to provide for measures of

both the amount of participation and the degree to which it is direct or indirect. See *The Civic Culture*, *op. cit.*, esp. pp. 105 ff.

32. See, for example, John M. Swomley, Jr., *The Military Establishment* (Boston: Beacon Press, 1964); C. Wright Mills, *The Power Elite* (New York: Oxford University Press, 1959), esp. pp. 274–278.

Among the popular presentations, see Fred J. Cook, *The Warfare State* (New York: Macmillan, 1962), esp. 162–201. For general related theoretical works, see Paul A. Baran and Paul M. Sweezy, *Monopoly Capital* (New York: Monthly Review Press, 1966); Paul A. Baran, *The Political Economy of Growth* (New York: Monthly Review Press, 1957). See also Victor Perlo, *The Vietnam Profiteers* (New York: New Outlook Publishers, 1966).

33. Samuel P. Huntington, "Interservice Competition and the Political Roles of the Armed Services," *American Political Science Review*, Vol. 55 (1961), pp. 40–52. See also his *The Soldier and the State* (Cambridge, Mass.: Harvard University Press, 1957). On "subjective" and "objective" civilian controls of the military, see pp. 189–192. On the limits of existing coordination see Paul Y. Hammond, "The National Security Council as a Device for Inter-Departmental Coordination," *American Political Science Review*, Vol. 54 (1960), pp. 899–910. The declining elitism of the United States military since World War II is documented by Morris Janowitz, *The Professional Soldier* (New York: Free Press, 1960), esp. pp. 54–75. See also Gene M. Lyons and John W. Masland on civilian influence on the education of military officers in the United States, *Education and Military Leadership* (Princeton, N.J.: Princeton University Press, 1959) and John W. Masland and Laurence I. Radway, *Soldiers and Scholars* (Princeton, N.J.: Princeton University Press, 1967).

34. See Sprecher, *World-wide Defense Expenditure* . . . , *op. cit.*, p. 7. Portugal ranks next in terms of percent of GNP invested in military efforts.

35. Vladimir I. Lenin, *Imperialism: The Highest State of Capitalism* (New York: International Publishers, 1933), esp. pp. 76–87.

36. Irving Louis Horowitz, "Noneconomic Factors in the Institutionalization of the Cold War," *Annals of the American Academy of Political and Social Science*, Vol. 351 (1964), pp. 110–120.

37. General Thomas S. Power, *Design for Survival* (New York: Coward-McCann, 1965), pp. 224–225.

38. Victor Perlo, *Militarism and Industry: Arms Profiteering in the Missile Age* (New York: International Publishers, 1963), pp. 21–22; 101. Victor Perlo, *The Vietnam Profiteers*, *op. cit.* The economic losses the war in Vietnam cost the U.S. are explored by Terence McCarthy, "The Garrison Economy," *The Columbia University Forum*, Vol. 9 (1966), pp. 27–32. See also Marc Pilisuk and Thomas Hayden, "Is There a Military Industrial Complex Which Prevents Peace?" *Journal of Social Issues*, Vol. 21 (1965), pp. 67–117; Merton J. Peck and Frederic M. Scherer, *The Weapons Acquisition Process* (Cambridge, Mass.: Harvard University, 1962); and Gene M. Lyons, "The Military Mind," *Bulletin of the Atomic Scientists*, Vol. 19 (November, 1963), pp. 19–22.

39. Kenneth E. Boulding and Emile Benoit (eds), *Disarmament and the Economy* (New York: Harper & Row, 1963), pp. 173–220.

40. According to this line of argument the United States avoided a deep depression only because of the Korean War and the rearmament which it entailed.

See, for instance, Organization for European Economic Cooperation, *Economic Conditions in Member and Associated Countries of the OEEC: Canada and the United States* (Paris: OEEC, 1954), p. 13. See also Thomas C. Schelling and Morton H. Halperin, "Arms Control Will Not Cut Defense Cost," Ernest W. Lefever (ed.), *Arms and Arms Control* (New York: Praeger, 1962), pp. 287–297.

41. For an overview as well as references to various studies, see Seymour M. Lipset, *The First New Nation: The United States in Historical and Comparative Perspective* (New York: Basic Books, 1963), pp. 321–340. For a discussion of Britain from this viewpoint, see Tawney, *Equality, op. cit.*, pp. 211–234. Victor R. Ruchs, "Redefining Poverty and Redistributing Income," *The Public Interest*, No. 8 (Summer, 1967), pp. 88–95.

42. Robert L. Heilbroner, "The Future of Capitalism," *Commentary*, Vol. 41 (April, 1966), p. 26.

43. For tables on eight countries, see "The Dispersion of Employment Incomes in Australia," *Economic Record*, Vol. 41 (December, 1965), pp. 558–561. See there also for references to other works. On Britain, see Tawney, *Equality, op. cit.*, pp. 211–215 (comparing 1958 to 1938). For Sweden, Göran Tegner is listed as assisting the editor, George R. Nelson, in *Freedom and Welfare: Social Patterns in the Northern Countries of Europe* (sponsored by the Ministries of Social Affairs of Denmark, Finland, Iceland, Norway, and Sweden, 1953), esp. p. 54. On Denmark, K. Lemberg, N. Ussing, and F. Zeuthen, "Redistribution of Income in Denmark," in Alan T. Peacock (ed.), *Income Redistribution and Social Policy* (London: Cape, 1954), p. 72.

The extent of reallocation one sees is affected by what one defines as a significant change. Studies which report significant increases in equality tend to focus on the proportion of wealth owned by the upper five per cent of the population. This group did "lose" significantly over the years. We prefer to ask to what degree did the total distribution move in the direction of a more equal pattern, as defined above. By this criteria, relatively little has been achieved. Note that by the first approach reallocation in favor of the upper middle class will register as a rise in equality even if no improvement has been made in the lot of the lower majorities.

Second, the level used as a basis for comparison is important. The inequality of modern societies seems much smaller than that of pre-modern ones, but little has been achieved in these societies since modernization was more or less completed. This is of special interest to us, as previous increases in equality were the "unguided" results of other processes, while more recent efforts—which have largely failed— have been deliberate attempts at reallocation.

44. Adolf A. Berle, Jr. and Gardiner C. Means, *The Modern Corporation and Private Property* (New York: Macmillan, 1933). See also Adolf A. Berle, Jr., "Concentrations of Private Power," in Edward Reed (ed.), *Challenges to Democracy: The Next 10 Years* (New York: Praeger, 1963), pp. 131–142; Robert Engler, *The Politics of Oil: A Study of Private Power and Democratic Directions* (New York: Macmillan, 1961).

45. Robert J. Larner, "Ownership and Control in the 200 Largest Nonfinancial Corporations, 1929 and 1963," *American Economic Review*, Vol. 56 (September, 1966), pp. 777–787.

46. Ernest Gruening, *The Public Pays—A Study of Power Propaganda* published a quarter of a century ago and republished, updated, three years ago, with an

addition to its original title —*And Still Pays*. Lee Metcalf and Vic Reinemer, *Overcharge: How Electric Utilities Exploit and Mislead the Public, and What You Can Do About It* (New York: McKay, 1967). Both authors were United States Senators when their books were written.

47. Frank Trippett, *The States: United They Fell* (Cleveland: The World Publishing Company, 1967). John C. Wahlke, William Buchanan, Heinz Eulau, and LeRoy C. Ferguson, "American State Legislators' Role Orientations toward Pressure Groups," *Journal of Politics*, Vol. 22 (1960), pp. 203–227. See also Rose on Texas, in his *The Power Structure, op. cit.*, pp. 359–381.

In a study of governments of nine American cities Edward C. Banfield showed that in all of them, organized business (and newspapers) have a great deal of political power, while minority groups and trade unions have very little. See his *Big City Politics* (New York: Random House, 1965).

48. See Allan Silver, "Military Repression and Political Reform: British Elite Perspectives Toward Parliamentary Reform and Catholic Emancipation (1828–1832)." Paper for the Working Group on Armed Forces and Society, Sixth World Congress of Sociology, Evian, September, 1966, and Moore, "England and the Contributions of Violence to Gradualism," in his *Social Origins . . . , op. cit.*, pp. 3–39. For a general discussion, see Chalmers A. Johnson, *Revolutionary Change* (Boston: Little, Brown, 1966).

49. Allan Nevins, *Grover Cleveland: A Study in Courage* (New York: Dodd, Mead & Company, 1944), p. 618. See also Hoxie, *Trade Unionism in the United States, op. cit.*, pp. 211–252.

50. *The New York Times*, August 3, 1965, p. 15. On the neutralization of U.S. city administration, see Lenski, *Power and Privilege, op. cit.*, p. 336.

51. David M. Potter sees "to level up" as an American orientation, in contrast to the European, radical approach which stresses reallocation. David Potter, *People of Plenty* (Chicago: University of Chicago Press, 1954), pp. 120–124.

52. See Trippett, *The States, op. cit.*, esp. pp. 3–4, and Banfield, *Big City Politics, op. cit.*, p. 13.

53. On the proposed Dirksen amendment, see T.R.B., "From Washington," *The New Republic*, Vol. 154 (April 30, 1966), p. 4. *Time*, April 29, 1966, p. 28.

54. See footnote 4, Ch. 17.

55. Jean E. Floud et al. (eds.), *Social Class and Educational Opportunity* (London: Heinemann, 1956). Four American studies are reviewed by Lenski, *Power and Privilege, op. cit.*, p. 408.

56. Torsten Husén (ed.), *The International Study of Achievement in Mathematics* (New York: Wiley & Sons, 1967).

57. $1120.0 billions in 1975 as compared to $662.7 in 1965 (in 1967 dollars). *A "Freedom Budget" For All Americans: A Summary* (New York: A. Philips Randolph Institute, 1967), p. 10; see also Leon H. Keyserling, "Guaranteed Annual Incomes," *The New Republic*, Vol. 156 (March 18, 1967), pp. 20–23.

58. The sociology of law has received recently a significant measure of revival but very little of it is devoted to the role of the law as an instrument of societal guidance. For a brief overview, see Philip Selznick, "The Sociology of Law," in Merton, Broom, and Cottrell, *Sociology Today, op. cit.*, pp. 115–127. See also William M. Evan (ed.), *Law and Sociology: Exploratory Essays* (New York: Free Press, 1962).

59. Lipset, *Political Man, op. cit.*, pp. 312 ff.

60. The Castro movement originated among university students and drew much of its initial support from relatively well-to-do middle- and upper-class people. Maurice Zeitlin, "The Cuban Revolution: An Attempt at Understanding its Causes, Course and Effects" (Ph.D. Dissertation, University of California, 1964), quoted by Lipset in Allardt and Littunen, *Cleavages, Ideologies and Party Systems, op. cit.*, p. 48. Later, of course, it gained a peasant and worker following. Talking about Protestant churches in the United States which have membership in both lower- and middle-classes, Liston Pope reports "even where the membership cuts across class lines, control of the church and its policies is generally in the hands of officials drawn from one class, usually the middle class." *Annals of the American Adademy of Political and Social Science*, Vol. 256 (1948), p. 89. H. Hyndman states the law of outside priming in somewhat excessively strong terms: "A slave class cannot be freed by the slaves themselves. The leadership, the initiative, the teaching, the organization, must come from those who are born into a different position and are trained to use their faculties in early life." Tuchman, *Proud Tower, op. cit.*, p. 360. Being an affluent graduate of Eton and Trinity College, Cambridge, as well as a leader of the Socialist Democratic Federation at the turn of the century in Britain, and surrounded by many of his kind, might explain his disposition. But it would hold for other movements too, from Moses—who had grown up in the House of Pharaoh before he led the Jews to freedom—to Central Europe, middle-class, initially assimilated Theodore Herzl, who was a leader for the lower-class, East European Jews. Of the outstanding figures of the Second International, only August Bebel and Keir Hardie were of working-class origin. Just a generation earlier, the middle-class political priming in Britain was still highly concentrated in aristocratic hands (*ibid.*, pp. 243–244) as it was in Germany at this stage.

61. See George Woodcock, *Anarchism* (Cleveland: Meridian Books, 1962), pp. 18–19 and James Joll, *The Anarchists* (Boston: Little, Brown, 1965), pp. 108–110.

62. *Ibid.*, pp. 193–192, 212–223. See also Jean Maitron, *Histoire du Mouvement Anarchiste en France, 1880–1914* (Paris: Société Universitaire, 1951).

63. Nathan Glazer, *The Social Basis of American Communism* (New York: Harcourt, Brace & World, 1961), pp. 169–180.

64. See the discussion of semi-deviation and second-best alternatives *supra* pp. 378–379.

65. *The New York Times*, February 16, 1966, p. 1; February 17, 1966, p. 67. For James Reston's comment on the resignation see February 18, 1966, p. 32. For Friendly's own account of the event and the criticism which he offers see his *Due to Circumstances Beyond our Control* (New York: Random House, 1967).

66. The late C. Wright Mills used to complain, only half in jest, that he could get Fulbright fellowships to study in Copenhagen but not in Paris.

Mr. E. Mazarak, a school teacher in Indiana was dismissed because he had gone to New York on his own time in order to participate in a demonstration against the war in Vietnam. He said: "You know, I really believe this will all turn out for the good," adding that he thought he could get a better paying job as a teacher elsewhere. *The New York Times*, June 4, 1967.

PART FIVE

BEYOND

TRIBALISM

TRIBAL SYSTEMS VERSUS *COMMUNITIES*

For a societal unit to be fully active, it must be able to transform not only its internal structure but also its external boundaries. This hold for villages or tribes in a modernizing society as much as it does for modernized societies late in the twentieth century. One major reason that the transformation of boundaries must occur is that many of the bases of unresponsiveness lie outside the boundaries of one societal unit, and if a societal unit's internal structure is to be made more responsive, external factors, especially those regarding its relations to external elites, must be transformed. A second basic reason is that the existing societal units are less encompassing than the processes which they need to guide if their values are to gain primacy over the instrumental orientations of processes such as economic exchange and technological development.

The modern, industrial technology was alienating in that it promoted an instrumental orientation. The post-modern technology adds new tools of mass manipulation and, above all, of warfare. The former tools magnify the inauthentic elements of societal being; the latter threaten its very existence. It is to overcome the unresponsiveness of the latter technology, to prevent war, that the central transformation this age requires is from a "tribalistic" international system to one of a community. A degree of intra-unit and supra-unit structural transformation will be needed before, will accompany, and will result from the reduction of the significance of the units of the international system, the post-modern tribes, and from the building up of the saliency of an international community. Internal structures and external boundaries are interlocked; one cannot be changed (and certainly not transformed) without also changing the other. Whether or not such a transformation will occur is an open question. In this part, we explore the conditions under which it may be advanced, and we hold that no society will be fully active unless it shares in such a transformation.

While the alienation resulting from the technologies of warfare appears in its most extreme form in the relations among nations armed with thermonuclear weapons, it is present in more limited forms in the relations between any two nations that may engage in large-scale war with each other and among subsocieties that are not sufficiently integrated to prevent civil wars. The latter is a widespread danger: There are more societies that do not constitute security communities themselves than those which are sufficiently integrated to preclude massive civil wars. And most of the societies which are now considered well-established communities have had a civil war in the past. Thus, the reduction of tribalism (or community-building) is a major macro-sociological subject.

By "tribal systems" we refer to those in which the units are stronger than the system; in "communities," the system is stronger than the units. More formally, *in a tribal system*, the acting units are more internally integrated than they are related to each other or bound into a supra-unit; in a *community*, the supra-unit relations which bind the units and regulate their relations to each other are more powerful than the intra- or inter-unit bonds. Typical international systems are tribal and have often been thus characterized;[1]* intra-society systems are either tribal or communal. When a system is in transition from a tribal to a communal one, the process is referred to as community-building. (Unification is a more generic term which refers to the processes which lead to an increase in the level of integration, whether it reaches the community level or stops short of this.)

This pair of concepts evokes appropriate connotations in that particular tribes do not have a central organization or supra-tribal bonds that are sufficiently strong to prevent wars among them, while these factors are present in a community. Tribalism connotes a primitive, savage world; community—a more civilized one. There are, of course, communities in the preliterate world (among the members of one tribe) and tribal systems in the modern world. In both situations, domestic relations are much more civilized than those with foreigners; while the modern communities are much more encompassing than the preliterate ones, so are the modern wars.

Sociological generalizations are often advanced as if they apply to any system; actually, they are often formulated with regard to communities and do not hold for tribal systems. One example will suffice: A rise in the assets, level of mobilization, and power of a collectivity within a well-integrated society will tend to lead to changes either within or of the society's structure. If the collectivity's new political demands are disregarded for a prolonged period, it is commonplace to observe that it will tend to work toward a revolutionary transformation. *But this, we suggest, holds only for communities; when such a collectivity is a member of a tribal system, we expect that it will tend to leave the system under these circumstances rather than attempt to remold the system's political organization or societal structure.* Secession and not revolution is the typical reaction.[2] Our discussion in Part IV dealt with action within communities. Part V deals with macro-action in tribal systems, especially with that leading to their transformation into communities where massive armed conflict is no longer practical.†

---

* Reference notes for this introduction appear on page 552.

† Two closely related subjects not explored here, both of which concern systems in which the levels of integration are higher than is required for the prevention of massive armed conflict within the community, are those of the containment of interpersonal violence and non-armed conflicts of a "harsh" or costly nature. The rates of some kinds of crime might be affected by the level of community integration, though the association may well not be as direct as is often expected, as the substance of the norms enforced is more important than the level of integration, which only indicates the effectiveness of enforcement. Where the norms substantively favor violence—e.g., when they call for bloody revenge when honor is thought to be violated, or a violent act is a mark of manhood— high integration would tend to produce a high rate of interpersonal violence.

Second, even where armed conflicts and interpersonal violence are avoided or prevented, non-violent conflicts might be weighed in terms of their societal costs—for instance, the frequency with which labor–management conflicts are settled normatively (say, by bargaining) as against those dealt with by utilitarian pressures (strikes, lockouts). We expect, though, that the higher the level of integration, the less "harsh" will be the conflicts—i.e.,

Our argument will proceed as follows: First, in Chapter 19 we assess critically the arguments that international interdependence is growing and leading to a world community. But the deflation of these arguments does not lead to the acceptance of the widely-held position that the main actors on the world's stage are nation–states; rather, we must recognize the importance of international power relations, in which scores of countries are linked by one controlling overlayer effected by elite-countries to form quasi-empires. These quasi-empires, as we shall see, are internally unstable and may war against each other; the question is, under what conditions may a more stable *and* world-wide war prevention system arise; these are the subjects of Chapter 20.

In much of the preceding discussion, we viewed collectivities as the units and societies as the supra-units. In this part, we "raise" the frame of reference to deal with societies as units and to explore their relations to each other (i.e., inter-unit bonds), and to study whatever supra-units have evolved above societies.* Chapter 19 deals largely with international flows and relations; i.e., the nation is the unit of analysis. The first section of Chapter 20 focuses on the relations of supra-units to units—that is, on the relations of supra-national elites to nation–states. The last section of Chapter 20 discusses changes in the supra-national system itself.

NOTES

1. Chadwick F. Alger, "Comparison of Intranational and International Politics," *American Political Science Review*, Vol. 57 (1963), p. 415. See also Ralph W. Nicholas, "Segmentary Factional Political Systems," in Marc J. Swartz, Victor W. Turner, Arthur Tuden (eds.), *Political Anthropology* (Chicago: Aldine Publishing Co., 1966), pp. 49–59; John Middleton and David Tait (eds.), *Tribes without Rulers: Studies in African Segmentary Systems* (London: Routledge & Kegan Paul, 1958).

2. Some evidence to this effect is presented in our comparative study of four international systems, Etzioni, *Political Unification, op. cit.* Two of them were responsive; two, which were not, suffered secessions rather than revolutions. In one case, even the more powerful member units preferred to secede rather than to try to change the system's structure.

---

the more likely they are to be normative and lower in societal costs. Neither kind of conflict is necessarily dysfunctional; a very high level of integration is likely to involve the suppression of conflict to such a degree that change will become overdue. Thus, by no means is elimination or limitation of all conflict desirable, even from the viewpoint of stability. We confine the textual discussion here to much lower levels of integration, to those which are required for preventing extensive armed conflict.

* Most of the propositions advanced here apply also to relations between collectivities and societies, as when community-building is a national rather than a supra-national process, but this application is not explored here.

CHAPTER 19

The Unifying Effects
of Rising Interdependence

T O INCREASE a society's capacity to affect its boundaries, it is not necessary to increase its power vis-à-vis other societies or more encompassing societies. Rather, such an increase often entails the development of the society's capacity to move toward those options which other actors also favor, to work out joint projects, and to share actively in the growth of more encompassing communities. After a brief discussion of matters of definition, we focus on the question of the conditions which lead to the evolution of new, cohesive supra-units whose member units are societies. The issue is not whether and the ways in which *any* kind of supra-unit may evolve, but rather the development of supra-units whose structures and actions are responsive to their membership.

Political Communities

Community Defined

A societal unit is a *community* when it has autarkic integrative mechanisms —that is, when the maintenance of its boundaries, inner structure, and political organization are provided for by its own processes and are not dependent upon external units, supra-units, or sub-units. The communities we deal with here are political and not culturally, religiously, or otherwise circumscribed in scope. A *political community* is a community which has three kinds of autarkic integrative processes: It has sufficient coercive power to countervail the coercive power of any member unit or coalition of them; it has a decision-making center that is able to affect significantly the allocation of assets throughout the community; and it is the dominant focus of political loyalty for the large majority of politically active citizens. A political community is, thus, a state, an administrative-economic unit, and a focal point of loyalty.

The control of the means of violence distinguishes a political community from other communities. This control protects the community from the arbitrary interference of member-units, makes the community the ultimate arbitrator among the members, serves to counter secessionist pressures, and makes the political community the focus of the defense against external units.

The ability to affect the allocation of assets is necessary for the financing of the activities of the community, especially its coercive organization (police, armed forces, other security agencies) and its administrative machinery. This capacity is also needed for the peaceful adjustment of the distribution of assets throughout the community in accord with the changing power relations among the member-units (e.g., classes). Finally, it serves to focus the attention of the publics and of interest groups on the community rather than on the sub- or supra-units; this encourages the formation of community-wide, horizontal cleavages that cut across the vertical, member-units, thus countervailing centrifugal forces.

Dominant political loyalty to the community serves to prevent a separation, and, hence, a potential conflict between the unit of coercion and administration on the one hand and the unit of political loyalties on the other. Nation–states meet this requirement of a political community, while empires —especially after the rise of nationalism—seemingly do not.[1]*

Loyalty to the community is necessary, we suggest, only in political matters. A more intensive identification in other matters (such as religious ones) with societal entities that are less or more encompassing than the

---

* Reference notes for this chapter appear on page 576.

community is quite possible without weakening the community's integration, unless, of course, these non-political identifications have or develop political corollaries. This proposition is in opposition to the widely held proposition that a general sharing of ultimate values (not only political ones) is necessary for a high level of societal integration. Actually, significant differences in religious and other "ultimate" values and identifications are found in societies which are otherwise considered highly integrated. Such diversity can coexist with community-level integration so long as the various religious (or other) foci of identification of most of the citizens are a-political or are compatible with the dominant political orientation. Even in political matters, commitment to a sub-community or to a member collectivity is not dysfunctional so long as loyalty to the community is dominant—that is, in a case of a conflict of loyalties, loyalty to the community is more powerful than loyalty to a sub-unit.

We emphasize again, in accord with the theory advanced in previous chapters, that the societal realm has three elements and that societal units are compositions of these and are not merely psychological or symbolic states; a "sense of community" and a community are not the same phenomenon. Full-fledged communities are held together not only by a set of shared symbols, values, and sentiments but also by utilitarian and coercive bonds. This threefold nature of the integrative bonds affects the dynamics of communities in two ways: if a member unit seeks to secede, it will face not only symbolic obstacles, but also the armed and economic sanctions of the supra-unit and of the other member units; and if the three kinds of bonds of a community are not coextensive, the pressures which these "discrepancies" generate will help to explain the community's action, inaction, and change of boundaries.

An Integration Continuum

The level of political integration is the main characteristic that distinguishes political communities from other political systems. While the member-units of a system are, by definition, interdependent, its level of integration—on each of the three dimensions specified above—can be high or low.[2]

Few communities are fully integrated, but the levels of integration of several established nation–states, such as Britain and Sweden, approximate quite closely the level required by the *community* model. If a system is less integrated but its members are able to act in unison on a wide range of matters, we refer to it not as a community but as a *union* (of cities, of nations, etc.). If the level of integration is still lower, the units are merely members of a system. Systems that are less than fully integrated may be less integrated in terms of each of the three variables or lower on some but higher on others. The "imbalance" which interests us here is that of systems whose coercive base is more integrated than their utilitarian base, and whose utilitarian base is more integrated than their political loyalties. Such an imbalance characterizes *empires*, while the opposite profile approximates that found in *commonwealths*.

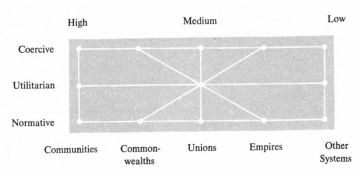

INTEGRATION CONTINUUM

Is World Integration Increasing?

The Unification Propositions

It has often been argued that the post-modern global tribal system is moving toward higher levels of integration; the world of nation–states is obsolescent and is being superseded. Others have countered that the nation-state is not declining; on the contrary, nationalism shows a new momentum, both as the disintegrator of empires and as the force which shapes the relations of new nations to each other and to their member units. It is as important in the Communist parts of the world as it is in the Western ones; it helped to transform monocentric blocs into poli-centric ones, if not to split them outright.

Many of the arguments advanced to support the first proposition—that the nation–state system is obsolescent—are phrased in dichotomous, imprecise, and a-sociological terms. The dichotomous approach can be seen in the controversy about whether or not the nation–state system is being superseded. Actually, the integration of the world as one system could increase, but the world would still constitute a tribal system; increases in world integration (until it reaches a high level) do not make nation–states obsolescent. Considerable *additional* increases in the level of integration might occur, but this additional integration, while it might be made somewhat more *likely* by whatever increases in the level of integration have taken and are taking place, is not automatically set into motion by them. So far as the nation-state is concerned, first, the sum of the new extra-national elements is still rather limited, and, in tests of power between these elements and nationalism and international organizations, most of the time the nation-state prevails. Second, the nation–state is not likely to disintegrate but rather to be transformed as additional layers of inter- and supra-national integration are imposed on top of the tribal system of nation–states. Transformation often takes this form of adding new elements to existing ones rather than closing one shop to open another.

Imprecision enters when future developments are confused with the presently available means, and the means available to super-powers are confused with those available to most other nations. Thus, much has been made of the modern means of communication—e.g., a world linked by one set of television satellites beaming the same programs to everyone.[3] But no such arrangement is yet available. To introduce it, not only are post-modern satellites needed, but also television sets will have to be distributed to people in countries where few of them can be found. While this, theoretically at least, can be accomplished relatively rapidly by a donor country, large local maintenance crews will have to be trained and spare parts be provided. Even if these were to become available, the peoples of the various nations will still have to learn to be able to absorb, in terms of their languages and cultures, the broadcasts. Similarly, much has been made of the decline of the significance of distance and territory as security factors in the age of long-range projectiles. The primacy of the nation–state, it is suggested, is based on its capacity to protect itself inside a shell from outside aggression, and this shell has been cracked by the jet bomber and the intercontinental missile.[4] But so far, very few nations have such long-range weapons, and those which have them have found them ineffective for most political purposes. It is small wonder that the missiles did not have the expected integrating effect. It is not that the argument is faulty, but that the missiles have not—or have not yet—cracked the national security shell of most nations. All this may well occur, but not in a few years as has often been implied, *and* one cannot expect to see in this decade the integrating effects of a trans-national system that may be introduced in the next.

Moreover, much of the increase in international flows—trade, tourism, communications—is concentrated in a few countries, mainly the "have" ones. The world is not shrinking; it is rather that the elite-countries are in more contact with each other and in relatively less contact with the "have-not" countries.*

---

* Between 1950 and 1963, receipts from international tourism more than tripled, to over \$9 billion. Most of the travel, though, was concentrated in twelve countries, which spent 82 per cent of the total and received 65 per cent. Only "have" countries, Western Europe and the United States, are included. (Figures are of the International Union of Official Travel Organizations, and were reported in *The New York Times*, July 9, 1966. See also *ibid.*, January 16, 1967.) For statistics and a discussion of other flows, see Robert C. Angell, "The Growth of Transnational Participation," *Journal of Social Issues*, Vol. 23 (1967), pp. 108–129. The November 1966 issue of *The Annals of the American Academy of Political and Social Science* is devoted to "Americans Abroad."

Still other arguments are a-sociological in that they assume that those sectors which are "integrating" have secondary-priming effects that they actually do not have. The logic, explicit or implicit, is as follows: The unification of one sector of several societies will initiate the unification of other sectors of these societies leading toward a community level of integration. That is, a change in the *inter*-societal boundary relations of one (or a few) societal sectors will affect—via their *intra*-societal bonds—the *inter*-societal relations of additional sectors.

While the concept of secondary-priming is of much value, and while some such secondary-priming of integration does occur, it is much less common than was expected by those who hoped for the development of regional if not world community from it. While there is practically no societal sector which has not been nominated as a major primer and as a take-off base for encompassing unification, an increase in international trade is one of the most often mentioned sectors. It seems, though, under most conditions, that increased international trade does not generate very much unification and certainly does not lead to the formation of new political communities. Countries which traded with each other *considerably* have not been prevented from warring—Germany and Britain, for instance, on the eve of World Wars I and II. In not so distant days, nations continued to trade *while* they were warring. The same, as we shall see, holds for most societal sectors. The sectors which do have a secondary-priming effect and the extent to which they have this effect, remain subjects for the future study of unification.

While similarly exaggerated, imprecise, and often a-sociological in its formulation, the "one-world" proposition is not without merit; it indicates the direction of a general trend or at least a rising option. Moreover, an examination of the reasons that the various unification developments and drives did not yield the expected results helps to specify some of the conditions under which unification may occur and can be advanced. We first explore international flows; then we deal with supranational activities, leading to the seemingly most promising approach to the subject—the development of inter- and supranational guidance mechanisms. As many international flows, activities, and guidance mechanisms develop in part unwittingly and in part as the consequences of deliberate efforts, the following discussion is both a comparative exploration of various international developments and an assessment of the merits of various community-building strategies.

International Flows

International flows include inter-nation exchanges of objects (international trade), symbols (via the mass media), and persons (tourism, cultural exchanges). The proposition that increases in such exchanges will have supranational unifying effects rests on a three-step notion: (a) that increased flows will change citizens' attitudes about each other's nations in the direction of more positive orientations; (b) that these changed attitudes and orientations are related to political attitudes and political behavior, especially political loyalties and voting; and (c) that changes in political loyalties and voting will lead to an increase in the level of supranational integration, especially in regard to the formation of political communities. While these three steps are specified in few studies, they are implicit in most of them.

Each of the steps raises some questions. The first step—that higher interaction "improves" the orientations of citizenries toward each other—has been advanced by Park, Homans, and Lerner.[5] A question should be raised, however, concerning whether or not such increased contact can be expected to have the same effects on two actors irregardless of their characteristics and relations prior to the increased contact. The evidence seems unclear on this point.[6] We would expect increased contact between actors to have a greater integrating effect on their relations the more similar they were in interests, values, and cognitive perspectives and the more integrated their relations were at the outset. Increased communication can make the actors aware of a latent congruence which they can use to build up consensus, procedures for limiting conflicts, and integration. But when the values, perspectives, and interests of the parties are incompatible, increased communication, we expect, will make them more conscious of that which separates them and will increase tensions and conflicts and, quite likely, decrease the level of integration. Increased communication may well *solidify* favorable relations, but it is doubtful that it can *produce* them.

Turning to the second step, even when, following increased interaction, attitudes change and other nations come to be viewed in a more favorable light, this, we suggest, will tend to have little effect on the political attitudes and actions of those involved so long as these changes have been in nonpolitical images (e.g., in cultural or aesthetic ones, which is often the case), because these tend to be greatly dissociated from political images. Germany, in 1870, 1914, and 1939, was not without knowledge of French culture and vice versa. As the Sino-Soviet conflict advanced in the early 1960s and became more visible, the American publics seem to have become more hostile toward China and less so toward the Soviet Union, but there is no reason to believe that Americans became less aware of the cultural traditions of China. Tourism, under most conditions in which no primary contact occurs between the tourist and the native populations, we expect, reinforces mutual stereotypes rather than leading to their change.[7] And whatever new insight is acquired is not likely to be political.

Also, the relative weight of national as opposed to international exposures tends to be ignored. For every citizen who travels abroad, there are many more who stay at home. And of those who travel, for every interaction with foreigners, there are many more interactions with fellow countrymen during their travels and especially after their returns home. So far as the mass media are concerned, for every exposure to international communications, there are many hundreds of exposures to national ones.

It might be said that we are measuring *changes* in exposure—i.e., that when we add to national transactions some international ones, the relative weight of the international transactions increases. However, the facts seem to present a quite different picture. Frequently, in the same period in which international elements are added, the intranational contacts and exposures also increase and to a greater extent. For instance, as international trade increased, intranational trade seems to have increased even more.[8] Intranational communication networks in general, and in developing nations in particular, seem to grow much more rapidly than international ones.[9]

Moreover, the ratio of international to national exchanges is so low for most citizens[10] that the absorption of international interaction can easily be shaped by national processes.* The ratio of international transactions and interactions to national ones would have to be much higher before the international transactions and interactions could be expected to have any but marginal effects.

When this ratio is substantially higher and the increased international flows affect large segments of a nation, as among the citizens of West European countries, this seems to be far more the result than the cause of greater affinity between the nations, and due in large part to the fact that the international exposures do not contradict the national ones. Under these circumstances, increased international contacts are to be expected to reinforce ongoing unification processes. Under most international circumstances, however, interaction among peoples of different nations seems to be far lower than the level required for it to have even these secondary unifying effects.

Turning to the third step—the effect of changes in the political attitudes of citizens on the relationships among their nations—two major mechanisms are implied. One is that direct contact among the citizenries will advance a world community *despite* their governing elites. Numerous anarchist, socialist, and federalist writers have held that the peoples of various nations increasingly favor a world community but that the political elites are obstacles to such a community, and that eventually the peoples will form a world community (via general strikes, revolutions, or the shifting of their allegiances to the United Nations) despite their governments.[11] Actually, there is little evidence that most citizens in most nations are more favorably disposed toward a world community than their respective governments. Nor has it been

---

* The meaning of the messages sent through the formal (mass) media is greatly affected (and, especially, their contexts are provided) by informal processes. As most of the international flows are via the formal (mass) media while their informal context is national, we would expect that conforming and not transforming messages are received and that the interpretation of international "bits" will be chiefly national.

demonstrated that the "people" could form a world community without first increasing the responsiveness of their respective societies and polities.

There is more validity in the notion of an indirect effect—i.e., that changes in the political attitudes of citizens will affect the actions of their elites. But changes in citizens' attitudes should not be viewed as autonomous changes to which their governments must adjust; there is an interplay between citizens and their governments in which, in many matters and especially those concerned with foreign policy, the governments play a key role.[12] Not only can a government impose a tribalistic policy even though its citizens are more favorably oriented toward a community-building policy, but the government can foster a tribalistic view on the part of its citizens.

Some observers, possibly reacting to the naive estimates of the power of such international contacts, have fallen into the opposite trap of under-estimating the role of such contacts and their attitudinal impact. While citizens have little influence on or even information about many specific foreign policy decisions, in democracies they do seem to have some—and possibly a growing—concern with foreign policy decisions, including their country's orientation toward a regional and a world community. Specifically, there seems to be a trend in which an increasing number of voters list foreign policy matters as first among those that determine their vote, even in non-war years.[13] The spread of education, while not automatically expanding the boundaries of the community of interest and commitment, seems to have had a net effect in that direction; that is, more educated people tend to have broader horizons.[14] We, hence, expect that as societies move deeper into the post-modern age, more of their citizens will be concerned with the foreign policies of their governments than in the modern age. At the same time, as foreign policy becomes more complex and technical, the effect of the citizens is likely to be, even more than was the case previously, contextuating rather than prescriptive; that is, their effect is expected to be one of setting limits on the policies that can be followed without high political costs and risks, leaving the elites a fairly free choice of options within these limits. So far, these contexts have often worked against community-building (inasmuch as they were nationalistic); once the opposite context is evolved or established—that is, a context favorable to community-building (probably first on a regional level)—the effect of the citizenry will be reversed. In general, how-ever, the main bases of international community-building seem not to be the expanding exchanges among the citizens of various nations.

Supranational Activities

A second set of theorems deals with the effects on the level of integration of supranational activities, such as a shared defense line or a joint research project. Unlike exchanges, which are *inter*-unit activities, these create a shared *supra*-unit sector, composed mainly of activities carried out through the medium of international organizations. The theoretical position that participation in some shared activities will lead to broader unification leading gradually toward a community level is often referred to as "functionalist."[15] The term is not used in the sociological or mathematical senses, but rather to refer to one or a few kinds of activities carried out by international organizations. Traditional writings on functionalism refer to functions such as postal services, public health, or labor relations. As a rule, the international organization assumes only a small fraction of the activities involved in servicing a particular function; e.g., few of the postal services are international. Second, as the activities which are unified by these organizations are highly segregated, the supranationalization involved has almost no secondary-priming effects. Most important, the foci of national governmental and political processes are not deflected from the national centers, as the internationalized function requires little control-integration and mobilization of consensus since it usually entails an increase in the volume of supranational activities while the centers of control of the activity remain national. The international organizations tend to have no decision-making power; they are controlled by inter-governmental bodies and have almost exclusively advisory and administrative capacities.

More recently, a new functionalist approach has developed which sees take-off bases for unification in new supranational activities, mainly military or economic ones.[16] The old and new versions of functionalism should not be confused; the fact that the unification of some military or economic sectors has a secondary-priming effect cannot be used to argue, by extension, that the functional approach in general is valid, and that, hence, supra-nationalization of almost any activity seriously enhances community-building. The differentiating criterion is the degree to which the specific activity involved is linked to other societal activities. Services (e.g., postal, public health), we suggest, are particularly segregated, and, hence, their supranational integration can be expected to have only little secondary-priming effect. Military services, under most circumstances, have more effect, for instance on defense industries, but military services can be unified to a considerable degree with little subsequent unification of other sectors occurring. Very little community-building occurred between Britain and the United States in World War II or among the NATO countries since 1951. More unification can be expected to result from economic integration, because economic processes affect all societal groupings and are closely related to other societal activities. Legal "unifications" have had, by themselves, only minimal impact; a far-reaching codification of the laws of Sweden, Denmark, and Norway generated little community-building in Scandinavia.[17] On the other hand, if the national political structures and organizations are merged (including those of consensus-formation), and if the major symbols of political loyalty (e.g., the flags, the heads of state) and the political units (interest groups, parties) become supranational, then a considerable amount of integration has already been achieved and much more is to be expected. The political processes have link-ups with all the major sectors and, hence, maximum secondary-priming and community-building effects.

International Control

Bonds among nations develop on two levels—action and control. Increases in international flows and supranational activities are bonds of action. We expect that they will tend to have few community-building effects (unless they are in those few sectors which are closely linked to others, or they trigger or entail the rise of international controls). The second route to community-level unification begins on the control level (as the preceding discussion of the political sector suggests). The unification of action is expected to follow more readily this unification of control than that of control to follow the unification of action.

The role that an increase in international flows can play in building international controls may be illustrated by noting the effects of increased international trade. Sheer increases in volume are not expected to have much unifying effect, but when the volume increases to the level at which the inter-governmental regulation of the process becomes cumbersome, pressure to introduce supranational controls increases,* and unification of the con-trolling overlayers may then be initiated. This is of central importance, since a supra-unit controlling overlayer is necessary *before* economic integration can advance to the community level. Thus, for instance, if X nations surrender part of their control of their economies by removing national tariff barriers, quotas, and export–import licenses (assuming that their remaining controls do not suffice for the nationalist regulation of the economies),[18] then supranational control will be needed. (We expect that if such control does not emerge, additional trade unification will be avoided and/or new nationalist controls imposed.) Once this is effected, the refocusing of interest groups toward this new center of control, the building up of legitimation symbols around it, etc., will lead to additional unification. Also, the well-established tendency of new centers of control—e.g., the Executive Authority of the EEC—to seek to expand their power works in this direction. While unification is by no means automatic under these circum-stances, the pressures toward it are greater than when only an activity is integrated or exchanges increase without changes in national controls.[19]

In the case of the kinds of international exchanges and supranational activities that usually have little community-building effect, when their

---

* We expect supra-unit decision-making and implementation to be more efficient than inter-unit ones. This is by no means an uncontested proposition. For arguments on the inter-unit side see Lindblom, *The Intelligence of Democracy, op. cit.*; on the supra-unit side, above Chapter 14, pp. 285–298. See also the next section.

volume is so high that they necessitate encompassing changes in the ratio of unit to supra-unit controls, they, too, have a unifying effect. Thus, international exchanges and decisions concerning shared activities are like fluids in a pipe; up to a given level, increased flow can be carried by the old pipes and has little effect. If, however, the volume increases further, broader pipes must be introduced, i.e., more supra-unit controls and unification are required.

Is Supranational Guidance Necessary?

Supra- versus International Guidance

The level and kind of integration and organization that are necessary depend on the societal goals the actors seek to realize individually and collectively. For instance, the economic welfare of the members of an international system can be advanced to a degree without a significant increase in integration beyond that which the activity itself entails by relying on international exchanges and controls. The prevention of large-scale war is the goal for which the following control models are explored. Two questions need to be answered: (a) What kind of controlling overlayer is needed? Must it be supranational, or can it be of the more easily developed international kind? (b) To stabilize a controlling overlayer, to construct a guidance mechanism, community support is needed—but must such a community and its consensus-formation structure be coextensive with the controlling overlayer, or could national communities support an effective world organization? We will now discuss these questions.

While there are many specific control models, they can be reduced to two major kinds. One has a supra-unit controlling overlayer, a system overlayer which has control capacities superior to those of the member units; the other draws on inter-unit controls rather than on supra-unit organization. While there are various mixtures of the two models of control, the discriminating factor is that of superiority as assessed in cases of a "showdown" between the supra-unit's center (if there is one) and the plurality of inter-unit controls. We shall treat as supranational those overlayers whose supranational control elements prevail in cases of conflict even though they may contain varying degrees of international control elements. We will view as international those overlayers in which there is no supranational organization or it is weak and surrenders in a "showdown." Among the mixed overlayers that are predominantly supra-unit controls are the political organizations of federations, such as the contemporary United States and West Germany; among those that are international despite some supranational elements is NATO. The United Nations is almost exclusively inter- and not supranational. The classification is based on actual control organizations and not on formal, legal arrangements. For instance, the fact that the United Arab Republic was formally a unitary state while the United States was a federation does not suggest that the United States' polity was less "supra"; indeed, a comparison of the respective polities suggests the opposite.

Our main arguments in support of the proposition that supranational controls are necessary for the prevention of a major war are based on the preceding discussion: Inter-unit controls leave the ultimate decision in the hands of the actors and, therefore, leave the option of war open; supra-unit controls foreclose this option. The controlling overlayers of inter-units can carry a limited volume of decisions and, hence, can control only a limited amount of supranational activities and international flows. If unification is to be advanced, a higher volume seems necessary. Last but not least, to build a community, a center of coercion, reallocation, and identification is needed, which requires supranational control. The community, in turn, is needed for the stabilization of controls able to regulate nation–states by providing consensus-formation.

Turning to our second question, we hold that no regional or world state can be stabilized without community support. While political organization and community-building need not develop in full synchronization, if a supranational state is imposed on a tribalistic, inter-society base and the gap is not narrowed, we expect that the political organization (the state) will not withstand the strain and will collapse. *For a supranational controlling overlayer to function effectively, it requires the support of a supranational community. Arrangements based on international control can function in a tribalistic societal context.* (Were international control imposed on a community—which is rare—it would lead to strain and, similarly, be followed by either deunification or collapse.)

The reasons we support these propositions are twofold: (a) empirically, many states without community underpinnings have, sooner or later, collapsed (e.g., the United Arab Republic, the Federation of the West Indies); and (b) theoretically, the enforcement of disarmament laws requires that the world government have a police force superior to that of any member unit or coalition of them so that it can control deviants if other mechanisms fail. Such a force requires a hierarchy of command and laws, rules, and policies to guide it. These would have to be formulated and enacted and their legitimation built up; i.e, a supranational consensus-formation structure and a central focus of loyalty seem necessary.* Consensus is needed because without it, no world state could have enough power to make the members comply. Legitimation is needed because a world state that relies on illegitimate power will be unstable and may experience civil wars as devastating as the worst international wars of the

---

* It is not implied that such a structure will allow for consensus if other conditions are lacking, but only that it seems necessary—even if the other conditions are favorable.

modern age. As legitimation is inherently normative and, in this· sense, non-rational, commitments to values supportive of the supranational community must be built up, a process which requires the mechanisms of identification. Thus, the elements that are needed are consensus-formation, the development of legitimation, and political loyalty to the supra-unit, as we know them from stable communities.

Consensus and legitimation, in turn, cannot be created and maintained without community activities over and above the enforcement of law and order and disarmament, because enforcement generates alienation which undermines commitment; consequently, additional and different activities are needed to build up and sustain positive involvement. Also, inasmuch as any pattern of law and order protects a stratification structure, there must be a mechanism for the reallocation of assets so that the societal structure and the political organization will remain articulated. Without a promise of an arrangement for the peaceful inter-societal reallocation of assets, the "have-not" nations are unlikely to support world-wide community-building; they cannot be expected to consent to the establishment of a world police force to protect and, thus, rigidify the existing world-wide allocative patterns.

These needs, it is important to realize, cannot be met by merely adding a few functions to a world state, e.g., by adding a development agency (as a means of assisting "have-not" countries to "catch up" with the "haves") to a supranational police force.[20] Societal transformations are needed, including the introduction into the political process of new collectivities, mainly non-white ones; the reduction of the more extreme forms of cultural heterogeneity; and the building of a broad-scoped, high-volume level of supranational activities and international flows to assist community-building. In short, to gain and maintain consensus for a disarmed world, supranational normative and utilitarian integration will be needed, because only such integration could effect the necessary reallocations and symbolize the world community values that the enforcement of disarmament requires.

Such an expansion of the scope of the projected world state and community places further burdens on whatever international consensus-formation structures already exist. Before autonomous nations will submit themselves to a political organization which has an effective and encompassing supranational authority, they will demand to know which policies that organization will follow. And the greater the differences between their perspectives and those of the new organization, the less likely these nations are to participate in or tolerate unification processes which lead to the community threshold. The fact that the member nations will be able to exercise political power over the world government is likely to be of little solace to them, so long as they cannot agree on the basic mold of the new state. In addition, the main nations are to be expected to fear a loss of power in the supranational transformation. It is an understanding of these very great difficulties in reaching consensus about a broad-scoped world state and community and the slow pace of unification up to now, while the need for disarmament seems urgent, that have led some scholars to favor a narrow approach: A world state limited to police functions only and, at least initially, without a community underlayer. The preceding discussion—which, in effect, applies to the world community the arguments against the nineteenth-century liberal conception of a *laissez-faire* "night watchman" nation–state—explains our position in favor of the broad-scoped state *and* community approach. We do concur that this option is a very difficult one to realize. The easier option, though, seems unavailable. On the other hand, it has been correctly suggested that the establishment of the supranational control of force may well lead to community-building;[21] however, other supranational controls and integration must follow shortly. The supranational control of coercion alone, even if it could be achieved, would be unstable and, while it lasted, might well be more like a world empire than a responsive state.

The debate between the narrow- and the broad-scoped approaches to the building of a world community is a family argument among those who agree that the world-system can be fundamentally transformed to build a new community. The acceptance of this approach comes easily to sociologists, who are accustomed to dealing with relatively integrated communities and well-established nation–states, many of which have emerged from subnational tribal systems. But many political scientists question the basic approach and argue that both the broad and narrow routes to supranationalism on the world level are Utopian. They suggest that most nations, whatever levels of integration the international systems of which they are members may reach, will not, in the foreseeable future, attain the community level of the supranational control of coercion and, thus, cannot be expected to undertake the task of preventing war; and that the load will have to be carried by the mutual adjustment system, one which has next to no supranational bonds and links but rather is maintained by the members of the system because it is to their respective advantages.

A strong argument in support of this tribalistic approach to the prevention of war is that the unification of nations has, in effect, never occurred. The many unification examples cited by those who favor the world community approach are not relevant. The cases cited are either pre-nationalist (for example, colonial rulers grouped tribes to form Nigeria), or instances in which the rising community (and not the member units) was sanctioned by nationalism (as in the unification of Germany and Italy). The more modern societal units became the foci of intense, secular political loyalties, the more the society and the state became co-extensive, and the more the control of coercion became co-extensive with the control of utilitarian and normative activities—all of which are the marks of a rising nation–state—the more difficult became supranational unification. The most advanced unifications of nation–states (for example, in contemporary Central America and Western Europe) have not even approached the community threshold. Even under circumstances that would seem highly favorable, unification has not greatly advanced. Unification has not occurred among the highly "homogeneous" Arab states or among those of Scandinavia; it has not taken place among states that had a considerable "head start," such as the members of the East African Common Services organization; it has not happened among states in a Communist system—a system which presumably is meant to supersede nationalism and has created a number of regional tools in the Warsaw Treaty Organization and the Council for Mutual Economic Assistance. There have been scores of attempts at regional integration, and many regional and even universal international organizations have been initiated, but none of these efforts has led to the formation of communities whose members are nations. These are important facts which support the tribalists. Their argument, though, rests not only on the persistence and viability of nationalism but also on the fact that various forms of international balance-of-power systems have afforded security from war for centuries. It is here that there is a place for a counter-argument.

Balance of Power and Its Limits[22]

As an historical concept, balance of power refers to a system in which states sought to maintain their independence through the establishment of an approximate equilibrium of power. The maintenance of peace was thought to require no central authority; rather, the balancing of power among states occurred as a result of the shifting of alliances in time of peace and coalitions against the aggressor in time of war. A would-be aggressor was either deterred from initiating a war by perceiving the odds against victory or, seeking to expand its power to a point at which it could unbalance the system and gain dominance, found that other states, unwilling to tolerate such a course, would wage war to maintain the balance or to restore it if necessary. War is, thus, seen as a temporary and limited phenomenon, as something necessary to insure the maintenance of the conditions under which no one state or group of states could dominate the others with impunity.

A balance-of-power system in interstate relations is comparable to a system of *laissez-faire* in economics. The assumption that no central political authority is necessary is the equivalent of the assumption that economic units, each seeking to maximize its profits, can be relied upon to generate a desirable state of affairs without a central control. Numerous interstate systems, from the Greek city–states to Renaissance Italy, have been viewed as approximating a balance-of-power system.[23] An examination of the ways in which a balance-of-power system functions is helpful for an understanding of its limitations in the post-modern period.

The conditions for the maintenance of a balance of power were particularly favorable during the nineteenth century, as attested by the absence of a general war from 1815 to 1914. Military power was diffused among several states. Diplomacy was conducted by skilled professionals, and there were few ideological impediments to the freedom of statesmen to lead their countries from one coalition to another on the basis of shifting power relations. The relative strengths of competing states could be calculated with some accuracy. War was seen as a method of implementing policy, but there was a consensus that its objectives should be limited and should not include the destruction of an enemy state, since yesterday's enemy might be tomorrow's ally. Important makeweights in the balance cannot be destroyed if conditions of equilibrium are to be preserved, and, for this, a peace of reconciliation—not alienation—was essential. Great Britain as an island power played the role of balancer, adding its weight to the weaker side when the threat of dominance arose. Most important, perhaps, the European states that dominated world politics shared a common interest in preserving the system itself, since they saw this as the best method of preserving the independence of each of its members and of safeguarding their domestic regimes.[24]

A classic example of a balance-of-power system is provided by the Congress of Vienna, where the statesmen of Europe met in 1815 to achieve a settlement after the chaos wreaked by the Napoleonic wars. The French domination of the Continent had finally ended due to the military success of a coalition led by England and including Austria, Russia, and Prussia. This coalition was formed to restore the European balance. The work of the statesmen meeting in Vienna was facilitated not only by the relative equality, in power terms, of their respective states, but also by their relative sociological homogeneity. They shared a normative orientation based upon the acceptance of monarchy and dynastic legitimacy, an aversion to popular democracy, and generally conservative political views. They were of the same social class, spoke a common language (French), and had long experience in dealing with their diplomatic counterparts. They had more in common with each other than with the masses of the people in their respective states. These social and cultural conditions, together with their shared interests in the restoration of the balance-of-power system, contributed to the relatively moderate peace terms imposed upon the defeated state, France. An indemnity was extracted and there was a period of military occupation, but, with a Bourbon king restored to the French throne (and with Talleyrand's skillful diplomacy), France was almost immediately readmitted to the councils of the Great Powers.

Since World War I, however, the conditions required by a balance-of-power system have undergone erosion at an accelerated pace. The power relations among states are no longer characterized by even a rough equality. Diplomacy is often practiced by amateurs. An age of opposing ideologies has supplanted the earlier periods of consensus. Statesmen no longer share common perspectives, less often speak a common language, and do not agree about either the nature of the order to be established or the length of time and the ways in which the *status quo* should be preserved. Under pressures of public opinion, they are no longer free to make policy independent of the views of their peoples. In contrast to the century of peace, 1815–1914, the period since 1914 is characterized by great political and sociological heterogeneity, by two world wars, and by numerous limited wars.

The year 1945 began a period of bipolarity: The European Great Powers of the past were overshadowed by two continent-sized superpowers, the United States and the Soviet Union. A true balance-of-power system was precluded by a bipolar division of power. There were no third, fourth, and fifth powers who could be relied upon to prevent either superpower from gaining dominance. Despite this new development, the old idea of balance-of-power continued to guide the statesmen and strategists who molded the relationships between the two superpowers and their camps: The two superpowers were to "balance" each other.

But in the early 1950s, there was added to the already bipolar pattern the element of *nuclear* bipolarity. Armed with nuclear weapons that were made increasingly invulnerable to attack by shielding and concealing devices, neither side could rationally launch a war against the other, since massive nuclear retaliation was likely to follow. The initiation of nuclear war, it was argued, meant national suicide. In this sense, the two nuclear giants "balanced" each other. As the balance achieved was based not on the actual use of strategic weapons but on threats of their use, the system was described as one of *deterrence*.

While the Communist camp may still have desired to extend its reign and the Western alliance may have wished to "roll" it back, neither side dared to engage in anything but marginal skirmishes—and even these were undertaken with considerable caution. Many American strategists in the 1950s and early 1960s believed that the deterrence system could be prolonged indefinitely, although they favored the elimination of especially hazardous elements through limited arms-control measures and the increase of conventional forces which would allow a military alternative to the usage of nuclear weapons and the policies of nuclear brinkmanship.

It should be emphasized that even before the advent of nuclear weapons and even when the socio-political requisites existed, the balance-of-power system could not be relied upon to preserve peace. What this system did was not to prevent war but to make major wars less devastating and minor wars less frequent. When wars occurred, procedures existed for restoring the balance and, thus, a state of peace. The object of war, as we have seen, was not the destruction of the opponent but a form of sanction that was intended to preserve the system—and all of its major members. With deterrence, however, where the total destruction of an opponent is technically possible, the fear of retaliation is relied upon to deter a nuclear attack. But whereas a rational statesman would not initiate a nuclear war, whether or not even nuclear weapons would deter a Hitler of tomorrow any more than the fear of a conventional response deterred the Hitler of yesterday is an open question. In addition, because of the unprecedented and continuing peace-time preparations for war and the instantaneous impact of post-modern arms, there is no longer any time lag between a major mistake and a major war. The enormous destructive capacity of thermonuclear weapons means that even a single breakdown of the deterrence system has to be prevented. Moreover, in a time of conflicting ideologies in which competing regimes seek not limited triumphs but each other's elimination, an international system with no margin for error and relying on the rational behavior of *all* its superpowers—and their allies, to the degree that they can involve the superpowers—is far from providing security from war.

An additional point must be considered. Control mechanisms and organizations operate on the basis of probabilities. Performances, safeguards, and supervision cannot be perfected. However, systems vary greatly in their relative emphasis on redressing an act, on imposing a penalty to deter additional violations or breakdowns (*post-hoc* controls), and on seeking to avoid violations or breakdowns in the first place (*preventive* controls). Guarantees issued by the automobile industry to their customers constitute *post-hoc* measures; the use of quality-control units at a factory are preventive. The relative cost and effectiveness of the two kinds of control measures can be calculated. The important proposition is that *for rational actors, the relative reliance on preventive versus post-hoc controls will be greater in proportion to the disutility of a violation.* Inasmuch as the disutility of nuclear wars—even of limited ones because they may escalate into all-out nuclear wars—is maximal, the investment in preventive control ought to be maximal. Balance-of-power systems provide *post-hoc* control; community-building and disarmament are *preventive.* Hence, while community-building is much more "expensive" in that it is much more difficult to evolve, the guiding of their efforts in this direction seems to be the course of action rational actors would prefer over that of attempting to perfect the balance of power, especially under the new technological and societal conditions.

The post-modern balance-of-power theorists, adherents of the deterrence approach, are not unaware of the dangers of tribalistic security systems. But, as they do not believe that the existing international system can be transformed, they advance various proposals for making it less dangerous; their proposals are referred to collectively as "arms-control."[25] Such controls, if implemented—which they were not by the time the nuclear age was in its twentieth year—could, at most, reduce the probability of war and limit its scope if it should occur; but they are very unreliable means for preventing wars. Such arms-control is like birth control by abortion rather than by contraception, and under conditions in which abortion involves a high rate of mortality. The system required if the alienation resulting from warfare technology and nationalistic relations is to be reduced is one which will prevent war rather than tangentially decrease the probabilities that it will occur or promise an opportunity for post-war repairs. Of course, it does not follow that just because arms-control is not satisfactory, disarmament based on world community and global law enforcement can be achieved. But, since the arms-control model does not meet the need even on paper, the discussion must return to the processes which may lead toward a world community and state.

Before we seek to explore the conditions under which this may be advanced, we point out that such a community is necessary as much for overcoming modern alienation, whose sources lie in production technologies and administrative techniques, as for liberating society from the additional post-modern alienation, whose roots are in the technology of armaments. Moreover, a global guidance system may be the next evolutionary step.

A Global Guidance System

A Sequential-Option Model

The ideas of social progress and evolution were rejected by social scientists during the last generation with the same degree of assurance with which earlier generations embraced them. Recently, though, a new interest in evolutionist conceptions has been discernible.[26] The neo-evolutionist models compare to earlier ones in that: (1) Although they forego a naive belief in mankind's progress from primitive darkness to rational enlightenment, they do attempt to establish history's patterns; (2) although they do not assume that all societies follow one pattern, they do expect a limited set of alternatives from among which societies choose; and (3) although the movement from stage to stage that the theoretical patterns specify is not expected to be one of unilinear progress but of developments which know regressions, an over-all "secular" trend is maintained. Thus, the elements that remain from old evolutionist approaches are mainly that societal change has a direction and a limited set of options which can be theoretically determined, among which the genetic processes choose in some discernible sequence. It is, hence, best referred to as a *sequential-option* model. It ties functional (the alternatives) and structural (the options chosen) analysis to the study of change (the propositions about sequences).* The concept suggests that earlier macroscopic choices constrain later ones,[27] and that there are relatively critical turning points at which the contexts for the next period are set. History is, thus, seen not as an endless sequence of piece-meal choices which accumulate,

---

* For heuristic purposes, it often is useful to assume one or more "target" states toward which the process may be evolving or be guided. We refer to these as future-systems. We used one in the study of a differentiation process (Etzioni, *Studies in Social Change, op. cit.,* pp. 6 ff.) and another one in the study of a unification process (*ibid.,* pp. 112 ff.). The active society is a future-system for the analysis of post-modern history.

but as a process in which periods of fundamental choices are followed by periods in which the effects of these fundamental choices must be confronted; they can be ameliorated or magnified but cannot be transformed[28] until a new turning point is reached or produced.

The Reintegration of Society

Our endeavor is neo-evolutionary in that we see the active society as an option of the post-modern period. We now explore one aspect of it that is directly related to the reduction of tribalism—namely, the reintegration of society. In studying this aspect of societal history, a three state sequential-option model seems fruitful. The first stage is one of a *fused society*, in which the various societal needs are served by one and the same societal unit with a minimal differentiation of activities, of power, and of normative principles, as well as with almost no controlling overlayer. Fused societies develop, but their change is largely unguided. Expressive considerations have marked dominance over instrumental ones, which are neglected if not suppressed. A small, illiterate, very primitive society most closely approximates this model.

The second stage is one of a *differentiated* society, in which each major function and sub-function has a sub-system, a structure of its own, a power center and organization, and specialized normative principles which legitimate it. There is only limited articulation of the various differentiated units and only a weak supra-unit regulatory capacity. In such a society, instrumental considerations outweigh expressive ones, because the latter are dependent on inter-unit and supra-unit bonds which are weak. Industrial societies in their relatively *laissez-faire* periods (e.g., Britain from 1840 to 1871) approximate this model.[29]

The third stage is one in which a previously differentiated society is *reintegrated*, in that, without refusing the differentiated structures, a large number and variety of potent inter- and supra-unit mechanisms evolve, largely expressive or political in nature, which bind the differentiated units into a complex but integrated whole. The reintegrated society differs from a fused one not only in that it has been differentiated, but also in that it is more organizational and less collectivistic, more political and less societal. Nor is it without differentiation in its present form: It has a fused overlayer and set of bonds on top of a differentiated underlayer of activities and lower-ranking controls.

The integration of the third stage is more artificial than that of the first one, as not only control but also consensus-formation is partially planned. But it is also a much more affluent, malleable, mobilized, committing, and transforming society. The first stage is marked by the primacy of societal values; the transition to the second—by the liberation of means and by the supremacy of instrumentality; the third—by the primacy of societal goals which, unlike vaguer values, entail the carrying out of specific societal tasks.

In the first stage, the society and the environment are taken as given; in the second, the main effort to change is focused on the environment and related societal alterations; in this stage, society is viewed as a means. Industrialization seeks to remold society so as to make it a more effective means for carving tools out of the environment; it is assumed that the affluent society will be a "good" society. In the third stage, society's own transformation is the central goal. It is a return to the questions raised by the ancient Greek philosophers of which societal organization will better realize collective values, and, hence, the emphasis is on the ways in which the societal parts are made into a whole—on reintegration and the political function. The third stage is an option open to mature, differentiated societies (though fused societies may try to shorten, if not avoid, the second stage), but it is not in any way "inevitable." Societies may remain differentiated, disintegrated, or at one level of fragmentation or another.

The differentiated society is the most alienating of the three kinds in that it is fragmented, does not form a whole, lacks in ultimate meaning, and is basically unresponsive to its participants. The plurality of power centers respond neither directly to the members nor to a universal political authority which might speak for them. And, as the differentiated society fragments its participants, even if it were to reflect their perspectives fully, they would be distorted perspectives. The fused society was a small whole. While it did not fragment, its rigid cultural and political patterns could not but be unresponsive. Its low capacity to act, its poverty of assets and guidance, forced many basic human needs to remain unmet. The reintegrated society has the capacities of a differentiated one and much of the wholeness of a fused one. While there is not automatic assurance that it will be responsive internally or transform its boundaries, at least it has the potential ability to do so because the members to which it responds—if it does—are less fragmented, and it has a sufficient political overlayer for it to act with minimal alienation. It can be an active society.

Differentiation, Reintegration, and System-Boundaries

The transition from one stage to another involves not only the differentiation of fused elements and their reintegration within each societal unit, but also a transformation of the relationships among societal units. The environmental system of each societal unit—that is, the other societal units with which it is interrelated—becomes more inclusive with the transition from stage to stage, though, again, the trend is not without "interruptions."

The transition from the first to the second stage involved the rise of the nation-state, which entailed—with some exceptions to which we turn below—the formation of a more encompassing societal unit of integration and of control and not just of interdependence. We suggest that a similar extension of the unit of integration and control is needed before the transition from the second to the third stage can be completed. The movement into the third stage involves, therefore, not only the reintegration of elements of a society that came apart with the impact of differentiation; it also involves the binding of elements of several societies, each of which is internally differentiated.

The first extension of the societal unit was necessary if the efficacy of means was to be increased (e.g., the broadening of markets). The second extension is necessary if the primacy of values is to be reestablished. The first extension was necessary because production required it; the second, because existence, on which all values are predicated, needs it. Moreover, unless the guidance mechanism encompasses the units that are already interdependent, the primacy of values over means cannot be reestablished, and interdependence is growing world-wide. We saw that the degree and importance of interdependence have been exaggerated and that its integrative capacity has been greatly overstated. But the degree of interdependence is growing and is expected to continue to increase, and, while this does not make for a community, it does require guidance if its dynamics are not to be arbitrary from the viewpoint of the actors.

We certainly do not suggest that that which is needed will happen. Many societies have not yet differentiated, and others will not reintegrate; a world community may well not evolve. We do argue that, first, modernization and, now, a stable peace and an active society each require an extension of the unit of guidance and, hence, of the boundaries of community. The failure of the ancient Greek city–states to form the supra-polis community that was needed for them to defend themselves against external threats is widely viewed as the decisive element in the destruction of Hellenic civilization. Whether or not a world community will eventually be built and the alienation of differentiation overcome are questions which, we believe, cannot in principle be answered, as they are concerned with the ways in which future actors will exercise their options. All we may be able to establish is the nature of these options and the directions in which alternative sequences of choices point. Societal actors can exercise the option of community-building, we argue, because we see, at present and in the future, the necessary developments in the techniques of the guidance of societal processes, just as, in the modern age, techniques of the control of work and machines evolved.

Both transitions—from collectivities to national societies and from nations to more encompassing communites—involve a change in the locus of guidance, not in terms of abolishing earlier loci but by imposing more encompassing levels on top of existing (though transformed) ones. The nation–state added a level of action, control, and consensus-formation to collectivities, while transforming them. The world community, if formed, would add a layer of action, control, and consensus-formation to the transformed nation–states rather than abolish them. Meanwhile, as we enter the post-modern period, international flows and supranational activities and organizations create some extranational elements. They are still very weak, much weaker than the national ones, but they seem to be slowly accumulating in the direction of increasing and strengthening the international bonds and links where there already exists considerable interdependence.

In the next chapter, we deal with the rise of several supranational systems; they fall far short of the model advanced here for active community-building because they are internally unstable and distorted and externally sub-global rather than world-wide. In the following chapter, we explore the conditions under which a more authentic and encompassing community may arise.

NOTES

1. See, for instance, Robert A. Kann, *The Habsburg Empire* (New York: Praeger, 1957), pp. 49 ff.

2. For a conceptual discussion of integration see Myron Weiner, "Political Integration and Political Development," *The Annals of the American Academy of Political and Social Science*, Vol. 358 (1965), pp. 52–64, esp. 53–55. See also Haas, *The Uniting of Europe, op. cit.*, p. 16; Deutsch et al., *Political Community and the North Atlantic Area, op. cit.*, p. 31.

3. "After World War II, with the development of nuclear energy, cybernetics, and the techniques of transportation in space, the world contracted . . . ," Helio Jaquaribe, "World Order, Rationality, and Socioeconomic Development," *Daedalus*, Vol. 95 (1966), p. 611. Note that by the time these lines were published in 1966, nothing was ever transported in space and cybernetics and nuclear energy were used almost exclusively to divide the world. "Historically, the most relevant fact of our times is the unification of the field of important political decisions, which occurred after the cultural unification of the world. . . ." "Western Culture finally became the universal culture," *ibid.*, p. 610.

Marshall McLuhan echoed in superlatives the often repeated statement: "Today [1964], after more than a century of electric technology, we have extended our central nervous system itself in a global embrace, abolishing both space and time as far as our planet is concerned." *Understanding Media, op. cit.*, p. 3.

4. John Herz, *International Politics in the Atomic Age* (New York: Columbia University Press, 1959), pp. 96–108.

5. Park pointed out that conflict generates interaction between the adversaries; the adversaries communicate with each other and come to know each other, which, in turn leads to the evolution of shared perspectives and bonds, until the conflict turns into competition. Park and Burgess', *Introduction to the Science of Sociology, op. cit.*, pp. 504–784. George C. Homans supports this line of analysis by suggesting that communication breeds affinity. *The Human Group* (New York: Harcourt, Brace & World, 1950), pp. 110–117; see also pp. 120, 133. A study by Daniel Lerner lends empirical support to the proposition. Lerner reports that French businessmen who travel, read foreign magazines, and have contact with foreign visitors are more likely to favor the formation of a European community than are those who are less exposed to foreigners. Among the businessmen with no exposure, sentiment in favor of such a community is about 2 to 1, while those who have had much contact with foreigners favor the community by a ratio of 6 to 1. The difference between these two groups might have been related to factors other than exposure, but

Lerner shows that such variables as age, birthplace, socio-economic status, size of firm, and location of firm do not explain the difference. Daniel Lerner, "French Business Leaders Look at EDC: A Preliminary Report," *Public Opinion Quarterly*, Vol. 20 (1956), pp. 212–221.

For a study of cross-cultural adaptations of foreigners who come to work in France, see Alain Girard and Jean Stoetzel, *Francais et Immigres: I. L'Attitude Francaise. L'Adaptation des Italiens et des Polonais; II. Nouveaux Documents sur l'Adaptation. Algeriens, Italiens, Polonais* (Paris: Presses Universitaires de France, 1954), two volumes. See also Claire Sellitz, June R. Christ, Joan Havel, and Stuart W. Cook, *Attitudes and Social Relations of Foreign Students in the United States* (Minneapolis: University of Minnesota Press, 1963).

6. Various studies are reviewed by Berelson and Steiner, *Human Behavior*, *op. cit.*, pp. 327–329. See also Raymond W. Mack and Richard C. Snyder, "Approaches to the Study of Social Conflict," *Journal of Conflict Resolution*, Vol. 1 (1957), pp. 105–110. Surveying earlier research, they suggest that a high degree of intimacy will intensify conflict. "The Analysis of Social Conflict—Toward an Overview and Synthesis," *ibid.*, pp. 212–248, esp. p. 225.

7. This subject deserves much more study. For some relevant data see Bruce Lannes Smith and Chitra M. Smith who provide a guide to the literature in their *International Communication and Political Opinion* (Princeton, N.J.: Princeton University Press, 1952).

8. Karl W. Deutsch and Alexander Eckstein, "National Industrialization and the Declining Share of the International Economic Sector, 1890–1959," *World Politics*, Vol. 13 (1961), pp. 267–299.

9. Bruce M. Russett et al., *World Handbook of Political and Social Indicators* (New Haven, Conn.: Yale University Press, 1964), pp. 105–133; Karl W. Deutsch, "International Communication: The Media and Flows," *Public Opinion Quarterly*, Vol. 20 (1956), pp. 143–60.

10. The group studied by Lerner, "French Business Leaders," *loc. cit.*, is highly atypical here, as transnational exposure is unusually high.

11. For a discussion of these views, see Inis L. Claude, Jr., *Swords into Plowshares: The Problems and Progress of International Organization* (New York: Random House, 1961), rev. ed. pp. 373 ff.

12. Almond, *The American People and Foreign Policy*, *op. cit.*, pp. 136–157; Holbert N. Carroll, *The House of Representatives and Foreign Affairs* (Pittsburgh: University of Pittsburgh Press, 1958); James A. Robinson, *Congress and Foreign Policy Making* (Homewood, Ill.: The Dorsey Press, 1962), pp. 102 ff. See Ch. 17 *supra* for a detailed discussion.

13. The percentage of those who answered that foreign policy, world affairs, and defense are most important ranged, in the period between November, 1935, and January, 1939, between 11 and 26 per cent, with the highest percentage obtaining at the outbreak of the Spanish Civil War. In the period between February, 1948, and October, 1959, those who felt that such issues were "most important ever" fell below 30 per cent, and in all but one survey (October, 1949), were at least 40 per cent of those polled. Data by the American Institute of Public Opinion.

14. John P. Robinson, "World Affairs Information and Mass Media Exposure," *The Journalism Quarterly*, Vol. 44 (1967), pp. 23–31. Milbrath, *Political Participation*, *op. cit.*, pp. 42–43 and *passim*.

15. For the functionalist position, see David Mitrany, *A Working Peace System* (London: Royal Institute of International Affairs, 1943). Curtis W. Martin, "The History and Theory of the Functional Approach to International Organization," unpublished Ph.D. dissertation, Harvard University, 1950. Harold E. Engle, "A Critical Study of the Functional Approach to International Organization," unpublished Ph.D. dissertation, Columbia University, 1957. For a study on the microscopic level which develops a useful conceptualization, see Frank W. Young, "Cooperative Cross-Cultural Study in Intervillage Systems," *Human Organization*, Vol. 25 (1966), pp. 46–50.

16. Ernst B. Haas, *Beyond the Nation–State: Functionalism and International Organization* (Stanford: Stanford University Press, 1964), especially Chapters I–IV, and James Patrick Sewell, *Functionalism and World Politics* (Princeton, N.J.: Princeton University Press, 1966).

17. *Political Unification, op. cit.*, pp. 184–228.

18. We take it for granted that economic processes are not self-regulating.

19. Cf. Joseph S. Nye, Jr., *Pan-Africanism and East African Integration* (Cambridge, Mass.: Harvard University Press, 1965), esp. pp. 241–247.

20. A suggestion to this effect was added to the second edition of Grenville Clark and Louis B. Sohn, *World Peace Through World Law* (Cambridge, Mass.: Harvard University Press, 1960).

21. Lincoln P. Bloomfield et al., *International Military Forces* (Boston: Little, Brown, 1964), esp. pp. 11–46 and 64–78. Hans J. Morgenthau, "The Political Conditions for an International Police Force," *International Organization*, Vol. 17 (1963), p. 403.

22. I draw here on my "War and Disarmament," in Robert K. Merton and Robert A. Nisbet, *Contemporary Social Problems* (New York: Harcourt, Brace & World, 1966), 2nd ed., pp. 723–773.

23. On the logic of these systems, see Morton A. Kaplan, *System and Process in International Politics* (New York: Wiley & Sons, 1957), pp. 100 ff.; and Richard N. Rosecrance, *Action and Reaction in World Politics* (Boston: Little, Brown, 1963).

24. Inis L. Claude, Jr., *Power and International Relations* (New York: Random House, 1962), pp. 90–91.

25. The best collection of articles on the subject is Donald G. Brennan (ed.), *Arms Control, Disarmament, and National Security* (New York: Braziller, 1961).

26. See George C. Williams, *Adaptation and Natural Selection: A Critique of Some Current Evolutionary Thought* (Princeton, N.J.: Princeton University Press, 1966); Parsons, *Societies, op. cit.*, pp. 2–3 ff.

27. See Chapter 4, pp. 79–83 for additional discussion.

28. See Chapter 12, pp. 291–293 for additional discussion of this aspect of societal decision-making.

29. Discussion of differentiation draws on previous works by Parsons and others cited in Note 20, Ch. 4. The models advanced in these works, with Riggs' being the main exception, do not deal with a third, reintegration state.

CHAPTER 20

From Many—One?

Historically, we suggested, the boundaries of societal units have tended to extend, and such extensions are necessary to overcome the modern and post-modern sources of alienation. But, it may be asked, what is the place of modern (and earlier) empires in this pattern? Has history not left the societal dinosaurs behind rather than face them in the future? And is the post-modern world system not one of numerous, small nation–states? We shall argue below (pp. 580–583) that empires were an "exception" that supports the rule, and that the emerging system is one of multiple blocs rather than myriad nation–states (pp. 583–586).

But even if it is granted that the major world actors are a few groupings and their supra-power elites, how, if at all, can a multiple bloc system be transformed into a world community? We first attempt to answer this question in analytic terms, to indicate that the transformation needed is smaller than might at first seem (pp. 586–590); we then suggest that post-modern historical trends seem, on balance, to move in the direction required for community-building (pp. 590–602).

Empires: The Grand Exception

The Collapse of Empires—Premature Expansion

The major exception to the proposition that the more differentiated and reintegrated a society, the larger the extent of its system is the collapse of pre-modern and early modern empires. While nationalism and modernization often entailed the rise of more encompassing systems or the transfer of control from the local to the national level, other systems deunified under the impact of these forces; scores of nations emerged where previously there were a few empires. Pre-modern empires, like Rome and China, were similarly unstable. If a theory cannot account for the collapse of empires, the proposition that history moves toward larger societal entities cannot be supported. Even though any proposition must allow for temporary lapses and digressions, empires were too common and existed for too long to be considered merely an "interruption" of a trend.

We suggest that a theory of societal guidance can account for empires by viewing them as premature and, above all, unbalanced reductions of tribalism, and by seeing their disintegration into smaller societal units as aiding in the building of mature and balanced supranational unions and communities. The reason that empires are considered anomalies can be explained in the basic frame of reference used here; and, above all, since the factors which retarded the earlier development of encompassing societal units are now disappearing or are being removed, early failures cannot be used to argue convincingly that post-modern global communities are not feasible.

The premature nature of empires has been demonstrated by showing that they did not have the cybernetic capacity and power, the communication and transportation means, and the consensus-formation structures necessary to keep a large or extending polity integrated and guided.[1]* (The Roman Empire at its zenith encompassed 50 to 60 million people and several million land acres, more than most contemporary nation–states.) Most pre-modern empires seem to have "faded" as the distance from the capital grew, in that the capital of the empire often had little information about and even less control of many of the provinces. The imperial policy was super-imposed on feudal or tribal local systems, without effectively committing many of their politically active citizens.[2] If one were to construct an index of controlling capacities which took into account the number of people included, the scope of the activities controlled, and the intensiveness of the control, much if not all of the "anomaly" of pre-modern empires would disappear: Their capacities

---

* Reference notes for this chapter appear on page 608.

were *lower* than those of the modern nation–states; these capacities only seemed larger because they were spread (more thinly) over a larger area. Historically, the capacity to control did grow, but not the extent of the territories which the empires attempted to encompass. Modern empires had more control capacities than earlier ones, but they still were not sufficient for effectively controlling a territory which spans many parts of the world. Above all, modern, like earlier, empires were unbalanced; they relied more on coercion than on the utilitarian reallocation of assets among the controlled units, and they were unable to commit many of the active citizens of their member units; their low levels of responsiveness and their deficient consensus-building capacities undermined them. In short, these empires had controlling overlayers, but not guidance mechanisms. Hence, when national-ism, a movement with mass appeal, appeared, it could mobilize the members and disintegrate the empires.

It might be said that this discussion offers a major anachronism: In the days of empires, it was not necessary to build consensus because most citizens played no active political role and could not be mobilized by political competitors. Our position would be anachronistic if we were interested in understanding the empires per se in their historical contexts. Here, though, we are concerned with the changes in guidance mechanisms, comparing those found in different time periods to a guidance model. The question for us is whether or not the failure of pre-modern and modern empires suggests that global, post-modern supranational communities are not feasible. Empires had a much smaller guidance capacity than nation–states and that which is available to post-modern, supranational communities. That empires could be maintained at all was due to the fact that they existed in the periods preceding mass mobilization; that is, they could function primarily on the basis of the control and consensus-mobilization of local elites. The advent of nationalism made this form of societal guidance obsolete and was accom-panied by a large increase in the capacities of societal guidance which makes much larger systems feasible. These systems, though, to be stable, as we shall see, will have to be communities and not empires.

The characteristics of a stable late-modern and post-modern political community are penetration into the member units, a balanced use of power, and relatively less inequality and unresponsiveness, as these features are found in several stable, well-established national communities. As nation–states arose where empires had prevailed, they tended to be less encompassing but more intensive and balanced. (Some nation–states were also less inegalitarian and more responsive.) This development is to be viewed as a regression on one front which prepares the foundations for a better-founded extension on others. The more developed parts of the world seem increasingly prepared to move into the next stage; the increased guidance capacities allow for communities to exist in areas as large as those covered by previous empires or larger. The United States is a prime example; it encompassed—

even before the post-modern development of guidance mechanisms—more people in one political community than many of the empires ever did.

Guidance First, Integration Later, Sequence

The capacities for a global controlling overlayer are much better developed than those for global integrative bonds and consensus-formation, but this is not necessarily a bad omen. When, during the process of the unification of two or more societal units, progress on various levels is unsynchronized, two main patterns tend to emerge, depending upon which level is "lagging." If the establishment of integrative societal bonds greatly precedes that of the guidance—in particular, control*—capacities, the supra-unit overlayer (to the degree that it has evolved at all) is likely to be overloaded and, when challenged, to collapse. On the other hand, control capacities may be developed, either by one or a few units or on the supra-unit level, before the intensity and scope of integrative bonds are greatly increased. When these are extended later, the success of community-building seems more likely.

Prussia, for instance, underwent internal administrative reform and economic development which provided it with a "surplus" of control capacity on the eve of German unification. There was, here, a supra-elite before a supra-organization, and the latter preceded the supra-society. The governments of several post-modern states now command, to varying degrees, the capacities needed for a global overlayer. The United States, for instance, manages with little difficulty a world-wide security force, with the direct communication of all the units on all continents and seas and in the air and space. Like Prussia among the German states, the United States is more able and more willing than other Western nations to invest in the role of a world military elite.[3] The USSR has similar capacities and ambitions.[4] Neither suprapower has mobilized the assets and skills to support effective global utilitarian systems; the foreign-aid programs of both of them so far have been poorly funded and managed. Their normative appeals vary but seem to be on the decline. Both must deal with the nationalistic tendencies of third countries as well as of those in their own camps. Other powers so far have provided mainly regional leadership. World-wide unification, it seems, will have to rely—if it is to occur at all—on some combination of the supra-powers and the mobilization of the support of others, rather than on the

---

* We stress control because we expect that supra-unit consensus-formation cannot be evolved before the unification of activities and societal (rather than merely political) processes. However, where there is a normative community on the supra-unit level—such as a widely and intensively held national identity—before there is a societal one, the chances of success are greatly enhanced. The beginnings of such a world-wide community may be discernible, especially among intellectuals and more educated persons.

imposition of the controlling overlayer of one supra-power on the others. A world community, thus, seems more likely than a world empire.

Post-Modern, Sub-Global Systems

Camps and Quasi-Empires

The main actors in the contemporary world are a few sub-global systems, camps (or loose blocs)—to each other, quasi-empires—to their members, The United States, the Soviet Union, and, to lesser degree, De Gaulle's France lead camps of smaller nations, camps which act in unison to some degree vis-à-vis each other. Within each sub-global system, the supra-power, often with the help of one or more secondary (or lieutenant) powers, is an external elite for the other members of its camp. The supra-power, as we shall see, controls with varying degrees of specificity several key internal processes of the member units and their relations to other camp members and to non-members, especially to other suprapowers. As compared to earlier sub-global systems, especially modern empires, the post-modern ones are more effective control systems, somewhat more advanced as consensus-formation structures, and least advanced in terms of integration and, consequently, community-building. There also seems to be a measure of increased responsiveness of the supra-elites to the members, as compared to earlier periods. To support these statements with empirical evidence would require a volume larger than the present one.* In the following pages, we attempt only to outline the main propositions and to discuss a few of the issues involved.

As we see it, the post-modern world is not one in which 130 odd nation-states are the main actors, in the sense that their attributes, their relations to each other, and the actions guided by them do not determine the directions of the main international processes; these are largely determined by a few suprapowers. The suprapowers have a good deal of control not only of such processes as international trade, foreign aid, communication, and the work of international organizations, but also of the relations among and within the majority of the other nations.

Before the countries affected by the control of one suprapower or another are listed, it should be noted that this control is often partial (i.e., limited in scope) and contextual rather than prescriptive. We state that a suprapower constitutes an external elite capable of controlling another nation contextually if: The boundaries of the unit subject to control are set and/or protected by the power or influence of the external elite; and the internal political

---

* Some evidence is included in the works cited below and in our *Winning Without War*, *op. cit.* We hope to make available additional evidence in a future work in preparation under the auspices of the Institute of War and Peace Studies at Columbia University.

organization and the processes of societal change of the unit are allowed to vary only within limits set by the external elite.

The intervention of the external elite may be coercive, utilitarian, or normative; it may be tight, day-to-day control, only an occasional exercise of control (when the units subject to control act out of context, or threaten to do so), or only indirect control (for instance, by inducing other small nations to intervene). Here, we are not concerned with the mode, frequency, or specificity of the intervention but with its macroscopic effects.[5] The majority of the countries of the world seem externally to be contextuated. The countries whose actions are contextuated by the Soviet Union and Communist China are well-known.[6] They include thirteen countries, if one counts the half-nations (North Korea, North Vietnam, and East Germany).[7] France's control over most of its former colonies in Africa seems to be great enough to include at least fourteen of them in its sphere.[8] Britain, acting in cooperation with the United States, plays a similar role for several of its former or present colonies, including Kuwait, Malaysia, Hong Kong, Malta, Jordan, and part of the West Indies. The United States exercises contextuating influence over most of the twenty-one members of the Organization of American States and over several Asian countries (especially Taiwan, Turkey, Iran, Thailand, and South Vietnam).[9]

Countries able to maintain a relatively autonomous position draw on economic assistance, trade, arms, and so forth, from two or more suprapowers. Egypt under Nasser, Ghana under Nkrumah, and Indonesia under Sukarno are typical cases. In these instances, attempts by one supra-elite or another to use its inputs into these countries for external control purposes led them to seek inputs from other suprapowers and, generally, to strive to avoid excessive dependency on any one of them. Nasser's turn to the Soviet Union when he was subject to American pressure over the Aswan Dam and his later reconciliation with the United States as well as his drawing on China, both Germanies, and, later, even Britain and France is a prime example of the policy of relatively autonomous "third" countries in a multi-camp world.

The nature of contextuating control needs to be specified. It entails the setting of limits on variations in foreign and domestic policies that the suprapower is willing to tolerate. For example, the Soviet Union showed in Hungary in 1956 and earlier in Poland and East Germany that it would not willingly tolerate secession from the Communist camp and the establishment of a non-Community government. In addition, pressure is exerted to follow—within the context of tolerable options—those policies favored by the suprapower. For instance, the Soviet Union exerted pressure on the East European countries to limit their contacts not only with the West but also with Yugoslavia. Of course, neither the in-context nor the contextuating pressures work with full efficacy, as Rumania's relatively independent position vis-à-vis China in 1966 and Yugoslavia's withdrawal from the Soviet-directed camp illustrate.

The United States' contextuation is, in most cases, less rigid and coercive than that of the Soviet Union, but there are similarities. The joining of the Communist camp in matters of foreign policy and the establishment of a domestic Communist government are options that the United States tried to eliminate for countries in its sub-global system. Cuba is the United States' only "Yugoslavia" since 1950. Within the foreign policy context, the United States has preferred countries to trade with it (or with the United Kingdom) rather than with France (the same holds for education and probably for other sectors). As far as domestic options within the anti-Communist context are concerned, the United States has shifted its preferences over time and from country to country, indicating preferences for left-liberal democratizing developing forces, or military governments, or conservative-aristocratic *status quo* regimes.[10] While the details differ, the basic patterns of contextuation of other external elites are similar.

Some countries are under the influence of a lieutenant-power which cooperates in controlling it (contextually) with a supra-power. Britain since World War II has increasingly coordinated its "overseas" policy with the United States and has relied on the United States for back-up power. Or, conversely, the United States has relied on Britain as the first line of control but has made it clear that Britain was supported—for instance, in Kenya and, even more clearly, in Jordan.[11] The United States became involved in Vietnam in 1954, when France was still a lieutenant and needed support. The unusual course of events in the 1956 Suez crisis—in which a subject won over two suprapowers—occurred not only because Egypt was no longer part of the US–UK–France sub-global system and had gained USSR backing and a measure of autonomy, but also because the United Kingdom and France did not "clear" the action with Washington, whose lieutenants they were at the time.

We, then, view the world as a small set of sub-global systems; at the center of each system is one suprapower and one or more lieutenant powers. At the margins of the systems and "in between" them are countries which belong to none. The sub-systems have an ideological tone (e.g., the Free World), a cultural flavor (e.g., French), and constitute a trade and aid sub-set and, above all, a military system.[12] Security mechanisms of the military, police, and "counter-subversion" types exist in all of these sub-systems and are used not only to enforce the limits of the contexts,[13] but also against internal opposition (less preferred in-the-context options).

These post-modern sub-global systems differ from earlier, especially colonial, empires in several ways: (a) Their power mix is relatively more balanced; they rely less on direct coercive control (though this is still used frequently as compared to its use in the intranational systems of the supra-powers themselves). (b) Utilitarian exchanges seem relatively less exploitive (though there is some "colonial" residue), in that relatively more genuine technical and economic aid is given, more indigenous development—

including some industrialization—is allowed, more of the benefits of production remain in the countries, and a considerable increase in autonomous local administration is tolerated.[14] (c) Relatively higher stress is put on normative control, in the forms of various extended elite-controlled educational and propaganda facilities, a rhetoric of equality, and a facade of multilateralism and formal equality of representation in the General Assembly of the United Nations and various regional bodies. (d) There is also an increase in the upward communication from the non-elite countries to the elite, more "downward" knowledge of the non-elite countries on the part of the elite,[15] and even some increase in responsiveness.

These are all shifts in the "right" direction in the sense that if these sub-global systems are to be stabilized and activated, the power mix has to be more balanced, responsiveness must be at a higher level, and so on. What is lacking most is a smaller power differential within each sub-system. Curiously enough, this is achieved in part by the transition from a bi-polar to a multi-polar (i.e., a multi-external-elite) world, which increases the options of in-between countries and creates more inter-camp penetration and counter-vailence, and—to a lesser degree—by the regional unification of non-elites against the elites.[16] (So far, most regional efforts are controlled, at least contextually, by an external elite).

Further solidification of the sub-global systems also would require increased tolerance on the part of the suprapowers of in-context and even contextual changes in countries in their sub-systems. Without such transformations, the external elites often maintain political organizations in the controlled countries which do not "fit" the underlying societal structures, which, in turn, generates intra-national, intra-bloc, and inter-bloc tensions and conflicts. But even assuming that each sub-system could become internally responsive and more like a community and less like an empire, we still must explore the conditions under which these sub-global systems can be united into a world system. This problem is first discussed analytically and then in historical terms.

Encapsulation—A Conflict-Containing Process

We first deal with a theory of conflict which applies to conflicts in general and not merely to international ones. We then apply it to a discussion of the post-modern world-system. Here, as we have seen, the superpowers play a large role. But their existence does not preclude the evolution of a world community, in part because of the dynamics of their relations and in part because of the roles played by other nations and processes. In this and in the following sections, conditions and strategies are explored jointly; thus, for instance, if we ask whether the development of supranational regional communities retards or advances the development of a world community, the tentative answer points both to a condition and to a strategy which those who actively seek to transform the existing tribalistic, multi-camp system may follow. The whole discussion may be viewed as an "optimistic but not unreasonable" scenario.

Encapsulation, Not Conflict Resolution

The prevention of war requires that a world community be advanced to the extent that it will be able to provide a "capsule" to limit the level of international conflict and to allow for peaceful outlets. Encapsulation refers to the process by which conflicts are modified in such a way that they become limited by rules (the "capsule"). The rules exclude some modes of conflict, while they letigimate other modes. Conflicts that are "encapsulated" are not solved in the sense that the parties necessarily become pacified. But the use of arms—or, at least, some usages of some arms—is effectively ruled out. Many observers doubt that the normative components of Communism and of the Western tradition could become reconciled, suggesting, therefore, that the basis for building a world community on which such rules must come to rest is lacking. They see two alternatives: Powers are basically either hostile or friendly. Encapsulation, however, points to a third kind of relationship. Here, basic differences in perspective, even a mutually aggressive orientation, may continue, but the parties agree to rule out some means and some modes of conflict and establish the organizational machinery necessary to enforce such an agreement. In this sense, encapsulation is less demanding than pacification, since it does not require that the conflict be resolved or extinguished, but only that the range of its expression be curbed. Hostile parties are more readily "encapsulated" than pacified.

At the same time, encapsulation tends to provide a more lasting solution than pacification. Pacified parties remain independent units that, after a period of time, may again find their differences provoked, leading to new conflicts or to renewals of the old ones. Once encapsulated, the parties lose some of their autarky by being tied into a community and some of their autonomy by being subject to a shared political organization. The community provides the societal foundations that the formation of consensus requires; this consensus, in turn, is the basis of the conflict-limiting organization (or "capsule").* That is, we deal with the institutionalization of conflict and, hence, with the transformation of its nature, which has political-organizational aspects (the development of the capsule) and societal aspects (community–building).

---

* The "capsule" includes legal rules, related values or legitimation, and enforcement machinery; it, hence, is parallel to the concept of the political shell, used in previous chapters to refer to the fully developed "capsules" of highly integrated state-societies.

If there is to be movement toward a world community, it must be self-propelling. Once an authority superior to the contending superpowers—a world government or a powerful United Nations police force—is viewed as a prerequisite, an authority is posited that can impose rules on the contending parties and, thus, keep their conflicts limited to those channels allowed by the world community. But such an authority is not presently available. The search for possible patterns to achieve a world community must, therefore, focus on those conflicts in which, through the very process of conflict, the participants initiate self-imposed limitations on the means and modes of strife, leading toward further encapsulation and community–building.

An Economic Analogy

A very useful analogy is found in a different area: the avoidance of price wars by large corporations in some industries. To obviate the necessity of discussing a multitude of irrelevant details, we draw on a hypothetical case. Let us begin with two superfirms competing for an automobile market; one firm seeks to capture a larger and larger share of the market, while the other firm is trying to maintain its share. The competition is waged (let us assume, in order not to complicate matters unnecessarily) through changes in quality and in prices; that is, the expanding company attempts to cut into the market of the other company by offering automobiles of higher quality for lower prices. The defensive firm counters by matching the offers of the expanding firm. Both companies realize that an all-out price war might be ruinous for both sides,[17] and the small price-markdowns might easily lead one side or the other to offer larger ones, soon passing the point at which cars are sold above cost and thereby undermining the economic viability of both firms. Quality contests are also expensive, but, for reasons that are not completely clear, they are much more self-limiting and much less likely to ruin the companies.[18]

For these reasons, it is more "rational" to limit the interfirm competition to quality contests; indeed, years pass without a price war, and the companies seem implicitly to have "agreed" not to resort to this devastating means of conflict. But the system is one of deterrence and is not preventive; a price war might erupt at any time. (Older executives tell of times in which such wars actually did occur.) The expansionist firm, set on gaining a larger share of the market, might turn to a price war if it finds that it is making no progress in the quality contest. The defensive firm, on the other hand, attempting to make the other firm accept a duopolistic sharing of the market, feels that it must not allow even a small fraction of the market to shift away from its controls; even a small encroachment would reward and thus encourage the expansionist efforts. The defensive firm, it is hard to deny, might have to initiate a price war to counter encroachments on its share of the market. Both firms realize that by resorting to a price war they might undermine their own viability, but both hope that the price war will be limited and that they will be able to use it to show their determined commitment to whatever policy they favor, be it expansionist or duopolistic. Theoretically, there are several escapes from this tense and potentially ruinous situation; in practice, it seems, the range of alternatives is much more limited.

The solution advocated by the defensive firm is to formalize and legalize the existing allocation of the market; each firm will hold on to its part, and, thus, both price and quality contests (the conflict *in toto*) would be terminated once and for all. The expansionist firm finds it difficult to accept this duopolistic solution; it feels that some buyers, given a free choice, would prefer its product. Whether or not its ambitions are justified or its feelings are valid does not matter; in either event, it refuses to accept the duopolistic settlement, and there is a danger that the implicit curbs on the conflict will be eroded.

The tension thus generated—either firm may suddenly find that a price war has begun—has led several executives on both sides to consider an all-out price war to drive the other firm to bankrupcy; but this, the cooler heads on both sides point out, requires taking some rather forbidding risks, actually endangering the very survival of both firms. Economics is not enough of a science and the information about the resources of the other firm is not sufficiently adequate to provide any assurance about the outcome of a showdown. Thus, while this alternative is constantly considered, it has been avoided so far because it is believed to be too risky.

Still another approach, favored only by a few, is to form a monopoly by merging the two superfirms. But practically everybody realizes that the two firms could never agree on the president of the merged corporation, its product, the way in which the profits should be shared, and so forth. This solution may not be dangerous but it seems unfeasible.

Finally, the existing precarious informal encapsulation might be extended, not by imposing new arrangements but by an institutionalization of the existing relations between the two firms. This would involve the formulation of an explicit *agreement* to avoid price wars and the establishment of limited *machinery* to enforce the agreement, while allowing—within broad limits—uninhibited *competition* through quality. This would formalize the implicit accommodation toward which the firms have moved by themselves, provide both sides with assurances that there will be no regressions, and alleviate the psychological strains and the economic costs of fear. Unlike the duopolistic approach, encapsulation does not forbid the continuation of the competition: While some means of conflict (price wars) are ruled out, others (quality competition) are legitimated.[19] It should be emphasized that *this conflict-under-rules, or competition, is not far removed from the existing relationship between the firms*, which was, in effect, limited to quality contests and avoided price wars but which involved no explicit agreement. The question is not whether the conflict is or is not imposing limits on itself (that is, encapsulating), but whether the capsule is to remain implicit or to be strengthened by being made explicit.

Among the conditions under which the firms are likely to be willing to shift to explicit curbs on conflict are the following: Each firm must realize (a) that its chances of driving the other into bankruptcy (winning a total victory) are minimal; and that (b) unless explicitly and effectively ruled out, price wars may occur and would very probably be ruinous to both—that is, informal encapsulation is unreliable, probabilistic and not preventive. (c) The expansionist firm must accept the limited outlet for its ambition provided by competition in quality, on the assumptions that trying to satisfy greater ambitions is too dangerous and that the only other alternative offered is a duopoly in which there would be no outlet at all. And (d) the defensive firm must be willing to forego its desire to frustrate completely the drive of the other firm, because it realizes that, in the long run, such an effort is unlikely to succeed, if only because buyers like to shift, and the other firm would probably not agree to pacification through a duopolistic division of the market. At the same time, the defensive firm must feel able and *be* able to compete in quality, to feel that losses of buyers will be at worst limited and probably temporary, and have some realistic possibility of regaining customers lost earlier. Thus, competition will jeopardize the defensive firm's control of its present share of the market, but it will also allow for potential gains.

An International Application

A Historical Perspective

The international analogies to the interfirm model are too obvious to need delineation. The Western responses to Communist challenges are largely dominated by a sharp conceptual contrast—that between parties in conflict and parties at peace. East and West, it is said, are in conflict; resolutions through the formation of a world government or all-out war are seen as either unfeasible or immoral alternatives, or as both. The main Western approaches are "protracted conflict"[20] and a search for pacification.[21] The first approach foresees no accommodation with the Communist powers and, hence, prepares for many years of conflict. The other approach implies the hope of full conciliation as the Communist camp mellows, or as its mellowness is recognized, or—as the West's aggression is mollified. Open competition in some spheres coupled with the elimination of conflict in others through effective international machinery is a third alternative, which is considered here as an evolving trend, an alternative solution, and a strategy.[22]

The fusion of containment with deterrence, a duopolistic policy which is the essence of the American strategy, means to the advocates of "protracted conflict" holding the line to gain time but no end to the latent conflict or its risks. For the advocates of pacification, this strategy offers a solution reminiscent of the stalemate of the Anglo-French conflict over Africa in the 1890s. It suggests, in effect, dividing the world into two spheres of influence along the containment line; each camp is deterred from challenging the other's sphere by nuclear, conventional, and subconventional arms. If such an arrangement were acceptable to the other side, then both camps could live happily ever after in a state of peaceful coexistence.

Duopoly, in this as in other cases, is a stance favored by the challenged side which seeks to preserve the *status quo*, its sphere of influence; it is one of the least attractive alternatives to the expansionist side, requiring it to give up its ambitions and settle for whatever it had gained before the agreement. The central question is whether or not there is any other approach that would be more attractive to the Communist powers and still be in accord with the basic values of the Western ones. Encapsulation of the interbloc conflict, so as to allow full and open competition in unarmed capabilities and rule out effectively armed competition, seems to provide such an answer.

Encapsulation requires the drawing of a sharp line between permissible and non-permissible means of conflict, but *where* the line is to be drawn is a different issue altogether. Theoretically, it can be drawn between all-out and limited wars, nuclear and conventional wars, inner and outer space, and so on. However, there are considerations of political feasibility, inspection technology, and the assessment of the probability and disutility of escalation of permissible into non-permissible conflicts. Here, we explore the characteristics of an encapsulated conflict in which the line falls between armed and unarmed means.

First, one may ask whether or not the superpowers do not already, in effect, rule out nuclear war and most other kinds of armed conflict and focus their sparring around space and development races—that is, around unarmed competition. In effect, they do, but the analogy of the two rival firms highlights the difference between an informal limitation on conflict and an institutionalized one. The present interbloc accommodation is of the first type. The limitations to conflict that have been introduced are based on expedient and probably transient considerations. There is little in the present world system to prevent a superpower from exploiting some major technological breakthrough (for example, in the field of anti-missile defense) through an all-out war against the other. Second, since the existing limitations on the conflict are self-imposed and have not been explicitly agreed upon, they are vague and ambiguous. Khrushchev, for instance, may not have anticipated the American reaction to his Cuban missiles;[23] yet the United States saw them as a major violation of the *status quo* (or duopoly) which it thought the USSR had gradually come to accept. Thus, violations *might* be quite unintentional and still trigger the spiral of responses and counter-responses that would break the capsule of informal limitations.

Third, since there is *no effective organizational machinery for adjusting* the implicit curbs on conflict, the principal method of seeking to alter their scope is to commit violations. For instance, in 1963 the United States found itself informally bound to allow Soviet guards to count the passengers in United States military vehicles on their way to West Berlin, by dismounting the passengers at the entrances to the East German routes. The United States, at this point, for reasons irrelevant to the issue at hand, wished to change this procedure. Since it was not agreed upon in the first place, and since there were no mechanisms or guide lines for renegotiation, the United States attempted to change the rule by a *de facto* change in conduct: It suddenly refused to dismount the passengers on a technical pretext.[24] The Russians reacted by blocking the passage. An American officer tried to break through. The Russians accumulated armored cars. An "eyeball to eyeball," front-page crisis was generated, working against the encapsulating re-laxation of tensions President Kennedy was developing. Further escalation was avoided in this case by an informal compromise (the passengers dis-mounted for purposes other than being counted), but the case illustrates the risks of arrangements which have no established procedures for revision. The lack of effective machinery also means that arbitration procedures have to be worked out each time on an *ad hoc* basis. Finally, practically *no machinery is evolved for the validation and enforcement* of the rules. The sides rely almost completely on their partisan reporting for validation and on the threat of retaliation for enforcement.[25] Thus, they hover only a few steps away from unlimited conflict.

The Effect of Various Power Constellations

There is a general tendency to associate the use of power with self-serving goals and to see the advancement of collective goals as carried by their own virtue. Actually, the building of communities and encapsulation, whether it be of labor–management conflicts or the disarmament of the Wild West, proceed more effectively under some power constellations than under others. Collective causes can be advanced by self-serving motives and can be supported by power.

A power constellation under which encapsulation seems to advance is one which allows the more powerful parties to protect their positions against the pressure for the reallocation of power to rising parties. The number of the members in a system has often been related to the stability of the system. The balance-of-power system seems to require at least four or five members.[26] Systems with three members tend to lead to coalitions, in which two join forces against the third.[27] Bi-polar systems (i.e., those with two members) have been shown to be particularly difficult to pacify. These highly analytic propositions do not take into account differences in power among the members. An outstanding characteristic of political reality (especially the international one), however, is that the members differ drastically in their power.

A realistic model must, therefore, take into account the relative power of the members involved in the issue at hand rather than focus only on their number. Encapsulation and community-building seem to be enhanced by the transition from a relatively duopolistic system to a more pluralistic one, a process that may be referred to as *depolarization*.[28]

International relations approximated a state of duopoly between 1946 and 1958. Depolarization generated a situation more conducive to encapsulation; between 1958 and 1964, in each of the two major camps, a secondary power rebelled. The effect of these rebellions was to draw the two superpowers closer together. Seeking to maintain their superior status and fearing the consequences of the inter-camp conflicts generated by their rebelling lieutenants, the superpowers set out to formulate some rules binding on all parties. The treaty for the partial cessation of nuclear tests, which the United States and the Soviet Union tried to make binding on France and China, was a case in point. American–Russian efforts to stem the proliferation of nuclear weapons was another. Russia, in this period, stopped whatever technical aid it was supplying to Chinese nuclear research and development,[29] and the United States refused to help France develop its nuclear force.[30]

These measures have in common the important characteristic that they serve the more "narrow" needs of the superpowers while they also advance the "general welfare" of the world and can, hence, be presented in terms of universal values and implemented through world institutions (i.e., extend the "capsule"). For instance, the primary superpower motivation for the 1963 test treaty might well have been the desire of the United States and Russia to remain the only two great nuclear powers, but the treaty also reduced the danger of nuclear war. It was presented as if the prime motive were the advancement of peace and disarmament and the reduction of fallout to protect human health. It is a familiar strategy of political interest groups to work out solutions among themselves and then clothe them in the values of the community-at-large. Indirectly, these values affect the course of action an interest group chooses from among the available alternatives and provide a common base on which the similar or compatible interests of divergent powers can be harmonized and the shared community broadened.

International "Floating Vote"

Another process that has enhanced encapsulation is the emergence of a "floating vote"—that is, a vote not permanently committed to any one of the adversaries. The value of the existence of a sizable floating vote for the *maintenance* of a political system is that it tends to moderate the conflict among the parties by making violent conflict less "attractive" and by reducing the temper of conflict, thus making all-out, capsule-breaking conflict less likely. So long as a significant portion of the voters is uncommitted, gaining their support tends to be preferred to a violent (and risky) "showdown"; moderation tends to appeal to the uncommitted voters who are, as a rule, "between" the parties of a conflict in terms of their interests. The emergence of a significant floating vote supports the *development of a* community by encouraging encapsulation. In the same period in which depolarization advanced and the solidarity of the Eastern and Western camps declined, the duopolistic system was further weakened by the increase in the number of nonaligned countries.[31] And the status of nonalignment rose as the main superpowers increasingly recognized this stance as legitimate.

The growth in the number and status of the non-aligned nations—a kind of international floating vote—made several contributions toward encapsulation and community-building. Around these nations began to develop a growing *shared norm*—the recognition of non-alignment—which limited the conflict between adversaries in that it increasingly defined one major sector of the world system as outside the conflict *so far as armed means were concerned*. While the norm was occasionally violated (e.g., in Vietnam and Laos), it was widely observed, and, over the years, violations became less frequent. At the same time, non-violent means of competition such as trade, aid, and propaganda composed an increasing proportion of the investments which the United States and the Soviet Union made in third countries.[32]

The norm supporting non-alignment is of special interest for the study of encapsulation, since it does not bar conflicts but only rules out armed intervention in non-aligned countries. Peaceful appeals are "allowed." This quality of the norm had a double effect: First, it forbade (quite successfully) the joining of non-aligned countries to a bloc, a joining that would have weakened the movement toward regulation of the conflict and, if continued, would have reduced and potentially exhausted the floating vote. Second, the norm allowed for the expression of the ambitions of the superpowers without their violating the rules curbing the conflict, a major attribute of encapsulation as distinguished from conflict-resolution or pacification.

Above all, the increase in the floating vote, like the decrease in bloc solidarity, significantly increased the range of political activities and sharply reduced the pressure to resort to military means. The more rigidly the instruments of power (e.g., votes) and prospective rewards (e.g., economic assets) are divided between two parties, and the more internally integrated each of these parties is, the less the weaker of the two can expect to gain a majority (in a parliament or the United Nations) and improve its share in the allocation of assets by nonviolent means. The more political efforts such as campaigning (to appeal to the floating vote) and bargaining (to take away a segment of the opposing party or bloc) are or seem to be futile, the greater the pressure toward an armed showdown. As has often been suggested, the more constitutional or otherwise legitimate avenues of effective action are closed, the greater the pressures toward change by force.

These general propositions, we suggest, apply with special strength on the international level. Here, the use of armed means is not considered as illegitimate as it is inside a national society ("war is the continuation of diplomacy by other means"). The normative bonds among the actors are weaker, and hostility among the parties is more encompassing. There are fewer constitutional avenues for the expression of conflict and no central force to curb the escalation of conflicts toward violent "solutions." Hence, a decrease in the solidarity of the blocs and an increase in the "floating vote" reduce the pressure toward unlimited armed conflict and increase the value of other political options.

Since the floating vote provides a reward that shifts to the superpower that is favored, the values according to which the floating vote shifts are among the values the sides seek to promote (or at least to give the appearance of promoting). In the period under study, the floating vote often rewarded superpower moderation, since this vote tends to be politically "between" the sides in a conflict. On balance, the non-aligned countries stand to lose from an American–Soviet war but to gain from peaceful competition between the superpowers for their support. Hence, it is not surprising that, between 1958 and 1964, the non-aligned countries tended to use their influence to encourage encapsulation. In general, the non-aligned countries favored the reduction of armaments and of cold war tensions, an increase in the capacities, power, and status of the United Nations, the cessation of hostilities in Korea and Vietnam, and the elimination of the superpowers' armed interventions in the internal affairs of other countries.[33]

End of Ideologization

The extent to which interaction among collectivities, especially among nations, was ideologically based increased in the modern age. The mass mobilization of citizens in macroscopic conflicts was common (in elections, strikes, or wars), and normative means were used to gain such mobilization because they are less expensive and more committing than the utilitarian ones that were used in earlier ages in which the level of mobilization required was lower and the concern with efficiency was smaller (e.g., the use of mercenaries and paid voters). The depiction of the other nation as evil and "ours" as good is part of this process of ideological mobilization. Against this general trend, however, there are important differences in the degree of the "ideologization" of international relations. At one extreme, the mobilized members of the nations involved understand the relations in highly ideological, moralistic terms. At the other extreme, international relations are viewed in calculative terms, as "power politics."

Among the factors which appear to influence the extent of a conflict's ideologization are the number and combinations of the adversaries. When they are divided into two opposing camps, ideologization seems to be greatest. This may be explained psychologically in that such a division makes dealing with the ambivalence inherent in every relationship relatively simple by projecting the positive on the ingroup and the negative on the outgroup. Accordingly, we would expect duopolistic relations to be highly ideological and depolarization to result in a reduction of the extent of ideologization. The period between 1958 and 1964 provides an opportunity to explore this proposition because the unity of the Communist and the Western camps declined sharply. In 1963, President Kennedy created and exercised the option to reduce the ideological content of Soviet–American relations This permitted some increase in reality-testing (largely in US–USSR relations), and a much broader span of political maneuvering as a new range of combinations rose in geometrical proportion to the increase in the number of autonomous adversaries. There were Franco-Chinese transactions, an American–Soviet treaty, Franco-Soviet negotiations, and even some increase in American–Chinese contacts. In short, it appears that depolarization (or an increase in power pluralism) reduced ideologization, opened the international arena to more political alternatives, and relegated the military approach to only one of an increasing number of options.

Consensus-Formation and Regional Bodies

Societal processes which reduce the differences in perspective among members (i.e., reduce the system's heterogeneity) and increase integration enhance unification by enhancing consensus-formation. The development of *intermediary bodies* seems of special value here. Regional organizations and regional communities and blocs can serve as "intermediary bodies" for the international community. To view every regional body as a step toward world community, however, would be incorrect. The following dimensions serve to characterize regional organizations in terms of variables that affect their capacity to serve as a "middle" tier in an evolving world-community consensus-formation structure.

(a) Regional organizations that serve only marginal societal functions, such as the European research organization on the peaceful usages of nuclear energy (CERN), are less effective than those that serve functions more central to the member nations or to the rising union, as the European Economic Community (EEC) has begun to do.[34] (b) Regional bodies intended to countervail other regional bodies, especially military alliances such as NATO and the Warsaw Treaty Organization, often retard rather than advance the encapsulation of conflict; they tend to reflect on a large scale the more deunifying features of nationalism. (c) Economic associations may serve as "antiblocs" rather than as a basis for a world community. For example, the British-led European Free Trade Area was formed to "counter" the French-led EEC. On the other hand, regional bodies aimed at internal improvement, such as "welfare" communities (a foundation of the EEC) or development associations (e.g., in Central America) which stress rapid economic growth or mutual assistance, are more likely to serve as intermediary layers in building a world community.

Upward Transfer

Above all, only regional bodies that allow for the process of *upward transfer* aid in the construction of a world community. Studies of structures as different as the American federal government and the Southern Baptist Association have shown that *once a new center of control is established, on the supra-unit level, it tends to grow in power and in command of loyalties* earlier commanded by the member units.[35]

Not every establishment of a supra-unit center of control automatically triggers such an upward transfer. Moreover, not every upward transfer necessarily advances unification to the community level. The conditions under which upward-transfer "takes off" and the conditions under which and the stages at which it is blocked or terminated, and whether the plateaux reached are stable or are only temporary stopgaps after which the process either progresses or regresses, are questions we have merely begun to explore.

When an upward transfer process is proceeding, several questions need to be asked: (i) How many tiers are being developed above the level of nation–states? Will there be only two tiers—regional bodies (OAS, OAU, and so on) and a global organization (UN)—or three tiers including supra-regional or subregional organizations? (NATO is a supraregional organization, relating North America to Western Europe; Central American organizations and LAFTA (Latin American Free Trade Area) are subregional in the OAS region.)[36] (ii) Will the tiers differ in their control power, in the sectors that are controlled, or in both? Corporations tend to provide more power to the higher tiers and to rely on the resulting hierarchy as a basis of organization. Highly decentralized corporations, however, often have the opposite distribution, with more power given to the lower levels. This seems to be the case so far with international structures: The UN is weaker than the regional organizations, and they, in turn, are weaker than the national tier. While such a distribution can be sustained for a transitional period, we expect that a hierarchical distribution is necessary if community-building is to be completed and stabilized.[37]

Another possibility is to distribute the control of sectors among the levels; e.g., education can be controlled on the lower levels, the economy on the middle levels, and force on the highest level. In present international systems, normative controls tend to be national even when some utilitarian or coercive controls are shifted upward.

It also has been argued that there could be multi-center control structures, each mono-sectoral but with coextensive jurisdiction,[38] as was the situation with the church and king in parts of Europe during the middle ages and as is now the case in the OEED and NATO, each of which include approximately the same countries with one organization dealing with economic and the other with military matters. We expect, however, that for a community to be integrated, the control of all of the main sectors will have to come from one center, though the delegation of control to the middle and lower levels can be very extensive. In other words, the top tier will have to possess the right to steer all activities but could transfer much of the actual control to lower levels. (The merger of three authorities—EEC, ECSC, and Euratom—as the unification of the EEC advanced is a case in point.) We do not suggest that such a structure is developing on a global level or is even likely to develop, especially in the first transitional stages of world-wide upward-transfer. But we do suggest that a community organized differently would be too unstable, underintegrated, and undermanaged to fulfill its basic encapsulation function, the prevention of war.

We are projecting the image of an integrated and responsive society. In this projection, nation–states or sub-regional communities serve as the sub-units. They may be tied into more inclusive, broad-scoped units (regions or supra-regions) or be cross-related by mono-sectoral organizations. All this is in addition to their being gradually integrated into a supra-unit and organization, the world community and state. The existence of cross-cutting loyalties[39] and organizations (i.e., those that are not coextensive in their membership with any cohesive unit or sub-unit) is expected to enhance the growth of a world community, but, as in a national community, too much leverage should not be expected from these factors, as the prime units of affiliation and action are collectivities and the organizations which express them.

The last phase of the upward-transfer process is particularly difficult to chart at this stage of our knowledge, because the development of intermediary bodies depends heavily on spreading the flame of regional and bloc chauvinism in order to melt away some national sovereignty in favor of regional organizations or states. Without the cold war, many of the efforts to form Atlantic and East European communities are difficult to imagine. A major driving force behind the attempts to form common markets in South America, in various parts of Africa, in the Far East, and elsewhere is the desire to counter the actual or anticipated consequences of the European Economic Community.[40] Progress, in short, might not be unilinear but dialectical, with nations moving apart and thereby providing the foundations for moving closer together.

Dialectics of Unification

The deunification of a particular system need not be deleterious to community-building, just as not every conflict reduces integration. In fact, when there are many heterogeneous units, one major way in which a community can be advanced is by the formation of subcommunities by subgroups of units, with considerable conflict among the subcommunities at this stage; only after such unifications of subcommunities are advanced are the member units ready to form one community. The conflict among the subgroupings helps each in its sub-system unification. Once such unification is advanced, the sub-communities provide the middle tier for a multi-tier consensus-formation structure. In this sense, the second stage, characterized by inter-subgroup tension, leads to the third stage, which could not be initiated by a jump from the first to the third because heterogeneity was at too high a level in the first stage.

Thus, in a dialectical pattern, subcommunities antithetical to each other lead to community synthesis; dissensus is a pre-condition of consensus. Historical examples of this process include the formation of a United King-dom for the European low countries in 1814–1830, which seems to have been a premature attempt to move from the first to the third stage. It collapsed when the southern provinces rebelled in 1830 and formed Belgium. The ensuing war between the two sub-groups helped in the integration of each but did not hinder the eventual unification of both in a structure that recog-nizes the distinctiveness of the two sub-groupings (i.e., Benelux). Similarly, the Civil War increased the integration among former colonies within the South and the North but did not prevent and, in a way, even helped the development of the American society. Actually, American integration is held to have reached a community level in the 1890s, after the Civil War.

From this viewpoint, the Cold War has sometimes been viewed as a preparation for a world community by advancing two camps.[41] It would appear, however, that each of these camps has been too complex and heterogeneous to integrate, and that each has broken into one or more sub-camps. But we may say, in general, that the rise of regional communities, so long as the specific counter-productive factors discussed above are not operative, is to be seen as a step in the transition from an 130-odd nation–state world to one with fewer actors which is more given to further unification.

We do not argue that dialectical unification is without functional alternatives, but this process is encountered often enough so that all de-unifications should not be construed as signs of increased tribalism. Our analysis assumes that the regional units which are formed in the second transition stage remain as a subordinate but nevertheless viable component of the third, community stage; otherwise, the rising community would lack a middle tier (intermediary bodies) in its consensus-formation structure. Thus, a genetic approach (three stages) is related to a functional analysis (the need for three tiers) and to a future-system: the community.

Homogeneity and Unification

Many tribalists argue that since homogeneity is essential for community-building and since the world is heterogeneous, a world-community cannot be built. On the other hand, advocates of world-community point to Switzer-land to show that diversity of religion, language, and culture does not prevent community-building. The tribalists counter that world heterogeneity is much greater; Switzerland, therefore, does not provide a convincing precedent. Actually, the proposition which both sides assume to be valid—a negative association between heterogeneity and unification—needs to be specified and revised; as usually advanced, it seems invalid.

First, some kinds of heterogeneity are conducive to unification, while homogeneity can thwart it. Countries whose economies are complementary can unify more readily than those whose main crops are identical.[42] Second, the relationship between unification and homogeneity is not unilinear; while a high level of heterogeneity hinders unification,[43] the difference between middle and low levels of homogeneity as predisposing conditions for unification is not large. Actually, most well-established political communities are, to some degree, heterogeneous.

Third, the level of heterogeneity should not be treated as a given: Groupings of units that seek unification can reduce their heterogeneity by efforts such as an inter-country division-of-labor (attempted in Central America) and a reallocation of wealth (which the EEC attempted to a limited degree). In general, the more a system is integrated, the easier it is to reallocate within its boundaries (not just wealth, but also power and status), and not just the other way around—the more egalitarian the allocations, the more likely is the unification. Once again, we see two mutually reinforcing processes: Some unification allows for some reallocation, which, in turn, allows for additional unification, thus reinforcing a dynamic relationship that continues until other factors block additional progress on one of the two "legs."

Finally, the existence or construction of a multi-tier structure provides for consensus-formation in the face of heterogeneity. Such a structure cannot bridge all diversity, but it can reduce the political effects of societal differences; hence, societal homogeneity is not a prerequisite of a stable and active community.

The Role of International Law

The major concern in the study of encapsulation, as distinct from most analyses of intrasocietal law and controls, is not with protecting the existing guidance mechanism from erosion but with accelerating its extension and growth. This points to the importance of formalizing implicit and "understood" rules into explicit and enforced international laws, which is neither obvious nor widely agreed upon. There are many who stress the value of implicit, unnegotiated "understanding."[44] Such understanding is valued because it can be reached with less interference from dissenting allies and domestic opponents.

But there are several disadvantages. The possibility of miscommunication is greater. It is similar to announcing one's intention to shift lanes on a highway by starting to move the car into an adjacent lane rather than by using the agreed-upon specific signal. The probability of miscommunication increases with the complexity of the issues, the extent of the cultural differences, and the level of hostility among the actors. When miscommunication occurs, it generates feelings of betrayal and mistrust in elites and citizens, which, in turn, are obstacles to future communication. And to the degree that the publics are unaware of the agreements because they are implicit, their communities-of-assumption remain intact and will tend not to support more encompassing agreements when those become possible and favored by the elites. Furthermore, to the degree that the publics become aware that a "deal" was made, they became distrustful of their elites.* Finally, the inter- or supranational organizations do not increase their tasks and power unless implicit understandings are codified and enforced by them.

When rules are formalized, effective verification and response machinery becomes necessary. The 1954 agreements to neutralize Laos and to limit arms supplies for Vietnam were supervised by an understaffed, under-financed, ill-equipped, and—above all—a politically deadlocked commission. (Its members were India, Poland, and Canada.) In 1959, East and West accused each other of violating these agreements; the enforcement machinery provided neither a clear picture of the first transgressor nor an appropriate response. On the other hand, United Nations troops on the Egyptian–Israeli Gaza strip successfully pacified this highly volatile border between 1957 and 1967. Multilateral inspections of scientific stations in the Antarctic helped to enforce the agreement to keep it a disarmed zone. It is not that such control networks, set up by world authorities, can, at this stage, prevent conflicts even among small powers, let alone among superpowers. But to the degree that the powers favor encapsulation, such networks provide a tool for its institutionalization, which, in turn, has some limited autonomous effect on the advancement of encapsulation and unification.

Like other developments discussed here, the formalization of superpower or world-wide agreements is an option. The conditions under which less tribal, more communal options arise and are chosen were briefly outlined here, in a hypothetical fashion. Each choice of a sequence of options is also to be viewed as a strategy for national actors, especially superpowers, to follow. These strategies may be either tribalist or communal in their cumulative effects. To the degree that the processes discussed here raise more options for regional and world community-building (which seems to be the historical trend) and the actors involved prefer these over tribal options (which is far less evident), a gradual build-up of a world community is to be expected. This requires that societies be actively engaged in transforming their boundaries and in supporting more encompassing regional and world

---

* We do not suggest that a single incident will have such an effect, but that a policy based on such procedures will.

organizations and communities. This entails reducing, to a degree, the societies' authority and autonomy but not their active quality, for to be active requires the reduction of the existential alienation which cannot be overcome without a world community. Moreover, sharing in a larger community will increase the economic and cultural assets of the members, enhancing their and the new community's activation. Such a community is necessary in the functional sense of the term, i.e., if societal needs are to be met; it is feasible—as such a development does not violate any sociological law. Whether or not it will be established is a question we cannot answer.

A Global Perspective

Tribalism in Normative Systems

A study of the factors that influence the growth of a world community is not complete without a sociology of values and ideas. This is a vast field, approached, on the one hand, by the tools of the humanities which analyze *leitmotifs* of cultural systems, their relations and dynamics,[45] and, on the other hand—often in a quite unrelated manner—by survey analysis studying the values and ideas to which people subscribe and changes in their commitment. The following limited introductory comments point to a few relationships between the study of the building of a world community and the sociology of culture. The key question is: Which creeds have sufficient transcendental force to overcome tribalism?

Only the most primitive creeds are tribalistic in that they sanctify the family, clan, or village with little or no universalistic abstraction. Most creeds draw on universalistic values to legitimate particularistic polities and societies—e.g., their community is the one chosen by a universal God; their polity is more democratic than others. The values and ideas in themselves are given to universalistic interpretations; others may appeal to the same God or claim that *their* polity ranks higher in terms of the same value—i.e., is more democratic. The very commitment to a universalistic creed provides a potential, however elementary, basis for de-tribalization. Other tribes, even all tribes, may be legitimated by it.

Next, any one creed, whether it be religious or secular, may tribalize or legitimate community-building, depending upon the historical and societal situation. From the perspective of an Indian village or a Nigerian tribe, nationalism is community-building; from that of *Europa*, nationalism is a tribal force. Our transcendental perspective is that of a global community.

Even as seen from the top of the United Nations, however, not all nationalism is tribalistic. Viewed dynamically and, especially, dialectically, creeds that sanctify the formation of new particularisms may support global community-building if the new particularisms are more encompassing than the earlier ones, and, above all, if the new positive evaluations are not based on a negative orientation toward outsiders and toward universalism. Similarly, particularisms which challenge distorted communities may lead to more authentic ones. Finally, there is no necessary opposition between nationalism and internationalism; one can complement the other. The tension is between absolutist conceptions of national autonomy, often telescoped into a rigid concept of sovereignty, and conceptions which recognize that national values can be advanced by supranational institutions. This is the major difference between "closed" and "open" nationalism.

Studies of the universalistic elements of creeds from Christianity to socialism have made much of the fact that these creeds have failed in their confrontations with nationalism—e.g., socialists joined in 1914 to support international wars, despite many previous statements about world-wide workers' unity, and Christian nations warred with each other.* However, it may be that, as in societal transformations in which new communal bonds first co-exist as weaker elements next to older tribal bonds, universalistic normative elements lost the first rounds but not necessarily the match. We hold as a working proposition that in the post-modern period, there is a secular trend which, despite much fluctuation, seems to indicate a rising commitment to universalistic elements. The increased interest among the clergy of many religions in world peace (e.g., the Pope's "Peace on Earth" encyclical) is a case in point. A rising preoccupation with world peace in secular ideologies (which, in the modern period, were more concerned with other aspects of humanity) can be discerned (e.g., within the non-Marxist left).

Surveys show fairly general approval of some form of world community.[46] These findings might well amount to nothing more than widespread lip-service to an ideal (we are not even confident that this lip-service continues to spread). Still, they may be of somewhat more significance than they seem, especially if this turns out to be not the kind of lip-service that remains as a vestige of a value which has lost most of its committing power, but is rather of the opposite kind—which precedes the evolution of deeper commitments.

The present commitments to universalism are secondary; most followers hold them in typical tribalist "open" fashion—i.e., they are willing to subscribe to global community so long as it does not conflict with their primary tribal commitments. Even in nations in which globalist sentiments are fairly strong, it seems quite easy for the national elites to mobilize a tribalist primacy. In that sense, most, if not all, nations are still in the 1914 stage. On the other hand, if community-building were to advance on other fronts, these inchoate, weak commitments to universalism could magnify

---

* So did nations whose citizens adhered to other religions. Jews, not burdened with two states, fought each other in the armies of France and Germany, Austria and Russia, and elsewhere, wherever the host state would allow them the privilege.

rapidly.[47] The existence of a legitimation of integration, even in a weak form, prior to the integration seems to make the integration both more likely to occur and to have a transforming impact.

When a new universalism arises and spreads rapidly, or an old one is revived and gains in following, there is still no assurance that it will provide the needed transforming creed. Many such creeds reveal a pathology that deserves closer study; they are born with a latent defect that sooner or later destroys their universalism before they reach maturity. Creeds, born globalist, tend to "tribalize" as they gain mass following, because they spread unevenly and are used to legitimate the particularism of those tribes which adopt them first against those in which they are not yet prevalent, often thus preventing the continued spread of the creed. Thus, Christianity was strongly globalist in its early days as a creed of a minority in ancient Judea and of slaves in Rome, but, once the Emperor embraced it, it was turned into a creed of the empire which labelled other societies as heathen. Similarly, communism was to unite workers of all nations, and all men but a few were to become workers. But once the revolution established itself in a few countries and its export or native expansion to other societies slowed down, it became tribalized, the creed of one set of societies against others. In both creeds, an element of universalism remained, as indicated by the belief that members of other societies can be saved, but tribalism registers even here in the belief that although those who saw the light first ought to help those still in the dark, they ought not to risk their tribe. On the contrary, the heathens should smash their own false gods and join with the saved ones.

Finally, both religious and class ideologies were and are used by true believers to justify holy wars against other tribes and to "legitimate" totalitarian controls and the suppression of minorities such as in Calvinist Geneva, Catholic Spain, and Stalin's USSR. Thus, tribalism, especially a "closed" one, often distorts the foundations of whatever universalism it professes to serve. The fact that as these creeds mellow, as true believers become apathetic followers, they are increasingly alienating[48]—does not bolster authentic communities; these require that political and societal responsiveness and international transformation be central and integral parts of the creed.

Most important is the perspective of treating all others as members of one's moral community. The community of those entitled to such a status seems to be expanding, a hypothesis which can be tested empirically. As the concept of a moral community is central to universalism, it deserves some elaboration.

Moral Communities

Every value to which an actor is committed can be characterized in three major ways: Its substance, the intensity of the commitment, and—a dimension usually neglected—the extent of the community to which the actor applies the value. For instance, two persons who hold that lying is a sin and hold it with the same degree of intensity may differ considerably in the boundaries of the community to which they grant the right not to be lied to. For instance, one person may feel that this norm is less applicable to children than to adults and more applicable to friends than to persons with whom he has only secondary relations. Another may hold, as Kant did, that it is a universal right. The extent of such "communities" is neither randomly nor personally determined; societal processes affect the extent of the moral community as well as the substance and intensity of the norm. For example, the boundaries of the moral community seem to be wider for educated than for uneducated persons. (They seem to be associated with the extent of consciousness, considered above.) One common way in which moral communities are limited is to define those who are excluded as not human or as less human.* The moral communities of members of a collectivity (who are similar in their activation scores) tend to be similar in terms of the part of humanity they encompass, and, in this sense, one can refer to a moral community of a societal actor.

The moral community of a given actor does not remain constant; it expands and contracts. The study of the factors which affect its limits is essential to the study of the rise of new communities. Here, an important difference among values is to be taken into account. Some values are more closely related to primary relationships than others and, hence, are more difficult to de-tribalize. Those associated with affection and love, despite such conceptions as universal love in the Christian tradition and free love in the socialist one, are inherently particularistic. The moral community of other values is more directly relevant to the boundaries of political communities— for instance, distributive justice. If *these* values are less encompassing than the political system, as they are in many new nation–states, they decelerate community-building; if they are more encompassing, they are a unifying force, as "European" sentiments were in six European nations at the height of the EEC popularity.

The Non-Violent Community

Of all of the values societal actors hold, the one most directly relevant to the reduction of tribalism is the non-violent (moral) community, which provides the normative foundations of peace. It is the community of those for whom the actor under study—if it be a person, an elite, a class, or a nation—

---

* The ancient Greek and white southerner used the same mechanisms—both limited the moral community of those who deserve to be treated as free men, excluding "barbarians" and "niggers" as sub-human. The Nazis used the same mechanism for Jews, gypsies, and other "non-Aryan" groupings.

holds that force is not to be applied even when differences of interest, values, and viewpoint are high and the need to reach an agreement on a joint course of action is great.[49]

Historically, the non-violent community seems to be extending, though there have been numerous and important regressions. The non-violent community of many primitive societies included only a few hundred people; outsiders were, literally, free game. In historical societies, this community was extended, but it rarely effectively encompassed all members of society.[50] The rise of the nation–state had a major extending effect; it focused the legitimation of the use of violence against outsiders, so that a much higher ratio of insiders was included in the non-violent community than in previous periods. But, as though the nation–state bit off more than it could initially chew, several hundred years passed before this non-violent community was effectively established for all the sub-societies included. Children, workers, and racial minorities, roughly in that order, only slowly gained places in it. The growing redefinition of deviants, the insane, and criminals as not morally bad but mentally ill and, hence, as morally entitled to treatment and rehabilitation rather than segregation behind bars if not annihilation,[51] is an expression of the same trend to expand the moral community of non-violence so that it becomes more and more coextensive with the political boundaries of the nation–state. As the modern period closed, practically all the major groupings in established communities had the basic human right of freedom from violence, while members of other national communities were largely excluded. As with other values, moral claims were much more widely established than realized, and some groupings continued to be excluded—e.g., minorities in Nazi Germany. Significantly, these were considered "exceptions" and violations of a widely held code, unlike the burning of widows in earlier generations in India or the amputation of the arms of thieves in eighteenth-century England, acts which seem to have been considered legitimate. The contrast is most evident nowadays if the use of violence against foreigners is compared to its use against co-nationals.

In most post-modern nation–states, there is latent but easy-to-mobilize legitimation for the use of force against other nations, under pretexts and for reasons that would not justify to the same citizens the use of force against members of their own societies. Such tribalistic "boxing" of values can be seen with regard to other values as well: Poverty in the United States (commonly defined as $3,000 for a family of four)* moves many Americans to support efforts to alleviate it, but it ceases to be poverty when the citizens' eyes cross the border. Ninety-eight per cent of the citizens of most societies are poor by the United States criterion, but they are considered entitled to much less help. Since the advent of the post-modern age, there seems to be some evidence that some supranational extension of the moral communities

---

* The reference is to annual income.

of various values may be taking place, as reflected, for example, in the support for the work of UNICEF and for genuine foreign aid. Even the ideological conceptions of the "free world" and the "brotherhood of socialist societies" contain such elements. While many of those who promote such conceptions do so on the basis of narrow, tribalistic interests, the creeds per se have a supranational (though sub-global) element and, for those who come to believe in them, justify making some sacrifices for citizens of other nations, extending to them some of the same rights earlier more exclusively reserved for members of one's own nation. The supranational elements of post-modern, cold war ideologies stand out when compared to modern, isolationist concepts (which implied that the world beyond one's own national borders had little moral status) or to those ideologies which openly justify intervention in terms of real or alleged self-needs (e.g., the protection of American investments). The *act* of intervention may be similar under all these banners, but the supranational elements of post-modern ideologies do provide an opportunity for authentic, globalist interpretations, which the tribalistic ones do not.

Social Science and a Global Perspective

For a social scientist, it should seem obvious, but it is not, that there is only one basis for a moral community—a global one. Subjects put various boundaries on their values, and social scientists record these boundaries as being those of the *subjects* and compare the boundaries imposed by various groupings of subjects and their changes. But for a scientist *qua* scientist, values have no inherent boundaries. The truth of science is not that of a tribe or nation; it has to be tested in the universal community of scholars. What is valid for an "American" experiment must also be valid for a Chinese one, and all restrictions on communication other than those which are themselves universal (like protecting the subjects from the effects of research) are anathema to science.

A social scientist, as a *citizen*, may be limited by the moral community of his collectivity or society or be liberated from its constraints to varying degrees, but, in his scientific capacity, there is no principle he can draw upon to justify his adherance to one moral boundary rather than to another. Hence, when it comes to studying the moral community of a group of subjects, the *objective* criterion—in the sense of being replicable, non-changing, transferable, inter-subjective—is the degree of distance between the subjects' community and the universal one. It is the only criterion on which all social scientists can objectively agree.

Surprisingly, many social scientists tend to overplay the nation–state as the unit of societal analysis and underplay supranational bonds and controls;[52] above all, they tend to take the nationalistic moral community as *the* community of values. Ostensibly, these social scientists use no values other than those of their subjects. In effect, though, they commonly compare the attitudes or behavior of a group of subjects to a set of values. But how are these values chosen? Many social scientists would answer that they are the values of the subjects themselves. White and blue collar attitudes are compared to those of average Americans, male and female values to those of average nationals, or those of one class or race to those of another. But on what grounds are the particular norms used as a model chosen? Why American values and not American–Canadian, or Western, or world-wide ones? So long as the answer is one norm of the subject or another, it is, in effect, arbitrary, and the comparison—"more" liberal, "more" tolerant—is an artifact of the comparative mode chosen by the researchers. It may be argued that national values are most often chosen because the nation is the community most meaningful to the subjects or the central seat of societal action. But such an argument is not supported by the same canons of evidence which these social scientists revere and demand that other assertions be submitted to, as our discussion of the prevalence of quasi-imperialism suggests.

The only systematic escape from such relativism and latent ideological commitments is to rely on the one foundation all social scientists, whatever their affiliations, can share and measure—values whose community is all men. Such values also provide the only immovable foundation: Tribes merge and split, but the community of man remains. This does entail a transcendental stand, as the realization of this community is lagging, but so do all other positions, with one difference—the global community is the only one which embraces all social scientists *and* all of their subjects.

The father of sociology may have been closer to a universal sociological perspective on this point than many of his sons. He saw "no reason for confining human development within the boundaries of sovereign national states. Its idea of a universal order is consummated only through the union of all individuals in mankind, and the positivist destruction of obsolete theological and metaphysical standards comes to fruition in the recognition of *humanity* as the *être supreme*. Humanity, not the state, is the real universal, nay, it is the only reality."[53]

NOTES

1. Karl W. Deutsch, *Political Community at the International Level* (Garden City, N.Y.: Doubleday, 1954), pp. 9–13.

2. There were, of course, significant differences among empires and in each empire over time but the statement seems to hold as a generalization. See S. N. Eisenstadt, *The Political Systems of Empires* (New York: Free Press, 1963), pp. 156 ff. For background on the main modern empires, see D. K. Fieldhouse, *The Colonial Empires: A Comparative Survey from the 18th Century* (London: Weidenfeld & Nicolson, 1966).

3. The United States defense budget, as per cent of GNP, amounted to 8.2 per cent ($51.3 billion). Sprecher, *World-Wide Defense Expenditures and Selected Economic Data, op. cit.*, p. 7.

4. Sprecher, *ibid.*, p. 8.

5. Cf. to other discussion of intervention which stress legal and ethical aspects: Manfred Halpern, *The Morality and Politics of Intervention* (New York: The Council on Religion and International Affairs, 1963); Quincy Wright et al., "Intervention under the Charter of the United Nations and under the Charter of the Organization of American States," *Proceedings of the American Society of International Law*, Vol. 51 (1957), pp. 79–115; Ann Van Wyneh Thomas and A. J. Thomas, Jr., *Non-intervention: the Law and its Import in the Americas* (Dallas: Southern Methodist University Press, 1956).

6. For a recent case study of such context setting, see George G. S. Murphy, *Soviet Mongolia: A Study of the Oldest Political Satellite* (Berkeley: University of California Press, 1966).

7. We include Albania and Cuba, but not Yugoslavia. Tibet is usually considered part of China. For a recent report, see Harrison E. Salisbury, "Chinese Consolidate their Control over Tibet," *The New York Times*, July 5, 1966.

8. Madagascar and French Somalia are included; Guinea is excluded. For France's role in the armies of African states, see William Gutteridge, *Military Institutions and Power in the New States* (New York: Praeger, 1965), pp. 117–129. See also Mamadou Dia, *Réflexions sur l'Économie de l'Afrique Noire* (Paris: Présence Africaine, 1960). Conor Cruise O'Brien, "The Limits of Political Choice in French West Africa, 1956 to 1960," *Civilisations*, Vol. 15 (1965), p. 217. Teresa Hayter, *French Aid* (London: The Overseas Development Institute, 1966).

9. For recent domestic studies which help to assess the extent of the effects of the external elite, see Ronald C. Nairn, *International Aid to Thailand: The New Colonialism?* (New Haven, Conn.: Yale University Press, 1966). For a report by an American participant, see John Bartlow Martin, *Overtaken by Events: The Dominican Crisis From the Fall of Trujillo to the Civil War* (Garden City, N.Y.: Doubleday, 1966). For a good journalistic account, Tad Szulc, *Dominican Diary* (New York: Delacorte Press, 1965). See also Frank C. Darling, *Thailand and the United States* (Washington, D.C.: Public Affairs Press, 1965), esp. pp. 214–228 and Leonard Binder, *Iran: Political Development in a Changing Society* (Berkeley, Calif.: University of California Press, 1962), esp. pp. 339–343. See also Norman Jacobs, *The Sociology of Development: Iran as an Asian Case Study* (New York: Praeger, 1966); Ronald Matthews, *African Powder Keg* (London: The Bodley-Head, 1966); and Robert Fitch and Mary Oppenheimer, *Ghana: End of an Illusion* (New York: Monthly Review Press, 1966). The developments in Vietnam are too well known to require a reference.

10. For a detailed discussion of our view, see "Intervention for Progress" in *Winning Without War, op. cit.*, pp. 115–163.

11. Similar cooperation has taken place in British Guiana, between 1964 and 1966. See Thomas Mathews, "The Three Guianas," *Current History*, Vol. 51 (1966), pp. 337 ff.

12. On the degree to which trade is intra-camp, see Russett, *Trends in World Politics, op. cit.*, pp. 33–37.

13. See Willard F. Barber and C. Neale Ronning, *Internal Security and Military Power* (Columbus, Ohio: Ohio State University, 1966); David Galula, *Counterinsurgency Warfare: Theory and Practice* (New York and London: Praeger, 1964) and John S. Pustay, *Counterinsurgency Warfare* (New York: Free Press, 1965). See also Robert T. Holt and Robert W. van de Velde, *Strategic Psychological Operations and American Foreign Policy* (Chicago: University of Chicago Press, 1960) and Blackstock, *The Strategy of Subversion: Manipulating the Politics of Other Nations, op. cit.*

For two informative journalistic accounts, see John Donovan, *Red Machete* (Indianapolis: Bobbs-Merrill, 1962); David Wise and Thomas B. Rose, *The Invisible Government* (New York: Random House, 1964). See also various articles on the work of the CIA in *The New York Times*, including April 26, 1966, p. 1; April 25, p. 20; and April 27, p. 23. George Morris, *C.I.A. and American Labor: the Subversion of AFL–CIO's Foreign Policy* (New York: International Publishers, 1967).

14. John D. Montgomery, *The Politics of Foreign Aid: American Experience in Southeast Asia* (New York: Praeger, 1962); cf. Tom S. Soper, "External Aid," *African Affairs*, Vol. 65 (April, 1966), pp. 148–159. Many client states sell to the metropolitan country at above the world-market prices. The United Kingdom and the United States, for instance, buy Caribbean sugar much above world-market prices. Nicholas Bosanquet, "At the Mercy of Sugar," *New Society* (June 23, 1966), p. 24. By 1965, the Soviet Union provided about three-fourths of the raw material requirements of East Germany, Czechoslovakia, Poland, Hungary, Rumania, and Bulgaria. *The New York Times*, January 16, 1967.

15. The United States, for instance, conducts regularly public opinion polls in allied and non-aligned countries. Those are not published. For a published study, see Lloyd A. Free, *Six Allies and a Neutral* (New York: Free Press, 1959).

16. For an American view of uniting Europe, see Emile Benoit, "The European Common Market: Rival or Partner?," *Business and Government Review*, University of Missouri, Vol. 4 (1963), pp. 5–13. On African unification to "countervail" Europe, see Arnold Rivkin, *Africa and the European Common Market: A Perspective* (Denver: Social Science Foundation, University of Denver, 1966), revised 2nd edition, Monograph 4, 1965–1966.

17. For another attempt to draw on economic models, see Ralph Cassady, Jr., *Price Warfare in Business Competition* (East Lansing: Bureau of Business and Economic Research, Occasional Paper no. 11, Michigan State University, 1963), esp. pp. 81–90.

18. John G. Fuller, *The Gentlemen Conspirators* (New York: Grove Press, 1962), provides an example of an encapsulation whose machinery was quite formal but extra-legal—the electrical industry's price-fixing attempts.

19. Cf. Coser, *The Functions of Social Conflict, op. cit.*, pp. 121–128.

20. For a further discussion of this concept, see Robert Strausz-Hupé et al., *Protracted Conflict* (New York: Harper & Row, 1959).

21. Typically represented by the search for conflict *resolution*.

22. We draw in the balance of the discussion on our *Winning Without War, op. cit.*, and an article, "On Self Encapsulating Conflicts," published in *The Journal of Conflict Resolution*, Vol. 8 (1964), pp. 242–255.

23. Sorensen, *Kennedy, op. cit.*, pp. 762–763.

24. Jean E. Smith, "Berlin, The Erosion of a Principle," *The Reporter*, November 21, 1963, pp. 32–37.

25. Lawrence S. Finkelstein argued effectively that partisan (or mutual) inspection can go further to verify agreements than was previously believed. See his "The Uses of Reciprocal Inspection," in Seymour Melman (ed.), *Disarmament: Its Politics and Economics* (Boston: American Academy of Arts and Sciences, 1962), pp. 82–98. Central inspection is still superior (when possible), and encapsulation cannot advance far without it.

26. See Kaplan, *System and Process in International Politics, op. cit.*, pp. 27, 34 ff.

27. Georg Simmel, "The Number of Members as Determining the Sociological Form of the Group," *American Journal of Sociology*, Vol. 8 (1902), p. 45.

28. I am indebted to Johan Galtung for this concept.

29. G. F. Hudson, Richard Lowenthal, and Roderick MacFarquhar, *The Sino-Soviet Dispute* (New York: Praeger, 1961).

30. American–Soviet negotiations to agree on inspection of atomic plants, mainly aimed at insuring the use of atomic research for non-military purposes in third countries, pointed in the same direction. The 1963–1964 *détente*, which isolated Communist China and France, and the Geneva disarmament negotiations in the same years, in which these two countries did not participate, were further reflections of this trend.

31. For a description, discussion, and references to other works, see Richard N. Rosecrance, "Bipolarity, Multipolarity, and the Future," *The Journal of Conflict Resolution*, Vol. 10 (1966), pp. 314–327.

32. For details, see *Winning Without War, op. cit.*, Ch. 2. These statements refer to the 1958–1964 period. Both the United States and Russia have re-increased their military budgets with the escalation of the war in Vietnam in 1965.

33. Francis O. Wilcox, "The Nonaligned States and the United Nations," in Laurence W. Martin (ed.), *Neutralism and Nonalignment* (New York: Praeger, 1962), pp. 121–151; Joseph L. Nogee, "The Neutralist World and Disarmament Negotiations," *Annals of the American Academy of Political and Social Science*, Vol. 362 (1965), pp. 71–80; Khalid I. Babaa, "The 'Third Force' and the UN," *op. cit.*, pp. 81–91; M. Samir Ahmed, "The Role of the Neutrals in the Geneva Negotiations," *Disarmament and Arms Control*, Vol. 1 (1963), pp. 20–32; Robert L. Rothstein, "Alignment, Non-alignment, and Small Powers: 1945–1965," *International Organization*, Vol. 20 (1966), pp. 397–418.

34. The function itself, use of nuclear energy, is not unimportant, but for the said societies in the said period it had only a marginal role. Had CERN disappeared, its absence would hardly have been noted in the period under study.

35. Lester G. Seligman, "Developments in the Presidency and the Conception of Political Leadership," *American Sociological Review*, Vol. 20 (1955), pp. 706–712; Paul M. Harrison, *Authority and Power in the Free Church Tradition* (Princeton, N.J.: Princeton University Press, 1959). See Guetzkow, *Multiple Loyalties, op. cit.* For additional theoretical discussion and data, see Henry Teune, "The Learning of Integrative Habits," in Jacob and Toscano (eds.), *The Integration of Political Communities, op. cit.*, pp. 269 ff.

36. Richard W. Van Wagenen's "The Concept of Community and the Future of the United Nations," reviews the various approaches to the question of the "top"

tier, in Norman J. Padelford and Leland M. Goodrich (eds.), *The United Nations in the Balance* (New York: Praeger, 1965), pp. 448–463.

37. For reasons, see above, pp. 285–298.

38. Susanne J. Bodenheimer, "The 'Political Union' Debate in Europe: A Case Study in Intergovernmental Diplomacy," *International Organization*, Vol. 21 (1967), pp. 24–54. See also J. W. Beijen, "United Europe: Federal or Supernational," *International Spectator*, April 8, 1965 (19th year, No. 7).

39. On "intrasocietal identifications that are transitional in scope," see Wilbert E. Moore, "Global Sociology: The World as a Singular System," *American Journal of Sociology*, Vol. 71 (1966), p. 480. See also Evan Luard, "The Growth of the World Community," *The Annals of the American Academy of Political and Social Science*, Vol. 351 (1964), pp. 170–179.

40. Jan Tinbergen, *Shaping the World Economy* (New York: Twentieth Century Fund, 1962), pp. 195 ff.

41. Talcott Parsons, "Communism and the West," in Eva and Amitai Etzioni (eds.), *Social Change: Sources, Patterns, and Consequences* (New York: Basic Books, 1964), pp. 390–399.

42. Even this needs further specification: When unification allows them to control the market, a condition which is approximated if together they produce a large enough fraction of the product to affect world prices significantly, homogeneity may assist unification.

43. Etzioni, *Political Unification, op. cit.*, pp. 19–21 ff.

44. For a discussion of this approach, see Robert A. Levine, *The Arms Debate* (Cambridge, Mass.: Harvard University Press, 1963), pp. 56 ff.

45. For one of the best sociological treatments in recent literature, see Robert N. Bellah, "Civil Religion in America," *Daedalus*, Vol. 96 (1967), pp. 1–21.

46. A world-wide organization, to carry on regular inspection of disarmament, was favored by 70 per cent of those surveyed from among citizens of the United States, 72 per cent of Great Britain, 85 per cent of France, 78 per cent of India, 92 per cent of West Germany, and 91 per cent of Japan. Surveys were conducted in 1958. See William M. Evan, "An International Public Opinion Poll on Disarmament and 'Inspection by the People': A Study of Attitudes toward Supranationalism," in Seymour Melman (ed.), *Inspection for Disarmament* (New York: Columbia University Press, 1958), p. 235.

47. The community commitments in Western Europe, which declined after a half-dozen attempts at unification failed to take off in the post-World-War II period, acquired a new vitality once the initiation of the EEC proved successful. For a survey, see U. W. Kitzinger, *The New Europeans* (Pleasantville, N.Y.: The Reader's Digest Association, 1963).

48. This is a central thesis in Bell's *The End of Ideology, op. cit.*

49. Most such communities include an escape clause, some specific conditions under which violence is justified, but they are very limited, somewhat like the limitation on freedom of speech that does not legitimate shouting "fire" in a crowded theater. They need not concern us here.

50. David Brion Davis, *The Problem of Slavery in Western Culture* (Ithaca, N.Y.: Cornell University Press, 1966), *passim*.

51. Hugh J. Klare (ed.), *Changing Concepts of Crime and Its Treatment* (New York: Pergamon Press, 1966).

52. C. Wright Mills observed correctly that "the nation–state is the frame within which they [social scientists] most often feel the need to formulate the problems of smaller and of larger units." His statement that "in choosing the national social structure as our generic working unit, we are adopting a suitable level of generality" is best understood in the context of his quest for a macroscopic sociology and his concern with American society. Both citations are from p. 135, *The Sociological Imagination, op. cit.* See also p. 137.

53. Marcuse, *Reason and Revolution, op. cit.*, p. 360 (referring to Auguste Comte, *Système de politique positive*, Vol. I, p. 334).

EPILOGUE

CHAPTER 21

Alienation, Inauthenticity,

and Their Reduction

T O BE active is to reduce alienation because it is to make society more responsive to its members. The post-modern society inherited from its predecessor an alienating structure—the product of modernity—especially industrialization, bureaucratization, and the legitimation of the priority of the logic of instruments (or "rationality"). The post-modern society has added to this basically distorted structure an increased capacity for macroscopic manipulation, for the generation of a *sense* of responsiveness where there is actually none. There have always been groups of men who were unaware of the basic facts of their socio-political lives and, thus, acted in opposition to their basic interests and private selves. It is the *scope* and *depth* of such false awareness and commitment that seem to be new.

The relative significance of manipulation becomes more evident as the non-symbolic, material bases of alienation decline in societal importance. The modernized societies command an enormous capacity for material production which can satisfy most of the material needs of most of their members. Inequality is maintained to a significant extent because of a

psychology of scarcity (which had a more realistic base in earlier ages)[1]*
and because of the prestige and power implications of increased equality. All
this points to the relative increase in the importance of the role of symbolic
distortions and of their resolution for post-modern activation.

The Basic Concepts: Alienation and Inauthenticity

Alienating and Alienated

There are many definitions and discussions of alienation.[2] It suffices to
say here that the concept has many levels, but, as we use it, it has one core:
The unresponsiveness of the world to the actor, which subjects him to forces
he neither comprehends nor guides. The early industrial society is the archetype of an alienating society. Market relations and administrative structures
which were developed and imposed ostensibly for the greater happiness of
the greater number in effect led to a society that stood between its members
and the service of their basic needs.

Alienation, it has been correctly stressed, is not only a feeling of resentment and disaffection but also an expression of the objective conditions
which subject a person to forces beyond his understanding and control.
Hence, even if a person is only vaguely aware of his own deprivation,
dependency, and manipulation, he is still alienated so long as he is unable to
participate authentically in the processes that shape his social being.
Alienation, thus, has structural bases and psychic consequences. As these two
aspects of alienation are often confused, we refer to the society as *alienating*
and to its members as being *alienated*.[3] It should be noted, however, that the
roots of alienation are not in interpersonal relations and intrapsychic processes but in the societal and political structure.

Both the structural and the psychic dimensions of the concept refer to a
holistic state—of society or of being in it. While we can refer to levels of
alienation and to some societies as being more alienating than others, it is
not within the intellectual tradition of the concept—as broad as it is—to use
it to refer to specific, limited structural distortions or personal dissatis-
factions. That a worker does not like his working place is not sufficient
evidence that he is alienated; when alienation exists, it encompasses most, if
not all, social relations. Moreover, a worker who is satisfied with his place of
work may still be alienated. The concept of alienation does not assume that
the alienated are aware of their condition. It is a concept of the critical
intellectual and the social scientist. The level of alienation can be empirically
measured and the members of a society can be made aware of it (two points
to which we return later), but the awareness of alienation does not create
it any more than a lack of awareness makes it disappear.

---

* Reference notes for this chapter appear on page 655.

Alienation is encompassing in still another sense: It affects both the excluded groups and those who exclude them. The excluded are affected because the society is particularly unresponsive to their needs. The excluding groups are affected because the process of exclusion creates a distorted social world which they cannot elude. Highly alienating structures, as we have seen, rely relatively heavily on coercion; this brutalizes the wielder of force as well as those who are whipped, as studies of concentration camps or police forces demonstrate. The modern market system places a high value on material objects; the incapacity of the participants for uninhibited and holistic affection for a human being, which results from such a system, deprives all the members of a market-dominated society and not just the workers.

An alienated man may be passive or active in his orientation toward his condition. A passively alienated man is subject to societal forces and, subconsciously or even consciously, acquiesces to his state; an actively* alienated man is similarly subject to such forces, but he is committed to a fundamentally different society and works to realize it. He is much more likely to be conscious of his condition and, above all, to strive to transform it. The passively alienated tend to be apathetic; the actively alienated tend to be mobilized but obsessive in their conduct.† Personal activation within alienating structures is always distorted and incomplete, as there cannot be personal realization without societal activation. We shall see, however, that personal activation can contribute to societal transformation and, hence, lead ultimately to an active society.

Alienation and Inauthenticity

The concept of alienation has been applied to such a variety of phenomena and such a range of ideas that it has lost some of its analytic power.[4] We attempt, here, to explicate a sub-category of that which has previously been conceived as alienation. We refer to this as *inauthenticity*, a term heretofore used primarily as a vague synonym for alienation.

A relationship, institution, or society is *inauthentic if it provides the appearance of responsiveness while the underlying condition is alienating.* Objectively, both alienating and inauthentic conditions are excluding, but inauthentic structures devote a higher ratio of their efforts than alienating

---

* Active here refers to his orientation only, and it too is never fully active in an alienating condition.

† Obsession is used here to characterize a psychological state typically observed in the "fanatic" commitments of radicals to their causes. No derogatory connotations are implied. On this psychological state, see Sandor Rado, "Obsessive Behavior," in Silvano Arieti (ed.), *American Handbook of Psychiatry* (New York: Basic Books, 1959), Vol. I, pp. 324–344.

ones to concealing their contours and to generating appearance of responsiveness. Subjectively, to be alienated is to experience a sense of not belonging and to feel that one's efforts are without meaning. To be involved inauthentically is to feel cheated and manipulated.* The alienated feel that they have no power;[5] the inauthentic feel that they have pulled a disconnected lever, without quite knowing where and how, so that shadows are confused with reality. The alienated are imprisoned; the inauthentic work at Sisyphean labor.

Authenticity exists where responsiveness exists and is experienced as such. The world responds to the actor's efforts, and its dynamics are comprehensible. We shall see below that authenticity requires not only that the actor be conscious, committed, and hold a share of the societal power, but also that the three components of the active orientation be balanced and connected. It is the fate of the inauthentic man that what he knows does not fit what he feels, and what he affects is not what he knows or is committed to do. His world has come apart. The alienated man, in comparison, is likely to be excluded to a greater extent from all three societal sources of activation, laboring in someone else's vineyard, laboratory, or army.

The relationship between the underlying societal condition and its superstructure or appearance is central to our conceptualization. There are four basic possibilities:

		Societal Super-Structure Responsiveness	
		CLAIMED	*NOT CLAIMED*
	HIGH	*Inauthentic*	*Alienating*
Basic Condition: Alienating			
	LOW	*Authentic* (manifest)	*Authentic* (latent)

---

* "If I wear a beard and a girl I love stays in my room all night and I sleep with her, I'm a beatnik and in a state of moral decline. If I shave and go to a whore house, buy stocks on the South African exchange that net me a large profit, and sign up for the CIA when I graduate from college, my behavior is unquestioned and my integrity assumed." A statement by a student quoted by Robert Coles, "Sex and Students," *The New Republic*, Vol. 154 (May 28, 1966), p. 21. Some such statements are surely made by many generations about the rhetoric of their elders. But the theme of "it's all a lie" seems stronger and more common since 1945. Lewis S. Feuer argued that point in "The Elite of the Alienated," *The New York Times Magazine*, March 26, 1967. See also Margaret Halsey's article in *The Village Voice*, April 6, 1967, subtitled "The Lying Society." She points out, "There have always been lies and liars," but the United States in the 1950s and 60s reached a new level. Its advent, Halsey says, is symbolized by Charles Van Doren, whose six figures' worth of intelligence proved to be rigged, and by Richard Nixon's manipulative "Checkers" speech.

These types refer to various relationships between the two societal aspects. When both the appearances and the conditions are non-responsive, we deal with outright alienation; when both are responsive—with an authentic relationship; when the appearance is responsive but reality is not—with inauthenticity. The fourth category is a rare one in which the conditions allow for participation, but this is not recognized and acted upon by the participants. We expect this to be usually a short-lived lag because it is difficult for the possibility of genuine participation to go unnoticed.

The difference between an active and a passive personal orientation may be added as a second dimension in terms of the orientation to the societal situation. For authentic relationships, the orientation is active (unless the authenticity is still latent); those caught in inauthentic or alienating relationships are active to the extent that they seek to transform their condition.*

The concept of inauthenticity is not without antecedents, and the term has been used by several existentialist writers. The most widely known antecedent of inauthenticity is false-consciousness, a much more constricted term. So far as inauthenticity is concerned, the consciousness of all collectivities and not just that of the working class may be affected. Further, as we shall see, all relationships and not only consciousness may be affected. Society itself may be inauthentic.

Existentialist writers have used inauthenticity as a synonym for alienation in the Marxist tradition to refer to the condition of being disconnected and of foregoing one's responsibilities.[6] If the term is used as a synonym for alienation, we have two words for one phenomenon and none to denote what seems to us a distinct sub-category. If inauthenticity is used to refer to being disconnected, it becomes a relative concept and an actively alienated person may be an authentic one. We attempt to use the concept as an absolute one in the sense that authenticity is not possible under alienating conditions. While the actively alienated man may play a significant role in transforming his condition and in creating the opportunity for authenticity, so long as this transformation is not advanced, he is not free from the effects of his alienating condition.

Finally, existentialists have used the concept for a highly voluntaristic theory, stressing the personal responsibility of the actor.[7] This ethical position is connected with their basically negative view of society which we do not

---

* For some purposes, a difference among kinds of inauthentic relations may be noted along these dimensions: According to the extent to which the objective base is alienating or manipulative. The more manipulative it is, the greater the role the subject plays in allowing himself to be "taken." Secondly, we may distinguish between inauthentic involvement in an existing regime (which is closer to the passively alienated) and involvement in an inauthentic effort at transformation (which is closer to the actively alienated). These need not concern us here. For a few additional comments along these lines, see the discussion of projects below.

share. It also leads to a paradox, as in both the religious and left existentialist writings, society and history tend to be viewed as largely predetermined by supranatural or economic-technological forces. The incompatibility between personal voluntarism and macro-determinism has characterized many of the writings on the subject.[8] We see the person as less free, though he has options which ethics command him to exercise in such a way as to increase the total sum of his freedoms;[9] we view society as less determined, as open to restructuring by the efforts of the members. Thus, in our conception, the gap between man and society is much narrower at the outset, and it can be bridged, we suggest below, by greater articulation of the relations between personal and societal projects.

Inauthenticity is a concept for which empirical referents can be formulated without more difficulty than for other basic sociological concepts. We discuss below "subjective" indicators (in overt personal behavior and of intra-personal tensions) and societal ones. First, though, the concept of basic human needs must be introduced.

Basic Human Needs

The concepts of alienation and inauthenticity assume the concept of basic human needs. While we cannot point to such needs in that we have never encountered them in a pure form, we can analytically separate basic from specific human needs and specify the empirical consequences of the basic ones.

The Analytic Status of the Concept

Alienation and inauthenticity refer to a lack of responsiveness, but unless we assume that those to whom the societal structure does not respond have needs which are independent of the needs produced by their relationship to the societal structure, the phenomenon of unresponsiveness is inconceivable. There can be some lack of coordination between a society's socialization system and its productive and allocative structure or some time lag in the accommodation of personalities to changing societies; these factors could account for some unresponsiveness. But this unresponsiveness could, in principle, be eliminated as readily by changing socialization as by changing the productive and allocative relations. Thus, without an analytic concept of autonomous needs, it must be concluded that there is, in principle, no limit to manipulability—that the members' needs are basically pliable in that they can be changed to fit the societal structure rather than require a transformation of the structure to achieve a higher level of responsiveness.

The Limits of Socialization and Social Control

The central point at which the prevailing theories of social action of both the Meadian and Parsonsian traditions differ from *both* the Marxist and the Weberian perspectives is that the former assume, in effect, that human needs are almost completely pliable within very broad limits set primarily by physiological tolerance, such as the need for heat, sleep, and food. Social needs—e.g., for affection—are recognized by these theories, but it is emphasized that such needs may be satisfied by a large variety of institutional arrangements. While social needs must somehow be satisfied, they have only very broadly contextuated properties of their own which affect the arrangements by which they are satisfied. This means (a) that most of the variance in the actual socio-cultural patterns must be accounted for by properties other than those of the basic needs; (b) that differences in the psychological costs of various patterns are not systematically taken into account; and (c) that there is no analytic place in these theories for an unresponsive societal structure.

Societies are expected both to provide one or more "outlets" for the basic needs of their members *and* to socialize their members to accept these "outlets." Some members, it is recognized, are not successfully socialized; they may be resocialized (e.g., in a rehabilitation institution) or "socially controlled" (which is a function of the courts, police, and jails). Further, although the possibility of broader malfunctioning followed by a relatively high level of deviance and pressure for societal innovation is recognized, it is assumed, in principle, that there are few if any limits to socialization and social control. The best indication of this assumption is the presence in these theories of conceptions of deviant individuals, sub-cultures, and even social movements, *but never of a deviant society*. The concept of a deviant society, however, is the key concept for the alienation tradition—a society whose structure is contrary to human nature and does not allow the satisfaction of basic human needs. If they are to be satisfied, *society* will have to be restructured *and* quite fundamentally.

We suggest that a "moderate" version of this approach is a more productive view of personality–society relations than the views which are prevalent in sociology.[10] We prefer this version because we certainly do not wish to return to earlier approaches which saw human needs as demanding one specific set of outlets or a very narrow range of them, or which viewed the socio-cultural patterns as reflecting "basic personality." Before we suggest the limitations which basic human needs impose on the structure of a responsive society, let us indicate the needs that we consider basic.

A Tentative List

The following list of basic human needs is far from complete; the revival of interest in this subject is very recent, and much more study is required.* Nor is the list a new one; similar lists have often been drawn up before.[11] Nor should we focus on the specific items on the list at this tentative stage of our knowledge. What we seek to illustrate are the opportunities to test *empirically* the key proposition that the *flexibility of basic human needs is limited in that they can be more readily and fully satisfied in some societal structures than in others.* Thus, *some societal structures, as a whole, are less responsive and more alienating than others,* and *there are significant limits to the manipulability of the members.*

We are dealing here with *human* needs and not with the physiological ones that are common to man and animal and are often discussed as "basic" in other contexts. We suggest six basic needs and briefly explain our choice of this list as a working hypothesis.

Human needs seem to include the need for *affection*, also referred to as the need for solidarity, cohesion, or love; and the need for *recognition*, variously referred to as the need for self-esteem, achievement, or approval. While recognition is a matter of the normative evaluation of achievements and tends to be specific and universalistic, affection is a matter of expressive relations and tends to be holistic and particularistic. Recognition flows down a status or rank structure. The need for affection tends to be satisfied in more "horizontal" relations, either in peer relations or among persons close in rank. Recognition tends to be asymmetrical; if A recognizes B, A will tend to derive his recognition from C, with C being higher and A lower in the status structure. (The validation of leadership is the main exception.) Affection tends to be symmetrical; if A gratifies B, B is likely to satisfy A's need for affection. (While triangular relations are often described, especially in novels, no claim is made for a stable source of affection for the three parties concerned.) Recognition is much less "scarce" than affection, in that any one actor can grant recognition to more people than those for whom he can have affection.

A third need is for *context*, variously referred to as the need for orientation, consistency, synthesis, meaning, or "wholeness." The various facets of the personality are related to various societal sectors and levels. Cognitions, emotions, and beliefs are all affected by inputs from these societal sectors (such as educational, economic, and religious sectors) on their various levels—sub-collectivities, collectivities, and society-wide. The person seems

---

* The prevailing view of the classification of human needs and the very concept is well expressed by the following quotation: "Nobody has ever been able to formulate an inventory of original or unsocialized tendencies that has commanded more than scattered and temporary agreement. In the second place, the very meaning of 'original human nature,' in any other sense than a range of possibilities, each of them dependent upon specific experiences for its development or maturation, has always proved exceedingly elusive and obscure." Albert K. Cohen, *Deviance and Control* (Englewood Cliffs, N.J.: Prentice-Hall, 1966), p. 60.

to have a need for some degree of "harmonization" among these various inputs and demands.

Fourth, there is the need for *repeated gratification*, an anti-neutrality inclination; that is, whatever the source of gratification, large lapses of time between instances of it are frustrating. People who vary in their personality structures, societal positions, and cultural backgrounds differ in the length of time they can maintain an activity (without a loss in commitment) if they are not rewarded. Once, however, the base is set for a person, the same "law" seems to hold: More frequent rewards are preferred to less frequent ones (unless they become very frequent).* Thus, the first and second needs relate the individual to his peers, superiors, and subordinates; the third one deals with the lateral and the fourth with the longitudinal organization of satisfaction.

Two "second order" needs arise out of these basic ones; one concerns the longitudinal and the other the lateral organization of gratification. The first is the need for a degree of *stability* in the pattern of the distribution of rewards—of their expectability independent of the level and frequency of gratification. If there is not sufficient stability, the level of anxiety is expected to rise and, with it, the opportunity for manipulability; that is, persons can be mobilized into roles incompatible with their needs, which they otherwise would not seek, in order to gain some emotional security. We expect that the effects of such manipulation will be limited because, in accord with our propositions about the existence of basic needs, the needs other than that for stability will not be gratified *and* will not adapt so that they can be satisfied in these roles. For instance, a person who seeks security by suppressing his individuality in a collective unit will suffer from deficient recognition.

The other "second order" need is the need for *variance in a social structure*. Because the members of any society are born and socialized in social statuses that differ, the ways in which the basic needs are specified in personalities tend to vary; incomplete or ineffectual socialization adds to this variance. Hence, there is the need for a variety of social roles and norms to provide outlets for the varied personalities. Alienation is higher, the greater the gap between the extents of the variance of personalities and of roles[12] and the more specified the norms. Secondly, alienation is higher, the greater the gap between the distributions of specific attributes of personalities and of roles and norms. For instance, a society whose production system demands many more highly skilled men than the I.Q. distribution can provide is likely to be alienating.

As a first crude approximation, it seems to hold that the more a societal structure allows for the satisfaction of the basic needs of its members, the less the structure will be alienating. The participation of the members in a

---

* Of course, other factors, such as the absolute size of each reward, its nature, and its expectability must be controlled.

societal structure comes to assure the responsiveness of that structure to the basic needs. *Ultimately, there is no way for a societal structure to discover the members' needs and adapt to them without the participation of the members in shaping and reshaping the structure.* Thus, participation, besides serving psychological needs, is a major societal instrument. But complete satisfaction is not possible; the gratification of some needs reduces the ability to gratify others[13] because of the limitations scarcity imposes on the capacity to satisfy even compatible needs and the devaluating effect of very frequent rewarding on the reward. If all the available societal energy were invested in gratification, assets would be consumed but not replenished, and anticipatory action—if only in anticipation of environmental changes—would be neglected. The realm of social life entails, as Freud stressed, some frustration, for the sublimation involved in the deferment of gratification is never completely successful and there always remains an element of suppression. Thus, there is no social life without some alienation; it is the degree and the distribution of this alienation that are important. If the reducible and irreducible kinds of alienation are discussed as one phenomenon, the distinction between the pains of being human and those inflicted by a particular societal structure and its political organization is lost.[14]

In short, sociability requires some irreducible deferment of gratification. As this is never fully accepted voluntarily, there seems also to be a residue of irreducible alienation. (In macro-systems, this can be seen in the need for organization and differential rewards.) Beyond this residue, however, *most alienation is the result of a specific societal and cultural pattern and can be reduced by changing that pattern.*

This holds as much for each basic need as it does for all of them taken as a group. Complete security, maximum affection and recognition are all impractical and probably self-contradictory. The range of societal options is more limited. But within it lie the possibilities for more as opposed to less frequent gratification—for more as opposed to less affection and recognition, varying degrees of security, and so on. While persons can be socialized into roles which provide low, infrequent, and uncoordinated gratification, the costs of such arrangements are high, which—we shall show—provides the empirical test of the existence of underlying, frustrated, basic human needs.

The Lessons of Comparative Analysis

The empirical verification of the validity of the concept of basic human needs ought to concentrate on comparisons of the socialization and social control "costs" of various roles, societal sectors, and total structures, and on the visible indications of underlying frustrations. (We refer to psychic costs as "personal" and to all others, especially socialization and social control costs, as "social.")[15] The fact that a man can be socialized and/or controlled to carry out almost any role is not a sufficient indicator of the extent of his flexibility, so long as the social and personal costs of the efforts are not taken into account. We suggest (a) that the socialization and social control costs as well as the levels of frustration of any two roles differ, and (b) that they are higher when the roles are less "natural"—i.e., allow for less satisfaction of the basic human needs.

Comparative anthropology has shown that a man may be socialized to be peace loving or aggressive, passive or hyperactive, monogamous or polygamous. These findings are usually interpreted as indications of man's pliability. But this is a correct interpretation only in so far as it does take into account the respective social and personal costs. If, for example, the costs of monogamy are much higher than those of polygamy, this finding is relevant for the question of man's pliability; however, these variables are disregarded in much of the literature on the subject.[16]

A discussion of persuadability in its broader sense further illustrates the point. The question is asked: Can the personality of an adult be deeply affected (i.e., can his "character" and not only his "surface" traits or attitudes be changed)? While there is no established answer to this question and a review of the literature on the subject would require a volume larger than the present one, the following statements seem to reflect the main findings. Most studies of efforts to affect "deep" personality variables—especially psychoanalysis, "brainwashing," and psychological experiments—show these efforts to have little effect.[17] "Brainwashing," the most encompassing and intensive of these efforts, seems to affect only a minority of those on whom it was attempted, and this minority included people predisposed to such effects and/or to the view they were "persuaded" to accept. Moreover, many of those who were affected remain so only so long as they remain in the particular environment in which the effort was made.[18] It is only when the "total environment" is changed and remains so, as when Communist governments established themselves in Eastern Europe or adults emigrate, that a deep effect seems to occur.[19] The great amount of literature about attitude changes, which may be said to be less "deep" than personality changes, seems to suggest that under most conditions, only bit changes rather than contextual changes are attained. Thus, adult persons can be made to shift from one consumer product to another brand which is very similar to it or even to accept new products which serve an already existing need, but the ability of the mass media to change attitudes about religious, racial, ethnic, or political matters seems to be limited.[20]

Most important, the great cost of successful persuasion is often not taken into account.* Very unusual social conditions must be constructed (e.g., isolation imprisonment), and a high level of frustration must be inflicted.

---

* For a good discussion of the high costs of maintaining a restrictive environment, see John Strachey's discussion of the costs of colonialism in his *The End of Empire* (New York: Random House, 1960).

Hence, if the concept of cost is added, we reach the opposite conclusion—not that man is "persuadable," but that, under most conditions, he is not.

The Measurements of Costs

Social and personal costs may not always be measurable by the research techniques which, as their advocates themselves point out, measure the manifest (or "superficial") aspects of personality. Here, the analysis of alienation and inauthenticity encounters unnecessary obstacles. Workers are alienated in capitalistic societies, it has been argued; why, then, do they exhibit no symptoms of alienation? Most workers say that they are happy both with their work and with the regime, and they do not support political movements which favor radical change. Similarly, it has been suggested that the citizens of modernized societies enjoy their mass culture, consumption gluttony, and suburbia. Alienation, it has been said, is a radical invention of an intellectual projection.

> By accepting the myth of suburbia, the liberal and left wing critics are placed in the ideologically weak position of haranguing the suburbanites precisely for the meaninglessness they attribute to the very criteria of their success. The critic waves the prophet's long and accusing finger and warns: "You may *think* you're happy, you smug and prosperous striver, but I tell you that the anxieties of status mobility are too much; they impoverish you psychologically, they alienate you from your family"; and so on. And the suburbanite looks at his new house, his new car, his new freezer, his lawn and patio, and, to be sure, his good credit, and scratches his head, bewildered. The critic appears as the eternal crotchet, the professional malcontent telling the prosperous that their prosperity, the visible symbols of which surround them, is an illusion: the economic victory of capitalism is culturally Pyrrhic.[21]

This "happiness" approach draws its information about the workers, consumers, or citizens almost exclusively from attitude surveys which show that most of them are "satisfied." For instance, 75 to 90 per cent of American workers are reported to be "reasonably satisfied" with their jobs.[22] However, even survey studies which use only somewhat more indirect questioning find numerous indications of alienation.[23] But, more important, in a society which spends so much on socialization and manipulation—escapist activities, patriotism that masks basic problems, the reinforcement of the consumption obsession, and tension-reducing drugs[24]—the symptoms of alienation could hardly be expected to lie on the surface. Actually, there is reason to believe that these symptoms are increasingly suppressed; it is precisely this characteristic that made late modern society not only more alienating but also more inauthentic than early modern societies and that makes the condition of the post-modern generation more inauthentic than that of the last modern one.

Some advocates of the alienation tradition have gone to the opposite extreme and maintain that alienation is an objective condition; hence, even if the members of a society exhibit no symptoms of frustration, they are nevertheless alienated because of the nature of the means of production, the property relations built around them, and the estranging state bureaucracy. Or, they have argued, the symptoms of alienation are buried so deeply that they cannot be measured by the methods of social science but must be sensed through empathy and "understanding."

We take an intermediary position. We do recognize the need to demonstrate empirically that those societal elements that the social scientist considers alienating do indeed incur personal and social costs, *but*, we suggest, *these may register only when those social science methods are applied which probe the deeper layers of personality.* If *no* instrument of social science can discover any consequences of alienation, or only those methods which are so uncontrolled that they amount to a euphemism for the personal intuition of the observer, we would have to eliminate alienation as a scientific concept. But this is clearly not the case. We have already seen that there is some evidence of alienation on the manifest level in terms of attitudes and manifest social costs (such as an increase in police forces). In addition, there are methods which measure the more latent aspects of personality—e.g., unstructured and stress interviews and psychological tests—which have yielded data that support the basic proposition.[25] The existing "depth" methods can certainly be improved; actually, this is one of the major tasks for the next generation of social scientists. But there is evidence that high personal costs are found when we look where we can expect to find them—below the surface of life in an inauthentic society.

The social costs of socialization and of the social control of similar roles in different historical periods or societies are more readily measurable. We find, for example, that systems which allow for no personal achievement—and, hence, frustrate the need for recognition—are so costly that they are unsustainable, such as *austere* communist states, kibbutzim, and other utopian settlements. Generally, austerity tends to erode in the direction of more frequent and higher levels of gratification—e.g., the transformation of communal settlements. Other "unnatural" systems are sustained but only with much "policing" (i.e., with high social control costs) or for very select groups (e.g., religious orders) so that the socialization costs are tolerable.[26] Such systems could usually not be sustained if they were society-wide.

To support fully the basic proposition, it is not enough for depth methods to show that people exhibit severe personal frustrations and anxieties in postmodern society, and for comparative studies of social costs to show that industrialized societies invest a good deal in manipulation or police activities: It is also necessary to show that these personal and social costs are the consequences of the structural distortions of modern and post-modern societies. It is not enough to demonstrate that there are high rates of crime, alcoholism, drug addiction, suicide, and so forth, in modernized societies; since it is occasionally argued they were "always" high,[27] we need also to show that they have risen with modernization. Most of all, we need to specify the ways in which unresponsive roles, institutions, and societal structures bring about these costs, and the ways in which an increase in the responsiveness of the roles, institutions, and societal structures decreases the extent to which they are alienating and brings about a decline in the severity and frequency of the symptoms.

The tracing of the consequences of unresponsiveness requires not only a demonstration of the association between a general rise or decline in the responsiveness of a societal structure and a rise or decline in the rates of neurotic symptoms or social disorganization, but also necessitates a delineation of the specific associations. It may be futile to search for a one-to-one relationship between one symptom and the unresponsiveness of one structure to one basic human need. Again, the theory of alienation does not imply such specific links. On the contrary, a divergence in reactions to the same alienating condition is to be expected, depending upon the internal constitutions of the various persons involved. These variations, though, are expected to be in terms of the basic needs; e.g., some people have a stronger need for affection and others have a stronger need for recognition (but all have both needs). Second, frustration may turn to a variety of outlets for its alleviation, just as the basic needs can be satisfied by a variety of outlets. But just as the basic needs can be more readily satisfied in some roles than in others, so we expect the frustrations resulting from the lack of opportunities to gratify one kind of need to be more likely to be expressed in some kinds of symptoms than in others. Hence, we may be able to link major kinds of unresponsiveness to major kinds of symptoms.

So far, the evidence on the more subtle points of the causal link is not satisfactory, because of the above-mentioned polarization of survey-methodology and empathy as well as the relative neglect of the concept of basic human needs. The association between modernization and an increase in various personal costs seems quite strong,[28] however, despite a few counter-studies, and there are some studies of the relationships between specific factors as well as some evidence that authentic activation reduces the rates of such symptoms as drug addiction, delinquency,[29] and the "culture of poverty."[30] This is as far as the prevailing methodologies have brought us.

So long as the language of sociology is collectivistic and social being and social knowing are sharply divided, no other methodology is likely to emerge. But from the viewpoint of a theory of societal guidance, social reorganization and research grow closer together in general and meet specifically in guided societal experimentation. Post-modern societies are increasingly experimenting with different forms of societal organization. Various social movements test different forms of mobilization. When various forms of organization and mobilization in the same society and historical period are compared, we are able to see their relative costs and, thus, test hypotheses about their levels of responsiveness. The term "practice" has been used to refer to this aspect of reality-testing, in which social action and scientific testing converge.[31]

Two Additional Elaborations

Only part of the cost of a particular social structure can be charged against the structure's incompatibility with basic human needs. While in stable societies this kind of cost is relatively high, in changing societies, a significant part of the cost results from the fact that the socio-cultural specification of the basic needs to a particular set of outlets has to be un-learned and a new relationship between the needs and the outlets acquired. Hence, the introduction of a new role, institution, or society incurs costs *even* if the new structure is more compatible with basic human needs than the old one. On the other hand, the new relationships cannot account for *continued* social and personal costs;[32] if the costs of a new societal element do not decline after the "novelty" of the element has worn off, they must be viewed as a result of the incompatibility of the element with human needs. The counter-argument has often been advanced to justify the imposition of collective institutions on resisting individuals and classes—that they will learn to appreciate their new life. This position has a measure of intrinsic validity so long as it is recognized that it can hold only during the transition period. If, after many socialization and social control efforts have been made, the costs of maintaining a pattern are still high, it seems highly likely—unless some special circumstances prevail, such as foreign intervention or special scarcity—that the new pattern is less responsive than the old one.

However, one cannot expect a "straight-line" progress in the sense that if the new pattern is basically more responsive, the costs of its introduction will gradually decline, and, hence, after a short period, some signs of its compatibility with basic human needs will become visible. As in psychoanalysis, the sequence of such change often takes some other form, such as high resistance at first and then a sharp decline in costs.

The length of time that must be allowed before it can be concluded that the high costs are due to basic rather than temporary incompatibilities is difficult to specify at this stage of our knowledge. In part, it is a question of the extent to which an adult person can be resocialized without regressing first to a childhood level. It seems not unreasonable to suggest that if the second generation of a new society still does not accept the new institution or some of its features, under most circumstances, that institution (or societal structure) is incompatible with basic human needs. There is nothing in sociological theory or findings of which we are aware to support the notion that a prolonged imposition of a social pattern on a group of men will bring them to adjust their *basic* needs to that pattern. It is in the meeting of these needs that social designing, planning, control, and education encounter ultimate limits within which they must respond if human costs are to be low—i.e., alienation is to be reduced.

In addition to the time lag that must often be allowed if the responsiveness of a new pattern is genuinely to be tested,[33] the structural context must also be taken into account. If a new pattern is merely a change of part of an old and incompatible context, the pattern cannot be expected to take root, at least not at the same pace and cost as when other elements of the context are also being transformed. The essence of alienating structures and inauthenticity is precisely in the whole, in the context, and their distorting effects tend to diffuse both via the personalities of their members which link their societal roles and via inter-sectoral ties. It is, thus, futile to expect to find a fully authentic life in a bohemian island in a capitalistic society, or to increase the responsiveness of universities in societies whose polities and structures are left unchanged. In short, if the alienating context remains, islands of authentic relations are difficult to establish and, especially, to sustain. This does not mean that all changes must be simultaneous or that they must be revolutionary. They may be gradual, but if they are not encompassing and accumulative, many additional costs will be incurred and there will be severe limitations on their effects.

Marxists have criticized psychological approaches that dealt with basic needs as a-historical:

"The real basis of the absolute 'essence of man,' of which German philosophers talked at such length, was, Marx said, the sum of forces of production and 'social forms of intercourse,' which every generation inherits as something given. In his later works, he showed that the ideal of the full-blooded, spiritually rich personality, well-developed in every direction, is not a dream or an abstraction but a real requirement of history and expression of the tendencies and possibilities within the social character of production. What capitalism crushes is not various characteristics alleged to be eternally inherent in man, but those possibilities that man himself constantly formulates as demands and inquiries."*

We see no empirical, analytic, or critical reason to accept this position. Basic needs are universal. All men are expected to have them and any theory which is not open to this possibility is open to racist ("superiority") interpretations. The opportunity to satisfy these needs is what is historically set. Post-modern societies have a greater opportunity to satisfy and a lesser objective need to "pacify." The extent they realize this opportunity depends greatly on their societal structure and political organization. But their members have the same basic needs as "primitive" men.

---

* A. I. Titarenko, "Erich Fromm in the Chains of Illusion," *Science & Society*, Vol. 29 (1965), pp. 319–329.

Inauthenticity: Personal, Sectoral, and Global

Here, we are especially interested in the differences between alienation and inauthenticity, because, we suggest, the transition from the modern to the post-modern period has been characterized by an increase in inauthenticity. At this stage, we can only tentatively suggest the differences in the indicators of the personal and social costs of an inauthentic as opposed to an alienated life, and the differences between those who are conscious of the inauthenticity of their condition and those who are not.

Personal Inauthenticity

When a person is unaware of the inauthenticity of his condition, he is likely to feel listless, uncommitted, apathetic, and unsatisfied in a generic way. While this disaffection may focus on specific issues, when those are corrected it only focuses on others. He is likely to be unable to articulate the cause of his malaise because he accepts the disguise as valid. Of course, there are other sources of inarticulateness, such as a low level of education, a low political content to education, and low IQs, but the extent to which inauthenticity contributes to this inarticulateness can be studied by comparing groups who have similar attributes but who differ in their activation and in the extent to which they are manipulated. Also, we expect that the inarticulateness of the members of a group whose condition is inauthentic will be particularly pronounced with regard to topics related to their inauthentic condition because they are caught in a cross-current of feeling, of accepting and rejecting the same structure—accepting it consciously and rejecting it subconsciously. The members of such a group suffer in their attempts to reconcile an incompatible public self with their basic needs.[34]

When mobilization removes, at least in part, the disguise which conceals the underlying reality, inauthenticity still does not simply disappear both because disguises tend to be reintroduced and, thus, continued effort is required to keep them away, and because the disguises themselves are part of the societal structure which resists change. The awareness of inauthenticity, however, introduces a strong sense of being "taken" or cheated.

The alienated man who is conscious of his situation senses that he is excluded and deprived; the man who is aware of his inauthentic condition feels that he has been manipulated and was made to bless his captors if not his tormentors. The alienated man sees before him a tall, unyielding wall. The man caught in an inauthentic situation feels entangled in a cobweb. It is much more difficult for him to define the source of his malaise and to fight against it. There is much more guilt, because there is a sense that one shares in one's own manipulation, in allowing gestures and quasi-solutions to substitute for real change. The alienated man may sense that reality has been distorted and that he has been affected. The inauthentic man—in addition—

will feel detached from reality and will question his ability to grasp it; a smoke screen has been erected between himself and his world. Hence, we expect the inauthentic man to exhibit greater anxiety and more neurotic symptoms as compared to the alienated one.[35] The former has learned to see the smoke, but he is unsure of where it ends and reality begins or of what reality is like.

Both alienating and inauthentic contexts are likely to be impersonal, such as market and mass media forces. But the alienating context provides, especially for the actively alienated, a clear enemy. In the inauthentic context, much more effort is invested in concealment and facades; while the members often have, because of the historical spread of education and rise of income, a greater potential ability to see, there is much less that can be readily seen. (These are ideal types; concrete situations vary in their "mixes." The term "inauthentic condition" is used here to refer to a situation in which the inauthentic element is relatively stronger, while an alienated condition refers to a situation in which it is relatively weaker. Both, it should be recalled, have an alienating substructure.)

It should be stressed that a person's acceptance, rejection, calculation, or even ambivalence in regard to a particular societal structure does not allow us to judge whether or not his commitment is inauthentic. A person who rejects the application of force, is moved by genuine warmth and affection, wheels-and-deals in the market place, and is ambivalent when faced with a mixture of these elements might well be relating authentically to all of them. It is he who loves the hand that beats him (in concentration camps) and is calculative primarily in his love relations (in promiscuous liaisons) who is inauthentically committed. Unlike the common ambivalence which appears in all social relations, inherent in inauthentic situations is the dichotomy between the facade and the underlying reality; that is, the actor is not being torn between two forces similar in quality but confuses a shadow and a wall.

The depth of the inauthenticity varies. It may be quite limited—some lip-service paid to a conflicting set of norms, such as a free thinker in the United States claiming that he is religious. Or it may run quite deep, such as a homosexual who pretends to be heterosexual, maintains a marriage, and accepts internally the societal prescription of heterosexuality but is aware to varying degrees that he "cannot" conform to it. Moreover, a person may be "split" three ways, aware of one level of inauthenticity and standing on another—which he considers authentic—that hides the deeper, underlying structure. This is found in persons who engage in "bit" criticism when it is really the context that is unacceptable to them, a situation shared by many liberals in the Soviet Union and the United States.

Inauthentic Institutions and Society

The inauthenticity of various sectors of post-modern society has often been described; here, we need only to relate these familiar discussions to our main line of analysis. Our central propositions are: (a) that post-modern society is inauthentic to a significant degree, though the scope and depth of its inauthenticity have not yet been established; (b) that this condition of post-modern society seems to be more the result of the inauthenticity of political processes than of the disintegration of cohesive units or technological–economic factors; and (c) that inauthenticity in one institution nourishes it in others, and, hence, while research may have to study one sector at a time, analysis—if it is not to be inauthentic itself—must explore the macroscopic context.

Inauthentic institutions seem to have (a) a comparatively high investment in manipulative activities (e.g., post-modern societies seem to spend more on public relations than did the modern ones); (b) inter-rank (or status) strains resulting from the split between the appearance of community and the underlying bureaucratic reality (*above and beyond* the strains resulting from alienation itself); and (c) the incapacity to mobilize adequately the energy of their members. Energy is either "bottled-up," generating various personal distortions, or it leads to uninstitutionalized ("mass") societal expressions.

In line with our propositions, we deal first and most extensively with vertical relations—macro-authority or political processes. Secondly, we are concerned with "community" (or, horizontal cohesive) relations and their position in more encompassing macroscopic units, especially the society and its polity. We then explore briefly relations to objects (at work) and symbols (culture and socialization), which leads us to a view of the society as a whole. We focus on post-modern democracies and only briefly mention the non-democracies. Unless otherwise specified, the following statements refer to democracies.

INAUTHENTIC POLITICS

In the history of modern democracies, the period of alienation was one in which large segments of society, often the overwhelming majority, were disenfranchised. Later, the scope of exclusion was reduced, but major segments of the population (such as the working class and various minorities) were still left unrepresented. These societies developed elements of inauthenticity when, in the name of democracy, excluded groupings were given the right to vote but—by various well-known mechanisms—the alternatives from which they were to choose were limited to those which expressed the interests of the power elites and related collectivities. This is somewhat like a town with two newspapers run by one man. It does not allow the collectivities which have gained in societal power to express themselves or the new societal power to be converted into political power (or, it does so to such a limited extent that such conversion is ineffectual). This new societal power, therefore, despite franchisement, seeks non-institutional outlets in "direct action" (from strikes to riots). A sense of frustration about the democratic procedure is also generated; distrust of politicians and politics is prevalent. "You have to hold your nose to vote," said the anti-imperialists in the 1900 election, after their candidate misled them.[36] This is only one step from not voting and two steps from rejecting the political system as a whole.

Early labor parties, which became so enamored of their being allowed to participate in parliamentary politics that they tended to neglect the representation of the economic needs of the workers who voted for them, soon showed the familiar signs of inauthentic political mobilization—dissatisfaction, factionalism, secessions, direct action, and so forth. The German Social Democrats' efforts to avoid offending the Kaiser in 1912 and the MacDonald involvement in "parliamentary games" in Westminster, replacing Keir Hardie's harder line, are cases in point, though British labor was more inclined to express its latent alienation than were the German workers.

Similarly, the post-modern period's increased reliance on the mass media and on other manipulative techniques to "sell" candidates on the basis of their appearances is successful in the sense that members of collectivities whose basic needs are not represented by these candidates do vote for them.[37] Studies suggest, however, a fairly widespread sense of not being fully involved in the political process or of being cheated.[38] This seems to increase in periods in which the candidate campaigns on one lead-theme only to carry out the opposite policy once elected, as Wilson did in 1916 and Johnson did in 1964. Both campaigned as peace candidates and engaged in wars. These shifts are widely reported to have "bewildered" the American people who seem superficially but not deeply convinced by the reasons that are given for a president legitimating one alternative when he faces the electorate and shortly thereafter pursuing the opposite one, though the situation has barely changed.[39]

A more extensive study of Western democracy from this viewpoint is necessary. One of the reasons for its considerable stability and continuity is that it was by no means in all periods unresponsive to the needs of new, rising collectivities and social movements. When the left, anti-monopolistic groups saw the United States, in the years before 1894, as so unresponsive that their commitment to the political system was weakened, the Democratic party responded to them and, for a while, under the pressure of the Populists, represented the anti-business alternative. On the other side of the political spectrum, as the conservatives became increasingly "dispossessed,"[40] the candidacy of Goldwater in 1964 gave them a political expression they had not had since Herbert Hoover. Before 1964, this grouping felt increasingly cheated by the democratic process. The fact that there was only little increase in non-democratic, right wing, direct action efforts after the 1964 election suggests that most of the conservatives felt that the system was "fair," however much they resented the outcome and "explained" it away. Thus, the conditions under which and to what degree the American polity is or is not responsive are still unsettled questions.

More generally, it has been widely argued that the "textbook" model of democracy, in which the needs of the people "percolate" upward and provide directives for societal action, is unrealistic. Most of the flow, it is said, is downward; alternative elites initiate and specify policy alternatives and gain endorsement by mobilizing the support of the population. Some upward flow is recognized, but it is considered much less significant than the downward flow.[41] There is much validity to this correction of the popular democratic model. In particular, it is true that the units of the process are not the millions of individuals that make up the society. Also, the downward model may well provide a fairly accurate picture of inauthentic democratic politics and inauthentic consensus-building;* however, it does omit the costs when it implies that this is a model of a well-functioning democratic system rather than of a distorted one.†

One major consequence of inauthentic democratic politics is that new societal power is not converted into political power, and, thus, new collective needs are not "proportionately" and quickly transmitted to the society's control centers. This leads to overdue and inadequate responses, direct action, the disaffection of the intellectuals and the collectivities they succeed in mobilizing, and—when extensive and continued—a violent transformation of society. Less perceptible but nevertheless costly are the widespread feelings of not being taken into account, of distrust, and of resentment.

No less important is the fact that inauthentic politics cannot mobilize sufficient energy for higher levels of societal activation. At best, they can contain the existing conflicts, but, as the differences among the various collective actors are not narrowed when consensus-formation is inauthentic, societal passivity pervades. It may be argued that passivity is functional for those who benefit from the *status quo*. But it seems to us incorrect to assume that the "have" groups and the power elites always seek to stabilize the *status quo*. Faced with rising societal demands, the more far-sighted powerful collectivities do try to adapt, even if this entails a loss of part of their assets in order to keep the "rest." For example, first the British aristocracy and later the British bourgeoisie showed that they understood this sociological point, at least better than their French brethren. But to

---

* "As many American political scientists have regularly deplored, the relation between action in the policy-making process and in the electoral process is frequently very tenuous. ... Differences which are highlighted in a campaign often concern dramatic but unimportant issues where one contestant has been maneuvered into taking an extreme or vulnerable position. Once a candidate is elected, his policies in office often have little relation to those which both he and his opponent advocated when they were campaigning for office." Brzezinski and Huntington, *Political Power: USA/USSR, op. cit.*, p. 192.

† On this point, see Jack L. Walker, "A Critique of the Elitist Theory of Democracy," *The American Political Science Review*, Vol. LX (1966), pp. 285–295. See also the rebuttal: Robert A. Dahl, "Further Reflections on 'The Elitist Theory of Democracy,'" *ibid.*, pp. 296–305 and Walker's comment, *ibid.*, pp. 391–392.

adapt in this way an effective political process must be operative to test and work out the limits of reallocation and to tie the authentic inclusion of the new collectivities into the democratic political process with their socialization to participate within it. In short, inauthentic politics hinder both conservative accommodation and radical socialization.

The inauthentic polity, despite its high investment in manipulation, requires some consensus-formation and responsiveness if it is to function at all. It seems to us that as an overreaction to the textbook model of democracy, the degree to which consensus-building can be effectively carried downward and citizens be manipulated has been greatly exaggerated. Studies of the American presidency illustrate that national political elites are quite "boxed in" by the contextuating images internalized by the active and quasi-active publics and by various highly institutionalized and often over-represented interest groups.[42] Of course, the inequality of the power distribution among these groupings results in over-responsiveness to some collectivities and under-responsiveness to others, but this is a societal "upward" fact; this distortion may be magnified by the slant of the state but is not created by it. Second, the elites and organizations which mobilize collectivities into the society's political process often are "downward" regarding their position inside their respective collectivities but not in their relations with the national elites; also, much more give-and-take among the sub-collectivities and factions in the organizations takes place than is recognized in the "downward" model. Third, the most "downward" relation seems to exist between the local sub-collectivity and its organizational arms and the individual citizens. But even this is mitigated by multi-affiliations, mobility, the universality of the state, and other factors.

So far as the whole polity is concerned, a distinction ought to be maintained between downward flows which specify the basic needs of the citizens and those which seek to legitimate a course which falls outside the context of these needs but pretends to be a specification of them. The first process, which is technically downward, is responsive to the limits set by the members and is, thus, an authentic mechanism, which the second one is not. For example, to offer a group of students demanding the right to control the educational program of a university significant representation in the university's decision-making bodies is to respond to their basic demand, though their specific request is denied. To suggest that students are only transient members of a university and, hence, have no right to participate in its decision-making is not to respond to their basic need (and newly-found power), even if the students are unable to articulate the reasons that the administration's argument and policy are invalid.

When the approach is unresponsive to *basic* needs, it may, of course, lead to a confrontation and a change of the elites or their policies. When this does not occur and inauthentic consensus-building is practiced for prolonged periods of time, it will incur the various costs of inauthenticity.

This is the element, to reverse the analytic perspective of our discussion, that consensus adds to responsiveness: Members' needs can be served in a variety of ways, and some concessions can be made without a sense of alienation, of generalized disaffection. Authentic consensus-building may "specify" the needs of the members in such a way that the differences among them will be reduced and, thus, increase the level of responsiveness of a policy to *all* the members, despite their divergent structural positions. This is the reason that we suggest that a significant part of politics is not reallocative but re-educative.

The difference between inauthentic politics and compromise politics, part of the authentic democratic process, needs to be highlighted. The essence of consensus-formation—especially, of responsive consensus-formation—is that actors who differ in their perspectives work out a "concurred" policy. This policy often will not satisfy their original demands and needs; the process entails some sacrifice of their initial positions. Hence, often after a policy is established, there is a sense of loss and a hope of gaining more influence the next time around. But so long as the procedure in which the policy was established is considered legitimate and some of the actors' needs are satisfied or are respecified through authentic participation, the sense of compromise will not lead to latent or open alienation and the politics are not inauthentic. Politics are inauthentic when (1) the appearance of a give-and-take masks a "take" but no, or only a token, "give"; (2) participation is manipulated and is not a genuine sharing in the decision-making process; and (3) the political superstructure does not represent the societal bases, though it tries to appear as if it does.[43]

In totalitarian politics, there is a similar limit to manipulation. Much has been written about the potency of downward political control in totalitarian societies. In democracies, it has been said, such control is curbed by the many elites and sources of mass communication which constrain each other. In totalitarian polities, with a monolithic source of communication and one elite and with uninhibited, state-controlled propaganda, there are very few limits to what can be legitimated and affected.

In contrast, we hold that (a) some proliferation of collectivities and organizations as well as inter-elite competition and upward flows exist in totalitarian societies; and (b) totalitarian persuasion does not gain authentic political endorsement, in that its legitimation is not deep and the members of such a society have a considerable residue of "internal" and behavioral resistance. Our position needs two kinds of reinforcement which cannot be provided here:

(i) In terms of personality theory, we need a better conceptualization of deep versus only superficial acceptance.[44] One indicator of this difference may be the readiness with which the acceptance "washes out" when the social pressure ceases; another may be the extent to which it is encompassing (e.g., is it operative in private sectors?).[45] Also, we expect that studies using depth methods will find signs of latent rejection and suppressed resistance, even while persuasion seems to "work" on the manifest level. Finally, we expect mobilization that is based on persuasion to yield much less energy than that which is based on authentic commitment, as is illustrated by comparisons of "drummed-up" demonstrations with spontaneous ones or of Party-required participation in a class on Marxism with a seminar in a free university.

(ii) We need many more empirical studies of the effects of mass persuasion. Studies of the totalitarian efforts in this regard seem to support both sides of the argument and usually ignore the social and personal costs. The findings of studies of advertising and other forms of mass persuasion in the West support our position, because, it is widely agreed, they tend to show that bits can be changed in a context (e.g., consumer products can be substituted for each other), but that it is extremely difficult to change contexts, especially when these have been geared to basic needs.

Some support for our position so far as totalitarian societies are concerned can be seen in that basic human needs seem to reassert themselves in these societies as soon as the early, revolutionary stage is passed. Actually, in terms of the organization of these societies, these needs may account in part for the societies' moving out of this stage. They seem to push the regimes, in spite of their enormous coercive and persuasive power, in directions in which they do not wish to move. Among the needs which most openly assert themselves are (1) the need for context, indicated by the search for realistic information (hence, the discounting of state-communication and an increased reliance on rumors—accurate, in comparison—and on foreign sources of news such as the BBC and the Voice of America in the USSR);[46] (2) the need for a sector in which individual achievement can be exercised and for differential rewards; (3) the need for less remote gratification and more personal security, and (4) the need for a less arbitrary change of norms. The fact that programs such as the collectivization of the farms or the assimilation of ethnic minorities which were supported by the full power of the Party–State had to be curtailed further illustrates the limits to acting against basic human needs. Even where such programs were advanced, their continued social and personal costs were large, which lends further support to our point.

To be committed inauthentically is to be passive in the encompassing sense of the term, because being passive in one or in a few realms of activity is not the mark of the uncommitted. Commitment requires being active in some spheres* and being mobilizable when the contexts of the other spheres are violated. The value of restraint and neutrality as pre-conditions for democratic politics has often been emphasized, and the "function" of apathy has been pointed out. The essence of the argument is that if all the members of

---

* For reasons discussed above, a political element is essential.

society were fully mobilized and committed, consensus-formation which requires a willingness to compromise (which is negatively correlated with the intensity of commitment) would not be possible. Thus, while democratic polities can function if some members are committed intensely on some issues, they cannot function if all members are committed intensely on all issues. And democracy requires a "floating" vote to reward the acceptance of the limits on partisan action which are institutionalized in the democratic process. The highly committed are unlikely to "float" and to allow "procedure" to take priority over the alternative they favor, *and* they feel intense about most issues. Thus, intense and encompassing commitment tends to be associated with "extreme" political conduct and extra-institutional action.

But the need for moderation and restraint can be overemphasized, especially when the problem is the widespread illusion of commitment rather than overcommitment. It is not only that when few citizens are actively committed to politics, the practice of politics is left to power elites or oligarchies (as studies of labor unions show), but also that the limitation of commitment must have a special structure before it is functional for democracy: The commitment must be low in regard to specifics but high in regard to contexts. Thus, democratic commitment is low to any party but high to the democratic process; i.e., democracy cannot be based on encompassing apathy. Similarly, there are basic values other than democracy that, when violated, bring the "contextually" committed out of their *partial* (or contextuated) apathy. Thus, the moderate who cannot become enraged about the violation of any value is as much of an anathema to democratic politics as are those who are extremely committed on most issues.

INAUTHENTICITY IN COHESIVE UNITS

It is well established that without diffuse, affective relationships, individuals cannot maintain their identity, emotional stability, and rationality. These relationships are found in micro-cohesive units such as the family, friendship groups, or school teams. In turn, these relationships need to be built into more encompassing cohesive units such as the village or community in order to enable a person to outgrow one group and move to another and to extend his loyalties to macro-units. Modernization is said to have created anomie by its undermining of both micro- and macro-cohesive units. We have already seen that this is not the case—that the old cohesive units have adapted and that new ones were created.

Both macro- and micro-cohesive, modern units, though, are said to be inauthentic. Modernization is alienating in that men treat each other as instruments; this undermines cohesive units which are based on a non-rational commitment, on treating people as goals. Inauthenticity enters when actors pretend that they are goal-oriented while actually they are instrumental, when they pretend that they seek friendship while actually they seek utilization (such as the quasi-friendship of the salesman or of the status-seeker). The falsification of friendship or community may be deliberate (as in advertising) or unwittingly built into the relationship (as in the status-competition in some suburbs).[47] Again, we would expect that living in an inauthentic community would result in a kind of neurosis different from that inflicted by living in a disintegrated one, though at this stage we can merely speculate about the differences.[48] The main point is that neither kind of community provides the social bases of active collectivities, as psychological energies are bottled-up and are not available for collective action,[49] and the psychological conditions for rational decision-making and authentic consensus-formation are lacking because these require the emotional stability that is found only in authentic, cohesive units.

The cohesive units of modern societies and their relations to other societal sectors seem to be in part inauthentic, with the degree of inauthenticity varying from country to country, within each country, and over time. The scope of the inauthenticity in any period should be determined empirically. We suggest that in the contemporary United States, there are significant elements of inauthenticity. While not all cohesive relations, especially those in the micro-units, are inauthentic, most relationships seem affected by inauthenticity to some degree (including the mother–child one)[50] and will need to be transformed before an authentic, active society can be evolved.

An authentic society requires authentic sub-societies and the authentic upward representation of their needs and societal power, an effective downward communication of the society's values and policies, and a broad sharing within each sub-society of the assets which the society's allocative processes set aside for it. If inauthentic leaders stand between the society and a collectivity, this tends to generate inauthentic political linkages even if both units are themselves authentic. This is a situation approximated in the following case: Israeli society is fairly authentic, though less so than it was in its "social movement" days. Immigrants who come from traditional societies, such as Yemen, tend to arrive in well-integrated sub-collectivities, headed by traditional leaders. In their attempts to integrate these sub-collectivities into the society, various Israeli agencies learned that breaking up these groupings and attempting to provide the immigrants with modern Israeli leaders generated much anomie and alienation. The prevailing policy is, hence, to transform the sub-collectivities from traditional to modern ones rather than to dissolve them, and to attempt to transform the traditional leadership. In the process of "modernizing" the traditional leaders, some tend to become highly self-oriented and to use their special access to the polity for self-aggrandizement to the detriment of their groups.[51] This is the danger of inauthentic leadership. While actively alienated leaders lead their groups toward "anti-social" behavior, they at least serve to help express the alienation and, occasionally, to transform the society. The inauthentic leader does double damage: He consumes the assets needed for the transformation of his group, and he does not fulfill the leadership function but rather takes the place of a leader, making it appear as if there were one.

INAUTHENTIC WORK AND WORK RELATIONS

In early industrial society, as has been stated by Marx and by many others,[52] the source of much alienation was the lack of responsiveness of the industrial organization to the needs of the workers or of the society. In comparison, work in the highly industrialized societies is less depriving and more remunerative but not more involving.[53] Above all, its organization is still basically nonparticipatory, and a good deal of the increased participation of the workers is inauthentic, as we shall illustrate below. At the same time, the distorting effects of work relations (and the related market ones) on other societal sectors have not greatly declined, though they have become less manifest. Inauthenticity is also generated in other sectors (e.g., education) and is carried over from these into work relations. The various sectors mutually support each others' inauthenticity, and pseudo-participation and not only the lack of ownership is central to the unresponsive structure. Thus, we expect that neither nationalization nor other forms of public ownership will remove unresponsiveness, as is illustrated by oligarchic unions, exploitive cooperatives, and, of course, factories in socialist states.

In *work relations*, the early, industrial management–worker relations mark the period in which open alienation prevailed. The introduction of Human Relations as a manipulative technique indicates the rise in inauthenticity.[54] Here, the participation of workers in management decision-making has provided little change of the underlying power or asset structure and no genuine sharing of goals, and it has often had the deliberate purpose of draining energy from conflict politics, especially unionization. Ideologically, this is supplemented by the emphasis on the shared goals and interests of workers and employers and by the denial of the existence of divergent ones.

In the realm of *labor organization*, open alienation prevailed in the period in which the right of workers to organize was denied. Early inauthenticity is marked by the organization of company unions which appear to be expressions of the workers but are actually run by the management. Many labor unions which originally provided authentic, upward representation gradually, by cooptation and other devices, came to act like an extension of the Labor Relations Department of the Company and are highly inauthentic.[55] The elements that make these aspects of work inauthentic are the facade of their appearance as compared to their underlying structure, their unresponsiveness to the members, and their ostensible openness to upward consensus-formation while they are actually tools of the downward mobilization of consensus or control. Symptoms of membership in an inauthentic union are the members' unrest (expressed by generalized dissatisfaction with the union coupled with an inability to specify its sources) and "wildcat" strikes, in which the unrepresented needs of the members and unabsorbed collective energies seek an outlet.[56]

Several studies show that American workers prefer high-paying, alienating labor to lower-paying, less alienating work.[57] But this does not show that these workers favor alienating work. They choose it to obtain the means to sate the consumption cravings and status anxieties that are rooted in their inauthentic off-the-job relations. Advanced capitalist economy, it seems well-established, needs the continued artificial stimulation of appetites and anxieties; advertising is the most obvious example. An economy which reduced the amount of inauthentic stratification (e.g., the obsessive concern with marginal differences in symbolic scales) would undergo a severe crisis if not collapse unless it simultaneously reduced alienating labor (by making its pace more amenable to the workers' needs, introducing shorter working hours, allowing more room for creativity, etc.). Thus, a smaller need for economic products would be combined with some decrease in economic effort, leaving more energy for other societal activities. Also, work will be more meaningful, the more it is geared to the public sector and to societal values (education, culture, health, welfare) rather than to private consumption.

It may be argued that the preference for a culturally and politically active life over the pursuit of consumption is a value judgment—an intellectual's projection of his preferences on the average citizen—and a Utopian expectation. It should, hence, be added, first of all, that the preceding statements refer to changes which are on-going; though they presently encompass only a fraction of the members of affluent societies, this fraction seems slowly to be growing and its growth will accelerate although it will not necessarily encompass more than part of the society. Second, we hold that a society will move in the active direction as more of its members exhibit preferences for an authentic life; i.e., we expect that more people will live like intellectuals. That other segments of the population cannot be expected to demonstrate needs similar to those of intellectuals in the foreseeable future suggests merely that the society will not be fully active in the foreseeable future, but not that it cannot be much more active than it has been to date. That inauthentic work and consumption have serious consequences for important segments of the population is a proposition that can be empirically tested; it does not rest on our projection but on the indications of restlessness, a sense of being cheated, and so forth, among the citizens of the inauthentic societies under study.

Initially, parts of the population may well have to learn to recognize the inauthentic elements of their work and consumption and acquire the taste for higher culture as well as for a more active political life, but this does not mean that these are artificial needs. The test lies in the ways in which men react once they have the opportunity for a more authentic life presented to them for a prolonged period.

INAUTHENTIC SOCIALIZATION

Socialization is a pivotal process in the determination of the condition of a society, for socialization shapes the character of its members. If merely authority relations are inauthentic, the estrangement is far less profound; if socialization is also affected, the split between societal appearances and reality is more likely to affect deeply the private self and "basic" personality.

Inauthentic socialization promotes self-images which are unresponsive and not committing. The post-modern school system has been accused (and, to a degree, documentation has been provided) of placing a public self between the person and the world which prevents the authentic expression of emotions and the development of authentic relations to others, thus eliminating the possibility of attaining a genuine arousal or release.[58] It prepares the child for pseudo-*gemeinschaft* and its officials. It fosters uniformity to such a degree that the members' need for variance cannot be satisfied.[59]

The discussions and studies of the inauthentic quality of mass culture, entertainment, and leisure activities are well known.[60] These have been countered with the notion that the criticism of mass education and culture is an elitist, intellectual projection, and that this culture *does* reflect the desires and needs of the mass.[61] Future studies will have to determine (a) the extent to which the acceptance of this culture is authentic (whether or not there are signs of rejection below the surface); and (b) the degree to which the acceptance of inauthentic culture is the result of inauthentic socialization, community, authority, and work, and of the lack of continued exposure to more authentic culture.

THE INAUTHENTIC SOCIETY

Ultimately, it is not a question of whether or not this or that institution is inauthentic; it is a question of the quality of the whole society. To what degree does the affluent society impose on its members work that is inauthentically involving—labor through which men day-dream in order to finance inauthentic leisure, neurotic status-races and consumption obsessions that sustain the inauthentic work structure? Thus, products are sold and the workers are able to release the strains of inauthentic work and authority relations, to buy more, and work more. We suggest (1) that no collectivity (or society) can lead an authentically rich life amidst the deprivation of others; and (2) that the more self-aware, educated, articulate, and mobilized members of the affluent society are clearly less committed to this society than those who are less endowed. Possibly, the majority of the membership have similar basic needs but are less aware of them and less able to express their disaffection. (3) The high rates of personal costs—neuroses and asocial behavior—are indicative of the inauthentic bases. And (4) no society that stresses material affluence can overcome the prevalence of the instrumental orientation among its members and, therefore, be authentic. A much greater focus on symbols and on a purposive orientation is a prerequisite. The affluent society may well be less alienating than early industrial society, but it is less authentic. Even if the affluent society offers the closest approximation to a responsive society achieved by any society it does not seem to be a highly responsive one.

In fact, inauthentic societies are less responsive than alienating ones in two ways: (a) There seem to be more limitations on the acquisition of valid societal knowledge and collective self-consciousness and, hence, on the mobilization of most members for political action; and (b) there seems to be a trend toward the increasing construction of the identity of the citizens around the rejection of some foreign power and the maintenance, in non-war years, of a semi-military mobilization of society which divides the members of one society from those of another.

It may be said that an increase in societal responsiveness—to allow for more authentic participation in shaping work, more adequate public services and facilities, decreased inequality, and so on—will undermine the conditions of instrumentality and the utilitarian system. One could propose that only a person who is authentically committed and gratified will be highly productive, and that rational decision-making is based on membership in genuine cohesive units. But even if activation entails *some* sacrifice of instrumentality, the citizens—if fully aware of the choices and options involved—may still opt for an active society.* And there seems no way to release the material and political and psychic energies necessary to reduce inequality, to transform ethnic status relations, and to overcome tribalism other than a growth in the consciousness and mobilization of the collectivities now caught on the economic, stratification, and political treadmills of the inauthentic society—i.e., other than an increase in their activation.

An active society would absorb the energies of its members, and in particular their political energies, in institutionalized (though not bureaucratic) structures. Societies tend to lose some of this capacity for the absorption of energy as their institutional structures become more rigid, especially as they become more complex, instrumentally oriented, and organizational (which are the tendencies of modernization). This development, in turn, reduces the degree to which the members' energies are committed and the legitimacy and efficacy of the institutional structure. If no mechanisms for activation and transformation are operative (or tolerated), and they are

---

* The dilemma of efficiency (rationality, instrumentality) and a less obsessive life and society is too often argued as though the choice were one of underdevelopment versus affluence. Daniel Bell avoids this mistake in his "Work and Its Discontents," in *The End of Ideology* (New York: Free Press, 1960), pp. 222–262. Without dealing with the choices underdeveloped countries now face, the choices of modernized societies are between additional escalations of the material consumption of the majority or the substitution of some of this for more symbolic activity, more social justice, and more personal activation.

substituted with manipulation in the broadest sense of the term, inauthenticity is likely to grow and to increase the potential for radical mobilization, which, in turn, becomes the mechanism for recommitment to societal institutions (though to a different set).

Reduction of Inauthenticity

A Dynamic Perspective

A central characteristic of the inauthentic society is that its structure and components are inherently unstable. While such a society may endure for decades—as the various elements help to sustain each other, especially in periods of rising utilitarian affluence and high national security—there is the possibility of rapid mobilization for transformation, because the inauthentic structure is not committing *and*—unlike the alienating one—hides from its own elites as well as from observers the extent to which consensus has been lost. In this way, inauthenticity blocks the recognition and treatment of societal problems—even those the interests of the elites would prescribe— and the elites which manipulate the membership manipulate themselves as well.

While the transformation of an inauthentic society is affected by many forces, it is useful for our purposes to distinguish two main kinds: forces which affect the underlying, alienating structure, and forces which affect the symbols and institutional facades. Both kinds appear in the forms of various modes and levels of mobilization, the process by which energy is made available for new societal action. Here, we explore these within the context of personal, collective, and societal projects.

The Project

A *project* is a concentrated act. It entails a relatively specific goal or goals and a heightened level of activity and, hence, usually a measure of mobilization. A project is a program that is usually limited to a given time period. While one project may lead to another or be combined with others into a more macroscopic one, an ongoing activity is not a project. Desegregation is a societal project; education is not.

While the concept of project is used here in its psychological and sociological senses, we deliberately draw on the connotations of the concept in existentialist writings because we accept many of their philosophical implications. For existentialists, man is viewed as a self-transcending being who has a measure of choice (often exaggerated in this highly voluntarist philosophy), and his being is expressed in the choices or commitments he makes and in the projects he undertakes. In these projects, man pro-jects himself; they are his existence. Man is, thus, not a thing but an action.[62]

An alienated man in the existentialist writings is a man who does not make choices, who evades his responsibility; as we prefer to put it, he is passive and is not engaged in his "own" projects. This may be either because he has been reduced to an object or because he has become entangled in unresponsive projects—those which involve treating others and himself as "things" and which prevent responsiveness to basic human needs.

Personal Projects

A person in an inauthentic society faces the basic option of committing himself to a project or of accepting passivity. While we reject the voluntaristic viewpoint of many existentialists, we do propose that even the most oppressed person has some measure of choice. Evidence would show that in all but rare limit-situations, there is no way fully to commit a man's psychological energies, intellectual capacities, and utilitarian resources; he can retain the capacity to commit some of them and, above all, some of himself, as he sees fit. That which he sees as fit is likely to be affected by his societal context and may be distorted. But there are moments, we suggest, in which each man sees the roots of his uneasiness, the shadows of his captors, and the hands of his manipulators, and he, thus, has an irreducible element of freedom which he can extend by committing himself to a project.

This may initially be rather limited—a small step toward some additional understanding of his societal position and of the society in which he is positioned, or some minimal participation in a societal action such as signing a petition.* This, in turn, may act as a catalyst leading to broader activation, though at each step the individual may relapse into passivity (this is increasingly less likely as he collectivizes and organizes his projects), or he may choose a project which in itself is not authentic.

A personal project that is materialistic and individualistic is most likely to increase inauthenticity, as it is likely to involve the treatment of others as instruments. Symbolic–individualistic projects[63] (e.g., a-normative art) will not lead to transformation because the transformation of the objective foundation of the inauthentic social condition is not energized by withdrawal from it. A collectivistic–materialistic project will entail the kind of objectivization commonly encountered in totalitarian production units. Both of these kinds of project are relatively closer to activeness than passivity or the locking of oneself into a personal, materialistic orbit, but both are inauthentic.

---

* The nature of a small as opposed to a greater step depends on the societal and historical situation. Signing a petition may be a major step in South Africa but a very small one in New York, and even in New York, it was a larger step during the McCarthy era than it was later. A major step in many personal chains of activation is the decision not to accept the system any longer, and that it must be changed basically.

A personal project which is symbolic *and* related to a collective project, such as participation in a social movement, is more likely to be authentic than the two kinds just described.[64] Its goal may be the change of one of the two elements of the inauthentic condition (or various combinations thereof): (i) *reducing the facade*, unveiling the underlying structure—thus increasing realistic societal knowledge and consciousness, foreshortening the distance between the private and public selves, and making personal energy available for societal action. On the one hand, this is expected to lead to a more authentic life, even if the underlying structure does not yield; on the other hand, it is extremely difficult to initiate, advance, and sustain, unless it is supported by projects on other levels. (ii) Such personal projects may lead to *changes in the alienating structure, if* they are linked to each other, and if they are collectivized and organized. In short, personal activation may lead only to new societal insight, or also to societal change.

Collective Projects

Most members of inauthentic societies are too deeply entrenched in the existing structure to initiate a symbolic–collective project. The initiation of transforming projects is, hence, the work of a selected few. Many more individuals, though, are able to participate in such a project once it has been initiated. The fact that for any individual who activates a social status, there are numerous others in similar statuses means that there are others who potentially can be activated in the same direction. This is the reason that macroscopic projects have an objective collective base rather than being merely aggregations of numerous microscopic or personal projects. Collectivization provides a basis for mobilization because it frees the participants from at least part of the guilt they experience in taking an "anti-social" step, releases energies spent in self-defense, allows for more rational conduct, and serves as a basis for building counter-symbols and ideals as well as primary relations to satisfy the members' needs for recognition and affection—without their having to conform to the societal norms.

Collectivities (or sub-collectivities) which are activated (or formed around a project) face all the traps which can ensnare a personal project—above all, a sub-collectivity's project may be "individualistic," concerned with the sub-collectivity rather than with the society which contextuates it. Notions of setting up "Utopian" settlements in an inauthentic society, popular among some segments of the New Left, are a recent example of this age-old escape.[65] There are many reasons that authenticity cannot be advanced in this way. The main bases of inauthentic mass communications, economic exchange, and political power rest in the society at large and, unless they are transformed, they tend to (a) intrude into the Utopian islands and undermine their authenticity, and (b) prevent the creation of a foundation for a new society which requires a set of communicative institutions, a productive base, and a state of its own—features which are not available to "islands" but only to autonomous societies. (c) The guilt of the inhabitants of the islands for those who are left at sea further distorts the former's situation; vicarious participation, it seems, works both ways: Just as the protest of the few does activate (if only a little) the spectator majority, so the continued inauthentic life of the many hampers the freedom of the few.

Societal Projects

From an amalgamation of activated sub-collectivities, intellectuals, service-collectivities, and unbalanced and alienated sub-collectivities, social movements rise whose project is the transformation of society. When the project is broad-based and reaches an unusually high level of activation, and if the circumstances are favorable (as explored above), such a project may suffice to tip the scales in favor of fundamental societal change. When mobilization does not attain a sufficiently high level and the alienating forces are too strong to be overcome, inauthenticity may still be significantly reduced, because in the confrontation, the underlying structure is unveiled. (This holds not just for social movements which seek more responsive structures but also for those which seek to establish less responsive ones, and not only for those who are future-oriented but also for those which seek to restore a past.)

Such projects, however, fail to achieve even an approximation of full societal activation. First, there is a tendency for activeness to rise temporarily to new plateaux only to subside again, either after the fundamental transforming act is accomplished or when it is blocked. In order to mold a permanent social-movement society, there must be the continued initiation of new societal projects which respond to increasingly more encompassing bases of membership and, as we shall see, to more symbolic and collective needs. The picture of a revolutionary jump into the euphoria of a fully responsive but static society is, thus, doubly misleading. History knows no such jumps, and the outcomes of one generation's projects require additional transformations by the next generation. The authentic quality can be maintained only by continued activation. This, though, is not a statement of despair, because each round of completed projects opens new and potentially "higher" options and the engagement in projects itself has an activating quality. Ultimately, there is no end but rather a continuous drive toward realization. This view of societal action may seem unduly pessimistic; it should, hence, be noted that it does not grow out of the analysis of the sociologist but rather out of the world which he analyzes—and which societal action encounters.

The relations between personal and societal activation may be highlighted by the following point: Data collected in a large variety of societies and cultures show that workers who were asked if they wanted additional material goods answered strongly in the affirmative.[66] This may be used to argue that it is "in human nature" to wish for a plethora of consumer goods. A quite different interpretation may be given to the same data, however. Every person may be ambivalent, attracted to material and individualistic rewards *and* to symbolic and collectivistic ones. When a person is asked about the desirability of material goods, the question captures one side of his ambivalence. If the same man were asked, for instance, if he favored the use of one half of 1 per cent of his tax money for raising the cultural *niveau* of his country, he may well also assent (especially after some explanation of the issue and if no campaign is conducted by opposing interest groups). Thus, we suggest, there is as much of a personal foundation for a symbolic-collectivistic choice as there is for a materialistic–individualistic one, *and* one factor which determines whether one option or the other is activated is the nature of the societal context. When societal institutions activate some symbolic and collectivistic choices, this lays the foundation for additional action in the same direction, which, in turn, lays the foundation for more symbolic and collectivistic societal institutions. The way in which West Europeans view social security and full employment as "inevitable" is a case in point.

Such mutual reinforcement of societal and personal activation is not without limits. In societies in which the emphasis on the collectivistic–symbolic approach is already strong, the process may well exhaust itself or even tend to move in the opposite, materialistic–individualistic direction. Thus, some societies are unrealistically[67] public and austere, while others stress too heavily self-oriented, object-producing activities if their values are to be realized.

Finally, like collectivities and their combinations, societies, too, have projects of their own. Moreover, these projects can have greater macroscopic consequences than most social movements. In the past, societies have been mobilized mainly to impose their wills on others or on member collectivities. Much of the analysis in the preceding chapters is concerned with the conditions under which the capacity for the attainment of a high level of mobilization for active self-change, for the realization of goals subscribed to by the authentic consent of the membership, may rise or be developed. Of special importance in this regard are increases in consensus-building capacities, responsiveness, and societal mobilization, and community-building on the supranational level (i) to prevent wars (and the preparation for wars) from draining the societal energy, assets, and attention required for intra-societal projects, and (ii) to gain resources with little societal strain by increasing the scale of the units of action.

Ultimately, the projects of a society cannot be advanced unless they affect the societal boundaries. Here, as we have seen, the contemporary reality is one of sub-global quasi-empires. The replacement of these with more egalitarian regional and world communities is likely to entail projects in which collectivities in "have-not" societies will join with those in affluent societies which seek the transformation of the whole system toward one which is more responsive internally as well as externally.

Mutual Reinforcing and Gradual Accumulation

Projects on each level, it seems, support each other up and down the micro-macro ladder. Projects of lower-level units may trigger and energize those of higher-level ones. While there is some "slack" on each level and leeway among them—conditions which allow for the initiation of projects on any one of the levels without the initiation and synchronization of projects on the other levels—only some gains in authenticity and in the reduction of alienation are possible unless all levels are involved. If a project is limited to the personal, collective, or societal level, sooner or later it will approach the boundaries set by the other levels and will be blocked.

On the other hand, when the activation of one level is accompanied or followed by the activation of the others, there is a mutual reinforcing process. When workers previously unrepresented in the legislature of a country are mobilized on a *collective* level and gain *societal* representation, they can use their new political power to spread education and render the polity more "neutral," which, in turn, facilitates further worker mobilization. When a person's view of society becomes more valid and he works for the mobilization of a sub-collectivity, he contributes to the societal transforming forces and makes the reduction of alienation more likely.

Projects are, thus, potentially like catalysts; they may set into motion chain reactions which go far beyond the initial action. When the initial priming is small, the effects may be very limited; in cases in which it is larger, at first only a latent change may accumulate. And even when chain reactions do "take-off," they frequently are exhausted before the society is transformed, especially when they meet countervailing forces on other levels. But rarely does the society remain the same after such an activation, because even if the chain of projects does not change the society's structure, the bases of mobilization are likely to have been affected, and a new foundation has been provided for future projects.

Maintaining the Connection

So far, we have focused on the inter-level links of societal action, stressing the role of the context, the whole. The same approach also applies to the links among the three components of the active orientation. We are aware of nothing in social nature that necessitates the development of links among the three components of the active orientation, and the necessity of a balanced mix among .the three components seems even less evident. Individuals and collectivities find their knowledge, commitment, and power dissociated under the impact of societal structures and political organizations which distort the distribution of societal knowledge, manipulate the focusing of members' commitments, and are unresponsive to the changing societal consensus. Such societies themselves—i.e., the society-wide level—are likely to experience dissociation of the three elements if they do not effectively mobilize their members. We saw that man is a being who penetrates all three realms, but there is a danger of his becoming dissociated or of his being reduced to one of them. His symbolic, social, and objective being—his knowledge and consciousness, his commitment and the objective base of his power—may become unrelated.[68] Or, he may cease to be effective in two of these realms and remain only a thinker *or* a committed being *or* a mover. Projects and, more generally, action are ways of keeping the elements connected, because they test knowledge, reveal and adjust commitments, and explore the foundations of power. But under alienating or inauthentic conditions, action is unable to serve its articulating function and increases the extent of the dissociation for persons as well as for societal units. The activated paranoic person may reinforce his paranoia, and Nazi Germany at war was more internally disconnected than before. It seems that only in relatively responsive societies are projects likely to reinforce the connections among the elements of the active orientation, and only projects oriented toward the reduction of alienation and inauthenticity are likely to build active societies.

We face here what seems like a closed circle: For action to be viable, it has to be promulgated in a free society; for a society to be free, it requires continued action. The escape seems to lie in a mutual reinforcement and gradual accumulation process; the use of the leeway each society has for some collective and symbolic projects reduces the scope of inauthenticity, which, in turn, allows for more activation. This leads either toward a freer society or toward a confrontation.[69] Confrontations lead either to a transformation or to a change in the base of mobilization. Neither alternative is definitive; a transformation is likely to necessitate further transformations as new and "higher" needs arise, even if the initial transformation was toward a more rather than a less responsive society. A change in the mobilization base affects the future plateaux from which projects will be launched. *In either case*, activation ultimately may be achieved only in societal projects aimed at increasing the responsiveness of society rather than seeking a "good" society. And, thus, in the articulation of the personal and the societal project of building an active society lies the resolution to the existentialist paradox of an over-voluntaristic view of the person and a deterministic picture of society.[70]

While the activation of some members of a society may increase rather than decrease the society's alienating character, we hold that if all the members of a society are activated, the society cannot help but become more responsive and authentic.[71] While a project may be misdirected and distorting, at least it has a potential capacity to test and improve the connections among the elements of the active orientation. No such hope can be held for those who are engaged only in the pursuit of knowledge, *or* the expression of their commitments, *or* the exercise of power, unless, of course, the elements of their activation are joined on some other level.

Differentiation and Reintegration

The rise in activeness tends to be associated with an increase in the division of labor, authority, and normative principles—i.e., with societal differentiation. This seems to be the inevitable basis for specialization. At the same time, differentiation entails the fragmentation of knowledge, commitment, and power and frustrates a basic human need, the need for a context. Thus, the three elements of the active orientation may not only be weakened or become dissociated, but each one may become internally fragmented— a main source of the sense of meaninglessness and of drifting on both personal and societal levels. De-differentiation, regression to simpler systems, entails the undermining of the instrumental gains of differentiation; the active solution, is, hence, reintegration—the establishment of a new, higher-level context—and not regression. Thus, there is a need for a synthesis of knowledge, for a synthesis of emotions and values, and for a holistic view of the use of power, as well as for the reinforcement of the connections among these elements. On the personal level, this requires a kind of holistic education and active experience which has been often discussed but rarely implemented. On the societal level, such syntheses entail the investment in and support for the units engaged in such activities (such as the intellectual and political units), even if some neglect of the instrumental units is required.

While the active society requires a higher level of articulation of instrumental and expressive elements rather than a lower one, such progress seems to entail a temporary and limited regression, especially when the fragmentation and differentiation process has developed considerably. This seems necessary for two reasons: (a) because the specific structures have evolved with little concern for their reintegration and (b) because the societal energy has so "dried up" by being scattered among many unrelated bits that unless it is released by some regression, not enough will be available for societal reintegration and transformation.

The first reason is illustrated in the realm of work. It may well be impossible to return to the fusion of a production unit with a family or a community—i.e., differentiation must be maintained (if modern instrumentality is to be sustained)—but the work arrangements may be reorganized quite fundamentally to increase the responsiveness of the organization of work to the workers *and* the family and community.

The second reason is illustrated in the rejection of a differentiated world, its organization, its norms and authority by members of some social movements, some intellectuals, and "bohemia" who lead a much more "fused" (or, oceanic) and intense life, carrying the seeds of a new whole. Before societies undergo transformations, especially rapid ones such as a social revolution or the gaining of national independence, they often experience a similar "regressed" stage. Typically, in this stage, differentiation is suspended, instrumental activities are held in low esteem and intellectual and political ones in high esteem, and the level of activation is high.*

There is a common danger in personal, collective, and societal regressions—that they will not serve as a transition period of "re-vitalization"[72] and as a basis for reintegration (which entails a return to greater—though not as great as the original—instrumentality and its relative neutrality) but will remain in the "regressed" phase. For persons in rehabilitation, this takes the form of a refusal to leave the sheltered world of the therapeutic community and an increase in child-like dependency. For social movements, it involves an increased emphasis on self-oriented activities, "social" activities, and tension release (from sexual orgies to narcotics), and an increased neglect of societal orientations and political action. For societies—new nations, for instance—it entails a deferral of economic and administrative development in favor of excessive political and even intellectual activity.[73]

.   .   .

In the inauthentic society, the majority of the members are caught in the typical cleavage between their private selves and public roles and manage by treating their neuroses with drugs, alcohol, professional counseling, and the like, thus reinforcing the inauthenticity of the society which caused their malaise. There is a minority of retreatists who ignore their public roles and build lives around their private selves. While these people are more authentic and, potentially, carriers of societal change, they have little societal effect. Finally, there are those who evolve new public selves which they collectivize and make the basis of their societal action. In these lies the hope for an initiation of the transformation of the inauthentic society. They are the active ones.

NOTES

1. Sociologists have tended to argue that material or physiological needs are very limited, and, hence, most material products are sources of symbolic gratification. From this viewpoint, both modern and post-modern societies have "abundant" economies. While we concur on this basic point, we suggest that in recent years the symbolic element has increased even more in relative importance. Thus, a 1945 car provides better transportation as compared to a 1925 model, whatever the symbolic implications. In contrast, the differences between 1965 and 1945 automobiles are much more related to status than to transportation. There have been some post-modern material advances, for instance, in the development of

---

* See Chapter 8 for a discussion of unlocking and recommitting, and of synthesis as a process.

artificial substitutes for fabrics and leather. But an increasing segment of post-modern production is symbolic (such as the knowledge industry, education, and communication). Second, there seems to be a declining marginal utility to material rewards in "affluent" societies and, hence, an increase in the motivational significance of symbolic rewards. On the first point, see Gerhard Lenski, *Power and Privilege* (New York: McGraw-Hill, 1966) and Ralf Dahrendorf's review of Lenski's book in the *American Sociological Review*, Vol. 31 (1966), p. 715. See also Riesman, *Abundance for What?, op. cit.*, pp. 300–308, and our discussion of symbolization of society, *supra*, pp. 198–205.

Several studies have been conducted which show that higher income groups aspire to an increase in their incomes similar to that desired by lower income ones. But this does not mean that there is no limit to man's commitment to objects, for a larger part of the higher income group's income is spent on symbolic items. Finally, in principle, there is no reason why $1,000 worth of symbolic gratification cannot be gained from an increase in "'social justice" as it can from gaining in status symbols.

2. For a review of the concept in Weber, Simmel, Durkheim, de Tocqueville, and, especially, Marx, and for references to their relevant works, see Robert A. Nisbet, *The Sociological Tradition* (New York: Basic Books, 1967), pp. 264–312. In regard to Marx, his early work is what concerns us here. See Karl Marx, *Die Fruehschriften* (Stuttgart: Kroener, 1953). For a selection of relevant readings, Eric and Mary Josephson (eds.), *Man Alone: Alienation in Modern Society* (New York: Dell, 1962). See also Fritz Pappenheim, *Alienation of Modern Man* (Paperback, Monthly Press Review, 1959) and Maurice Stein and Arthur Vidich (eds.), *Identity and Anxiety* (New York: Free Press, 1960). For a book of literary criticism, see Marcus Klein, *After Alienation* (Cleveland: World, 1964) and a literary selection: Gerald Sykes (ed.), *Alienation: The Cultural Climate of Our Time* (New York: Braziller, 1964, 2 vols). For a recent study and references to several empirical works, see Jack McLeod, Scott Ward, and Karen Tancill, "Alienation and Uses of the Mass Media," *Public Opinion Quarterly*, Vol. 29 (1965–1966), pp. 583–594.

3. Cf. Nisbet, *The Sociological Tradition, op. cit.*, p. 265.

4. Lewis Feuer, "What is Alienation? The Career of a Concept," *Sociology on Trial*, Maurice Stein and Arthur Vidich (eds.) (Englewood Cliffs, N.J.: Prentice-Hall, 1963), pp. 127–147. See also Melvin Seeman, "On the Meaning of Alienation," *American Sociological Review*, Vol. 24 (1959), pp. 783–791.

5. A study of auto workers shows that individuals who feel socially alienated (as indicated by a lack of confidence in other people and in the future) also tend to feel personally impotent, at least with regard to political matters. Arthur W. Kornhauser, Harold L. Sheppard, and Albert J. Mayer, *When Labor Votes: A Study of Auto Workers* (New York: University Books, 1956), p. 194.

6. This hold for the major works of Martin Heidegger, Jean-Paul Sartre, and other existentialist writers. For specific references, see below.

7. Martin Heidegger, *Being and Time* (London: S.C.M. Press, 1962), especially pp. 184, 264–268; Jean-Paul Sartre, *Being and Nothingness* (New York: Washington Square Press, 1966), especially pp. 591, 678–679, Sartre uses the term "bad faith" as a synonym to inauthenticity.

8. Cf. André Gorz, "Le Vieillissement," *Les Temps Modernes*, No. 187 (December, 1961), pp. 829–852. See also his *La Morale de l'Histoire* (Paris: Editions du

Seuil, 1959) and Emmanuel Mounier, *Introduction au Existentialisme* (Paris: Gallimard, 1962), pp. 52 ff. Jean-Paul Sartre, *Situations* (New York: Fawcett Crest, 1966), pp. 16–20 and his *Saint Genet* (New York: Mentor Books, 1964), pp. 43–45. Marjorie G. Grene, "Authenticity: An Existential Virtue," *Ethics*, Vol. 62 (1952), pp. 266–274. Sartre published in 1944 an article on the Jewish problem in which he says that the Jew is authentic if he identifies with Jews and inauthentic if he claims that Jewish problems will be solved through world assimiliation. *Reflexions sur la question juive* (Paris: P. Morihien, 1946).

9. Simone de Beauvoir seems to hold that a person must choose the greater freedom for himself which will also increase that of others. But the underprivileged, in monopolized or overmanaged societies, may have to curtail the freedoms of the privileged to increase the total sum *and* to make the freedoms of those now at the top more authentic. Cf. Simone de Beauvoir, *Pour une Morale de l'Ambiguite* (Paris: Gallimard, 1947), pp. 56 and 71 ff.; and Grene, *Ethics, op. cit.*, pp. 269 ff.

10. Our position here is closest to that taken by Alex Inkeles, *What is Sociology?* (Englewood Cliffs, N.J.: Prentice-Hall, 1964), pp. 49–61. See also Dennis Wrong's discussion of "The Oversocialized Conception of Man," *op. cit.*

11. Karl Mannheim, Arthur Maslow, Vilfredo Pareto, Talcott Parsons, W. I. Thomas, Max Weber, and Florian Znaniecki have such lists.

12. Role variance may also be higher than that of personalities.

13. On this point, see Thomas S. Szasz, *Pain and Pleasure: A Study of Bodily Feelings* (New York: Basic Books, 1957), *passim*.

14. Existentialists, utopian socialists, and anarchist writers often do not recognize this distinction. It is advanced by Marcuse, *Eros and Civilization, op. cit.*, pp. 32–35. See also Gustav Bally, *Vom Ursprung und den Grenzen der Freiheit* (Basel: Benno Schwabe, 1945).

15. For an important conceptual discussion which provides a theory for treating costs in the context of role analysis, see William J. Goode, "A Theory of Role Strain," in *American Sociological Review*, Vol. 25 (1960), pp. 483–496. Studies which measure personality variables as distinct from those of the roles occupied include: Doris C. Gilbert and Daniel J. Levinson, "Role Performance, Ideology and Personality in Mental Hospital Aides," in Milton Greenblatt et al. (eds.), *The Patient and the Mental Hospital* (New York: Free Press, 1957), pp. 197–208; Morris Rosenberg, *Occupations and Values* (New York: Free Press, 1957); George G. Stern, Morris I. Stein, and Benjamin S. Bloom, *Methods in Personality Assessment* (New York: Free Press, 1956). Kornhauser suggests that mass society, culture and pressure for conformity do not allow for enough variance. William Kornhauser, *The Politics of Mass Society, op. cit.*, pp. 100–103.

16. Ruth Benedict, *Patterns of Culture* (Boston: Houghton Mifflin, 1934). Cultural variety is the theme of well-known works of Margaret Mead, *Coming of Age in Samoa* (New York: Morrow, 1928) and *Sex and Temperament in Three Primitive Societies* (New York: Morrow, 1935). There is much less emphasis on variability in her post-World War II work. See also recent post-1945 work by Clyde Kluckhohn and by Alfred L. Kroeber, especially their *Culture* (New York: Vintage Books, 1963). "In the prewar anthropology, the psychobiological design of man seemed irrelevant. The design was open; it could be made to subscribe to any culture." Wolf, *Anthropology, op. cit.*, pp. 33–86.

17. For a review of findings on psychotherapy, see Kenneth Mark Colby,

"Psychotherapeutic Processes," *Annual Review of Psychology*, Vol. 15 (1964), pp. 347–370; Allen T. Dittmann, "Psychotherapeutic Processes," *Annual Review of Psychology*, Vol. 17 (1966), pp. 51–78. For the limited success of brainwashing, both in terms of depth and permanence, see Edgar H. Schein, *Coercive Persuasion; A Socio-psychological Analysis of the "Brainwashing" of American Civilian Prisoners by the Chinese Communists* (New York: Norton, 1961) and Robert J. Lifton, "Thought Reform of Chinese Intellectuals," in Marie Jahoda and Neil Warren (eds.), *Attitudes* (Baltimore, Md.: Penguin Books, 1966), pp. 196–209. Lifton interviewed in depth 40 intellectuals who had escaped from Communist China on the process of "thought reform" and its results. He describes this process as one which "harnesses the most powerful human emotions in the total manipulation of the individual" (p. 208). Given the force of this effort, Lifton asks whether or not the Chinese methods achieve their aims. He concludes that "the great majority . . . [are] partially convinced" (p. 208), but only a small minority undergo complete personality change. On psychological experiments, see William J. McGuire, "Attitudes and Opinions," *Annual Review of Psychology*, Vol. 17 (1966), pp. 475–514.

18. Lifton, "Thought Reform . . ." *op. cit.*, and Schein, *Coercive Persuasion, op. cit.* See also Glen H. Elder, Jr., "Role Relations, Sociocultural Environments, and Autocratic Family Ideology," *Sociometry*, Vol. 28 (1965), pp. 173–196. It is shown that placing authoritarian personalities in non-authoritarian settings does not reduce greatly their authoritarianism.

19. See Czeslaw Milosz, *The Captive Mind* (New York: Knopf, 1953).

20. For review of the literature, see Berelson and Steiner, *Human Behavior, op. cit.*, pp. 557–585; Paul F. Lazarsfeld and Elihu Katz, *Personal Influence* (New York: Free Press, 1964); Joseph T. Klapper, *The Effects of Mass Communications* (New York: Free Press, 1960); Charles R. Wright, *Mass Communication: A Sociological Perspective* (New York: Random House, 1959), pp. 90–112.

21. From Bennett M. Berger, *Working-Class Suburb: A Study of Auto Workers in Suburbia* (Berkeley and Los Angeles: University of California Press, 1960), p. 102. In a footnote, Berger adds that a typical example of this view is Erich Fromm's discussion of Park Forest in *The Sane Society* (New York: Holt, Rinehart & Winston, 1955), pp. 152–162. Cf. Jack L. Walker, "A Critique of the Elitist Theory of Democracy," *American Political Science Review*, Vol. LX (1966), pp. 289–290.

22. Blauner, *Alienation and Freedom, op. cit.*, p. 29.

23. Melvin Seeman, "On the Personal Consequences of Alienation in Work," *American Sociological Review*, Vol. 32 (1967), pp. 273–285. Melvin Seeman, "Alienation, Membership, and Political Knowledge: A Comparative Study," *Public Opinion Quarterly*, Vol. 30 (1966), pp. 353–367; Arthur G. Neal and Salomon Rettig, "On the Multi-dimensionality of Alienation," *American Sociological Review*, Vol. 32 (1967), pp. 54–64; Gwynne Nettler, "A Measure of Alienation," *American Sociological Review*, Vol. 22 (1957), pp. 670–677; John P. Clark, "Measuring Alienation Within a Social System," *American Sociological Review*, Vol. 24 (1959), pp. 849–852; Dwight G. Dean, "Alienation: Its Meaning and Measurement," *American Sociological Review*, Vol. 26 (1961), pp. 753–758. For a measurement of satisfaction, see Norman M. Bradburn and David Caplovitz, *Reports on Happiness: A Pilot Study of Behavior Related to Mental Health* (Chicago: Aldine Publishing Co., 1965). The study draws on interviews and self-administered

questionnaires. See also Alex Inkeles, "Industrial Man," *American Journal of Sociology*, Vol. 66 (1960), pp. 1–31.

24. 80 million persons in the United States have used drugs containing meprobamate (one kind of tranquilizer) in the eleven years since they began to be marketed. *The New York Times*, June 28, 1966. On sexual escapism from politics, see Herbert Marcuse, *Eros and Civilization* (Boston: Beacon Press, 1955), *passim*.

25. Edgar Z. Friedenberg, *Coming of Age in America* (New York: Random House, 1965). He used depth interviews and projective tests. Ely Chinoy, *Automobile Workers and the American Dream* (New York: Doubleday, 1955). "A small sample was chosen so that the investigation could probe deeply into men's aspirations; qualitative richness was desired rather than statistical coverage" (p. 24). Interviews, observations, and group sessions were used by Argyris. See Chris Argyris, and with a chapter by Roger Harrison, *Interpersonal Competence and Organizational Effectiveness* (Homewood, Ill.: Dorsey Press, 1962). Kenneth Keniston, *The Uncommitted: Alienated Youth in American Society* (New York: Harcourt, Brace & World, 1965), pp. 1–206. Keniston studied intensively 12 highly alienated students, 12 non-alienated ones, and 12 who were not extreme either way. He used Thematic Apperception Tests, various psychological experiments, and intensive interviews.

26. For the reasons why selection reduces socialization costs, see Etzioni, *A Comparative Analysis . . . , op. cit.*, pp. 154–160.

27. Some question has been raised about whether or not the decline of religion, rise of mental illness, and increase in escapistic literature are really related to modernization. Leo Lowenthal, "Historical Perspectives of Popular Culture," *American Journal of Sociology*, Vol. 55 (1950), pp. 323–332. Goldhamer and Marshall, in their study of differing rates of incarceration for mental illness during the last century, show that in some cases and for some groups, the rates of admission to mental hospitals in Massachusetts are "just as high during the last half of the nineteenth century as they are today." Herbert Goldhamer and Andrew W. Marshall, *Psychosis and Civilization: Two Studies in the Frequency of Mental Disease* (New York: Free Press, 1953), p. 91. The occurrence of severe mental illness among Hutterite communities was roughly comparable to the occurrence of hospitalization for mental illness in New York State, according to Eaton and Weil, *Culture and Mental Disorder, op. cit.* In the Middle Ages, as much or more leisure time existed as at present. See Harold Wilensky," The Uneven Distribution of Leisure: The Impact of Economic Growth on 'Free Time,' " *Social Problems*, Vol. 9 (1961), pp. 33–34. In pre-modern periods, work was viewed as an unpleasant burden or punishment. Adriano Tilgher, *Work: What It Has Meant to Men through the Ages* (New York: Harcourt, Brace & Co., 1930). Referring to the *traditional* Chinese family, Yang stated: ". . . a feeling of a closed universe from which there seemed to be no escape, except perhaps death. The large number of suicides resulting from the strain of family relations among women is a reflection of this situation." C. K. Yang, *Chinese Communist Society: The Family and the Village* (Cambridge, Mass.: M.I.T. Press, 1965), p. 7. See also pp. 107–109. Many propositions relate highly effective socialization and social control to great personal costs; e.g., the Japanese are said to be well-mannered but have a high rate of ulcers. The problem with studying such propositions is that they require measures of all the various costs because if, let us say, the Japanese do not have more ulcers but

rather a high rate of hypertension, the proposition would still hold. In industrial research, where a similar problem is faced in that any two working conditions may differ on numerous dimensions, we avoid the issue by asking, "All said and done—do you like this job better than X?" But this technique could not be applied here, as many of the costs are not consciously experienced. A comparison of a large number of rates of various costs, both psychosomatic and others, may allow this problem to be handled. See Herbert Hendin, *Suicide and Scandinavia* (New York: Grune & Stratton, 1964).

28. For instance, ". . . Between 1836 and 1890 suicide increased 140 per cent in Prussia, 355 per cent in France. England had 62 cases of suicide per million inhabitants in 1836 to 1845, and 110 between 1906 and 1910. Sweden 66, as against 150 respectively. . . ." Maurice Halbwachs, *Les Causes du Suicide* (Paris: Felix Alcan, 1930), pp. 92 and 481. Such figures have been often questioned, especially because of improved reporting but they seem to be the "hardest" data available.

29. For a story of a deviant who becomes a political innovator through mobilization, see *The Autobiography of Malcolm X*, with the assistance of Alex Haley, Introduction by M. S. Handler, Epilogue by Alex Haley (New York: Grove Press, 1965). A study of narcotics addiction among Negroes in the United States for a decade by the Federal Bureau of Narcotics showed a 15 per cent decline (27,321 as compared to 29,482) from 1955 to 1965; the first factor listed among four was "growing racial pride among Negroes has accompanied the fight for civil rights." *The New York Times*, March 6, 1967. See also Clark, *Dark Ghetto, op. cit.*, p. 216. On similar evidence for Los Angeles, see Ed Cray, *The Big Blue Line* (New York: Coward-McCann, 1967), p. 131. It is said that rates of neurosis were much lower during the London Blitz, and that those mobilized by a social movement have a low criminal record. See George Rudé, *The Crowd in History* (New York: Wiley, 1964), especially Ch. 13, pp. 195–268; Donald D. Reid, "Precipitating Proximal Factors in the Occurrence of Mental Disorders: Epidemiological Evidence," *Causes of Mental Disorders: A Review of Epidemiological Knowledge, 1959* (New York: Milbank Memorial Fund, 1961), and Joseph W. Eaton and Robert J. Weil, "The Mental Health of the Hutterites," in *Man Alone, op. cit.*, pp. 498–504. It is necessary, though, to use as indicators anti-social behavior as defined by a social science model and not by the middle class or the alienating society. Thus, it is not clear at all that the smoking of marijuana (as distinct from heroin or opium) is more anti-social than moderate drinking. Its prevalence in a mobilized group is not a sign that activation does not reduce deviancy. But interpersonal violence, for instance, seems more anti-social, and we would expect a lower rate in active groups, unless this is part of the pattern the group picks up as its rebelling symbol. The question of an absolute base for the study of deviant behavior will be explored further in a later publication.

30. "On the basis of limited direct observation in one country—Cuba—and from indirect evidence, I am inclined to believe the culture of poverty does not exist in socialist countries. In 1947 I undertook a study of a slum in Havana. Recently I had an opportunity to revisit the same slum and some of the same families. The physical aspect of the place had changed little, except for a beautiful new nursery school. The people were as poor as before, but I was impressed to find much less of the feelings of despair and apathy, so symptomatic of the culture of poverty in the urban slums of the U.S. The slum was now highly organized, with

block committees, educational committees, party committees. The people had found a new sense of power and importance in a doctrine that glorified the lower class as the hope of humanity, and they were armed. I was told by one Cuban official that the Castro government had practically eliminated delinquency by giving arms to the delinquents!" Oscar Lewis, "The Culture of Poverty," *Scientific American*, Vol 215 (Oct., 1966), p. 23.

31. This is a meaning which can be given to the term within the Marxist tradition. There may be more validity in this methodological position than in many of Marx's substantive sociological predictions. Karl Marx, "Theses on Feuerbach," in Karl Marx and Friedrich Engels, *Selected Works*, Vol. II (Moscow: Foreign Language Publishing House, 1955), pp. 402–404.

32. For a recent discussion of this subject by a Soviet sociologist, see Y. Zamochkine, "La Sociologie et les problemes de l'orientation sociale de l'individu dans la societe contemporaine," *La Sociologie en U.R.S.S.* (Moscow: Editions du Progrés, 1966), pp. 63–77.

Marx refers to a "general" human nature: "To know what is useful for a dog, one must study dog-nature. This nature itself is not to be deduced from the principle of utility. Applying this to man, he that would criticise all human acts, movements, relations, etc., by the principle of utility, must first deal with human nature in general, and then with human nature as modified in each historical epoch." Karl Marx, *Capital* (Chicago: Charles H. Kerr & Co., 1906), Vol. I, p. 668. Cited by Albert Szymanski, in "Individual Needs and Systematic Sociology," in *G.S.S. Journal* (Columbia University), Vol. 6, No. 3 (May, 1967), p. 5.

33. Of course, the more effective theory becomes, the more we can forecast the outcome and spare the social and personal costs. Social experimentation is "necessary" as long as such theory is not available or not heeded.

34. The following statement puts the burden exclusively on the withdrawing ego: "Under what circumstances might the Ego withdraw from cathectic commitment to role occupancy—might it, in a word, become *alienated*?" Role occupancy is only one aspect of role in which pathological situations might be found; another is role performance. "Under what circumstances," we ask, "might the informational controls internal to the system itself become inadequate? Under what circumstances, that is, might the Ego find itself in an *anomic* situation?" Charles Ackerman and Talcott Parsons, "The Concept of 'Social System' as a Theoretical Device," in Gordon J. Direnzo (ed.), *Concepts, Theory, and Explanation in the Behavioral Sciences* (New York: Random House, 1966), pp. 19–40, quoted from p. 34. Compare this to Anne Marie Rocheblave-Spenlé, *La Notion de Rôle en Psychologie Sociale* (Paris: P.U.F., 1962). Note here that in the prevailing American sociological traditions, role is a "positive" concept, mobilizing members into society; in the European one, it is a negative concept, constricting the person.

35. For useful discussions of indicators and related propositions, see Harry Stack Sullivan, *Conceptions of Modern Psychiatry* (Washington, D.C.: William Alanson White Psychiatric Foundation, 1947); Karen Horney, *Neurosis and Human Growth* (New York: Norton, 1950); Isidore Portnoy, "The Anxiety States," in Silvano Arieti (ed.), *American Handbook of Psychiatry* (New York: Basic Books, 1959), Vol. I, pp. 307–323; and George K. Zollschan and Philip Gibeau, "Concerning Alienation: A System of Categories for the Exploration of Rational and Irrational Behavior," in *Explorations in Social Change*, George K.

Zollschan and Walter Hirsch (eds.) (Boston: Houghton Mifflin, 1964), pp: 152–174.

36. Tuchman, *The Proud Tower*, *op. cit.*, p. 165.

37. Kornhauser et al., *When Labor Votes*, *op. cit.*, pp. 194–196. Concluding an examination of the power elite in Pittsburgh, Auerbach stated, "The community power elite ... has shed its blatant ostentatiousness, its naked violence, its total disregard for civic and community welfare. It has become suave and sophisticated, secure and mature, and sensitive of its public image. It does not engage in loud diatribes against social security, labor unions, communism, or the 'welfare state.' Community leadership sees its interests linked more and more with the welfare of the total community. True, it still carries a big stick; but it speaks softly."

Arnold J. Auerbach, "Power and Progress in Pittsburgh," in *Trans-action*, Vol. 2, (Sept.–Oct., 1965), p. 20. For a case study of inauthentic politics, somewhat over-interpretative, see Murray B. Levin, *Kennedy Campaigning* (Boston: Beacon Press, 1966). The study is of Edward M. Kennedy's election to the Senate from Massachusetts in 1962. See also Murray B. Levin, *The Alienated Voter* (New York: Holt, Rinehart & Winston, 1960). On the sense of impotence, see p. 58. On the use of public relations firms in election campaigns, see Stanley Kelley, Jr., "Whitaker and Baxter: Campaigns Inc.," in his *Professional Public Relations and Political Power* (Baltimore: The Johns Hopkins Press, 1956), pp. 39–66. See also pp. 170–235.

38. See Seeman, "Alienation, Membership, and Political Knowledge," *op. cit.* Almond and Verba, *Civic Culture*, *op. cit.*, esp. pp. 49–51 and *passim*.

39. Arthur S. Link, *Wilson: Campaigns for Progressivism and Peace, 1916–1917* (Princeton, N.J.: Princeton University Press, 1965), Vol. 5, and T. R. Fehrenbach, *F.D.R.'s Undeclared War* (New York: David McKay, 1967).

40. Daniel Bell, "The Dispossessed—1962," *Columbia University Forum*, (Vol. 5, Fall 1962), pp. 4–12.

41. For reference see above, footnote 7, Chapter 16.

42. See Truman, *The Governmental Process*, *op. cit.*, p. 260. On a similar condition in Britain, see Samuel H. Beer, *Modern British Politics* (London: Faber & Faber, 1965), Chap. IV and pp. 240–242.

43. For empirical case studies see a study of "cooptation" of local interests in a federal body, the Tennessee Valley Authority, Philip Selznik, *TVA and the Grass Roots* (Berkeley: University of California Press, 1953). For a study of a community political structure in which those who appear to have power are actually controlled by national corporations, see Arthur J. Vidich and Joseph Bensman, *Small Town in Mass Society: Class, Power, and Religion in a Rural Community* (Princeton, N.J.: Princeton University Press, 1958). An interesting variation is found in the politics of the left, when those who engage in them do so not for power purposes but for release of emotions. Thus, what appears as political action really is social psychotherapy. See discussion of pseudo-power in Clark, *Dark Ghetto*, *op. cit.*, p. 201.

44. On "surface conformity" and "character change," see J. Milton Yinger, *Toward a Field Theory of Behavior* (New York: McGraw-Hill, 1965), p. 175. See also studies of persuasion cited above. For a discussion of related concepts, see Erving Goffman on "role distance" and "working the system," *Encounters* (New York: Bobbs-Merrill, 1961), p. 85–152.

45. See Milosz, *The Captive Mind*, *op. cit.*, for a discussion of opposition

members in Eastern Europe. Patterns of overt-conformity without inner commitment develop. But, it is suggested, those sometimes lead to what seems like full internalization (p. 55). Stanley M. Elkins in his book *Slavery* proposed that absolute dominance in North American slavery and in German concentration camps produced in the victims child-like "Sambo" personalities (New York: Universal Library, 1963), p. 82.

46. Alex Inkeles, "Mobilizing Public Opinion," in Alex Inkeles and Kent Geiger (eds.), *Soviet Society: A Book of Readings* (Boston: Houghton Mifflin, 1961), pp. 219–228. The author first describes the Soviet system and then analyzes its effectiveness (pp. 226–228). On the one hand, the system is said to "have been extraordinarily effective in shaping the pattern (sic) of thought about public issues among Soviet citizens" (p. 227). On the other hand, this is said to be so only as long as it does "not challenge their basic values" (p. 228). The author warns about the difficulties of studying this matter. There are references to "extraordinary hunger for honest and straightforward information . . ." (p. 228). See also Alex Inkeles and Raymond A. Bauer, *The Soviet Citizen: Daily Life in a Totalitarian Society* (Cambridge, Mass.: Harvard University Press, 1959), pp. 234–238, 243–245, 252, and 321.

As there are very few studies of life under communism, we must turn to less than completely satisfactory ones and to literary sources. The study by Paulson is about life under a local Communist government in Italy. As idealists give way to bureaucrats, the study shows that personal alienation grows. Belden Paulson, with Athos Ricci, *The Searchers: Conflict and Communism in an Italian Town* (Chicago: Quadrangle Books, 1966). For a view of a Chinese village in 1948 by a foreigner favorable to the regime, see William Hinton, *Fanshen: A Documentary of Revolution in a Chinese Village* (New York: Monthly Review Press, 1967). For a later study, see Jan Myrdal, *Report from a Chinese Village*, translated by Maurice Michael (New York: Pantheon Books, 1965). See Barrington Moore, Jr., *Terror and Progress USSR* (Cambridge: Harvard University Press, 1954); I. L. Janis et al, *Personality and Persuasibility* (New Haven: Yale University Press, 1959); Carl Hovland, I. L. Janis and Harold H. Kelley, *Communication and Persuasion* (New Haven: Yale University Press, 1953).

47. For a typical report, see William H. Whyte, Jr., "The New Suburbia," in Peterson and Matza, *op. cit.*, p. 793–304.

48. August B. Hollingshead and Fredrick C. Redlich, *Social Class and Mental Illness* (New York: Wiley & Sons, 1958). The study found that "a definite association exists between class position and being a psychiatric patient; the lower the class, the greater the proportion [of patients]" (p. 216); and the lower the class, the higher the rate of psychoses (as opposed to neuroses) (p. 248). The diagnostic classifications were determined by the patients' therapists. See also Srole et al., *Mental Health in the Metropolis, op. cit.*, and for an earlier study, Robert E. L. Faris and H. Waren Dunham, *Mental Disorder in Urban Areas* (Chicago: University of Chicago Press, 1939).

49. "That we shall be able to truly increase the innate energy or intelligence of man seems unlikely. What we can do, however, is to free the psychic energy that is bound by inner conflicts and emotional turmoil. Thus we can add to the available energy and ability to think." From a letter by Alfred Denzel, entitled "Energy: Release, Not Increase," to *Science*, Vol. 151 (March 4, 1966), p. 1036.

50. John R. Seeley et al., *Crestwood Heights* (New York: Basic Books, 1956), p. 203; Maurice R. Stein, *The Eclipse of Community* (Princeton, N.J.: Princeton University Press, 1960), p. 214.

51. S. N. Eisenstadt, "Processes of Communication among Immigrants in Israel," *Public Opinion Quarterly*, Vol. 16 (1952), pp. 42–58; S. N. Eisenstadt, "Conditions of Communicative Receptivity," *Public Opinion Quarterly*, Vol. 17 (1953), pp. 363–374; S. N. Eisenstadt, "Analysis of Patterns of Immigration and Absorption of Immigrants," *Population Studies*, Vol. 7 (1953), pp. 167–180.

52. Siegfried Giedion, "Mechanization Takes Command," in Gerald Sykes, *Alienation: The Cultural Climate of Our Time*, *op. cit.*, pp. 5–16; J. J. Gillespie, *Free Expression in Industry* (London: The Pilot Press, 1948); Chinoy, *Automobile Workers and the American Dream*, *op. cit.* For a good review of the literature and analysis, see Blauner, *Alienation and Freedom: The Factory Worker and His Industry*, *op. cit.*, pp. 166–186. See also Daniel Bell, *Work and Its Discontents* (Boston: Beacon Press, 1956) and Peter L. Berger (ed.), *The Human Shape of Work* (New York: Macmillan, 1964).

53. Robert Blauner, "Work Satisfaction and Industrial Trends in Modern Society," in Walter Galenson and Seymour M. Lipset (eds.), *Labor and Trade Unionism* (New York: Wiley & Sons, 1960), pp. 345–349.

54. Bendix, *Work and Authority*, *op. cit.*, pp. 308–318. See also Loren Baritz, *The Servants of Power* (Middletown, Conn.: Wesleyan University Press, 1960). Some inauthentic elements existed in earlier periods. See Pollard, *The Genesis of Modern Management*, *op. cit.*, esp. pp. 142–147.

55. For a description based on a study by W. R. Dymond, see William F. Whyte et al., *Money and Motivation: An Analysis of Incentives in Industry* (New York: Harper & Row, 1955), pp. 149–165.

56. More than 10 per cent, or about 800, of the cases of "labor troubles" which required government action in the United States in 1966 were cases where the union rank-and-file spurned agreements accepted by the leaders. A. H. Raskin, "Why Labor Doesn't Follow its Leaders," *The New York Times*, January 8, 1967. Like other concrete indicators, the statistics on wildcat strikes can be misleading, and some are caused by other factors, such as factional problems and low settlements by union leaders in the face of rising costs of living (*ibid.*). But "communication gaps" among leaders and members are a recognized fact (*ibid.*). These would be smaller if the existing union structures, elites, and policies were responsive to the members.

57. See, for instance, Charles R. Walker and Robert H. Guest, *The Man on the Assembly Line* (Cambridge, Mass.: Harvard University Press, 1952).

58. Friedenberg, *Coming of Age in America*, *op. cit.*; Kenneth E. Eble, *A Perfect Education: Growing Up in Utopia* (New York: Macmillan, 1966); Keniston, *The Uncommitted*, *op. cit.* For an extreme expression of this view, untroubled by data, see Paul Goodman, *Growing Up Absurd* (New York: Random House, 1960). Cf. Frank P. Besag, *Alienation and Education: An Empirical Approach* (Buffalo, N.Y.: Hertillon Press, 1966).

59. Whyte, "The New Suburbia," *op. cit.*, reports that in a survey conducted by the high school of a suburb, most parents wrote that the *prime* aim of the school should be to teach people how to get along with other people. This goal allows for much less variety than such goals as "growth" or "self-expansion." The same holds for the relative lack of privacy in suburbs (*ibid.*, p. 297).

60. Bernard Rosenberg and David M. White (eds.), *Mass Culture* (New York: Free Press, 1957); Harold Rosenberg, *The Anxious Object: Art Today and its Audience* (New York: Horizon Press, 1964); "Mass Culture and Mass Media," *Daedalus*, Vol. 89 (Spring, 1960), entire issue.

61. Edward A. Shils, "Daydreams and Nightmares: Reflections on the Criticism of Mass Culture," *Sewanee Review*, Vol. 65 (1957), pp. 587–608. Gary A. Steiner showed that people like the TV shows they watch and that intellectuals watch basically the same "mass" shows, only that they express more guilt about doing so See his *The People Look at Television* (New York: Knopf, 1963).

62. For additional discussion of our position, see Chapter 3, *op. cit.* For that of existentialists, see William A. Luijpen, *Existential Phenomenology* (Pittsburgh: Duquesne University Press, 1963), pp. 279–281; John D. Wild, *The Challenge of Existentialism* (Bloomington, Ind.: Indiana University Press, 1959), pp. 129–130. On freedom to choose (existential) see also Otto Von Mering, *A Grammar of Human Values* (Pittsburgh: University of Pittsburgh Press, 1961). See there also for voluntaristic statements.

63. For a typical account of a personal "solution" to a collective situation, see Sammy Davis, Jr., and Jane and Burt Boyar, *Yes I Can: The Story of Sammy Davis, Jr.* (New York: Farrar, Straus & Giroux, 1965). See also Maria de Jesus, *Child of the Dark: The Diary of Carolina Maria de Jesus*, translated from the Portugese by David St. Clair (New York: Dutton, 1962). Compare this to the thesis that the artist must be political, which is a central idea in Günter Grass's play, *The Plebeians Rehearse The Uprising* (in Günter Grass, *Four Plays*, New York: Harcourt, Brace & World, 1967) as well as in his own personal project.

64. Cf. Kornhauser, *The Politics of Mass Society*, *op. cit.*, p. 111. He sees autonomous man as both self-related and self-oriented. David Riesman, Nathan Glazer, Reuel Denney, *The Lonely Crowd* (New Haven: Yale University Press, 1950), sees a need for a balance between self and collective orientation. See also Yrjö Littunen, "Social Restraints and Ideological Pluralism," *Cleavages, Ideologies and Party Systems: Contributions to Comparative Political Sociology*, ed. by E. Allardt and Y. Littunen (Helsinki: Transactions of the Westermarck Society, 1964), pp. 70–77. We stress that collective articulation of the project is necessary to make it macroscopic and fully authentic. This is not to deny the autonomy of the choice, the act, and other values attached to personal projects, individualistic in orientation, such as certain forms of art.

65. See, for instance, B. F. Skinner, *Walden Two* (New York: Macmillan, 1961).

66. Alex Inkeles, David H. Smith, Howard Schuman and Edward Ryan, *Becoming Modern* (Boston: Little, Brown, in progress). Inkeles adds, in a personal communication, that "If you show people a consumer good—a radio or tape recorder, or camera—the majority, sometimes the great majority, say they want it. Also, if you ask whether a man who is comfortable enough to feed and clothe and house himself and family should still strive for more money to get still more of the good things the majority again—except for Israel where it is 50–50—says 'yes, strive for more.' But if you ask whether getting more and more material possessions brings a man happiness after he has some minimal comfort, the majority says 'No.' "

67. Unrealistically, in the sense that there is an expectation that a regime which is that public and austere can be stabilized.

68. Lionel Trilling, criticizing modern criticism, stated that it "has taught us how to read certain books; it has not taught us how to engage them." *Beyond Culture: Essay on Literature and Learning* (New York: The Viking Press, 1965), p. 231. This is also a key point of his *Matthew Arnold* (New York: Norton, 1939), *The Liberal Imagination* (New York: Viking Press, 1950), and *The Opposing Self* (New York: Viking Press, 1955). Much of the writing about the dissociation of the "two cultures," science and the humanities, reflects a different aspect of the same core issue.

69. Here, the question of the need for violence arises. Frantz Fanon, among others, argued that it is both inevitable and liberating—i.e., desirable. *Annals of the American Academy of Political and Social Science*, Vol. 364 (1966), p. 12 and p. 10. See also his *The Wretched of the Earth* (New York: Grove Press, 1965). See especially Series A, cases 3, 4, and 5, pp. 213–219. For additional discussion and references, see above, pp. 320 f. We hold that it may be avoided, and that if relied upon, it is likely to have more distorting effects than liberating ones. It cannot be viewed, hence, as without costs. But its costs must be weighed in any historical situation against those of continuing the existing structure and the possibilities of changing it without macroscopic violence. (We argued above that there is almost no instance of societal transformation without some incidence of violence.)

70. Cf. Sartre, "Reply to Albert Camus," *Situations* (New York: Fawcett Crest, 1966), pp. 66–67, 76, 207. See there also for a definition of project as "ourself" (*ibid.*, pp. 66–67). Compare to the concept of "project" as used by Alfred Schutz, *Collected Papers* (The Hague: M. Nijhoff, 1962–1964), Vol. II, p. 11 ff. For another discussion of the societal futility of the personal project, a tragic rather than merely pessimistic view of man, see Albert Camus, *The Myth of Sisyphus* (New York: Vintage Books, 1955), esp. pp. 62–68. On the existentialist difficulty of reconciling man and society, see especially Jean-Paul Sartre, *L'Être et le Neant: Essai d'ontologie phénoménologique* (Paris: Gallimard, 1966).

71. Reasons for this statement, see *supra*, pp. 415–418.

72. Anthony F. C. Wallace, "Revitalization Movements," *American Anthropologist*, Vol. 58 (1956), pp. 264–281. See also R. Bastide, "Messianism and Social and Economic Development," in Immanuel Wallerstein, *Social Change: The Colonial Situation* (New York: Wiley & Sons, 1966), pp. 467–477.

73. Within the knowledge system: high investment in "generalists" versus experts.

Glossary

Active Public—Citizens who are both politically informed and act politically. Contrasts with *passive public*.

Assets—The possessions of an actor. See *utilitarian assets, coercive assets, normative assets*.

Associations—Social units whose main functions are to create and sustain normative bonds among the members.

Atomistic Approach—A conception of societal states as the consequences of mechanistic relations among a large number of units.

Autarky—Functional self-sufficiency.

Authentic—A relationship or structure whose appearance and underlying reality are responsive to basic human needs.

Autonomy—Self-control.

Bit (of Knowledge)—A concrete, specific item of knowledge.

Coercive Assets—Weapons, installations, and manpower which the military, the police, or similar agencies command. See *assets*.

Collectivistic Approach—A conception of societal states as the consequences of quasi-organic relationships among the components of a societal whole.

Collectivity—A macroscopic unit that has a potential capacity to act in unison by drawing on a set of normative bonds which tie together the members of a stratification category.

Commonwealth—An imbalanced system which relies more on normative power than on utilitarian and coercive power.

Community—A system in which the supra-unit relations, which bind the sub-units and regulate their relations, are more powerful than the intra- or inter- sub-unit bonds.

Community of Assumptions—A set of assumptions shared by the members of a social unit which sets a context for their views of the world and of themselves.

Community, Moral—The segment of humanity for which an actor holds his values to be applicable.

Community, Political—A community which has three kinds of autarkic integrative processes: (1) it has sufficient coercive power to countervail that of any member unit or coalition of them; (2) it has a center of decision-making that is able to affect significantly the allocation of assets throughout the community; and (3) it is the dominant focus of political loyalty for the large majority of politically active citizens.

Community-building—The processes by which two or more units are integrated to form a community.

Compliance Structures—The typical patterns of relations that result between power wielders and their subjects which are affected by the kinds of power used and the orientations of the subjects to the power-wielders.

Consciousness—A generalized capacity to be aware, to pay attention.

Consensus—Congruence in the perspectives of a set of actors.

Consensus-building—The upward and downward processes by which consensus is created and sustained.

Consensus-formation—The process by which the perspectives of the members of a societal unit are transmitted upward to the controlling overlayers and the differences among them are reduced.

Consensus-mobilization—The processes by which society-wide perspectives are transmitted downward from the controlling overlayers to the members, to reduce the differences among them.

Contextuating Control—A kind of control which sets the limits within which those who are subject to control are free to alter their conduct and make their own decisions. See *prescriptive control* and *control*.

Contextuating Orientation—An actor's orientation which provides a context for bits.

Contextuating Symbol—A symbol around which a context is built.

Control—The process of specifying preferred states of affairs and revising on-going processes to reduce the distance from these preferred states. See *normative control, specification of control, contextuating control, prescriptive control*.

Control, Specification of—The extent to which control is detailed. *Prescriptive* control refers to the relatively highly specified segment of the specification continuum, while *contextuating* control refers to the relatively less specified segment.

Conversion Pattern—The distribution of the assets of an actor which are converted into power among various kinds of utilization.

Conversion Ratio—The proportion of an actor's assets that is converted into power, as opposed to his total assets.

Cross-sectoral Links—Links between functional sectors. See *sector, functional*.

Decision—A conscious choice between two or more alternatives.

Elite—A control unit that specializes in the cybernetic functions of knowledge-processing and decision-making and in the application of power. See *external elite, internal elite, system-elite, unit-elite*.

Elite, External—An elite which is not integrated into the supra-unit of the units it controls.

Elite, Internal—An elite which is integrated into the supra-unit of the units it controls.

Elite, System—An elite which accommodates to most if not all of the member units of a system. See also *unit-elite.*

Elite, Unit—An elite which accommodates only to one or a few member units of a system. See also *system-elite.*

Emergent Properties—Properties which appear on one level of analysis and are not present on another level.

Empire—An imbalanced system which relies more on coercion than on utilitarian and normative power.

Encapsulation—The processes by which conflicts are modified in such a way that they become limited by rules.

Functional Sector—See *sector, functional*

Fundamental Criticism—Criticism of a community of assumptions.

Guidance—See *societal guidance, societal guidance approach.*

Identity—An actor's position in a normative-cognitive pattern.

Inauthenticity—A relationship or structure whose underlying reality is unresponsive to basic human needs but whose appearance is as if it were responsive.

Influence—The encouragement of a course of action which is in line with the preferences of the actors involved.

Intellectuals—Those members of a unit who engage in fundamental criticism.

Interpretation, Cognitive or Evaluative—The provision of one or more cognitive or normative contexts for a bit. See also *synthesis.*

Macro-analysis—The theoretical study of macroscopic processes and units.

Macroscopic—That which affects societies, sub-societies, and combinations of societies.

Macro-units—Units the majority of whose consequences are macroscopic.

Mechanisms, Interwoven—Processes which are sustained mainly by units whose primary functions differ from those to which these processes are primarily devoted.

Mechanisms, Segregated—Processes which are sustained mainly by units whose primary functions are the same as those to which these processes are primarily devoted.

Micro-analysis—The theoretical study of microscopic processes and units.

Microscopic—That which affects families, peer groups, instrumental teams, and other small groupings.

Micro-units—Units, the majority of whose consequences are microscopic.

Mixed-scanning—A strategy which combines encompassing and undetailed scanning with detailed but limited scanning.

Mobilization—The processes by which a unit gains significantly in the control of assets it previously did not control.

Mutually Reinforcing Processes—Two or more processes which enhance the advancement of each other.

Normative Assets—Symbols, values, sentiments.
Normative Control—Persuasive power and/or influence.

Perspectives—Interests, values, and cognitive orientations.
Political Intensity—The ratio of societal activities which are politically controlled as compared to those which are not.
Power—The capacity to introduce change in the face of resistance; a capacity to overcome part or all of the resistance.
Power, Political—The capacity to control the state and other downward political processes.
Power, Societal—The capacity of a societal unit to gain its way in the face of resistance by other societal units.
Project—A concerted effort which entails the focusing of energy and comparatively intensive and guided activity related to limited and specified tasks.

Rationality, Comprehensive—The optimal selection of means, taking into account all the goals of a societal actor.
Rationality, Instrumental—The "open" (relatively or completely uninhibited) selection of means taking into account only one goal.
Reality-Testing—The revision of knowledge in accord with experience.
Responsiveness—That which takes into account the needs of the units involved.

Secondary-priming—The process by which the introduction of changes in one sector brings about changes in other sectors.
Sector, functional—Activities and structures which are devoted chiefly to the service of one function of a given unit.
Social Entropy—Absence of social order and social bonds.
Societal Analysis—The substantive aspect of macro-analysis.
Societal Guidance—A combination of downward control and upward consensus-formation processes.
Societal Guidance Approach—The combination of a collectivistic and a voluntaristic approach with power analysis.
Societal Knowledge—A set of symbols which provides a societal unit with a relation to reality and interprets this relationship. See also *reality-testing* and *interpretation*.
Synthesis—The organization of bits into contexts. See also *interpretation*.

Transformability—The capacity of a unit to change fundamentally its structure and boundaries.
Tribal System—A system in which the acting units are more internally integrated than they are related to each other or bound into a supra-unit.

Unbalanced Collectivity—A collectivity whose members' statuses are unbalanced.

Unbalanced Statuses—Statuses of persons or social units which differ in their ranking on various stratification dimensions.

Unification—The processes which lead to an increase in the level of integration of a unit, whether or not it reaches a community level.

Union—A grouping of units able to act in unison on a wide range of matters; less integrated than a community and more integrated than a tribal system.

Utilitarian Assets—Economic possessions, technical and administrative capabilities, and manpower.

Variables, Hierarchical—The properties of interlevel relations.

Variables, Inter-unit—The properties of the relationships of two or more units on the same level.

Variables, Universal—Variables that characterize all units, including micro- and macro-units. See also *emergent properties*.

Voluntaristic Approach—The conception of societal states as if they were the expression of one macroscopic individual's will or mind.

Indexes

Index of Names

Index of Subjects

A

Abstraction, 123-124
Action, as blind force, 12
  constraints on, 5
  freedom of, 5, 12
  mechanical aspects of, 27, 28
  realm of, 24, 26, 27
  societal, 99, 223-244
  value of, 12
Activation, of society, 6ff.
  personal, 619, 650-651
Activeness, relation to consensus-
    building, 468-469
Active orientation, components of, 4-5,
    12, 15, 73
  concepts necessary to explore, 77
  of social scientists, 16
Active-passive distinction, 4
Active society, 5ff., 467
  as a social movement society, 526
  difference from democratic society,
    517
  relation to modern society, 7ff.
Action autarky, 111-116
Action underlayer, 110ff.
Algeria, 369
Alienated, 618
Alienating, 618-619
Alienating structure, 617
Alienation, 350, 352-353, 357,
    361-363ff., 373-381, 389, 475, 480,
    486, 503, 504, 512ff., 538, 541, 550,
    566, 571, 572, 602, 617-622ff.,
    628ff., 633ff.
  costs of, 633
  level of, 618
  passive and active, 619
  relation to inauthenticity, 619-621,
    633
  relation to power, 352-353, 361-364
  relation to power mix, 362
  relation to responsiveness, 8

sources of, 376-377
  subjective and objective facets of, 353
American Medical Association, 436
Americans, affiliations of, 448
Americans for Democratic Action, 396
Analytic approach, 435
Anarchists, 540
Anarchy, 441
Anomie, 14, 356
Apathy, 400
Argentina, 299
Arms-control, 571-572
Assets, 7, 10, 11, 315, 323-329ff., 335,
    340ff., 351, 359, 365, 388ff., 401,
    438, 470, 471, 517
  allocation of, 554
  control of, 421
  conversion into power, 357, 358
  reallocation of, 532-533, 535-537, 566
  relation to power, 322-323
  utilitarian, 532-533
Atomism, 272
Atomistic approach, 61-65ff., 75ff., 162
  examples of, 62-64
Atomistic view, of democracy, 510
Atomization, 445
Austro-Hungarian empire, 108
Autarky, 115-116ff.
  action, 111-116
  defined, 115
Authentic consensus, 351, 352, 471, 482,
    505
Authenticity, 620-622 (*see also,*
    inauthenticity)
  of commitment, 634
Authoritarianism, defined, 522
Authoritarian government, 507-523
Authority, 355
  charismatic *versus* legal-rational, 450
  defined, 360-361
  rational, 354
  relation to force, 356